A History of Byzantine Civilization

A History of Byzantine Civilization

H. W. HAUSSIG

translated by

J. M. Hussey

169 illustrations, 22 in colour

THAMES AND HUDSON

Translated from the German, *Kulturgeschichte von Byzanz,*
second revised edition © 1966 by Alfred Kröner Verlag
in Stuttgart
English translation © 1971 by Thames and Hudson
Limited London
Text filmset in Great Britain by Filmtype Services Ltd, Scarborough and
printed offset in Switzerland by Druckerei Winterthur AG
Illustrations reproduced in West Germany by
Klischee-Werkstätten der Industriedienst
GmbH & Co, Wiesbaden
Bound in Holland by Van Rijmenam n.v., The Hague
ISBN 0 500 25023 5

Contents

Foreword

The English translation of my book on Byzantine civilization is not just a reproduction of the German second edition which came out in 1959. It goes further than the German edition in that it makes use of illustrations on a scale not possible in the original. The 169 illustrations in the English edition serve a real function for they have been selected in order to provide a historical comment on Byzantine life in all its varied aspects. The analysis of the subject-matter of these illustrations given in the text demonstrates the extent to which they can be used as original sources providing evidence on the nature of Byzantine civilization.

Finally I should like to express my warm thanks to the publishers for making it possible to produce a translation with such a wide range of illustrations and for taking so much trouble in tracking down comparatively inaccessible material. I am equally grateful to those who gave me similar assistance with my first German edition. I also acknowledge with gratitude the institutes and scholars who have provided plates for the English edition.

HANS–WILHELM HAUSSIG
April 1970

Πάντα χωρεῖ καὶ οὐδὲν μένει
HERACLITUS

Introduction:
The phenomenon of Byzantine civilization

This book tells the story of a civilization. A civilization lives and dies as does a human being, and for it, too, death does not mean simply the end of everything, dust unto dust, vanishing without trace, bequeathing no legacy. Man lives on in his achievements. And so does a civilization, for its creations through the centuries survive as a spiritual heritage whose influence passes from generation to generation. Different civilizations are connected each with the other, like links in a chain. And so Byzantine civilization is one of the links in that very chain to which our present-day civilization belongs.

Many will ask, 'What has Byzantine civilization got to do with our present-day world? How can there be any connection between us?' To question thus is to be unaware of the debt which we owe to Byzantium. What would western art be without the figure of the Saviour dying on the Cross, his features showing the deep suffering which alone can give his face that human expression which moves us all so deeply? Who would wish to renounce the figure of the Madonna bending over her Child in all her tender motherhood? Those were gifts to the West made by Byzantium during its thousand years of life. It might be argued in reply that it was only the West which was able to give the representation of the Saviour and the Mother of God that final perfect form which is found in the figures of Gothic and renaissance art. None would deny this. But this does not give us the right to pass over Byzantine prototypes in silence. What kind of a son would deny his mother?

What would western music be without the organ which was first brought to the Frankish king in the eighth century by Byzantine ambassadors? But here many would reply that it was only the West which perfected this instrument. True enough: the perfection of the organ was the work of the West. But in paying tribute to those who develop an invention none would wish to forget the original creator.

What would the West be without an instrument with which to measure time? The clock, that is, the water-clock, was also a Byzantine gift to the West. And our mechanical clock is only the old Byzantine instrument developed and perfected.

Byzantium lived on in the West, just as something of the Rome of Cicero and Virgil survived in Byzantium, and the Greece of Phidias and Pericles in Rome. Each handed on to the other something of its very essence.

When a man is standing on the threshold of old age he likes to dwell on the past, but he also looks with anxiety at the ever decreasing span of time still left to him. He sees old age as the precursor of death which must follow swiftly in its wake. And in this respect a civilization may be likened to the human beings which it has formed. When the end of an epoch is in sight, it is not by mere chance that there is a proliferation of oracles, prophetic dreams, astrological predictions and religious visions. When antiquity was in its death throes, prophets and astrologers raised their voices. An enormous amount of so-called apocalyptic literature was produced at this time. The commentaries on the dream of the prophet Daniel and the Revelation of St John come from the days when antiquity was in decline.

Every civilization, like all living organisms, is subject to the laws of growth and decline. Failing powers, the heralds of old age in mankind, are also experienced by great civilizations. But they differ in the manner of their death. When a living being dies, its organs fail and life swiftly departs from its body and soon it is no more than inanimate matter. The end of a civilization is accompanied by many phenomena: some of these belong to the process of disintegration, but some reveal the new emergent forces of life. For it is indeed impossible to pin down the precise moment when a civilization comes to birth or dies. And so late antiquity lived on far into the middle Byzantine period, just as Byzantium itself has survived in the modern world. The transition is defined by no firm line of demarcation. And indeed none of us know where we stand, whether at the end or at the beginning of a civilization.

It is in the nature of all historical writing to attempt to evaluate its own age in the light of the past. We of today cannot tell whether an internal crisis is imminent or whether it is already in process. The path which lies before us has become obscure, and it is understandable if now at this moment we look back at the stretch of road lying behind us. The way which leads from late antiquity to Byzantine civilization, and from thence to the renaissance, is part of the road along which we have travelled. To understand the present it is first of all necessary to know about the past.

The intellectual heritage of humanism which our fathers and forefathers grew up with is today no longer the formative influence in the thought and work of the greater part of mankind. The industrial revolution which began two centuries ago has penetrated during the last few decades into the class now taking the lead in intellectual matters. The human being, the be-all and end-all of antiquity and the humanism which grew out of it, is now increasingly losing his former dominating position. This dehumanization, or anti-humanist attitude, in things of the mind finds its strongest expression in representational art. In the eyes of some of us, living nature, as well as mankind, is no longer represented in painting or sculpture in its long accustomed form. The gases in the retort, the various forms of crystal into which inorganic matter can be split, the spectrums which certain given conditions can produce from metal or mineral—today these are for many the manifestations of a far more genuine reality. It is in forms of this kind that man seeks his objective, representing it as the essence of a new image of the world. The material begins to influence art and to determine the way in which it is expressed. In music too there are developments which ignore accepted and traditional modes of expression. The world of sound is changing. The time is not far distant when the discords of today will be regarded as perfect harmony. Change of this kind is affecting every aspect of our civilization. But the small group of pioneers using these new and so far unknown modes of expression are faced by the vast masses who are still hesitant. Mankind is uncertain. Can the inclination towards the material, those pictures in abstract form, grip the beholder in the same way as did those old creations fashioned after the actual reality? And herein lies a dichotomy like that which characterized Byzantine civilization during the early centuries of its existence, though under another guise. For the Byzantines, pictures, though in a much more religious sense, were the vehicles of grace and the transmitters of the energies of the Godhead. In many ways the crisis of mankind in Byzantium was very like that of our own day. The rise of a small group of extremists, coming from the periphery of the Empire in the form of the monastic movement, within a few decades had undermined the old way of life and the old civilization, but the attitude of their contemporaries towards them differed very little from that of the present day towards our changing values and new forces. When the monks left the desert and became bishops and patriarchs

14

in the cities some of their contemporaries thought that the end of the civilization of antiquity was at hand. Subsequent developments proved them right. Monks took over university chairs, ecclesiastical workshops, artists' ateliers. Thus a new civilization came into being. This was incomprehensible to the older generation brought up in the tradition of classical antiquity, men who had been to the universities where the spiritual heritage of the classical world was still being handed down. Homer remained their literary ideal and in representational art they looked back to the Greek masterpieces of the fifth and sixth centuries B.C. Their musical taste had been formed by the voluptuous polyphony of the composers of western Asia Minor. The pictures created for the churches by monastic artists meant nothing at all to them. Indeed they regarded these as a distorted representation of human beings in a primitive form characteristic of barbarians from beyond the frontiers. And their musical susceptibilities were offended by the unison singing without instrumental accompaniment which was now used in the church services.

Against all this background of contemporary opposition and discord Byzantine civilization made its entry into the world of late antiquity. The intrusion of this new development was regarded as something revolutionary and destructive. And yet this new world, which seemed at first so strange, was later to be regarded as the well-established way of life which guaranteed the security of mankind.

It is not easy to determine the nature of Byzantine civilization. Like the West and Islam, the other medieval civilizations which grew up in what had once been the *imperium romanum*, Byzantium lived to some extent under the shadow of late antiquity, but it was also preparing for a new age. It is difficult to draw the line here and to grasp what was indeed peculiar to its own particular way of life. The creations of its representational art were to begin with only crude compositions made up of a medley of motifs taken from the works of late antiquity. They still lacked finish. It was only later that assimilation was gradually achieved. Thus Byzantine civilization was to a great extent overshadowed by that of late antiquity, and yet at the same time it did in the end develop its own modes of expression. When these circumstances are borne in mind, it is clear that the criterion for this civilization must be different from that applied to the modern world whose development has been determined by different conditions.

Byzantine civilization had much in common with the West. Literary works in the western world in the middle ages were also more or less artistic mosaics consisting of sentences or phrases taken from the writings of Latin prose or poetry from the classical Roman period. The origin of these individual mosaic fragments was clearly recognizable. But this technique in no sense deprives the world chronicle of John Zonaras, or the *Alexiad* of Anna Comnena, of the high place assigned to it in the field of Byzantine literature, any more than a similar method detracts from the value of Otto of Freising's world chronicle or Einhard's *Life of Charles the Great*.

The characteristics of the literature of this period are also present in representational art. Here the same mosaic-like technique is found. Parts of an older work, usually belonging to late antiquity, were selected and combined with borrowings from other works of the same period to produce something new. This method was used in mosaic and fresco as well as in miniatures and small-scale sculpture.

But this is no answer as to the nature of the peculiarly individual quality of Byzantine civilization. What is it that distinguishes Byzantine civilization from that of the West, of antiquity, of the modern world? Here a comparison can be made with the succession of mankind generation after generation. The personality of each human being is largely determined by the qualities handed down to him by his fathers and forefathers and it is from these that his own individual character is developed. It is the same with a civilization. The parents of Byzantine civilization were the two formative influences of late antiquity, the Greek and the oriental. Byzantium drew on Greek, Egyptian and Syrian sources and at the same time on Iranian-Islamic and Mesopotamian-Islamic. The result of the fusion of these various cultural influences was Byzantine civilization. Even in its last and most vigorous expression it still clearly showed its debt to outside civilizations.

In the modern conception of historical development Byzantine civilization has only a very small place. Such an assessment seems to ignore its very considerable contribution to the gradual development and advancement of western civilization. Today this might be put down to carelessness or ignorance but it was originally due to a very conscious sense of resentment. This is true not only of more recent historiography but of the medieval world chronicles which did in fact colour our historical views on late antiquity and the early middle ages. The authors of the world chronicles considered that their own western Empire was the legitimate successor of the *imperium romanum* while the 'heretical' East Roman, or Byzantine, Empire was deliberately omitted from any historical consideration. This is why there was scarcely any mention of the significance of the long drawn out defensive Byzantine struggle against Islam. And then the western historians of the day completely ignored the importance of the Byzantine blockade of Arab merchandise to which the Arab states at once retaliated by attempting to prevent the delivery of Byzantine goods to western ports. Yet that blockade created conditions which stimulated the rise and growth of the West's own economy. It forced the West gradually to outstrip Byzantine culture and techniques, and it prepared the way for the development of an independent western culture. As a result of the Byzantine blockade and the Arab counter-measures only very limited quantities of goods from Byzantium and the East reached the West and this created favourable conditions for the growth of cities which were to become the centres of an independent industrial development. Western urban industries, which had hitherto supplied goods only for modest daily needs, were now freed from competition so that they could develop and gradually meet the demands created by the blockade, and in many areas they eventually supplanted the Byzantine and oriental merchants. Thus on the basis of a new urban economy conditions favourable to the development of western civilization were created, for the *polis* has always been the essential factor in the cultural evolution of a people.

For us today Byzantine civilization is a phenomenon like a celestial body in the cosmos which disappeared millions of years ago and yet whose light still continues to reach us. Byzantium was destroyed more than half a millennium ago. But the reflection of its civilization can still be traced in our day and even if unnoticed by most is still with us in many a guise and form.

1 San Vitale, Ravenna

2 *The Ascension;* 12th-century
miniature

3 Tekfur Saray, Istanbul

4 Mosaic depicting palace of
Theodoric the Ostrogoth;
Apollinare Nuovo,
Ravenna

5, 6 Frescoes of the Brumalia and country life; Qusayr Amrah, Jordan. (See pls. 58, 59, 79.)

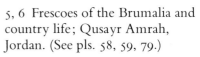

7 Charioteer in the Hippodrome; silk textile of late 8th-9th century

8 Session of a church council; 9th-century miniature

9 Pilate; early 6th-century miniature

10 Emperor Basil II as *triumphator*; miniature from early 11th-century Psalter

11 *The Last Judgment*; mosaic, Torcello cathedral

PART ONE

Factors leading to the emergence of Byzantine civilization

The collapse of the West

The shortcomings of private capital

The *imperium romanum* met its first crisis at the moment when Italy lost its position as a major economic power. In the days of the earlier Emperors Italy was not only the political but also the cultural centre of the great Roman Empire. There industry and agriculture flourished side by side and, unhampered by competitors, found markets not only in subject territories like Gaul and Africa but also beyond the frontiers of the Empire in free Germany and in the Far East or in India. Different goods were exported to different regions. In India there was a market only for luxury goods and valuable industrial products. Germany and Gaul however absorbed agricultural produce as well as industrial goods. The chief exports to Gaul and Germany were wine, wheat and olive oil.

Italian industry was concentrated in the smaller and medium-sized towns. There industry was carried on by families of craftsmen whose work by reason of its quality achieved almost a monopoly in world markets. Thus Arezzo enjoyed a world-wide reputation for the manufacture of special ceramic ware. The *terra sigillata* ware which was made there was as much coveted in India as it was on the German market. The manufacture of artistic glasses and oil-lamps was in similar case; here it was Aquileia that acquired a monopoly in the West. Towns in Campania were noted for the manufacture of delicately worked table silver and other metal goods. In Florence there were textiles. These products were made in the medium-sized and small towns of Italy and assured the prosperity of the peninsula. Archaeological finds in Germany, Afghanistan and India witness to the vast extent of this trade in Italian manufactured goods; similar finds in the north in Scandinavia and the Baltic islands, and in the east as far as the Vistula and Passarge, give a picture of the range of the export trade of the Italian peninsula. *Terra sigillata* from Arezzo reached the east coast of India. Fine thread glass ware from Aquileia found its way to Korea and Japan, and in north-west India and the north-east of Afghanistan the import of the work of Italian craftsmen was responsible for introducing Roman styles into Bactrian-Indian art.

This peak in Italian agricultural and industrial development was followed from the mid-second century onwards by a clearly recognizable recession which gradually affected every field of economic activity. The first symptoms point to the effect of an all too liberal economic policy on the part of the Roman imperial government.

The economic monopoly of the Italian peninsula in Europe and North Africa was gradually broken by the opening up of the as yet undeveloped provinces of the Roman Empire, at the instigation of private entrepreneurs. This began with Roman speculators getting olive trees planted in large quantities in Gaul and Africa. Not a few Italian landowners bought property in the Rhone valley in Gaul or in the recently pacified areas of the Roman province of Africa (present-day Tunisia and Algeria), in order to introduce the culture of the olive tree there. They thought to increase profits derived from the culture in Italy, profits that were considerably diminished by freight costs, by now laying out plantations in the very areas to which the exports were sent. The same sort of thing happened with the wine trade. The consequence was that after a time the Italian peninsula saw itself faced by steadily increasing home production in North Africa and Gaul. The result was a decrease in Italian production and therefore also a decline in prosperity.

This setback, which hit in the first instance Italy's agricultural exports, also affected the peninsula's industrial exports. Even though the pottery produced in the ceramic works of the Rhine valley was not equal in quality to genuine *terra sigillata* ware, yet the cheapness of these products virtually succeeded in driving the fine Italian pottery off the German market. The monopoly of the city of Aquileia in supplying Gaul and Germany with glassware was seriously affected by the glass-works newly established in areas which had formerly been markets for exports. Thus glass-works at Cologne by degrees met German needs and even found openings as far afield as Scandinavia, thereby depriving the glass industry of Aquileia of an important export market. The new industries grew out of the workshops of the so-called *cannabae,* the barrack suburbs of the legionaries' camps. Originally they supplied only the needs of the legionaries, but soon, with the encouragement of export entrepreneurs, they switched to exporting to the independent areas of Germany.

By reason of this development the trade-routes leading from Italy to the north lost much of their economic importance. Only the road that went via Carnuntum east of Vienna, up the river March and then westwards through Bohemia to Central Germany, or the trade-route that swerved east through Silesia to the Samland, maintained their former trading status on account of the import of amber to the Mediterranean lands. With the development of new industries the route down the Rhine to Vectio (Wechten near Utrecht) now gained ever-increasing importance. It was via Vectio that Frisian merchants supplied not only the Scandinavian market but also, from the estuaries along the North Sea coast, the trading centres in northern and eastern Germany.

The loss of economic superiority was however only one of the causes that precipitated the great crisis in the *imperium romanum.* A far heavier blow was dealt by the migration of Germanic tribes; even in its first phase, the descent on Italy of the Marcomanni, it had already touched off the development which in the end deprived Italy of economic and cultural as well as political supremacy within the *imperium romanum.* The great turning point came with the Marcomanni wars of A.D. 166 and 183. Through the inroads of the Marcomanni into northern Italy the fertile plain of the Po was laid waste. It was decades before the fruit trees and olives that had been hewn down or the vines that had been destroyed could be replaced. But a more serious loss which could not be made good came with the destruction of rural life in northern Italy, when the imperial government decided to convert this important agricultural region into a frontier district with military defences. It was not merely that the towns of northern Italy, which had previously taken in large areas of the plain of the Po, hastened to demolish the peripheral parts of the town and to encircle the central city core with walls and fortifications. The decisive factor was the settlement of soldiers detailed to defend the area. This settlement scheme was mainly at the expense of the large estates which were split up into small lots for the military settlers, most of them of Germanic stock.

The predominance of foreign troops

The new military settlers, known as 'laeten' (Frisian *led*) or 'gentiles', now determined the lines of agricultural development in North Italy. This agrarian district, which had previously been an area of large estates under intensive cultivation by means of slave labour aiming at large crop yields, was now turned into a land of tenants and small farmers. The new settlers, accustomed as they were to extensive farming, failed to till the soil efficiently; their helpers were mostly the members of their own families. The consequences were inevitable. The yield of the land decreased. There was no more question of exporting. The surplus yield was so small that it was no longer adequate to meet even the needs of the local towns. Areas formerly known for highly developed specialized farming, such as the hinterland of Ravenna, famous for its extensive asparagus beds, now declined under the hands of the new Marcomannian or Sarmatian settlers. North Italy, which a few decades earlier was exporting agricultural produce, now had to import grain and oil from neighbouring countries in order to supply its own needs.

Prices for agricultural products therefore rose and the standard of living declined. Large cities, such as Rome, Ravenna or Milan, were less hit than the small and medium-sized country towns. This reacted on the various industries located in the smaller towns. Important concerns were transferred to the eastern regions of the Empire. Well equipped workshops and smaller industrial enterprises closed down because the constant deterioration in conditions made the continued running of the workshops uneconomic. Master-craftsmen, journeymen and labourers flocked into the cities where imports from over-seas, from Sicily, Africa and Egypt, still kept alive a strongly industrialized urban economy. A further, not inconsiderable number of these craftsmen elected to go east, to Syria and Egypt. A visible result of this movement of craftsmen was the rapid appearance on Syrian glassware or Egyptian metal goods and textiles, of shapes and patterns which had previously been characteristic of the West.

As trade and industry in the small and moderate sized towns of Italy withered away, so capitalists too lost their natural field of economic activity. Hence it soon happened that men of large means either turned their backs on the Italian peninsula and invested their capital in the new industries beginning to flourish in the East, or if they stayed in Italy sought to safeguard their wealth, threatened by the menacing spectre of general devaluation in the Roman Empire, by land purchase. These capitalists bought up small, comparatively unproductive farms and left the previous owners of the land as tenants of the property; in many cases these were the descendants of soldiers who had received the land as part of the policy of military settlement. In the end this development saw the soil of Italy in the possession of a few large property owners with innumerable tenants.

The recession in agrarian and urban economy in Italy was accompanied by a reduction in the circulation of money in the country. This meant further difficulties for the financial administration. The imperial government therefore handed over the collection of taxes (*capitatio*) in a large part of Italy not only to autonomous civic administrations but also to the new large property owners. In the long run this meant a limitation of the power of the state in favour of the predominance of a single class. Once in possession of the privilege of levying taxes, the important land owners could proceed to build up the farming districts into virtually independent rural units with their own authority based on armed force. This armed force was exercised with the help of mercenaries recruited for the purpose (*bucellarii*) and in the end was bound to lead to the overthrow of the authority of the central administration. Every special imperial tax-levy (*indictio*) became a trial of strength with the large property owners. Often enough the announcement of a new *indictio* was the occasion of a levy by the landed magnates. So in the West, in contrast to the East, considerable limits were set to imperial absolutism (*dominatio*). Here the Emperor had lost most of his authority even before he resigned it of his own free will to a co-Emperor.

28

Foreign workers in city and countryside

Alongside the downward trend in the economic sphere Italy's loss of leadership within the *imperium romanum* was clearly indicated by the decline of Roman culture. The disintegration of Roman culture, rooted and grounded in Italy, began even before the economic regression. In this case the causes lay for the most part in the great shifts of population which affected Italian cities, especially at the beginning of the imperial era. The economic boom and the growth of industry had led at that time to a shortage of labour. It was soon evident that foreign labour would have to be brought in if industry in the Italian peninsula was to be extended and maintained. To overcome this labour shortage artisans were recruited from the industrial enterprises of the East and numbers of slaves were imported. The first of these expedients was used particularly when it was a question of procuring highly qualified craftsmen. So for example Syrian glass blowers were taken in by the glass industry of Aquileia and artisans from Alexandria by the workshops of Campania making table silver. This influx of people of various nationalities gradually transformed the population of the cities. It is therefore no chance that even in the early days of the Empire the surviving funeral inscriptions of slaves and freedmen provide more examples of Greek than of Latin names. This does not constitute proof that the majority of the slaves imported into Italy were of Greek nationality. The language of trade, including the slave trade, was Greek. Slaves from Syria, Asia Minor, Egypt or the Roman province of Africa were given Greek names regardless of their country of origin. Greek served as a common language for the slaves as well as for the slave traders. It is the Greek of the Gospels, the *koine* of the Mediterranean world. The spread of the Greek language in central Italy proves how great the number of the immigrants into Italy must have been. Not only were the names of slaves and freedmen Greek, but Greek was also the language of a wider circle. Thus the leaders of the Christian Church in Rome wrote in Greek at this time. Even Hippolytus of Rome used Greek in his writings in the middle of the third century. As late as this Greek was the language of the Christian liturgy and also of the Roman Christian world, which at that time was largely made up of slaves and freedmen.

From year to year the proportion of slaves of eastern extraction and their descendants in the population of the Italian cities increased. In the process of integration necessitated by the continuing growth of the foreign element the national character of the old Roman population was fused into a Latino-Greek civilization. This development was not confined to the cities alone. The great landed estates made use of the same expedients as the factories of the large cities. They too obtained trained slave labour from the East. Such workers were well versed in more advanced agricultural methods than those commonly used in Italy. They were entrusted with the care of fruit trees and useful plants previously unknown to Italian agriculture. The mounting proportion of these slaves in the population of the Italian countryside encroached more and more on the Romano-Italian element, so that town and country were almost equally affected by a development which ended by changing the old Italian and the old Roman population into an agricultural and industrial proletariat of uncertain ancestry.

Decline of the Roman ruling class

Events in countryside and town did not leave untouched even the Roman ruling class. The old Roman nobility, the members of the senatorial families, had been liquidated in the treason trials of the Emperors Tiberius and Domitian. The new ruling class came from the officer corps of the army. Military leaders rising from the army or the guard troops to the position of Emperor brought into the senate their most trustworthy and most capable officers. In a Roman senate recruited from army officers Romans gradually became rarer and rarer, since by no means only Italians served in the Roman army but men of the most diverse nationalities. Even the Emperors were no longer drawn from the Italian nobility but were by origin of Berber, Arab and Illyrian race. An Emperor like Septimius Severus, a Berber, spoke Latin extremely badly; his sister, who did not understand this language at all, used her native Berber dialect even in Rome. The Roman art of portraiture, with its characteristically keen observation of nature, preserved for posterity in marble the physical features of this new ruling class. These Roman portrait heads bear witness that neither among the new Emperors nor among their generals were to be found any Italians.

As a result of all these changes in the ruling class and in the urban and country population there came into being a general Latin civilization no longer closely lined with the Italian people. Latin, like Greek some centuries earlier, became the language of a cultural community which embraced alike Italians and Illyrians, Gauls, Iberians and Berbers. Latin was the language of command in the army, the language of law, the language of the Emperor. It was the rivet which held the Empire together.

This transition to a Latin civilization that was no longer sustained by Italians was first accomplished on the periphery of the *imperium romanum*. Here, in provinces such as Gaul and North Africa, the adoption of Latin civilization meant the beginning of a new cultural era, but for the Italian peninsula it was a period of decline, of the loss of its own individuality in literature and in art. In the Italian peninsula the third century is characterized by the almost complete eclipse of higher literary activity. Of writings surviving from this period, the little that was written in Italy, such as the work of Solinus (about 250) and of Censorinus (238), is dry, pedantic and dependent on models which were often misunderstood and inaccurately reproduced. Art was dominated by the bad taste of the ruling class which was still semi-barbarian. The rooms in the villas of the Emperor (Piazza Armerina in Sicily) and of the senatorial ruling class were decorated with mosaics representing scenes from the Circus in which the killing of men by animals was portrayed in a manner bordering on the intolerable. The old Roman traditions of architecture were abandoned in favour of foreign styles developed in Syria. Thus the palace of Diocletian in Spalato (Split) has close affinities with the carved stone architecture of Syria. Even late Roman portrait sculpture, which with its keen observation of nature appears to be in the old Roman tradition, reveals in such details as the treatment of the hair and the portrayal of the eyes the influence of eastern, and particularly Syrian, portraiture.

The rise of the East

2

The centre of economic and military life shifts to the East

In the West the crisis of the *imperium romanum* was triggered off by the economic and cultural decline in the Italian peninsula. But this was only one of the determining factors giving rise to the emergence of Byzantine civilization. An even more powerful factor was the shifting of the cultural, economic and military centre of gravity from Italy to Asia Minor and the provinces on the lower Danube. This meant that the Italian peninsula with its capital Rome lost the vital position which it had so far held as the very core and centre of the Empire. North Italy was now on the periphery of the Empire, as the imperial centre of gravity shifted more and more towards the straits of the Bosphorus and the Hellespont.

This development too was primarily dictated by military needs. The Persian Sassanids were driving westwards (from 225 onwards) and as well as this the main thrust of the migratory Germanic tribes was aimed at the provinces on the lower Danube. The new Persian dynasty of the Sassanids committed itself to the restoration of the old Achaemenid Empire and proclaimed the re-conquest of Asia Minor and the control of the Bosphorus as its political goal. The western campaigns of the first Sassanid kings, in particular Shapur I, clearly demonstrated that this claim was more than a vague theoretical aim and was to be implemented by military conquest. Such a development turned Asia Minor into a vital military area. A large part of the army now had to be transferred to this region. But there was also a second strategic centre, located on the other side of the straits, in the area corresponding approximately to modern Bulgaria and Turkey. This was due to the attacks by Germanic tribes on the lower Danube frontier, attacks which occurred at almost exactly the same time as the Persian advance.

In the East there were then two fronts which had to be held at all costs: the European front along the lower Danube, where the river forms the boundary between present-day Bulgaria and Rumania, and then the battle-front in Asia. The frontier under attack here was that part of Syria where the Euphrates and the Mediterranean are only 125 miles (200 km.) apart.

The Persian expansion took the West by surprise and was occasioned by a change in the political leadership of that country. But, on the contrary, the Germanic advance into Bessarabia, Rumania and then finally into the territory south of the Danube as well, certainly came as no surprise to leading statesmen in the *imperium romanum*. The new objective and route of the Germanic migration towards the south-east had been recognized right from the beginning with the easing of pressure on the Rhine frontier and the increase of acts of aggression on the upper Danube in the sector between the present-day towns of Bratislava and Gran. Although the attacks of the Marcomanni and the Quadi on North Italy showed up the weakness of the Roman frontier defences in this area, yet at the same time they underlined the new objective of this Germanic migration. Only a small part of the migratory tribes broke through into North Italy then: the main body pushed further on beyond the Carpathians towards the south-east. Iranian tribes, such as the Jazygi and Sarmatians, were displaced by them and were therefore diverted into Roman territory, leaving the Roman government in no doubt as to the course which the migration was likely to take.

As a result of this, military units were moved in ever increasing numbers from the frontier zone on the Rhine to the lower Danube, as is shown by surviving inscriptions. Moreover, the two existing roads in the Balkan peninsula, the Via Egnatia, connecting the Adriatic port of Dyrrachium (Durazzo) and Thessalonica on the Aegean, and the military road from Byzantium (Istanbul) to Singidunum (Belgrade), were linked by means of secondary and transverse roads into a strategic network of communications for the deploying of troops. With the help of this network of roads it was possible to carry out troop movements to strategic points from any direction in the shortest possible time and thus successfully to counter surprise attacks. The most important road from this point of view was that between Byzantium and Singidunum, with intermediate posts at places like Viminacium, Naissus (Niš), Serdica (Sofia), Philippopolis (Plovdiv), Hadrianopolis (Adrianople), and Perinthus (Eregli) on the Sea of Marmora. Even today it is this road which is largely followed, with only minor deviations, by the rail track along which the Orient Express travels. This road, together with the Via Egnatia, was the backbone of the later Byzantine military frontier in Europe.

In Asia Minor too the change in the military centre of gravity led to the construction of a number of roads of vital strategic importance. For reasons of defence the area between the upper Euphrates and the Mediterranean required new roads so that troops from western Asia Minor could be moved to this danger zone in the shortest possible time. The old network of the roads from the Persian–Achaemenid period had provided adequate communications between Susiana, which had been the centre of Persian power, and the straits and the west coast of Asia Minor; but it was not good enough for defence purposes in the threatened territory between the upper Euphrates and the Mediterranean. The Roman Emperors had therefore to create a new system of communications, with a road running across the salt steppe of Tus Tshölu and with transverse link-roads to give more rapid access to the passes over the Taurus into Cilicia. This road linking Byzantium with Antioch via Anatolia formed from then on the most important route for troop movements to the East. Other roads, like that along the south coast of Asia Minor, made troop movements possible in case of naval attack. It was with the same objective that the north coast of Asia Minor was also opened up at that time by a road system. Here too the aim was to be independent of the fleet, so that an enemy in the Caucasus could be engaged at any time by troops sent by a land route. Thus it would be possible to counter any Persian attack in this area.

It is not however only the transfer of troops and the building of a network of roads which provide evidence for the shift of the centre of military gravity to the lower Danube and Asia Minor. Closely associated with these measures is the creation of an industry working to supply military needs, as well as the opening up of new agricultural areas to provision the troops. In the development of this armaments industry in Asia Minor a distinction must be made between enterprises which were set up with the express object of supplying the troops and the not inconsiderable group of factories whose production was diverted to military needs. The first group consisted mainly of arms factories erected at that time which owed their existence to the presence of considerable iron ore deposits in Asia Minor. Thus crude ore for the arms factories of Nicomedia came from the mines of Mount Olympus, while the supply of iron ore for a similar factory in Caesarea in Cappadocia was derived from the mines in the Anti-Taurus range.

The Roman armaments factories set up in Asia Minor were so organized that no one establishment manufactured every type of weapon. Hence the factories of Nico-

32

media were confined to the production of shields and swords. In Sardis and Caesarea in Cappadocia only armour was manufactured. In Irenopolis in Cilicia nothing was undertaken but the production of spears and lances. The distribution over a wide area of the works where the various types of weapons were manufactured was certainly not a matter of chance. Perhaps the intention was to ensure that enemy occupation of some of these factories and transportation of the specialist craftsmen would still not put the foe in a position where he could control the whole Roman armament system to his own advantage. It is probable that all Roman arms factories in Asia Minor were part of a definite armaments programme supervised and co-ordinated by a central board in the capital.

The second group of military factories included existing textile industries on the west coast of Asia Minor and in Cilicia. In this case production was switched to meet the army's requirements. These factories now manufactured items of soldiers' uniform such as cloaks and headgear, but they also turned out blankets and tents for the equipment of the army. As far as the wool of sheep and goats was concerned, the textile industry of Asia Minor did not depend on imports. Its raw materials were provided by the great flocks of the Anatolian uplands, which at the same time could contribute in part towards the provisioning of the army by providing sheep for slaughter. The troops were also catered for by the products of countless dried fish establishments on the coast. It was only grain that had to be imported, and this came from Thrace and the provinces on the lower Danube.

From the defence of the straits to the creation of a new capital

Asia Minor then, with the Danubian provinces of the Roman Empire, formed a self-sufficient economic unit which never had to contend with difficulties of supply, even when imports from other parts of the Empire, such as Egypt, were cut off. The fact that Syria and the territory on the lower Danube were both vital military areas meant that Asia Minor and the European territory round the straits always received preferential treatment, both in economic and military matters, in the scheme of imperial defence. The close economic and military interdependence of these two parts of the Empire thus provided the basis later on for the foundation of the Byzantine state. Even at this period the southern exit of the Bosphorus must have commended itself as the obvious place from which to govern the two parts of the Empire.

But the creation of a great fortified city on the Bosphorus was not only suggested by its position commanding one of the most important routes between Europe and Asia. The need to defend access through the Bosphorus to the Mediterranean area was a further reason for the establishment of a strong and sure centre of control on this sea route. As early as 220, Germanic tribes had appeared in south Russia and their efforts to penetrate into the Roman Empire were not confined only to the land route. A large fleet of Goths had thrust forward through the Bosphorus into the Sea of Marmora and had forced their way into the Aegean. The large industrial towns on the west coast of Asia Minor and the places on the east coast of Greece were all of them without defences and could therefore be plundered by the Germans at will and some of them were destroyed. These strong Gothic war-fleets, the forerunners of the Varangian raiders, could only be countered by the construction of a strongly fortified naval base on the straits and a fleet ready for immediate action. So from the particular military problem of preventing the Gothic fleet from breaking through into the Sea of Marmora and the Aegean there emerged the preparations for the foundation of Constantinople, later to become the capital of the Byzantine Empire. Almost a century before the founding of Constantinople a beginning had already been made in the city area of the old Dorian settlement, Byzantium, with the establishment of fortifications, barracks and naval bases, all of which did much to further the later development of Constantinople into a metropolitan city.

The growing military importance of the straits of the Bosphorus as a connecting link between the two centres of gravity of imperial defence, that is, the provinces on the lower Danube and the area between the upper Euphrates and the Mediterranean, made it essential to concentrate in the straits area a number of élite troops who could be used either on the Danube or in Syria as military needs dictated. Previous political experience of the imperial government had shown that a concentration of picked troops far from the capital at Rome meant the risk of a revolt against an Emperor ruling in far-off Italy. It was essential that the Emperor should be where his strongest and best armies were stationed. This obviously implied the transference of the imperial residence, and with it political and military government, to the Bosphorus area. But on the other hand, in view of the worsening military situation on the western frontiers, a prolonged absence of the Emperor from Italy was equally undesirable. The solution was therefore not the transference of political and military government of the Empire to a city on the straits but the division of the imperial power. And so, beginning with the shift of the centre of military defence and continuing with the building of a new capital city, there came about the development which was to lead to the division of the Empire into two, followed by the rise of the Byzantine state.

The birth of the Christian imperium

3

The heritage of illegality: individual Christian developments

The decline of Italy and the shifting of the centre of political and military gravity to the region round the straits had prepared the way for the Byzantine Empire, but Byzantine civilization had not yet come into being. The beginnings of the development of this civilization were only possible with the elevation of Christianity to the position of the state religion. Without this close relationship between the Roman state and Christianity, Byzantine civilization would have been inconceivable. The Emperor Constantine may indeed have acted more from reasons of state than as the representative of a religious movement. Still, realizing the portentous nature of his decision which went far beyond political day to day events, he only completed the foundation of the capital on the Bosphorus after he had proclaimed Christianity a permitted religion. The new capital was to mark the beginning of a new epoch. It was similar to the action of Peter the Great when he left Moscow and founded St Petersburg as the capital of a new Russia.

It was not without reason that soon after its foundation the East Romans called the capital founded by Constantine Nea Roma, New Rome. Here there was a reference to II Corinthians 5, 17: 'The old things are passed away; behold, they are become new.' Three hundred years later Andrew of Caesarea in Cappadocia clearly expressed this in his commentary on the Apocalypse. For him the Old Rome was the apocalyptic kingdom, the great Babylon, and after its downfall the rule of 'the Christ-loving Emperor' was established in the New Rome.

Before it became a permitted religion, Christianity was developing along different lines in the various provinces of the Roman Empire. These differences reflect the extent to which Christianity had assimilated existing popular religions. Towards the end of the third century, at a time when there was no thought of recognition by the state, it was possible to speak of Anatolian, Syrian, Egyptian and Roman Christianity. From the outset these branches of Christianity were distinguished by linguistic differences; for instance, the beginnings of a Christian Syriac literature appeared in the middle of the second century A.D. and the first Coptic (Egyptian) translation of the Bible belonged to the end of the same century. But they were far more distinguished by the character of the liturgical service, the type of religious cult and the formulation of the creed.

As well as these individual developments in various provinces, from the second half of the second century onwards there was a movement which attempted to eliminate such differences within Christianity and to work for the unity of the Christian Church. Its adherents were drawn from the circles of the philosophers and sophists, that is, from the still surviving Graeco-Roman paganism. The foundation of a Christian theological school in Alexandria gave this movement its first real intellectual centre and this was followed in the third century by the establishment of a Christian academy at Caesarea in Palestine. The new movement was characterized by vigorous philological research into the sources of the Christian religion, that is, the Gospels and the Old Testament, and by its efforts to establish authoritative directives for the understanding and exegesis of the divine Word by providing an accurate commentary on the Holy Scriptures. A few decades later Christian schools of this kind were set up in all the important cities in the Roman Empire as well as in Alexandria and Caesarea. Thus the old city of Edessa in Mesopotamia became the seat of a famous Christian school of learning. In many respects these Christian theological centres were not in agreement on matters of the exegesis of the Holy Scriptures. These contrasts were heightened by regional differences in local religious cults arising from the assimilation of the popular religions into Christianity. Even the theological doctrines of the academies, purged as they were by Hellenistic philosophy, showed traces of these popular religions.

But a more potent attack on Christian unity than these individual developments was the threat of the new religious movements which brought the Church face to face with the danger of schism. The new religious movements were to some extent indebted to Christianity. This is very true of the Manichaeans as well as of the Gnostics and Neopythagoreans. Other movements arose in lands beyond the frontiers of the Roman Empire and then established themselves within the Empire, as for instance the cult of Mithras or of the sun god of Emesa. These were all forces calculated to diminish the attraction of Christianity for the masses. Christianity attempted to meet this danger, even though it had itself to some extent adopted certain religious usages from these movements. For instance, eastern Christianity in particular owed to the new religious movements much of its liturgical usage, as well as its religious literature (Pseudo-Dionysius the Areopagite) and certain forms of cult. This is why eastern Christianity is distinguished by many forms different from those of the West. The Christian movements of the East were a far more formative influence in Byzantine culture than those of Roman Latin Christianity. Any analysis of the forces conditioning Byzantine civilization must necessarily take into account those elements in eastern Christianity which originally lay outside the Christian religion.

The growth of the cult of icons shows how strong eastern influence was on the formation of Byzantine culture. Here were the icons, the pictures of Christ, the Mother of God and the saints, becoming almost the sacral centre of the divine services. It is impossible to visualize the life of the Eastern Church without icons, which are amongst the finest creations of Byzantine art, but they originated outside Christianity. Their position in early Christianity was determined by the commandment laid down in the Decalogue (Exodus 20, 4): 'Thou shalt not make unto thee a graven image, nor the likeness of any form that is in heaven above, or that is on the earth beneath, or that is in the water under the earth'. Early Christianity thus repudiated not only the veneration of the pictures of the saints but figural representation in general in the divine cult. This command was not however obeyed, particularly in Egypt and East Syria. This was not only true of Christians. Thus the Jewish faith also had had to make concessions in these regions. In the middle of the third century in Dura-Europos both the Jewish synagogue and the Christian place of worship were richly decorated with pictures. This is why a special iconographic programme for the Holy Scriptures grew up in Syria and Egypt and was used in the cities of Antioch and Alexandria. From now onwards both these iconographies determined the choice and form of representation used in illustrating the Bible. The Antiochene cycle of pictures of the saints came from East Syria where there was strong Iranian influence. The Christians of the Parthian Empire and of the *imperium romanum* had much in common. The cycle of pictures coming from this region shows many characteristics pointing to this Parthian-Syrian border district. In a picture on an arcosolium in the Catacombs of Priscilla the three young men in the fiery furnace are shown in the dress of Persian nobles, and in a picture in the Capella Greca the Magi wear the clothing and headdress of the Persian priests of the Ahura

Mazda religion. Both pictures clearly demonstrate the strength of Syro-Iranian icono-graphic influence on the Christian cult in Italy in the early fourth century. It exercised an even stronger influence over Byzantine culture, which was gradually emerging in the area round the straits of the Bosphorus and Hellespont.

There is no doubt that this oriental influence, emanating from the two sources Alex-andria and Antioch (whence they take their names), determined both form and content of religious representational art in Byzantine culture for almost a millennium. Take for instance the scene showing the resurrection of Lazarus. In one tradition Lazarus was represented in an open coffin bound as a mummy, indicating Egyptian influence. In the Antiochene cycle of pictures Lazarus steps out of a funerary monument raised above the ground and is in the act of descending a ladder. This representation presupposes the wide tower-shaped funerary edifices known in Palmyra and Dura-Europos, and also widely used in Irak. These two traditions are not found side by side until the Palaeologan period, that is, the last phase of Byzantine art.

From the outset these two iconographic cycles also show marked differences in portraying Christ. The bearded Christ with hair reaching to the shoulders was inspired by the external appearance of the Parthian kings in Irak. On the other hand the por-trayal of Christ as a beardless young man comes from Egypt. Its prototype was the god Horus who is shown in Egyptian pictures in the form of a young man.

This eastern influence of Christianity was not however limited to the externals of the divine cult. In Syria and Egypt, where popular religion had largely overgrown the original Christian message of the Gospels, these pictures were soon accompanied by a cult of special veneration towards them. So there grew up in the liturgical services and the divine cult a conception that was not to be found in any of the teaching of the Gospels. The Christians of Egypt and Syria persisted in representing the Son of God and the Persons of the Holy Trinity although this had been condemned by early Chris-tianity and the church fathers, such as Clement of Alexandria (†before 216) and Origen of Caesarea in Palestine (†254). They went further than this. The next step was the cult of venerating these pictures. Plotinus, the founder of neoplatonism, is said to have enunciated the doctrine that by the law of sympathy the image copied by the hand of the artist was bound to the divinity and partook of its divine essence. His pupil, the Syrian Jamblichus, developed this further by a theory of emanation. According to this, the Godhead through a hierarchial scale of manifestations could penetrate the material object and communicate to it something of its own essence. When this was applied to the pictures of the saints and the portrayal of Christ and the Mother of God it meant that these pictures contained in themselves something of the divine power of the person represented. The icons were the vessels of the Godhead and could impart their power to the faithful. In this particular icon veneration, which has characterized eastern Chris-tianity almost up to the present day, the neoplatonic theory of the divinity and old Egyptian popular beliefs meet. It was not by mere chance that Plotinus was an Egyptian. And at once there come to mind the mummy portraits of the Fayum which in tech-nique and form correspond so closely to the Christian symbols. Here too are found the same staring eyes which seem to fix the beholder and refuse to release him from their gaze. The pictures, which, like little windows, penetrate the winding of the mummy bandages at the head of the dead man, were held by the Egyptians to be the seat of Ka, the indestructible substance of the departed.

The new religions, such as neoplatonism and Manichaeism, had taken over almost unaltered the traditions of the popular religions, and herein lay their danger to Chris-tianity. Thus the development of the cult of Mary within the Christian religion was of extraordinary importance. This was true in Egypt where the Isis–Horus relationship had foreshadowed certain aspects of the Christian relationship between the Mother of God and the Son of God. It was equally true in Syria where the widely practised Syrian-Arab solar worship knew of a virgin who gave birth to the sun god. December 25, the Christian festival of Christmas, was in Syria the birthday of the sun god (*heliou genithlion*). On the same December 25 (in Egyptian reckoning the 29 Chojak, the day of Kykellia, the rite in honour of Isis) the Egyptians celebrated the birth of the god Horus, the son of Isis.

Thus the effect of popular religion was not only felt in the Christianity of the East. But, as already emphasized, it was on Byzantine Christianity that eastern influence was strongest. Eastern Christianity was far more affected by the forms of the old oriental solar worship and the cult of a mother of gods than the West.

It was not only that the birthday of the Christian Saviour was placed on the day on which many festivals already celebrated the birth of a great sun god. The representation of Christ was also linked with that of the oriental sun god; this has determined the portrayal of Christ and his apostles up to the present day. Thus Christ is now shown with the circular ring of the sun and in some pictures He is even standing in the chariot of the sun. This solar disc in the form of a nimbus has remained a permanent feature of Christian iconography. The nimbus encircles the head of the figure represented like a round disc. Not only Christianity, but the Roman imperial cult before it, had taken over the solar disc, the symbol of the sun god. Here too this adoption was linked with the acceptance of the usages of the solar cult. Thus in the eleventh and twelfth centuries the *prokypsis* took place on December 25. This was a festival marked by a mime in which the Emperor impersonated the figure of the sun god. This transference of the worship of the sun god to the imperial cult accounts for the fact that Constantine and his family were portrayed with the nimbus. The most recently discovered fresco in the cathedral of Trier also shows the members of the imperial household with the nimbus. With the adoption of the cult of the sun god into the cult of the ruler, the Roman Emperor acted as did the Sassanid kings. They too were represented with the solar disc. On the great rock pictures and on some Persian silver bowls the Sassanid king is given the nimbus, the solar disc. The Emperor's personification of the sun god which is thus expressed was the result of Hellenism. The old Achaemenid kings of the Persians, like the Egyptian Pharaohs, were only represented in an attitude of adoration before the sun god.

With this fusion between the cult of the ruler and the cult of the god derived from Hellenism there also opened a new era in Christianity. The Seleucids and the Roman Emperors had made use of such an era, and in the same way the Christians followed the ruler cult and, like Manichaeism in the Iranian world, created their own era. Both Christianity and Buddhism adopted from the Hellenistic ruler cult the figure of the Greek goddess Nike. In pictures of Roman Emperors and Persian kings a being in the form of the goddess of Victory (Nike) is seen accompanying them, and in the same way the sacred pictures of Buddhists and Christians portray their two religious founders with this same figure. It is the Christian angel which has taken over the form of the Greek goddess Nike.

The influence of Christianity on the formation of an individual Byzantine civilization within the *imperium romanum*, through the acceptance of the religious conceptions and the cults of popular religions, was not the only factor to be taken into account here. The struggle for right belief, orthodoxy, was of the greatest significance in the formation of this civilization. Byzantine Christianity claimed that it alone was in possession of orthodoxy, that is, the true Christian faith. This was of basic importance in determining the unique position of the late Roman state vis-à-vis the various different developments within Christianity. The Roman state sought to preserve the unity of Christianity on the basis of right belief. If the *imperium romanum* failed to achieve this task, it must disintegrate, for it was not a nation, but a cultural entity. Its strongest bond lay in its common religion, and in the period before the acceptance of Christianity this had been obligatory for all imperial subjects alike in the form of the ruler cult. After the acceptance of Christianity the Christian state religion supplied this bond. Every rejection of orthodox Christianity inevitably endangered the well-being of the Empire. Such deviations, which soon developed into separatist movements, were already present in Christianity before it became the state religion.

The acceptance of certain elements from popular religions, which occurred especially in Asia Minor, Syria and Egypt, inevitably led to deviations from orthodox Christian teaching. These deviations had long been developing in various sects, which had built up their own body of theological belief, and it was necessary to bring these into line with the traditional teaching of the Gospels. This task fell to the Christian scholars educated in the pagan philosophical academies and the schools of rhetoric. This explains the close relationship between the terminology and scholarly methods of these new Christian theologians and the Greek philosophical schools. So it came about that, together with the assimilation of elements from the old popular religions, various theological schools and trends began to appear. They were faced with the task of using their philosophical weapons to justify and defend the various individual developments in Christianity in different parts of the Empire. Even before the alliance of Christianity and the *imperium romanum* there had arisen a special Christian movement in Asia Minor having its spiritual centre in Ephesus. This was related to the old popular religion which worshipped Artemis and the Great Mother Cybele, and also the followers of Atargatis. Other Christian trends appeared in Syria. They were based on the theological schools of Antioch and Edessa. In these currents the association of Christianity with the old, but still living, worship of the sun god was evident. Similarly in Egypt, on the basis of its deeply rooted popular religion there developed at the same time a special Christian emphasis which was represented in its own theological school of Alexandria.

The first task of the imperial government after the alliance of the *imperium romanum* with Christianity was to impose some kind of unity in all these various trends. Thus the first three centuries of the union between Christianity and the Roman state were occupied in the attempt to formulate a compromise which would satisfy all parties. This attempt to find some approach acceptable to all which would reconcile the various deviating Christian trends in Asia Minor, Syria and Egypt did however lead to an estrangement between the imperial government and the Latin Roman Christianity of the West. The concessions made by the imperial government were in the long run unacceptable to the West and were the occasion for the separate development of western Christianity with the Roman Pope at its head.

The imperial cult and the Christian faith

The association between Church and state inaugurated by Constantine proved to be not only the basis on which the Christian Church was built but also provided the conditions determining the growth of Byzantine civilization. Thus any consideration of this must therefore begin with the origins of the Christian state Church under Constantine and the opposition of the Roman Emperors to the separatist movements within

Christianity. The alliance between Christianity and the *imperium romanum* inaugurated a new era. This association arose as the result of an internal development which can be characterized as the reorientation of the Empire, and it was the basic problem during the first three centuries after Constantine. To understand correctly future developments, it is necessary to start from the premises which determined the decision of the Roman imperial government.

Before Christianity had been raised to the status of the state religion the most important provinces of the Empire, Asia Minor, Syria and Egypt, with most of their population, had accepted Christianity. The economic, military and cultural reorientation had therefore to be paralleled by similar proceedings in the state religion. The cult of the ruler, the unifying religious bond, that was binding on all subjects of the Empire irrespective of their race, first began this eastward orientation by linking the cult of the sun god with the imperial cult. It was only when Christianity proved itself stonger than solar worship that it was decided to associate Christianity with the imperial cult.

Constantine showed beyond all doubt that even as Christian Emperor he wished the imperial cult to remain a focus and an obligation for all subjects of the Empire. The fundamental principle of continuing the cult of the ruler lay behind all his efforts to create a united Christian imperial Church out of the different Christian communities. It was perhaps because of this feeling for the uniqueness of his position that he had refrained from appointing an imperial bishop who would be the spiritual head of the Christian *imperium*. As object of the imperial cult the Emperor was both spiritual and secular head of the Empire. It was considerations of this kind that laid down the future position of the Emperor. The era by which dates were reckoned was from the regnal year of the Emperor. The burial place of the Emperors used to be connected with a pagan temple, the place of his divine cult, but now it was a Christian church. In Christian times at first almost all Emperors and Empresses were understandably canonized, just as in pagan times they had been deified. This was true of the great Emperor Constantine and his mother Helena (21 May) and then of the Emperor Theodosius (17 January) and his wife Flaccilla (17 January and 14 September), then Theodosius II (29 July) and the Empress Eudoxia (13 August), then the Emperor Marcian (17 February) and the Empress Pulcheria (17 February and 7 August) and finally the Emperor Leo I (20 January). This conception of the position of the Emperor was reflected in the fact that the ruler summoned the Oecumenical Councils, presided over them and promulgated their *acta*.

Constantine, the creator of the imperial Church

In the age of Constantine the performance of the prescribed sacrifices of the imperial cult and loyalty towards the *imperium romanum* were inseparable. He who refused to subscribe to the imperial cult was no loyal subject. He who denied the doctrine pronounced by the Emperor was a traitor to the Empire and had sinned against the person of the Emperor. The question of the unity of the Christian faith and the position of the head of the Christian Church were thus of supreme importance. The Roman papacy's claims to primacy were therefore resisted as a danger to the unity of the Empire and a threat to the position of the Emperor, and similarly there was equal opposition to the attempt to form separatist Christian Churches in the East based on doctrine differing from that of the imperial Church.

This is what lay behind some of the measures to try and create a united Christian Church for the whole Empire. This was the reason for the formulation of a Christian creed binding on all, which would resolve as far as possible the different developments in the various provinces of the Empire and would at the same time create a common Christian cult closely linked with the person of the Emperor.

These measures arose from the effort to maintain the cult of the ruler in as unified a form as possible throughout the Empire. It was this that first determined the architecture of Christian buildings for worship. Before Christianity had been legalized there was no special form for such buildings. Christian services had at that time generally been held in rooms in private houses or in underground chapels like the so-called Pythagorean basilica discovered in 1917 near Porta Maggiore. There were of course the liturgy and hymns, but these had not been much developed by the Christian community, which was understandable in view of their modest premises and the danger of discovery. In its essentials the Greek mass had indeed originated in the period before Christianity became the state religion, but it still lacked the musical parts which were particularly dependent on a choir. The substitution of an ecphonetic system for reading prose was introduced only later. Some parts must have been sung quite early on, such as the supplication 'Kyrie eleison' ('Lord, have mercy') derived from Biblical concepts of the world and from the cult of the sun god. But other parts were simply in spoken prose and not sung. Thus as yet no definite demands on church architecture had been made in connection with the performance of the liturgy. This explains why almost without exception the basilica was the architectural type of building adopted for Christian worship in nearly every part of the Empire. Constantine's churches in Rome, Constantinople, Jerusalem and Bethlehem helped to serve as prototypes and thus spread this style of architecture.

But as well as the basilica the architectural form of the simple domed church was also found. Both types of building had previously been used in close connection with the imperial cult. The domed buildings erected either by Constantine or directly after his reign served at first as mausoleums for the imperial family. For instance there were the churches in Rome which were originally mausoleums of the Empress Helena (Torre Pignatara) and of Constantine's daughter (Santa Costanza), and if these are compared with the domed churches built by the early members of the Constantinian dynasty, the connection is obvious. Thus the church of the Dormition (*Koimesis* or The Falling Asleep of the Mother of God) built by Constantine's mother is a domed church. Similarly churches (*martyria*) erected at this time over the graves of the martyrs were domed buildings. In pagan days the deified Emperor had been worshipped in the imperial funerary buildings, but once Christianity had been officially recognized, the Christian mausoleums became the centres of the cult of the dead Emperor and of the relics of the martyrs.

The basilica was also closely related to the imperial cult. The secular use of this type of building stretches right back to the days of the Roman Republic. But surviving remains going back to the second century B.C. are noticeably different in structure from the Christian basilica. Between these two types of building stands the basilica which was part of the official imperial residence. It is here that the apse is first found. This was originally part of the pagan temple, and it was only with the palace buildings erected by Augustus that it became an integral part of the basilica. The imperial throne stood in the apse of the basilica in the imperial palace; the episcopal throne stood in the apse of the Christian basilica. The seats round the apse in the imperial secular building were occupied by high office holders and in the Christian basilica by the bishop's close advisers. Thus the way led from the apse of the pagan temple, where the picture of the god was housed, through the apse as the place for the throne of the divine Emperor, to the Christian place of worship where the bishop's chair was placed in the apse. Constantine had the Christian basilica fashioned after the pattern of the imperial audience hall. Just as the praetor in the provinces administered justice in the name of the Emperor, so the bishop was to conduct the church services as the representative of the spiritual and secular overlord, the Emperor. He therefore sat on a throne raised up in the apse as did the Emperor. As priest, he received this seat by the same imperial *auctoritas* which empowered the praetor or provincial governor to sit on a throne and administer secular justice as the temporal judge and representative of the Emperor. When the praetor presided over the sessions of the tribunal, the portrait of the Emperor, the symbol of the omnipresence of the omnipotent ruler, was always in evidence, and it was the same when the Christian bishop took part in the divine liturgy. Even in the sixth century the mosaic portraits of the Emperor Justinian and the Empress Theodora were still found in the sanctuary in San Vitale in Ravenna. The ruler's picture inside the church symbolized the close links between Empire and Church, between the spiritual and secular powers. For Constantine and his successors, the bishop, like the praetor, was an imperial official.

The unity of architectural style provided by Constantine was destroyed before the break-up of the unity of the Christian Church. The new liturgical developments coming from the monastic movements in the East introduced a different kind of interior into church buildings in parts of the eastern provinces. This meant changes in ecclesiastical architecture, and within the Byzantine world this led to the development of the domed church, and later on the domed cross-in-square church. The West, on the other hand, continued to use the basilican form of church architecture promoted by Constantine.

Though Byzantine culture did not adopt the architectural style of building favoured by Constantine, unlike the West, it did preserve certain essential characteristics connected with the interior arrangement of the church. For instance, this is true of the imperial portrait in the church and also for the place assigned there to the Emperor. The imperial portrait of Justinian and Theodora in San Vitale in Ravenna stands not at the end of this development, but midway. The portraits of the Emperors and Empresses in Hagia Sophia in the eleventh and twelfth centuries point to a different religious conception of the imperial office, but they still witness to the close connection between Empire and Christian worship as manifested by the presence of the imperial portraits within the church.

The struggle for the unity of the Christian Church, a fundamental principle of the new Empire

In the question of ecclesiastical architecture Constantine was able to impose the type of building which he favoured without meeting any noticeable opposition. This was because before it was officially recognized Christianity did not possess its own particular style of architecture. But when it was a matter of establishing a Christian creed binding on all Christians the position was immeasurably more difficult. The different developments in the various provinces had early on sent down deep roots. In his desire to create a single creed binding on the whole Empire, without which it would be impossible to speak of one Christian Church, Constantine had to weaken resistance. In such circumstances the imperial command was not always the best weapon. The Emperor had other means at his disposal. In 325 he summoned the highest representatives of the Christian community in the Empire to Nicaea in Asia Minor. Here within the Christian Church there met face to face the supporters of the neoplatonic movement, who were especially numerous in parts of the Empire such as Egypt and Syria, and the Christian community of Asia Minor with views strongly influenced by the old popular religions. It looked as though these opposing views were irreconcilable. The populace of Asia Minor, as Christians, strongly supported the conception of the perfect equality of God the Father and God the Son. To them it was unthinkable that God the Father and God the Son were not of like substance. On the other hand there were the Christian neo-platonists of Syria and Egypt who had also been influenced by indigenous popular religion. They had no doubt that God could only be a single substance. In their view Christ the Son partook of only so much divine substance as had been imparted to him by God the Father, the original source of all. In their eyes Christ the Son was only a creature of the Father and not of the same substance. The leader of the Christians who took this view was the presbyter Areios (Arius) and his followers were therefore called Arians. Those opposing him were led by the deacon Athanasius, later raised to the episcopate.

At Nicaea supporters of the Asia Minor-Hellenistic view formulated the doctrine of the consubstantiality of God the Father and God the Son and prevailed. But their victory lasted only a short time. When Constantine realized the strength of Arian teaching in Syria and Egypt, he favoured this party and withdrew his backing from the supporters of consubstantiality. In 337 it was an Arian bishop who administered the Christian sacrament of baptism to the dying Emperor. This Arian victory did not, however, prove decisive for the future. The General Council held in Constantinople in 381 gave the victory to the previously suppressed supporters of consubstantiality. The Arians who refused to accept this were condemned to an existence outside the law. It was only in the German migrant tribes in South Russia and Bessarabia converted by Arian missionaries from Asia Minor that these beliefs persisted. And by the middle of the seventh century the last of these German peoples, the Lombards, had given up their Arian Christianity and had been converted to the Catholic doctrine.

The conflicts within the Christian imperial church created by Constantine did not cease with the condemnation of the Arians at the Council of Constantinople in 381. They came to the surface again in 431 when Cyril of Alexandria, supported by Pope Celestine I and the Egyptian monks, proclaimed in Ephesus that Mary, the mother of Jesus Christ who was both God and Man, was the Mother of God and demanded that she should be venerated as the bearer of God (Theotokos). Was it mere chance that this request was made by the Arian and by some of the Egyptian members of the Council? Asia Minor was the home of the Great Mother goddess. Here Artemis, Cybele, the Great Mother and the original Mother goddess Atargatis were still being worshipped. In Egypt the goddess Isis quieting the boy child Horus was still the all-powerful Mother goddess in what was a living popular cult.

Christianity could only overcome the old religions in Egypt and Asia Minor if it had something similar to offer in their place. When both Egypt and Asia Minor demanded that not only God the Father and God the Son but the Mother of the Son of God should be honoured, this was contrary to the Christological views of Nestorius Patriarch of Constantinople, who thought that Mary was only the mother of the human person of Christ the Son of God. This view was contested by the opponents of Nestorius, who maintained that he was denying the true Godhead of Christ, since he was dividing the one Christ into two persons. Nestorius was condemned by the Council of Ephesus in 431 and was deposed from his patriarchal see. Twenty years later he died in a lonely monastery on the edge of the Egyptian desert.

But part of the Syrian Christian community refused to recognize the decision of Ephesus. They firmly supported the teaching of Nestorius and completely seceded from

This is all wrong

the imperial Church which they now held to be heretical. By reason of the close bond between Christian Church and Roman state, this step meant withdrawing from the political entity represented by the Empire. Thus religious secession was followed by political immigration. The followers of the banned Patriarch Nestorius went to Persia. Here the Nestorians, as they were called, were permitted to set up their own ecclesiastical organization. The Nestorian Church in Persia had its own Patriarch whose seat was in Seleucia near Ctesiphon, the residence of the Sassanid kings.

Side by side with the Christian Roman Church there was now a Christian Persian Church. So the Christian Church had only kept its unity for a hundred years, although the emigration of the Nestorians had at least removed the danger of the coexistence of two Christian Churches side by side within the Roman Empire. But with the formation of an independent Nestorian Church the Emperor could no longer claim to be the protector and liberator of the Christian subjects of the Persian Empire.

The East Roman imperial government had at once recognized the dangers implicit in the decision of Ephesus and had sought to counter this. With such an aim in view a new General Council was called at Chalcedon in 451. The doctrine formulated here, namely that Christ has two natures, the Divine and human, distinct in person yet inseparable in substance, had all the characteristics of a compromise. It was necessary to meet the still powerful Arians who denied the consubstantiality of God and Christ. Hence the deliberate emphasis on the human nature of Christ. The small word 'distinct' was conceded to the Nestorians who saw two natures in Christ. It was hoped to conciliate the victors of Ephesus by the insertion of the word 'inseparable'. But the compromise formulated at Chalcedon could not preserve the unity of the Church. The radical wings of the different Churches did not accept it. The result was a split in the Church in Egypt. The radical wing here organized their own Coptic Church with a Patriarch at its head (457). But as well as this there was also the melkite Egyptian Church, loyal to the Emperor and the doctrine of Chalcedon (*Malka* corresponded to the Greek word Basileus and stood for the East Roman Emperor). In the sixth century the Syrian radicals round Edessa followed the Egyptian example. Under Jacob Baradaeus they formed their own Christian Church in the region of Edessa and seceded from the imperial Church. Their supporters were called Jacobites after their first leader. At the same time, in the first half of the sixth century, the Armenians also broke with the imperial Church at a synod' held in Dvin, the capital of the part of Armenia under Persian rule.

Thus began the development which was ultimately to lead to the dissolution of the *imperium romanum*. The three Churches which broke with the imperial Church and were called monophysite, because in opposition to the Chalcedonian compromise they affirmed the one inseparable nature of Christ in their profession of faith, found most of their supporters in the countries on the route to India. Their missionaries won over the southern lands on either side of the Red Sea to the monophysite belief and they became its loyal adherents. Abyssinia and the Hamitic tribes in the Sudan regarded the Coptic Patriarch of Alexandria as their spiritual head. South Arabia, East Syria and the Arab tribes of Irak and Syria adopted Christianity of the Syrian monophysite brand and they were under the Patriarch of Antioch. The Christians in Irak and in Iran, under the leadership of the Patriarch resident in Ctesiphon, followed Nestorian doctrine. In Armenia after the synod of Dvin a national Armenian monophysite Church was formed with its own Patriarch who was known under the title of Katholikos. As well as the Syrian monophysite Patriarch, there were now also four other Christian Patriarchs in the East who did not acknowledge the imperial Church.

This situation had its effect not only on the ecclesiastical policy of the Empire. To use violence against these schismatic Churches would inevitably have closed the gates to the eastern world. Byzantine oriental diplomacy necessarily had to take these Churches into account and avoid a break with them if it wished to keep open the route to India. It was therefore necessary to come to terms with these separatist Churches in some kind of doctrinal compromise. On the other hand this created difficulties in the Emperor's relations with a large section of his own imperial Church, which viewed any attempt to meet these separatist Churches as a deviation from orthodox belief. Hence it was constantly necessary for the Empire to employ strong forces to maintain the internal peace of the official Church. Necessary measures of this kind sometimes almost took on the character of a civil war. Police action against rebellious bishops, imprisonment of high ecclesiastics, the intervention of the military against ecclesiastical underground movements were the order of the day. It was moreover inevitable that the ecclesiastical policy of the Byzantine government, in its preoccupation with conciliating the separated schismatic Churches, alienated the western Byzantine provinces. These for their part considered the Byzantine imperial Church to be heretical. Thus a chasm opened out. The West now repudiated the Byzantine Emperor and his Church as something alien. This alienation was gradually converted into the desire to separate, and this led to the formation of a western and a Byzantine Church. The same process which occurred in the East soon after the creation of an imperial Church, was repeated later on in the West. Thus there came about the separation of the Byzantine Church from the Christian Churches in the East and in the West, and this separation must be regarded as the formative influence in the rise of Byzantine civilization.

The new state and its non-Christian subjects

The Roman state's close connection with Christianity not only meant the secession of the Eastern Churches but also emphasized its condemnation of non-Christian religions. This also left its mark on the character of Byzantine civilization, for this exclusiveness can be regarded as one of its most outstanding features. Among non-Christian religions pride of place was taken by the Jews who had a larger number of followers than any other non-Christian faith in the Roman Empire. At the time of Constantine and his successors the Jews were about 8 per cent of the population of the Roman Empire, that is, about four million. Relations with this important religious minority were certainly worsened when the Roman state was linked to Christianity. The laws of the early Christian Emperors showed this quite plainly. The edicts promulgated during this period determined the position of the followers of the Jewish faith in the western and eastern states for almost fifteen hundred years.

The Roman Empire, and later the western states, defined as a Jew anyone who professed the Jewish religion. Before Christianity became the state religion Jews were only forbidden to proselytize. Thus Roman citizens could never be fully converted to Judaeism, obeying all its precepts and even being circumcised. But there was nothing to prevent them from becoming half-proselytes, as it was called, who worshipped only Yahweh and shared the Sabbath festival with the Jews. At this time Jews were no worse off than other imperial subjects. They could obtain Roman citizenship and occupy public offices. In Palestine and other places where there were large Jewish communities they enjoyed a certain—even though limited—autonomy which secured to them their religious organization and their own judiciary and penal system. The only exception was capital punishment. The religious head of all Jews, the Patriarch, resided in Palestine. The Roman Empire had granted him the highest Roman titles of honour, such as *vir spectabilis* and *vir illustris*. As well as secular rights which were conceded to him, he had to collect the taxes from all Jews living within the Empire. He also had the power to levy from them a contribution in the form of the *aurum coronarium* to defray his own expenses.

The first Christian Emperors, supported by their spiritual advisers, were quick to abolish the judicial equality of Roman citizens of the Jewish faith with other citizens of the Empire, as well as existing Jewish autonomy. This began with the prohibition against proselytizing. Then followed restrictions on building new synagogues. Old synagogues could only be repaired if they were in danger of collapsing. Further imperial laws deprived the Jews of the right to hold office, forbade them to plead causes in a law court or to contract mixed marriage or to possess Christian slaves. Other edicts altered the Jewish laws of inheritance in favour of Jews converted to Christianity, who by Jewish law were excluded from inheriting. Christian synods forbade the consultation of Jewish doctors; and Christian priests, both in preaching and in their writings, called for a boycott of the Jews. The next step was to deprive the Jews of their Jewish administrative autonomy. The Patriarch lost his powers of jurisdiction (415) and finally his honorary prefecture was abrogated. When the last Patriarch from the family of Hillel died in 425, measures were taken to prevent the election of a new Patriarch, and the patriarchate was abolished. The payment previously made by all Jews to the Patriarch now had to go to the Roman state treasury. With the abolition of the patriarchate, ecclesiastical direction of the Jews fell to the so-called Academy, a council of elders established in the sixth century in a location on the sea of Tiberias. The supreme ecclesiastical power of the Patriarch was vested in this Academy which had the right of appointing elders and establishing the Jewish calendar. There was no appeal from their decisions in matters of interpretation of the Holy Scripture and the application of ecclesiastical law.

Roman legislation on the Jewish question revealed very clearly the degree of social and human degradation imposed on the Jewish communities living within the Roman Empire. The Christian pogroms which were constantly occurring were not only aimed at the destruction of the Jewish places of worship whose rebuilding was forbidden by law, but they also claimed many human victims. Thus the Jews living in the Roman Empire gradually developed a feeling of intense hatred towards the state which was persecuting them. The Roman Jews had far-reaching connections with the Jewish communities outside the frontiers of the Empire, and this meant that the hostile measures against the Roman Jewish minority soon proved an embarrassment in relations between the Roman Empire and its neighbours to the south and to the east. This involved not only the Persians but the Arab states. From time to time kings converted to Judaeism were ruling in the Hijaz and some Arab tribes had gone over to the Jewish faith. Moreover the little island of Jotabe at the entrance to the gulf of Akaba was the centre of a small Jewish state. These Arab Jewish states retaliated against the persecution of the Jews in the Roman Empire by taking measures against Roman traders. The trade route from Gaza in the Mediterranean via the South Arabian sea ports leading to the Indian Ocean was almost exclusively in the hands of these Arab states. This meant that if they imposed a blockade against Roman trade the import of raw materials from the Arabian and East African coast regions would dry up. The Roman trade with India which used the sea route could also be brought to a halt if the Jewish South Arabian Himyarite kingdom blockaded the straits of Bab al-Mandab. Almost every hostile measure against the Jews in the Empire was answered by retaliatory action on the part of the Jewish Arab states, resulting in considerable harm to the Roman economy.

Relations with Persia were also greatly damaged by the persecution of the Jews within the Roman Empire. In Persia the Jews were not subject to special restrictions. Like the Nestorian Churches they had their own ecclesiastical organization here. The head of the Persian Jews, established in Irak since the days of the Babylonian exile, had the title of *Exilarch*. He ranked next to the Patriarch in Jerusalem and as leader of the oldest and largest Jewish diaspora he possessed great authority. There were also celebrated Rabbinic schools here, famous for their Biblical exegesis, and the *Mishnah* and the *Midrash*, together with the works of the Palestinian schools, were regarded as authoritative. It is significant that there was a *Talmud* of Babylon as well as of Jerusalem and this took precedence of the older Palestinian *Talmud*.

The Jewry of Irak supported their oppressed brothers and co-religionists in the Roman Empire. The common ties of nationality and faith led the Jews of Roman Palestine, together with those of Irak, to give their political support to the Persians. Thus almost every Persian attack on Syria and Palestine was accompanied by a rising of the Jewish communities in these regions. The Persian conquest of Jerusalem, and later the Arab attacks on the city in the first half of the seventh century, were accompanied by Jewish pogroms against the Christian Roman population living there.

The anti-Jewish policy of the Roman government had been further intensified in the sixth and seventh centuries. Justinian I had not only altered the Jewish calendar when the Jewish Passover came just before the Christian Easter but he also interfered in Jewish worship. It was he who decreed that the prayer and scripture reading (the recitation from the *Torah* and the books of the Prophets) should be not only in Hebrew with an Aramaic *targum* (translation) but also in Greek and Latin as well. The Greek translation was only to be taken from the Septuagint, or in exceptional cases from the translation of Aquila. From this time onwards the Greek *targum* was used in the Byzantine Empire as well as the reading from the Hebrew. The Greek language was also used in other parts of the service. This Graeco-Jewish ecclesiastical language was affected by general linguistic developments. At Corfu *targumim* in vernacular Greek used by Byzantine Jews in their services are still preserved. The use of the scriptural exegesis of the great Rabbinical schools, the *Mishnah* and the *Midrash*, was in general forbidden. Perhaps Justinian thought that these measures would counteract the Jews' tendency to isolate themselves from the rest of the Empire as a separate community, with their own language and their own religion. It is impossible to tell. In any case the attempt failed. Repressive imperial measures, such as those taken by Heraclius after the Jewish massacre of the Christian population when the Persians took Jerusalem, were not such as to endear the Byzantine state to the Jews. The Emperor's call to persecution was not directed only against Jews within the Empire. He also tried to attack those in the Germanic kingdoms of his day, and he sent special embassies to broach this subject to the Germanic rulers, as for instance the king of the West Goths. The Byzantine Empire did not succeed in solving the problem of integrating the Jews into the Christian Roman state. The Jews remained an alien body within the Byzantine Empire, maintaining their own nationality and their own faith. The Jewish ghetto in Constantinople on the Golden Horn was little different from the ghettos of the medieval cities of the West.

Nevertheless, in spite of these apparently insoluble disputes between the Jews and the Empire, the Jews did have a considerable influence on Byzantine civilization. This was particularly true in the field of Byzantine hymnography, which could hardly have developed without the Jewish tradition. Legend says that the greatest of the Byzantine hymn-writers, Romanus, was of Jewish stock and yet he is the real creator of the Byzantine hymn. Romanus was a contemporary of the Emperor Anastasius, and his influence spans the two first decades of the sixth century. Those of his hymns which have survived point to considerable influence from the psalmody of the Jewish synagogue as well as from Syriac sources. Among the finds at the Geniza in Cairo there is a fragment of an ecclesiastical canticle which appears to provide a Jewish prototype for one of Romanus' hymns. The full effect of this Jewish influence on the formation of the Byzantine liturgy and Byzantine church hymns was first felt in the sixth century at a time when the Roman state was making its relentless attack on the Jews. This was also the period when the Byzantine Church first made a break with the old Hellenic culture of late antiquity. This is particularly true of the form of the church service. It is known that the older form of Christian worship, the *agape*, the love feast, had no hymns, as is evidenced by the descriptions of both Theodoret and Tertullian. Musical instruments and choral songs were now used as part of the service. The singing of the congregation was accompanied by clapping of hands, rhythmical movements, and the ringing of bells. The tunes of the songs sung during the service were in part secular in character. It was said that during the services the followers of Arius sang spiritual songs to the tunes of sailors' chanties. A not unimportant role in the oldest church music was also played by the influence of the so-called Alexandrine music brought into the Roman Empire by Negro slaves from the Sudan. Clement of Alexandria was critical of this Negro music which in form and origin was something like present-day jazz. The church fathers complained of this music that it was loud, harsh, rhythmical, and more instrumental than vocal. They condemned its sentimental and chromatic harmonies which were penetrating into church music, like the ornamental coloratura. In contrast to this early Christian form of service, Jewish worship had neither instrumental accompaniment nor choral singing.

This form of worship based on hymns sung in unison (Gregorian), inspired by the Jewish usage, became obligatory for Christian services in the sixth century. But this was not the only field in which the Jewish tradition influenced Byzantine culture. The execution and style of the Jewish *Torah* manuscripts were the sources from which the hand (*ductus*) and the form, such as the abbreviation of words (*contractiones*) and the calculation of the syllabus and letters, were derived. The extent of this influence can be judged from the fact that Byzantine manuscripts of the Bible used the same lectionary divisions as in the ritual reading of the *Torah* and the writings of the Prophets. Thus the lectionary markings in the Isaiah manuscript of Qumran were identical with the pericopes in the Byzantine *Prophetologion*. It was the same with the notation regulating the details of the ecphonic intoning of the reading of the *Torah*; the Jewish models were followed when the Holy Scriptures were recited in the Byzantine Church. This notation was the forerunner of the Byzantine neumes which were a means of assisting singers in performing church songs. Thus, all things considered, it is true to say that Jewish culture played a considerable part in the development of Byzantine church poetry and in the development of the Byzantine liturgical service.

Other non-Christian religions suffered just as much as the Jews in having their faith denounced and in being subjected to persecution. They also exercised no less an influence on Byzantine culture than the Jews. Thus it was from the Gnostics that Christian music took its eight modes, the eight *echoi* (four *kyrioi*, and four *plagioi*, plagal). All this did not prevent the Byzantines from attacking these religious movements, which still persisted in the country regions as well as having many adherents in intellectual circles in the big cities. The blow against the university of Athens was aimed at neoplatonism as a philosophy and not as a religious movement and was a sign of the times. Justinian's decree announcing the closure of the doors of the university followed the attacks of the

48

Christian sophist school of Gaza on the neoplatonic philosophers in Athens, the disciples of Proclus. There can also be no doubt that Justinian took decisive steps against neoplatonic religious meetings. In the person of bishop John of Ephesus, who wrote the Syriac *Ecclesiastical History*, Justinian had indeed found an agent well suited to root out and liquidate these sects and pagan conventicles.

For Roman paganism the sixth century was a period of decline. During the first fifty years after the edict of Milan, paganism had remained unharmed, for this edict of toleration made it clear that both Christianity and the Roman state religion were on the same footing. Hence the offices for the Roman priesthood were still being regularly filled until the last decade of the fourth century. It was not until then that the property used for the maintenance of the pagan priesthood was confiscated. Later decrees against the temple establishments of Roman paganism followed. It was Justinian in Constantinople who with his usual vigorous approach decreed the destruction of all pagan statues. It was only to be expected that some members of the patrician families, such as the Symmachi and the Anicii, at first continued their strong support of paganism and spoke vigorously in the senate in defence of the old Roman pagan institutions. But the government gradually broke down their opposition and the measures directed to this end included exclusion from the senate and the confiscation of property. The significance of this struggle of the government against Roman paganism lay in the exclusion of its supporters from teaching and education. Towards the end of the fifth century teachers in the universities of Alexandria, Beirut, Athens and Constantinople were largely pagan. When their salaries were cut off and their buildings confiscated a severe blow was directed at those hitherto largely responsible for maintaining the links with ancient Hellenic civilization.

The transformation of the
political structure

4

The reform of the central administration:
the signal for the transition to a planned economy

Having discussed the conditions which made possible the emergence of an individual Byzantine civilization, we shall now examine its first phase. In this respect the division of the Empire and the founding of the capital Constantinople seem at first sight to be the most clearly visible signs of the new development. But what happened on 17 January 395 under the influence of the westward migration of East Germanic tribes was only the cutting of the cables of a ship which had for a long time been ready for its voyage. Through the displacement of the economic and cultural centre of gravity within the *imperium romanum* everything had already been prepared for this day. Thus it cannot be maintained that Byzantine civilization began with this division of the Empire and with the foundation of the capital Constantinople. Rather we should consider first the internal development of the *imperium romanum* before 17 January 395. This prepared the ground for decisive changes under Justinian and his successors which helped the new spirit on its way to the break-through before which the civilization of late antiquity gradually had to yield. But here it must not be forgotten that the civilization of late antiquity, through the division of the Empire, had developed differently in the West and in the East. Essential characteristics of Byzantine civilization had already emerged in this period. And so before considering the decisive encounter of the new movements with the cultural heritage of late antiquity in the age of Justinian, this phase of preparation must be examined. The inner structure of the state and the urban and agrarian economy, which assume a new shape in this period, must be seen as a preparation for the Byzantine epoch. Thus in the sphere of urban economy the structure of this preliminary phase remains preserved even in Byzantine civilization. In the case of agrarian economy, where new forms grew up, consideration of this preliminary stage is essential in order to understand the new reforms which began in the time of Justinian and led on to the Byzantine period. The imperial reforms under Diocletian and Constantine must therefore be taken as the starting point. The reforms reshaped the inner structure of the state and by introducing changes in the form of the economy finally led to a social transformation. These reforms began in the central government; subsequently they embraced the provinces and cities and thus also affected the life of the individual in both town and countryside.

The new ordering of the central government, which began under Diocletian and reached its first conclusion under Constantine and his immediate successors, was not a new creation, but a reorganization of already existing institutions. The old Roman central authorities of the imperial epoch, which had carried on into the time of Diocletian, were reformed and were assigned new duties. A model for this reform was the central administration in Egypt, economically the most strongly developed part of the Empire. It had existed since the conquest of the country by Alexander the Great, and even in the time of the Roman occupation it had not been interfered with, and by and large had been able to carry on its work as before. This central administration, which in the time of Diocletian was able to look back on a history of almost six centuries, formed the backbone of the Egyptian economy, for the Egyptian economy was from the outset a planned economy. This was a result of its dependence on the inundations of the Nile. Planned distribution of labour, compulsory delivery, control of agricultural production, state monopolies for almost all branches of economic activity—all these had been the rule since ancient times.

In the Roman Empire, in view of the great economic crisis at the end of the third century, which included not only the Italian peninsula but almost the whole of the Mediterranean area, resort was had to the planned economy which had proved its worth in Egypt. The economic reforms that had to be made in the central government of the Empire were aimed at solving various problems. There was the question of countering ever-increasing inflation by the stabilization of the currency. But on the other hand agricultural and industrial production had also to be increased. Agricultural produce had to provide for the army and the population of the cities engaged in industry. Industry had to increase export with its products and thus to ensure the amassing of greater stores of precious metals, which alone made power-politics possible.

These measures in the central government were intended in the first place only to bring about a division of responsibilities, not of political authority. The Emperor as holder of the *imperium* still retained the highest power. Although this power had originally been conferred on him as an office, his *imperium* was soon designated in Roman political law as *imperium merum*. That means that the decision of the Emperor was not limited by the law (*rex legibus solutus*). The officers of state, including the highest ministers, in contrast to the Emperor, possessed only the *imperium mixtum*, i.e. in their decisions they were bound by the law. In spite of these far-reaching privileges, even in late antiquity the imperial position was still conceived of as an office, as is shown by the separation of the Emperor's private wealth from the finances of the state. Ideas such as those of the European princes of the seventeenth and eighteenth centuries, who regarded the states as their personal property, were as foreign to the Roman, as to the Byzantine, Emperor.

The division of competences within the imperial reform of Diocletian and his successors affected five different spheres. There was a central ministry which exercised control over the entire economic life of the state, two special ministerial offices or commands for the army, a ministry with departments for administration of justice and foreign affairs, and ministries for the imperial finances and the private estates of the Emperor. It is tempting to see in this development the prototype of a modern cabinet, but there is a certain difference between the cabinet of the nineteenth and twentieth centuries and the representation of the Roman imperial offices as a single body or committee (*gremium*). The leaders of the Roman imperial offices had neither the responsibility of modern specialist ministers, nor was their work done in strictly demarcated departments whose representatives co-ordinated their work in cabinet meetings and passed resolutions on the basis of votes. Between individual offices relations probably existed as were occasioned by the nature of the duties being conducted, but there was no fixed demarcation of the competence and authority of each. The Emperor's council, at which all heads of these imperial departments met together whenever necessary, is comparable as an institution with the prince's council of the sixteenth and seventeenth centuries in Central and Western Europe. This new organization of government offices, which can be regarded as a point of departure for the development of later Byzantine civilization, was not concerned with the creation of a council of ministers which might deprive the Emperor of some of his power. Instead of that, it was intended to relieve the pressure on the Emperor, so that he could do justice to the multifarious tasks imposed on him in the carrying out of imperial reform. For these reasons a new division of departments was undertaken and the former council of the Emperor was also reorganized.

In the period before this reorganization of government offices the most powerful man, after the Emperor, was the *praefectus praetorio*. He stood at the head of all authorities and military units belonging to the *praetorium*, the headquarters of the Emperor. Of these functions it was particularly his control of the imperial bodyguard that gave him political prominence. Besides these military duties, he had to assist the Emperor in the performance of his administrative work, and also to act as his representative. This duty was now taken from him. In the new division of authority he was given control and administrative authority over all branches of the economy. In this sphere the prefect had the power of unlimited jurisdiction and at the same time he was the highest instance for appeal. This meant that it was impossible to appeal in the last instance to the Emperor against a judgment made by the prefect in economic affairs to obtain a reversal of his ruling.

Among the most important spheres of duty of the *praefectus praetorio* was the control of agriculture. This consisted in the supervision of the receipt of the *annona*. The *annona* was the delivery-target imposed on the rural districts and was determined by the provisioning needs of the cities and the army. The prefect supervised urban economy through control of prices and the assignments which urban industry had to make to the state (*canon vestium*). Among the other duties of the prefect were the supervision of the postal system and of public works, and the control of urban corporations (obligatory guilds), schools, government munitions works, and factories, so far as they were working within the scope of a state monopoly. Similarly, the stores of supplies and arms depots were under his command. He was also responsible for the levying of recruits (*tironum praebitio*).

By virtue of his full powers the *praefectus praetorio* was therefore in a position to control all spheres of public life that were even remotely connected with the economy. Thus, as head of the department of public works, he could take charge of the installation of canals, water-supplies and reservoirs, which indirectly were necessary for the further development of industry and agriculture. Being in command of the imperial post made it possible for him, by appropriate measures, to ensure, if necessary, the rapid dispatch of agricultural produce for the provisioning of the army and the urban population.

With the aid of these full powers the prefect was able to build up within the *imperium romanum* a planned economy similar to the Egyptian one, which had already been working successfully for six centuries. The office of *praefectus praetorio* had been in existence for three centuries before its reorganization under Diocletian and Constantine. It is true that in the time of Justinian, two and a half centuries after Diocletian, important duties were removed from it. But its significance remained, since the offices to which these duties were transferred—such as the office of the *logothetes tou stratiotikou*—pursued the same course of planned economy. The adoption of the Greek administration developed in Egypt, which was apparent in the reorganization of the office of the *praefectus praetorio*, considerably strengthened the Greek influence within this department. In some of the central authorities Greek had established itself as the language of the chancery since the beginning of the fourth century, in contrast to the army, which retained Latin as the official military language until the beginning of the seventh century. Other imperial authorities, above all the ministry of justice, kept to the Latin language until the beginning of the seventh century.

The military commanders with departments within the central government were, under Constantine, at first divided according to the nature of their equipment. There was a separate high command of the infantry under a *magister peditum* and a high command of the cavalry under a *magister equitum*. The Emperor remained commander-in-chief of both parts of the army, as before. This divided high command for the two branches of the army was disbanded in the fourth century and the troops co-ordinated under common positions of command set up in accordance with regional needs. Thus a high command of the European troops was established under a *magister militum per Illyricum* and a command of the Asian troops under a *magister militum per Orientem*. Both commands, which remained in force until the beginning of the seventh century, were of great importance for the development of the Byzantine state. In the course of this development still more areas of command were created. At the beginning of the seventh century there were already five; from these developed the later regional subdivisions of the Byzantine Empire.

Besides the offices of the central government responsible for the economy and the army, there were four other leading ministries; their heads had to share the administration of the remaining departments and of finance with a council composed of professional officials and permanent members. These four ministers, together with the council under the presidency of the Emperor, formed a body which conducted the foreign and home affairs of the Empire. One of these, the *magister officiorum*, through the departments administered by him, already occupied a leading position, so that, with the reservations made above, he can be compared to a Prime Minister. The *magister officiorum* was in charge of the departments of protocol and foreign affairs; he was also head of the political police (*schola agentium in rebus*) and commanded the palace guard. His colleague, the minister of justice, *quaestor sacri palatii*, had among his duties the preparation of the imperial laws and documents, for which he took over part of the responsibility with the authorization *legi* ('I have read'). Besides the minister for foreign affairs and the minister of justice, there were two ministers of finance, the *comes sacrarum largitionum* and the *comes rerum privatarum*. The *comes sacrarum largitionum* was in charge of taxes and attended to the monetary obligations of the Empire, such as the payment of wages to the troops and salaries to the officials, and the payments of money to foreign princes, in so far as these had to be provided in accordance with political agreements. The *comes rerum privatarum* was in charge of the great income which accrued to the Emperor from his estates and demesnes (*domus* or Greek *oikoi*). He was the head of the *curatores*, of whom each was in charge of the Emperor's estates in one part of the Empire. This revenue provided the means for the maintenance of the Emperor's private armies, such as the cavalry troop known as the *scholae palatinae*. The revenue from the Emperor's estates also had to cover the cost of his building activities, public charities, the circus games instituted by him, state receptions and the current expenses of the imperial household. These estates were private property. Each Emperor was also the heir to the private property of his predecessor. Since no dynasty had grown up in the late Roman Empire, under normal conditions the private property of the Emperors was bound to increase with every new reign.

Within the central authorities transformed or newly created by Diocletian and Constantine, the Emperor's council, the *consistorium*, also played an important part. This council already existed in the earlier times of the Emperors in the form of the *consilium principis*. The new character which the reforms of the two Emperors gave it consisted in the regularity of its meetings and the participation of permanent members. It was no longer the same as before, when changing members from senatorial families, summoned erratically to the meetings, gave the assembly more of the character of a representation of a social class. Permanent members (*comites*), of whom each was in charge of a definite department, now attended to an ordered administration. The division of these councils into ranked classes was also carried out. So here there was a development similar to that which took place in Europe in the fifteenth and sixteenth centuries, when the prince's hereditary councillors were replaced by a body of professionally trained experts.

The council composed of professional officials was also preserved in the Byzantine state. This distinguishes it from the western states of the middle ages. It must not of course be overlooked that this council of special ministers and councillors tied to departments, often meeting irregularly under the chairmanship of the Emperor, was limited in its capacity for work in comparison with modern institutions of this kind. To a considerable extent the fault lay in the strictly conducted imperial ceremonial, which had to be observed, even at the meetings of the Emperor's council. It was not for nothing that this Emperor's council reorganized by Constantine bore the name of *consistorium*. It was the custom, therefore, to stand (*consistere*) at the meetings of this council. It was obvious that at meetings of the council conducted in this way it was scarcely possible to settle matters which had to be discussed in detail between Emperor and councillors before a resolution was passed. New offices inevitably sprang up and joined in rivalry with existing arrangements. The beginnings of this development are recognizable, above all, in the immediate entourage of the Emperor.

Within the limits laid down by the ceremonial, it was only very rarely that the Emperor was still able to make extempore decisions during the course of the council. He had to acquaint himself with the ministers' and councillors' proposals before the meetings, in order to be able to prepare himself for them. Hence the actual meeting became a matter of protocol in which things already decided and agreed upon were solemnly restated in a ceremonial setting. Thus liaison staffs and new departments were formed for the purpose of working over the agenda before the official meetings of the *consistorium*. These new offices soon developed into an imperial private chancery, which was named *cubiculum* after its workroom in the imperial private apartments. As its derivation shows, *cubiculum* corresponds to terms such as 'chamber' and 'cabinet'. The members of this office were called *cubicularii* (chamberlains) and *secreti* (private secretaries). The head of this Emperor's private chancery bore the title of *praepositus sacri cubiculi* (head of the imperial cabinet). The *cubiculum* thereby soon developed into an authority that surpassed the imperial council, the *consistorium*, in political importance. It was no coincidence that Narses, commander-in-chief of the imperial army in Italy, wielding the most extensive powers, had held the office of *praepositus sacri cubiculi*. Thus, in the period of transition from the late Roman to the Byzantine Empire there was a development similar to that which took place in the European national states of the sixteenth and seventeenth centuries. What was signified in the former case by the contrast between *consistorium* (council) and *cubiculum* (chamber) is found in the latter case in the institutions of council and chamber. In the latter case the prince's chamber became the cabinet, i.e. the central point of government, while the council later became a more parliamentary body with only indirect influence on the affairs of state. Therefore in the sixteenth and seventeenth centuries, too, a new organ of government, the cabinet, had been brought into being through a change in the ruler's position in relation to his councillors.

If ceremonial now played a more important part within the organs of central authority, then this, like the reorganization of various offices of the central government, points to the influence of Hellenistic methods of government coming from Alexandria. Under the successors of Alexander the Great, the Seleucids and the Ptolemies, this ceremonial had already grown out of the cult of the ruler introduced at that time. The Roman

Emperors had taken over this cult of the ruler. The Emperor thereby became a sacred person, a god of the state, to whom every subject owed divine reverence regardless of his personal religious belief. It was the incompatibility of the Christian faith with the fulfilment of the public duty of the cult of the Emperor which gave rise to the conflict between the Roman state and the Christians.

In the later days of the Roman Empire the forms of the Emperor-cult underwent a further development. Through the Roman state religion's adoption of solar-worship, which had taken place under Constantine's immediate predecessor, the Emperor became the emanation of the sun-god. As part of his elevation to divinity he personified the disappearance and reappearance of the sun at the *prokypsis*, the festival celebrated at the time of the winter solstice, the birthday of the god. This *prokypsis*, in which the Emperor had to represent the reappearing sun in the setting of a mime, was solemnly observed until the last days of the Byzantine Empire. The elevation of Christianity to the state religion was unable to make any difference to this ceremonial, as is shown by the continued celebration of the *prokypsis*, and the Christian Emperor, just like the pagan Emperor, claimed sacred privileges after his death. Therefore, by analogy with the dead pagan Emperor's elevation as *divus augustus*, Constantine claimed for himself the position of a *protos apostolos*, the 'first of the Apostles'. In designing his burial place he therefore had the cenotaphs of the twelve apostles set up around his sarcophagus. This Emperor's mausoleum, the Church of the Twelve Apostles, then became the centre of special services, like the mausoleum of Alexander the Great and his successors in Alexandria. In Alexandria, too, on certain days religious festivals took place for the deified kings in the temples erected beside their mausoleums. It was not for nothing that St Peter's position as Prince of the Apostles was emphasized in Rome under Pope Damasus, to counter the Emperor's claim to equal status with the Apostles.

It was obvious that this Emperor, who wished to be regarded as the emanation of the sun-god and claimed the same veneration as the Apostles of Christ, could not give up the sacred ceremonial of his predecessors either, unless he wished to expose himself to the danger of a profanation. Thus the imperial ceremonial had to be kept up even in the presence of the highest dignitary of the Empire. This explains why even the highest dignitaries had to remain standing before the Emperor during the council, and had to conceal their hands from him as from a deity. Even the Christian Emperor, from the point of view of the ceremonial, was still a god. His arrival was heralded by the raising of several curtains, like the appearance of the deity in the oriental mystery religions. Hence the meetings of the Emperor's council held in this sacred setting were able to announce only decisions which had been discussed and settled outside this body (*gremium*).

The struggle for the increase of agricultural production

From the central government the reform movement encroached on the provinces. To transform the Roman state on the basis of a planned economy after the Egypto-Hellenistic model meant above all the abolition of the hitherto existing form of regional government. The provinces were too large to guarantee adequate control of the population by the state executive. The first step towards the introduction of planned economy in the territory of the Empire therefore had to be taken by means of a new arrangement of the provinces. The old large provinces were abolished and a hundred new ones created in their place. By the fifth century they had even been increased to 120. The provinces, combined into twelve larger units, formed so-called dioceses. This provincial reorganization made the administrative network more close-meshed. There were now better administrative bodies for the enforcement of those fiscal measures which, together with the currency changes, constituted the core of the imperial programme of reform.

This programme aimed at increasing production in urban industry. That however was not possible without sufficient agricultural produce to provision the city population. Hence the hitherto irregularly requested delivery of corn to the organs of the state, the so-called *annona*, was changed under Diocletian into a regular delivery. At first it was reassessed every five years and later every fifteen years. The basis of the required delivery that had to be produced every year was the declaration of those obliged to deliver. Every man who owned land of more than one *iugum* was under this obligation. A *iugum* was the amount of land that a single man could cultivate, taking into consideration local conditions. Hence the tax-return to be made every five, and later every fifteen, years had to declare the *iuga* (yokes) and *capita* (heads) for every property.

The criterion in assessing the quantity due was the amount of manpower involved. The farmers and landed proprietors were thus compelled to increase their production. What was produced in excess of the fixed amount of the *annona* remained for their own free use. The declaration for purposes of assessment for the *annona* had to take account not only of the number of existing human labourers (*capita*) but also of draught animals which came under the heading of *capita animalium*. This obligation to deliver provisions included cereals, oil, wine, and meat. The receipt of goods owed under the *annona* was entrusted to officials of the *praefectus praetorio* who were responsible for provisioning the city population and the army.

This reform placed at the disposal of the state a fixed quantity of natural produce at definite intervals and was based on a given amount of human labour. It was the beginning of the planned economy of the late Roman Empire and it laid down the lines of economic development almost up to the conquest of Constantinople by the crusaders.

A characteristic feature of this planned economy was the introduction of a fixed labour norm which could vary up or down according to the current yield and which was used in fixing the *iugatio-capitatio*. This inevitably led to the formation of new social classes among the populace. To begin with, the *annona* favoured the great landowner because in its assessment of the obligatory delivery of produce, although it took into account the extent of the cultivable land and the number of available hands, it did not include the agricultural plant and the buildings concerned with agricultural produce. The big landowner who possessed mills, wine presses, olive presses, granaries and disposed of a vast supply of labour in the form of slaves and tenants could more easily fulfil his obligations than the small farmers and those who were originally military settlers. These often had to hire their draught animals and agricultural implements and could only use mills, wine and olive presses in return for payment. Further, their labour was supplied almost entirely by members of their family. If there was a bad harvest it was impossible for this class of farmer to fulfil his obligations.

Consequently many peasants who had formerly been free came under the lordship of the great landowners. Such men then cultivated their acres as tenants, and payment of their *annona* was taken over by their landlord. It looked as though this balancing of the *annona* in favour of the big landed proprietor corresponded to a deliberate intention on the part of the lawgiver. It is probable that the small farming concerns of the peasantry were regarded as being unviable from the point of view of the economy as a whole, for a small farm produced far less proportionally than a large estate. Possibly the *annona* system was used as a weapon against the small farmer in order to accelerate the absorption of this class into the large private and public estates. For the imperial government was primarily concerned in increasing the production of food to meet the growing needs of an expanding urban population. The increase in consumption could not be met by the efforts of the small peasantry, many of whom were descendants of the military settlers. The expansion of urban industries demanded a great drive in the countryside conducted on national lines. Imperial laws tying to the soil those who had lost their farms supplied the landed magnate with a secure source of specialized agricultural man-power in these peasants dispossessed through failure to pay the *annona*. Thus the *annona*, in addition to its original purpose of provisioning the army and city, provided the government with the means of winning the battle for increased production of grain in order to meet the growing demands of expanding industry.

In order to offer urban industries greater possibilities for development, important agricultural regions formed special economic links with large industrial cities. Thus Egypt provided for the capital Constantinople, Sicily and Africa for Rome, Liguria (the western region of the Po valley) and Apulia for the great city of Ravenna. The wants of the industrial population of these cities were supplied by these provinces. There was a connection between the agricultural produce and the industrial products. A falling off in provisioning meant a setback in industrial production with a consequent regression in commercial exchange of industrial merchandise with various other states. This resulted in a reduction in the city's income from taxation, for it lived off its manufactured wares. Whether factories were in private hands or were a state monopoly, their workers had to be provided with sufficient to eat, otherwise there was danger of losing them. It was for this reason that the government exercised direct surveillance over all businesses concerned with providing the populace with oil, meat, bread and dried fish. They were obliged by law to belong to compulsory gilds and their activities and price-fixing were closely supervised. On fixed days certain people could get cereals and oil on presentation of special tickets (*tesserae*). In Rome there were about 2,300 centres for the distribution of oil.

How did industry work?

The measures of the central government which aimed at strengthening the development of urban industries by the introduction of the regular delivery of the *annona* benefited almost exclusively the big cities. Thus a process was begun which led in the final instance to the formation of a city economy limited to the capital Constantinople. Not the least of the services of this city economy was the preservation of the heritage of antiquity. Thus the Byzantine civilization of the middle ages kept in safety something which was lost to the West in the storms of the barbarian migrations.

The city economy for which Constantine and his immediate successors had toiled was quite different from the economy of the present day. It had no heavy industries like the modern combinations of iron works and coal mining. The industries of antiquity concentrated on the production of textiles, papyrus, glass, ceramics, lamps, iron utensils, arms, drugs, perfumes, leather wares and various kinds of ornaments. Such food indus-tries as there were at this time were primarily concerned with the conservation of pro-visions such as fish, meat and fruit. Fish for export was partly dried, partly treated with fishflour, and was placed in linen sacks for sale. Other businesses in the same line prepared for export delicatessen items such as highly prized fish sauces. Meat was salted or made up into sausages. Fruit was either dried, such as dates, apples and plums, or was bottled with honey as a conserve.

57

The most important branch of the late antique economy was the textile industry. It managed to keep its pre-eminence in economic life up to the eighteenth century and it was only then that it gave way to heavy industry. The raw material for the textile industry was supplied only in part by the Roman Empire and it was necessary to import, particularly for luxury products. This was especially true of the silk industry which up to the beginning of the seventh century had to import raw silk from China. The Chinese silk had to be spun in Syrian and Egyptian workshops before it could be woven and made up. Side by side with Chinese silk there was Indian cotton which was another essential raw material used by the late antique textile industry. Then there was indigo, an important dye used in the textile industry, which had to be imported from India. It was therefore vital for the late Roman Empire to keep open the trade routes to those countries producing the more important raw materials needed for its industries. Thus the aim of Roman imperial policy was directed towards securing the route to India and providing its own industries with access to the countries supplying it with its raw material.

As well as the textile industries which had to rely on imported raw material, there were other establishments in the same industry which were independent of such imports. Among these were the factories (*ergasteria*) on the west coast of Asia Minor and in Cilicia whose raw material was the sheeps' wool supplied from the uplands of Anatolia. Workshops using dyes to tint their materials and garments only relied in part on foreign imported dyes. At this time there was indeed a chemical industry which produced successful imitations of the Indian indigo and the still more costly Phoenician purple. The genuine purple came from the murex, a shellfish yielding purple dye, which was found off the coast of Tyre, where there were special works producing this dye. Its manufacture was an imperial monopoly and its sale was severely restricted. A chemical substitute for this purple, called 'scarlet', was manufactured on the west coast of Asia Minor.

The textile industry of late antiquity was not confined to workshops engaged in spinning the raw material or weaving and dyeing the cloth. It also had a flourishing industry which made up the cloth. Some factories concentrated on particular types of cloak copying garments worn in the British Isles and therefore known by the Celtic name of *birroi*. Other factories manufactured cloaks following Gallic fashions; others were said to follow the models of the Belgic Nervii.

In contrast to the Italian peninsula, the smaller provincial cities in Syria, Asia Minor and Egypt were able to develop important industries. This was particularly true of the textile industry which possessed a long-standing tradition going back to pre-Hellenistic times. Thus the centres of the linen industry in Syria, Cilicia and Egypt were found in the smaller cities and were by this time highly specialized. Cyprus produced only napkins and sheets. Syria had a monopoly of fine spun materials. The products of the factories of Byblus, Scythopolis near Damascus, Laodicea, Tyre, and Beirut enjoyed an international reputation; they were largely exported and commanded a very high price on the foreign market. With luxury goods it might happen that widely separated cities shared in the production of a single article. Thus Chinese silk imported from Persia via Palmyra was woven to western taste by silkweavers (*serikopoioi*) in Syria; it was then dyed purple in the famous dye factories of Tyre in Phoenicia, and finally embroidered in gold in Alexandria in Egypt. Purple silk was twelve and a half times dearer than the thread spun from Chinese raw silk and three times as dear as purple wool. The price for this kind of luxury product remained high, though it was possible to get cheaper imitations, such as the scarlet wool manufactured with chemical dyes in Nicaea in Bithynia. Goods of this kind also had an important market.

The position of the workers in the textile industry was poor. It was only the specialist in particular demand who received a high wage. Slave labour depressed the wages of the free workers. Payment was usually for piecework. Only women were not on piece-work but on a daily basis. In the textile industry piece rates were based on the weight of the woollen woven material. With embroidery, payment depended on the weight of the gold thread used. There were in any case great contrasts. Wages varied from 25 *denarii* for simple embroidery to 1,000 *denarii* for embroidery in gold thread which was particularly difficult and highly prized. Here the 1,000 *denarii* would be paid for one ounce (27–28 grammes) of embroidered material. Usually in classifying individual workers engaged on the same type of work there were degrees of individual skill which affected the rate paid. It was only in dyeing concerns that the rate was so much per piece. The payment for each piece was laid down according to an exact tariff.

The victory over inflation: the issuing of a new currency

Measures to ensure that the population engaged in industry were adequately provisioned was only one requisite for the intensification of urban economy. Equally important was the stabilization of the currency and well organized directives to urban economic activities. Regulation of the currency took precedence over all other measures designed to control prices and direct production.

In the Roman Empire at the end of the third century, inflation had set in and had completely overturned the existing price structure, doing particular damage to Roman foreign trade. By A.D. 303 the devaluation of the silver *denarius* was about 4,400 per cent and by A.D. 324 it had dropped twentyfold to 88,000 per cent. The cause of this inflation lay in the vast military undertakings of the later imperial era which had completely exhausted the reserves of precious metal accumulated in earlier centuries by tribute and the opening up of new mines. The result was a continual reduction in the proportion of silver in the silver *denarius* and a considerable variation in the weight of the gold coins. It was, then, a decisive factor in currency policy when the change from silver to gold currency was completed. The gold minted *solidus* with a weight of 4.48 grammes of gold provided a firm basis for a new economic policy. Special measures were taken to guarantee the weight and sterling quality of the *solidus*. When paid into the state treasury the gold coins turned in were at once melted down and minted anew. This was to avoid loss of weight and consequent devaluation of the coin piece. It was with this in mind that instructions were issued directing that gold pieces paid into the state treasury had to be weighed and any deficiency in weight made good by the depositor. Thanks to these measures the Byzantine gold *solidus* kept its place as an international currency up to the twelfth century.

This stabilization of the currency not only met the needs of export trade but served to establish a greater equilibrium in domestic economy, since measures were also taken to stabilize the smaller units of currency and to fix their relationship to the gold *solidus*.

The contraction in circulation of small value coins, which had been marked in the third century and had seriously affected agrarian economic life, was now ended. For more important financial transactions such as those involving payments between states—for instance, the payment of tribute or subsidies—the pound (*litron*) was created. This was a higher unit than the *solidus* and one gold pound consisted of 72 gold *solidi*. The old *denarius* of the inflationary period provided the lowest unit of currency. This was reckoned in 'purses' (*folles*). If compared with modern European currency [1966], such as the Swiss franc, the value of individual Byzantine coins would be as follows: 1 gold pound=72 gold *solidi* (*nomismata*)=1,080 Sw. fr.; 1 *solidus* or 1 *nomisma* (this was the Greek term for a *solidus*)=12 *miliaresia*=24 *keratia*=15.43 Sw. fr.; 1 *keration*=12 *folles* =0.64 Sw. fr.; 1 *follis*=0.05 Sw. fr. (5.33 centimes). The current value of Roman silver coins varied in different parts of the Empire; in Egypt, for example, it was higher than in other imperial provinces.

The first restrictions on private employers

Closely connected with the currency policy was the control of prices and markets. In late Roman and Byzantine economic policy, as in all planned economies, civilian needs were of secondary importance. An increase in exports was regarded as the most vital task of industry. In this connection it must be remembered that the Roman Empire had to import both raw materials and precious metals. On the other hand severe measures were taken to prevent the export of basic food products or important raw materials and partly manufactured industrial goods. Export licences for goods in these categories were only granted in the context of exceptional economic agreements. Thus in the seventh century grain was exported to the British Isles in return for an agreed quantity of tin.

Within the Empire, state control of markets was vigorous and bore hardly on the rights of individual Roman citizens. Thus certain kinds of purple garments never came on the market. They were exclusively reserved for the Emperor and his needs.

Not only the sale of goods but the money market came under the strict surveillance of the government. Above all the state tried to control the money market by measures limiting the rates of interest. In the fourth century the legally permitted rate of interest was $12\frac{1}{2}$ per cent. This did not however mean that a higher rate could not be obtained. Short term loans for foreign trade which involved higher risks could command more than 50 per cent. The law did not however recognize this rate and it could not be enforced in a law-court. These difficult conditions on the capital market were particularly damaging to the export trade which was often attended by considerable risk. Here too the state had to intervene and take steps to provide adequate funds. This took the form of an export duty which was used in financing trade with India. For particular financial transactions of this kind application was made to banks which could be found in all big cities. It appears that bank credit was often used, particularly for covering the cost of military undertakings. In this connection the state frequently used the expedient of pledging the taxes as security. After Justinian's death his successor had first to cover the banking debts of his predecessor. One way of dealing with such problems was by means of confiscating the property of political opponents who had to face prosecution after a change of government.

A characteristic mark of this rigorously planned economy, which controlled not only agrarian economy and urban industries but imposed its grip on commerce and industrial markets, was the division of the economy into different categories. Each of the categories had its own corporation or gild (*systema*). The setting up of a new business depended upon acceptance into the appropriate gild, membership of which could only be granted with permission of the state authority, in particular the *praefectus urbis*. An employer could not carry on simultaneously business activities involving more than one gild. In this respect late Roman and Byzantine planned economies showed how strongly they had been influenced by the Hellenistic Egyptian economy. In Hellenistic Egypt, and indeed in the period of the Empire, the greater number of the artisan activities were state monopolies. If anyone wished to engage in a business or craft which was a monopoly he had to pay a fixed tax to the state before he could do so.

In the late Roman and Byzantine periods, during which the change-over from free to planned economy was really completely effected, new solutions to problems had to be found, and here state supervision was closely modelled on Hellenistic Egyptian practice. In Egypt use had long been made of corporations of workers and artisans. These corporations were organized, and their character determined, by the state. It was officials of the city prefect who made decisions concerning the admission of new members and gave rulings on the quantity and nature of the goods to be assigned to the workers for completion. They decided the services owed by the members of the corporation to the state in the light of their technical proficiency. All this was a return to the liturgy, or civic service, which was well known in the economy of the ancient world and had from earliest times taken the form of employing citizens in the great labour tasks of the state.

In the early stages of developing this planned city economy the emphasis was on the corporation's responsibility for branches of artisan activity of particular importance for the state. Later on, in the seventh century, with the introduction of the theme system and the radical modification of agrarian policy, the city economy saw the complete extension of compulsory membership of a corporation to all branches of its economic activity. In the sixth century, that is, in the age of Justinian, apart from provision businesses, there were only a few other industrial activities important to the state which were obliged to be organized on the compulsory gild system. Among these were businesses concerned with the sale or manufacture of silk. Doctors, bankers (*argyropratai*), notaries, jewellers, ointment and spice merchants, were probably already organized in corporations. Notaries and doctors were indeed to a certain extent supervised by the state. Some control over legal transactions and documents registered in a notary's office, as well as in matters of public health, was understandable, even in a state which was not based on a planned economy. A new factor, introduced in the late antique and Byzantine periods, was the supervision of all concerns depending on the import of raw material from foreign countries, such as the various branches of the silk industry, businesses for ointments and spices and jewellery. And in view of the close connection between capital and foreign trade it was also essential to control banking which was organized into a compulsory corporation. In this connection it was inevitable that merchants engaged in foreign trade and shipowners also had to belong to corporations of this kind. It was laid down by law that when preparing for an enterprise abroad connected with foreign trade, the members of both corporations had to make an agreement stipulating in detail the rights and responsibilities of either party.

The Empire fettered to its balance of trade:
the objectives and routes of Roman export and import trade

The risk that inevitably attended foreign trade with distant countries can be measured by the fact that ships were far too small for their long and arduous journeys. In this connection the relatively small surface of the sails should be compared with the heavy cargo carried. A moderate sized merchantman carrying a cargo of 200 tons had sails only 140 to 160 square metres in extent. The average speed of a ship of this kind was about 5 knots. Thus internal sea traffic going from the coast of Campania, via Sicily and Malta, to Alexandria, took about twelve days if conditions were favourable. From the coast of the Sea of Azov to Rhodes took ten days. Distant trade to foreign lands had to reckon on considerably longer for the journey. Merchandise destined for India first went by caravan down the Nile valley to the port of Berenice near present-day Ras Benas. This route was taken because unfavourable winds made a journey from Clysma on the gulf of Suez, or Aila in the gulf of Akaba, too lengthy. From Berenice ships for India had to leave by 1 July at latest because the journey to Ocelis on the strait of Bab al-Mandab took thirty days. If this harbour was reached after 1 August it was not possible to use the south-west monsoon to India. This wind could take ships to the south coast of India in forty days. The return journey from India was easier. The Indian ports were left in September and the north-east monsoon was used for the voyage to Ocelis. The prevailing Red Sea wind made possible a through journey to Clysma near Suez or Aila on the gulf of Akaba. It was in the Red Sea that shipwrecks most frequently occurred. All too often ships came to grief by missing the narrow navigable channel between the coral reefs so that the vessel was wrecked on the rocks, or else they were captured by Arab pirates when travelling down the coastal waters.

Whether it was luxury goods for export or imported raw material, the value was so great that the loss of a single ship inflicted such a disaster on the firm concerned that it often meant bankruptcy. Here the state had to intervene to subsidise export businesses. Such state subsidies meant that individual firms would not be burdened with losses quite beyond their means. Thus the losses of individual shipowners and merchants could be easily balanced by the usually generous indemnity paid by the state.

Foreign trade, particularly with India, was a matter of special interest to the state in the late Roman and Byzantine Empire. Foreign policy was largely determined by the needs of foreign trade. Thus in the sixth century behind the conflicts between Persia and the Byzantine Empire lay the struggle over the route to India, which was at the same time a struggle for free access to the markets for Chinese silk in Central Asia. China, India, South Arabia and Abyssinia took Roman luxury goods in exchange for vital raw materials. From China came silk, from India came spices such as pepper, cinnamon, ginger, and the valuable indigo dye. From India also came valuable woods (ebony), precious stones and gold. South Arabia and Abyssinia produced incense, myrrh, and African ivory. The export list of the East Roman Empire included products of the ceramic industry as well as glassware, textiles and highly wrought ironwork which was particularly valued.

In exporting industrial products from the *imperium romanum* or importing raw material and manufactured goods Byzantine trade did not rely solely on its own merchantmen since a considerable proportion of commercial exchanges between the *imperium romanum* and other countries took place inside the imperial frontiers. Caravans or foreign ships came to the more important trading and industrial centres of the Empire. Here the foreign merchants had at their disposal special quarters, cut off from the rest of the city by high walls, where they received board and lodging. These quarters contained not only dwelling houses but storage room for their goods and stalls, and foreign merchants had to pay a fixed sum for their use which included their food and lodging and fodder for their animals. As soon as they arrived they had to provide the Roman officials with an exact list of the wares which they had brought with them. Then they received a residence permit limited to three months at most. These quarters for foreign merchants, which were called *mitata*, survived right down to the end of the Byzantine Empire. Thus the establishments of the Venetians, the merchants of Pisa and the traders of Amalfi were found in Constantinople on the Golden Horn, next to the Jewish ghetto. These colonies of foreign merchants often influenced Byzantine decisions in matters of policy, as when they were granted the right to carry on foreign trade in their own ships: their influence on the culture of the Empire was ever deeper and more lasting. In the second half of the sixth century an important role was played by the Sogdian and Turkic *mitata* in Constantinople; later it was the establishments of the Italian maritime cities.

As early as the oldest *mitata*, quarters were allotted according to nationality. The most frequented quarters were those belonging to people living at a considerable distance, such as the Turkic races from Central Asia in the sixth century. At the time when Byzantino-Turkic relations were broken off in 581 the Turkic *mitaton* was housing about 100 people who were then sent home. Among the merchandise sold in Constantinople through the Sogdian and Turkic *mitata* were Chinese silks and precious stones, such as rubies from Badakhshan in north-west Afghanistan. There was a considerable export into Byzantium of textiles and beautifully woven tent hangings, the products of home industries. These products known today as Central Asian carpets, were called 'the Huns' weave' by the Byzantines. In Constantinople in the sixth century there was a great vogue for 'Hunnic' fashions. Adolescents had their hair cut after the style of the Huns and wore clothes in the Hunnic fashion. But of course the real importance of the Sogdian and Turkic establishments lay in the silk trade where they acted as middlemen. The prosperity of the Sogdian state was founded above all on the Chinese silk trade.

The *mitata* of the Persians were incomparably greater in number than those of the Central Asian states. They had settlements in other cities of the *imperium romanum* as well as in the capital Constantinople. There was a Persian *mitaton* in Caesarea in Cappadocia. Here it was particularly the products of the highly developed leather industry of Irak which were sold. These goods, such as the favourite red coloured sandals, were known as 'Babylonian leather' and were among the most highly prized articles of merchandise. Not everything marked as 'Babylonian leather' came from Persian Irak, just as today most of the leather marked 'Moroccan' has never seen Morocco and is merely a clever imitation. It was the same with the so-called Babylonian leather on sale in the Byzantine Empire. In the province of Phoenicia there was a very productive shoe industry specializing in the imitation of this kind of Persian leather.

Imitation of popular Persian goods was not confined to leather work. Chinese silk spun in Irak with its exquisite artistic designs was imitated in Byzantium and, like the leather goods, was then sold as Persian. At that time Persia was the arbiter of fashion. In the fifth century women's clothes with their artificially stiff-standing gowns were an imitation of Persian models.

But trade between Persia and the Roman Empire was not limited to luxury articles. The Roman Empire was one of the principal customers for the date crop from Persian Mesopotamia. In turn the Roman Empire exported a wide range of Phoenician wines to Persia; this was brought in special boats along the Euphrates up to Seleucia. There was also a not inconsiderable export of ceramic ware from Persia to the Byzantine Empire. Green coloured ware from Rakka, which was still being produced in the early Islamic period, at this time reached the Roman Empire by way of the East Syrian cities. The import of Persian materials made from Indian wool was also of considerable importance. On the other hand the export of the products of the Syrian armament industry, centred in Damascus, was strictly forbidden by law. However, in spite of existing prohibitions, the highly prized swords of Damascus were smuggled into Persia with the help of the Bedouins.

Trade with Persia, Abyssinia, India and the South Arabian and Central Asian states used the monetary system common to all these countries in which payments were made on the basis of the exchange rate of the country's own currency with the Roman gold *solidus*. On the other hand most of the Altaic peoples traded on the basis of exchange of goods. This was true for Persia as well as the Empire of late Roman and Byzantine times. It was an exception, since these two Empires, which could be regarded as the great powers of late antiquity, each exercised indirect control over the monetary economy of the group of states belonging to their currency block. This meant that these states minted their money according to whether they were in the Persian or Byzantine sphere of influence. The visible sign of this was whether the legend on the coin was in Persian or Greek lettering. The Persian currency block included all the Central Asian states (that is, the kingdoms of present-day Afghanistan, Sogdiana and the basin of the Ili) and the East Caucasian states (that is, the greater part of present-day Georgia and the whole of Azerbaijan). The Byzantine currency block embraced the Mediterranean countries with the Germanic kingdoms, as well as South Arabia, Abyssinia, and at certain periods India. The Abyssinian Negus coined money with Greek legends, which were accepted as currency in South Arabia. The states in the eastern part of the Caucasus had indeed legends on their coins in their own language but the minting of these coins showed affinities with Persian currency.

Both the great powers traded with the Altaic tribes in Russia and Siberia and this was done on an exchange basis. Table silver was the Persian and East Roman medium of exchange. Silver was chosen because it was highly valued by these tribes, who already had an abundance of gold. So Persian and Byzantine silver vessels were accepted in exchange for furs from Russia and Siberia. It is not mere chance that these silver bowls have been found particularly in the district of Perm and along the course of the Kama, for this was the end of the famous trade route from Siberia via the Urals to the West. In the region of the Kama and present-day Perm valuable skins from Siberia and Persian and Byzantine silver vessels exchanged owners. Hunnic merchants (the Onogurs), who lived to the east of the Sea of Azov, brought the furs to Cherson and Bosphorus, the Byzantine ports on the northern shores of the Black Sea. From here they reached the great cities of the Mediterranean. It was the city states of West Turkestan, including Samarkand and Khwarizm, which acted as middlemen for the Persians in their trade with the Siberian peoples. As well as valuable furs, particularly the coveted ermine, Siberia produced seal skins. These last were used on ships' masts for protection against thunder.

Trade with the Germanic peoples and with the Gauls had almost been the monopoly of the Italian peninsula during the early imperial period. But with the great economic crisis in the second half of the second and in the third centuries Italy had lost it to Syrian and Egyptian merchants. From the fourth century Coptic textiles with ivory and wood work and Syrian metal and glass ware dominated the Germanic market. These imports from Egypt and Syria, which also reached Scandinavia and the British Isles, exercised a strong influence over the Germanic art growing up in the fifth and sixth centuries during the migratory period. Coptic ornamental motifs appeared in Germanic forms, and, as the development of the arrow ornament shows, they influenced a wide range of early Germanic art. Coptic textile designs were copied on the decoration of Germanic helmet clasps. Coptic ivory carvings showing St George on horseback provided the model for the rider found on early Germanic gravestones (Hornhausen). This Coptic and Syrian influence on the art of the Germanic peoples replaced that of Asia Minor in Gaul and of Rome in Germanic Central Europe. The effectiveness of this influence corresponded to the degree of economic penetration.

ΝΥΞ ΗϹΑΙΑϹ ὁ ορθρος

12 The prayer of Isaiah; miniature from
10th-century Psalter

13 The prayer of Isaiah; miniature from
11th-century Psalter

14 Christ with St Menas; 6th-century icon

15 Christ the Pantocrator; mosaic, Church of Hosios Loukas of Stiri, Phocis

16 Mother of God with Child; 6th-century icon, monastery of St Catherine, Mt Sinai

17 Mother of God of Vladimir; icon

18 *Descent of Christ into Hell*;
fresco, Kariye Cami, Istanbul

19 *The journey to Bethlehem*;
mosaic, Kariye Cami, Istanbul

20 *The raising of Lazarus*; fresco, Church of Pantanassa, Mistra

21 Pala d'Oro; altarpiece, San Marco, Venice
22 The cross of Justin II

PART TWO

The emergence of
Byzantine civilization

Justinian: the man between two worlds

The age of Justinian marks the second stage in the development of Byzantine civilization. The foundations laid in the time of Constantine were a particularly formative influence in moulding the economy and political institutions, and it was on these foundations that an individual self-contained civilization grew up in the eastern half of the Roman Empire. Above all, two movements in quite different spheres played a notable part in influencing the new developments. These two movements together heralded the end of the world of late antiquity. But history does not indeed record only those movements which use men as their apparently compliant tools. As the stream of time relentlessly sweeps all before it towards new developments, great personalities exert an overwhelming influence. Such men seize the tide in their affairs and are carried forward on the crest of change. Therein lies the significance of Justinian and of the more outstanding of his successors, Maurice and Heraclius. They guided the vital new movements along the lines which were to be followed during succeeding centuries. It is indeed impossible to consider the monastic movement and the reform of the army without taking into account the personality of the Emperor Justinian who laid his imprint upon his age as no other did. And it is essential to begin by first considering what Justinian's role really was. In the past this Emperor has usually been regarded as the man of the *renovatio* who destroyed the young growing Germanic polities—the kingdoms of the Ostrogoths and the Vandals—and attempted to reverse the trend of events by restoring the *imperium romanum*. Can this be maintained? Or did Justinian himself already mark the turn of the tide and the transition from the world of late antiquity to that of Byzantium?

Judgments of this kind have hitherto been made with the Italian policy of the medieval German Emperors in mind. From the point of view of German imperial policy Justinian's destruction of the Ostrogothic kingdom meant the weakening of a Germanic stronghold in Italy. Justinian was therefore held to be indirectly responsible for the failure later on of the Italian policy of the German Emperors. And so the political divisions of Italy down to the mid-nineteenth century had to be regarded as the result of the Byzantine conquest of the peninsula in the first half of the sixth century. But this evaluation takes no account of the imperial policy which was directed towards the East, establishing relations with India, South Arabia, Abyssinia, the kingdom of the Berbers and western Turkestan. Justinian is thus judged not by his policy in its wider context but simply as a factor in Mediterranean affairs. This is seen as the crucial point, and therein lies the weakness of such a view. The age of Justinian and his successors—including the reign of the Emperor Heraclius (610–641)—must be regarded as belonging to world politics. It was a heritage from the ancient civilizations of Syria and Egypt which dominated the institutions of the Hellenistic states and the Roman Empire, including Justinian's Empire.

The new movements were a formative influence in civilization but they did not ignore the East Roman imperial office, nor did they work in opposition to it. It was Justinian and his immediate predecessors and successors who determined the course of these new movements, a path along which Byzantine civilization was to travel for centuries to come. On the other hand, neither the monastic movement nor the military reforms belonged exclusively to the East. They affected the West as well, where they brought about changes similar to those in the East. In the East they created Byzantine civilization; in the West they were responsible for the growth of western civilization. In the West the personality of Charles Martel at once comes to mind, and his connection with the military reforms leading to the development of vassalage, thus indirectly creating the hierarchical society which dominated the central middle ages, or one thinks of the movements fostered by monasteries such as Corbie or Luxeuil. Developments such as these mark the beginning of a new age, of a period of western civilization whose influence has lasted up to the present day. But there was an essential difference between the military reforms and the monastic movement in the East and in the West. This lay in their relationship to the civilization from which they sprang. And here East and West parted company. In the East the personality of the Emperor Justinian laid its imprint on an era hitherto regarded as the last phase of late antiquity. This is just as mistaken as the assertion that Justinian acted with the intention of restoring the Roman Empire. According to this view, the Gothic and Vandal wars of the Emperor are a last attempt to restore at the expense of the young rising Germanic kingdoms an *imperium romanum* long sunk in the dust, and in the same way Justinian is looked upon as the last ruler under whom the cultural life of late antiquity survived. The epoch of Justinian doubtless bore many marks of late antiquity but it also showed just as many signs of the new Byzantine civilization that was coming into being. The age of Justinian is essentially the time of transition from the world of late antiquity to that of Byzantium.

A detailed analysis of the period of transition is essential if the beginnings of Byzantine civilization in Constantine's day and its further development are to be rightly evaluated. It is necessary to know about the social classes which played their part in the evolution of this culture at this time. But it is also essential to consider the growth of the external forces which influenced its decisive transformation.

In the preceding chapters the economic, military and internal politics of the state at that time have been considered. But there has been no discussion of the social groups of the day. Each section of society must be regarded as a factor which influenced civilization, provided Emperors, or recruits to high ministerial office or to the ranks of the civil service. Then there is the question of the social background of the writers and artists whose work has survived. And in the context of these considerations must be sought the basic reasons for the differences in East and West which resulted in the emergence of a western and a Byzantine civilization as two distinct and contrasting developments. There is the question as to why and how the representational art and the literature of Justinian's epoch moved away from lines laid down by late antiquity and where the first signs of change are to be found. Finally—and this is a matter of extreme importance —the development of the two new movements must be considered together with the social revolution which followed in their train. This raises the question as to the way in which the old civilization and the social classes supporting it conflicted with the new movements. The monastic movement must first be considered.

The monastic movement: a revolution from within

The birth of the monastic way of life

The beginnings of monasticism go back to the period before Christianity was made a state religion. To begin with, the outstanding personality of the great ascete Antony pointed the way. He exercised an irresistible attraction over those men who were revolted by the ways of the world and sought to find a vision of God in the solitude of the desert. It was this *visio Dei* that distinguished the new movement (which first began in the Nitrian desert in Upper Egypt) from the Christian Church of the day. These ascetics in the desert repudiated the world. They had not made their peace with the secular power as the majority of the Christians had done. All their strivings were directed towards things beyond this world. Through their ascetic practices they hoped to achieve knowledge of God. Everything they did was directed towards the vision of God. The great church fathers had learnt from the old philosophers both methods of thought and the desire to formulate with clarity the principles of faith hammered out in the theological workshop. But this was quite alien to the desert hermits. They devoted themselves to prayer; many said the same prayer more than a hundred times a day, employing their hands the while in plaiting mats. It was not indeed any incapacity that would place them below the great theologians of the Christian Church. Their path towards the knowledge of God lay through ascetic practices and not theology, for them a way beset by doubts. Many will call this autosuggestion. But the historian is not required to make judgments on matters of this kind. His function is to witness to the profound influence which this apparently simple and primitive form of religion exercised on the development of the new culture, whether on religious pictures where the monastic artist seemed to simplify everything, or in church music where polyphony vanished to be replaced by hymns sung in unison, varied only by a certain choice of melody. Anything in late antique art reminiscent of the high achievements of Pompeian painting, such as the background shown as a landscape or with buildings in perspective, was ignored. Drapery became stiff with ornament and the sculptured fullness of the human form disappeared. Faces began to shine with an inner light, and in spite of all their rigidity figures moved with a compelling and convincing sense of urgency which was much more effective than the skill and refinement in the pictures of the early Christian period.

The eastern and western monastic movements were united in their opposition to the existing social order. The Church which was in alliance with the Roman state supported this social order, but in the eyes of the monks it was incompatible with the commands of the Gospel. On the basis of this conviction there grew up a radical Christian wing which sought to fulfil the despised commands of the Gospel in the arid deserts of Palestine, Syria and Egypt. No doubt in the East the *katochoi* of Serapis and the neo-pythagorean communities provided the Christian extremists with a precedent. All the same, this Christian movement produced something new which cannot be compared to any phenomenon of the past.

Monasticism grew up during almost the same period when Church and state were concluding their alliance. Its leaders, Pachomius and Apa Shenoute, were the creators of the monastic community. Here they differed from Antony, who sought God in the lonely way of solitude. Pachomius also devised the first monastic rule which provided detailed regulation for the life of the monastic community. He began as an anchorite (hermit) and it was not until 320 that he attempted to found a cenobitic house. Apa Shenoute, who died in 450, was the head of the famous White Monastery in the Thebaid. Out of the different monastic communities he built up a separate church. His personality pointed the way to a secession from the imperial Church. Here he may be distinguished from Pachomius, whose rule was used by Basil and laid the foundations of monastic life in the Byzantine Empire. The West also knew this rule. In his *Rule* St Benedict of Nursia borrowed a good deal from Pachomius. The form of monastic community which Pachomius had in mind in his writings did however also recognize hermit life, unlike Benedict's rule which was framed for an exclusively cenobitic house. Before his conversion to Christianity Pachomius had been a soldier. This is still apparent in his monastic rule which regiments the monks in a strict organization reminiscent of military life. At the outset each monk possessed his own dwelling. Later a number of monks lived together in a single house; each had his own cell which could not however be shut. All the monks did the same manual work, plaiting mats, weaving linen, acting as fullers, tailors and shoemakers. Like settlers, they worked in the desert or in reedy swamps. Their houses were divided into *tagmata,* like the military divisions. One house of the monastic community would be responsible for cooking, another for the infirmary, a third would have the duty of looking after the sale of wares produced by the monks, with the responsibility of supervising contracts with the outside world and providing hospitality for guests. The personnel of these three houses was changed every three weeks, when those who had been assigned to them again resumed their manual work. Within the monastic community there was a group concerned with the distribution of materials for manual work, and another group to look after the organization of the services of prayer. Here too there was a rota for the work. On Saturdays and Sundays all met together for a service. The liturgy with the Eucharistic Sacrifice was only celebrated once a week, together with catechetical instruction from the abbot. On fast days this instruction was given by the house father. This was the name given to those in charge of the houses of the monastic community. Even when listening to this instruction the monks did not remain idle; while attending to the house father's words the monks would plait mats or work their spindles.

The essence of monastic life, particularly in the Nitrian desert, was its asceticism. The goal of the ascetic was the attainment of *apatheia,* tranquillity, freedom from passion, that out of which love was born. The monks thought that this state was the means whereby real knowledge (*physike gnosis*) could be attained. The final goal was *gnosis,* or *theoria,* the vision of the Holy Trinity. Asceticism meant the mortification of everything corporeal, the renunciation of all contact with the outside world. Physical appearance and the care of the body were despised. Only the barest necessities were permitted and it was thought that this would effectively combat the suggestive attacks of the tempter.

This ascetic way of life led to excesses. In their quest for the vision of God some attained a state of ecstasy in which they believed that they had achieved union with God. Features of this kind are found throughout later mysticism. On the other hand there were some monks whose asceticism was so extreme that they repudiated the world and everything human as sinful. Representatives of this view regarded the well-to-do as damned and considered the married as excluded for ever from eternal salvation. These monastic extremes were specially prevalent in Asia Minor at Sebasteia (Sivas). Other monks, the so-called *saloi,* behaved like fools when they were not really so, and believed that they were serving God by their foolishness. But it was not only the extremists who repudiated the world. The monks in general adopted a deprecatory attitude towards the state and its Church. In their view the world was full of demons. They saw temptation everywhere. They even went so far as to regard it as positively sinful to take any care of the body, such as washing and having baths. In the monasteries the Holy Scriptures were not read because they were considered dangerous since they were capable of more than one interpretation. Spiritual nourishment was provided by the sayings of the fathers or of meritorious monks and abbots. There were some monks who said three hundred prayers a day. St Paul of the Scete was one of these; he was profoundly disturbed when he heard of an anchoress who achieved as many as seven hundred prayers a day. At a sign from the Patriarch of Alexandria they would hasten to the Egyptian capital to defend threatened orthodoxy. The weakness of Byzantine theology, which consisted of *catenae* and commentaries on the Bible made up of quotations from the fathers, was a legacy from the Nitrian monks. In the Egyptian monasteries Greek was not spoken. The Bible was written and read in the Coptic language. For the few Greeks in the monasteries there was a special interpreter who translated the homilies and the orders of the abbot into Greek.

And yet this Egyptian monasticism was to give its imprint to the Byzantine civilization which grew up later on. The direct influence of the monastic communities of Palestine and Syria was no doubt stronger, but Egyptian monasticism had greatly influenced the formation of a Greek-speaking monastic movement, particularly through the Greek adoption and remodelling of Pachomius' rule which was achieved by Basil in the fourth century. Greek monasticism had founded houses, mostly in Palestine, but it had also penetrated into the Syrian desert. Monks often established themselves in old forts, once part of the Roman defence system. The devout from Rome and Constantinople thronged to these centres to observe the edifying life of the monks. Palladius, bishop of Heliopolis, described the life of these monks in a special work, the *Historia Lausiaca,* so called after the imperial chamberlain to whom it was dedicated. Even the great theologians visited these monasteries. The Dalmatian Jerome, who translated the Bible into Latin (the Vulgate), went into the Syrian desert to live a life of solitude with the monks. Later on he founded a monastery in Palestine. Rufinus, another well-known theologian, the continuer and translator of the works of Eusebius, made the journey from Rome to the Nitrian desert in company with a distinguished lady, Melania; he wanted to get to know about the life of the monks there.

The crisis in the imperial Church: ecclesiastical organization in the hands of the monks

The monastic movement repudiated the imperial Church, considering that this Church, which had gradually become part of the state, had been secularized. Under its banner were found the same demands which were raised by later monastic reform movements. The Cluniac movement in the early middle ages denounced simony and demanded clerical celibacy. These two demands were also made by Byzantine monasticism. The abuses then to be found in the Church against which the monastic movement launched its attack are well attested by the ecclesiastical reforms of Justinian. Men without religious training were raised to the episcopate, former civil servants whom the Emperor wished to reward by giving them a see. The Church was encumbered with debts.

78

Newly ordained clerics had to pay considerable sums to the priest of the church as a kind of admission fee. All too often church property was sold in order to extricate the churches from financial difficulties.

Many churches had to follow a trade and take part in economic life in order to gain a livelihood. It was generally known that some churches had rights of monopoly and they ran industries which were exempt from taxation. An instance of this was the business connected with funerals. The church of Hagia Sophia in Constantinople possessed the very lucrative monopoly of the undertaker's work for the whole capital. The income went towards the upkeep of the numerous priests and deacons in this church's establishment. Hagia Sophia alone had 60 priests, 100 deacons, 40 deaconesses (infirmarians), 90 sub-deacons, 110 readers, 25 singers (*psaltai*) and 100 door-keepers. In spite of economic activities of this kind it did sometimes happen that churches got into financial difficulties and the state had to intervene to assist them. Such help was given to the church of the Ascension in Jerusalem, in this case through a state commission, which was not however able to obtain the necessary sum by means of a collection and therefore had to resort to a loan. It did not prove possible to raise this, and so it was decided to sell property near the holy place of the Ascension of Christ and therefore highly prized and able to be sold for a good sum. The money realized was used to purchase other property which would bring in a regular income for the church and could be used to wipe out the existing deficit.

It was not only the financial entanglements of the Church which the monastic critics attacked. One of the targets for their criticism was the clerical way of life. It was considered inadmissible that bishops should attend theatres, take part in shows of horse-racing or gladiatorial fights, or be involved in gambling or even marry. Priests of the lower ranks were allowed to marry. The canonical ruling was that the lower clerics, psalm-cantors and readers were permitted marriage without any restriction. Married priests could only continue to perform their spiritual offices as long as they were not married to a widow or a divorced woman. Bishops had in any case to renounce the married state.

The Emperor Justinian was anxious to put right these abuses among the clergy. His laws show how concerned he was with church reform. The imperial attitude made it possible for the monastic movement to come out of isolation and to penetrate deep into the life of the Christian state Church. From the second half of the sixth century members of the monastic movement secured a firm footing in the ecclesiastical hierarchy. In 579 the romanized Goth Pelagius was the first monk to occupy the Chair of St Peter. His successor Pope Gregory (590–604) also belonged to the monastic movement. The same development took place in the East where a monk, John the Faster (†595), became Patriarch. Anastasius (†599), Patriarch of the imperial Church of Antioch, had also exchanged the monk's cell for the patriarchal chair, and at the same time a monk from the monastery of St Sabas became Patriarch of Jerusalem. This meant that the monastic movement, which was in effect the radical wing of the Church, at the turn of the century was in possession of the patriarchal chairs and therefore had the ecclesiastical hierarchy under its control. Secular ecclesiastics, educated in the schools of rhetoric and in the universities, such as the Patriarch Severus who was in office in the first half of the sixth century, gradually disappeared. Thus the Christian Church moved a step further away from its late antique foundations.

The victory of the monastic movement signified the beginning of a new age. It was however more than this, for the break between East and West was also intensified by the monastic movement. Greek and Latin monasticism were as different as the

Syrian and the Coptic-Egyptian monastic communities. The fundamental difference between the rule of Basil, who had adopted and elaborated the rule of Pachomius, and the rule of Benedict of Nursia lay in the position of the individual monk in the community. Basil, following Pachomius, tried to reconcile the cenobitic and eremitic ways of life. The monk lived in a monastic community, but as an anchorite. Asceticism, that is work for oneself, led to a life pleasing to God, that is, a life which fulfilled the commandments. The rule of Benedict placed work for others above work for oneself. The monk was an essential part of a monastic community. 'Ora et labora', 'Work and pray', and each was of equal importance. In the West the function of the abbot was to command as well as to advise and exhort as the *hegumenus* of the Basilian monastery did. The Basilians also had work to do, but this was more the work of the anchorite performed in the quiet of the cell. The Greek Basilian rarely turned his hand to the plough as the Benedictines were accustomed to do. But they performed a lasting service in preserving the Greek character of the populace; they were strongly rooted in the urban and rural populations and thus assisted in warding off the danger of assimilation by the Slavs or Turks.

In the days of Justinian the monastic movement was split up into various regional groups—Greek, Syrian, Coptic-Egyptian, Armenian, Latin. In the sixth century these different regional monastic groups all had their own rules whereby their community life was regulated. The rule of Pachomius for the Egyptian-Coptic monks in the first half of the fourth century was followed in the second half of that century by the Greek rule of Basil and in the middle of the sixth century by the rule of Benedict for Latin monks. It was not until the first half of the sixth century that Syrian monasticism produced its rule. Here the great monastic law giver was Abraham of Kashkar (†588), the founder of the monastery on Mount Izla, and his successor Dadisho (†607).

The monastic movement takes control of the universities

In those monasteries where there was ethnic solidarity amongst the inmates there were no social distinctions. Simple folk, artisans, peasants and soldiers, lived side by side with men well versed in late antique culture and trained in the schools of Hellenistic philosophy, rhetoric and grammar. The gradually increasing influence of these monasteries on the ecclesiastical hierarchy inevitably affected its spiritual life. Above all, this influenced the schools and universities of late antiquity. The closing of the Academy in Athens was a sign of this. Through the episcopate and the patriarchates the monastic movement had gradually conquered the Hellenistic and pagan orientated universities. Thus a deadly blow was struck at late antique culture.

The late antique university only survived as a faint reflection of the splendid institutions of the age into which Christ was born. The Stoa and Museion were long since dead, although in the sixth century there was still an Alexandrian university and an institute of higher education in Athens which proudly traced its ancestry back to Plato's Stoa.

The question now arose as to the form in which universities and schools could still be maintained in view of the attack of the monastic movement. There was first of all the university of Constantinople. This was situated in the forum of Constantine and was then transferred to the Stoa on the old Capitol of the city. It bore the title of Stoa Basilike, that is, the imperial portico. The name is indicative of the close connection between this institute of learning and the imperial household, and with good reason, for this university was supported by imperial endowments. There was a library in the

Stoa Basilike where by order of the Emperor Valens four Greek and three Latin scribes devoted their entire time to the writing and copying of manuscripts. These figures reveal the poverty-stricken situation of this university in the fourth century which bore no comparison to the Alexandrine library. With such a limited staff it was impossible to copy even the most frequently read authors such as Homer, the tragedians, and Herodotus and Thucydides. The perishable nature of books at that time (papyrus codices) meant a continual loss of classical works. In 476 this library was destroyed by fire. But what really damaged the survival of ancient culture was not so much the difficulty of obtaining copies of books as the limitations imposed on intellectual freedom by the Christian state of late antiquity.

In contrast to Hellenistic times, teaching in the universities was closely supervised by the state. Teachers could only give instruction if they had a state permit. Philosophers and academic teachers who were not acceptable to the Emperor had therefore to leave the Stoa. An edict of 15 March 425 promoted six of the oldest university teachers to a higher rank and correspondingly higher salary. In future all university teachers could reach this grade after twenty years' service. The range and composition of the teaching body was stabilized at this time by imperial decree. The teaching staff henceforth was to consist of ten Latin and five Greek grammarians together with three Latin and five Greek sophists. In addition there were to be two jurists and one philosopher. This allocation of chairs showed that the university as it existed in the first half of the fifth century, had sunk to the level of an institution for professional training. The universal nature of a real university had been lost since the days of the Alexandrines. Here young men now received the education necessary to equip them for the higher offices in the civil service. The urge for real knowledge was scarcely ever found among students. It was significant that the teaching body contained only one philosopher. The result was that the solitary representative of philosophy did not lecture in any of the schools of philosophy then in existence or known, but limited himself at most to the philosophy of Aristotle and then confined his teaching here to certain selected works.

This brings home the close connection between Emperor and university. The Emperor had the last word on the appointment to a chair. All too often the specialist appointed by him was some favourite, a retired tutor of the imperial princes or a deserving imperial private secretary who at the same time held high office in the state. Thus the fortunes of the imperial university in Constantinople were not always happy. Under the Emperors Leo I (457–479) and Anastasius the university enjoyed considerable imperial support. Justinian adopted a different policy. Money which his predecessors had used for financing the university, he spent for other purposes so that the salaries for the different chairs were held up. Here the decisive factor was not so much the difficulties experienced by imperial finances, but rather the desire to apply financial pressure in order to silence university opposition to the government's measures. The situation in other universities was the same. In Athens the philosophers of Plato's school with the financial support of the old city endowments maintained their independence a little longer, until the university was shut by Justinian because of its alleged excessively pagan character. Until the middle of the sixth century the university teachers were pagan. In this respect the universities of Alexandria and Beirut were like Athens. It was only in Constantinople that the majority of the university lecturers were Christian.

The system of education towards the end of the fifth century was described in the biography of Severus, later Patriarch of Antioch, written in Syriac by his friend Zacharias the Rhetorician. According to his account the teachers in the university of the city of Alexandria were pagan. The students were divided into two groups, Christians and pagans. Lectures took place every day except Friday which was set aside for private coaching by university teachers. The monks started an agitation against the universities in pagan hands. It was learnt through informers that pagan rites were still practised in a place near Alexandria and that university teachers took part in them. Before officials launched an attack on this an attempt was made to make the temple unrecognizable by rapidly putting up walls. But to no avail. The temple was destroyed, the pictures of the gods laden on camels and taken to a public square in order to be burnt there. The priests of the temple, taken prisoner, had to explain the significance of these as they were thrown into the fire. The university teacher Horapollon, who was compromised by this scandal, had to resign his chair and leave Alexandria. He then went to Constantinople where he was converted to Christianity. Half a century later the university of Alexandria had already been largely clericalized and members of the monastic movement were mentioned as teachers there. John Moschus, who visited the university in the middle of the sixth century with Sophronius, later Patriarch of Jerusalem, told how the lecturer in philosophy, Theodore, also held the office of an abbot. This clericalization was not however entirely complete, for Theophylact Simocattes, the last representative of the late antique rhetoricians to be found among the historians, was also a student at this university.

The famous university of Beirut was but a shadow of its former self. About 490 the Severus mentioned above studied here together with Zacharias the Rhetorician. Both had left the university of Alexandria in order to pursue further their legal studies in Beirut. According to Zacharias the Rhetorician there were at that time only two professors there and these were responsible for all the teaching. There were two courses: one was for the *dupondi,* the first year students (the name was taken from the fees which they originally had had to pay), and the other comprised the next year, the *edictales,* the students of Roman law. The *edictales* were in the habit of attending for a second time the first year classes. The whole course took four years.

À propos of the life of the students it was said that to begin with the Christians were not considered the social equals of the rest. Work went on throughout the week, except on Saturday afternoons and on Sundays. Unless like Zacharias and Severus they preferred to work, students spent their free time in pubs, gambling dens and brothels. But in Beirut complete clericalization had also been achieved by the second half of the sixth century. This clericalization was not the work of secular clergy who had themselves attended the pagan university, but it was achieved by those belonging to the monastic order. Since the fifth century the monasteries had undertaken elementary teaching and now they were striving to gain control over higher education as well and to occupy university chairs. There were also exclusively theological schools for higher education. The catechumens' school at Alexandria was famous. It had been founded about A.D. 200 as a Christian institute of higher learning and from the mid-third century it had only Christians on its teaching staff. The theological school of Nisibis was built with a similar end in view. Until 363 Nisibis had been in the Roman Empire, and then after the Emperor Julian's unsuccessful campaign it was handed over to the Persians. Statutes of this theological school dating from 496 have been preserved. The school was in the hands of the Nestorians who had seceded from the imperial Church in the middle of the fifth century. The teaching language was Syriac. It is clear from the statutes that the students had to live in a monastery and it was only if the monastery was full that they could get permission to reside in the city. These theological students had to wear prescribed clothes; they could not be completely shaved nor could they grow their hair long. They were forbidden to take part in out-of-door festivals and excursions, and taverns in the city were also out of bounds. Nor were they allowed to fraternize with the students at the medical school in the same city. The course in this university lasted for three years. Part of their instruction consisted in taking down the Bible from dictation. Nisibis enjoyed an international reputation. Students from Italy and Africa attended lectures at this university. Cassiodorus, who had visited Nisibis, wanted to get the support of Pope Agapetus for setting up a similar university in Rome.

As well as institutions exclusively concerned with theology, there were universities which undoubtedly had a Christian orientation, notwithstanding their retention of the rhetoric and philosophy of late antiquity. The school of rhetoric of Gaza belonged to this category. It was from here that the attack on the university of Athens, which finally resulted in its closing by Justinian, was launched. In Gaza, as in Alexandria, the city supported the university. The city council made new appointments to chairs and their nominations were confirmed by the Emperor and at the same time the stipend settled. At this period half the salary of a university teacher was in kind.

The triumph of the monastic movement meant the downfall of the universities. Towards the end of the sixth century the patriarchal sees in Constantinople, Antioch, Jerusalem and Rome were occupied by monks. Only a generation·later the culture of the ancient world had been overthrown. It is true that in about 628 Theophylact Simocattes wrote the history of the Emperor Maurice, but he was the last of a long line of great imperial historians. During the same period George of Pisidia, the last great epic writer, composed his panegyrical poem on the Emperor Heraclius and his victory over Chosroes. In spite of the fact that the metre of this poem sometimes echoes forms used in the liturgy, it is still completely in the tradition of antiquity. Thus the victory of monasticism was synonymous with the decline of the culture of late antiquity whose last strongholds had been the universities. It is indicative of the change of the times that the later university of Constantinople, founded under the Emperor Theophilus, was sited in a church. The old university of Constantinople had used part of the Stoa, and then buildings on the Capitol. The content of the lectures given in this university had been through a theological filter. It consisted of chosen excerpts from the tragedians Aeschylus, Sophocles and Euripides together with Homer and the historians Herodotus and Thucydides. Of the philosophers only Aristotle was permitted and then only selections from his works; for instance, only the *Organon* up to the *Analytica* I, 7 was included in the curriculum.

The new sacral forms, the outward expression of the separation of the monastic movement from the West

The annihilation of the universities by the monastic movement meant the dissolution of the common culture of late antiquity. Regional separatism now became still more marked. This was true of Syria, Egypt and Greece as well as of the Latin West. This process did not stop short even at the Christian Church. The Christian Church had grown up in the first centuries in the tradition of late antiquity and its writings were in Greek or Latin, but now it gradually began to break up into regional churches. During the early centuries the forms of Greek thought had determined the way in which the Christian gospel was proclaimed and expounded. But now this was completely changed. The Graeco-Hellenistic phase of antique culture had continued even after the elevation of Christianity to the status of the state religion in spite of the rifts manifested in the first General Councils, but this now came to an end. The separatist movements coming from Hellenistic antiquity were intensified by the rifts in the Church.

The first indications of this were the translations of the Holy Scriptures from Greek into regional languages which were part of this separatism. The translation of the Bible into Syriac, Coptic, Armenian, Latin and Gothic belonged to the first stage of this movement. In the same context there was the new interpretation which the Coptic, Syrian and Iranian artists gave to Greek models. Thus Greek representational art, whether of mythological or Graeco-Christian subjects, was given an individual interpretation in Coptic and Syrian art, and this was found everywhere in ivory carving, on textiles and glass goblets, frescoes at Dura or pictures in Coptic monasteries.

These movements in the fields of literature and representational art were the first external manifestations of the beginnings of a cultural split. This was to a great extent the result of the shifts in population which had taken place within the *imperium romanum*. And so those manifestations, particularly in the sixth century, which point to a contrast between East and West, Constantinople and Rome, must be traced back to their origins which are revealed as early as the second century. It is possible to speak of a slow but clearly perceptible penetration of eastern religious forms into the West. Thus icon veneration can be traced to the traditions of the old Egyptian religion. It spread from Egypt to Asia Minor and Greece where it developed into one of the essential characteristics of the religious practice of the Eastern Church. On the other hand, the veneration of relics so characteristic of the Latin Church is clearly seen to be derived from the Greek hero cult in Asia Minor and Greece. This form of religious veneration passed from there to Italy, Gaul, Spain and Germany.

The spread of both these movements, the cult of icons and veneration of relics, which was one of the main differences between religious practice in East and West, can probably be traced back to the shift of population in the early Empire. People moved from Egypt and Syria to Asia Minor, and from Greece and Asia Minor to Italy and Gaul. Both movements can be related to the spread of Christianity in the first two centuries A.D.

Greek Asia Minor was first won over to Christianity from Syria and Palestine. But the further spread of Christianity was due to Egyptian and Syrian specialist craftsmen connected with industrial developments in Asia Minor which were part of the imperial economic policy of that period. In accordance with this policy Egyptian and Syrian Christians were settled in Asia Minor and they exercised a decisive influence over Christianity in that region, introducing the icon veneration which was common in their own countries. On the other hand, artisans from the coast of western Asia Minor, then in possession of a highly developed industrial and cultural life, migrated to Italy and Gaul, taking with them to those regions the Christian veneration of relics which was linked to the Greek hero cult. It was in this way that the cult of relics derived from the Greek hero cult from Greek western Asia Minor was brought to Italy and Gaul, and on the other hand the veneration of icons, part of the Egyptian folk tradition, came to the then undeveloped regions of parts of Asia Minor, such as Cappadocia and Isauria. These provinces became so important in the East Roman Empire that the west coast of Asia Minor, the capital Constantinople and parts of the Balkan peninsula followed their example. It also happened that some of the Emperors came from these provinces. Thus the Emperor Zeno was an Isaurian and Maurice a Cappadocian from Caesarea. It is known that Zeno brought Isaurian workmen to Constantinople and had churches built there. As early as Maurice's time the domed church had definitely established itself in Constantinople.

Thus there was a marked change in church architecture. It was in the East that the basilica, the original type of Christian church as decreed by Constantine, was first abandoned. It is not mere chance that the relinquishment of this Constantinian form of ecclesiastical architecture coincided with separatist movements within the imperial Church. Here again monasticism was a major factor in this architectural development. Connected with this were changes introduced into the liturgy and the form of the divine services in general. Ecclesiastical architecture was essentially conditioned by the development of the Christian liturgy and the Christian services. The five-part mass of the West (Kyrie, Gloria, Credo, Sanctus, Agnus) was not found in the East. There the prayers of the first centuries had been firmly integrated into the Divine Liturgy. In the nave of the church stood the faithful, men and women, and both had their own door of entry. The position of everyone was regulated down to the last detail. Old and young men, married and unmarried women and widows, all had their special place in the church. Children stood close in front of the altar. Bishops and priests sat in the apse behind the altar, the bishop on a special throne. The mass of the catechumens came first. This consisted of a reading from the scriptures, a sermon and prayer. Then after the catechumens had left the church the *missa fidelium,* the mass of the faithful, followed. At the opening of the service the doors were shut. The central eucharistic prayer (*anaphora*) is a splendid thanksgiving for God's promise of salvation, for the creation of the world, for the redemption of mankind by Christ. During the priest's prayer of thanksgiving came the Thrice-Holy, sung by the people, Then followed the description of the institution of the sacrament by Jesus at the Last Supper, the *anamnesis*, a remembrance of Jesus' death and resurrection, and finally the *epiclesis* in which God is besought to send the Holy Spirit to bless and change the earthly gifts of bread and wine. After the communion the mass ended with the blessing of the faithful by the priest.

Between the third and sixth centuries under monastic influence certain changes were made in the old form of the Christian mass. The so-called Entrance was introduced. This was a solemn procession of deacons and priests carrying the Gospels and the holy icons at the opening of the mass of the catechumens, and then with the holy gifts at the beginning of the mass of the faithful (*missa fidelium*). This was held to symbolize the preparations for the Sacrifice of the Lamb of God. The Eucharist previously celebrated in the sight of the whole congregation became a secret mystery performed in the *sancta sanctorum*. Now the holy celebration was for the most part withdrawn from the eyes of the faithful. The climax of the mass, the actual divine transubstantiation whereby the holy gifts became the Body and Blood of Christ, took place behind the iconostasis, the partition covered with icons, which was found as early as the sixth century, and was to begin with a curtain, as in Hagia Sophia. The processions allowed the faithful to take some visual part in the celebration but its climax remained hidden from their eyes. Without doubt Syrian influences were at work here, as they had been in the changes occurring in the form of the liturgical hymns. The basilica, the Constantinian type of the Christian church, was unsuited to this new development in the Christian mass. In the basilica it was difficult to arrange the processions with the holy gifts and also to separate the sanctuary from the congregation. This is why the architectural structure of the domed church came into use again at this time. It had originally been used for mausoleums of the martyrs and saints and it provided the kind of building needed for the new form of service. The domed cross-in-square church which developed later was likewise not a completely new type of ecclesiastical building but, like the domed church, was also to be found in pagan times. In basic essentials it is for instance similar to the building which the great traveller and art collector Hadrian erected in his villa at Tivoli. It was Hadrian's custom to build in the park at his villa replicas of all the notable buildings which he encountered on his travels. Thus at Tivoli he had built the prototype of a cross-in-square church and at least its main walls have survived to the present day. It would appear that this form of building was used for mausoleums before it was adopted by Christian ecclesiastical architecture. Thus the cross-in-square church of the sanctuary of Sergius in Rusapha in East Syria dating from the sixth century was originally the mausoleum of a Ghassanid prince.

It was only with the victory of monasticism that the domed church, and the cross-in-square domed church developing from it, became firmly established in the East. In this field too Justinian stood half-way between Hellenistic late antiquity and the Byzantine middle ages. He was the first to introduce the domed church to Constantinople. There were Syrian models for this in the type of church found at Qasr ibn Wardan. But with the aid of the achievements of late antique mathematics Justinian was able to build this kind of church on a monumental scale. The science of statics as developed by the mathematicians made possible for the first time the construction of a vaulted dome without supports. Moreover up to this time traditional building methods had offered no possibility of constructing a dome in which the drum was pierced by windows. The dome obtained by means of vaulting ribs of terracotta pipes fitting into each other, plastered with stucco and quick drying mortar, was in use, but not the dome in which the arches over the windows served to convey the lateral pressure downwards to the walls. This was first achieved by Justinian in Hagia Sophia. Here for the first time in almost modern fashion the external form was determined by the constructive data. At the same time Hagia Sophia was characteristic of the opening period of the new ecclesiastical architecture which accompanied the victory of monasticism.

The construction of the dome had to take account of the needs of the new form of service. In the new service there were no accompanying instruments, no polyphonic voices. There was only unison singing. Hymns were sung, and these were combined with the recital of the psalms. The verses of the hymns were meant to be inserted between the psalms and were linked to these by subject matter. There were a limited number of tunes for the hymns. The form and performance of the hymns were determined by metric rules, the number of syllables in each line, and the word stress. There were recognized collections of versicles *(sticherarion)* and hymns *(hirmologion)*. Later on the form of the canon was used and this consisted of eight or nine odes (hymns). In the harmony of the hymns the congregation believed that the angelic songs could be heard. For the Byzantine faithful these were a manifestation on earth of the celestial choirs. This is why new tunes were not composed for new hymns. In the simplicity of its melodies this church music can be compared to icon painting. In the case of both icons and hymns the creation of the artist was strictly limited to following certain accepted models. Just as it was held that icons were the receptacles of the divine power, so it was with melodies. In the words of Pseudo-Dionysius the Areopagite, these melodies were the echo *(apechema)* of the divine beauty.

The birth of Byzantine art under the formative influence of the monastic world

The strength of monastic influence on ecclesiastical architecture, and indeed on urban architecture and thus over the organization of much of the city's social life, was clearly demonstrated when the capital was rebuilt after its destruction in the Nika revolt.

Up to the Nika revolt of 532 the capital city of Constantinople was largely a Christian imitation of Old Rome. It too had its imperial fora. The great triumphal avenue, the Mese, linked the forum of Constantine with those of Theodosius and Arcadius, and not least of all with the new forum of Justinian, the Augusteum. Here the example of Old Rome was followed with its fora of Caesar, Augustus, Nerva and Trajan. The centre of Constantinople was the region round the Milestone where stood the buildings of the Senate, the imperial palace, the guards' barracks, the great baths and the temple of Mars, the Hippodrome and the church of the Holy Wisdom. Everywhere the resemblance to Rome was striking. It is true that Hagia Sophia had replaced the temple of Jupiter. But the temple of Mars still stood and the triumphal columns of the Emperors followed Roman models. The column of Constantine and the column of Arcadius were inspired by the monuments of Trajan and Marcus Aurelius in Rome. The Hippodrome in Constantinople corresponded to the Circus Maximus in Rome. Both Rome and Constantinople possessed a Field of Mars (*campus Martius*) where the election of the Emperor took place. In Rome this was the place where consuls were chosen in the republican period. It was the starting point of the great ceremonial avenue, the *via triumphalis,* which led to the Capitol where the consul and *triumphator* sacrificed to the gods in the temple of Jupiter. Constantinople also had its triumphal avenue. This led through the Golden Gate (*Porta Aurea*), where the city goddess was represented by a statue of Tyche holding a cornucopia, by way of the imperial fora to the church of Hagia Sophia which here took the place of the temple of Jupiter. But the city goddess remained: in Rome it was the Dea Roma whose statue was placed by the city gate, in Constantinople the city goddess presided over the Golden Gate.

Justinian, essentially a man of transition, did not make any complete break with the past. Like Marcus Aurelius, he had himself represented on horseback, as *triumphator,* in his forum in the middle of the Augusteum which he had rebuilt. This same Emperor did however reject the basilican type of building when he erected the church of the Holy Apostles, the churches of St Irene and of Hagia Sophia, and he chose for the new churches the domed style of ecclesiastical architecture which had developed in Syria. In the church of the Holy Apostles the characteristics of the late domed cross-in-square church were already perceptible. The appearance of this church, now destroyed, can be seen from the building of San Marco in Venice which closely followed the famous model in Constantinople.

It was not only in ecclesiastical architecture that monastic influence was predominant. There was a change in the lay-out of the city. When Constantinople was rebuilt at this time it no longer copied pagan Rome. The imperial fora and such of the arterial streets connecting them as had not been destroyed by the great fire at the time of the Nika revolt were not rebuilt. The area between the aqueduct of Valens and the Golden Horn now began to be filled with great churches and secular buildings. This was the region containing the streets along which the procession to the church of the Assumption of Mary (*Koimesis*) passed on its way to the Charisian Gate, which was situated in the quarter later known as the Blachernae. This church was a copy of the *rotunda* said by tradition to have been erected by the Empress Helena in Jerusalem and it was originally outside the city walls. With the growing cult of the Mother of God it attained a special importance. To begin with, an imperial palace was built in its neighbourhood, and then under Heraclius this region, which had originally been outside Theodosius' fortified city wall, was incorporated into the city's system of defences by means of a special wall. The growing significance of the church of the Assumption of Mary in the Blachernae quarter was evidenced by the increasing number of monasteries and churches founded along the processional route to this church. Imperial nobles vied with the Emperor in erecting monastic houses and churches. The church of the Chora (Kariye Cami), famous by reason of its Palaeologan mosaics and frescoes, was founded near this processional road perhaps by Crispus, a relative of Phocas, at the turn of the sixth and seventh centuries.

So, then, in the matter of ecclesiastical architecture the period of Justinian was also a time of change. The Emperor had introduced the domed church as the new architectural model for the Empire. The domed basilica which probably first developed in Cappadocian and Syrian regions had developed here from the cult of the *martyrium* (the martyr's tomb). In the capital this was first found towards the end of the fifth century, probably first introduced by the Isaurian Emperor Zeno. During his reign he had builders sent to Constantinople from his native land. To begin with this new architectural form does not seem to have acclimatized itself. It was only really established in its characteristic form with Justinian's erection of Hagia Sophia, the church of St Irene, and the church of the Holy Apostles. But although he consciously adopted the domed church as an expression of the new religious feeling engendered by monasticism, he did indeed still attempt to retain in this church architecture some connection with the culture of late antiquity. So in developing the domed basilica on a monumental scale he made use of the highly developed science of late antiquity. For it was only by means of late antique knowledge of the laws of statics that Hagia Sophia could be crowned by a dome of span larger than anything ever previously known and with a drum pierced by windows.

The form of the interior in Justinian's day also showed the transition from the late antique to the Byzantine period. The iconoclast controversy left undestroyed very little of the old mosaics in Justinian's churches in Constantinople and Asia Minor, but the church of San Vitale in Ravenna provides evidence of the ecclesiastical mosaic decoration of this period. Here the imperial artists used mosaic decoration in quite a different way from the iconographical programme for the interior decoration of churches visualized and subsequently introduced by monasticism. Naturally the interior decoration of San Vitale shows the scenes from the Bible used in later churches, representations of Christ, of the Mother of God, of the Holy Spirit, of the prophets and the saints. The difference lies in the style. In San Vitale the religious picture is inspired by the traditions of the old Hellenistic wall paintings; these paintings are reproduced in the medium of the mosaic. This is particularly true of the treatment of landscape backgrounds, which in pictures influenced by the monastic movement are either completely missing or are almost translated into a kind of ornamental arabesque.

One picture in which this comes out very clearly is the representation of the sacrifice of Isaac. In San Vitale it is set against a spring landscape, broken by groups of trees ranging from intense green to the dark fir trees in the background, and in between—with a sense of colour almost like that of Van Gogh—flowering trees break through the green like burning torches. Another mosaic shows Moses on Mount Sinai. The setting is a wild cleft of rocky mountainous terrain. In the distance, almost hidden in the clouds, is the outline of a fortress. The heavens breathe thunder. The landscape is bathed in the colour of the sky. The rocks reflect the yellow sulphurous tinge. Only the dark branches of the trees tossed hither and thither by the approaching thunderstorm can be seen. Some giant seems to have piled the rocks on top of each other. The dynamic of this landscape, whose analysis of objective reality strikes us moderns, is something very far superior to the illusionism of the later Pompeian landscape painters. The creators of the mosaics of San Vitale had a feeling for atmosphere and space which the Hellenistic landscape painters lacked, at least in their surviving work. The magic of a landscape like that of the artist of San Vitale was not seen again until the fourteenth-century master who created the mosaic in Kariye Cami (church of the Chora) in Constantinople.

88

That was the period when learning and literature gradually began to reach once again the cultural heights of the age of Justinian. In the mosaics of San Vitale the landscapes belong to the school of secular painting then flourishing, of which nothing now exists except faint traces in Syria. The mosaics in the courtyard of the Great Mosque in Damascus from the early Umayyad period belong to this tradition, which drew its inspiration from Justinian's day. Here there are to be found mosaics comparable with the scenes in the church of San Vitale. Here the artist succeeds in recreating the atmosphere of the landscape. The mosaics of Damascus show well cared-for parks with all the rural accompaniments of a landed aristocracy enjoying *dolce far niente*. They can be compared to the Zuccarelli baroque landscapes of the eighteenth century.

There was a marked contrast between the religious painting of Justinian's day with its strong secular associations, such as is found in the mosaic pictures in San Vitale, and the painting of the monastic movement. An excellent illustration of this later style of painting is found in the miniatures of the Bible in the *Codex Rossanensis* and the Vienna *Genesis*. There are no landscapes in the Vienna *Genesis*. Scenes which take place in front of the city walls are so represented that the city seems to be like a kind of pictographic indication in the middle of the page without any need for being placed in a landscape. It is the same in the *Codex Rossanensis*. In one of its scenes Christ stands before Pilate as though on a modern stage; behind Pilate there is only an empty wall. Both the *Rossanensis* and the Vienna *Genesis* probably belong to the beginning of the sixth century, that is, fairly near to the period of the mosaics of San Vitale. The striking contrast is to be explained not by the different mediums used—mosaic and parchment—but by two entirely opposed conceptions of representational art. This contrast is conveyed in modern terminology by the words naturalism and expressionism. This break with tradition is also found in the secular painting of the day. The miniatures in the manuscript of the *Iliad* in the Ambrosiana in Milan dating from the same period make as little use of the landscape backgrounds as the Rossano manuscript or the Vienna *Genesis*. There is no question of this form of artistic representation having first arisen in the sixth century. It is found as early as the middle of the third century in the frescoes in the synagogue at Dura-Europos. It is, then, a case of an old form of art originally found on the periphery of the Empire, regarded by the ancient world as being barbarian art. From the sixth century the chosen means of expression for this kind of art was the icon.

The form of religious painting inspired by the monastic movement was inseparable from the icon. The oldest icons came from the monastery on Mount Sinai or from Coptic monastic settlements. Thus the icon of John the Baptist preaching in the wilderness in the possession of the Sinai monastery was a piously venerated symbol of monks and anchorites living in the desert rather than a holy icon of city dwellers. The picture of the martyrs Sergius and Bacchus, in whose honour Justinian had a church erected in Constantinople in the first half of the sixth century, appears on an icon of the same date in the Sinai monastery. As well as figures of the saints there were icons showing pictures of the Mother of God and Christ. Because of the special veneration owed them, these pictures were transferred to the church and repeated in mosaic or fresco on the walls or in the dome. Such pictures were so venerated that definite rules and prescriptions were laid down which had to be scrupulously observed in their reproduction. The position of the pictures of Christ, the Mother of God, the Holy Spirit, the apostles, prophets and saints, was determined by the degree and form of their veneration. During this period pictures in the interior of the church acquired a different significance from that which they originally had. The picture as an explanation of the Holy Scriptures, repeating within the church scenes from the life of Christ, now gave way to the picture as an object of veneration and cult.

The iconographic programme and the form of the interior of a church were not determined only by the adoption of the icon and its artistic conception as represented in fresco and mosaic. Icons had already been influenced by the popular religious practices of pre-Christian Egypt, and similarly the form and sub-division of iconographic material showed non-Christian origins. In such an iconography, developed under monastic influence, Hellenistic cosmology was abandoned. The world was no longer represented as a sphere with a single heavenly space, but an eastern cosmology of the heavens was adopted, and in particular an old Jewish conception, which thought that there were several heavens and corresponded to an Akkadian–Chaldaean tradition, now found expression in the monastic movement.

The way in which these views were transmitted is known. Cosmas Indicopleustes, who wrote a Christian cosmography of which at least the preface has survived, tells how his views on the creation of the universe came to him from Mar Aba who was then the Nestorian Katholikos. On the basis of this, he attempts to explain the cosmos as symbolized in the Mosaic tabernacle which was a copy of it. This view of the cosmos also reflects Mesopotamian sources. Cosmas had assimilated Akkadian with Christian views of the cosmos. This also brought about a change in Christian iconography. Christ is shown by Cosmas as the universal judge enthroned in the first heaven, the angels occupy the second heaven, mankind is assigned to the third zone, and the fourth is reserved for the underworld. These four heavens are the scene of the event known as Christ's descent into hell, when the Saviour of the world entered hell (the underworld) to redeem the souls there and bring them to everlasting life. There is no trace of this scene in the Holy Scriptures and it is first found in figural art in the seventh century. It comes from the apocryphal *acta* of Pilate and the equally apocryphal Gospel of Nicodemus, works which appeared in Syria and Palestine between the end of the second and the fifth centuries. They illustrate the Christian adoption of Akkadian myths still living in Mesopotamia. Christ's descent into hell can be paralleled by Ishtar's descent into the lower regions, by the resurrection of Tammuz and the assumption of Etana. The old Jewish and Akkadian views on the existence of four heavens later influenced the structure and form of the domed cross-in-square church, when four secondary domes were added to the main dome. So here too the old Jewish conceptions of the creation of the universe influenced Byzantine civilization through the monastic movement.

The revolution from without: 2
the dictatorship of the army

First moves towards new methods of frontier defence

The monastic movement had achieved the transformation of the late antique into a Byzantine civilization. In this, however, it could not claim sole responsibility. The reform of the army had an equal significance for the development of the new Byzantine civilization. It was this which had first disrupted Hellenistic society and built up a new social order in its place. The transformation brought about by the reform of the army was felt in two directions. First, it meant a change in the nature of the frontier defence, and then it altered the financial administration previously in force.

The appearance of fresh peoples on the imperial frontiers gave the impetus for changing the old form of frontier defence. In the face of these peoples the old inflexible system of defence consisting in a fortified line, the *limes*, proved ineffective. The Persian attacks, and then the Arab onslaughts in the regions of Syria and Palestine, and those of the East Germans in the area of the lower Danube, had probably given the first impulse to reorganization of the frontier fortifications.

Here the great reformer was Diocletian. The powerful line of fortifications stretching from the gulf of Akaba on the Red Sea to the upper reaches of the Euphrates near Kirkesion and beyond to the Tigris, were owed to him. But this line of defence differed from the German *limes,* or Hadrian's wall in Britain, which consisted of a fortified wall for it was based on a system of fortifications connected by roads. The roads linked up the forts which were situated far out in the desert. They enabled troops to be moved to any threatened point in the defence zone in the shortest possible time. In connection with this changed system of defence the old names of *vallum* or *limes* were no longer applied to Diocletian's work. This was known as the *strata Diocletiana*, Diocletian's road.

The new element in Diocletian's frontier defence was the settlement rather than the stationing of troops. The *castellum* was no longer a garrison but the central point of a district where the troops held land which each soldier could cultivate with the help of his family. Land was reclaimed from the desert by means of an extensive system of irrigation which served the animals of the Arab nomads as well as the fields of the inhabitants of the *castellum*. Land thus won from the desert was granted to the soldiers, who each received their own portion to cultivate and could bequeath this to their heirs. There were no civil officials here. Everything concerning the ownership of the land, even legal rulings, was registered or decided by the military authority of the *castellum*, at the office of the commandant or of a tribune, or in case of appeal from the section commandant, by the *dux*. The soldiers had to pay a tax for the land which they held. Being outside the competence of the civil taxation departments they paid it to an office of the district commandant whose head was called a *numerarius*. Soldiers thus had the *pronomion,* a right which allowed them to pay their tax direct to the office of the *dux*.

The garrison of the *castellum* did not consist exclusively of military settlers for there were men of other professions. Here geographical factors played a decisive role. If the place where the *castellum* was sited was on a river there was need for some of the soldiers to look after the boats. Men belonging to the higher professions, such as doctors, were also called to be members of the garrison. Membership of the garrison of the *castellum* only became valid after entry on the military muster roll. Every military unit of the imperial army had its own muster roll which provided information about date of entry into the service, arms and equipment. These had been used earlier on by the legions in the early imperial era. Pay was issued on the strength of information in the muster roll. After entry on the muster roll each soldier received a document, the *probatoria*, which attested his enrolment in the service. The garrison of the *castellum* at first had a muster roll which gave the original designation of the division. But this was soon replaced by the name of the *castellum*. Thus troops belonging to the *castellum* founded at the beginning of the sixth century under Anastasius in the southern tip of Palestine at Nessana were originally called *numerus Theodosianorum* but this was soon changed to the name of the place. The method of enlarging the manpower of military divisions settled in the zone of the *castellum* was new. Normally recruits to field divisions were sent from entirely different districts to receive military instruction in reception camps, but the garrison of the *castellum* got its recruits from its own area. Members of the families holding land in the zone of the *castellum* had to supply their sons as recruits for its military force.

In normal times soldiers who belonged to the military garrison were not greatly hindered from following their civil professional calling. Even in the form of judicial procedure the nationality of each member of the *castellum* was taken into account. The Arab form of oath as usually employed in judicial procedure was not called in question. Thus when the Arab soldiers of the *castellum* at Nessana took an oath they did not swear by the name of the Emperor as was usual, but they were permitted to continue to use the old Arab form of oath. The spoken language during judicial proceedings was certainly also Arabic, even though the protocol and documents deposited in the archives of the *castellum* were drawn up in Greek. This was very important for the continuity of foreign ethnic groups. Arab soldiers were not assimilated into the Hellenistic-Roman culture of late antiquity. Though they were Roman soldiers they remained Arabs.

Developments here on the Romano-Arab frontier can be paralleled by similar manifestations in the frontier *castella* on the Danube. What the Arabs were in Syria and Palestine, the Germans were in this region. This explains why German words and expressions penetrated into the language of the East Roman army. Many *castella* bore German names which even found their way into official military phrase-books. Thus here on the lower Danube, in the region of present-day Bulgaria, there were *castella* with names like Mareburg, Stileburg, Tulkaburg, Halikanburg and the barrier zone near the Shipka pass was called by the German word Werigawi (defence or protection zone) which the Greeks called the *kleisourai Berigabon*. The military units also used Germanic designations. Thus a small military unit was called *Foulkon* which was how the German word Folk (Volk) was written. The subdivision of a *numerus* was called by the German word *Band* (field banner), which became *bandus*. This process even went so far as to adopt part of the military organization of the German army. In the ninth century the Byzantine army still had the troops of the Optimates; this was originally the designation of a crack corps of the Gothic army. In the territory of the lower Danube the racial characteristics of the soldiers in the frontier zones were entirely respected. The tribal chieftains were even granted the position of Roman officers and in this capacity continued to rule over their people.

Castella on the lower Danube were not built in the same way as the forts on the edge of the desert in Palestine. Behind their walls the houses stood closely packed together. They usually had only two rooms, one for cattle, the other to sleep in. The houses were of a single storey, unlike those in Egypt where, as at Syene, dwelling houses often had several floors and considerably more comfort than those on the lower Danube. Here all the *castella* had common granaries for corn and stables and space for the country populace who might take refuge there. There was also usually a church.

These *castella* were constructed in all military frontier zones which were specially exposed to danger. But with the increased threat of external danger, the range of the defence zones was extended. By the time of Anastasius several provinces were included in this region needing protection. Thus the military instructions issued by this Emperor for the defence of the province of Libya, present-day Cyrenaica, provided for a network of *castella* extending over the whole province. Surviving edicts show that Justinian took similar measures for the military reorganization of the re-conquered Roman province of Africa.

The existence of these frontier zones for defence, as they were up to this period, that is, up to the middle of the sixth century, had not yet changed the character of the individual regions of the Empire. It was only on the periphery that a new social order had been formed which, to judge from conditions in the Empire, was at first something of a foreign element.

The further development of the imperial army: its reorganization after the pattern of the frontier troops

It was the Lombard conquest of part of Italy in the second half of the sixth century that first made it necessary to extend to a whole province a system which had previously only been used on the frontiers of the Empire. The Lombard invasion of Italy was the result of the great migration of the Altaic peoples known as the Avars which had forced the Germans to abandon their homes in the Danube basin. It would appear that the Lombards had begun by settling in North Italy with the consent of the local authorities and they were to be integrated into the Roman defence zones there. But a successful uprising on their part made this impossible. They penetrated beyond the areas assigned to them and took possession of a large part of North Italy, as well as two regions in Central Italy (Tuscany and Spoleto) and an isolated area towards the South (Benevento). The needs of the hour demanded energetic measures from the imperial government designed to meet the threatened loss of the whole of Italy.

To deal with this difficult situation the East Roman Emperor Maurice resorted to the policy of applying the defence system of the frontier zones to the whole of Italy, threatened as it was by the Lombards. To this end the most strategically important roads were fortified with *castella*. Thus in order to separate North Italy from Central and South Italy fortifications were made on a road running from Padua, Monselice, Modena, over the Apennines to Luni and Genoa. The road linking Rome with Ravenna was also secured by *castella*, and this cut off the Lombards attacking Tuscany from Spoleto, which was also in Lombard hands. Finally a similarly fortified road between Rome and Naples prevented the Lombards of Benevento from reaching the sea.

The setting up of these *castella* led to an agrarian revolution in Italy. This was because conditions of ownership of land suitable for cultivation here were quite different from the frontier zones where there were scarcely any large landed proprietors. As well as extensive imperial domains, in Italy there were a very considerable number of both ecclesiastical and private landowners. To establish *castella* and military settlers meant dividing up these large estates. The method adopted was expropriation without compensation, but the soldiers stationed in the *castellum* were granted land in the form of an emphyteusis, that is, a hereditary lease. The actual ownership of the land remained with the proprietors and the soldiers had to pay them a fixed annual rent in return. This relationship with the landowners meant that the garrison of the *castellum* did not form an independent community, for the *castellum* was established on private property.

The development of this relationship between the soldiers and the landed proprietors, based on leasehold, was of extreme importance for the West. Under Germanic influence the nature of the emphyteusis began to change and what had been a Roman legal concept now turned into a relationship of vassalage. The relation between soldier and landed proprietor, which from the Roman point of view was regarded as a private contract, began to be interpreted as a relation between lord and vassal. The reasons for this development lay in similar Germanic relations, which on their side went back to old Roman institutions which had passed into Germanic law. This is particularly true of the Lombard *arimannia* which influenced the process whereby an emphyteutic relationship was changed into that of vassalage. A personal bond existed between the *arimanni*, settled on royal land with the obligation of doing military service in the royal army, and the ruler, and this can be regarded as the first stage towards commendation in the sense of medieval feudal law. In the case of the Roman system of frontier defence, the soldiers holding in emphyteusis felt that they were in the position of retainers, particularly in the case of ecclesiastical property. This meant that the two largest landlords in imperial Italy, the Pope and the archbishop of Ravenna, now became territorial rulers. In the case of the papacy this situation was given legal validity by the Franks, so that the Pope was at least *de jure* ruler of the land of which he had formerly been proprietor.

Under the influence of strong Germanic elements, this process had initiated a policy which was to direct Italy away from the social structure of late antiquity into the feudal world of the West. This was of great significance for Byzantine civilization. It was not only that a considerable part of Italy was finally cut off from the world of late antiquity. There was also the fact that the agrarian revolution, which began in Italy with the application of the system of frontier defence to part of the Empire, affected the Roman Empire in the East as well.

What the Lombards were to Italy, the Arabs were to the Roman Empire in the East. With the defeat of the Byzantines at Yarmuk in the middle of the seventh century, the Roman Empire in the East was left with little more than Asia Minor with Constantinople controlling the narrow straits, and in Europe with the coastal areas of Greece. The Arab onslaught aimed at capturing Constantinople and breaking through the Byzantine lines of defence along the summits of the mountain ranges in eastern Asia Minor. In this difficult situation the imperial government had no choice but to apply the frontier zone defence system to Asia Minor. Consequently a large part of the existing field army were settled there. The *comitatenses*, the field troops, became *limitanei*, the garrison troops of the *castella*. Historians describe this policy as the establishment of themes. This word originated from the Greek *thesis*, which also had the meaning of 'a bundle of documents'. Thus the word *thema* indicates the custom of calling the new military units after the officials who kept the soldiers' muster roll. The designation of the older military units, *catalogus* and *numerus*, had pointed to the officials keeping the pay lists. But in the case of the themes it was no longer a case of individual units, but of whole armies which were concerned in the process of settlement. All these armies had been concentrated in Asia Minor to meet the attacks of the Arab invaders. The Opsikion (*Obsequium*) theme, the Emperor's private army, was assigned to Bithynia and the region of the narrow straits. Earlier on this army had been stationed in Thrace in the European region of the Empire. The second European army which used to be

94

under the command of the *magister militum per Thraciam* was charged with the defence of the area round Smyrna. The third European military unit, the Danube fleet, was responsible for the defence of the Lycian coast against Arab attacks. This Danube fleet was called the Carabisianon theme, after the *carabi*, a kind of widely used light ship originating in Cyprus. The two Asia Minor armies, the one commanded by the *magister militum per Armeniam*, the other by the *magister militum per Orientem*, undertook the defence of the mountain passes on the eastern frontier of Asia Minor. These armies later formed the Armeniakon theme and the Anatolikon theme. Their stationing in Asia Minor was, then, to meet the needs of a clear-cut military situation, for the Arabs, in preparation for their planned attack on Constantinople, had provided themselves with a chain of stations from Cyprus by way of Rhodes, Cos, Chios, Smyrna to the peninsula of Cyzicus in the Sea of Marmora. It was the responsibility of the Opsikion, Thracesion and Carabisianon themes to ward off attacks from these Arab strongholds. The two eastern themes, the Anatolikon and the Armeniakon, undertook the protection of the eastern frontier of Asia Minor.

This military situation, which lasted for several decades in the mid-seventh century, was a decisive factor in the internal development of Asia Minor and therefore also in the formation of Byzantine culture. For in Asia Minor the same course was taken as in the home provinces. Soldiers were settled in *castella* placed at strategically important points which had to be defended against attack. As in Italy, the military units were instrumental in building up a new structure in the state and became the dominating social class. The military zones took the place of the provinces and the military commanders became the provincial governors.

In the end the new measures also changed the character of the agrarian populace. The troops settled in the themes very largely came from districts on the periphery of the Empire which had only very slight contacts with the Hellenistic culture of late antiquity. This was true not only of the troops but of the officers, who under the new system were entrusted with the government of the themes and thus became the ruling class of the new Byzantine society.

The Italian lands can be cited here as an instance of what happened. In Italy a large proportion of the troops were from Armenian units and were indeed to a great extent divisions which had been recruited from that part of Armenia belonging to Persia before 591. Others came from the defence zones in the lower Danube and were German in origin. Some, in any case a smaller group, came from Syrian garrisons and some, especially cavalry units, were recruited from Turks originating in South Russia or West Turkestan. It was the same with the officer class. Some of the commanders in Italy were Armenian. Thus the military governor in the highest rank (*dux*) bore the name Arsicinus which pointed to the well-known Armenian family of the Aršakuni. Another Armenian commander had the name Wahan (shield). The Germanic peoples were also always strongly represented among the officers. These officers often changed their army and consequently their scene of action. Thus the high-ranking German Guduin (Godwin) was sent first against the Avars in the Balkan peninsula, then to Italy, to Campania, against the Lombards in South Italy, and finally to Africa to the west bank of the Nile delta. Another German commander, Droktulf, a Sueve (Suevus) who came from the present-day Ukrainian Carpathians, fought first in Italy against the Lombards, then in the Balkans against the Avars and Slavs, and lastly in the African theatre of war, against the Berbers in present-day Tunisia. A third German leader served in East Syria under Roman command, then changed sides and went over to the Lombards.

Individual careers such as these well illustrate the predominantly multi-racial character of the Roman army and bring home the extent to which the settlement of these soldiers on Roman soil brought about radical changes. In Asia Minor, in contrast to Italy, the German element in the Roman army was not large. The predominating role in Asia Minor was played by the Armenians, as is evidenced by the names which have survived. After them came the Syrians, and then the Slavs. This influx of men of a different culture belonging to a feudal type of society quite unlike that of the ancient world inevitably meant a gradual change in the social structure of the Empire. Like the Germans in the West, the Armenians gave the first impulse towards the development of a new social order in the Byzantine Empire. In Armenia from time immemorial there had been a greater and a lesser nobility. The greater nobility, the *nakharars*, not only supplied the most important officials in the administration of the Armenian regions of the Empire, but, which was of great importance for the future, they also held the highest command in the army. The settlement in Asia Minor of a considerable number of troops of whom by far the most were Armenian inevitably had the same results there as had occurred in Italy in connection with the German troops. The foreign element in the Byzantine Empire was indeed not so strong as to effect here, as in the West, the introduction of a feudal system which gradually destroyed the structure of the state inherited from late antiquity. But on the other hand it did indeed provide a class of magnates derived from the feudalized corps of army officers, and after a long development of several centuries this eventually produced a solution similar to that adopted in Central and Western Europe soon after the end of the Germanic migrations. The relationship of vassalage which existed here between soldier and officer, and between lower and higher officer, could only weaken the central administration. Moreover it also came about that this Armenian feudal organization was gradually imposed on troops who were not Armenian in origin. This meant that the officer class was now interposing itself between the soldiers and the central government as a landowning aristocracy.

The beginnings of this system can be perceived in the Roman army as early as the sixth century when it was usual for higher officers to have a personal following. At this period officers had their retinue (*obsequium*), as the Germans did. The members of this bodyguard were called 'sword-bearers' (*spatharii*) or 'spear-bearers' (*doryphoroi* or *hypaspistai*). Besides this retinue there were the *bucellarii*, engaged for a limited time and a definite purpose, who were soldiers serving individual officers in return for their pay and without any personal ties. In contrast to the *bucellarii*, the personal bodyguard owed loyalty to their lord and were pledged to protect him even at the cost of their own lives. The lord for his part provided for the maintenance of his followers and gave them his protection. It was largely this institution of bands of personal followers which made it so easy for the process of military settlement to enable individual officers to acquire the position of independent territorial magnates.

The introduction of the themes in Asia Minor meant the end of Hellenistic late antiquity and the beginning of the Byzantine world.

As in Asia Minor, the themes in Europe took shape in response to a particular military situation. This was occasioned by the threat to the Empire from the Turkic Bulgars. It was essential to protect the vital link with the West, the Via Egnatia. It was with this in mind that the most important European themes were established. Thus the first three set up at the beginning of the ninth century, Macedonia, Thessalonica and Dyrra-chium, were to begin with only military sectors of the Via Egnatia protected by *castella* and troop settlements. When the most important *castella* on this road fell into Bulgarian hands about 900 the only territorial link with the West still left intact, the coastal road, was fortified by a chain of strongholds. Thus the last European themes were set up:

the Strymon theme to protect the passes over the Rhodope mountains; the theme of Nicopolis to secure the coastal region on the gulf of Patras; and the Dalmatian theme to secure Byzantine access to the Dalmatian islands.

The change in social structure

Soldiers were originally settled on the land on the periphery and then, to give security to a larger area, this policy was extended into the interior and ended by providing the basis for the complete militarization of the Empire. But this was not the sole reason for the change in Byzantine society. An almost more powerful influence was the change in administrative practice. The military settlements alone would not have led to a change in the social structure; it was the handing over of part of the civil administration to the military which brought about this development. It was Justinian whose edicts first showed signs of moving in this direction. He introduced changes which under his successors led to a complete alteration in the administration of the state.

The problem began with the difficulty of provisioning large armies on imperial soil during the winter months. All too often it was found that provinces were not in a position to supply the demand. And moreover military needs often meant that the armies had to be stationed in the same regions. Thus individual areas were economically exhausted by the prolonged presence of troops. This situation was aggravated by the fact that the *annona*, originally allocated to the provisioning of the troops, had been commuted to a money payment (*adaeratio*) in some of the provinces. In order to manage to provision the troops in their district the military command had to resort to forced purchase, the *coemptio*. The price of goods requisitioned for the army through the *coemptio* was fixed by the state at the beginning of the year, thus taking no account of possible bad harvests. The provisioning could only be deducted from the tax on the basis of the food prices fixed by the state. The demands of the troops were usually so high that they could not be met by the resources of a single province. Food had therefore to be purchased at a higher price from another province in order to be provided for the troops at the lower state fixed price on the basis of the *coemptio*. Added to this, the regions in which the armies wintered were particularly exposed to enemy attacks.

Realizing the impossibility of this situation, Justinian resorted to the device of handing over to the military command part of the civil administration, namely, the collection of the taxes. Thus he entrusted the commander of the Danube fleet and the units under him with the responsibility for getting in the tax (*annona*) from the region assigned to him for winter quarters. This meant that the army was now responsible for the civil administration of the provinces on the lower Danube, that is Scythia Maior and Moesia I. The military commander in these provinces received the title of *quaestor Iustinianus exercitus* and within the area of his command he assumed the duties of the *praefectus praetorio* and his officials in matters of financial administration.

The imperial government considered that in this way it would be possible to get a fair evaluation of the annual supplies to be provided by the *coemptio*. The military commander, better informed about the financial burdens of his district, would be more inclined to grant a postponement in the date of tax payments if occasion arose than the *praefectus praetorio* residing in the capital. Thus there grew up this fusion of military and civil authority which spread over the whole Empire with the introduction of the themes and undermined the control exercised by the state.

The changes in organization connected with this were soon felt in the central administration where the fusion of taxation and military administrative arrangements took place about 680. What had applied to individual provinces in Justinian's day was now extended to the central administration, and thence to the whole Empire. The inauguration of the new régime coincided with the introduction of the office of logothete *tou stratiotikou*. Holders of this office are first found in the second half of the seventh century, that is, at the same time as the appearance of the first five themes. In this office, taxation and military administration were made the responsibility of one minister in the central government. The officials concerned with the muster rolls of the soldiers and with the collection of the *annona* were thus combined in a single functionary. Arrangements corresponding to those of the central authority were introduced in the provinces. The logothete of each individual theme corresponded to the logothete *tou stratiotikou*. The old offices in the central administration were abolished. The *praefectus praetorio* vanished, and also the government departments under him, the *genike trapeza*, which collected the general inland revenue, and the *idike trapeza*, the department responsible for the income from the imperial estates. The logothete *tou stratiotikou* now took over the collection of revenue both from the military settlers and the ordinary taxpayers. Further, not only did these two departments disappear but the ministerial office of *comes sacrarum largitionum* responsible for expenditure was abolished during this period. This minister had had the task of presenting the public budget and finding the funds whereby the army was paid and other vital financial needs of state met. His place was taken by the imperial treasury, the *sacellum*, which developed in the seventh century. The *sacellum* only dealt with actual money, so that a special department, the *vestiarium*, was created for payments in kind. The ministerial office for the imperial estates was also abolished for obvious reasons: in the process of establishing military settlers the great imperial domains had been largely parcelled out and the taxes of the new owners, the soldier-farmers, could now be more appropriately paid to the newly created office of the logothete *tou stratiotikou*.

It was an ominous sign that this fusion of taxation and military departments had placed the whole provincial administration under the control of the military authorities. Here too there were the same officials as in the central offices. For the military leaders, the officers, were excluded from the grants of property. They received no soldiers' farms but had only the right of supervision over the military settlements. They were however in the position to buy property in the region under their command and could thus increase their own power. An officer's pay was so high that even the lower commissions had large sums of gold at their disposal. They also had a very substantial share in war booty, which was theirs by law. With their capital and the powers at their disposal in connection with the collection of the taxes, these officers could rapidly enlarge their estates in the provinces under their control and thus further reinforce their position in their zone of authority. From the tenth century they could also act as tax farmers, that is, in return for a fixed sum they had the right to collect the taxes within their zone. This meant that by means of unfair taxation and ruthless methods of collection they could bring pressure to bear on owners of peasant farms and agricultural property, thus forcing them to sell the land which they wanted in order to enlarge their own estates. A century after the establishment of the theme system officers were acting in their zones of command exactly like landed proprietors. It had become almost impossible to dismiss officers without stirring up a revolt. Commissions gradually became heritable. In the end this meant that certain families, as the Ducas, the Phocas, the Maleini, the Scleri and the Rangabe, had established themselves in the Asia Minor provinces of the Empire as great landed magnates and were powerful enough to determine the succession to the throne.

The great war between the Empires of East Rome and Persia as pacemaker of the expansion of Islam

3

Mood of crisis: intensification of planned economy: decline of money economy

The East Roman Empire developed on lines similar to those of the West. There too the reform of the army, which in the West is coupled with the name of Charles Martel, had created a new social class, the landed nobility. But in spite of this development a good deal of late antique civilization persisted in the East Roman Empire and this is due to its urban economy. It was because of this continuity that Byzantine civilization in the East Roman Empire was able to develop from that of late antiquity. In urban life too there were signs of the beginnings of a new planned economy as early as the time of Justinian. Justinian had introduced a strongly monopolist character into existing corporations of manufacturers and craftsmen and this was to determine the nature of the Byzantine economy for many years to come. He made a beginning with the branches of industry connected with foreign imports, such as those of the silk weavers, the silk dealers, the sellers of unguents and the spice merchants. Through existing associations he established far greater control over these craftsmen and merchants than his predecessors had done. Associations of craftsmen and dealers had existed since the time of the early Roman Empire. They were known as *collegia* and grew up contemporaneously with the antique city economy. At that time they were found with responsibility for 'liturgies', or civic duties, that is, the service of the community in the work projects of the state. In Roman times membership of these *collegia* was determined by birth. Members of a particular family therefore had to follow the same calling as their fathers and forefathers. Later on, in Justinian's time for instance, this limitation had disappeared. Membership of the association of craftsmen and dealers was now no longer determined by one's father's calling but depended upon a licence from the state.

Justinian's reforms in economic policy aimed at restricting the free market. Under this Emperor, the sale of certain goods on the free market was absolutely forbidden. This particularly affected branches of industry concerned with the manufacture of certain luxury textile goods. But these measures also touched those businesses which were concerned with the weaving and dyeing of silk. Procopius, a contemporary of Justinian, describes in his *Secret History* how by reason of a decree of the Emperor all shops in this branch of industry had to close down. It was now the rule that these luxury goods went to the state authorities and were distributed by them in lieu of salary to certain specified imperial officials of the highest rank. This new turn in economic policy necessitated the creation of a special authority charged with the management of the luxury goods produced by the industry and also with the supervision of their distribution. Subsequent developments led to a state of affairs in which not only luxury goods but a large proportion of the products of the industry had to be delivered to the authority set up by the state. The official in charge of this bore the title *chartularius tou vestiariou* and was of equal status with another high-ranking official, the *chartularius tou sakelliou*, who controlled the state treasury. The officials entrusted with the issue of cash payments were now joined, on an equal footing, by those responsible for the distribution of these goods used in lieu of cash payment. These imperial measures, with their control over production, amounted to the creation of a kind of second currency through these payments in kind alongside cash remuneration in the form of gold and silver coins. As a result of never-ending wars considerable strain had been put upon the Empire's economy, and this led to a decline in gold reserves and therefore in the circulation of money. As export trade did not earn the Empire sufficient gold to cover all the needs of the state, the circulation of money was inevitably restricted. The whole economic life of the Empire was indeed beset with increasing difficulties. The attempt to create a kind of second currency by using manufactured goods or foodstuffs is a mark of the difficult economic situation in which the East Roman state found itself in the sixth century. Not only were the high officials of the Empire now given part of their remuneration in the form of luxury clothes; even the pay of the ordinary soldier was changed into this new form of payment. The proportion of a soldier's pay that took the form of cash became increasingly smaller and smaller. It was not just that he received extra allowances in the form of rations of grain; even clothing and equipment were issued to him and reckoned as a part of his pay. These measures aroused fierce discontent. There was mutiny among the soldiers as well as conspiracy in high financial and economic circles. It seemed as though the changes aimed at a return to natural economy. In contrast to the West, Byzantium succeeded in the sixth century in scotching this trend in time by means of a planned economy which was consistently carried out.

This shift from payment in cash to payment in kind is also characteristic of further Byzantine development. This can be defined as an intensification of the planned economy of late antiquity. The economy of the free market was increasingly excluded. On the home market it was now only possible to obtain the comparatively cheap objects of daily use and requirement. All articles and goods of particular value could only be got in the form of allowances. They were tied up with office and social status. Everybody, from the ordinary soldier to the most exalted patrician (*patricius*), lived on allowances from the imperial government. Even the export trade was more and more withdrawn from the ring of foreign traders. The marketing of Byzantine industrial goods was determined by export licences and monopolies.

Within the existing compulsory associations a clear distinction was now made between manufacturers and retailers. Both had their separate associations and had to deal with each other under state supervision. But it was not only traders and artisans who were bound together in these obligatory associations. Members of the learned professions, such as lawyers and doctors, were also organized in associations (*scholae*). Here too the exercise of state control seems to have been the main reason for gilds of this kind. On the other hand, as members of these corporations they received allowances from the state, for both doctors and lawyers were not really members of a free profession but were state employees. Often enough they were drawn on for government posts. Thus lawyers were employed in the imperial administration and doctors in the imperial army.

Certain kinds of workers were also grouped together in compulsory associations. Thus there was a gild of leather-workers. In the case of workmen it was through the tariff contracts that the state supervised conditions of work. The remarkably low wages which men received at this period are explained not only by the competition of slave labour but also by the fact that a large proportion of them received their pay in the form of goods.

Thus the age of Justinian stamped its imprint on the urban economy of later Byzantine civilization as well as in other fields. In agrarian life it was the reform of the army that led to reorganization and a change in the social classes of society: in urban economy, it was the economic crisis which heralded the change-over to a thorough-going planned economy. And this continued in the main to characterize the economy of the Byzantine period.

The world as the Byzantines knew it

The causes of this large-scale economic crisis are to be found in the place of the East Roman Empire in world politics. Like Sassanid Persia, the East Roman Empire was an economic world power. Through their trade both powers controlled a large part of the contemporary world.

What is the significance of this? The world of Justinian's time was certainly small compared with that which is known today. It was only part of the world. But it was larger than the world which the West knew even in the middle ages. In Justinian's time men were well acquainted with Scandinavia and could distinguish between Sweden and Norway as individual countries. They used the trade route through Russia to the Baltic. The peoples of Russia, from the Finns and Letts in the north to the Morduini and the Iranian and Altaic nomads, were no strangers to the Byzantines. The British Isles too, including Ireland, lay within their horizon and they had knowledge of political events there. The tin trade, which carried the coveted metal from Cornwall through the Straits of Gibraltar to Alexandria, also brought information about the country and its people to the East Roman Mediterranean. But on the other hand in Africa the great Berber immigrations had led to the severance of links with the south. The Byzantine Empire knew scarcely anything about the political conditions in Morocco, which was in the hands of Berber tribes, and nothing at all about the areas beyond the Sahara. The link between Timbuctu and the ports on the North African coast, which had been maintained throughout the period of the Roman Empire, was cut in the Byzantine period. There are still traces of this development in the remains of the old Negro cultures in the lower reaches of the Niger, in Ife and Nupe. The earliest examples of bronze plastic art still show clearly the influence of the late Roman world—indeed the late Roman imperial globe and the Christian cross were adopted by these peoples as stock motifs. But later development is characterized by a decline of the old culture. Today there only exist isolated traces pointing to the route which still led to the West African coast in the late Roman period. For instance, even now the Tuareg in the highlands of Tibesti happen to have preserved in their vocabulary a number of Latin words, such as *angelus*, thus indicating that even in the fourth century A.D. the cultural influence of western Christendom was active far into the Sahara.

The question of the Sudan and the exploration of the sources of the Nile is another matter. Imperial Rome had no first-hand knowledge of the Sudan or of the basins of the rivers forming the sources of the Nile. In the age of Justinian some advance was made here. In the sixth century in particular, economic considerations emphasized the importance of having access to a practicable overland route to Abyssinia. And so both the Sudan and the territory of Atbara were visited by Byzantine merchants, soldiers and missionaries. At that time Christian missionary work and the extension of political and economic influence worked together. The Sudan was no exception and here too political and economic advances were followed by conversion to Christianity. It was however the monophysite form of Christianity to which the Sudanese kings were converted. A special Nubian, that is, Sudanese, literary language was created. It was then that various translations were made from Coptic, most of which are now lost.

But fragments of the story of the finding of the bones of St Menas have survived in Nubian. The Byzantine authors of the sixth century, especially those who wrote in Syriac, were very well informed about this region. They knew the kings of the two most important tribes of the Sudan, the Noba and the Blemmi. Inscriptions of the kings of the Noba written in the Greek language witness to the fact that Greek was used alongside Nubian as the administrative language. The kings of the other Sudanese tribe, the Blemmi, also made use of Greek and some of their sixth-century documents have survived in this language.

The East Roman Empire of Justinian's time had first-hand knowledge of Abyssinia as well as of the Sudan. Abyssinia's connection with the Roman Empire was older than that of the tribes of the Sudan. As early as the time of Constantine, Ezana, who was then Negus of Abyssinia, had adopted Christianity. Ezana and his successors used Greek as the language of the court and the administration. Abyssinian coins used the Greek script for the name of the ruler who minted them. Ge'ez, the oldest language of the Abyssinians, is full of Greek loan-words, thus revealing the strength of Byzantine influence. Almost all words that designate objects connected with a higher standard of living are derived from Greek words. Many translations were made from Greek into Ge'ez. Even the old script in which Ge'ez is written is probably the work of East Roman missionaries. Thus in Ezana's time the old consonantal script was abandoned and was replaced by one in which the vowels could be denoted by strokes and hooks attached to the basic letter form. This script was the work of Roman missionaries who had probably previously worked in India and learnt there of this method of perfecting the script. The cultural penetration of Abyssinia took place against the background of East Rome's economic opening up of this country. For Abyssinia was one of the main sources of supply of incense, myrrh and elephants for East Rome. So in Adulis, Abyssinia's chief trading centre, the churches stood side by side with the warehouses of Syrian and Egyptian merchants.

As in the case of Abyssinia, it was economic developments which introduced South Arabia to Romano-Byzantine culture. And in the time of Justinian more too was known about South Arabia than in either the western or Byzantine middle ages, or indeed even in the nineteenth century. It was not for nothing that Byzantine diplomats went to and fro between the palaces of the Arab sheiks in South Arabia. These diplomats, who at the same time were visiting the island of Socotra in the Indian Ocean and Abyssinia, brought to the west very accurate information about conditions in South Arabia. On the other hand Byzantine culture penetrated into the South Arabian world. In actual fact Islam has left scarcely a stone standing of the numerous Christian churches which once existed in South Arabia. Only the barest ruins and spoils now in Arab mosques survive to point to the Christian period in South Arabia. Here too, as in Abyssinia, there are inscriptions which describe the deeds of the kings, relating political events in these kingdoms. They tell of enterprises known otherwise only through the Byzantino-Greek tradition. In contrast to Abyssinia where the cultural roots went deeper, in Arab territory the Greek script did not in fact succeed in establishing itself as a literary medium.

For the Byzantines, the world did not end with Arabia or Abyssinia. They regarded both countries merely as posts on the route to India. According to Cosmas Indicopleustes, a Byzantine merchant from Alexandria who wrote about his travels, India, as well as Ceylon, was known at least as to its west coast and the Indus valley (the Punjab). Cosmas gives a most detailed account of the country and its people; he mentions the Turkic nomads who were then in control of northern India; and he reports on the silk trade. India made a deep impression on the Byzantines, as is shown by the special monograph on the fauna of India, which was composed by Timothy of Gaza at the beginning of the sixth century. The *Chronicle* of Malalas, written in Antioch during that same century, contains an account of the reception of a Byzantine diplomatic mission by a maharajah in South India.

But India itself did not mark the end of the Byzantine world. In the second half of the sixth century, with the Turks of Central Asia as intermediaries, even China came within the ken of the Byzantines. Theophylact Simocattes, writing at the beginning of the seventh century, tells of the struggles between the two parts of the Chinese empire of Pei-Ts'i and Pei-Chou, already in existence in the second half of the sixth century, which led to the formation of the Great Chinese Empire under the Sui dynasty. Theophylact's report contains detailed information about the life of the Chinese, for instance a coronation festival at the court of a Chinese emperor, or a Chinese imperial funeral. These vivid descriptions originated from ambassadors who had themselves actually been present at these ceremonial occasions as representatives of their people. And it was through them that these reports reached the Byzantines. After a spell as envoy at the Chinese imperial court they would be sent by their khan to Byzantium to serve in a similar capacity at the court of the East Roman Emperor. These Turks, standing in their turn on the purple circle let into the floor in the imperial Byzantine Audience Hall, made their report to the Byzantine Basileus, and it was in this way that this information reached Constantinople. They told the Basileus how the Emperor of the East, the 'Son of Heaven', lived. They even mentioned to him the Chinese title 'Tai-Shang', 'sublime lord', borne by this Emperor, and the stenographers of the imperial civil service took it down, thus preserving it for posterity. Much is to be learnt from this Byzantine report about the life of the Chinese; one hears of the expensive oxen-drawn carriages in which men of rank travelled, and listens to tales of the harem in the imperial capital Chang'-an. The Chinese annals of the empire of Pei-Chou record that west of the Huang-ho practically the only currency in use was gold and silver coins from the west. In Turfan, and even in the Chinese capital Lo-Yang, East Roman gold coins with the likeness of Justinian on them have survived. Coptic buckles too, with words inscribed on them, have been found in China.

However, it was not only China that came within the horizon of Byzantium at that period, but Central Asia as well. The Byzantines knew the great Turkic realm which stretched from Persia to China. They were acquainted with the four khans who ruled in this empire, and this from their own observation. Byzantine officials of the highest rank, such as Zemarchus, the *praefectus praetorio per Orientem*, journeyed in person to the seat of the Turkic khan in the neighbourhood of Kutcha in present-day eastern Turkestan. His report was read out in Constantinople in the imperial presence, and in it Zemarchus described in considerable detail his reception by the Turkic Great Khan in a *jurta* decorated with gold, and how the khan, sitting there on a throne richly adorned with gold, granted an audience to the Byzantine envoy. The reports of the East Roman diplomats also include detailed descriptions of the life of the Turks. Apart from Chinese accounts these are the first reports describing these people. Stories about an exorcism by a shaman alternate with descriptions of the funeral of the Turkic chief and details about the climatic conditions of the country inhabited by the Turks.

It goes without saying that the Byzantines also visited West Turkestan including Sogdiana. Here too there were economic and political reasons to account for the opening of diplomatic relations with these peoples. For one thing it was imperative to safeguard the silk trade, and on the other hand there was the desire to encircle Persia in the political and military sense by means of an alliance with the Turks.

The connection with Sogdiana also has deeper roots than the encounter with the Turks occurring in the second half of the sixth century. Important trade went on between the Black Sea ports and Sogdiana, by way of the caravan routes going round the Caspian Sea to the north. Chinese silk has been found in the graves of Kersch which are as early as the first century A.D., thus showing that even at this date there was silk trade with China passing through Sogdiana. On the other hand, coins of the second and third centuries B.C. from towns on the Black Sea, such as Pantikapaion and Olbia, have been found in western Zungaria; and in the Chinese province of Shen-si copper coins of Roman Emperors from Tiberius to Aurelian have turned up. Roman coins were also very common in Sogdiana. Thus the portrayal of the young Romulus and Remus with the wolf appearing on coins minted by Constantine, was copied on Sogdian *brakteati*. The strength of western economic influence is also shown by the occurrence of Greek loan-words, such as the word *stater*, in the Sogdian language.

The reports of Byzantine diplomats in the second half of the sixth century also give full information about western Turkestan. The Byzantines knew about the Sogdian city-states which existed at that time, and in many respects they were better informed about these regions than the Chinese were. But the decline of the East Roman Empire meant a break in relations with Sogdiana. In Central Asia very little was preserved from that great age when East and West saw more of the world than ever before. There is a faint memory of this great period when two worlds met reflected in the inscriptions of the later Turkic khans which were discovered in Mongolia at the end of the last century. They still tell of diplomatic missions from Rome which had taken part in the funeral ceremonies of the Turkic khans. The truth of these reports is confirmed by the mention of the same khan who is named in the inscriptions and of the envoys who were present at his funeral. This is practically the only trace remaining in the Far East of seven decades of close Byzantino-Turkic relations. The title of Caesar which survives in the old Tibetan chronicles in the form *Gesar* is yet another reminder in Central Asia of the days when the Byzantine Emperor bestowed on the Turkic khan the title of Caesar.

It was the same with the peoples of the Caucasus as with West Turkestan and Central Asia; economic factors led the Byzantines to open up relations with them. The Caucasian peoples lived between the Caspian Sea and the Black Sea in what was in fact a key area for communications with West Turkestan. Here too strong Byzantine infiltration into the Caucasian states is found. The Iberians in particular among the Caucasian peoples had formed a strong attachment to the Byzantines, while Azerbaijan and the eastern part of Georgia remained under Persian influence. In the Caucasus the East Roman Empire had retreated somewhat in contrast to the days of the *imperium romanum*, for during the early years of the Empire the political influence of Rome had sometimes extended as far as the district of Azerbaijan.

The peoples of the Caucasus had in part accepted Christianity as early as the first half of the fourth century and hence stood in an extremely close cultural relationship to the East Roman Empire.

Byzantine histories also contain detailed information about the Altaic peoples living to the north of the Caucasus. The cavalry units of the East Roman army were reinforced by recruits from people of this Altaic stock. The same is true of those Altaic peoples who had settled in the region which is now Rumania and later, in the second half of the sixth century, in the lower Hungarian plain. Byzantine envoys frequented the court of the Hunnic khans there. The Byzantine diplomat Priscus gave a famous account of his visit to the court of the Hunnic chief Attila. Here too there are plenty of vivid pictures of the life of people and nobles, of ceremonial receptions and solemn funeral rites.

The drive for world domination:
the fatal disease of the Empires of East Rome and Persia

Such was the world as the Byzantine Empire knew it. Such were the regions which occupied the thoughts and plans of Byzantine diplomacy. By the sixth century the great economic expansion, begun in late antiquity, had assumed the proportions of a life-and-death economic war, and it was inescapably bound up with these geographical factors. The Byzantine needed the Indian market for his products. India possessed sufficient funds to absorb the whole output of luxury goods from the industries of Syria and Egypt. The profits from trade with the East were not even remotely counter-balanced by the German market, which Byzantium dominated at the same time. This is shown by the far-reaching plans which Byzantine diplomacy contrived in order to ensure that the gateway to the East remained open to its trade. Hence the building up of a chain of stepping stones leading from the Red Sea to India via the highway of Bab al-Mandab. This explains why the Byzantines fought for positions in the Caucasus with such unfailing tenacity. It provides the clue to the lavish payments of money made to the Altaic tribes in South Russia. The prime aim behind all this was to counter Persian ambition. The great power of Persia, being fully aware of the implication of the situation, strove to bar to the Byzantines the route to India and access to the silk countries. A considerable source of Persian wealth was derived from the transit of Indian and Chinese goods to the Roman Empire. The difference in the cost of goods reaching the Byzantine Empire via Persia and those bought by merchants in India and West Turkestan was enormous. It was profits from this entrepôt trade which financed the equipment of the Persian army, the recruitment of Arab mercenaries and, in the event, the military expansion of the Persian Empire towards the west. Both the great powers fought with equal bitterness. Each knew the potentialities of the other. The dispute between them gradually took on the proportions of an all-out war which finally brought about the downfall of both these mighty powers.

The immediate occasion was trivial. The great conflagration was sparked off when the Byzantines cancelled the autonomy of a small Jewish community on the island of Jotabe, which lies at the entrance of the gulf of Akaba. This measure, decreed by Justinian, resulted in sanctions being imposed in 527 against Roman merchants by the ruler of South Arabia. This Arab king of Jewish faith, who ruled a territory corresponding approximately with the modern state of the Yemen, closed the caravan route which led to Gaza in Palestine. This affected the great trade route from the ports on the Indian Ocean via Mecca and Medina to the Mediterranean port of Gaza. It was used by much of the trade in incense and spices. And as if that were not sufficient this South Arabian ruler, who had close political alignments with Persia, had the narrow navigable channel leading through the route from Bab al-Mandab closed with the aid of a chain. Obviously he was helped in this by Persian technicians. There is no question but that his policy was determined by his Jewish faith. He decreed the closing of the straits at the very time when the Roman authorities passed laws discriminating against the Jews in Palestine and Syria, as reprisals for the blocking of the route to Gaza. There followed anti-Christian excesses in South Arabia. The Christian churches there were set on fire, the believers, men, women and children, murdered. These incidents were by no means widespread, but they were played up by East Roman propaganda. In Syria, Palestine and Egypt so-called open letters were circulated exaggerating the extent of the massacres and demanding a campaign to avenge them. Despite the fact that semi-official propaganda had thus paved the way for intervention in South Arabia, the Roman imperial government did not in the first instance undertake direct military action in that region because of Persia. The removal of the South Arabian adversary was contrived by means of an alliance with the Negus of Abyssinia, who was lavishly equipped with money and ships to ensure the command of the sea. Surviving eye-witness accounts tell how an expeditionary fleet gradually collected in the Abyssinian port of Adulis, thence to set sail for South Arabia. An Abyssinian and Sudanese expeditionary corps jointly broke the resistance of the South Arabians. A government friendly to Byzantium was set up and with its help the Persian possessions in the Arabian peninsula were attacked. A South Arabian inscription mentions this undertaking, which failed to achieve its object. In the face of this threat to their standing in Arabia, the Persians did not remain inactive. In 568 a Persian fleet sailed from its base in Bahrein for South Arabia and there overthrew the pro-Byzantine sheik. South Arabian envoys were still waiting for an audience with the East Roman Emperor to ask his help, while their country was meeting its fate. South Arabia became Persian and this meant that the Byzantine sea route to India via the Red Sea fell under Persian control. The prices of imports from India immediately rocketed. There were signs of an extremely grave economic crisis. At this moment when the choice lay between war and peace it is understandable that the East Roman imperial government chose war.

Nevertheless the conflict in Arabia was only one of the reasons why war broke out. The Persians were also threatening the northern route through South Russia and the Caucasus to West Turkestan and so to the silk-producing countries. Persian involvement in Arabia and the consequent risk that they would block the sea route to India meant that the Roman imperial government had to seek an alliance with the Sogdian city-states. Therefore relations with the Caucasian states and certain of the Altaic tribes in South Russia were intensified. Roman gold flowed into the treasury of the petty kings of the Caucasus and of the Hunnic chiefs of South Russia. But the Persians did not sit back with folded hands. Persian emissaries brought about a coalition between Persia and some of the Caucasian states and Hunnic tribes in south Russia. This resulted in raids on Byzantine caravans coming from West Turkestan. By means of bribes the Huns on the Danube were induced to attack the Roman frontier. Attempts were even made on the lives of Byzantine diplomats returning from Sogdiana.

In this difficult situation the East Roman imperial government made an alliance with the khan of West Turkestan against Persia. This alliance, encircling Persia by a pincer movement from East and West, shows that Byzantine government circles had become accustomed to think in terms of world politics.

The course of the war between Persia and East Rome was uneven. On both sides a decisive role was played by internal conflicts and by the peoples on the frontiers. The resulting difficulties were a warning that the downfall of these great powers was imminent. In both Empires the nature of the internal conflicts was predominantly social and economic. In 590 the Persian king fell a victim to a conspiracy largely the consequence of a harsh tax policy which drew into the tax collector's net even the field of the humblest peasant. In the Byzantine Empire the same sort of thing happened. Here the revolution of 602 was brought about by an attempt to increase further the proportion of soldiers' pay given in kind, thus reducing their cash payment. This can in fact be said to be due to an excessive escalation of the government's war budget. In both Empires the economy was overstrained and on the brink of collapse. In such a state of affairs it was immaterial who finally emerged as victor in the military sense. Both were defeated. To begin with East Rome was beaten by the Persian armies supported by Arab troops; the next time the Byzantine Emperor was the victor with the help of Turks from

Central Asia. Fate decreed that on either side decisive military success or otherwise was determined by races on the periphery, the Turks and the Arabs. The upsurge of the Arabs immediately after the last Byzantine victory was the logical consequence of this development. The 'wonder weapons' of the two great powers, Persia and East Rome, the armoured troops, the divisions of archers and the great array of siege-engines, no longer impressed these peoples. They had themselves fought under the Roman and Persian flags. They knew the weapons with which victory had been achieved and so had no hesitation in deploying them themselves against their one-time masters. All that Mohammed did was to point the direction and the goal.

The secession of the West

4

The formation of the western states, the result of the Germanic tribal migrations

The conflict between Persia and the East Roman Empire to all outward appearances ended the late antique period. The loss of the provinces of Egypt, Syria, Palestine and Armenia drew the boundary-line for Byzantine culture in the East. And the separation from the West, though not yet complete, had nevertheless reached a decisive stage. The causes were various. There was already a national Roman reaction, which even in the age of Constantine stood out clearly in its opposition to the new Greek capital, Constantinople. This movement was intensified as a result of the Germanic tribal migrations and it finally created the atmosphere for the break of the West with the Byzantine world.

In the great migration of Germanic tribes, it was particularly the second phase, which began in 375, that shaped the West. The impetus for this movement did not come from Europe. What happened there was only the last link in a chain of tribal movements, whose origins must be sought in the eastern Asian region, in the province of Jehol. The westward migration of the people named in Europe 'Huns' brought about the second phase of Germanic tribal migration, the thrust to the West of the Germanic peoples from southern Russia and Hungary. More than half a century before, one group of the Huns had already taken the Chinese capital Lo-Yang and conquered a great part of China. Another horde of Huns marched along the northern edge of Tien Shan to West Turkestan and from there occupied northern India. A third group had finally advanced as far as southern Russia, had subjected here the Iranian Alans living as nomads east of the Don, and had then advanced against the Germanic kingdoms to the west of the Don.

The attack of the Huns broke up the great Ostrogothic kingdom in southern Russia, but even the Visigoths living in Bessarabia and the territory of present-day Rumania had to vacate their homeland. By 375 the Huns had crossed the Don, and in 378 the Visigoths penetrating the Empire across the Danube came face to face with the imperial troops. The ensuing battle at Adrianople was lost. The East Roman Emperor fell and powerful bands of Goths now marched through Roman territory without hindrance and laid waste the most valuable provinces. In this situation the expulsion of the Goths from the territory between the lower Danube and the Aegean Sea—equally important from both the military and the economic point of view—became a vital question for the Empire.

From the demands of this situation then grew the decision to divide the Empire. Constantine had avoided division: he had only wanted to take account of the development whereby the political, military and cultural centre of gravity had been shifted to the East and for this reason he had transferred the capital of the Empire to the Bosphorus. But now separation was carried out for the sake of political self-preservation. The Empire was cut into two politically autonomous regions, the eastern part and the western part of the Roman Empire. As further development shows, from the point of view of the eastern part it was not a real division but rather the amputation of a diseased limb destined to decay to save the life of the other part still capable of surviving.

The western part of the Empire had to die, in order that the Roman Empire might remain preserved in the East Roman Empire. This was why the Germanic invaders, who since Adrianople had been constantly laying waste the provinces of the Balkan peninsula like a consuming blight and threatening to undermine the defensive power of this part of the Empire, were now diverted to the West. There they overran the western part of the Roman Empire and in a comparatively short space of time brought about its downfall. The sequence of events makes clear the inevitability of the fall of the western Roman Empire.

Between 395 and 396 Alaric's Goths marched through Greece and the Balkan peninsula, leaving a wide trail of destruction behind them. By 401 Alaric was in Italy. In 410 Rome, the old capital of the ancient world, fell into his hands. In the same year he attempted to conquer Apulia and Sicily, the regions which supplied the Italian cities Rome and Ravenna. But the attack on Sicily failed. When the conqueror subsequently died in southern Italy, Gaul was allotted to his successor by the western Roman Empire. Thus there was now a Germanic kingdom on the Mediterranean which soon afterwards, from southern Gaul, was even to encroach on Spain.

Yet this movement of Germanic peoples unleashed by the Huns was continuing to spread in another direction. Under pressure from the Ostrogoths pushing westwards from South Russia over the Carpathians some of the Suevi living there left their homeland. These were the Suevi who had previously belonged to the kingdom of Vannius between Waag and March and whose last remnants were annihilated by the Lombards in the first half of the sixth century. Similarly, the Vandals settled in Transylvania were now yielding to the pressure of the Gepids. They themselves had in turn retreated before the Goths—the Goths who had been driven to the north-west by the Huns. Thus a movement took shape here, fed from two main sources—from the Suevi and Quadi retreating from Hungary and from the Vandals expelled from Transylvania; and to these were joined the Iranian Alans. These 'Alans' were not the Iranian nomads living beyond the Don, who were subjected by the Huns, but the Sarmati living on the Theiss in the eastern Hungarian area. They too—like the Iranians of southern Russia —called themselves 'Alans', i.e. 'the nobles'.

This combined group of Suevi, Vandals and Alans reached the Rhine in 406 and crossed it on 3 December of the same year. By 409 they reached the Pyrenees and broke through the inadequately fortified passes into Spain. Here they met the Visigoths sent to Spain to fight them by the western Roman imperial government. Under pressure from the Visigoths, the Vandals and some of the Alans left Spain and moved over to Africa. Only the Suevi succeeded in holding their own in the Asturian mountains and founding a kingdom which existed until the end of the sixth century.

In 429 the Vandals advanced further to the east along the North African coast of the Mediterranean. The western Roman provincial government of the African part of the Empire handed over to them the duty of defending the frontier in the province of Numidia and allocated them settlements there. But instead of fulfilling the task assigned to them and fighting off the attacks of the Berbers, they fell upon the Roman province and in 439 by a surprise attack captured the capital, Carthage. This brought under their control the Latin-speaking western Roman provinces in Africa, present-day Tunisia and western Algeria. Only the Greek-speaking Pentapolis (from 1912 to 1945 the territory of the Italian colony Cyrenaica) remained in the hands of the East Roman Empire.

The strategic situation of the Vandal kingdom was unique. Situated at the narrowest part of the Mediterranean, opposite the rich island of Sicily, with the aid of a fleet it was able at all times to control communications between the eastern and the western Mediterranean. In further military enterprises this led the Vandals to take to the sea. The North African territories, still well-wooded at that time, provided the materials for ship-building, and before long Vandal fleets ruled the western Mediterranean. Sardinia and Corsica were conquered and then not only the Italian coast but even the towns in the interior of the peninsula were raided. On 2 June 455, the Vandals succeeded in capturing Rome. No other event heralded more clearly the imminent collapse of the western Roman Empire. Only Italy, Dalmatia and a few parts of Gaul were still spared from the Germanic peoples. The provisioning of the cities of Rome and Ravenna now depended solely on the willingness and capacity of Italian areas of supply, Sicily, Apulia and Liguria. African olive-oil and African grain were no longer shipped to Rome and Ravenna. Even the oil supplies from southern Gaul no longer reached Italy after the Germanic occupation of Provence. The supply situation of the two cities became daily worse and worse. More and more skilled workers emigrated to the eastern parts of the Empire.

The remnants of the western Roman Empire were then swept away by a second Germanic tribal migration. This too was only the final consequence of the Altaic tribal migration from the East. In the second half of the fifth century these Altaic peoples reached the steppes north of the Caucasus and drove the Hun tribes nomadizing here to the West. Under the name of 'Bulgars' they then came into the field of vision of East Roman historical writing. The result of this second great Altaic migration was that those Germanic tribes which hitherto had still stayed in southern Russia and Bessarabia, such as the Sciri, Heruli and Lombards, now retreated over the Carpathians into the Hungarian plain. Under pressure from them, the Ostrogoths living here moved south into the European provinces of the East Roman Empire and attempted to make new settlements there. But in the year 488, East Roman politics succeeded in diverting even these Germanic invaders to the West, where they conquered Italy and on the the soil of the western part of the Roman Empire founded a Germano-Roman state. The area vacated by the Germanic peoples was occupied by Slav tribes. The Slav Antes moved into the country between the lower Dnieper and the lower Dniester; the new home of the Slav Slovenes was further west between the Dniester and the Danube. In the Danube plain Heruli and Lombards took the place of the Ostrogoths who had emigrated to Italy. Thus under the pressure of the Altaic tribes pushing west, events led to the formation of a chain of migrational movements converging on the Balkan peninsula, and these movements included both Germanic and Slav peoples alike.

At almost the same time as this tribal redistribution set in motion from Central Asia, the tribes in northern Europe also began to move. It began in Jutland and on the Danish islands. A Danish advance to the south led to the migration of the Saxons and Angles, hitherto living in Schleswig-Holstein. One group of these tribes left their homeland by sea and occupied the eastern part of Britain. Other bands of Saxons and Angles, which had already penetrated beyond the Elbe, now moved on further to the west. Under their pressure, other Germanic tribes, including the Cherusci and Bructeri (who had joined together under the name of Franks since the end of the third century and the beginning of the fourth), retreated from the region of the Rhine estuaries into Gallic territory (present-day Belgium). This led to the conquest of Gaul associated with the name of the Frankish king Clovis.

The West was now almost completely occupied by Germanic tribes. Tribal alliances developed into Germanic states under the leadership of tribal kings, and these kingdoms set up on the soil of the West Roman Empire gradually began to assimilate the culture of late antiquity. These Germanic kingdoms existing at the beginning of the sixth century were of course still far from possessing any inner solidarity. This could not be achieved without the fusion of the Germanic conquerors with the native population. Such a development remained impossible so long as the two elements were in disagreement over religion and followed different laws. The Germanic population was in fact mostly Arian, while the native population belonged to the orthodox faith. Legal disparity arose because of the existing imperial laws which forbade intermarriage between the two peoples. It is true that the imperial law proclaimed in 375 had not expressly mentioned the Germanic element, speaking only of foreigners; but it was certainly the intention of the legislators, the Emperors Valentinian I and Valens, that it should be directed against the Germans (*Cod. Theod.* III, 14, 1). The Germanic population repaid in the same coin this attitude of the Roman Empire and for their part drew a line of demarcation between themselves and the Roman population by proclaiming laws which were valid only for their own people. These laws soon developed into legal codes. They even went as far as openly to release the Roman population of their own territory from allegiance to the Empire and they issued laws valid only for these sections of the Roman populace. Thus among the Visigoths there was a Germanic law and a Roman law, both deriving from decrees of the Visigoth kings. Here the *Codex Theodosianus* was rendered powerless.

The old resentment against the East.
The separatism of the West, fed from pagan and Christian sources

In view of the marked contrast between the Roman provincial population and the Germanic state which found its expression in differences of law and faith, these two ethnic groups could not come together in a common resistance to the Byzantine East. This contrast was still so marked in the first half of the sixth century that Justinian in his campaigns against the West was able to count on it as his best ally and it was one of the main causes which brought about the collapse of the Vandal and Gothic kingdoms. But in the end, despite the successful reconquest of North Africa and Italy, these campaigns showed only too quickly how much East and West had already grown apart. It was only a question of time before this contrast would inevitably find its political expression in a new, and this time definite, separation of the two parts of the Empire.

The contrast between West and East was older than the Germanic conquest of the former West Roman territories; it had become quite evident even in the time of Constantine in the fourth century. It showed itself first in a return to the old Roman traditions. At the head of the movement were the aristocrats of the old capital, Rome, so far as they held to their paganism; their literary salons became the organs of a new intellectual trend. An effort was made to rescue the Latin language from the barbarity into which it had sunk in the third century. Aelius Donatus wrote a Latin primer and commentaries on the comedies of Plautus. The historian Ammianus Marcellinus, who came from Syria, found in Rome not only the stimulus to write in Latin but also the possibility of so doing, and he produced his history of the Roman Empire continuing Tacitus' work up to 378. It is characteristic of the situation that here in Rome the Syrian Ammianus wrote Latin, not Greek. At that time the Latin classics were no longer written on easily perishable rolls of papyrus, but on parchment—the parchment which the Christians of Asia Minor had brought to the Latin West as writing material for the holy books. Hence the oldest manuscripts we have, even of Roman classics, the works of Virgil and Plautus, date no earlier than the fourth century.

Even the Christian Church in Rome had to take heed of these aristocratic circles with their thoroughly pagan orientation. The church, too, had good reason to be dissatisfied with political developments. After all, the new capital on the Bosphorus seemed also to be laying claim to be the religious centre of Christianity. Not without reason did Constantine designate himself 'Proto-Apostolos', 'the first of the apostles'. He had indeed placed his own tomb in the middle of the cenotaph of the Twelve Apostles. This was rightly regarded as a threat to Rome's apostolic mission. And so Peter was raised to the status of Apostle-Prince and a consecutive list of Popes was drawn up, beginning with Peter. A search was now begun for the apostle's tomb, and its discovery was claimed. A cult of the relics of the two great apostles Peter and Paul began to develop. At the centre of these endeavours were the Pope Damasus and Jerome, the translator of the Bible and historian. Both of them were held in esteem by a section of the Roman nobility. It is no coincidence that at the same time as Jerome began the translation of the Bible into Latin (the Vulgate), Ammianus Marcellinus wrote the history of the Roman Emperors. The contrast between Byzantium and Rome did not however diminish. The Roman Church's cult of Peter was countered in Byzantium by a cult of Andrew. Here too an apostolic succession was created. The apostle Andrew, whose relics had been transferred to the new capital, was allegedly supposed to have consecrated a certain Bishop Stachys as first bishop of Byzantium. And here too a list of bishops was created which was declared traditional.

But in Byzantium, continuing from philosophical interpretations of history, things were taken still further. The new weapon was the *Apocalypse* of Daniel. The theory of the three Empires and the promise of the Messianic Empire was now applied to the new capital of Constantinople and its state. With a distinctly disparaging slant against the old Rome, the new capital was proclaimed as the 'New Rome' (*Nea Roma*), the new city of Rome. The sense of this interpretation was quite plain: the new Rome was supposed to be the capital of the Messianic Empire promised in the *Apocalypse* of Daniel; Constantine had ended the era of the old pagan Rome and through the founding of Constantinople had ushered in the new Messianic Empire. This policital theory had been developed by Bishop Andrew of Caesarea in Cappadocia in the fifth century. The West did not receive without comment this new interpretation of Daniel's *Apocalypse* by the East. The West's reply gave the prophecy a different interpretation. To counter the ecclesiastical politics of the East Roman Emperors, which aimed at an understanding with the monophysite eastern Churches, the West now developed the thesis of the 'Orthodox' Church. Rome was the *caput fidei*, the head of the faith, while the Eastern Emperors were tainted with the error of favouring heresy. Since Rome at the time belonged politically to one of the Germanic tribal kingdoms, the Ostrogothic state, the Roman Pope was more independent; he could speak more freely than a bishop under the political rule of the Emperor. Thus in Rome, under the Ostrogothic régime, there developed the thesis of the primacy of the spiritual over the temporal power. This also laid the foundations for the Roman Pope's claim to primacy.

In the development of the West's independent position *vis-à-vis* the East Roman Empire an important part was played by North Africa. Here the claim of the Pope to primacy and the western Christian standpoint in relation to the ecclesiastical politics of the imperial government were still defended, even when the Roman Pope had to submit to the political pressure of the Emperor after the conquest of the Ostrogothic kingdom by the Byzantines. There in the Roman part of North Africa was a group of Christian theologians who managed to uphold convincingly the standpoint of the West. The greatest of these was Augustine (354–430). Through his philosophy of history, he determined for centuries to come the lines along which the controversy developed. Augustine possessed the ability to assimilate the most conflicting opposites and reconcile them within himself. His theology of love was Christian and from the New Testament, his teaching about God was neoplatonic, his doctrine of sin Manichaean, his rhetorical self-analysis Roman, his metaphysic of the two empires was derived from the reforming Donatist Tyconius, his critique of religion can be traced back to Varro, and his psychology and metaphysics are derived from the neoplatonic Porphyry. In his work *De civitate Dei* he interprets history as the struggle between the city of God and the city of the world, thereby indirectly laying the ideological foundations for the idea of the primacy of the Roman bishop. Thus his philosophy of history stands in direct contrast to Byzantine theology. Byzantine theology knew nothing of the antithesis between the city of God and the city of the world; it unreservedly regarded the Emperor as supreme head of the Christian Empire. The religious pessimism preached by Augustine, his assertion of man's total incapacity for good and of the predestination of certain men for salvation also shows how much the Christianity of the West differed from that of the East. Augustine initiated a great movement of Christian historiography. Orosius, a Spaniard, wrote his history with the historical perspective of Augustine. Even the historian from Trier, Salvian (400–475), is influenced in his work by the African Augustine. Salvian, in a truly Augustinian spirit, justifies the distress and affliction of the West as divine retribution.

The Roman province of Africa, by reason of its common frontier with the Christian Berber states of North Africa, played a special part in the religious separation of the West from the Eastern Empire, simply by virtue of the fact that the African theologians, in their resistance to the ecclesiastical policy of the imperial government, knew that they had the Christian Berbers behind them. They were able to assert their independence even after the subjection of the Vandal kingdom. The Berbers were orthodox; like a section of the Roman provincial administration, they were opposed in faith to the Arian Vandals.

In North Africa Christianity had intensified existing social and regional conflicts. Even in the fourth century, under the influence of Christianity, events had led to the formation of a partisan movement, whose members called themselves *milites Christi*, 'soldiers of Christ', but were called *circumcelliones* by their opponents on account of their habit of raiding isolated farmsteads and settlements. The revolt of the *circumcelliones* arose through unhealthy social conditions, a consequence of Roman colonial rule, which had driven back the Berbers from the fertile part of the country into the inferior and less productive regions. The rich plantations, often with tens of thousands of olive-trees, were owned only by Latin Romans. The Christian Berbers, in contrast to the Vandals, were not Arians. The period of the Berbers' and the Roman Christian populace's common resistance to the Arian Vandals determined also the Romano-African clergy's subsequent relations with the Berbers. Hence, in its opposition to the imperial leadership, the African Church could rely on the Christian Berber states beyond the territory which was then under Byzantine sovereignty. Thus in the so-called controversy of the Three Chapters, Ferrandus of Carthage was still in a position to defy the East Roman Emperor Justinian, even when the Roman Pope Pelagius had complied with the imperial demands under pressure from the régime of the Byzantine occupation.

But what was decisive in the development of an independent western culture was the fusion of the Germanic and the Roman provincial population. Only when this was achieved did it become evident that the long-standing relationship between East and West was broken—the relationship which, despite all conflicts, had persisted within the framework of late antique culture. This fusion was attained not by the Church, but by the monastic movement which also existed in the West. It is significant that the foundation of Benedict of Nursia included Gothic as well as Roman monks. Gregory the Great's predecessor as Pope, Pelagius II, was a Gothic monk. This process of fusion began towards the end of the sixth century and was completed by about the middle of the seventh. In the last decade of the sixth century there were still historians in Gaul, such as Bishop Gregory of Tours, and poets such as Venantius Fortunatus, both members of the Roman population; but with them the Roman element ceased to lead a life of its own and to be the sole representative of literature. This transformation was due to outside influences. It was the Irish monks who passed on the foundations of Roman culture to the Germanic population in Gaul and northern Italy. The monasteries of Bobbio and Corbie, the one in Italy, the other in France, were in both countries milestones in this development. The culture taken over from the monks was one-sided; it was filtered through their taste and religious viewpoint. It is relevant to mention here that at Bobbio they erased Cicero's works to provide sheets of parchment on which to write down the decisions of the Council of Chalcedon. The intrusion of a new ethnic element, that of the Germanic world, was inevitably associated with a cultural regression. The crude handwriting in the manuscripts from the Gallic monasteries of the seventh and eighth centuries is sufficient evidence of the fact that the Romans had long since retreated from their cells. Similarly, the clumsy Latin and violations of grammar in the first literary works of this era—historical and hagiographical works—bear witness to the fact that here an alien national element was hesitantly beginning to speak the language of an ancient culture. The partitioning of land by the Germanic conquerors had gradually deprived the Roman class of its social standing; thus in many provinces it could no longer assert itself as an active upholder of culture in the literary field.

The beginning of the new age took place in the form of a transition, not a break with the past. But even if monasteries still reckoned according to the years of the reigns of the Emperors in Byzantium, a sense of being something different had nevertheless grown up. The *imperium romanum* was no longer the obvious form of political existence, as in the times of the Germanic kings or even perhaps of Theodoric. Things had now reached the point when there was an awakening of an individual sense of nationality which was to find its political expression in the rise of the Carolingian dynasty. When the Frankish annals of this time speak of the *gentes Romanorum et Graecorum*, 'the peoples of the Romans and of the Greeks', the line of demarcation is thereby quite consciously drawn between the new Germanic national state and the *imperium romanum* of the Byzantines.

The transition from late antique to Byzantine civilization

5

New forms of expression side by side with old traditional ones

Contrasting western developments, created by the Germanic tribal migration, by the idea of the Roman Pope's primacy and by Augustine's philosophy of history, had built up a barrier against the Byzantine Empire. The boundary-line in the East, resulting from the expansion of the Arabs, now went further and joined up with that of the West. Nor did these external changes spare the culture of late antiquity. The monastic movement and the army reform had destroyed the unity of late antique civilization on the soil of the Roman Empire. This poses the question of the survival and tradition of late antiquity in the new Byzantine world. Here too the change comes in the time of Justinian. Late antique culture and the new forms that develop out of the monastic movement stand face to face. John Moschus and Procopius are contemporaries; monks and philosophers live side by side. But the end of the universities brought with it the decline of late antique culture as the dominating element in life. At the beginning of the seventh century a period of great silence began. No literary work has come down from this period; a gap of almost 150 years yawns between the point when the last historian of the old late antique school laid down his pen and the moment when the account of past and present was resumed in the form of a monk's chronicle. To obtain the solution of this riddle, we must go back to the person of the ruler, to Justianian. That man, with his dual personality, half monk, half Emperor in the pagan sense, was in himself a symbol of this period of transition. His contemporary, Procopius, says of him that he lived like a monk, worked through the night by a feeble lamp, received old priests and sustained himself with only the bare minimum of food. He was in no way a man of the senate, i.e. a descendant of an aristocratic line. Only after the death of the Emperor Anastasius did Justinian's uncle Justin exchange the uniform of commander of the guards for the imperial robes. The family's home lay in the valley of the Morava in Tauresium, near Bederina (Usküb). Justin, his uncle, a humble Macedonian peasant, had risen from the ranks to commander of the guards despite his lack of education. Then when he came to power and made his reputation he remembered his family and had his nephew brought to Constantinople. After attending elementary school, probably a monastery school, and receiving extensive private tuition, Justinian went to the university. Through his uncle's eminence he was admitted to the civil service and then, particularly after he had seized power, was able to hold the most influential positions in the state.

Justinian was physically weak—no general, more of a thinker, active as theologian, statesman and legislator, similar in many respects to Philip II of Spain. In him, too, an almost mystic piety was combined with a strong streak of sensuality. His relationship with the actress Theodora, which he legalized by marriage, was from the political point of view a heavy burden for imperial prestige. Like his uncle he had risen to power as an agent of reconciliation; he too was to mediate between East and West. The Emperor Anastasius, who came from Syria, followed a monophysite policy influenced by the

East, and this had to be repudiated and the danger of the Empire's disintegration removed. The threatened revolt of the North, that is of the Balkan peninsula, had to be prevented. Justinian carried out all these tasks. He secured the unity of the Empire; over and above that, like Constantine—who determined developments for almost a hundred years, until beyond the time of Theodosius I—he gave the ship of the state the impetus which directed the course of its voyage for more than a century. That applies not only to political development. The late antique heritage also bore his stamp in so far as it survived during the time of the Byzantine middle ages, living on in representational art and in literature.

Justinian is renowned for the significant part which he played in the development of church architecture, in determining the lines along which Roman law was to continue and in the literary work of his time. But Justinian was also the man who had the universities closed and thereby began to deprive late antique culture of its lifeline.

No civilization can be understood in isolation from the society which carries it. In the time of Justinian it included landed proprietors, foreign merchants, craftsmen who had become entrepreneurs, as well as intellectuals and artists. The intellectuals—pupils of the grammarians' and rhetoricians' schools or of the law-schools—no longer stood in the tradition of the classical age. What they were brought up on was the form of education which was established in the sophists' schools of the second or third centuries A.D. These were schools of an inferior grade. Neither the Stoa of Plato in Athens nor the Museion in Alexandria have anything to do with this form of learned education. The classics, the teaching material of these schools, were no longer those of the professors of Alexandria; the sophists' selection had laid down which extracts should be used for teaching purposes. Euripides, Sophocles, and Aeschylus were no more read than they are today. The great Menander belonged to the private reading of literary salons; he had disappeared from the teaching programme. What the dictionaries recorded was the language and expressions of a certain class. The Attic legal language was preserved and made into the literary *koine* of late antiquity. This shaped the nature of the literature of the age. Even the greatest figure among the writers of this time, Procopius of Caesarea, fits into this picture. Procopius did not belong to the immediate entourage of the Emperor; he came from the circle of the discontented military. Not a soldier himself but a lawyer by profession, he wrote for the Emperor's generals; in their service he wrote as a critic of the age of Justinian and not as its eulogist. In his critical attitude to his own time he has affinities with Tacitus; he too is full of hatred of the powerful men of his day. And yet there are many differences between the Roman patrician Tacitus and the Syrian Procopius from Caesarea in Palestine. The work of Tacitus has a positive aim: the ancient freedom of the Roman republic, and this lies behind all his criticism. But with Procopius there is nothing which he loves, nothing for which he is fighting. He practises criticism without knowing any ideal of his own.

Three writings compose his literary work. He begins with the history of Justinian's wars, then in a second work describes the Emperor's public buildings and finally, after these two works, he publishes yet another which purports to be the *Secret History* of the Emperor Justinian. So Procopius begins with a partisan work, writing for the general Belisarius as one of his adherents, then follows a panegyric work on behalf of Justinian, and finally a pamphlet against the Emperor's régime.

Procopius' manner of writing history reveals the strength and weakness of the late antique culture of Justinian's time. In the preface to his history of the Emperor's wars Procopius speaks of the tasks of the historian. According to him, he is concerned with the causes (*aitiai*) in history—it is these that he wishes to elucidate. He says that his history is more important than any other: what has happened here has never occurred before, and he is qualified to perform this task, for he has taken part personally in the events which he is depicting. This introduction shows more than anything else how far removed things were from the age of Polybius. Admittedly Procopius stresses the importance of writing history from personal experience, like Polybius, and thereby attacks those armchair-historians who record history in their small studies without having had any personal connection with the events concerned. What is true for Polybius however cannot be claimed by Procopius for himself. Certainly he took part in the Emperor's wars in Belisarius' retinue, but he lacks what Polybius had—insight into the great political interactions of cause and effect. No documents came into his hands; he had no close acquaintance with any contemporary diplomats from whom he might have got information. He sees things only from the standpoint of the soldier. And so the causal connections and the chronological data are the weakest parts of his work. Even his assertion that his age was the most important of all, because it had tried out amazing and hitherto unknown weapons proves to be rhetorical nonsense; the 'amazing weapon' he mentions—mounted archery—had been known to the Roman army since the early imperial era. He is probably following the introduction of a Hellenistic work which has not come down to us. Nor does his assertion that he has striven only for recognition of the truth hold water; the Emperor of the *History of the Wars*, who manages to hold together a crumbling Empire, conquers new Empires, drives off the barbarians, becomes —in the *Secret History*—a murderer, a demon, and then again a henpecked husband, the puppet of Theodora, the whore raised to the rank of Empress.

The strong as well as the weak points of the historian Procopius lie in his psychological grasp of peoples and persons. In his contradictions, in his inconsistencies, he is quite the man of late Hellenism. Hence the baroque traits of his historical writing: the *deinotes*, the *terribilità*, which today we at first find disconcerting. Even if he judges the battles of the Goths from the standpoint and with the criteria of the Homeric age, he goes far beyond this apparently primitive basic attitude. Thus the Vandals are seen with a regard for the *condition humaine* that is almost modern, as though modelled on Taine. Similarly, he sees the Frankish intervention in North Italy and the double game of the Franks as a characteristic attribute of the people.

From the literary point of view if seen in the context of the age of Justinian, Procopius was an outsider who nevertheless combined in himself all the weakness and strength of that final late antique period. His complete opposite was the diplomat Peter. Peter was one of the highest imperial officials and, unlike Procopius, was able to write history from first-hand knowledge and personal participation in imperial politics. Whereas Procopius, as a member of the political police and a tool of Belisarius, had a social status that kept him well in the background, Peter was one of the most esteemed men of the Empire. At first he had started no differently from Procopius; he too had chosen to study law, but then, in contrast to Procopius, he had risen rapidly and very early on entered the imperial chancery. After the usual career in the service of the chancery, he soon became an ambassador and because of his skill was entrusted with the most difficult diplomatic missions. In 534 he was ambassador at the Ostrogothic court in Ravenna and here had to conduct the none too easy negotiations with Amalasuntha. As a result of his diplomatic services, in 538 he was raised to the office of *magister officiorum*. This office corresponds to that of a foreign secretary combined with the duties of the head of the ministerial council. In 550 he represented the Emperor as ambassador in Ctesiphon; in 552 he negotiated with Pope Vigilius in Chalcedon, and in 568, again as the Emperor's representative, conducted important political discussions with the Persian king in

Ctesiphon. By all accounts Peter was an outstanding diplomat, an accomplishment which in those days required both brilliant oratory and expert legal knowledge. His service to the state had made him a rich man; from the accusations of his opponents, to whom Procopius lent his ear, it appears that he owned important whetstone quarries as well as vast estates. Unfortunately only a little of this man's work has come down to us; above all, Peter left no writings concerning the time when he himself was active. His only historical work, part of which has been preserved, concerns the period from the second Triumvirate to the death of the Emperor Julian. He also wrote about the state and state institutions. Parts of this work were incorporated in the *Book of Ceremonies* of the Emperor Constantine Porphyrogenitus.

Besides the writer Procopius and the diplomat Peter, there is still however the grammarian John the Lydian. Unlike Procopius and Peter, he was a representative of civilization and not of culture. Admittedly his work has no lasting value, but it deserves attention as a valid statement about the literary interests of the general public. John the Lydian had gradually worked his way up from a minor imperial clerk to the office of chief secretary and then at the end of his career was given a chair at the university of Constantinople. John wrote without any real understanding of events. In his writing *De Magistratibus* he draws on an abundance of notes and quotations from works which are now lost. In so doing he displays great erudition which however cannot conceal his inability to understand what he has read and put it across clearly. Nor is this judgment disproved by his other writings—his work on mathematical omens and his little treatise on the months. His whole literary output shows how inadequate the state of education was in the higher education establishments of late antiquity during the last years of their existence.

Procopius, Peter, and John the Lydian, each in his own way gives a picture of the literary class that determined intellectual life during the age of Justinian. The social status of the pillars of literature is also reflected in the picture they give of their own times. Those who wrote history were diplomats. To these circles, besides Peter and Nonnus, belonged Priscus, the man who had visited Attila; his diplomatic career had taken him far round the world still ruled by Rome and Byzantium at that time. From the Balkans he hurried to Alexandria, then he was in Arabia and Upper Egypt, and finally even on diplomatic service in Rome. These diplomats were able to see much of their world with their own eyes and thereby gained insight into the conditions of many peoples.

Another class engaging in literary activity was composed of imperial chancery officials. Through their knowledge of the documents they were in a position to give accounts of extremely important matters. To this class belonged John of Epiphania, Evagrius, and Theophylact Simocattes. To judge from the documents reproduced by them, in part verbatim, they wrote the history of the Empire and Emperors by official appointment. Yet another group was formed by members of the court and it included historians as well as poets. An officer of the guards, Menander, wrote the history of his times by imperial commission, and the chamberlain Paul the Silentiary lavished his praise in verse on the Emperor's public buildings.

But the legal profession, which was not tied to the service of the state, also won literary fame at that time. One of its members was Agathias, who made a name first as an epigrammatist; later he was commissioned to write a history of the Empire. In this work he continued the description of Justinian's wars, begun by Procopius, up to the year 562. Agathias' continuation of Procopius' history of the wars is an indication of the recognition and assent which must have been given to Procopius' historical work quite soon after its appearance. Literary success was still decisive at this time; without it Procopius would not have received the imperial appointment to write the *De Aedificiis (On Buildings)*, nor would his history of the wars have been continued by Agathias and then later by others up to the year 602.

This raises the question of the historian's commission. At this period there was imperial historiography, contemporary history written to order. The Emperors always took care to have their own times recorded by a worthy historian. It is not known who first received the commission to depict the age of Justinian. In any case, in the face of Procopius' well-known work, it could not have had any success. Tradition rejected it.

In the case of another form of historical record—the annals—the position is different. Even the Christian Emperors had not given up the ancient Roman custom whereby the Pontifex Maximus had to look after the calendar and also, in connection with this office, to record the most important events of the year, such as appointments of officials, festivals, and public works. In the Christian epoch the priests of the court churches had taken the place of the Pontifex. Thus the annals of the western Roman Empire, whose Emperors resided from time to time in Ravenna, were now recorded by eminent churchmen in the entourage of the archbishop of Ravenna, and the eastern Roman annals by priests who belonged to the clergy of the church of Hagia Sophia in Constantinople. Alongside this however there still existed a secular form of annals recorded by a higher imperial official (*comes*). The extant outline of this work is connected with a *comes* Marcellinus; and in the only surviving manuscript this, with its continuations, extends into the middle of the sixth century. The western Roman annals were kept regularly until the beginning of the second half of the sixth century. The eastern Roman imperial annals extend into the first half of the seventh century. Both these annals are of great significance in the development of western and Byzantine historical writing. In East and West these annals formed the chronological framework of the so-called world chronicles.

The world chronicles became the literary form of expression of the monastic movement. In them the history of the world is viewed critically from the monastic standpoint. But even these chronicles were not new as a literary form. They go back to the Hellenistic period of the first and second centuries A.D. The chronicle of Hesychius of Miletus is still a history of the times in the sense of the Hellenistic models, but in its structure it already points the way to the later monastic chronicles of the Byzantine period. Hesychius of Miletus was a contemporary of Justinian. His story began with the Assyrian king Belos and continued up to the death of the Emperor Anastasius. Judging from what little remains of his work, his language was simple and clear and different from that of the later monastic chronicles. This is not the case with the chronicle known under the name of John Malalas. John Malalas belonged, as the epithet 'Malalas' indicates, to the broad class of rhetoricians. But despite the secular status of its author, his chronicle of the world is dominated by a primitive religiosity that is characterized more by superstition than belief. He was probably not the first to write in this manner; his models, which have not come down to us, belong to the second half of the fifth century. With John Malalas it was content and form that distinguished him from his literary contemporaries. His language was not new, but it had not previously been used in literature. His Greek was the language of the people, which otherwise has been preserved only in papyrus documents and the records of barbarian princes beyond the borders of the Empire. In content his work also marks a break with the late antique tradition. Whereas Procopius still declares his intention of reporting events as they were in reality, Malalas presents everything that he has picked up from the most varied sources. Thus with him the gossip of the market place is found side by side with quotations from the official imperial annals. Malalas' presentation is that of the novelist; he aims at entertainment, and so anecdotes clearly bearing the stamp of fiction and falsehood are introduced into the historical description. His standpoint is a didactic one, but he has no sense of the historian's responsibility. Procopius' work or Agathias' history of the Empire, and even the literary work of Theophylact Simocattes, was written for a comparatively limited circle which gathered in the literary salons of the capital for the reading of these works. On the contrary, Malalas wrote for the people, for the monks, who came from the most diverse social circles. His chronicle was read out aloud in the monasteries of the deserts and not in the salons of the capital. Hence the use of the vernacular, hence also, however, the wide dissemination of the work which put the writings of Procopius and other imperial historians entirely in the shade.

With this literature in the language of the people, a new period started, a new social class rose and began to come of age. The same thing happened in regions where the Latin language was used. The Alan Jordanes wrote a chronicle for monastic circles and a history of the Gothic peoples. Both are written in a barbarian language, but this was indeed the vernacular of the time. It is known that Jordanes adapted to the vernacular a composition in the literary language, and this was one of the writings of the great historian Cassiodorus. Cassiodorus wrote a Latin that was schooled on the style of Cicero. Not for nothing did he count as leading 'minister' of the Ostrogothic king Theodoric. But his fastidious presentation, his affected Latin expressions, meant nothing to the popular ear; hence the editing by Jordanes, which brought the work down to a lower level.

In another instance, that of the Roman Pope Gregory, the vernacular was chosen by a man who in other literary works made use of the literary language. Thus Gregory the Great's dialogues on the miracles of the saints—intended for the circle of Italian monks and minor clergy—were written in the vernacular, while his lofty theological works were composed in the literary language.

Thus in Justinian's time the vernacular and the literary language were found side by side. The literary language lasted as long as the universities of antiquity. But the two of them did not live side by side without mutually influencing each other; even hymnology and liturgical language influenced the otherwise highly conservative poetry of late antiquity which was based on classical models. George of Pisidia, who in the first half of the seventh century described the deeds of the Emperor Heraclius in epic form with formal perfection of language, took over in his metre certain forms deriving from the liturgy, and from that form of liturgy used by the monastic movement. Now George of Pisidia was a deacon at Hagia Sophia in Constantinople. He was no secular poet. This explains why he adopted certain ecclesiastical forms in his poetry. But for the rest, his epics are modelled after late antique patterns; his metre is the hexameter, which Nonnus had already used. Of his three epics, the first concerns Emperor Heraclius' campaign against the Persians, the second deals with the attack of the Avars on Constantinople in the year 626, and the third extols the Emperor's victory over the Persian king Chosroes; and in other respects they are no different from the classical form of the epic. But in addition to his epics the same poet also wrote poems which differ in content from late antique models. Thus George of Pisidia wrote a hymn on the Resurrection of Christ and a poetic work dealing with the creation of the world. It was characteristic of this age that its poets face both ways. On the one hand they stood in the classical succession, and on the other they produced Christian work which was quite different. Thus Nonnus, who at the beginning of the fifth century had depicted in 48 cantos the birth of Dionysus, his journey to India and his return and arrival in Greece, had at the same time written a paraphrase of St John's *Gospel*. The position was such that even in individual literary personalities both movements were found side by side. Another poet, Paul the Silentiary, composed a description (*ekphrasis*) of Hagia Sophia and at the same time wrote love-poems whose tone is strongly reminiscent of the later Greek erotic poets.

The end of late antiquity:
restrictions and prohibitions in learning, literature and art

The characteristic of this age is an inner break with the past. This impression dominates the picture of literature and representational art. But it was not only the split between an old dying civilization and a new one growing up that stamped the artistic expression of that time; there was in general a constriction of artistic and scholarly activity which is bound up with that epoch. Neither scholars nor artists enjoyed complete freedom to engage in creative activity. Behind everything there lay a powerful obligation, either to duties of state and religion or to the taste of the masses.

Consider the Emperor Justinian's order prohibiting commentaries on the laws and decrees laid down in his famous legal code. A prohibition of this kind meant nothing less than the suppression of any kind of creative jurisprudence. Justinian's *Codex* was supposed to remain for all time the absolute legal code of the Empire, untouched by critical scientific scrutiny. Jurisprudence was thereby forced to confine itself to the adaptation of this Justinian legal code to the demands of the time, without applying any original interpretation to the statutes. This means that the jurists either arranged selections of the most important and most frequently used laws, or undertook translations of the code into the Greek language spoken at that time in the East Roman Empire. Jurisprudence was therefore left with very limited possibilities for further development. The paraphrases of Theophilus and Stephanus, the *Epitomai* of Cyril, and the *Summa* of the Anonymus grew out of the very limitations in which jurisprudence was then trapped. These commentaries of Roman law in later times, very much akin to the theological commentaries on the *catenae*, were the result of the restriction on jurisprudence caused by Justinian's prohibition. In this activity in writing commentaries, later jurisprudence can be compared to the exegesis of the Holy Scriptures which the theologians produced. A theological commentary on the interpretation of a passage in the Bible consisted of strings of quotations from the fathers without any attempt at independent intellectual interpretation. It was exactly the same with a legal commentary. In the interpretation of a statute, only related legal texts were put together; it was rare to find any attempt at an original interpretation.

A fate similar to that of jurisprudence befell the so-called natural sciences: mathematics, astronomy, physics, and medicine. Here too scientific research-work gave way more and more to explanation of older writings. The tendency of the development was to make astronomy gradually degenerate into astrology and chemistry into alchemy. Theoretical concern with the sciences receded; everywhere practical application took precedence over theory. The chemical works of the ancients were consulted only in so far as was considered necessary for reaching the solutions of important practical problems in contemporary industry and military science. This kind of interest in the sciences, as early as the beginning of the seventh century, had led to the development of Greek fire, the miraculous weapon which may have saved the life of Byzantium in the struggle against the Arabs. Here again, the theoretical premises for the new weapon had already been worked out in Hellenistic times, and the same is true of other discoveries of late antiquity. Thus Ptolemy mentions the astrolabe, but the definitive perfection of this instrument did not take place until the time of Justinian. The astrolabe made it possible to read off longitude and latitude with the aid of its dioptra. Mathematical research took the same course; late antique work carried out in this field exhausted itself in the interpretation of older writings. Seldom was any step made towards original research which went beyond the achievements of the Alexandrians. The famous neoplatonic philosopher at the university of Athens, Proclus (410–485), wrote a commentary on Euclid; likewise his contemporary Marinus, and somewhat later Simplicius. All these works are lacking in the development of original theories; they simply make use of what the Hellenistic age had achieved.

Medicine presents the same picture. Works of this period on anatomy, pharmacology, dietetics and gynaecology contain scarcely any original observations; almost everything is derived from the works of the Hellenistic medical men, particularly of the Alexandrian school. On the whole the great encyclopaedic medical works of Justinian's time, such as Alexander of Tralles' twelve-volume account of pathology, simply reiterate—very imperfectly—the knowledge of the Hellenistic doctors (e.g. Galen).

The development of Greek fire from the theoretical groundwork of Hellenistic times is comparable in the field of mathematics with the calculation of free-standing cupolas of great dimensions. Here again the premises had been worked out in earlier times. Hagia Sophia, with the vaulting of its immense dome, was the result of the application of mathematical science to architecture. Hence it is not surprising that the two great architects of this church, Anthemius of Tralles and Isidore of Miletus, also distinguished themselves as mathematicians. Anthemius has left essays on the construction of burning-mirrors; Isidore was prominent as a teacher of mathematics.

The limitation of the scientist's freedom, when he was forced to devote himself to practical application in his research, was paralleled by the pressure to which the representational artist and the writer were subjected. Neither in sacred nor in profane art was the artist free. There was no freedom in the choice of themes and even the iconography was bound by strict rules. This limitation was caused by the artist's firmly defined commission. In church-building the architect was dependent on the demands of liturgy. Further limitations came with the establishment of a definite iconographic programme. An example of this is the inclusion of the cupolas in the pictorial decoration of the interior of the church; the arrangement of the windows was directed by the conditions essential for the illumination of these pictures. The transition from the basilica to the domed church was determined not by the architects, but by the demands of liturgy.

Even the composition of the religious picture had well defined forms by the sixth century. It makes no difference that the way of depicting Christ remained diverse for a long time. In the mosaics of Ravenna the beardless Christ is found beside the bearded Christ. For the depiction of certain episodes in the Bible definite models were also being evolved at this time. In the form of miniatures for the Holy Scriptures these models were widely disseminated in illuminated manuscripts. The makers of mosaics and painters of frescoes had to work from these. Such a development led to the exclusion of the secular artist from the field of religious representation; the religious picture was already felt to be so sacred that its creation could only be entrusted to artists and mosaic-workers ordained as priests. The churches and monasteries were soon maintaining their own artists' ateliers and building works. Thus representational art reveals a development similar to that which took place in higher education, when universities and academies disappeared and were replaced by episcopal and monastic schools.

Even in secular representational art there was hardly any freedom to speak of in the artist's choice of subject, or even in his style of composition. The artist was no more free here than he was in the execution of sacred pictures, and this applies above all to the pictures that belong to the cult of the ruler. In Justinian's time the cult of the ruler still took almost the same form as in the time of the Roman Emperors. This means that even in representation, definite schemes of composition, which had already developed to some extent in the first century A.D., had to be followed. There was the equestrian statue of Justinian in Constantinople which is now known only from pictures. In the stance of the horse and the depiction of the Emperor, it corresponded exactly to the equestrian statue of Marcus Aurelius which is still preserved. It is the same with another picture from the cycle of representations of the Emperor-cult: the East Roman Basileus as leader of a procession. This scene shows the Basileus with the Empress, the highest imperial officers and the senior clergy, on the way to divine service in church. Justinian chose this form of the ruler's picture for his own portrait in the church of San Vitale. Even towards the end of the eleventh century the grand duke Yaroslav of Kiev used this form of the imperial picture. Here too a parallel can be drawn with the early period of the Empire; one is inescapably reminded of the frieze in the temple of the *Ara Pacis Augustae* in Rome, with the relief showing the Emperor Augustus and his family on the way to the sacrifice.

With yet another form of the picture of the ruler, the scheme of composition is fixed within the compass of the cycle of representations of the Emperor-cult. This is the picture of the Emperor sitting in the imperial box at the Circus. The depiction of the Emperor on the ivory diptychs is the same as on the reliefs on the Obelisk of Theodosius I in Constantinople; in the latter the Emperor is also enthroned in the box of honour in the Circus. In just the same way, the position of the Emperor standing as a general has scarcely been altered. The Giant of Barletta, which dates from the beginning of the fifth century and is probably a portrait statue of the Emperor Marcian, has the same stance as the statue of Augustus at Prima Porta. Yet another form of the imperial figure shows the Emperor as *triumphator*. Here he is seen with the enemies of the Empire offering him their submission. Here again the portrayal of the Emperor has remained unchanged up to the time of Justinian; on the ivory tablets of the sixth century the subjected princes prostrate themselves in homage (*proskynesis*) in the same way as on the base of the Obelisk of Theodosius I.

Only after the time of Justinian did the victory of the monastic movement lead to changes in the way in which the ruler was represented. This produced the mosaic in the antechapel of Hagia Sophia in Constantinople, where the Emperor offers *proskynesis* in the same form as the subjected princes on the Obelisk of Theodosius and on the ivory tablets. This was a sign of the monastic movement's victory, for with its radical aims, as seen in the monastery of Studius, it wished to place the Emperor in a position of subjection. Later on this was again given up: the Emperor was then no longer prostrate before Christ, but stood beside the throne on which Christ had taken his place. That was how he was depicted in the eleventh century. In such pictures the Emperor stood in the place which was occupied in the old pictures by the Caesar, the junior Emperor. Moreover in the later pictures of the ruler-cult, dating from the time after Justinian, the Emperor was no longer crowned as *triumphator* by the goddess of Victory but by Christ.

The strict control of the artist was still laid down by this commitment to the state even when he was not concerned with pictures connected with the cult of the ruler. At this time compulsion was present in almost all artistic work. For instance in the illuminated manuscript of the *Iliad*, which dates from the beginning of the sixth century and is now in Milan, the pictorial representation of individual episodes was probably determined by a definite model. It seems that this model applied to all illustrations of Homer; it included all the famous pictures of episodes from the Trojan war. Hence there is no alternative for the artist but to imitate these prototypes. So here too the same development is found as in sacred art; for the manuscript of the Gospels, the *Codex Rossanensis*, which dates from the same time as the *Iliad* manuscript, reveals just as plainly its dependence on a model of this kind in which famous pictures of stories from the Holy Scriptures were collected. For instance, the picture of two Emperors at Pilate's table during Christ's meeting with the Roman governor points to a time when two Emperors were ruling, that is, to the fourth century, whereas the *Codex Rossanensis* dates from no earlier than the beginning of the sixth century.

This imitation of definite classical models also dominated literature. *Mimesis*, i.e. imitation of the ancients, remained the fundamental concept of Byzantine literature. Here too there was no possibility of any original creation. And yet it was never a slavish imitation. The interpretation of the model varied. This does not always point to the strong individuality of an individual artist; often it points to definite racial groups whose ethnic character was now beginning to make itself felt more strongly even in literature and art. The depiction of mythological scenes on ivory tablets of the sixth century may still reveal their relation to the Hellenistic prototypes, as in the picture of the sacrifice of Iphigenia or the rape of Europa, but the reproduction is nevertheless different. Art has become more realistic; the influence of new social classes can be detected. But a great deal of this change also points to the demands of contemporary civilization. Ivory tablets and textiles were designed for merchants and customers; their tastes had to be taken into consideration. Since the oriental element in the population had become stronger, iconographic concepts were bound to change too. What the Sudan was for Egypt, South Arabia was for Syria and Palestine; the settling of immigrants in Syria and Palestine corresponded in Egypt to the civilizing of the nomadic population coming from the Sudan. On ivory tablets and textiles, in the depiction of mythological scenes, feminine beauty was interpreted in accordance with the taste of the later Muslim Arab authors; so too many of the wood-carvings produced in Alexandria are believed to be recognizable as the work of Negroes because of exaggerated emphasis on certain parts of the body.

Music also showed that this was no isolated phenomenon. It had that loud, strongly rhythmical quality which has always characterized Negro music. What is known today as jazz was then named after the city of Alexandria. The artist was dependent on the taste of the masses. The factors which were present at this time also explain the regression of the classical theatre. It is true that classical tragedy and comedy had already declined long before the victory of Christianity, but the great change of taste in theatrical performances was primarily a result of the Greek assimilation into a late antique oriental civilization. The urban masses wanted to see something different from the tragedies and comedies which had delighted and inspired the communities of Athens, Corinth and Rome. Pantomimes and farces of the lowest kind belonged to the sort of play tolerated by the people of Antioch, Alexandria, Constantinople and Rome. What people wanted to see were entertainments of the revue type, with almost naked girls, wild beast fights, horse-racing, and acrobatic performances. In vain was this kind of entertainment opposed by Christian moralists, such as Jacob of Sarugh (d.521) with his *Memra* on the theatre, or by defenders of cultivated taste, such as Procopius. When Procopius deals with the past of the Empress Theodora, a former chorus-girl, and describes the nature and manner of her public appearances, he reveals the intellectual's contempt for the passions of the masses.

During this period it was poetry and representational art, where they were still free, which reached the highest levels. Portrait sculpture attained a rare height of achievement; the so-called marble head of the Empress Theodora in Milan catches the type and character of its subjects with rare perfection. In literature, the same level was reached by Procopius. But this kind of art was on the verge of decline; the breakthrough of the monastic movement banished this sort of sculpture from art. Sculptors could not carry on their work except in isolation on the periphery of the Empire in Armenia and Italy, or as carvers of ivory tablets and wooden doors. In literature, love-poetry was suppressed. Paul the Silentiary could still freely write love-poems that sometimes bordered on the frivolous and the obscene, but a little later this was no longer possible. Here too the monastic movement had intervened. The status of women had changed, a development which can be deduced by a comparison between the marriage law of Justinian and the marriage laws on the imperial statute-books of the ninth and tenth centuries. Under the rule of the Emperor Justinian, women still retained independent control of their own property; separation and remarriage were not subject to any restrictions, and even the keeping of mistresses and concubines was still acknowledged as lawful at this time. In the later statute-books the Christian moral conception of marriage made itself felt more strongly; a man could not even remarry after the death of his wife except with great difficulty. Women were no longer present in public life. Since the love-lyric was concerned least of all with married love, the publication of poems with erotic content ceased altogether in the later period.

A people at the turning-point.
Carnival (Brumalia), superstition and fashionable crazes

Change in taste produced a transformation in literature and art; even artists now submitted to it. Representational art and literary works were thereby given a definite direction. The growing influence of lower social classes cannot be evaluated purely negatively, but from the point of view of the overall development it did bring about a lowering of standards. The disappearance of the novel and the decline of the old Roman comedy were dictated by the taste of the people. One detects the concessions which even such illustrious minds as the writer Ammianus Marcellinus had to make when they included information about astrological pursuits in their historical works, or mentioned superstitious practices and even devoted considerable space to such matters. The simple-minded people loved miraculous tales of this kind; and they were steeped in superstition. Thus there were people who could read one's hand, others who foretold the future from the dregs at the bottom of pots, as well as the whole crowd of astrologers and dream-interpreters. These people were fiercely attacked by the Church, but the great mass, and not only the simple folk, listened to them. This explains the vast circulation of this pseudo-literature, the books interpreting dreams, the astrological prophecies, the oracle-books, and the so-called thunder and lightning books.

But this was not the only thing that appealed to the people. The solemn cortèges of the Emperor, the church processions and the circus entertainments were popular festivals, just as the festivals of the old gods had been. The Brumalia were celebrated on the feast-days of the Saturnalia during the period from 24 November to 17 December, rather as Carnival is today, with splendid processions, 'soap-box speeches' and fancy-dress. Indecent pantomimes in which people imitated animals alternated with obscene dances by both sexes in which men dressed up as women and women as men. Comic, satiric, and tragic masks were worn. Even the Emperor and the highest officials were ridiculed in the Brumalia processions. Thus in the year 600, in one of them a man wrapped in a black robe and wearing a wreath of garlic was led through the streets on a donkey and hailed as the Emperor Maurice. But this mockery was not all: ditties were sung which attacked the private life of the Emperor. The Emperor Maurice, already an elderly man, had married a very young princess; the union had produced numerous children. This marriage made him the target of the carnival ditties. One of these satirical songs runs as follows:

'A cow he found, dainty and delicate,
And like young cocks do, he set about her;
He now makes children without number,
Like the shavings of a carpenter.
But no-one's allowed to grumble; he's shut their mouths up.
Holy Father, Holy Father! Terrible and Mighty!
Give him one over the head, to bring him down a peg or two!
Then I'll offer up this great ox as a sacrifice to You!'

Besides the Brumalia, the circus games were a way of getting to know the mood of the people. Here the circus parties of the Greens and the Blues, the organizations of the people of the capital, conducted discussions with the Emperor through their spokesmen. These circus parties existed in all the cities; thus they are heard of not only in Constantinople, but also in Antioch and Alexandria. Their power and influence were so great that they could even threaten the Emperor. They communicated with him through 'criers' (*kraktai*). In rhythmically delivered speeches, these speakers addressed the Emperor, who answered them in the same form through his own spokesman. At this time they controlled the distribution of food and seem even to have played an important part in the self-government of the big cities, although the number of registered members of both parties was never very great. The leaders of the parties were regularly received by the Emperor. In the illustration of the *Iliad* in the Milan manuscript, the painter of the miniatures adopts the uniform of the Greens for the depiction of battle-scenes, thus giving an indication of how powerful the influence of these urban circus parties must have been on the whole of public life.

City life at this time naturally had excesses as well, which were not unlike those of the present day. There were gangs of youths who made the streets unsafe and distinguished themselves from others by a particular form of clothing and hair-style. People spoke of the 'Hun hair-style' and similar fashionable crazes. These partly criminal gangs, particularly evident in Constantinople in the sixth century, are quite different from the merry students' processions which accompanied the academic end-of-term celebrations with all sorts of comic scenes. The latter only aroused the displeasure of the stern fathers of the Church Councils in the second half of the seventh century. These pious clerical gentlemen criticized the activities of these students and took offence at the so-called Greek clothes of the participants. Of all the manifestations of that epoch, the life of the people seems to have been affected least by the great break with the past signified by the decline of late antiquity.

The attack of the Arabs gave the death-blow to late antique culture. It was not that the Arab conquerors destroyed with their own hands the culture and institutions of late antiquity; they brought about a different form of decline. The centre of gravity of late antique culture lay in Syria and Egypt, the territories which were the first to be conquered by the Arabs. But whereas here the monks, the orthodox bishops and some of the Byzantine military officers emigrated before the Arab invasion to Asia Minor, and above all to the capital Constantinople, the greater part of the merchants, exporters and industrial magnates, quite apart from the rural population, stayed in their homeland. They did not take part in the great trek to Asia Minor. They willingly placed themselves at the disposal of the Arab conquerors, and the latter gratefully availed themselves of their administrative abilities and their cultural institutions. The imperial officials of the first Arab dynasty of Caliphs, the Umayyad, were Christian Syrians, men who spoke Greek and who had been educated at Greek schools of rhetoric. Indeed, the most important theologian of the Byzantine Church, John of Damascus, who lived in the first half of the seventh century, began by being one of the highest finance officials of the Umayyad Caliph; only later did he exchange the palace in Damascus for the monk's cell in the monastery of St Sabas near Jerusalem.

This Arab empire of the Umayyads stood right in the shadow of the East Roman Christian culture of Syria. In a Syriac fragment it is reported that Muawiya, the first Umayyad, after his elevation to the Caliphate, said his prayers on the site of Golgotha in Gethsemane and at the tomb of Mary. Consistent with this is the fact that the Dome of the Rock, the earliest great Arab mosque still preserved, had mosaics like those in Christian churches, and that in the hunting and spa palace of Qusayr Amrah frescoes in the style of late antique Syrian secular art were painted. But East Roman imperial art with pictures belonging to the Emperor-cult was also taken over. Hence the Caliph was depicted like the East Roman Emperor, sitting on the throne while the kings of the subjected nations paid him their homage.

Thus it is possible to speak of a continuation of late antique culture in Arab territory. This continuity however came to an end with the fall of the Umayyads and the foundation of Baghdad by the new dynasty of the Abbasids. The Greek language of the administration lived on in isolation into the middle of the eighth century. The process of the assimilation of late antique culture was a gradual one. The turning-point came with the decree of the Caliph Walid at the beginning of the eighth century. He ordered the tax-register of the empire, up to now kept in Greek, to be translated into Arabic immediately. As late as about 700, however, the Greek bishop of Nikiu in Lower Egypt wrote a world chronicle which continued the work of Malalas and brought its history up to well into the Arab epoch. Even the Patriarch in Alexandria went on for a long time using Greek in his chancery. But certainly, as time went on, the Greek administrative language was displaced more and more by Arabic. The progress of this development is shown by the Egyptian papyri that have been preserved. The first attempts to create an Arabic administrative language were made in the central branches of administration. Thus a knowledge of Greek could not be expected from the Arab governor in al-Fustat (Cairo); an Arabic version was therefore added to all documents submitted to him for signature. In this way there grew up a private chancery using Arabic for the governor, which at first was concerned only with the production of Arabic translations. After the beginning of the eighth century the Arabic translation was replaced by the original document in Arabic, which was now provided with a

Greek and a Coptic translation. This meant that it could also be read and understood by the regional authorities. But by this time Arabic had become the language of the central authorities, and towards the end of the eighth century the Greek translations disappeared even in the country districts; an Arabic administrative language had established itself in regional administration. Thus it is possible to speak of a continuation of late antique culture under Arab rule in the seventh and eighth centuries, while at the same time this culture was being extinguished in the Byzantine Empire by the monastic movement and the military reform.

BYZANTINE VERSION OF THE CREATION

23 The creation of man;
11th-century miniature

BYZANTINE VIEW OF THE WORLD

24 Symbolic map of Abyssinia;
9th-century copy of a
6th-century manuscript

BISHOPS

25 The consecration of St Gregory of Nazianzus as bishop; 9th-century miniature

26 St Matthew; 12th-century miniature

27 St Gregory with the sick; 9th-century miniature

28 The exposition of the Holy Cross by the patriarch; late 10th-century miniature

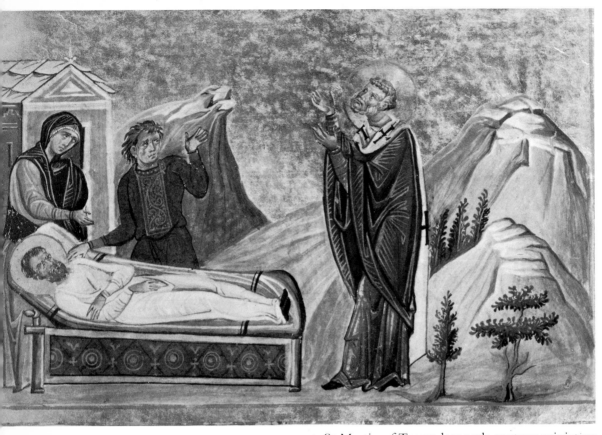

29 St Martin of Tours; late 10th-century miniature

DEATH OF A BISHOP

30 Transferring the relics of St John Chrysostom to the church of the Holy Apostles in Constantinople; late 10th-century miniature

CONSTANTINVS MAIOR IMPERATOR
HERACLII ET TIBERII IMPERATOR

PRIVILEGIA

31 Constantine IV giving privileges to the Bishop of Ravenna;
mosaic, Sant'Apollinare in Classe, Ravenna

32 The *Prokypsis*; an Emperor (possibly Leo VI) and Empress; 10th-century miniature

33 St Gregory in conversation with the Emperor Theodosius; late 9th-century miniature

34 Coronation of Emperor Constantine VII Porphyrogenitus by the patriarch; miniature, *c.*1300

35 Elevation of the emperor on the shield; miniature, *c.* 1300

PROCESSIONS

36 The emperor processing; ivory
tablet, 5th or 6th century

37 The four daughters of Yaroslav;
11th-century fresco, Hagia Sophia,
Kiev

38 The emperor in triumph; gold
medallion of Constantine II (337-61)

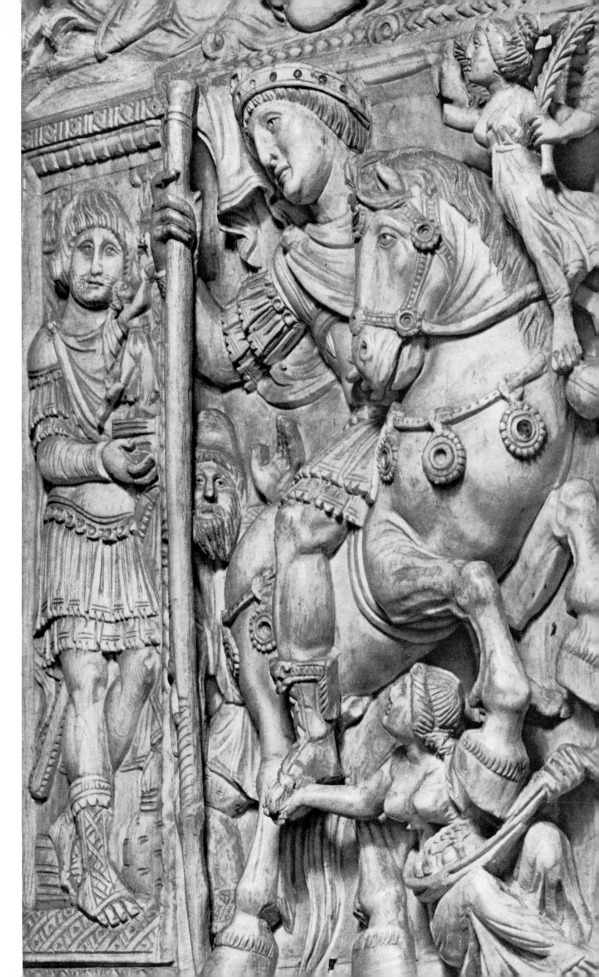

42 Emir Pinzarach (Ben Zarah) being received by Romanus III Argyrus (1028–34); miniature, c.1300

43 Constantine VI at the seventh General Council (787); late 10th-century miniature

44 Michael V Calaphates (1041–42) with representatives of the people; miniature, *c.*1300

45 Empress Theodora restoring the icons; late 10th-century miniature

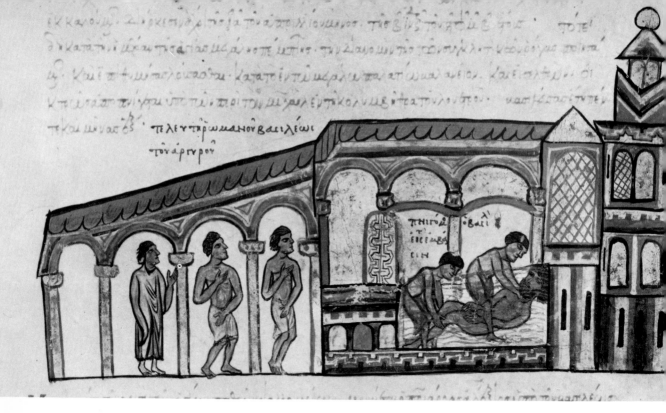

46 Romanus III Argyrus being drowned in the palace bath in 1034; miniature, *c.*1300

47 Herod as a Byzantine emperor; mosaic, San Marco, Venice

48 Elephants; late 10th-century silk cloth

49 A consul signals the beginning of the circus games; early 4th-century marble inlay

50 Breaking in horses; late 11th-century miniature

51 Lion and elephant; detail of mosaic in Hormisdas palace, Istanbul

Dancing girl on crown, c.1050

53 Miriam's dance; miniature from late 9th-century Psalter

ⲱⲟ ⲟⲣⲅⲩⲗⲱ ⲓⲁ ⲓⲁⲛ ⲟ ⲡⲣⲟ ⲟ ⲇⲣ ⲟⲣ ⲓⲛ ⲱⲱ ⲁ ⲃ ⲏ ⲧ ⲟ ⲓ ⲙ ⲁ ⲟ ⲓ ⲟ ⲁ ⲓ ⲥ :·

ⲠⲈⳞⲞⲒ ⲆⲈⲒⳞ ⲦⲀ Ⲛ ⲨⳞⲀ Ⲛ ⲦⲞⲒ ⲠⲞⲖⲒⲒ ⲚⲞⲒ Ⲟ ⲦⲀⲠⲒ ⲆⲢⲞ ⲘⲞ ⲚⲒⲈ Ⲗ Ⲕ ⲞⲤ

60 Hunting lion with a spear; late 11th-century miniature

61 Hunting lion with a net; late 11th-century miniature

64 Hunting scene; relief on 10th-century ivory casket

62 Castor hunting a lion and a stag; late 11th-century miniature

63 Pollux hunting a wild boar and a gazelle; late 11th-century miniature

66 Byzantine cavalry fighting the Seljuks; miniature, *c*.1300

65 Constantine triumphant with the help of the Cross; late 9th-century miniature

THE ARMY

67 The Emperor's German bodyguard; *missorium* of Theodosius I (detail)

68 St Demetrius as an army officer; 13th-century marble icon, San Marco, Venice

69 Battle scene; detail of ivory casket, 8th-10th century

71 Reception of foreign emissaries in a military headquarters;
10th-century relief on ivory casket

72 Joshua as a general in battle; 7th-century (?) miniature

70 Soldier-saint in cavalry
uniform; 15th-century fresco,
Brontocheion monastery, Mistra

73 Battle outside a city. General Maniaces defending Edessa (1032); miniature, *c.* 1300

う μιχ ωμοτ καὶ δρα ξ ερ ν σπκε ωο τα

74 A naval battle; 11th-century miniature

ο ο βένεθλι

IMPERIAL PALACES

75 Plan of the palace in Qasr ibn Wardan, North Syria

76 The so-called Theodoric's Palace, Ravenna; 6th and 7th centuries

77 Church and palace of Qasr ibn Wardan from the south

78 Ruins of the imperial palace in Constantinople

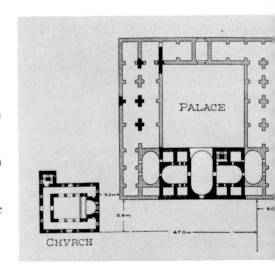

79 Desert castle Qusayr Amrah, Jordan (see Pls. 5, 6, 58, 59)

80 Tekfur Saray, Istanbul (see Pl. 3)

81 A country palace; mosaic from the Great Mosque, Damascus

82 Ploughing with oxen; 11th-century miniature

83 Sheep-shearing; 11th-century miniature

84 Three fishermen in a boat; late 11th-century miniature

ὸ οἰκο...

85 Bailiff paying labourers in presence of landlord; 11th-century miniature
86 Swine herding; 11th-century miniature on the prodigal son

143

ιοβαιτορ Νϲ δλθιαιομ. ϛιωθμ ✝ ποδοοιμιοθιοιτοῦ
τῶρʹ μουτωθρισοδουνοῖμᾶρʹππρʹ ᷉ϛιοο Νϲ μμιωδᾶπᾶς
λυμαι ✝ αραγαιο. τωρʹδιοσμαιπορʹ ππϛτορʹωρμε

87 Pestilence, fire and destruction;
miniature from the book of Job, 905

88 The destruction of Sodom; 12th-century mosaic,
Monreale cathedral, Sicily

PART THREE

The rise of
Byzantine civilization

Byzantium and the West: affinities and contrasts

The new Byzantine age proclaimed itself with revolutionary manifestations at home, connected with a social and an ethnic regrouping. At the same time the fight for self-preservation raged from the borders of the Empire to the heart of the countryside. This period of internal disturbances and hard external battles did not end until the beginning of the ninth century. By this time Byzantine culture had already reached maturity and was completely self-contained. The age of the great cultural expansion began on a religious basis which is associated with the names of the two missionaries Cyril and Methodius. But it was also an age characterized by a reconsideration of the knowledge of antiquity; the name of the Patriarch Photius became symbolic of this movement. Thus the ninth century was the golden age of Byzantine culture. And yet, even then, symptoms of decay appeared in the social order which foreshadow the later decline. Hence it is difficult to draw the line between the peak and the downfall. The period of cultural ascendancy was quite often also a period of political and social set-backs.

The beginning of this new Byzantine age was conditioned by the great political upheavals. The Arab attacks brought the introduction of the theme organization, a reform of the army that led to a social regrouping affecting almost the entire Empire. With the conquest of Syria, Palestine, and Egypt there began the great stream of refugees which almost swamped Asia Minor, the capital Constantinople and Byzantine South Italy. These refugees, who had given up their homeland in the conquered provinces and now poured into the areas of the Empire which were still Byzantine, were predominantly monks and supporters of the monastic movement. The Christian secessionists, who included the Syrian monophysites and the supporters of the Coptic church, did not renounce their homeland. This led to a strengthening of Orthodox monastic influence in Constantinople, Asia Minor and South Italy. In the monasteries of the capital, names from Syria and Palestine were now predominant. From this time on, church services in South Italy used the Syrian liturgy and not, as in Constantinople, the liturgy of St Basil and St Chrysostom. The domed church, whose definitive style had been developed in northern Syria (Sergiopolis) in the second half of the sixth century, now established itself in the capital and in the Byzantine provinces. Syriac iconography and the normal Syriac arrangement and divisions in the manuscripts of the Holy Scriptures (canonical tables of Rabula) became accepted throughout the remaining Byzantine world. Thus seen in the light of later developments, the Arab advance led to a stengthening of monastic influences in Byzantine culture.

At almost the same time, the influence of the West, the Latin world, which had been using the route over the Balkan peninsula, ceased in the Byzantine Empire. In the second half of the sixth century the advance of the Altaic nomads, who have gone down in history under the name of Avars, had already set in motion the world of the Slav peoples. Under the protection of the Avars these Slavs, the Antes between the Dniester and the Dnieper, and the Slovenes between the lower Danube and the Dniester, now crossed the border of the Empire. Macedonia became Slav at this time, likewise Bulgaria, in so far as the territory of the present-day state is concerned. Further Slav advances affected Greece, and here even reached the Peloponnese. From the end of the sixth century onwards it is possible to speak of an increasingly strong occupation, particularly of the Peloponnese. In the Peloponnese at this time the same tribal names are found as on the eastern German frontier in the tenth century. In view of the powerful threat to Asia Minor, first by the Persians, then by the Arabs, the Byzantine Empire could only conduct a defensive policy against the Slavs. The Emperor Heraclius transferred the last armies from Europe to Asia Minor: the Danube fleet, the Thracian army, and the later Opsikion (*Obsequium*) theme which was composed of men from the imperial guards regiment. The Slav occupation of the Balkan peninsula was even recognized by Heraclius; this is reported by a later but reliable source. According to this source, the Emperor is supposed to have settled the tribes of the Morava valley and those of the Croats between the Drava and the Sava as *foederati* of the Byzantine Empire.

The Slav tribes remained at first under Avar sovereignty; this lasted until the end of the seventh century, but it did not prevent the Slavs from advancing further to the south, west, and north, even beyond the actual sphere of Avar influence. Around 600 they had occupied in the north the whole of the upper Drava valley, far into the eastern Alps. In the west they were able to reach the Dalmatian coast. In the south they possessed almost the whole of Greece except for some coastal places. In Macedonia they pushed right up to Thessalonica, and even in Thrace it was only the fortifications on the Balkan passes that prevented them from further advance.

The Roman provincial population had managed to hold its own against the Slavs only in scattered places in the interior of the country, among which was the area around the present-day Bulgarian capital Sofia, which remained Byzantine almost down to the ninth century. Similarly, Roman enclaves held out in the towns on the lower Danube until as late as the ninth and tenth centuries. These Graeco-Latin minorities exercised a very strong influence on the first Bulgarian Empire, which was governed by a Turkic ruling-class. But the greater part of the Roman provincial population abandoned their homeland under this pressure from the Slavs. They consisted predominantly of Romanized Illyrians, who now left their small farms and went into the mountains, taking with them part of their herds and flocks. Here they lived as wandering herdsmen, moving from one place to another; they had abandoned their former settled way of life. Despite the Slav immigration, these Romanized wandering herdsmen managed to maintain themselves in the mountainous areas of the Balkans. At the end of the twelfth century, some of them once again changed their way of living and came down from the mountains to the plain, to become farmers there and cultivate the land again, as their forefathers had once done, half a century before. This process by which the wandering herdsmen, called Vlachs, moved out of the Carpathian mountains into the plain and settled there between the lower Danube and the Dniester, led to the formation of the present-day Rumanian people. The Vlachs found homes in this area because the Slavs had abandoned it on account of the attacks of the Altaic nomads coming from southern Russia. The settlement of the Vlachs led politically to the creation of the Rumanian principalities of Moldavia and Wallachia, later to become the present-day Rumanian state.

In Greece, developments were similar to those in Bulgaria and Macedonia. Here too, especially in the Peloponnese, a large part of the peasant population retreated into the mountains, and they too gave up their former way of life and became wandering herdsmen. The Tsaconians belong to this group, and even to the present they have preserved in their dialect very marked traces of ancient Greek (Doric) forms. Another section of the Greek population took to the sea and fled to South Italy. At the same time Greek refugees were also arriving from Syria and Palestine, so that the Greek element in South Italy was considerably strengthened.

Thus the Slav advance in the Balkans neutralized Latin influence on the culture of the Byzantine Empire, while the Arab advance led to a strengthening of Graeco-Oriental influence. Of course the Hellenism of the sixth century and the first half of the seventh century was not yet at the stage when it could be described as nationhood in the sense of conceptions current today. This Hellenism was a cultural community. Membership of it was determined by identity of religion, education, loyalty to the Emperor. Anyone who moved away from the state religion and confessed to one of the heretical Christian movements, such as monophysitism, thereby left this cultural community. The sign of his falling away was that he then no longer spoke Greek, but Syriac, Coptic or Armenian, that is to say, he used his original native speech instead of the Greek imperial language. It was a long road from a cultural community of this kind to the state of nationhood. This journey is not known to us in detail and we can only indicate a few widely separated stages. Certainly the migration to Byzantine territory of the Greek-speaking population from the provinces conquered by the Arabs contributed a great deal to the development of a Greek vernacular.

It was not without good reason that the monastic movement strongly championed the Greek vernacular, thus lessening the previously existing gap between the official formal language and the spoken Greek in daily use. The great monastic chronicles of the beginning of the ninth century used a style midway between the formal literary language and the vernacular. Nevertheless at this period, that is, the ninth century, it was not yet possible to speak of a genuine Greek vernacular. This only developed in the second half of the eleventh, and still more during the twelfth, century when the first great literary works in the vernacular were produced.

Byzantine civilization which began to emerge in its own right in the second half of the seventh century was partly the result of internal processes caused by reason of external issues, but it was also in no small degree the consequence of developments in other parts of the world. The rise of Byzantine civilization must be seen in the context of these great movements which changed the face of Europe and Asia. These must therefore be considered before evaluating the individual constituents within this framework.

Arab expansion did not affect Byzantium alone. It had a wider range, stretching out to the west and embracing Africa, Spain, and finally the Frankish kingdom. The same is true of the migrations of the Altaic peoples, known as the Avars. The Avar drive towards the south which resulted in the Slav occupation of most of the Balkans was followed by further advances to the north-west. The Avars and the Slavs who were tributary to them thrust forward into the valleys of the eastern Alps. They penetrated still further in the north-west, crossing the Elbe and following the course of the Main downstream. The attacks of the Arabs and the Slavs meant that the West was in danger of being encircled in a pincer movement. It was therefore essential to meet the onslaughts of the Arabs coming from Spain and the Slavs from the east pouring into the regions settled by the Germanic tribes. The reaction of the West differed very little from that of Byzantium.

The external threat led to changes in social structure, for the Frankish kingdom, like the Byzantine, was forced to introduce military reform. This is associated with the name of Charles Martel. Here the reform of the army was as important for the development of feudalism and the rise of a new aristocracy in the West as the introduction of the theme system under Heraclius' successors was for the Byzantine Empire. There is a clear parallel with the Byzantine world. Both the western reorganization of the army and the theme system resulted in the emergence of a military aristocracy. The growth of the power of this military aristocracy in Byzantium gradually led to the crippling of the central administration, and this led to the disintegration of the state. The same happened on Germanic soil. The military reform of Charles Martel and the resulting system of feudalism produced a similar development. It resulted in an ever-increasing burdening of the central authority and thus led to almost the same phenomenon as was apparent in Byzantium.

Together with military reform, the monastic movement was the other formative factor in the new era. In Byzantium, as in the Frankish kingdom where it pursued a similar course, it left its stamp on the new civilization. In the West the Irish monks with their network of foundations were of paramount importance. Then they were followed by the Anglo-Saxon monks who were the formative influence in the development of Germanic cultural and spiritual life. What would the Carolingian renaissance have been without the Anglo-Saxon Alcuin?

LEGEND FOR THE PLAN OF THE CITY

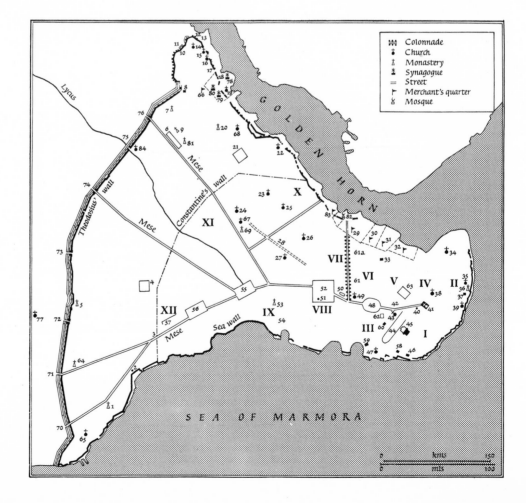

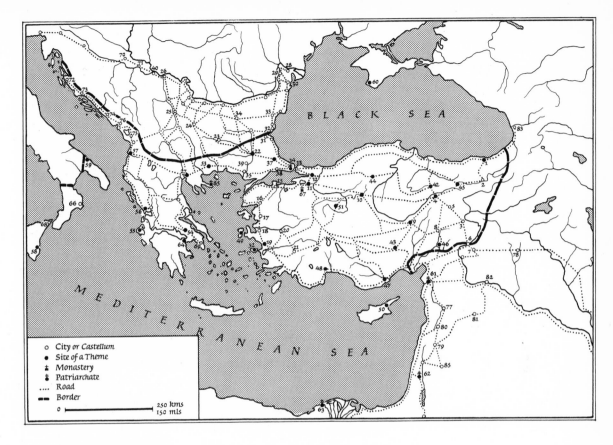

KEY TO TOWNS AND FORTIFICATIONS
BYZANTINE EMPIRE IN THE
TENTH AND ELEVENTH CENTURIES

1	Trebizond (Chaldia Theme)	29	Troesmis	58	Syracuse (Sicily Theme)
2	Satala	30	Istrus	59	Bari (Longobardia Theme)
3	Melitene	31	Develtus	60	Cherson (Cherson Theme)
4	Sebasteia (Sebasteia Theme)	32	Anchialus	61	Antioch-on-the-Orontes
5	Tephrice	33	Marcianopolis	62	Jerusalem
6	Samosata	34	Nicopolis	63	Alexandria
7	Edessa	35	Traianopolis	64	Corinth (Peloponnese Theme)
8	Arabissos	36	Kabyle	65	Mount Athos (monasteries)
9	Caesarea (Charsianon Theme)	37	Arcadiopolis	66	Crotone (Calabria)
10	Ancyra (Bucellarion Theme)	38	Heraclea	67	Mount Olympus in Bithynia
11	Nicaea (Opsikion Theme)	39	Didymotichus		(monasteries)
12	Nicomedia (Optimaton Theme)	40	Singidunum	68	Messina
13	Chalcedon	41	Sirmium	69	Athens
14	Constantinople	42	Amasea (Armeniakon Theme)	70	Sirmium
15	Cyzicus	43	Tyana (Cappadocia Theme)	71	Cibalae
16	Atramyttion	44	Gangra (Paphlagonia Theme)	72	Zara
17	Pergamon	45	Nicopolis (Colonea Theme)	73	Spalato
18	Smyrna	46	Germanicea (Lycandus Theme)	74	Ragusa
19	Ephesus (Thracesion Theme)	47	Seleucea (Seleucea Theme)	75	Scadar (Scutari)
20	Sardis	48	Attaleia (Cibyraiot Theme)	76	Dekatera
21	Laodicea	49	Chios (Chios Theme)	77	Apamea
22	Adrianopolis (Macedonia Theme)	50	Constantia (Cyprus Theme)	78	Nisibis
23	Philippopolis	51	Amorion (Anatolikon Theme)	79	Damascus
24	Serdica	52	Samos (Samos Theme)	80	Heliopolis
25	Naissus	53	Serres (Strymon Theme)	81	Palmyra
26	Viminacium	54	Thebes (Hellas Theme)	82	Rakka
27	Thessalonica (Thessalonica Theme)	55	Cephallenia (Cephallenia Theme)	83	Poti (Phasis)
28	Noviodunum	56	Nicopolis (Nicopolis Theme)	84	Aila
		57	Dyrrachium (Dyrrachium Theme)	85	Bostra

Urban economy: I
Byzantine superiority over western states

Labour market and workers' wages

Common ground in major issues should not be allowed to obscure a difference in one respect. This was the maintenance in the Byzantine Empire of certain forms of economy from late antiquity. Here Byzantine civilization can be compared to that of Islam. There too economic life was determined by the pillars of late antique urban economy, that is, the gilds and corporations. This was true both of the gilds of the former Roman territories and for the gild-types found in the Persian Empire where they were closely linked to the religious life of the cities. Their representatives confirmed synodal protocols in Nestorian church councils together with the clergy. In the Muslim period the gilds of craftsmen and merchants lived on, partly in the form of religious confraternities. In Byzantium this ecclesiastical relationship is not found to the same extent. The state took its place. Here the city gilds (*systemata*), originally the autonomous organs of the craftsmen, had now become government controlled. On the whole the essential difference between Byzantium and the West and the Germanic world lies in the continued development in Byzantium of the city gilds and with them of the urban economy. In the Germanic West the city gilds of late antiquity, like the towns, disappeared. The military organization left no place in its new structure for urban settlement with its own organization for its craftsmen and merchants.

Byzantine economy was a planned economy. The difficult situation of the Empire which arose by reason of the Arab invasions led to a change in economic life. State control, already decreed by Justinian for certain branches of craftsmen and merchants, remained and was further extended. The city prefect (the eparch) possessed almost dictatorial powers. He granted the permit for new industrial activity; he determined the number of workers in individual employments; he decided prices and the size of the stocks to be kept. His surveillance also extended over the workers' wages.

The wages of workers were extraordinarily low so that it seems doubtful whether they ensured even minimal subsistence. But surviving figures are deceptive. The remuneration calculated in money was only part of the wage paid to the worker by the employer or the state. By far the greater part was paid in kind. From the middle of the sixth century the Byzantine Empire had only a very restricted money economy. A high proportion of payments due were made in kind. This was true of university teachers and officials as well as of soldiers and artisans.

Naturally the presence of slave labour played a considerable role in determining the wage structure. It is only thus that wages such as the following can be explained. In 709 a ship's carpenter got 2 *nomismata* a month (that is, about £3★). A joiner was paid 1⅓ *nomismata* for the same time and the wage of a ship's caulker was 1½ *nomismata*. This was the payment for a short term contract of not more than three months. A notary (in this case meaning a clerk of the court) received for a year's service a monthly rate of 2 *nomismata* and 15¼ *keratia* (a *keration* was worth about 1/2d.). Here it must be taken into account that this notary for the most part was assigned definite half voluntary, half compulsory, specified special allowances which were in addition to his agreed salary (this work contract dates from 576). A stone mason worked in Egypt during the same period for a *keration* a day; a basket maker got slightly more. As the lowest

★*Translator's note:* Calculated before devaluation of the pound sterling in 1967.

168

classes of the populace at most modest reckoning needed about 10–15 *folles* (1/1d.–1/4d.) a day to maintain a bare subsistence, the wretched condition of these men can be appreciated. The miserably low wages of the period can be explained by the cheapness of slave labour (despite a high state purchase tax). The cost of purchasing slaves can be briefly summarized as follows.

In the sixth century the price for a slave of either gender under ten years old was 10 *nomismata*. Slaves over ten years without any special training or skill cost twenty *nomismata*. Notaries (slaves who could write) might fetch fifty *nomismata*. But the trade treaties with the Russian princes at the beginning of the tenth century gave much lower prices for slaves. The campaigns in the Balkans, often more in the nature of slave raids, sometimes threw thousands of slaves on to the market in Constantinople.

Oriental specialist workers among the leading Byzantine craftsmen as exponents of Islamic-Arab influence on Byzantine civilization

The conquest of Persian, and later Arab, cities meant above all that a considerable number of their inhabitants were enslaved and sold in Constantinople. In this way the Byzantine Empire acquired highly qualified craftsmen and doctors from the East. It was through these specialists that the West gained from the Arab world knowledge of the carefully guarded secret of how to manufacture paper from rags. The Arabs themselves were able to exploit this method of production because of Chinese experts in this field who had been deported to Irak after the capture of Samarkand. Once the Byzantine Empire had obtained information about this secret process they no longer needed to import expensive writing material from Arab countries as they had previously done. (The oldest Byzantine paper manuscripts still carry indications as to their place and date in Arabic script.) Despite this, special luxury paper was still being imported from the Arabs at a later date. The imperial chancery itself used this expensive material which was known as 'Baghdad' paper. Byzantium also learnt from Arab specialists the technique of making faience (majolica) and ceramic wall plaques then used to decorate churches. But oriental influence was not confined to the use of the secret manufacturing processes of the Arabs which had been divulged by Syrian or Persian prisoners of war, for the Byzantines also made use of certain elements from Arab art.

In the ninth and tenth centuries Arab culture was greatly admired in Byzantium. It would however be misleading to speak simply of a more or less short lived oriental fashion in the Byzantine Empire. The Basileus Theophilus (the Emperor who put up the greatest number of buildings in Constantinople after Theodosius II and Justinian I) was greatly attracted by the Arab world. This Byzantine Basileus therefore wanted to have residences, live the same kind of life, hold court after the manner of the Caliph in Baghdad and Samarra. To realize this dream he built in the imperial quarter a palace in the Moorish style with stalactites and domes. In the immediate neighbourhood of this palace there was a vast area for the Persian game of polo. Here Emperor, princes and nobles used to play this cavalry game even in the last days of the Byzantine Empire.

As well as Persian games, Arab music reached Byzantium at this time. The Byzantines particularly delighted in the performances of Arab dancing girls and this opened the door to Arab music. Representations of these dancers are found not only in secular art. The Chludov Psalter shows the prophetess Miriam as an Arab dancing girl, and even the crown of Constantine Monomachus, which was made in Byzantium and presented to the Hungarian king Andrew I, had enamel plaques showing two Arab dancing girls in their star turn, the serpent dance.

Dancing brought back into fashion the old Greek musical instruments, such as the lyre, which today is still used in folk music. The art inspired by Arab sources was particularly rich in ornamental designs of high excellence, since artists were driven to concentrate on this field by reason of the religious veto on the portrayal of the human figure. The space to be decorated was divided up by means of ornamentation in which animal motifs were skilfully interwoven with Kufic script. This form of art was adopted by the Byzantines in the eighth and ninth centuries. They copied the Kufic lettering and decorated their churches with the marvellous ornamental relief plaques. It even happened that Byzantine artists when using Islamic models in the production of relief plaques copied inscriptions in Kufic script in praise of Allah. Three hundred years later the same thing happened in the West when the crusading movement brought men there into close contact with the Muslim East.

The partiality of the Emperor Theophilus for the great decorative art of the Islamic East is related to his attitude towards icon veneration. He was the last iconoclast Emperor. Since he had forbidden icons to the Church he tried to put in their place ornamentation, as Islam had done. This explains the introduction of ornamental motifs which are found together with animal representation.

Influence of this kind, demonstrated by the relief plaques in churches, was reflected in the Canonical Tables in manuscripts of the Bible. Here, as in the case of the relief plaques, oriental Islamic motifs have been used. Animal figures are found and, according to the *Physiologus*, the Byzantine animal and plant book, they were given the meaning of Christian symbols. Even stronger than in the religious field, was the effect of the Islamic East on the art products of the Byzantines. With the help of Arab specialists who had been captured into slavery, Byzantine ceramics took over the shape and decoration of the celebrated ceramic products of Irak, and were so similar in glazing and decorative motifs, as well as with Kufic lettering, that it is often virtually impossible to decide whether a piece is from a Byzantine or Islamic atelier.

The Byzantine money market

The monopolist position which Byzantine industry held in the Mediterranean for almost half a century cannot be explained simply in terms of a slave-based economy. The mercantile enterprise and the capacity to save of a large section of the Byzantine populace played a part in this development at least equal to that of the specialist slave craftsmen concerned in production. It must be remembered that much of city industry was financed by loans made through bankers (*argyropratai*). These sums were raised from private individuals who had saved and counted on being able to live on interest from their savings. The capital circulating in the Byzantine economy was mainly obtained from private sources of this kind.

The importance of the money market to the Byzantine economy made state control here also essential. Thus the state supervised the rate of interest demanded and laid down compulsory regulations for this. Interest was not rigidly fixed but varied with the social position of the lender. For instance loans made by high officials and anyone holding the title of *illustris* only earned $4\frac{1}{6}$ per cent for their money. Other people, as long as they were not in trade, got $6\frac{1}{4}$ per cent for their money. Those in trade were allowed as much as $8\frac{1}{3}$ per cent. These relatively low rates of interest could easily be met by industrial enterprises. In any case the Byzantine Emperor undertook when necessary to finance expensive commercial projects and could enforce compulsory acceptance of state credit. Thus the big shipowners of Constantinople were induced to accept state credit in the form of bonds with a nominal value of 12 *nomismata* each and at a rate of interest of $16\frac{2}{3}$ per cent. And so shipbuilding, which was difficult to engage in because of the great financial outlay needed, was specially favoured. The graduation of permitted interest was based on salary scales in the Byzantine Empire. Thus the higher imperial officials got a lower rate for their money than other people because they had more capital at their disposal since higher salaries were paid in actual money.

As far as salaries went the military were generally better off than civil servants. Officers were exceedingly well paid. And an ordinary soldier also received more pay than an artisan could earn. According to Arabic sources every soldier received a year's wage of one *nomisma*. If so, then the daily remuneration of a soldier roughly corresponded to that of an artisan at the same period. But here it must be remembered that a soldier received maintenance and equipment for the duration of the campaign as well as his military grant of land (soldier's farm). Normally he would not therefore need to draw on any of his pay. He might also add to his cash remuneration by selling his share of war booty. All the same, he was far worse off than officers in the lower grades. According to the same Arabic source the group of officers including *comites*, pentekontarchs and dekarchs were paid from one to three gold pounds annually, that is, between 72 and 216 *nomismata*. In contrast to this, an ordinary soldier after twelve years service was only paid 12 *nomismata* a year (his pay was raised by one *nomisma* for each year of service). The *strategi* of the themes, whose rank was similar to that of a present-day commander-in-chief, received salaries ranging from 5 to 40 gold pounds according to the strategic importance of the theme. Here it must be borne in mind that higher ranking officers were themselves responsible for certain outgoings, such as the payment of their clerks —copyists and secretaries. Later in the second half of the thirteenth century a mercenary's annual pay was from 24 to 36 *nomismata*, but this reflects the fact that from the eleventh century onwards the *nomisma* used within the Empire was debased to a quarter of its original value. The wages then paid were only worth between 6 and 9 *nomismata* of the old currency. This highly preferential treatment of officers was due to the realization that the army led by these officers conducted campaigns combined with slave raids which brought highly qualified craftsmen and technicians to swell the ranks of native specialist workers, thereby securing the superiority of Byzantine industry over other Mediterranean countries and the supremacy of the Byzantine export trade in European markets.

Outlets and agents for the sale of Byzantine industrial goods

The marketing of industrial products, mainly luxury goods in so far as export was concerned, was almost entirely done by sale on commission. This was largely in the hands of the Byzantine Jews, especially the great Jewish communities of Constantinople, Thessalonica, Corinth and Bari. They had their own quarters where they were permitted to settle outside the walls of these cities. In Constantinople after the Blachernae region was brought within the fortifications of the city walls, their quarter was separated off from the rest of the city, like the *mitata* of foreign merchants. After the last great persecution under Heraclius, the Jews had been granted a certain measure of autonomy within their own city quarters. As with Jewish communities in Arab lands they were governed by their elders. The restrictions suffered by members of the Jewish faith during the late antique period had to a great extent been relaxed. Thus the Jewish quarter in Constantinople possessed several synagogues. In general the Jews were not forbidden from entering other professions and trades as they were later on in the West. Thus from the end of the seventh century the trade blockade of exports from Muslim-occupied Syria to the West favoured the economic ascendancy of Byzantine Jewry.

With this blockade great changes came about. Foreign trade to the West had previously been in the hands of Syrian merchants and traders. Settlements of Syrian businessmen were found in almost all the larger towns of the Frankish kingdom, in Paris as in the Rhine valley. It was the same in Italy. In Rome and Ravenna almost all the eastern trade was controlled by Syrian traders. But with the trade blockade carried out from the end of the seventh century by the Byzantines, who had an excellent fleet, Syrian and Egyptian goods stopped coming to the West. Anything from the Orient to the West had to come through the Byzantine Empire. This meant that pepper and other spices, medicinal herbs, materials for colouring, myrrh, precious stones and silks had first to go to Constantinople and were then taken to the West. The route by which oriental goods came is well known. All ships coming from Syria and Egypt had to go to Attaleia, the great harbour in south-west Asia Minor. Only then were they allowed to continue their journey to Constantinople. At Attaleia the customs officials came on board and entered against the list of goods the duty payable to the customs. The rate of duty was very high. In the tenth century the annual revenue from the customs dues at Attaleia was still about 300 gold pounds. The equipment of the Byzantine fleet was paid for out of this revenue. Attaleia was the centre of the espionage system directed against the Muslim countries. It was the ships coming from the Arab cities which provided the best source of information.

The re-routing of the eastern trade through Byzantium presented Byzantine trade with considerable problems. It was a question of arranging for the disposal of oriental goods worked up in Byzantium as advantageously as possible. Here the Jews were of use, for they had connections throughout the West. They were in a position to estimate correctly the sales value of oriental goods in the various countries. So from the end of the seventh century Syrian merchants in Europe were replaced by Jewish traders. The Jews kept their position as foreign traders in Europe up to the eleventh century and it was only then that they were increasingly displaced by European foreign merchants and in the economic field were almost entirely relegated to the sphere of money lending. In the West, Christians were strictly forbidden to take interest, which ensured the Jews this economic activity until in the fifteenth century they were supplanted in this branch of business by the Italian banking houses.

The disposal of Byzantine goods was done by sale on commission. Jewish agents took the goods and shared the profits obtained on an agreed percentage basis. For instance, a Jewish agent in the early seventh century sold textiles in Africa (Carthage) and Gaul (Marseilles) for 144 *nomismata* and he himself got 15 *nomismata*, that is, about 10 per cent profit.

A considerable amount of selling was done through trade monopolies. About 894 a firm in Thessalonica held the monopoly of trade with Bulgaria. Businesses in the Italian maritime cities, Venice, Amalfi, Gaeta and Naples, had the monopoly for the sale of certain Byzantine luxury goods to the West. It was above all Venice which took the lead in selling these products. In contrast to Genoa, Pisa and Luni, which belonged first to the Lombard, and then to the Carolingian kingdom and were therefore in hostile foreign territory, Venice had the advantage of an exclusive trade treaty with Byzantium. Venice, Gaeta and Amalfi had their own settlements in Constantinople which, like the Jewish quarter, lay directly on the Golden Horn with their own quays (*skalai*). Through their commercial colonies the merchants of these Italian cities bought up luxury goods, such as silk and purple, with the permission of the Byzantine official exports controller who was under the *logothetes tou vestiariou*. Once the permit was granted these luxury goods could be shipped off without further trouble from the customs officials. On the other hand these maritime cities had managed to get concessions from the western Emperors allowing them to send Byzantine luxury goods to the fair held each year in Pavia. Here in Pavia and also in Rome, Gaeta and Amalfi supplied the wares which were bought by the Frisian merchants. At that time the Frisians controlled the greater part of the western trade and arranged for the distribution of goods in Europe. In this way Byzantine products reached the great Frisian entrepôt of Doorstad near Utrecht. From here some found their way to the British Isles (the funeral ship of Sutton Hoo in Suffolk illustrates the extent to which Byzantine art was transmitted through export channels), some went to Scandinavian territory, such as Haithaba near Schleswig founded about 800, and to Lillö (or Birka) in Sweden. The find in the market place on the island of Lillö in the Mälar lake near Stockholm shows the distance which Arab goods could travel through the channels of international trade, despite the Byzantine blockade at that time. There is not only evidence of a lively trade with the Byzantine Empire and the Mediterranean countries, but there are also traces of trade relations with the Far East and Central Asia. On Lillö was found the figure of a Buddha originating in one of the oasis towns of the Tarim basin, thus showing that during this period Central Asia was still the middleman for luxury goods from the Far East, which reached the Far North by way of Arab and Byzantine markets. Chinese silk and Chinese porcelain reached the West, as did ginger from South Asia and pepper from the Indies. Chinese porcelain may not have been found beyond the frontiers of the Arab Empire, yet it can still be assumed that this was known to the Byzantine Emperors, as to the Caliphs in Samarra. Chinese silk was found in a Frankish prince's tomb of the seventh century near Cologne. Indian pepper as a stimulant was specially popular with the beer-drinking Germanic and Slav peoples at this time and was a source of great profit to Arab and Byzantine merchants.

In the West, including the Frankish kingdom, money was in very short circulation. Small change disappeared in the seventh century. Coins of legal tender, the Gallic *trientes* or the silver *denarii*, frequently contained a percentage of other metals. Here too the Byzantine *solidus*, or *nomisma*, maintained the greatest stability. It was in this coinage that the penalty fines of Germanic customary law were calculated, as in the edict of the Lombard king Rothari. From the beginning of the eighth century only silver currency was used in the Frankish kingdom, thus recognizing the supremacy of the Byzantine gold *solidus*. This considerably facilitated the sale of Byzantine goods.

The Byzantine economy had virtually stopped its eastern import trade from bringing Syrian or Egyptian manufactured goods into the Empire. Only raw materials were allowed to be imported. In this way its own industries and sales were safeguarded. After the introduction of these measures, Syrian and Egyptian textiles and glassware, or ivory work, no longer reached western markets. Coptic textiles and Egyptian and Syrian ivories, which had been particularly important in the development of early Germanic art after the migratory period, disappeared and their place was taken by Byzantine goods. This gave a new orientation to Germanic art. The oldest medieval fresco painting which is particularly indebted to the Irish monks and their pupils, was almost entirely inspired by Coptic originals. (The frescoes from the late eighth century in the church of Naturno in the South Tyrol illustrate this. Like the ornamental motifs of the Irish manuscripts it would be difficult to imagine these without the inspiration supplied by the Coptic exports.) In contrast to this the Carolingian painting of the succeeding period was notably under Byzantine influence.

The retreat of the state from rural economy:
the abandonment of the country populace to an almost autonomous administration

The essential basis of the Byzantine economy with its flourishing industries was the ample food supplies from the land. Here the Byzantine state avoided the mistake of the Roman Empire in the East in withdrawing the *annona* and at the same time applying the *coemptio*. The obligation to deliver to government stocks was relaxed, probably under pressure from the great landowners who were still powerful, but prices on the rural market were controlled. The prices of basic provisions, corn, oil and meat, were controlled by the state and remained almost constant practically up to the middle of the tenth century. This also applied to the price of land. Ownership of cultivated land therefore brought in a safe income. This accounts for the fact that the classes with capital were so eager to acquire landed property.

But the countryside was far from possessing a free economy. This is seen from the development of the Byzantine village community. Unlike the West, it did not originate as an independent peasant community with common meadowland and distribution of arable land, but was a taxable unit whose boundaries were defined by the fisc. The Byzantine rural community was only an economic unit in so far as this served the purpose of taxation. Membership of the village community resulted from inscription on the tax list. It was this principle which determined other forms of peasant settlements, individual farmsteads and hamlets. In Byzantine rural economy the most important role was played by the typical village settlement in which the farmsteads formed a close nucleus round which the arable land of the peasants was grouped. The Byzantines called this kind of settlement a *chorion*. In addition there were also individual farms situated in the middle of an agricultural estate. These were called *ktesidia* and for purposes of taxation were linked with the nearest village settlement as a taxable unit. The so-called hamlets (*agridia*), consisting of a widely distributed group of houses and farms, were treated in the same way.

In the Byzantine Empire the tax system was therefore based on the administrative framework of the village. This did not exclude the possibility of the further development of the rural community or the founding of new villages. There were farms where the inheritance was divided, or where woodland was reclaimed, thus forming independent farmsteads which were grouped together with other farms to form a new tax unit. This must have been of common occurrence and it meant that the tax-assessment list (*kataster*) was always being enlarged. Therein lay one of the greatest differences between Byzantine rural economy and that of the West. In the West there were no regional officials to superintend the tax collection, nor was there a central tax list covering all the cultivable land. Thus there was no agrarian policy in the West. The central authority had no means of assessing the economic capacity of the various parts of the kingdom.

In contrast the Byzantine Empire up to the end of the eleventh century possessed a regional administration which responded to every nod of the central authority. As well as the military authorities in the chief city of each theme, there were the offices of the *protonotarius*, the *chartularius* and the praetor. The praetor was the senior legal official of the theme. The *chartularius* was the head of the taxation offices and his subordinates were in charge of the *kataster* of the peasants as well as the soldier-farmers. The *protonotarius* was in charge of financial administration. In regional administration there was a division between departments for receipts and disbursement. The taxes collected by the tax-collectors (*dioiketai*) in the various tax zones were paid into the *chartularius'* office, entered and checked and then handed over to the *protonotarius'* office. From these receipts the *protonotarius* had to cover the expenses of the theme. These outgoings included the soldiers' pay, the salaries of officers and officials as well as expenditure for the upkeep of public welfare services, such as geriatric homes, orphanages and infirmaries. Expenditure for this was by no means small whether for provincial or central needs. It was only after the fulfilment of all financial obligations that any surplus was paid into the office of the *sacellum*, the imperial treasury in Constantinople. This system had the disadvantage of making provincial administration financially independent of the central authority. However great the contrast between the western states without any regulated financial administration and the Byzantine Empire, the setback as compared with the late antique period cannot be overlooked. The central administration now no longer possessed control over the whole system of taxation as it had done two centuries before. It was dependent on the provincial administration for part of its income. This inevitably had political repercussions.

This setback suffered by relations between central and regional financial administration was still more obvious from the methods of tax levying and assessment. The Byzantine surveyor, the *anagrapheus*, the official responsible for the precise valuation of land for purposes of taxation, could in no way compare with the Roman *agrimensores*. His knowledge of plane geometry was inadequate. His measurements contained the grossest errors. He was not in the position to calculate even approximately the area of the land being measured. In the tax lists there was often recourse to the usual descriptions of land also found in documents in the West. There were regular inspections but instead of correcting errors previously made, these were usually simply accepted. The whole work of surveying was therefore superfluous and useless. The villages were also penalized by having to give hospitality to the *anagrapheus* while he was carrying out his survey.

But the assessment of the property to be taxed, the method of valuation, was the most inadequate imaginable and revealed the extent of the decline in the Byzantine period in comparison with late antiquity. The Byzantines only had two categories of land valuation. The criterion for classification was the type of cultivation. For purposes of taxation a distinction was drawn between vineyards and agricultural land. Thus 6 *modioi* of vineyard paid the same tax as 50 *modioi* of agricultural land. In certain particular kinds of cultivation land was however divided into three classes, and here land reclaimed by irrigation had a special assessment. As may be imagined, Byzantine agricultural tools were primitive. Byzantine ploughs had neither earth board (*aures*) nor wheels. Miniatures show that almost up to the modern period the Byzantines were using the hook-shaped plough of the ancient world practically unchanged. In this respect the West was in advance of Byzantium, for as early as the Gallo-Roman period it was using the earth board and wheels.

In the Byzantine economy cultivation concentrated on the production of cereals and oil, that is, sunflower fields and olive trees. Next came wine and fruit and vegetables. In Asia Minor the greatest emphasis was on pastoral farming. The great flocks of sheep provided wool for the textile industry. But a highly developed use of land, particularly by means of irrigation, as in Egypt and Syria, was unknown to the Byzantine economy, where no progress had been made in working and cultivating the soil. The great manuals of agricultural economy of the Hellenistic age were enlarged by additions and circulated in Syria and were translated into Syriac and Arabic. They were indeed incorporated into the Byzantine encyclopaedias, but the errors in these supplements show that scientific interest in rural economy had long ceased. The military reforms certainly played a part here. The penetration of barbarian elements into the ranks of the Byzantine peasantry had also depressed agricultural standards. It was significant that after the reform of the army, Galatia, which in Hellenistic times had been a highly developed rural economy, was settled by soldier-farmers coming from regions where primitive methods predominated. Galatia was settled by military men of the *optimates* and the *bucellarii*. These last were almost entirely composed of Isaurian soldiers. Isauria was the mountainous region of the Taurus range and was of a very low cultural level. These mercenaries (*bucellarii* means 'private soldiers') were given land in Galatia as a result of the military reform. The detachment of the so-called *optimates* was not much better. They originated as Germanic auxiliaries, supplemented by Slavs from the region of Thessalonica. These Slavs and Germans settled in what had once been the highly developed agricultural region of Galatia. This soon led to a decline in production. It was the same in the Armeniakon and Anatolikon themes in eastern Asia Minor. Soldiers mainly from Syria were granted land in the Anatolikon theme. Those settled in the Armeniakon theme were to a large extent from the mountainous regions of the Caucasus. These army reforms naturally introduced changes in the structure of rural economy. Most noticeable was the disappearance of the economically viable great estates, and it was some time before the army officers produced a new breed of great landowners.

The structure of the peasant houses of these settlers in Asia Minor also seemed to have been determined by the fact that the country was still insecure by reason of the Arab attacks. Byzantine miniatures show peasants' houses looking like fortified towers and they can be compared with the type of peasant settlement still found in Albania today where peasants' houses are found with the living rooms several stories high only reached by a ladder.

The distribution of public land to soldier-farmers was determined by the construction of forts, which were set up in all important strategic points in the seventh century as part of Byzantine defence measures against the Arabs. The soldiers, the military settlers, were grouped round the forts. An officer resided in the fort. These officers were usually tribunes. A tribune corresponded to the rank of lieutenant or captain in a modern army, and, as is known from Italian sources, he possessed rights of jurisdiction in minor cases. Jurisdiction in higher matters (involving both capital punishment and the more severe penalties) was reserved to the praetor himself, who was the highest judicial authority in the theme. The position of the peasantry was altered very much for the worse because of this linking of military authority with jurisdiction in less important cases and the creation of regional financial administration. The gradual conversion of officers into big landowners completed the process whereby independent regions grew up corresponding to the earlier military zones under the control of officers.

The soldier-farmers became the dominating element in the rural population. But they did not form a separate group within the village community. Like all the other peasants they belonged to the village as a fiscal unit and they enjoyed the same form of land ownership as the rest. Among the Byzantine peasantry there was not only individual ownership, but also common property (*koinonia*) shared by several peasants. This kind of ownership was the result of subdividing an inheritance, which was found among the military settlers of the sixth century, as the military archives of Nessana in Palestine show. As well as property shared in common by several peasants, villages in the Byzantine Empire also had common property which to some extent corresponded to that found in villages in the West. This consisted of the right to use a wood, or a pasture meadow, or a mill.

The fixed price of cereals constituted the chief danger for the free peasant. This fixed price, secure from any diminution, led a large number of officers, as well as rich merchants, to acquire landed property. The farms of the soldiers were indeed at first protected from being swallowed up by the great landowners, but this did not apply to the property of other small farmers. This gave great scope to those officers who had joined the ranks of the landowners. They controlled regional finance and jurisdiction. The raising of taxes gave the local administration the opportunity to levy these in such a way that the main burden fell on the free peasant. Thus the peasant owners were all too soon faced with debt and compelled in the end to sell their property to the landowners. Taxation and its manipulation were chiefly responsible for the gradually increasing hold of feudalism over the Byzantine state.

Byzantine officialdom. The path from office to privilege

The development of the Byzantine system of taxation was in the last resort the development of Byzantine officials into a class of the privileged. It is true that its civil servants gave the Byzantine Empire a cultural advantage over the West, but all the same it was they who were to a great extent responsible for the decline of the state. Their standards were extremely low. Officials regarded their office only as a means of amassing as much wealth as possible. Responsibility towards the state and integrity were non–existent.

It is, however, difficult to speak of direct guilt. It was not only a question of human failure and lack of forethought on the part of the state. The basic reason lay to a large extent in the decline of bureaucratic organization in late antiquity. The technical conditions necessary for controlling the official apparatus became progressively worse. Taxation arrangements in the late Roman Empire based on surveyance of taxable land assumed a knowledge of plane geometry. The assessment called for a regulated system of valuation. The primitive economic division of land according to its suitability for a certain type of production (wine and cereals) was a retrograde step compared with the late antique method of land evaluation, where scientific observations on the necessary conditions determined the suitability of the land for the cultivation of a particular crop. In the Byzantine period it was not possible to survey the land properly nor to assess its potential accurately. There was no limit to the arbitrary decisions of individual officials and the central power was unable to exercise control over the financial activities of regional authorities.

The transfer of financial autonomy to the administrative officials of individual themes was not at first a concession to regional particularism, already clearly in evidence at that time. But it was a confession of the incapacity of the central authority and its officials to deal with the financial obligations of individual provinces. It was content with the surplus after these obligations had been met. Its measure of control consisted in comparing the annual surplus from the provinces with that of the previous year and then, after considering this and such circumstances as bad harvests or devastation through war, it attempted to assess the accuracy of the sum handed over.

In a state where the declining standard of education had led to a deterioration in effective control it proved impossible to maintain a sense of responsibility in the civil service. The first signs of a deterioration in standards appeared in the late antique period.

To begin with there were the economy measures of the government. Although the soldiers' pay was raised, that of civil servants remained unaltered despite the rise in the cost of living, and therefore they took to taking fees and perquisites of office. These fees began to be legalized. Thus on legal authority the judge could take fees for giving his ruling, the taxation officer for the compilation of the tax list, the commissariat officer for his supplies to the army. Thus a system was introduced which completely undermined the responsibility of the official towards the state.

But there was another factor which precipitated the deterioration of the bureaucracy. It became increasingly the custom to give the higher official positions as honorary titles with substantial remuneration to loyal supporters of the Emperor or to members of the imperial household. The so-called honorary officials, who received their *brabeia* (signs of office) and ivory tablets (diptychs) together with the document of commission from the Emperor in person, did not regard their office as involving any work but merely as a form of remuneration for their services. This group of so-called honorary officials continually grew larger and was responsible to the Emperor alone. The sources at times note as many as sixty of them. These office-holders in turn nominated the greater number of their subordinates, for only a relatively small proportion of the more important subordinates was directly appointed by the Emperor. It can be well imagined that the same consideration governed their nomination as had held in the appointment of their patrons. Bureaux were filled with the partisans of the departments' heads. New posts were created to provide for dependents. Hence the remarkable spectacle of the reduction in state machinery while the number of officials was continually being increased. As in the army, Byzantine officialdom began to show indications of incipient feudalization. An instance of this is the mounting differentiation of rank which was very rarely determined by an individual official's field of activity. This had already begun among the commanders (*strategi*) of the themes. The commander of the Anatolikon theme took pride of place, followed by the other theme commanders from Asia Minor. Then came the commanders of the European themes and lastly the heads of the central bureaux. The custom grew whereby particular families claimed military commands and civil service posts by reason of birth. This system giving preferential treatment to certain families was particularly widespread in the provinces, so that in those regions it was almost possible to speak of a break-up of the civil service.

It is in the context of this development that the tendency in the Empire to sell offices must be seen, and this set in from the beginning of the eleventh century. In the given circumstances this was the only possibility of getting any revenue. This was particularly true of financial administration. Here regional taxation was leased out for double the sum entered on the assessment lists. The tax contractor was answerable for the annual sum for which he had to pledge his own property. He usually succeeded in collecting three times the tax for which his area was assessed. Government and contractor knew very well that the assessment lists never corresponded to actual fact and provided only an approximate valuation.

Even more serious was the selling of offices in the spheres of justice and general administration. The office of judge had to be bought by paying a definite sum and this usually had to be obtained by getting credit from a bank. The judge had therefore to see that his professional activities brought him in sufficient money to repay this loan as quickly as possible, for it was only thus that he could avoid the burden of the heavy interest on the original loan which had bought him his office.

Where the judge accepted an honorarium from the parties in a case for pronouncing sentence, the tax-officials took fees for making entries in the tax register. But it should not be thought that everything was bad in the official world and that the state completely abandoned its civil servants. It did provide salaries which were paid yearly, but this remuneration was far too small.

Those who aspired to public office came from that still fairly considerable class of city dwellers who had a measure of general education. In Byzantium higher education was not the monopoly of the clergy, unlike the West from the seventh to the first half of the twelfth century where they were often the only ones who could read and write. Here in Byzantium general and specialist education was still largely in secular hands. After attending an elementary school run by a monastery, it was possible either to go to a Law Faculty or to follow a so-called philosophical course. There was also the possibility of concentrating on theology in a theological seminary. The legal establishments had become particularly important in the seventh and eighth centuries. The philosophical schools were mostly linked with the theological ones. It looks as though the theological seminary connected with Hagia Sophia in the eighth and ninth centuries also gave courses in so-called philosophy, that is, instruction in grammar, rhetoric and philosophy (Aristotle).

These schools were attended by practically everyone who wanted a public appointment. There were for instance the notaries. They began as legal copyists of documents (donations, wills) and deeds of sale. After a lengthy private practice they would then get an appointment as judge in one of the provinces and then, after some years in office, with the help of influential friends would enter the imperial chancery. Some officials came from banking circles (*argyropratai*). They were entrusted with book-keeping and accounts, and had to spend many years as money changers or transacting loans before they ventured to jump into state service. They mostly got posts as officials in the taxation department, first in provincial administration, and then, if they were successful, they would be recalled to the central offices in Constantinople. From the eleventh century onwards many of those with sufficient private means contracted to collect the taxes in the rural areas.

The bureaucracy was one of the greatest weaknesses of the Byzantine state. It had much in common with the French state of the ancien régime. In France too the judge bought his position, the office of giving counsel to the Parlement. As judge he had then the same interest in recouping himself for the cost of his office through his fees, just as his Byzantine colleague did. And in eighteenth-century France tax collecting was also farmed out.

With the relentless deterioration in general education and the lack of basic specialist knowledge, both results of the decline of the universities and the victory of the monastic movement, the absence of sufficient lower and middle grade civil servants was the reason for the weakness of the Byzantine state. The remuneration of the civil servant came from the fisc in the form of money or in kind, that is, the so-called fixed salary and the roga, a gift of money and garments on special occasions. Thus the officials' main income consisted of the fees (*sportula*) which he exacted for services performed, and these were soon legalized by the state. Even in the army fees of this kind were expected. Thus the *optiones* (the quartermasters) in the army took from the soldiers a fifteenth of their rations as *paramythia* and did this with the state's consent. The actual deduction would have been much higher. The Byzantine Emperors made frequent attempts to remedy this state of affairs. Leo III (717–741) explained in his *Ecloga* (legal code) that all judges would be paid from the state treasury so that the oppressive system of fees might be rooted out. This had no effect. Even the copyists got writing fees from the taxpayers for alleged transcription of the tax lists.

The fall of the last bastion of the late antique state:
the disintegration of the central administration

In Byzantium the administration of taxation, together with that of the army, was one of the most important central departments. To understand the effect of taxation on the transformation of the Byzantine rural population, it is necessary to start by considering those reforms of the central administration which show what the legislator had in mind in introducing changes in the tax system.

Development in Constantinople was along the same lines as in the provincial offices. Here too the general decline in education played an important part. The decline of the office of *praefectus praetorio*, the economic dictator of the period of Constantine and still so in Justinian's day, was due not so much to reforms and political considerations as to the realization that it was no longer possible to appoint anyone to fill an office which involved the control and direction of the economy of the whole Empire, simply because suitable candidates were not available owing to lack of specialist training. It was therefore necessary to transfer to the provincial departments some of the authority hitherto exercised by the central administration. Thus the management of the revenue from taxes was handed over to each province and the central government only reserved control over this. Similar measures had to be taken with regard to the cities. Here the *praefectus urbis* (city prefect) took over the former responsibilities of the central authority, and indeed of the *praefectus praetorio*.

In the seventh century the office of *praefectus praetorio* completely disappeared and its place was taken by the departments of the logothete *tou stratiotikou*. This office combined the departments of tax collection and the valuation lists with that concerned with the army pay roll, but even here a well-qualified personnel was essential and it was already becoming difficult to find this. Thus the more important responsibilities of the logothete *tou stratiotikou* fell to the *chartularius* of the theme who also received the title of logothete. As a consequence of this development the logothete *tou stratiotikou* lost a good deal of his importance in the central departments. In order to exercise some effective control over the themes, and particularly to safeguard the general interests of the state against the particularism of individual provinces, the office of logothete *tou dromou* was created. This high imperial official had the position of a commissioner with extraordinary powers. One of his most important duties was to provide for the army on the march. His work began from the moment when the soldiers received the order to mobilize and assembled at the given posts or theme, formed into companies, and then marched to the appointed meeting place where they would join the regiments of the other themes and the imperial army. His competence included the supervision of the imperial roads and post, and he also had the right to impose on any theme economic measures considered necessary to secure provisioning, maintenance and movement of troops on all routes within the Empire. With such authority this office attained so great an importance that the logothete *tou dromou* soon became the first minister of the Empire. The powers assigned to him made it possible for him to counter to some extent the rising particularism of the individual themes.

The transference of important powers and competencies from the central authority to the regional departments was closely connected with the reorganization of the imperial estates and financial administration. In Justinian's day the collection and checking of revenue was the responsibility of one of the departments in the office of the *praefectus praetorio*, the so-called *idike trapeza*. This corresponded to the department of the *genike trapeza* which dealt with general taxes. The *idike trapeza* paid its intake over to the office of the *comes rerum privatarum*. After the introduction of the theme organization the office of *idike trapeza* was abolished. The logothete *tou stratiotikou* certainly controlled the tax lists of the general taxes but had nothing to do with the revenue from crown lands. The *curatores*, the heads of the great estate zones, now paid this revenue direct to the imperial *sacellum*, the imperial treasury. Within the treasury, as in all financial departments of state, there were two departments, the *sacellum* for money payments and the *vestiarium* for payments in kind.

This development strengthened the dissociation of even the private imperial treasury of this period from the central state departments. The relationship of the imperial private offices to the general financial administration showed a tendency similar to that reflected in the granting of almost complete financial autonomy to provincial administration. Thus the imperial financial offices became autonomous during this period. Imperial administration now had its own organization. On the productive side of this vast economic activity were the imperial estates with their own economic organization— the imperial perfumery factories, the court pharmacy and interests in a number of industrial concerns, for instance the great bakeries which provided bread for the navy. On the debit side there were not only the various needs of the court but the imperial charitable foundations. There was an imperial administrative department for orphanages and for old peoples' homes. Both these had their own special officials. The department for the imperial possessions had a number of functions: there was the office responsible for the private wardrobe of the Emperor, the office for the care of the imperial table-silver, the imperial art room, and finally even the imperial library.

There was a very sharp division at this period between the property of the state and the private property of the Emperor. In the ninth and tenth centuries there grew up a third distinction, that of crown property. This differentiation between crown property and the private property of the Emperor arose because of government by co-Emperors who from time to time took over from the legitimate Macedonian Emperors, often against their will. Thus a line was drawn between the private property of a ruler and the property of the legitimate Macedonian dynasty designated as crown property.

The division between Emperor and state in administrative organization is seen even more clearly in military matters. The initial movement in this direction came from the development of the theme into an autonomous entity over which the central administration was not always certain of exercising control. It began with the reinforcement of divisions of the imperial bodyguard. Here a distinction must be made between the units serving the palace and the regular guards. Protection of the imperial person was first of all entrusted to Germanic troops, then later on to Turks from Ferghana in West Turkestan, then to Varangians, Normans, and finally Germans. But these did not belong to the regular units of the guards, which were divided into four divisions and called *tagmata*. The command of these troops stationed in Constantinople in the immediate neighbourhood of the imperial palace and the Hippodrome was in the hands of officers with the title of *domesticus*. The *candidati*, a cavalry troop, belonged to the companies of guards. They wore white trappings over their gilded armour and during public ceremonies were on parade with their long lances. The second division was called the *excubiti*. Unlike the *candidati* who mostly appeared on public occasions, the *excubiti* had police duties. They carried out important arrests and were responsible for the safety of the Emperor. The third division was the so-called *arithmus*. The title of the commander-in-chief of these troops was usually that of *drungarius* (admiral), thus indicating that they were drawn from the infantry companies of the marines. They probably escorted the Emperor when he travelled by sea and looked after his security. The fourth company was the *hikanatoi*, charged with responsibility for the Emperor when he was present in the city. They were particularly concerned with controlling street disorders and breaking up undesirable demonstrations. These companies formed the basis on which the Emperor's own army and navy were built up. It became increasingly necessary for the imperial authority to develop its own strong military force in place of the army of the themes which had become unreliable and less and less under its control.

This development of a private imperial exchequer and the creation of a special imperial army and navy in Byzantium was not very different from the situation in western states. There comes to mind the struggle of the German Emperor to build up his own military strength in order to combat the power of unruly princes. The dukes of Lotharingia, Bavaria and Saxony in the German Empire find their counterparts in the Byzantine Empire in the commanders-in-chief (*strategi*) of themes such as the Armeniakon, the Anatolikon or the Opsikion. In the Byzantine Empire too there was a decline in the central authority; as in the West, the imperial power was deprived of an efficient administration and now had to compete with the governors of the powerful themes for supremacy within the Empire.

It is not possible to follow this process of administrative change in all its detail. The names of some of the former offices certainly survived as honorary titles for deserving court officials, though their actual functions and responsibilities had been taken over by the newly created departments. Inherent in the movement revealed by the creation of new offices was the struggle between various interests to gain control in the state. It often happened that certain particularly energetic civil servants through their unusual activity in the central departments gave their office far greater importance than really belonged to it. They took great care to ensure that the importance gained by this usurpation of the responsibilities of other departments was retained, and with this in mind they appointed suitable successors, colleagues or men drawn from their own circle of relatives. This explains the fact that insignificant departments often acquired such great influence in the conduct of affairs of state. The officials brought into association with the central administration in this way were not only the members of certain privileged families. They were often men who had risen from lower social classes by reason of their own ability. The growth of a special city aristocracy, or city patriciate, resulted from a subsequent development, which enabled some of the provincial aristocracy, such as the Ducas, to get a foothold in the capital.

The privileged classes as leaders of the new social order: a process of transformation in the countryside

If this development is regarded as a whole, the impression is gained that a small minority maintained a very high standard of living while the vast majority of the populace lived in conditions of poverty very near the minimum subsistence level. The wages of artisans have already shown that the free worker could scarcely maintain himself in modest comfort. The presence of slave labour and the restrictions which economic control placed on every economic activity, including that of artisans, prevented any normal betterment. Those who got their livelihood from the cultivation of the land were no better off than the urban populace. The main characteristic in rural development was the increasing rate at which the old indigenous peasant population became dependents of the new privileged classes.

These privileged classes did not at first simply consist of the group of officers in the themes, in so far as they became transformed into land-owners. A much larger section of these privileged classes was composed of the soldier-farmers settled on the land. Forts were set up wherever military needs demanded. Round the fort land was made available for the new military settlers (*stratiotai*). The result was that almost all Byzantine villages had a more or less large group of military settlers who were distinguished from the other peasants by reason of their army connections. It was not only that they were better off because of their pay and their share of war booty, which was considerable in the navy. They had a particular advantage in the protection afforded by laws applying only to soldier-farmers, and this assisted their rapid economic advance. Further, their farms were usually larger than the lands of the old peasantry which had been reduced in size by partition among heirs and by forced sales. It is known that the lands granted to the *stratiotai*, particularly the cavalrymen, were of considerable extent. Similar conditions held for the property granted to sailors. Finally, the rural population who did not serve in the army had to take financial responsibility for the *stratiotai* doing military service.

But it was not only the military settlers who belonged to the privileged classes. The advance of the Arab conquest and the difficult situation on the frontiers meant the evacuation of a considerable part of the frontier populace. These evacuated peoples were settled in other parts of the Empire. They were granted privileges whereby some of their old rights which they had had over their lost frontier land were transferred to their new property. The concessions to new arrivals were necessarily at the expense of the old established population. For instance, a considerable group was evacuated from the island of Cyprus and given new dwelling sites near Cyzicus on the Sea of Marmora. Similarly the Mardaites, a Christian tribe of robbers living in the region of Amanus, were evacuated. They were suspect by reason of their political views. Some of them joined the Arabs. It was thought necessary to settle them at a distance from the frontiers. As sailors in the navy they were given service farms, some near Attaleia in south-west Asia Minor in Pamphylia, some in the Peloponnese, or on the island of Kephallenia, or near the harbour of Nicopolis in Epirus.

Another resettlement operation carried out at the same time concerned the Paulicians. They were a sect which thrived among the Kurdish tribes living in East Syria and North Mesopotamia. There were about 650 of them and the Syrian Silvanus was one of their first leaders. The name 'Paulician' was derived from the sect's reverence for the Apostle Paul, and their followers and churches nearly all had names from the writings of St Paul, such as Tychicus or Philippi. Their religious system was strongly dualist and they believed in two conflicting worlds, the realm of good and the realm of evil. The Old Testament and the writings of St Peter were rejected. The religious outlook of the Paulicians was somewhat similar to that of the Marcionites. They had been favoured by the iconoclast Emperors and while these were ruling they had spread into the eastern provinces of the Empire. But the iconoclast Emperor Theophilus was forced to take military action against them with the result that many Paulicians crossed over into the territory of the emir of Melitene where they formed their own cavalry division in the Arab army.

In 872 a campaign was directed against them and they were defeated and their capital Tephrice was taken. The conquered sect was transported to Thrace and settled there. Under the name of Bogomils later on they created difficulties there for the Byzantine Empire. In the days of the crusades the Bogomils even won support in the West. Their religious beliefs lived on in the Albigensians in the south of France. They were also known as Cathars; *katharoi* meant 'the pure' and was the sect's own designation of its members. From *katharoi*, by way of Italian, the word *Ketzer* (heretic) developed which was later generally applied to those who by reason of differing religious views were cut off from the official Church.

In contrast to the privileged classes of officers, soldier-farmers and new settlers evacuated from various parts of the Empire, the original peasantry were at a great disadvantage. This was particularly true in matters of taxation. It must be remembered that the local finance offices had the right not only to collect but to assess without much effective control from the central authority. It is true that the central offices possessed lists of taxes payable for the capitation tax, later known as the *kapnikon* or hearth tax, as well as the land valuation list for levying the land tax, but it was hardly likely that these would be used in order to check up on the regional authorities. From the eleventh century the actual tax collection was farmed out to solvent contractors on terms whereby the contract was limited to a single year. Later on in France of the ancien régime the taxes were similarly farmed out. In the Byzantine Empire, as in France, this system was open to abuse which bore most hardly on the small tax-payer. The main Byzantine taxes, levied from the rural population, were the land tax and the capitation tax. The land tax was levied from all land owners, including monasteries with property and the holders of soldiers' farms. The capitation tax was only levied on dependants, the *paroikoi*; landowners were exempt from this tax.

A further tax also borne by the landless *paroikoi* was the tax on draught animals. Most of them possessed draught animals as these were necessary for the working of their rented land. The term draught animal covered horses, draught oxen and donkeys. The cattle of the *paroikoi* were subject to a special grazing tax. In the case of cows, horses and donkeys, there was a tax on each individual animal; for sheep the smallest fiscal unit was a hundred. These taxes pinned down the *paroikoi* who were not subject to the land tax and who had been recruited from the ranks of the once free peasantry. As early as the sixth century an ever increasing class of *paroikoi* was coming into existence. These had originally belonged to the independent peasantry, but they had been forced to sell out to the great landowners because of the oppressive taxation on their property and they had then become tenant-farmers. Every attempt was made to transfer the main burden of taxation from the privileged classes to the *paroikoi*.

A further imposition on the *paroikoi* was the *synone*. This was the obligation of a landowner or a tenant farmer to hand over part of his harvest or his cattle to the military at a rate fixed by the state. In contrast to the *coemptio* of late antiquity, the *synone* was intended only for the needs of troops en route for the place of battle. It was not used, as the *coemptio* was, for the provisioning of troops in winter quarters, since with the introduction of the theme organization these were mostly abolished. Later on the *synone* was commuted. It was possible to buy exemption from the obligation of the *synone* by paying an annual agreed sum, and most tax payers availed themselves of this alternative.

The state was unable to arrest the process whereby the free peasantry were changed into a class of landless *paroikoi* and this continued after the institution of the theme system. The burden of taxation was too unequally distributed. On the one hand there were the privileged classes, on the other, the country population, defenceless and abandoned to the arbitrary will of the tax machine. The land tax was also raised still further by a series of unavoidable services which the small landowner could not pass on. These services are admirably described in the Byzantine sources under the heading *epiria*, burdens. Among these 'burdens' the most important was the obligation to furnish billets and maintenance for army departments, officers and men and the requisitioning of draught, saddle and slaughter beasts. These exactions were at first due when the army was on the march to the front. If a defensive war was being waged, that is, if the troops withdrew to prepared positions within the Empire, then the cost of maintenance throughout the campaign had to be borne by the populace resident there. Thus those burdens, which the introduction of the theme organization was supposed to eliminate, gradually crept back again.

The custom of farming out the taxes, which had become established since the middle of the eleventh century, also imposed a still further burden on land owners, since the tax farmer collected a rake-off for himself as well as what was due to the state. The big landed proprietor took care to pass on the burdens imposed by subtle methods of tax calculation thought up by a clever tax collector. Here he made further use of his *paroikoi*. Thus the main pressure from taxation was felt by the little man. In the Byzantine Empire the peasantry, the backbone and core of every state, were systematically destroyed by tax legislation which denied them the possibility of working on an economic basis. This, rather than the number of lost battles, offers a more illuminating explanation of the decline of the Greek population in Asia Minor and the rapidity with which the Turks assimilated the heart of the Byzantine Empire.

In conclusion, the Byzantine society which gradually emerged after the Arab attacks and the closely connected army reforms consisted of only a small class of the rich and powerful in contrast to the great mass of the exploited and propertyless. The rural and urban middle class were sacrificed to the new reforms which resulted in the most rigorous supervision in the economic sphere. The state-directed corporations and slave-worked industrial enterprises were for the city artisans what the class of privileged soldier-farmers and the new settlers from the frontier regions were for Byzantine rural economy. And so changes in culture came about. Out of the late antique arose the Byzantine. The soldier-farmers and the new settlers introduced into rural society a different element, largely from the periphery of the Empire, and this completely altered the character of the old populace. This transformation was accelerated by the social depression of the old established peasantry. In the cities the change was especially due to the influence of the slaves brought in as specialist craftsmen, which meant that the old artisan populace was reduced to a low social level. If the new oriental religious views got a foothold in Asia Minor and in the capital, it was largely the result of this internal social change.

*Imperial ceremonial and evidence of the many influences
going to form the Byzantine imperial conception*

At the apex of the social hierarchy constituted by Byzantine society stood the Emperor. He was the symbol of the state. Even in the Christian period he was the object of a cult whose roots stretched back to the republican era. The imperial cult determined both the form which the imperial elevation took, and particularly the nature of the imperial portrait, and it was rooted in the institutions of the Roman republic, in the Roman Empire and not least of all in Hellenistic oriental antiquity.

The imperial elevation to the throne was at first the exclusive concern of the army. The soldiers raised their victorious military leader on the shield. He was then granted the triumph and as *triumphator* he received the *corona aurea,* the crown of the *triumphator,* or the *corona laurea,* the laurel crown. This crown, which became the symbol of imperial authority, consisted in the sixth century of a double strand of pearls worn across the forehead broken only by a small shield. This earliest form of imperial crown is better described as a diadem. The massive gold crown made up of a number of plaques joined to each other by links first dates from the time of Heraclius. The Persian king wore a crown of this kind. This Persian royal crown with a kind of nimbus in the form of the sun surrounding the sovereign's head penetrated both eastward and westward. The kings of Kushana in North India and Afghanistan were portrayed with it, as were the later Byzantine Emperors. It is not by chance that this kind of crown first made its appearance in the Byzantine Empire with the Heraclian dynasty (610–711) which went back to the Armenian branch of the Persian Arsacids. In Persia it was God who crowned the Emperor and not the army. On the massive Persian rock reliefs in Iranian lands the Persian kings received power and crown from the supreme god Ahura Mazda. When the Sassanid kings were raised to the throne they received the insignia of royal authority from the chief Mobedh who held the highest religious office. In this the Byzantine Empire did not follow the Iranian model. It was only with the acclamations during the imperial elevation that a Christian element was introduced, Jesus Christ has raised —then followed the name—to be ruler of New Rome (Constantinople). The imperial coronation of the Emperor and Empress by Christ only appears in the iconography of the ruler after the time of Heraclius. This shows the long survival of the old conception of the ruler which had grown out of the elevation of the *triumphator* in Roman times. It is not until the ivory tablets of the tenth and eleventh centuries that the Byzantine Emperor is portrayed being crowned by Christ. The conception lying behind this was that Christ crowned the Emperor, and the Emperor in turn crowned kings, and this found visible expression on imperial and royal crowns. This was the reason why an eleventh-century German imperial crown showed the enthroned Christ on the centre plaque while the crown sent by Constantine Monomachus (1042–55) to the Hungarian king had the portrait of the Byzantine Emperor on this centre plaque in place of Christ.

The kings of the Ostrogoths and Franks wore as the insignia of royal office the *kamelaukion,* a bejewelled headdress, which the Germans in South Russia had taken over from the Iranians. In a little equestrian statue now in the Musée Carnavalet, copied from one of Theodoric the Ostrogoth in Pavia, Charles the Great is still seen wearing a *kamelaukion* and not a crown. The *kamelaukion* was not replaced by the Byzantine imperial crown until the Ottos adopted the Byzantine insignia of imperial authority; this becomes clearly noticeable after the marriage of Otto II to the Byzantine princess Theophano. The German crown now in the treasury in Vienna was made for Conrad III by Byzantine craftsmen in Sicily.

The Byzantine Emperor had the same attributes as the sun god: the nimbus. Sun and moon and the terrestrial globe were the symbols of his universal authority. The globe in his hand was his attribute down to the sixth century in the East; it was also carried by the Caesars on a silver shield of Theodosius I and by an Empress in the consular diptych preserved in Florence. It was in the seventh century that the terrestrial globe as a symbol of power was taken over by Byzantium at a time when it was turning its back on the old cosmology of late antiquity. In the West the terrestrial sphere survived as a sign of authority in the form of the imperial apple. The sun and moon, used as the symbols of universal authority in representations of the Persian kings, are first found in the Byzantine Empire at the time of the Emperor Heraclius I of Armenian origin who traced his descent back to the old Parthian and Armenian royal dynasties.

The victory of the monastic movement changed the symbols of imperial authority. The usual attributes of terrestrial globe and sceptre found in earlier representations of the Emperor disappeared and in their place appeared the *akakia*, a parchment roll, signifying orthodox belief, and a pouch containing dust, the sign of mortality. Down to the fall of the Byzantine Empire imperial personages were portrayed with these symbols.

In elevating an Emperor to the throne, the secular act of acclamation by army, people and senate remained the most important factor. Once acclaimed Emperor, the monarch was possessed of imperial authority. The distinction between imperial elevation and imperial coronation which was particularly noticeable in the West, was unknown in the Byzantine Empire. The Emperor received the crown immediately after he had been raised on the shield. The coronation by the Patriarch, which in the later period immediately followed the elevation, had no legal significance. The imperial elevation took place in the campus, the Mars Field of Constantinople near the Hebdomon, or in the palace. Later on, the Hagia Sophia was the place of elevation and coronation. From the middle of the fifth century the Patriarch took part in the imperial elevation by performing the coronation ceremony. He placed the acclaimed Basileus on the throne and bestowed the imperial insignia on him. From the middle of the seventh century Hagia Sophia had become the accepted place for the imperial coronation.

In the Byzantine Empire the army almost always took a regular part in the elevation of the Emperor to the throne. Here the old Roman origins of the ceremony were far more strongly preserved than when Emperors and kings were raised to the throne in the West. It throws significant light on the character of the act of elevation that in the earliest period coronation was often performed with the *torques*, the neck chain worn by a centurion. The *torques* was often used instead of a crown in imperial coronations. The imperial elevation, even in later days, was always performed in accordance with the old traditions of the Roman army. Before the elevation of the Emperor, the field banners remained lowered and they were only raised after the elevation. Under the shelter of a shield held high above his head the Emperor was clothed with the *chlamys*, a Macedonian warrior's garment, and the *paludamentum*, the old Roman general's cloak. He also put on the imperial purple spurs, the spurs of the commander-in-chief. Then he was raised on the shield and shown to the army, the people and the senate. He was now Emperor.

The imperial insignia were a combination of the costume of a Macedonian warrior king and a Roman general and they were still being used in the fourteenth century. It was not until this period that the *chlamys* was replaced by the tunic consecrated by the Patriarch. Empresses also wore this military costume when they went in state on ceremonial occasions to Hagia Sophia or to the Hippodrome. And so in the eleventh century Empresses were still taking their place in the imperial box in the Hippodrome in the *paludamentum* of a Roman general.

There is an obvious comparison between the elevation of the Byzantine Emperor and the election of the German king which brings out the fundamental difference between East and West. The West recognized the claims of the *stirps regia* and the royal dynasty, which could not be ignored without good reason. The election of the German king involved selection only from among the members of the royal family. But in the Byzantine Empire it was not until the period from the early seventh century onwards that the strength of a military state permitted the formation of a dynasty. And even with the dynasties of the Byzantine Emperors the hereditary succession was not determined by reason of the existence of an imperial dynasty but by the principles of Roman law. The Empire was regarded as private property subject to the laws of hereditary succession.

But the Byzantine imperial elevation, like the German choice of a king, recognized the right of designation. It was also possible for an Emperor to have his son crowned Emperor during his own lifetime. He could not however do this without the approval of the personages involved in the act of elevation. Before he carried out any such designation the Emperor had therefore to call together the senate and representatives of the army and the people to the imperial elevation, and only then could the person designated by him be acclaimed as Emperor. In the case of a German election, the Emperor or king also had to have the agreement of the electors.

This raised the problem of choice. No doubt feelings of sentiment played a major role here. But in the Byzantine Empire, as in the West, there was always something in the nature of a directive behind the process of elevation which apparently took place as the result of divine inspiration. It must not be forgotten that the development of the process of elevation was influenced by the method of choosing a consul in the republican period as well as by the elevation of a commander-in-chief. Thus it was usual for the senate to make a preliminary choice and then to present the chosen candidate to the palace guard and the people. This preliminary choice was made by taking a vote and it was noted down in writing how each vote was cast, that is, for which candidate.

The process of elevation to the imperial office remained closely related to general political conditions. It was not without significance that from the time of Arcadius and Honorius in the early fifth century down to the beginning of the seventh century the Emperors did not themselves command their army in the field. Thus the military factor in the elevation to the throne became far less important. The decision as to who was to be Emperor lay with the senate and the palace guard. In the later period designation played a highly important role. This is true from 610 to 711 when the Heraclian dynasty was in control, and later on in the eighth century it was also used as a means of elevation to the throne. It was only gradually that the idea of a royal stock, or a princely house to whom loyalty was owed, penetrated into the Byzantine Empire; this came from the East and was especially well established in Armenia and in the Caucasian lands.

The Emperor was the central focus of a whole series of ceremonies. These had to a great extent grown up during the time before Christianity became the state religion. These ceremonies are described in two works, one dating from the tenth, the other from the fourteenth century. Under the title of imperial ceremonial was included not only the imperial elevation to the throne, the imperial role in the circus games, the ceremonial entrance of the Basileus and his presence at the liturgical services, but a great deal about the everyday life of the Emperor. The daily round of the Emperor was divided up by a series of ceremonies. The tenth-century *Book of Ceremonies*, compiled by order of Constantine VII Porphyrogenitus, describes the daily round of ceremonial. The Emperor was woken at six o'clock in the morning by three knocks on the silver door of his apartment in the palace. He got up, then went to the *chrysotriklinos*, the Golden Room, and offered a prayer before the icon of Christ in the niche, the *concha*. Then he took up his seat on the golden throne. After breakfast he received the logothete *tou dromou*, the leading minister in the Empire, who made a report on important events. After seeing the logothete he held audiences for other imperial ministers and state dignitaries. They were called to the audience by an official specially appointed for this purpose and until the actual moment of the audience had to wait in an ante-chamber.

When they were received in audience high officers and imperial officials were clothed in special ceremonial garments, purple mantles embroidered with peacocks and shell-fish. They stood while the Emperor sat. Only when the Patriarch paid a visit was this ceremonial somewhat less formal. The Emperor and Patriarch would sit together at table and eat together and during the meal they laid aside their splendid ceremonial robes. After the meal the Patriarch would kiss the Emperor, put on his mantle and take a final farewell before he left.

At general audiences, which took place specially at Christmas, civil servants were promoted. They received their promotion in the form of a diploma, a deed of appointment which was ceremonially presented to them together with the *brabeia* (sign of rank) and the ivory tablets (like the consular diptychs). At the audiences which were concerned with the office of *magister officiorum*, and later of the logothete *tou dromou*, a special form of ceremony was used. The *cubicularii* received the suppliant and led him into the imperial apartments. Here he made a special form of *proskynesis* (prostration) which varied according to his rank. If he was not of senatorial rank he cast himself to the ground with outstretched arms and kissed the Emperor's feet. Foreign visitors, such as the Persian ambassador, made the *proskynesis* in a half-kneeling position. Senators had the right to use a more personal form of greeting and on entry all senators kissed the right side of the Emperor's breast. The Emperor returned the salutation by kissing the top of the senator's head. Foreign ambassadors had a special ceremonial reception.

Foreign ambassadors were met at the frontier by high officials. This meant that a Persian ambassador travelling to an audience in the capital was met by a high official from the central government and by the military commander-in-chief of the district as soon as he reached Kirkesion on the Euphrates. Here gifts were presented to him which he reciprocated in the name of his king. This was repeated in all the larger provincial cities through which he passed on his way to the capital. The high officials in the provincial government received clear instructions as to the protocol to be observed on these occasions and this varied according to the rank and importance of the ambassador and the nature of his mission. It was for instance fairly exactly laid down how many gifts each city was to present to the ambassador and what civil and military ceremonial was to be used at the reception. In the capital the ambassador was greeted by the Roman imperial chancellor, in early days the *magister officiorum*, then later on the logothete *tou dromou*. The first visit made by this high official was of a purely formal character as laid down by protocol. Conversation was confined to enquiries after the health of the monarch and his family and so on. Before the audience there was a formal exchange of gifts which the ambassador had brought for the Emperor and which the Emperor in turn wished to present to his sovereign. Then followed the ceremonial reception in the imperial palace. The ambassador was fetched from wherever he was lodged and given an imperial escort by guardsmen, the *candidati*. These guards wore dress uniform, gilded armour and helmets with white banners, white cloaks, and were armed with lances. On his way to the palace the ambassador rode a specially selected and decorated horse sent by the Emperor for the occasion. When the cortège had traversed the festive and bedecked streets of the capital and had reached the Magnaura, the reception palace in the complex of imperial buildings, he dismounted. He was received at the entrance by high imperial officials who conducted him and his party to the reception hall. Here at the moment of his entry the great hangings concealing the imperial throne raised on a pedestal were drawn back. The Emperor was revealed to sight and all present knelt while the ambassador advanced to the *rota*, a disc of red porphyry let into the stone paving of the floor directly in front of the imperial throne. Here he knelt and made a threefold *proskynesis*. Then he formally communicated the good wishes of his monarch to the Emperor and Empress and presented a personally written letter. Handwritten communications from his sovereign were presented to all influential personages as well as to the Emperor. After this epistolary presentation the Emperor informed himself about the well-being of his 'brother', if it were the Persian king or the Arab Caliph. If the ambassador came from a European prince, then the term 'son' was used. At this audience no business was discussed but the Emperor closed the formal conversation and bade the ambassador come to another audience to be held on the next day. The ambassador was then conducted out again in the same ceremonious manner.

In addition to these audiences, state banquets were held for foreign ambassadors to which most of the high office-holders and the other ambassadors in the capital were invited. Sitting at table was determined by most carefully regulated protocol. The table was in the shape of a half circle and the Emperor sat at the head with the most distinguished guests. In contrast to the other tables in the banqueting hall the Emperor's table was of gold. Men sat on the left of the table and women on the right. The Emperor's seat was in the middle of the table and behind him stood the chamberlains, the *silentiarii*; they held a staff, their sign of office, in their hands. Behind the Empress, who sat beside the Emperor, stood the ladies-in-waiting who each carried a wand. Foreign ambassadors who came from a sufficiently important country would have a seat at the head of the table near the Emperor. Other ambassadors whose princes did not loom so large on the Byzantine political horizon were given seats at the lower end of the table. Thus the tenth-century Liutprand of Cremona, the ambassador of the German Emperor, was offended because he was assigned a lower place, while the representative of the Bulgarian khan was placed higher up the table. During the meal the orchestra played. In addition to the organ, the musical instruments normally used were the cymbals and various stringed instruments. Chorus and soloists also performed during banquets. In the tenth-century *Book of Ceremonies* a spring song performed on these festive occasions is recorded. But these distinguished guests were not only entertained by musical performances. It is known that displays of dancing as well as mimes were provided.

At the audiences subsequently granted to ambassadors, it was usual for ministers to take part. The discussion was minuted by the imperial stenographers. During the negotiations the ambassador used his own interpreter while the Emperor put question and answer through his translator. At the final audience the ambassador received a letter from the Emperor for his sovereign. This consisted of two parts: the good wishes for the health and well-being of the foreign monarch, and then the second part concerned with the various political questions under discussion.

The ceremonies governing the reception of a foreign ambassador originated in Iranian-Hellenistic soil. This is true not only of the *proskynesis* which had to be made to the Emperor but also of the curtains before the imperial throne and the raising of the throne with a baldachino over it. All this goes back to the Achaemenid period. The great relief of the treasury of Xerxes in Persepolis shows an audience given by the Persian Great King Darius and here the *proskynesis* is being made to him as he sits on his throne over which there is a baldachino. Like the Persian Great King, the Greek Emperor was separated from his counsellors by curtains.

Other ceremonies were derived from Roman sources. This is true of the elevation of the Emperor which comes from the period when the guards of the capital, the praetorians, were the decisive factor in power politics. It is also true of the role of the Emperor as leader of the performances in the Hippodrome.

The imperial direction of the circus games went back to the time when the chief magistrates took charge of the management of the games and at the same time distributed free corn, thus attempting to win popular support. This was during the period of the Roman Republic. The distribution of corn was later established as an institution. It was known as *annona civica*, that is, political bread, and survived until the first half of the seventh century. The people, who were present at the games as spectators, had by then organized themselves into the so-called circus parties. Each circus party had its favourites who, like the charioteers, wore their party's colours. The parties had their own charioteers, wild animal keepers, players. At their head were the demarchs. The political authority of the circus parties was broken by the first half of the seventh century but they still kept some of their ceremonial functions in the Circus when the Emperor was present. And the imperial box in the Hippodrome was occupied until the late middle ages. The victory of orthodoxy with its hostility towards everything secular could not alter this.

The imperial connections with the Hippodrome are also reflected in the representation of the Emperor. On the base of the obelisk erected in the Hippodrome in Constantinople by Theodosius I (379–395) the Emperor is shown as taking part as a spectator at the circus games and as honouring the victor in the Circus. These circus games included not only chariot races but performances by dancing girls accompanied by organ music and wind instruments. Extant consular diptychs mostly show the consul as the chosen president of the circus games. This tradition survived until the middle Byzantine period. It is not until the second half of the eleventh century in the paintings by Byzantine artists on the staircase of the Hagia Sophia church in Kiev that the circus games show the Emperor presiding. The crown sent by the Emperor Constantine Monomachus to the Hungarian king belongs to the same period and together with the imperial couple this shows circus dancing girls. The association of these dancing girls with the crown, the highest symbol of the imperial office, indicates the close association of the Emperor with the imperial ceremonial of the circus games.

It was not only in the imperial elevation to the throne and in the circus games that old Roman traditions lived on. The way in which the vintage was celebrated went back at least to Roman times. At the festival of the blessing of the vines which took place on 15 August the Emperor and Patriarch left the city and took part in the liturgical service for the blessing of the vineyards. In Roman times, too, the blessing of the grapes was connected with a liturgical ceremony. The beginning of the vintage was announced by the *flamen Dialis* who sacrificed a lamb to Jupiter. The Byzantine Emperor was present at the ceremonies both for the blessing of the grapes and for their actual gathering which began in September. At this last festival, which took place in Hiereia on the Asian coast of the Bosphorus, the Patriarch and the highest imperial officials took part together with the Emperor who presented them with bunches of grapes during the ceremonies.

There was also another imperial ceremonial practice which dated from the Roman period. This was connected with the ceremony of the so-called empty throne. On Sundays and festivals the Emperor sat on the left side of the throne and on ordinary weekdays he occupied the right hand side. This was based on the fact that Christ was represented as having his seat on the right hand side of the throne. So on festivals and Sundays this was left unoccupied in his honour. On working days the Emperor sat there because he was the representative of Christ. The empty throne, like the imperial portrait, was shown in church decoration, as in the fifth-century mosaic of Santa Maria Maggiore. The empty throne went back to the pre-Christian Romano-Hellenistic institution of the so-called *sellisternium*. Caesar had been granted the honour of the empty throne. With the union of Christianity and the Roman state this institution was adopted and the honour bestowed on Christ.

The ceremonial which took place at the Emperor's funeral revealed its Romano-Hellenistic origins. Here there were indications pointing to the apotheosis, the deification of the Roman Emperors. The apotheosis in the pagan sense was still portrayed on ivory tablets in the fifth century. They show the Emperor, like Christ, ascending to heaven. This conception of the apotheosis of the Emperor also determined the ceremonies which took place at the funeral of an Emperor. The dead man was first of all laid on his bier in full coronation robes in the Room of the Nineteen Divans in the imperial palace Chalke. Then the funeral psalms were chanted, and the imperial master of ceremonies turned towards the dead man with the words 'Go forth, O Emperor, the King of kings, the Lord of lords, is calling you'. This was repeated three times. Then the bier was borne into the room in that same place where the Emperor, while he lived, had done justice. The bier with the corpse was set down here on the circle of red porphyry inset in the paved floor. The whole ceremony which had just taken place in the Room of the Nineteen Divans was then repeated. Then the procession passed through the great bronze door which gave its name, Chalke (bronze), to this part of the palace, and proceeded past Hagia Sophia and the Hippodrome along the Mese, the splendid main avenue, to the church of the Holy Apostles. The procession was accompanied by the guards and made its slow way to the chanting of the funeral psalms. In the Holy Apostles church the master of ceremonies approached the dead Emperor for the third time and bade him take off his crown. Then the *praepositus sacri palatii* came up to the bier on which the imperial corpse lay and took off the crown from the dead man. A purple band was now placed in its stead. The ceremony was based on the conception that the Emperor had left earth only to continue his office as ruler with Christ in heaven. Then the burial ceremony began. The corpse was placed in a coffin of cedarwood before it was deposited in the great porphyry sarcophagus in the imperial mausoleum. The form of these imperial obsequies is still preserved today in the funeral ceremonies of the dead Popes. Here too, as in ancient Roman times, there is the nine day period of mourning and the call addressed to the corpse on the open bier.

Hellenistic, as well as oriental-Iranian and ancient Roman, elements played a great role in imperial ceremonial. This is true of the festival connected with the so-called *prokypsis*. This *prokypsis* went back to the worship of the sun-god, whose birthday was celebrated with special mimes. These mimes were meant to signify the rebirth of the sun. This solar worship was grafted on to the imperial cult by Aurelian. In the Byzantine *prokypsis* the Emperor became an emanation of the sun-god. Earlier on, the Roman Emperor had been represented like the sun-god with the nimbus and the sun-chariot, and the worship of the sun-god was transferred to him. The linking of solar worship with the imperial cult remained in imperial ceremonial even after the adoption of Christianity as the state religion. In the mime on the day of the winter solstice the Byzantine Emperor personified the rebirth of the sun. This mime kept its place in Byzantine ceremonial until the late Byzantine period. The Emperor stood on a special platform decked with hangings. He was accompanied by the Empress, the princes, the court of the imperial nobles, who took their places on the platform in order of rank. Before them paraded companies of regular troops and the palace guard in the white parade dress of the *candidati*, preceded by the ensigns of the troops carried two by two in groups of twelve, together with the banners of the members of the imperial household and the colours of the demes (the circus parties). Before all in a special place stood the imperial standard and the imperial shield. Trumpeters, horn-players, cymbalists and flautists began to play and thus the ceremony began. Then the signal for silence was given. The *protovestarius* made a sign to indicate that the climax of the spectacle was approaching. At this point the curtains were drawn back and in the dark night could be seen the brightly illuminated figures of the Emperor and the imperial family. The Emperor wore his coronation robes. In his left hand he held the *akakia* and the pouch of dust, the symbol of mortality, in the right hand the sceptre with the cross. The Emperor wore his crown during the ceremony and so did the heir to the throne and they were illuminated from the knees up, while the rest of the imperial family who were standing at the back of the platform remained in the dark from the breast down. At the moment when the curtains were drawn back on the platform, songs accompanied by music broke out. On a signal given by the Emperor both song and music ceased. Then after a few moments silence the Christmas hymn was sung, 'Christ is born, He who has crowned thee, O Emperor.' Further hymns and songs followed and then there was again silence and the curtains were drawn together. To the sound of music the banners and colours were placed in front of the regiment to which they belonged. As the troops marched away the ceremony ended.

Ceremonies of this kind make clear the strong link between the Byzantine Emperor and the old priestly, even divine, functions which Christianity had not dared to attack. These old Roman traditions give the Byzantine Emperor a far stronger position than that of western kings and Emperors. It is true that the Byzantine Emperor when he preached did not possess sacerdotal powers and authority. Nevertheless he could enter the sanctuary, once reserved for priests. The Patriarch was nominated by the Emperor and he possessed scarcely any means of opposing the occupants of the throne. If he did so he would be deposed and would have to pay for his courage by exile or imprisonment. It was different in the West. Here the secular character of the act of coronation receded more and more into the background. The very placing of the imperial crown into the custody of the Church had developed into the papal right to refuse to bestow this crown, and the papacy's temporal authority over Rome and a large part of central Italy delivered into the hands of the princes of the Church not only the coronation but the raising to the throne which had originally been the secular part of the ceremony.

It became usual in the West to exclude the Emperor from the spiritual functions of his office which the Byzantine Emperor continued to retain, and this gave the papacy the possibility of imposing ecclesiastical penalties in order to force a troublesome Emperor into compliance or submission.

There were then three factors which accounted for the dependence of the western imperial office on the Pope in Rome: first the authority of the Pope over a large part of central Italy which secured him influence over the secular part of the imperial elevation, that is, the acclamation by senate, people and army; then the widespread belief in the West that the crown and other imperial jewels had special magic powers which conferred on the possessor an otherwise unattainable position, and since the imperial crown was kept in the sanctuary of the church these powers were believed to reside in the Pope; and finally the priestly functions which the western Emperor did not retain, contrary to his Byzantine counterpart. In the West the Emperor took pride of place among the laity but he was subject to the spiritual authority of the Pope.

The Emperor in his secretariat

The Byzantine Emperor was not so much occupied by his position as figurehead in an all-pervading ceremonial system that he had no time for personal direction of imperial policy. Doubtless ceremonies claimed a good deal of the Emperor's time but he still had to satisfy the very considerable demands which the direction of imperial affairs necessarily made upon him. To begin with there was an enormous amount of office work to deal with. The Basileus had to affix his signature to all state documents of any importance and was spared just as little as a twentieth-century head of state. This concerned those documents to which the Emperor gave legal validity, either by affixing his signature or by inserting the date. It followed from the conception of the sacred character of his person that all documents with which he was concerned had a special form distinguishing them from other secular documents. This also held for their external format. From earlier times down to the beginning of the tenth century papyrus had provided the writing material used by the imperial chancery. Then its place was taken by a special creaseproof bombycine which came from the Arab realm. It was called 'Baghdad' paper after its place of origin. To judge from the extant originals dating from the middle of the eleventh century, this was a soft, downy, fine kind of paper which was tinted with purple. The first line with the invocation to the Holy Trinity and the titles of the Emperor was written in a special hand in which the letters had to be a certain number of centimetres high. Besides this script there were a number of others in use.

The Emperor's signature was in purple ink and the documents were signed in a special room in the imperial palace. When he formally affixed his signature he was assisted by an official bearing the title of Keeper of the Imperial Writing Materials. The literal translation of this title seems to imply that he had charge of the pen (and the imperial ink). The holder of this office was a high-ranking official with great political influence. He can be compared to the Keeper of the Great Seal in western states. The question of the sealing of imperial documents also had to be dealt with. The Byzantine Emperor only used a seal for certain types of documents and that was a ring seal. Otherwise the Emperor used a chrysobull (gold seal) whose weight and size varied according to the importance of its destination. The bull bore on one side the portrait of Christ and on the other that of the Emperor. The Basileus was shown crowned and clothed in the imperial robes. The custom of sending the imperial portrait with the document indicates the continuity of the early Roman tradition. The Roman Emperors used to send foreign princes their portrait in the shape of a gold medallion.

But in yet another connection the Byzantine imperial document showed its indebtedness to the old Roman tradition. The imperial documents drawn up in Greek, still used Latin letters when they were addressed to all his subjects and were exhorting obedience to the imperial will, which was reminiscent of the Latin text not given up until the eighth century. In this way the Roman element in the imperial chancery was conserved until the downfall of the Byzantine Empire. It still survived there when Greek had long supplanted it in other branches of government administration. Latin had been abandoned as the legal language as early as towards the end of the sixth century. It was used as the language of military command until the eighth century and individual phrases in the army and in military manoeuvres lingered on for several centuries. In certain cases the signature to a document was preceded by confirmation by the head of the chancery, thus assuring that the contents of the drafted document corresponded to the imperial decision recorded according to protocol in the official minutes. Before the signature was formally affixed, there was a conference during which counsellors gave the Emperor their advice on the matter being dealt with. He made his decision immediately after the meeting and it was then put on record in the minute book and on the basis of this the text was drafted for the proposers or the proposed recipients. After countersignature by the head of the chancery the Emperor affixed his own signature. For the drafting, which was known as the 'dictation' of the document, representatives of special departments were called in; for instance, on matters of foreign correspondence it would be the logothete *tou dromou*. If the imperial decisions had a legal content, the quaestor was called on, and in financial matters it would be the head of the state taxation department or of the private imperial financial department, according to the nature of the document. There was a special translation department for letters sent to foreign countries. These had not only to translate the letters of foreign potentates into Greek and provide translators for conferences but to translate into the appropriate language imperial letters to foreign statesmen. Thus in 968 an imperial letter to Ar-Radi was produced in Arabic. This translation was attached to the Greek original and it was just as splendidly set out as the Greek version.

Still more time-consuming than the normal chancery work were the demands made on the Emperor by the diplomatic exchanges which took place in Constantinople. The central aim of most conferences was to reach an understanding on economic problems. The control of two sea-straits ensured to the Byzantine Empire a unique international position and for almost the whole of its existence its foreign policy included economic agreements. Even in the Palaeologan period, which was a time of political decline, Byzantium took part in the great coalitions of the important powers. It might be a question of an understanding with the Egyptian sultan whereby he was prepared to support the Byzantine Empire against its opponents, Charles of Anjou and the Seljuk emirs, in return for economic concessions, such as preferential customs duties for Egyptian merchants and free transit through the straits for ships importing Egyptian slaves, or it might be a matter of negotiation with the Italian maritime cities. Discussions of this kind always took place in the imperial palace. Even in the late middle ages, the diplomatic protocol observed mostly went back to the late antique period. It was taken over first by the Venetians and then by the great western states and has survived to the present day.

The first prerequisite for negotiations was the presentation of valid ambassadorial credentials and these were later deposited with the written agreement once this was concluded. Ambassadors also brought letters of introduction from their sovereign to almost all influential personages in Byzantine government circles. For their own guidance they had instructions clearly defining the maximum and minimum demands in connection with their mission. Discussions on important matters were first directed by the logothete *tou dromou*, who later on had the designation of *megas logothetes* (Grand Logothete). It was only when the discussions had reached some measure of agreement that the Emperor took part in the proceedings. In the imperial presence the agreements reached in the preliminary proceedings were sworn to. According to protocol the oath was inserted into the text of the treaty which had now been drawn up. Then at this session in the presence of the Emperor the ambassadors had to sign and seal the draft of the treaty. It was only then that the Emperor gave the order for the treaty to be prepared in both languages. The two copies were signed by the Emperor in a ceremonial session. One copy remained in Constantinople, the other went with the ambassadors who now began their homeward journey accompanied by a Byzantine legation. When they arrived the foreign head of state had to swear to the treaty in the presence of the Byzantine envoys. It was only with this ratification that the treaty was held to be binding on both sides.

Like the Hellenistic ruler, the Byzantine Emperor was regarded as the Basileus Soter, the ruler and saviour. He brought salvation and he was at the same time the *mimetes theou*, the imitator of God. This found special expression in the proems to his documents. Quite unlike the formless and stereotyped *arengae* of western rulers which did not get beyond hackneyed moralizing, these announced the programme for a new world order. In the introductions to his documents the Byzantine Emperor developed aspects of his governmental programme, at the same time very cleverly linking it to the special content of the document. These proems were drawn up by the leading statesmen in the Empire. They were for the most part the same men who were responsible for writing the history of the Emperor's rule.

The Emperor was still regarded as the personification of the old God of the heavens, as is shown by the symbol of imperial power, the eagle, the attribute of Jupiter, which became the double-headed eagle in the fourteenth century. This decorated the ceremonial garments distributed by the Emperor, as well as the imperial standard. It was the symbol of universal authority. Thus it was adopted by Frederick II at the height of his power and later, after the fall of Byzantium, by the tsar of Moscow as heir of the Byzantine Emperor.

Common elements in the development of the imperial palace and in ecclesiastical architecture

The special position of the ruler found expression both in the imperial palace buildings and in contemporary church architecture. As early as the days of Constantine Christian church architecture had adopted the same architectural type of building as that used in the imperial palace for the audience halls. The Christian basilica was a copy of the imperial throne-room. Whereas the Emperor's throne stood in the apse, in the Christian church this was where the altar was placed. This connection between the imperial palace and the Christian sacred building remained unaltered during the following centuries. But while in Constantine's day the imperial palace had provided the model for the church architecture, in the time of Justinian and his immediate successors the reverse was probably true. The *chrysotriklinos,* the so-called Golden Throne Room, begun under

Justin II (565–578) and completed under Tiberius II (578–582), copied almost down to the last detail the ground plan and form of the churches of St Sergius and St Bacchus in Constantinople and of San Vitale in Ravenna which Justinian had built. The imperial throne stood in the apse, the vaulting of which was decorated by a mosaic showing the enthroned Christ. In the tenth century the throne room was still the centre of the complex of the imperial palace buildings. Here stood the famous *pentapyrgion*, a splendid repository of immense dimensions in which the imperial crowns and crown jewels were displayed, as well as two organs richly set with precious stones and gold, and finally a golden tree with singing birds.

With the end of Justinian's era a new development set in. The iconoclast movement had greatly restricted the life of the Church, and with the victory of the iconophiles all the more powerful was the stimulus given to church building. Then once again the situation closely approximated to that of Constantine's day. Church architecture adopted the forms of palace architecture, for it was only in this field that progress had been made. Here the last highlight had been the building activities of the Emperor Theophilus (829–842). Theophilus repaired the walls of Constantinople (and today there are still inscriptions on certain towers commemorating this work); he also undertook a good deal of building within the city. He was a great admirer of Arab culture; many of the palaces built by him were inspired by models in Samarra and Baghdad. There was the Tzykanisterion Palace, which stood in front of the polo ground which he had made, and the Triconchus Palace built in 838. This last palace took its name from its three half domes which were constructed over the building's three apses and it had walls only on the south and west sides while the interior was supported by four pillars, thus showing a close affinity with later church architecture. The palace could only be entered through the three doors which led to the three apses; the centre door was silver, the two side doors bronze. In the three apses under the semi-domes the thrones of the Emperor, his son and his wife probably stood. This building, surmounted by a dome, differed from the church architecture then in use, and also from the throne-room (the *chrysotriklinos*) constructed after the same pattern, by reason of its four pillars which bore the whole weight of the dome. The pillars which supported the main dome were free standing in the nave of the church, the *naos*.

This Triconchus Palace built by the iconoclast Emperor Theophilus in 838 was probably the model for the famous *capella palatina*, the so-called Nea. It was dedicated to the Mother of God, the archangel Michael and the hermit Elias. It also had the three apses, but in place of the thrones there were altars. As in the Triconchus, the main dome of the Nea rested on four pillars. A new feature was the raised drum of the main dome, introduced for the first time in order to give more scope to the demands of icon veneration in the interior of the church. This raising of the drum, which was out of proportion to the rest of the church, allowed more light to enter and made it possible to place mosaics or frescoes in parts of the interior which had previously been in shadow and therefore unsuitable for this purpose. The Nea was the model for Byzantine ecclesiastical architecture of the tenth and eleventh centuries. Neither the *capella palatina* of the Nea nor its probable inspiration, the Triconchus Palace of Theophilus, have survived. Some idea of their structure may perhaps be gathered from the monastery church of the Myrelaion (Budrum Cami) which was built in the first half of the tenth century. Thus in the ninth century as in the sixth and fourth centuries there was a close connection between ecclesiastical architecture and that of the imperial throne room; the explanation lies in the fact that the sacred position of the Byzantine Emperor remained unassailed during the Christian period.

The palaces of the Emperor: state rooms and places for relaxation

The imperial palaces in Constantinople were an integral part of the sacral existence of the Byzantine Emperor. He lived in few of these, mostly only two, a winter and a summer palace, and yet he had to use a great many of them for certain ceremonial purposes. There were of course the so-called imperial pleasure palaces, such as the Tzykanisterion, the palace at the imperial polo ground, or the Palace *ton pegon* (of the Springs) just outside the city from which hunting expeditions set out, or the Hiereia Palace built by the Empress Theodora on the Asian side of the Bosphorus. This last was sometimes used for ceremonies; it was here that the Emperor had to receive the procession of high secular officials and ecclesiastics on the occasion of the vintage festival. Other palaces, such as the Bryas Palace built in Arab style by the Emperor Theophilus or the Mouchroutas (*machruta*=Arabic for 'vaulting'), were not so much used for ceremonial as for imperial relaxation. But this was only true of a small number of the palaces in the capital.

Ceremonial duties were centred in the so-called Great Palace. This was the name given to a whole complex of buildings, including a large number of individual palaces and churches. In this respect the 'Great Palace' may be compared with the Hradčany in Prague or the Kremlin in Moscow. In Constantinople there was, too, a clear demarcation between the 'palace' and the rest of the city; the Byzantine complex of the Great Palace had its own water supply, its own cisterns, baths, sports places and gardens. It was a fabulous city. In the West, as in the Islamic East, stories were told of the marvels of this great imperial palace. But in general visiting strangers saw little more than a few state-rooms or the celebrated clock on Hagia Sophia which told the hour of the day and night by a door opening to show a figure which remained visible for the duration of an hour. (This clock was later remodelled by Arab mechanics. Its appearance is known from an Arabic miniature dating from the beginning of the thirteenth century.)

It is significant that the greater part of our knowledge about the use which was made of the palace rooms comes from the *Book of Ceremonies*. This palace city was usually entered through the Chalke, a large building taking its name from its bronze entrance doors. By the eighth century the vestibule of the Chalke was only a museum containing statues of great generals and Emperors of the sixth century as well as famous sculptures of the Hellenistic period. Here were to be found the four heads of the Gorgon and the two bronze horses which Justinian had brought to Constantinople from Ephesus. There were also the statues of two men raising their hands, which came from Athens, perhaps a statue of the two tyrannicides, Harmodius and Aristogiton.

Beyond the vestibule was the tribunal room which was illuminated by an immense candelabra. This is where legal sessions were held. Adjacent to this room on the right and the left were the various rooms of the imperial guard. Through these the so-called Tribunal or Room of the Nineteen Divans was reached. It took its name from the great banquets held here when the Emperor and his guests would be served reclining on divans, as was usual up to the end of the sixth century. Each divan took twelve people and the tables were in the form of a semi-circle. The Emperor's table was of pure gold. Beyond this room was a chapel and the assembly rooms of the imperial counsellors, the large and little *consistorium*. The little *consistorium* was for consultations which took place in winter, since the great *consistorium* probably had no heating. From here the *sacellum* was reached, the imperial department of finance with the treasury and the state archives. Close by was the famous domed room in which the Church Council *in Trullo* held its sessions from 691 to 692, and the so-called *Delphax* where the Emperor ceremonially invested the highest imperial officials. In front of the Room of the Nineteen Divans was a passage leading to the Palace of Daphne, so named after a statue of the nymph Daphne standing here which had been brought to Constantinople from Rome. This palace was the oldest part of the imperial complex. It dated from the time of Constantine. In addition to a magnificent state room, it contained the imperial reception rooms and next to these was the so-called Octagon, containing an imperial bed-chamber.

The church of St Stephen was connected with the Palace of Daphne. Here imperial coronations and burials often took place. In the neighbourhood of the Palace of Daphne there was the Triconchus throne-room which has already been mentioned; this was used for receptions. Not far away from this building was the ramp where the horses of the two circus parties, in gold embroidered caparison, were led before the Emperor. Further to the east lay the great palace buildings of Theophilus. According to surviving descriptions these consisted not so much of large, many-storied buildings as pavilions decorated in excellent taste with mosaics and inset marble in the oriental style so fashionable in Byzantium at that time. The Empress's apartments were in the so-called Pantheon and these too can be likened to a pavilion, but an even larger one, like the still extant palace buildings of the Ottoman Sultan in the old Serai (Topkapu Serai) in Constantinople.

The Magnaura belonged to the old palace buildings going back to the era of Constantine. Here state receptions frequently took place. It was not until later in the second half of the ninth century that this building was assigned to the university, newly founded by Caesar Bardas, and lectures were held there. Like the throne room, the Magnaura was a basilica, thus keeping to the type of building which provided the pattern for Christian churches in the Constantinian period. The Magnaura had three aisles and, as later became usual in Christian churches, they were separated by rows of pillars. At the end of the main aisle there was an apse surmounted by a half-dome. Here, raised up and approached from the centre aisle by six steps flanked by golden lions, was the famous throne of Solomon from which the Emperor presided at state receptions. This room was splendidly lit by seven candelabras. In the Magnaura there was also the imperial nuptual chamber and a special bath for the Empress, and there were special ceremonies connected with its use three days after her marriage. A great terrace extended round the Magnaura and on it stood the statues of various Emperors of the sixth and early seventh centuries. The last statue to be placed here was that of Phocas (602–610) and after him this custom was abandoned.

Another palace, called the Porphyra, had a special role in the ceremonial which concerned the Empress. In it was the porphyry walled bed-chamber in which Empresses gave birth to their children. Porphyry was the imperial stone. It was in a porphyry room that the future Emperor first saw light and it was in a porphyry sarcophagus that the body of the dead Emperor came to rest. It was here in this palace on the first day of the Brumalia, that is, on 26 November, that the Empress distributed the purple to distinguished court ladies.

Besides the complex of the Great Palace buildings there were other palaces where the Emperor had ceremonial duties. Such was the palace of Hebdomon. In Hebdomon was the celebrated Byzantine Field of Mars where the European troops assembled before going on campaign. The Emperor would be present to encourage them and to take the march-by. It was in the palace of Hebdomon that the senate and the Patriarch and high ecclesiastics gathered to meet the Emperor returning from campaign and to join in the triumphal procession which followed. This triumphal cortège passed along the coast road, then entered the city by the Golden Gate and took the Mese, the central avenue, through the imperial forums, to the church of Hagia Sophia and the Hippo-drome. It was in the Hebdomon Campus that the ceremonial elevation of the Emperor took place almost down to the end of the sixth century. After the elevation the Emperor was crowned by the Patriarch in the church of St John the Baptist which was next to the palace.

The old Roman tradition lived on in the ceremonies connected with the Hebdomon Palace but there were Christian traditions associated with the ceremonial which took place in another palace. This was the Blachernae Palace which owed its position to the annual imperial procession to the Blachernae church. This church was dedicated to the Assumption of Mary and it was a copy down to the last detail of the church built in Jerusalem by the Empress Helena. It was built by the Emperor Marcian (450–457) and his wife Pulcheria in honour of the holy veil of the Mother of God. To begin with it was outside the city walls. With the increasing cult of Mary from the end of the fifth century onwards, the first palace buildings were erected and these were expanded because of the institution of the annual imperial procession. The inclusion of the region round the church within the city fortifications further strengthened imperial building activities at the palace. A decisive factor in future building operations was the route taken by the Emperor in the procession. Unlike some of the officials and the populace, the Emperor took the sea route and, as the church stood higher up, it had to be approached by steps leading from the place where the imperial barge was moored. For this reason *triklinoi* (rooms, salons) connected with the church were built on the land route in between. These *triklinoi*, designed for the reception of office-holders taking part in the procession, took their names from the fine mosaics in them. Thus there was a *triklinos* of the hunt, another of the Danube, and perhaps an Ocean *triklinos*. On 2 February the festival of the Purification of Mary was celebrated in the Blachernae church. After the procession and the church service there was the imperial ceremony when some of the officials who had taken part in the procession were invited to a state banquet. Lower ranking officials who were not at the banquet celebrated the day in special rooms put at their disposal.

The Byzantine Emperor and the other holders of an imperial title

The question arises as to why the Byzantine Emperor was superior to the Emperor of the West or the Bulgarian Basileus. There had been a western Emperor since Charles the Great, who was given the imperial crown by the Pope in 800. The Bulgarian khan had taken the title 'Basileus Romaion' in 913.

Charles the Great had avoided assuming precisely the same title as the Byzantine Basileus. He made use of the formula 'Carolus magnus pacificus imperator, Romanorum gubernans imperium.' As the title shows he only regarded himself as Emperor ruling the Roman Empire. He was not the Emperor of the Romans. He made no claim to universal authority. He did not describe himself as *Caput mundi*, as was done by later western Emperors. This was first found under Frederick Barbarossa who wrote in the *arenga* to his documents 'Quia divina providente clementia urbis et orbis gubernacula tenemus.'

In the western conception of the imperial office the secular elements found in the Roman Empire were ousted by Christian and ecclesiastical influence. The western Emperor called himself *serenissimus augustus a Deo coronatus*. This was not inspired by the Empire of Augustus, based on certain republican offices and ruling the state by its *auctoritas*. But in the West the Christian element was much more strongly emphasized.

It relied on the interpretation of the dream of the prophet Daniel given by the church fathers Hippolytus and Jerome. According to them the four great beasts of the dream corresponded to the four great empires, namely, the Assyrio-Babylonian, the Medo-Persian, the Graeco-Macedonian and the Roman. This last, the Roman, would endure until the end of the world. In Byzantium against this view of the apocalypse of Daniel was set the interpretation of the *Revelation* of St John by Andrew of Caesarea. According to him, on the fall of Old Rome, which was comparable to that of the great Babylonian Empire, its authority was transferred to New Rome. To meet this interpretation of the imperial conception the West took refuge in the weapon of 'orthodoxy'. In contrast to the heretical Byzantine Basileus, the western Emperor was the representative of the true faith. This further emphasized the link with the papacy.

No doubt the German rulers were moved to assume the imperial office for reasons of policy. The conquest of the Lombard kingdom in North Italy could only have any hope of permanency if it were made by a German king who also wore the imperial crown. The German king had to intervene here and secure for himself the imperial throne in order to prevent the dukes of Bavaria and Swabia from forestalling him. Attempts of this kind had already been made in the twenties and thirties of the tenth century. Thus the Italians had invited the kings of Burgundy to accept the imperial crown. A king of Burgundy who was also Emperor would introduce grave complications on Germany's western frontier. It would mean that the fate of Lotharingia, coveted by both the kings of France and of Burgundy, would be settled in a sense unfavourable to Germany. At the same time the eastern expansion of Germany was only within the power of a king who also wore the imperial crown and was therefore in a privileged position *vis-à-vis* the papacy.

The Bulgarian position differed basically from that of the Empire of the West. The adoption of the imperial title was also a matter of political importance for the Bulgarian tsar. He wanted to become the Christian ruler of the Slav world who by reason of his *auctoritas* could take the lead among all the Slav tribes. For this reason he needed the charisma bestowed by the Byzantine imperial crown. The Byzantine Emperor could continue to rule but not as universal sovereign. The Bulgarian tsar did not wish to control the Byzantine Empire when he took the title *Basileus Romaion* in 913. His attitude here was comparable to that of Louis the Pious who accepted the title *Imperator Romanorum* without intending to supplant the Byzantine Emperor. For the Carolingians the imperial title meant securing Frankish pre-eminence over the other German peoples, and in the same way the imperial title of the Bulgarian prince implied his own suzerainty over the Slav tribes such as the Croats, Serbs and Moravians.

The Byzantine Empire recognized neither the western Frankish Empire nor the Bulgarian Emperor. It spoke of the *archontes Boulgaron*, the princes of the Bulgars, and the *reges Francias*, the kings of Francia. The Byzantine Empire never gave up its claims to universal rule. It claimed to be at the apex of the family of kings; it was the father, they were the sons. It was thus that it addressed the western kings and the Bulgarian tsars. It was only with the Arab rulers that there had long been some recognition of equality, and also with the Persian kings, which was reflected in the title of 'brother' used in official documents. But between the title of universal ruler and real authority over the world there was an unbridgeable gulf. The Byzantine Empire of the eighth and ninth centuries could no longer make any claim to take the lead in the world on political grounds. In the field of culture it was a different matter: even in this period it was still possible to speak of the world supremacy of the Byzantino-Roman Empire.

Byzantium, its position in the world: 4
its resources and its opponents

Arab opponents

The Graeco-Roman heritage as the decisive factor in the political formation of the Arab Empire of the Umayyads

After the Arab invasion the Byzantine state had to fight for its existence. During this period on more than one occasion the Empire was saved by Constantinople, the creation of Constantine, with its walls and fortifications constructed with all the technical expertise of late antiquity. During this period the myth of the capital as the saviour of the Empire became a reality.

When the centre of gravity of the Arab Empire moved from the Hijaz in the Arabian peninsula to Damascus in Syria, the Byzantine Empire was faced with a powerful neighbour on the shores of the East Mediterranean, and moreover with one which could draw on the resources of the ancient world in Irak, Syria and Egypt. At the same time in the north the Slav tribes were overrunning Thrace, Macedonia and the greater part of Greece. In Europe the Byzantines held little more than the coastal regions. It was thus only Asia Minor and the capital Byzantium which could bring salvation to the Empire and secure its existence.

At this time the Byzantine territories in the West, Italy with Sicily and North Africa, were particularly valuable. Sicily, separated from Africa and Europe by only a narrow sea strait, was in an unusually strategic position. Under continuing pressure of attacks from the north and south-east the idea of transferring the capital and the imperial centre of gravity back again to the West must certainly have seemed a practical possibility. The Byzantine imperial government did indeed consider the idea. During the last decade of his reign the Emperor Constans II (641–688) was persuaded by Arab and Bulgar attacks to take the decision to transfer the centre of the Empire back to Italy in order to withdraw from the direct range of activity of the Umayyad fleet and the Bulgar and Arab cavalry. His attempt failed. He was not successful in mastering the formidable mountain strongholds of the Lombards in South Italy, particularly their main fortified centre of Beneventum. Thus the road to Rome from South Italy remained under Lombard control and a Byzantine Emperor who was not master of the Lombards could hardly appear as *triumphator* in the old capital. The Byzantine army, which the victories of Belisarius and Narses had taught the Italians to dread, had now lost its aura of invincibility with the defeat of the Basileus. Thus the belief in the reunion of Italy by means of an East Roman victory over the Lombards evaporated. The country was henceforth divided between the East Romans and the Lombards and the last traces of this division were not obliterated until the rise of an Italian national state in the middle of the nineteenth century. The Byzantine Emperor had to go back to Sicily where he shortly fell a victim to the murderer's dagger. Thus ended the Byzantine Emperor's attempt to put back the clock and to begin again at the point when Constantine had introduced his epoch-making changes.

Generally speaking, Byzantium, which was battling for its own existence, had lost the initiative to the powerful aggressors in East and West. The two attacks hurled with full force against the Byzantine Empire were independent of each other. The forward thrust of the Slav peoples resulted from a migration of the Altaic peoples whose home was in Central Asia. The Arab offensive, led by the Umayyads of Damascus, was due to the removal of the centre of their Empire from the purely Arab cities Mecca and Medina to Syria, the richest and culturally most highly developed province of the East Roman Empire. Thus the Umayyads came under the influence of the late antique world. Their imperial officials were Christian Syrians, men who spoke Greek and had been educated in the Greek schools of rhetoric. The most important theologian of the Byzantine Church, John of Damascus, was originally a high financial official of the Umayyad Caliph before he exchanged the palace in Damascus for a monk's cell in the monastery of St Sabas near Jerusalem. What could the Caliph, a member of the noble family of Umayya in Mecca whose political horizon was limited to the feuds in the Hijaz, be expected to know about international political relationships in the Mediterranean world? He was not accustomed to thinking on such a grand scale. It was the high imperial officials at the court of the Arab ruler who laid down the lines of his international policy for him. In their eyes world empire, whether Roman or Arab, was inevitably linked with the possession of the capital city of Constantinople, and it was with this in mind that they directed the Arab offensive. It was for this reason that the Umayyad navy was built and the Greek islands were occupied as the first move towards their objective. It was only when control had been established over Rhodes, Cos and Smyrna and up to Cyzicus on the Sea of Marmora that the attack on the capital Constantinople could be planned. This was the route taken in Justinian's day by the supply ships from Syrian and Egyptian ports on their way to Constantinople.

For the Christian Syrian counsellors of the Caliph the Mediterranean world was the heart of the universe. Hence the Arab attacks along the coast line of the Mediterranean. The first objective was the North African coast up to the straits of Gibraltar, then Spain and finally Gaul. This meant no less than the reconquest of the old *imperium romanum*, this time directed not from Constantinople but from Damascus. So Justinian's plans for a western *reconquista* were taken up again in Damascus.

Thus the western orientated plans of the Umayyads were evolved on Syrian territory where their Empire's centre of gravity was. The Christian Syrian advisers of the Caliph, steeped in the old East Roman traditions, had compelled the Umayyads to adopt a similar conception of universal power, so that a usurper from Syria could launch an attack on the Emperor in Constantinople. The capital Constantinople had first to be captured before the Caliph could aspire to rule the world (*oikoumene*) as Basileus.

The re-orientation of the Arab Empire under the Abbasids.
The breakthrough of the Iranian heritage

The great break in this development came about when the Abbasids supplanted the Umayyads as rulers of the Arab Empire. They overturned the Umayyads in the middle of the eighth century, and they too came from a tribe in Mecca belonging to the kin of Quraysh. In Mecca they enjoyed the very lucrative privilege of making the water from the holy spring of Zamzam drinkable by the addition of fruit juice and aromatic essences and selling this doctored water to pilgrims. Their political horizon was limited to the precincts of the city of Mecca. It was only when they came into contact with the Barmakids who originated in Central Asia that they were introduced to the conception of world power.

The Barmakids came from Balkh in North-East Afghanistan. They were hereditary priests in the great Buddhist religious centre there, in the Nawa Bahar (the New Monastery). The family later moved to Merv and adopted the religion of Ahura Mazda.

Then after the Arab conquest they were converted to Islam. The Barmakids came from territory which before the Arab conquest had belonged to the South-West Turkic khanate which included both the Tarim basin and North-East Afghanistan. There in Balkh, or in the more easterly Qunduz, was the residence of the Turkic khan. The Buddhist sanctuary in Balkh used to be visited by pilgrims coming from both the Tarim basin and North China. They brought the priests ample information about the powers then predominant in Central Asia, China under the Tang dynasty, the great Tibetan kingdom, and the federation of tribes being formed under the leadership of the Turkic Kök. The Central Asian policy of Harun al-Rashid, who allied in 798 with the Tangs in China against the great Tibetan kingdom under Mu-ne btsan-po, would have been inconceivable without the political vision of the Barmakids. The struggle with the Tibetans in Turkestan was extended to Sogdiana under the successors of Caliph Mamun —and indeed Tibetan troops even got as far as besieging Samarkand—but the conflict was then settled by a Tibeto-Arab agreement. In this war the great Arab Empire had secured for itself the Kabul valley and thus the way to India was open. The Barmakids initiated the Abbasid foundation of Baghdad, which was begun in 767 according to the calculations of astrologers. With the Barmakids, scholars from West Turkestan came to Irak.

Since the middle of the fourth century West Turkestan had ceased to be under the control of the Persian Empire. It had finally come under the nominal suzerainty of the North-West Turkic khans which meant that it was really under the Chinese Empire of the Tangs. Chinese and Indian influence were about equally divided in this region. Paper, a Chinese invention, was being used in Sogdiana and was also made there. Chinese porcelain was also found there. Copper minted coins of the princes of the Sogdian cities copied the small Chinese coins with square holes in the centre. But in Sogdiana the works of Indian scholars could also be read. Indian numerals were introduced in the ninth century by the mathematician al-Khwarizmi of Khwarizm south of the Aral sea. (These were adopted by the Arabs and later by the West where they were known as Arabic numerals.) Linear and quadratic equations and the introduction of a new system of calculation, logarithms, were also owed to al-Khwarizmi. West Turkestan, the point of entry of both Chinese and Indian culture, was also the centre of the new Islamic art. The religion of Islam forbad any representation of the human figure, but artistic inspiration coming from China and India had no difficulty in adapting itself to this and in concentrating on ornamental design. There also seems to have been painting on lustre and under glass, influenced by highly developed Chinese ceramics. Thus in place of the gold and silver vessels, banned from the tables of the rich by the fanatics of the faith of Islam, was substituted faience ware with lustre painting, which in its splendour could rival the fabulous Byzantine enamel work (émail cloisonné). This faience art, together with the techniques borrowed from Chinese ceramics, found its way into Byzantium. Thus faience icons were made, and here the enamel was used over a much greater area of the surface. Finds at Patleina (in Bulgaria) and in Istanbul show that this Byzantine lustre painting had reached the peak of its development by the beginning of the tenth century.

It was, however, not only the Barmakids who had stepped into the shoes of the Syrian Christian advisors of the Umayyads and had imbued the Abbasids with their views on political power. As well as the Barmakids from Central Asia, there was another, and no less important, formative influence in the Arab political outlook, and this came from the Nestorians. In particular, it was they who were responsible for directing Arab expansion towards Asia Minor.

Unlike the West Syrian monophysites who had been in the Roman Empire before the Islamic conquest and who then entered Arab service, the Nestorians had been under Persian domination for more than two hundred years. Thanks to the Persian kings they enjoyed freedom of worship and an uninterrupted religious development which had led to the growth of a native Nestorian church in Persia. Thus they regarded Arab policy from the Persian-Sassanid point of view and this meant that the attack on East Rome was now launched by way of Asia Minor. Harun al-Rashid, the same Caliph who had attacked the Tibetan kingdom in alliance with China, now succeeded in breaking into Asia Minor. In 798 the Byzantines were decisively defeated near Dorylaion by Harun al-Rashid's troops; and were forced to make peace and pay tribute.

While the Barmakids held office as viziers of the Caliphs, the Nestorians as the Caliphs' personal physicians were also able to influence the ruler's policy. It was above all the heads of the famous medical school of Gundi-Shapur who played a leading role as physicians of the Caliph's court. Gundi-Shapur was founded by Shapur I (241–272) in the neighbourhood of Susa and was almost entirely occupied by specialists, scholars, doctors, technicians, who had been compelled to live here. The city had a Nestorian bishop and could only be governed by a Persian official who was of the Christian Nestorian persuasion. In the proclamation drawn up for Gundi-Shapur and other Roman specialist foundations, the Greek language and Greek writing were used. Here in Gundi-Shapur and other settlements for the deported Roman experts and forcibly removed scholars the complete Ptolemy and Euclid were still read and commented upon. It was in these circles that the first Arabic translations of the learned works of Greek late antiquity were made, works which at that time had mostly disappeared in the Roman Empire or were known there only from excerpts or summaries. The influence of the deported scholars and specialists lasted up to the beginning of the second millennium. The Persian astronomer Abu Wafa (940–998) even had such a perfect knowledge of Greek that he could translate Greek mathematicians. But generally speaking the influence of late antiquity was not transmitted by translation from Greek into Arabic, but came by way of Syriac. In the middle of the ninth century Greek words were still being translated into Syriac and were then translated later on from Syriac into Arabic. It was in this way that the works of Hellenistic doctors and mathematicians reached the Arab world.

North Africa, a wedge between Byzantium and the West

The removal of the centre of the Arab Empire from Damascus to Baghdad meant that North Africa was now on the periphery of the Empire. Thus it was possible to build up in North Africa an Islamic political system which was independent of Baghdad. The Caliph Harun al-Rashid recognized the existence of this development taking place in North Africa when he conferred the dignity of emir on Ibrahim ibn Aghlab, the governor of this territory. This was the same Harun al-Rashid who had fought on one frontier against the Tibetans and the Chinese and on the other against the Byzantines in Asia Minor. Thus a process began in the Arab world which can be paralleled in Byzantium. Here in Islam interests in the eastern parts of the Empire were also considered more important and given pride of place over those in the West. Here too events brought about a division of the Empire, though this was indeed concealed by the nominal suzerainty of the Caliph in Baghdad over the emir in North Africa.

This new policy also determined relations with the West. There were not only embassies from the Arab Caliph, but North Africa sent its own diplomats to the court of the Frankish kings. These were the ambassadors of the first emir who resided in Qairawan in present-day Tunisia. In 797 they presented an elephant, the gift to the emir, to Charles the Great. The North African emir and the forces at his disposal were in the same strategic position *vis-à-vis* Italy and the Frankish Empire as Carthage had been at the beginning of the first Punic war against Rome. Any attack from North Africa had first to strike at Sicily and South Italy. Behind any plans for attacking Italy lay not only an inherited strategy but the religious fanaticism of the Berbers. As *circumcelliones* these Berbers had fought bitterly against the Roman landed magnates and now under Islam they fought equally fiercely for the green banner of the Prophet. Under their influence Islam had built up a religious theocracy in North Africa which meant that the emir was closely bound by the views of the religious leaders of Islam. The direction of Arab policy in North Africa emanated from the council room of the cadi in Qairawan. It was he who proclaimed to the faithful the *jihad*, the holy war against the non-Muslim coasts of the Mediterranean. This theocratic organization threw into strong relief the position of Islam in contrast to that of the non-Muslim peoples. The government of North Africa was in the hands of Arabs and of the Berbers who had been converted to Islam. The great Roman estate-owners who had long been settled here were expropriated and eked out a livelihood in dependent positions. The same was true of the descendants of those Greek-speaking Byzantine officials who remained true to the Christian faith. Both these sections of the populace succeeded in surviving for several centuries in Africa before they renounced their faith and their language and became merged into the Arab civilization of North Africa. The position of these non-Muslim groups, of which the Jews were one, was far worse here than in any other part of the Arab Empire.

The holy war had determined the growth and siting of the North African towns. The greater part of the old cities had been destroyed in the bitter struggle between the Berbers and the Byzantines. The new urban foundations grew up in the shadow of military bases, as indeed also happened in the Byzantine Empire and later on in the West. The original nucleus of the new urban settlements in North Africa, the *ribats*, were the fortresses founded by the Arab conquerors to secure their lines of communication with Spain. Both in layout and in function these *ribats* resembled the fortresses of the orders of chivalry in the later middle ages, only instead of a church and altar within their walls there would be a prayer hall and mihrab. And the city organizations which grew up there were also in keeping with the religious character of the *ribat*. The gilds and trades which developed there took the form of religious confraternities.

The enigma of Byzantine self-assertion

The victory of the 'wonder-weapon'

The Byzantine Empire was even further isolated by the formation of a great military Arab power in North Africa. The break with the West became even more serious. The Arab fleet occupied Sicily, and it devastated the islands of Corsica and Sardinia and indeed even Rome. The Byzantines were powerless to do anything. The western Mediterranean became a new battleground and the Byzantines now had a foothold only in South Italy. It was towards the north and west that Italy now looked, and gone were the days when its fate lay in the hands of Byzantium. The beginning of the Frankish state was at first strengthened by the threat from North Africa.

The European situation at this period was characterized by further Altaic attacks, the result of tribal movements in Central Asia. The Khazars, a tribe who until 670 had lived in the region between Terek and Sulaq in the immediate neighbourhood of the pass of Derbent on the west coast of the Caspian Sea, now moved to the north-west and broke into the country north of Kuban between the Don and the Volga. The Khazar migration was due both to Arab penetration into Azerbaijan and to the Altaic tribes who fled westwards from North-East Afghanistan before the Tibetans, and it led to the break-up of the Bulgar kingdom which had existed in Kuban since the second half of the fifth century. Some of the Bulgars left the region round the Kuban mouth and went westwards towards the Roman Empire and crossed the lower Danube to settle to begin with in what is present-day Dobruja.

In the Balkan peninsula, once the Emperor Heraclius had carried out the transference of the Roman army from Europe to Asia Minor, the way was clear for the widespread penetration of the Slavs. This resulted in the settlement of the Croats and Serbs, and of the Slav tribes in Macedonia and Greece. The Roman peasant population in the countryside either fled or took refuge in the mountains, living the life of nomad shepherds.

The retreat of the Roman army from the Balkan peninsula at first resulted in the formation of an Avar hegemony. From their strongholds in the Hungarian plain the Avars ravaged not only the Balkans but North Italy and Central Europe. The Bulgar invasion of the territory south of the Danube once again overturned the balance of power established between Byzantium and the Slav peoples. In place of the Avars who were relatively distant in the Hungarian plain—at least in Byzantine eyes—there now appeared the Bulgars. Their presence in the Dobruja and later in present-day East Bulgaria was a direct threat to Constantinople. It was separated from the Bulgarian horsemen by only a few days' journey. Thus the military situation of the Byzantine Empire in Europe had worsened. The capital Constantinople now had to suffer almost daily attacks by the Bulgars. At the same time in the east the Byzantines had to face the Muslim offensive of the Abbasids. The battle of Dorylaion against the Arab spearheads in Asia Minor resulted in a defeat. In this struggle the Byzantine Empire, unlike the Roman Empire, could not rely on any ally to attack the Islamic Caliphate in the rear. The only allies of the Byzantines in this contest against the Arabs were the Khazars. Their attacks against the Arab Empire came from Derbent over the Caucasian passes and penetrated deep into North-West Persia. Thus the Arab victory over the Byzantines at Dorylaion in 798 was followed by a Khazar attack on Armenia in 799. This at once jeopardized the Arab success against the Byzantines.

The political and military situation of the Byzantine Empire was determined by the Arab conquests during the second half of the seventh century and it was only possible to retrieve this by means of a tenacious military defence. It was essential to defeat the blockade which was being attempted by the Altaic and Slav tribes in Europe and by the Arabs both on the Asia Minor land front and by sea. The Arab siege of Constantinople from 674 to 678, which was preceded by the conquest of Chalcedon (Kadikoi), indicated the gravity of the situation. Cyprus had already fallen to the Arabs in 649. Crete and Rhodes were occupied in the same period. The Arab ships built in Syrian and Egyptian dockyards were superior to the Byzantine navy. In the battle off the Cilician coast, near Mt Phoinikos, a relatively weak Arab unit demolished a fleet led by the Emperor himself, thus demonstrating the technical superiority of the Arab aggressors.

In a situation such as this, the possession of a so-called wonder-weapon, that could alter the course of a battle, introduced a great change of events. This weapon was the Greek fire, the manufacture of which was then a secret in Greek hands. It was a chemical substance composed of petroleum, sulphur, saltpetre and unburnt quicklime. With the help of a copper siphon it could be hurled against the enemy if they were fairly near. This mixture possessed the property of burning in water and could therefore not be extinguished by this means. The quantity of smoke and the stench given off by this explosive proved terrifying to the enemy troops against whom it was used. The Umayyad court was not at first aware of the significance of this discovery which was made by the Syrian engineer Callimachus of Baalbek. But the head of the Roman army sitting in Attaleia was more far-sighted and he helped the inventor to escape from the Umayyad Empire to Constantinople. Here the new invention was quickly put into effect. The new weapon was carried in a fairly light type of boat called *karabos* after the light boats used in Cyprus. When the squadron of heavy Arab dromons blockaded the narrow straits during the great siege of Constantinople in 674–678, the light Byzantine boats using Greek fire forced the Arab fleet to retreat.

Greek fire introduced a revolution in the field of naval warfare. It was not long before the Arabs obtained the new secret weapon's composition and then used it against the Byzantines. This meant that defensive counter measures had to be taken on the Byzantine side. In these circumstances small boats were no longer considered suitable for hurling the fire against the enemy whose ships were now armoured. Lead plates were fastened to the bottom and sides down to the water line. The dromons themselves now carried the weapon and were armed with heavy siphons and were thus able to hurl the fire against their opponents. They also carried a number of small siphons for use in nearer combat. The complement of this kind of ship was about 200 men. Of these 100 were rowers, usually arranged in two banks of 25 each side. Then there were the sails to be looked after and the necessary nautical personnel, so that the actual fighting force of a heavy ship, the dromon, hardly totalled more than 70 men. As well as the equipment with siphons for hurling Greek fire at the enemy, the ship always had battering rams. The dromon as a man-of-war was in use only for a limited period, and later in the ninth century it was the structure of the Northmen's ships which exercised a particularly strong influence on Byzantine ship-building.

The new element in the situation as it now developed was the much more important role which naval warfare began to play in military conflicts. The Byzantine Empire had to maintain several fleets always ready for action. The Roman Empire in the East had relied mainly on a strong Danube fleet. But it was now necessary to have four fleets: one in Constantinople which, like the guards, was under direct imperial control; a second constituting the naval theme of the Carabisiani on the south-west coast of Asia Minor; a third in Sicily; and a fourth covering the area between Sardinia and the Balearics. This naval warfare needed much more expensive equipment than land warfare. The subsequent increase in defence expenditure intensified the element of control in the Byzantine economy. For the need to equip the fleets meant in the long run the earmarking of enormous masses of material and the supervision of a whole range of industries. Thus naval warfare indirectly exercised a not inconsiderable influence on the intensification of the measure of control in the Byzantine planned economy.

The rise of the Greek element. Byzantium in process of becoming a Greek state

The Arabs in North Africa forced on Byzantium an epoch-making decision. They realized that expansion into the interior of North Africa would be checked by the desert and Sicily therefore became the goal of their offensive. Thus the weight of the North African military attack was directed against Sicily and Italy. Asia Minor, thanks to the introduction of the theme system, was gradually becoming able to defend itself against the Arab attacks. Imperial policy therefore saw itself faced with the need for taking a decision: it could either launch its full strength against the Arab offensive in Sicily or it could turn to the reconquest of the lost provinces in the Balkan peninsula. With the decision to turn to the Balkans and fight against the Bulgars then penetrating the countryside there, yet another step was taken towards separating the Byzantine state from the West. For the distribution of military strength whereby the struggle in Italy had to be conducted with fewer forces than in the Balkans was interpreted in Italy as a step hostile to the West. Hence the Italian maritime cities, Venice, Pisa, Gaeta and Amalfi, were alienated from the Byzantine Empire. From the point of view of Constantinople this decision meant the renunciation of Italy as a centre of a new western policy having as its aim the restoration of the old *imperium romanum*.

In the Balkans it was a question of broadening the European bridgehead of the Byzantine Empire, of recovering the Greek territory lost through the Slav invasions in the seventh century. And so began the reconquest of the Greek motherland overrun by the Slavs, territory which constituted the greater part of present-day Greece. In the Byzantine Empire a policy was carried out very like that of the German colonization on its eastern frontier in Central Europe two centuries later. Here, as there, it was a question of winning back the land of the native peoples which had fallen into the hands of the Slav invaders. But the method of this *reconquista* in Greece differed from that used in Central Europe. In the Byzantine Empire the Church was the bearer of a spiritual mission rather than a colonizer, and yet the Byzantine episcopal sees Lacedaemon and Monemvasia had a significance for the reconquest of the Peloponnese similar to those of Magdeburg and Salzburg in East Germany. But the task of colonization in Greece was undertaken by the forces of the themes. The development of new themes in Europe pointed to the progress made in the Byzantine reconquest of Greek soil occupied by the Slavs in the seventh century. Whereas in Central Europe archbishoprics and bishoprics, margravates and counties, penetrated even deeper into Slav-occupied territory, so in Greece this was achieved by the themes. The Byzantine reconquest began with the erection of military strongholds, in the form of forts where soldiers and their families could settle. Thus the soldiers were the backbone of the Byzantine colonization. Byzantine military forces were indeed far from being an ethnic unity; they included many different races, and Slavs, Armenians, Caucasians, Syrians, Kurds, all served under the imperial standard. Nevertheless, the character of the army regiments was unquestionably Greek. By the second generation these soldiers no longer spoke their own language but only Greek. This process was favoured by a clever posting of newly enlisted soldiers to garrisons far from their native land. This was part of a deliberate imperial policy which aimed at integrating individual races into the single unity of the Empire. In this respect the Byzantine army performed the same function as the big industrial centres in the great states of our day, where often within two generations the immigrant has forgotten his racial origin and has become assimilated into Russian or American civilization. The Graeco-Byzantine Church also favoured this integration. And this poses the problem of the new Graeco-Byzantine civilization which emerged out of the collapse following the Arab attacks.

The monastic impulse in Byzantine civilization

The leaders of the Byzantine monastic movement
in Constantinople and Palestine

The monastic movement had rooted out everything secular which in late antiquity still had strong links with paganism and it was this monasticism which was a formative influence on the new Byzantine civilization. The followers of the monastic movement came from Syria or from Egypt. It is hardly surprising that these men from Syria and Egypt took the lead in spiritual matters, even in Constantinople. But there were others as well, for some had not chosen to emigrate to the Byzantine Empire. In particular, some Syrian and Egyptian intellectuals had not only stayed in the offices of Antioch and Alexandria but had also remained behind in the monasteries of Jerusalem and Mt Sinai. Though they were under Arab rule these monks also influenced the monastic movement.

This is particularly true in the field of theology. The outstanding theologians of the Byzantine period, John of Damascus and Anastasius of Sinai, lived and worked under Arab rule. Here development proceeded on lines laid down in Greek late antiquity. This was in contrast to the Byzantine Empire where decisive changes had been introduced into vast areas of economic and cultural life by the organization of the themes and the new planning of urban economy. Under the Arab domination the East Roman civil servants continued to work for the government. The Byzantine theologian, John of Damascus, belonged to the well-known family of Mansur and under the first Umayyad Caliph Muawiya the financial administration of the Caliph had been controlled by Sarjun ibn Mansur. These Christians, formerly in the service of the East Roman exchequer, carried through vital financial reforms for the Caliphs. As the East Romans had done in the case of the great imperial army, they divided up the Arab tribes into separate katasters which registered all members of each particular tribe. At the beginning of the eighth century the Umayyad Caliph ordered that the katasters, which up to now had been in the Greek language, should in future be in Arabic. And so a firm foundation was laid for the central government's control over the tribes. They also had the idea of departing from Byzantine military precedent which divided the land among the soldiers and settled them on it as military farmers. But they grouped them together in strongholds which were set up in districts which could supply their economic needs. Thus military establishments were placed in Kufa, Basra and Cairo (al-Fustat) because the troops garrisoned in these places could easily be provisioned from the fertile and highly developed countryside.

This intellectual circle, whose members carried out major administrative tasks for the Caliphs in Damascus, provided some of the leaders of the monastic movement. Thus John of Damascus started by being vizier of the Umayyad Caliph before he exchanged the minister's office for the monk's cell and laid down the theoretical foundation for the orthodoxy supported by the monastic movement. But another group belonged to the Byzantine governing class. These intellectuals exercised decisive influence on imperial administration as ministers of the Emperor. Such was Maximus, the offspring of a distinguished family in Constantinople, though his spiritual home was indeed Syria from which the monastic movement received considerable stimulus. Maximus was the secretary to the advisory council of the Emperor Heraclius.

So it came about that, though separated by a great gulf, the close adviser of the Byzantine Emperor and the first minister of the Umayyad Caliph found themselves successively at the head of a movement which had indeed been begun by very simple folk untouched by any theological training.

The great spiritual turning point which introduced the new age and gave it its distinctive characteristics was the struggle over the veneration of icons. The veneration of icons grew up in the circle of those Egyptian and Syrian monks who had been a formative influence in the development of the iconography and style of the oldest icons. The iconoclast controversy was the struggle between the iconophiles and the so-called iconoclasts who turned against the cult of venerating the holy icons in churches. The position of the West in this matter was determined by the pronouncements of Gregory the Great. Gregory regarded icons in the house of God as the Bible of the illiterate but not as objects of veneration.

It was different in the East. John of Damascus, as the spiritual leader of the monastic movement, had lifted on to a higher spiritual level, and gave theological support to the relationship between the holy icon and the worshipper, which formed the popular religion in Syria and Egypt and which taught that the grace and strength of the represented figure passed over to the worshipper. He used the formula 'I see the human form of God and my soul is saved'. What did this mean? John declared that the Godhead could not indeed be represented in a picture because it was invisible and incomprehensible. But in so far as the Son of God had become Incarnate, man could and must represent him in his human form. For such representations confirmed the perfection and reality of his manhood. This is salvation in the flesh, ἡ ἔνσαρκος οἰκονομία. Here one can trace the connection between the perceptive spiritual views of John of Damascus and the goal of the monastic movement which found the redemption of the soul in the corporeal vision of Christ.

The iconoclast controversy was not the first phase in the great religious clashes of the monastic movement with the older Christian conceptions. It had been preceded by the struggle over the human and divine natures of Christ. Heraclius, in view of the threatening disintegration of the Empire before the Persian onslaught, tried to end this dispute by producing a new and final formula of compromise which was supposed to restore unity to the Church and prosperity to the Empire. The new formula was worked out in 619 by theologians in Lower Egypt, which province was in fact still under Persian occupation. It maintained that Christ had two natures but only one will and one energy. This was formulated by the Egyptian bishops and was accepted by the Patriarch Sergius, a close adviser of the Emperor. It was contested by the monophysite bishops of Arsinoë on the Nile and of Pharan in the neighbourhood of the Sinai peninsula. The Akephaloi, the monophysite secessionists in Cyprus, were won over, as well as the monophysite Patriarch of Antioch. The monophysite Church of the Armenians also agreed to the compromise formula in 633. Thanks to this formula the Christian Church seemed to show signs of unity, but the orthodox reaction then set in. Its leader was Patriarch Sophronius of Jerusalem, backed by the important monasteries of Palestine, headed by the Lavra (monastery) of St Sabas. In view of the difficult situation caused both by Sophronius' opposition and by the Arab attacks which were then beginning, in 638 the compromise formula was altered in an attempt to win over opponents. The final act in this effort to restore once more the unity of Christian belief within the Empire came with the Council of Constantinople in 680–81. Even so, the formula worked out here, namely that Christ had two wills and energies existing side by side without mingling, could not prevent the split between the different Christian confessions in the East.

In this struggle over ecclesiastical agreement in matters of doctrinal teaching, Maximus showed his qualities of leadership. He realized that any attempt to meet the monophysites would only introduce still deeper rifts and so he attached himself to the extreme right wing which was the party favoured by the monastic movement. For this movement had two distinguishing features: asceticism and mysticism. The ascetic element required sexual abstention, which was not taken for granted in the eastern Church where lower clergy (including priests) were allowed to marry. The great monasteries were in Syria and Palestine and on the Sinai peninsula. Here the ascetic life was pursued. From the end of the sixth century onwards the Syrian monasteries had close connections with the West. Benedict of Nursia's ascetic programme, his *Rule*, was known in the Syrian houses in the same century. The *Pastoral Rule* which Pope Gregory the Great wrote was translated into Greek by Patriarch Anastasios II of Antioch (599–609) in Gregory's own lifetime. The Pope's *Dialogues*, translated into Greek at the beginning of the eighth century, was one of the most frequently read works of edification in Byzantine monastic circles. John Climacus, the abbot of the monastery on Sinai, makes mention in his ascetic writings of Pope Gregory, Benedict and Cassian. As extant papal letters show, he had corresponded with this Pope. John Climacus was the leader of the ascetic movement on Sinai. His life was described in most vivid terms by the monk Daniel from the monastery of Raithu on the Red Sea. The leader of the Syrian group was John Stylites (521–596). He and another ascetic leader wrote in Syriac. But much of his work was known to a wider public through the Greek translation by the monks of the monastic house of St Sabas.

This ascetic training did not appeal to Maximus. He was a man who had studied the philosophers in his younger days. He particularly prized the neoplatonic teaching associated with the name of Plotinus. Thus he was less attracted to the ascetic training of the monastic world than to the call of mysticism. It is true that mysticism and asceticism were closely linked in monastic circles. And the mysticism which set foot in monastic cloisters was in the last resort rooted in neoplatonic philosophy which Jamblichus had produced in a characteristically Syrian form. The thought-world of this neoplatonism was impregnated with Christianity. Thus at the end of the fifth century a work which had made use of various neoplatonic writings appeared and was said to be from the pen of Dionysius the Areopagite. (This Dionysius, a member of the Areopagus of Athens, was known to St Paul, according to the *Acts of the Apostles*. Later on he was said to have become the first bishop of the city and to have suffered a martyr's death.) This Christian neoplatonic work played an important role in Syria. At the beginning of the seventh century there was a whole series of Nestorian mystics, and writings from their circle have survived in Syriac. Maximus got to know of these mystical conceptions which were circulating in Syria among Nestorians, monophysites and Orthodox. And this was how he came to write his commentary on the work of Dionysius the Areopagite. This influenced Byzantine liturgy and mysticism for nearly half a millennium. It was through Maximus that the Areopagite's writings became the common property of the Greek Church. But it also became known in the western Christian Church, where its circulation was made possible by the Latin translation of John the Scot (Eriugena). Western mysticism was no less strongly influenced by this work than was the mysticism of the Byzantines.

*The iconophile and iconoclast movements as the dies which
stamped their imprint on the new Byzantine world*

The compromise of the Council of Chalcedon in 451 had laid down that a distinction
was to be made between the divine and human natures of Christ, but this was not able
to offer any solution to the controversy over the two natures of Christ which came
to the fore both in the monothelete struggle and in the dispute over the veneration of
icons. This last dispute also had a major share of responsibility for the break between
Byzantine and western Christendom.

The Byzantine Emperor, like the Umayyad Caliph, had indeed begun by under-
estimating the strength of the extremist iconoclasts. This movement was given support
by certain sections of the populace. Behind the iconophiles stood the monks. The army
was for the most part iconoclast, particularly those soldiers who came from the eastern
frontiers and from eastern Syria. The home of the iconoclast Emperor Leo III was at
Germanicea in eastern Syria. There was a distinctly hostile attitude towards icons in
Syria at this time. This was also clearly noticeable in Islam. And so there was a break
with the tradition of portraying the human form which had been tolerated by the
Umayyads. Representation of the Umayyad Caliphs in the medium of reliefs or wall
paintings, or on coins, vanished at one fell swoop. This movement for religious reform
had then brought about the downfall of the Umayyads in the mid-eighth century and
had assisted the Abbasid bid for control. It was not for nothing that Leo III's enemies
called him the friend of Arab culture and religion (*saracenophron*). By 723 the Caliph
Yezid under pressure from the reformers had ordered the removal of pictures from
the sacred and secular buildings of Islam, as well as from all Christian churches. Seven
years later the Greek Emperor did likewise. A council meeting (*silentium*), attended by
the highest secular and ecclesiastical office holders, was held in Constantinople in the
imperial palace. Here an edict was issued forbidding icons. The Patriarch, who opposed
this, was forced to resign. The patriarchal school (the *oikumenikon didaskaleion*), naturally
favourably disposed towards icons, was closed. The religious implications of the ban
against icons only came into question later on. Running counter to the decisions of
earlier synods, the iconoclasts justified the ban on icons by accusing their opponents of
monophysitism. It was said of the iconophiles that, like the monophysites, they merged
the divine and human natures of Christ since they represented both together. And the
supporters of icons were also accused of the Nestorian heresy, since, like the Nestorians,
they stressed the human nature of Christ. The new laws forbad any religious representation. In the place of pictures of Christ and the saints there appeared scenes of war and
hunting, of chariot races and theatrical performances. And landscape scenes again came
into general usage.

The majority of the iconoclasts were to be found among the troops of Asia Minor.
Phrygia was the centre of the movement. The presence of soldiers from the East who
had been settled in this region dominated the religious outlook of the whole province.
The ecclesiastical leaders of the opposition to the veneration of icons, Thomas of
Claudiopolis and Constantine of Nacolea, were bishops in a countryside which had
been apportioned out to troops coming from the East. In the capital the pressure of the
army also assured victory to the iconoclasts here. Among the iconophiles there were
many victims. Military courts worked swiftly. The condemned were the supporters
of the monastic movement which had remained loyal to the veneration of icons. They
had no choice and were condemned to death or exile. The great leader of the iconophiles, Abbot Stephen of Mt Auxentius, was lynched by the mob in Constantinople.

The governors of certain themes boasted that they had closed all monasteries in their provinces. The iconoclast decrees gradually took on an anti-monastic flavour. In these circumstances most of the iconophile religious chose to emigrate. They turned towards those parts of the Empire which did not submit to the imperial policy and where even under military duress they refused to carry out the laws against the iconophiles. Among such areas were orthodox Georgia, the Byzantine and Gothic parts of Crimea, the Latin-speaking region on the lower Danube, the territory round the present-day capital of Sofia and the greater part of Italy.

The imperial government failed in its attempt to use force to compel the West to recognize the ban on icons. For the Byzantine army which had been settled in Italy since the end of the sixth century resisted the imperial commands and actively opposed those loyal troops who tried to enforce the imperial orders. The attempt to take Ravenna with the help of the Byzantine fleet came to grief in the face of attacks from the rapidly assembled bands of iconophile Byzantine soldiers in Italy. There was also the fact that by the mid-seventh century the Lombards had given up their Arian beliefs and they supported the papacy and the rampaging Byzantine army. When the Emperor succeeded in crushing the opposition of the Byzantino-Italian troops and gained control over some parts of the Italian peninsula, the rebellious troops handed over to the Lombards the strongholds which they had previously garrisoned. Thus almost all the Byzantine fortifications in the Apennines came under Lombard control. The Lombard army took up the fight against the Byzantines and in 751 captured Ravenna. It looked as though Italy would become a Lombard kingdom and it was in these circumstances that there came about the epoch-making alliance between the Pope in Rome and the Frankish ruler.

Thus the influence of the iconoclast controversy was particularly noticeable on the periphery of the Empire. It resulted in the separation of East and West, of the Byzantine Empire and the western lands, and was eventually followed by the formation of a separate western Empire. And side by side with this was the fact that the periphery exercised a decisive influence over the future development of Byzantine culture. This was particularly true of the provinces of Palestine and Syria, now under Arab control. These regions now influenced the trends of the new development even more than in Justinian's day. This is true of theology as well as pictorial representation in the religious field. The mosaics of the monastery of Mt Sinai, like the icons and the illuminated manuscripts of the Palestinian monasteries, provided the models for the religious art which dominated Byzantine culture after the end of the iconoclast controversy.

The Abbot Theodore of Studius (758 to 826) was one of the leading personalities of this new Byzantine culture. He was the Abbot of the famous monastery of Studius in Constantinople. The ruins of its basilica still survive. As a result of Theodore's work the house of Studius achieved a position in the Byzantine monastic world like that of Monte Cassino in western monasticism. The monastic rule, which he introduced and tried out, had a far-reaching influence in establishing these principles of cenobitic life in other houses. And in addition to this Theodore exercised very considerable influence over cultural developments. His *scriptorium*, like that of Monte Cassino, developed its own script which provided a model for other *scriptoria*. Since the beginning of the ninth century the Greek minuscule style of writing had set its stamp on Greek handwriting and this was closely connected with the monastery of Studius. And it should be remembered that the generation of monks who had influenced not only monastic life but the whole cultural life of the capital at the beginning of the eighth century had indeed been deeply aware of the traditions of the monastic immigrants from Syria.

The Arab attacks in Palestine and Syria had driven these to Constantinople where they had introduced the rules of the original houses from which they had fled, thus influencing the cenobitic life of the capital.

For these reasons there was a distinct break with the culture of late antiquity. Secular art was now banished to textiles, the old pagan motifs survived only on ivories. In literature, the history of the Empire vanished and its place was taken by world chronicles written by monks. Learning took a retrograde step. Astronomy became astrology; chemistry became alchemy. Above all, a certain superficiality became noticeable. The whole cultural life was affected by that monastic repudiation of beauty and art which had originally been the characteristic of a group of Christian extremists antagonistic to the society of late antiquity. Beneath the uniformity of literary activity a certain narrowness of outlook is clearly discernible.

History was written in the form of the world chronicle. As in the case of monastic rules, the antecedents for this are found in Syria. The work of John Malalas provided one such model. Malalas wrote in the first half of the sixth century. Another historian, John of Antioch, a contemporary of the Emperor Heraclius, belonged to these Syrian monastic circles, as also did the author of the *Easter Chronicle* (*Chronicon Paschale*), a man closely connected with the Patriarch Sergius. All three world chronicles were written by the religious for the religious. In the days of Theodore of Studius there was a return once more to this type of historical writing which had owed much to Syrian influence. In the early ninth century, George, the patriarchal *syncellus* (an official corresponding to the coadjutor of a western bishop) collected material for a world chronicle. When he died in 810 his chronicle covered the creation of the world to the year A.D. 284, that is, to the beginning of Diocletian's reign.

His friend Theophanes undertook the continuation. Like George, Theophanes was a bitter opponent of the iconoclast policy of the Emperor Leo V and an ascetic and monk, a fighter for the faith. But he was no historian. As with other Byzantine chroniclers coming from similar circles, with him one misses the exact evaluation of the truth, the concern for an individual view of history. The chroniclers collected their material from the most varied authors, then rearranged it and dished it up with crude theological explanations. This was not historical writing as we understand it, but the production of works for Christian edification. A certain spiritual inertia manifests itself in these monastic world chronicles, and this is also found in the *catenae*, or series of excerpts from patristic literature, which provide almost the only form of theological commentary on the Bible during this period. It seemed as though the sword of Greek intellectual activity, which Procopius had wielded to such good effect, had now become blunted in monastic hands. And yet these chronicles, such as the work of Theophanes, or the somewhat younger George the Monk, are notable for the way in which they hit the mark as far as the Greek populace were concerned. They changed the Greek language in that they effected a synthesis between formal Attic style (which was still being used by Procopius and Theophylact) and the colloquial language of the people in their daily life. This assured extensive influence throughout a broad section of society. They were translated into Latin, Church Slavonic and Georgian. They were the mirror through which Byzantines viewed their history. But they also transmitted the story of Byzantine history to other peoples—Bulgars, Serbs, Russians, Georgians and Latins. This proved a decisive factor in building up the myth of the Byzantine Emperor and Empire.

The chronicles were not regarded as literary works of art. Their texts were not scrupulously copied as the classics were. On the contrary, with each new version the text of the original faded further into the background. Additions or omissions were made. Thus the chronicle of George the Monk has to be disinterred from a considerable group of individual redactions. In preserving the chronicles there was not the same respect for the work and for the personality of its author as there was in the case of the imperial histories written by Procopius, Agathias and Theophylact where great care was taken to avoid textual inaccuracy.

The leading figures of the monastic movement lacked the academic training which the old universities gave. For the most part they had been to ecclesiastical schools, which had now taken the place of the universities closed in the sixth century. Thus the ecclesiastical patriarchal school in Constantinople played a role in the monastic world similar to that of the universities of Athens, Alexandria and Beirut in the world of late antiquity.

The work of George, called 'the Syncellus' from his ecclesiastical office, reveals the intellectual equipment of the monastic historian. The decisive factor in determining the structure and intellectual orientation of his work was the Christian philosophy of history put forward in the commentary on Daniel's *Apocalypse*. The theory of the three empires determined the presentation of the historical material. It therefore followed that the development of the Assyrian and Babylonian Empire down to the Roman *imperium*, amply documented and presented with a Christian slant, was regarded as the preparation for the final consummation of the Messianic kingdom. This explains why George undertook a detailed study of the sources for his world chronicle. He made a careful examination of Egyptian and Babylonian histories in order to present an interpretation of historical development which accorded with Daniel's *Apocalypse* and its commentators. And this is why Byzantine world chronicles contain digressions from Alexandrian historians and chroniclers of the fifth century, Hellenistic accounts of Egyptian dynasties, such as the work of Manetho, and various writings on the Babylonian kings. But the monastic chroniclers did not confine themselves to scholarly works which recalled the events of a bygone age for future generations. They deigned to draw on the history contained in Hellenistic romances. Thus John Malalas used Dictys, a romantic story claiming to be the diary of someone who took part in the Trojan war, and George the Syncellus used the romance of Alexander which dates from the first century A.D. The use of these romances side by side with genuine historical sources in order to produce a specifically Christian interpretation of world history, clearly reveals the kind of cultural outlook which was characteristic of leading personalities in the religious world at the beginning of the ninth century.

The continuation of the tradition of late antiquity
in the literary salons of Constantinople

The legacy of the rhetors and sophists exercised a stronger influence than the scholars of the old Alexandrian university. It was not for nothing that the first great theologians of the Eastern Church diligently listened to the lectures of the famous Libanius, a pagan rhetor. In the schools of late antiquity, which survived down to the end of the sixth century, the influence of the rhetors and sophists was paramount. And in the circle of Photius, where men deliberately sought to pick up the threads of antiquity, they did not find their way back to the real classical world, but only got as far as the sophists and rhetors who had dominated the schools of late antiquity. It was the same with Photius himself, for he was completely under the spell of the great Hellenistic rhetors

Dionysius and Hermogenes. Both in style and presentation he was closely linked with these two. Even his so-called *Library* reflected the literary tastes of the rhetors. In his judgments on the works reviewed in his *Library* he showed how he had been influenced by the stylistic teaching of Hermogenes. The actual descriptions of the books were almost invariably nothing more than hastily constructed sketches. The judgments expressed dealt with problems of composition or style. The real content was of secondary interest. Photius thus revealed the inadequacy of his understanding.

It was, however, remarkable that in the ninth century, when the monastic movement was beginning to enjoy its triumph over the iconoclasts, a man such as Photius could come to the fore, and this was indeed characteristic of the new Byzantine culture. It was different in the West, where the Church controlled all branches of cultural life. In Byzantium there were still law schools to be found where laymen taught and commented on Justinian's legal code. There were also private circles where classical books were read as well as the Hellenistic rhetors and sophists. The personality of Photius presupposed nothing less than the existence of a definite literary salon in the capital.

The *Library* of Photius was a work which circulated in a definite literary circle. Photius commented on the books read aloud there. These were generally historians, poets and literary works of a secular character. Ecclesiastical authors were excluded from the readings in this salon.

It was characteristic of this literary world that in addition to reading various works a good deal of copying of old manuscripts was promoted. The famous Patmos manuscript of Plato belongs to this period. It was commissioned by Arethas, a friend and intellectual kindred spirit of Photius. The manuscripts of the tragedians and the anthology of Greek lyric poetry also belong to this age and to the same circles. Photius was to the ninth century what Constantine Porphyrogenitus was to the tenth, and made the same impression as did the personality of Psellus in the eleventh century. All three were the leaders of particular literary circles which had always flourished in Constantinople and which knew how to hold their own even in the face of the monastic movement.

The influence of Christian hermits and pagan sophists on the theological literature of the monastic movement

The monastic movement found its intellectual expression in commentaries on the Bible and the church fathers. But herein is revealed its great weakness. Byzantine theologians never succeeded in getting behind the Greek translation of the Old Testament which they had inherited from antiquity. The Hebrew original was unknown. The *Septuagint,* the Greek translation of the Old Testament, was the original text for these theologians. There was no attempt at textual criticism either here or in the Gospels. Even the canon of the Scriptures was not fixed until Photius' day. Biblical exegesis took the form of *catenae* and commentaries. The *catenae* (links or chains) only strung together the different glosses of the church fathers on a given biblical passage and excluded any expression of individual views. Even in a commentary it is most exceptional to find any independent explanation of the Holy Scriptures. Commentaries were almost always drawn from older works of this kind. In the matter of biblical exegesis the Byzantine theologians were scarcely any better than their western contemporaries. Their strength lay in polemic. This, together with the prevalent weakness in biblical exegesis, was rooted in the early days of the monastic movement. The Egyptian monks practised asceticism but they used the words of Holy Scripture to protect themselves in the face of intellectual controversy. They fought shy of any such thing as doubt. In contrast to this, there were increasing disputes and conflicts which had strong links with the rhetors and sophists, even in the days of the great church fathers, and which clearly revealed their affinity with the practice of the law courts.

This dependence of theological polemic on the language of the rhetors and sophists can be seen in the dictionaries used. The words and expressions of the Attic legal world were collected and made into dictionaries. These were partly produced in the second century A.D. and they provided the basis of the lexicons which have survived from Photius' day. The formal literary language of that time was drawn from these hand-books, and it was in sharp contrast to everyday language and indeed to the language of the monastic chronicles. One such dictionary has survived under the name of Photius and it heralds a whole series of works of similar character. These reached a high standard, particularly in the so-called *Suda* which belongs to the second half of the tenth century. This *Suda* (= stronghold) was the trusty guide of the Byzantines in matters of grammar, lexicography, history and literary history. The mass of detailed subject articles almost provides an encyclopedia and they have their own peculiar arrangement. This method may seem awkward to us, for individual articles are not arranged alphabetically but under letters with a similar sound. Thus 'a' is not followed by 'ae', because 'ae' is grouped with the similar sounding 'e'.

Polemic was from time to time a brilliantly wielded weapon of the theologian, but its efficacy was by no means confined to serving the needs of the individual. The state made use of the theologian for political ends. In the fourth century days of Gregory of Nazianzus polemic was the weapon which this argumentative church father used to attack the régime of the Emperor Julian. In the sixth century the polemic of the Christian theologians was pressed into the service of the government; Procopius of Gaza, head of the school of rhetors in his city, wielded his polemic against neoplatonic tendencies in the university of Athens, very probably at the imperial request. Though opponents might change, the weapons of polemic remained the same. They were drawn from the arsenal of the Hellenistic rhetors. In the sixth century theological polemic was directed particularly against the neoplatonists and the Christian opponents of orthodoxy, the monophysites and Nestorians. From the ninth century it was charged to attack Armenians, Muslims and Latins, the ecclesiastical and political opponents of Orthodox Byzantium. The Latins—then represented by the Frankish Emperor and the Pope—were the political rivals of the Byzantines in the struggle for control of the Balkan peninsula. This is the meaning of the concern with Latin Christendom as well as the political orientation towards the West, that is, towards the East Frankish Empire. This explains Photius' missionary policy in the Balkans and his reaction to the ecclesiastical and political claims of the West. The Byzantine government also used polemic against Islam. One of its exponents was Nicetas, a contemporary of Photius. He undertook to answer certain *suras* from the Koran by means of Orthodox theological arguments. From his writings it is clear that at this time a knowledge of Arabic was not unusual among scholars in Constantinople. It is worth remembering that treaties with the Arab Caliphs had an Arabic translation. The theologians also directed their polemic towards the Armenian question, a burning point of contention in Byzantine politics on the eastern front. It was hoped to make the Armenians give up their national Church and accept union with the Orthodox Byzantine Christians.

In comparison with Biblical exegesis, Byzantine polemic has real literary significance, but even so with all its brilliance of expression and originality of thought, it remained imprisoned in its age. And with this age it lived and died.

Music and hymns at the time of the monastic movement

Out of the great bulk of theological literature admittedly only the hymns have survived their day and generation. It is true that in content they are polemic and dogmatic, but their presentation allows us to forget the theological limitations of their subject matter. As with the chronicles and *typica* (monastic foundation charters), their beginnings and prototypes are to be found in the Byzantine monasteries in Syria and Palestine. Stimulus was provided by movements outside Christendom, by the Gnostics and the Manichaeans. The initial impetus probably came from the Syriac hymns of the gnostic Bardesanes in the second century A.D. and the liturgical songs of Manes in the third century A.D. which had found their way into certain collections of church hymns. The Christian Church had begun by being inclined to oppose the singing of spiritual songs during the services. This is shown by the decisions of the fourth-century synod of Laodicea on the Lycus on the borders of Phrygia and Caria. But this ruling did not last long and was limited to part of Asia Minor. The East, that is, Syria, Palestine and Egypt, encouraged hymn singing during the liturgy at this time. But it was not until the early sixth century that a revival of spiritual songs began to spread from Syria and to find its way into the Byzantine Church through the monastic movement. By the beginning of the sixth century in Syria there were collections of church songs (antiphons) in Syriac. One of the most widely used compilations of this kind came from the monophysite Patriarch, Severus of Antioch.

It was this circle of Syriac hymn-writers, such as Jacob of Sarugh and Simon the Potter (Quqāya), which produced Romanus, the greatest writer of hymns in the Greek language. He came from Emesa and tradition has it that he was of Jewish origin. He had been a deacon in the church of the Resurrection in Beirut before he came to Constantinople at the beginning of the sixth century. According to tradition he is said to have composed about a thousand *kontakia*. A *kontakion* (little stick) was a form of Greek hymn and was so called because it was written on parchment rolled round a small stick. (The roll continued to be used in the Byzantine middle ages for liturgical writings. This was not derived from the usage of classical antiquity but from the customs of Jewish practice which survived in the Christian world. In Jewish services the liturgical books as well as the Torah were only on rolls.) The kind of poetry which Romanus composed was a hymn in the form of a *kontakion*. This type of hymn reigned supreme over Byzantine church music for nearly a hundred and fifty years. One of the last great hymn-writers was Patriarch Sergius of Constantinople, a contemporary of the Emperor Heraclius, who, like Romanus, came from Syria. Then there was a change and the *kontakion* was succeeded by another kind of hymn, the canon. Andrew of Crete (650–720) was the first to use this particular form of hymn-writing. Like the *kontakion*, the canon also originated in Syria and Palestine. John of Damascus and Cosmas of Jerusalem, both belonging to the monastery of St Sabas, composed their hymns in the form of a canon. Later on in the ninth century the monastery of Studius in Constantinople became the centre of hymn-writing.

Byzantine music and the development of a notation were inseparably linked with these hymns. This notation at first only indicated the rise and fall of the voice (ecphonetic notation) and was known from the eighth century. To begin with, the exact intervals were not indicated. The same sign could stand for an interval of a third or a fourth. It was not until the great cultural changes at the end of the eleventh and beginning of the twelfth centuries that music developed its notation. As in literature and representational art, music returned to late antiquity. In turning away from the simple form of chant (which was like the Gregorian plainsong) there inevitably followed a development of the notation hitherto in use. Signs were invented to indicate intervals. New signs for steps, or intervals of an ascending or descending second (*somata*, bodies), and for leaps, or intervals of the third or fifth (*pneumata*, spirits), were introduced. And signs were added to indicate repetition, tempo, dynamic and rhythmic nuances. This was the only way of replacing a simple recitative by melody and coloratura singing. With the development of coloratura singing it was rare to find one note for a single syllable and usually it would be anything from two to ten notes (neumes). Church music in the twelfth century was reminiscent of the elaborate coloratura of late antiquity which had been denounced first by the church fathers and then by the monastic movement.

Even after the great changes at the beginning of the twelfth century, as far as church services were concerned Byzantine music remained monophonic and had no instrumental accompaniment. Secular music on the other hand had a rich instrumentation. Classical Greek music had the cithara as stringed instrument and the flute (*aulos*) but the Byzantines had the pneumatic organ, a development from Hellenistic techniques, and this was accompanied by the percussion instrument, the cymbal. Secular music found its place in imperial ceremonial. Shows in the Hippodrome, imperial processions and court ceremonial afforded full opportunity for musical performances.

Nothing remains of this secular music. And practically nothing has survived from the secular poetry which was sung. The fragments of this kind which have survived, such as a spring lyric from the repertoire of court ceremonial songs, or satirical verse from the festival of the Brumalia, the Byzantine carnival, are too few to give any idea of the real nature of this secular poetry.

Music and poetry were closely related to the great spiritual and intellectual movements of Byzantium, such as the monastic movement of the sixth century and the humanism of the eleventh and twelfth centuries. They were an integral part of these movements and cannot be considered independently. This is also true of church hymns. The liturgical reform carried out by the monastic movement in the sixth century was decisive for the development of the *kontakion* as also for changes in church architecture. The replacement of the *kontakion* by a new form of hymn, the canon, was closely connected with the significant liturgical changes inaugurated in the ninth century by the monastery of Studius in Constantinople. The final stabilization of the liturgy saw the end of Byzantine hymnography.

In composing hymns, poet and musician were one. The number of syllables and the accentuation determined the nature of the rhythmical verse of the hymns. Syllables were counted without regard to quantity (i.e. long or short). There was no uniformity in length of line, as in the so-called 'political' verse of secular poetry where each line usually had twelve syllables. It was only musical feeling which determined the length of the short lines and their grouping together into longer lines. Sometimes the verses of the hymns proceeded in regular steady measure, sometimes they rushed forward like a stream in spate. The pattern verse, the *hirmus*, determined the metre of the remaining verses of the hymn. Each verse repeated one or two short lines as a refrain which was sung by all those present at the service.

The canon, the second kind of Byzantine church poetry, was distinguished from the *kontakion* by its length. It often had eight or nine different odes (or hymns) each of three or four verses. Each ode had its own pattern verse, or *hirmus*.

Each *kontakion*, and each canon, was a work of art in itself which could easily be destroyed if new verses were interpolated which the poet-musician had not had in mind. Hence the safeguard of the acrostic which was made up of the initial letters of each verse and formed a sentence, sometimes a note on the author, sometimes a pious maxim, sometimes both.

The field of secular literature: epigrams and satirical poetry

Some secular poetry has survived. In the form of the epigram a not inconsiderable amount of secular poetry was able to continue even under the Orthodox régime. The epigram, though limited in length by its very form, preserved some faint glimmerings of the great tradition of secular poetry which was extinguished with the advent of the monastic age. The epigram bears the same relation to this secular poetry which had died out as does the ivory relief in the world of representational art to the great sculpture of late antiquity, which had disappeared when three-dimensional sculpture was no longer tolerated after the victory of monasticism. The epigram affords insight into the intellectual atmosphere of library salons of the kind to which Photius belonged. The populace in general played no part in these epigrams. Their interests were reflected in the many books on oracles or thunder and lightning, which were more in the nature of collections of popular superstitions than literature. Satirical farces which appealed to a wider circle belong to these more popular collections. These did not, however, originate in the Byzantine period but are found in late antiquity and have their spiritual home in sophist circles. One such collection has 264 satirical farces arranged according to their different points of view. There is one group in which the Scholasticus, that is, the learned and clever lawyer, bears the brunt of the jests. This reflects the tense relations between sophist and jurist in the two last centuries of late antiquity when they formed two distinct groups. Then in another group the satire is directed at the citizens of particular cities, the men of Abdera or of Sidon or Cyme. The very names show that this group of satires could not have originated in the Byzantine period. On the other hand, it is in the very nature of satire at any time to produce certain constant types, such as the miser, the swindler and the blockhead. And to this extent characters and situations of the Byzantine period are portrayed. Linguistic evidence in these collections of satires points to the ninth century.

The literature of spiritual entertainment: saints' lives and edifying stories

The monastic movement did not suppress all intellectual activity, particularly in the field of literature. It possessed theological works and church poetry, though these were in a language which was gradually moving further and further from the spoken word. It also had other kinds of literature whose content and language, like those of the world chronicles, had considerable vogue among the common folk. These were the saints' lives and the *acta* of the martyrs which had originally been written to keep green the memory of these holy men and women. But they developed into a kind of folk literature and their influence soon extended far beyond the narrow circle for which they were originally intended. This bridge between monastic circles and the great majority of the faithful in Byzantium was provided by the vast collection of saints' lives in the *Menaia* and *Synaxaria*. It was customary to celebrate the date of a saint's birth or death by a reading from an account of his life. In this way there gradually grew up an extensive collection of material which provided for each day in the year suitable extracts about the saint, or saints, whose festival was being kept. These accounts (*synaxaria*) were read during the service of Orthros and were taken from the appropriate liturgical book for the month (*Menaion*).

Syria and Palestine took the lead in producing this kind of literature. Cyril of Scythopolis in Galilee wrote the first Greek series of lives of holy monks. He had in mind particularly those saints who were connected with the monastery of St Sabas near Jerusalem. John Moschus produced a different kind of literary genre. At the end of the sixth century under the Emperors Tiberius and Maurice he travelled in Palestine, Egypt and the Sinai peninsula. In his work *The Spiritual Meadow* (*leimon*) he presented the fruits of his journey, the experiences, characteristics and sayings of the monks whom he had met or whom he had been told about. In contrast to Cyril, he expressed himself in a popular style and, like the western Pope Gregory the Great in his *Dialogues*, he did not address himself exclusively to monastic circles but to a wider and more popular public. The lives of saints and monks continued to be written in the seventh century. Bishop Leontius of Neapolis in Cyprus, who belonged to the circle of Archbishop John the Merciful of Alexandria, composed a life of Symeon the Fool (*salos*). Symeon was one of those 'fools' (*saloi*) who, despite their name, were not really crazy at all. They were men fully aware of the world around them who deliberately set out to cause offence by their behaviour. This was in protest against the clerics and monks who were regarded as lavishing their spiritual offices on the powerful and the rich at the expense of the despised poor. These 'fools' were surrounded by many of the outcasts of society, the despised and the scorned; they haunted sailors' taverns, prostitutes' houses and markets of ill-repute. The populace held them in superstitious reverence and even the departments of state and the clerics of the Church dare not oppose them when they angrily interrupted ecclesiastical and secular processions with their storming and mocking, as was the case with Nicholas the 'Fool' who threw himself down in front of an old Jew instead of before the miracle-working icon of the Mother of God at a great procession in her honour. Other 'fools' were found in the company of prostitutes and they publicly violated the laws of fasting. The 'fools', like the *santons* in the Muslim world, were a manifestation of popular religious feeling.

In addition to much that is edifying, many saints' lives also abound in details from the lives of ordinary men and women and form a kind of substitute for the non-existent secular literature.

The folk story belongs to the same religious literature which served as a substitute for the missing, or still-born, popular secular literature. There were many translations of these folk stories and in this way they also became part of the common stock of the literature of the West. The oldest folk story came from John of Damascus who as theologian and hymn writer had been a formative influence in the development of Byzantine culture. John of Damascus' activities as finance minister of the Umayyad Caliph had given him opportunities for getting to know the literary work of the East. The Umayyad caliphate included not only North Africa, Egypt, Syria and Palestine, but Persia as well. For John the route to India was not barred, as it was for Byzantines the other side of the Taurus frontier. He was therefore in a position to come across a story circulating in Damascus in an Arabic version which had been translated from the Sanskrit original into middle Persian towards the end of the sixth century. In the leisure of the monastic cell John translated this story into Greek and he also transformed it into a work of Christian edification. It was known as *Barlaam and Joasaph* in John's Greek version but it really originated in the world of Buddhism. John only knew it in an Arabic version circulating at the court of the Umayyad Caliph and not in the Persian translation of which parts have recently turned up in manuscripts from Turfan.

The story tells how a pagan king in India had a son Joasaph distinguished by his beauty and intelligence. He learnt through astrologers that his son would become a Christian and in order to prevent the fulfilment of this prophecy he built a wonderful palace for his son. Here Joasaph lived in gaiety and pleasure, far from the evils of life in surroundings where all strangers were banned, served only by those who were good to look upon. But in spite of all these precautions he did nevertheless one day see a sick man, a blind man, and then another time an old man, and finally a corpse. These made such an impression on him that he experienced a spiritual conversion and after a meeting with a Christian ascetic he turned to Christianity. The king thought to dissuade his son and sent messengers to him, but they too were converted to Christianity. Finally the king himself became a Christian and gave half of his kingdom to his son. But Joasaph went to live in solitude and died a devout hermit. His bones were laid in a magnificent church near by and they later worked great miracles.

It is true that the story is faithful to its Indian prototype—for Joasaph is none other than the Buddha and his father is the king of Kapilavastu—but all the same in his handling of the story John of Damascus produced a real literary masterpiece. It was in the form which John gave it that this story went from the Byzantine world to circulate in the West. The first Latin version is found in the twelfth century. By the thirteenth century there was a German version. Other versions are apparently based on a Syriac translation of the work deriving directly from the middle Persian; the Hebrew and Armenian accounts of the story belong to this family.

The early monastic picture. Miniatures and icons

The influence of the monastic movement provoked the creative spirit of both the literary world and representational art. To begin with, while Byzantine monasticism was gradually gaining momentum, the culture of late antiquity still held its own. It was in the seventh century that the complete breakthrough came. It can be seen as early as 642 in the newly built church of St Demetrius at Thessalonica. On a large mosaic Christ embraces two patrons of the church with a gesture the same as that already seen on a sixth-century icon from Bawit. An almost contemporary silver dish from Cyprus with scenes from the life of David on it, shows just that statuesque portrayal of the human form borrowed from the icon which was later to dominate the decoration of church walls in fresco and mosaic. Similarly icons can be seen today in the monastery on Mt Sinai which can be dated to the late sixth century and which foreshadow the portrayal of the Mother of God to be found in Santa Maria Antiqua in Rome at the end of the seventh and beginning of the eighth centuries. In miniatures, as with icons, Egypt and Syria played a formative role. The practice of illustrating the margin of the pages of a manuscript, as in the Chludov Psalter, was known to Syriac biblical illuminations. It is found as early as 585 in the manuscript of the Gospels written by the monk Rabula in the Mesopotamian monastery of Zagba.

This raises the question of the origins of icons and miniatures and their relation to each other. The earliest extant icons come from the middle of the sixth century; the oldest miniature belongs to the fourth century. Icons, particularly the early encaustic ones, have an obvious relationship to the memorial portraits. These memorial portraits are found in Egyptian tombs where they were placed on the coffin to remind relatives and friends of the physical appearance of the dead person. But the ancestry of the miniature goes back to the manuscripts of the classical writers of antiquity, particularly the comedians. Many of these miniatures are found in ninth- and tenth-century manuscript copies of the Roman comedies of Terence and Plautus and they served to provide stage directions to producers. They provided information as to the stage directions and properties required by the actors in each scene. It was from these pagan prototypes that the illustrations of the Gospels were borrowed. Christians even went so far as to place the portrait of each evangelist in front of his Gospel, just as the portraits of classical playwrights had been put on the edition of their works. There were probably no pictures of the evangelists, especially at the beginning of the third century when Christians, ignoring the command of the Decalogue, were turning to figural representation of Christ and the Apostles, and so pagan prototypes were also used here. Christ was portrayed as a Greek philosopher holding a book or cross, and the evangelists even had the appearance and clothing of the ancient philosophers as portrayed in the manuscripts of classical authors.

Two versions of the illustrations of the Gospels soon gained general recognition, the Alexandrian and the Antiochene. They were even followed during the last great period of creative activity in Byzantine art in the fourteenth century. Thus the iconography of the figures in the mosaic of the journey of the Virgin to Bethlehem in the Chora Church in Constantinople, dating from about 1300, is similar to that of the seventh-century fresco portraying this at Castelseprio. And the illustrations provided for the purpose of giving stage directions in ninth- and tenth-century manuscripts of Terence and Plautus are almost identical reproductions of individual scenes on contemporary phylactery vases and terracottas of the second century B.C. Here a thousand years passes like a flash.

In contrast to the illustrations of the Gospels, where the miniatures very closely followed the two existing schools, to begin with there was no guide when it came to portraying scenes from the saints' lives. Nor does the liturgy show any definite connection of this kind, as had long been the case with the Gospels, Epistles and Old Testament writings. But Byzantine pericopes (i.e. the passages from the Bible read in the services) from the Old Testament which were being used in the eighth century do indeed derive in part from a pre-Christian era. The scroll of the writings of the prophet Isaiah found in Qumran was already divided in the same way as in the later pericopes of the eighth-century Byzantine manuscripts of the Bible. The connection between the Holy Scriptures and the liturgy of divine worship which resulted from this use of pericopes necessarily determined the nature of the illustrations. Each pericope had its own particular picture so that the pericope divisions of the Bible carried with them a predetermined series of illustrations. This is preserved in the two early Christian traditions, the Antiochene and the Alexandrian, which in their oldest form go back to the first half of the third century, the time when pictorial art was introduced into Christian worship. The pericope divisions had an exceedingly strong and conservative influence on these pictures, as is obvious from a comparison of the illustrations of the seventh-century Joshua Roll with the corresponding twelfth-century manuscript of the Octateuch. They show marked similarity down to the minutest details of composition. Even clothing and weapons are reproduced almost exactly as in the original model. The same is found in the tenth-century Paris Psalter (Cod. gr. 139) where garments and military equipment date from the third century. The extent to which the division into pericopes was responsible for preserving these pictures unchanged can be seen by looking at the few extant miniatures of the Itala manuscript, the oldest Latin translation of the Bible. This was a private translation outside ecclesiastical control and it has no division into pericopes. In his pictures the artist's style and composition reflect the directions given by the copyist of the manuscript. This is why these independent illustrations of the

Bible do not turn up again, unlike the pictures linked with the pericopes and their two traditions which survived for more than a thousand years.

Hagiographical literature did not enjoy favourable conditions of this kind. It was subject to strong regional influences which at first proved an obstacle to the development of recognized cycles of pictures for all the saints' lives and the *acta* of the martyrs. An established series of pictures really first began to develop with new work on the liturgy, and these illustrations covered all the saints' lives and martyrs' *acta* now included in the liturgy. The new arrangement of the liturgy was closely connected with the contents of the *typica*, i.e. the directions for all the liturgical arrangements covering the cycle of the ecclesiastical year. This ordering of the church services was the work of the great reformed monasteries of Constantinople, such as the house of Studius, and it took place in the ninth century. These *typica* included the *menaia*, the twelve books, one for each month, containing excerpts from the lives of the saints and martyrs with their respective hymns (in the form of a canon). The excerpts from the hagiographical works and martyrs' *acta* were collected together separately in the so-called *synaxaria*.

This liturgical reform of the ninth and tenth centuries necessarily involved working over the whole collection of hagiographical material, and this meant sorting out the scenes from the lives of the saints which were traditionally linked with the texts. It is obvious that only those scenes which played an important part in the liturgy, and above all the hymns in the form of a canon, were introduced into the *menologion* (the book containing the outline of the lives of saints whose feasts occur in the calendar). Like the illustrations to the pericopes from the Gospels, the illustrations to the lives of the saints were introduced into the *menaia* which date from the ninth and tenth centuries. They were however 500 years later than these Gospel illustrations. They were also to a far greater extent the creations of Byzantine art since, unlike the miniatures for the Bible, the iconography of these various scenes dates from Byzantine times. It was at this period that Byzantine miniature painting reached its zenith, as the *Menologion* of the Emperor Basil II demonstrates. Contemporary manuscripts of the Psalter, such as the famous Paris Psalter (Bibl. nat., cod. gr. 139), show late antique influence, but in contrast the *Menologion* has already broken with this tradition and developed its own individual style. The explanation lies in the fact that the Psalter (*Psalterion*), the breviary of the Byzantines and the basis of private and of public liturgical prayer, remained immune from liturgical reform.

The miniatures in the *menologion* are closely related to the text of the *synaxarion* and the canon for each saint's day and their abstract style is sometimes reminiscent of twentieth-century expressionism. Reality, in so far as this is related to naturalistic representation, is thrown overboard. Quite contrary to the rules of antiquity, the miniatures of a *menologion* show two representations of the same figure when they wish to portray two different moments in the same life. The unities of time and place, the basic principles of classical painters, were here abandoned. Thus in Basil II's *Menologion* St Eudoxius is portrayed twice in the same picture, once under the executioner's sword and then with his head actually severed from his body. The laws of time and place were so completely ignored that a single miniature could show such widely separated events as the placing of the infant Moses in the Nile and his death.

Older models had indeed been used in these miniatures. They were completely transformed by the liturgical reform and by the remodelling of the saints' lives which Symeon Metaphrastes undertook at the imperial command. Often the new revised text of a saint's life was not available and then the miniatures were composed with the old text in mind. Very occasionally these were altered, as in the case of the portrayal of the martyrdom of St Anastasia in the *Menologion* of the Emperor Basil II. The version of the *acta* of this saint approved by the commission of Symeon Metaphrastes contains the information that Anastasia had her hands and feet cut off before her execution. The account used by the painters of the miniatures did not have this detail and in this case the mutilation has been added later to the picture of the kneeling saint.

The illustrations in Basil II's *Menologion* were undertaken by well-known miniaturists from monasteries in Constantinople. According to the signatures eight masters were involved in this work. They were distinguished by their style but did not differ in their conception of their art, which contrasted sharply with the naturalism of late antiquity. As seen through the eyes of late antiquity, the style which found its expression in the *menologia* was a denial of reality, and not only by ignoring the limits imposed by time and space. In movement and figure, human beings were portrayed in a manner far removed from familiar reality as visible to the eye. Bodies were elongated and seemed to follow the movement of the arms, thus abandoning the laws of proportion. These beings were not placed firmly on the ground and they seemed to execute their movements almost as though they were floating, held up by invisible wires.

This break-through in Byzantine art in an expressionist direction must be evaluated as part of a European phenomenon. The Carolingian renaissance had shown Byzantine influence together with a marked tendency to return to late antiquity. But after this western art also developed on expressionist lines, as Byzantine art had done, and it took a very similar form. The miniature paintings in Ottonian manuscripts abandon naturalistic portrayal, and as in Byzantium there is a marked leaning towards an almost expressionist style. This included the Gospels as well as pictures for the lives of the saints. The reason is found in the influence of the very abstract Coptic representations of the human form transmitted to the West by way of Ireland. But at the same time, as in the case of Byzantine manuscripts, there was also work which closely followed the models of late antiquity. And so in this respect art is not always entirely consistent.

Like the miniature, the icon was influenced by liturgical changes, and the liturgical reform of the ninth and tenth centuries brought about changes here, just as it had done for some miniature painting. But in contrast to the miniature, in the case of the icon there was at first no connection with the pericope divisions. Icons had developed outside the imperial Church in the monasteries of the Nitrian desert as a speciality of what was regarded by the Church as a whole as being a small group of extremists. It was not until the second half of the sixth century that the monastic movement gained a firm footing within the imperial Church and began to penetrate throughout the East.

Icons were originally really only memorial pictures designed to preserve for future generations the actual appearance of famous abbots and hermits. They probably derived from the widespread Egyptian use of portraits on mummies. There is practically no difference in technique between the oldest sixth-century encaustic icon and the mummy portraits. The portraits of abbots and hermits were cherished, together with the collection of their sayings. It was customary to place these portraits on the altar on the anniversary of their death while short extracts from their lives were read and hymns in their honour sung as part of the liturgy at the church services. It was only gradually that the repertoire of the icons was extended to include pictures of Christ, the Mother of God and John the Baptist, which purported to derive from authentic originals. This development had been long settled by the sixth century, to which the first extant icons are dated. The connection between icons, saints' lives and hymns, found in their earliest use in the services of the Egyptian monks, was not to disappear later on. It strongly influenced the arrangement of the interior of the church and particularly the altar itself. When the monastic movement infiltrated into the Church of the Byzantine Empire towards the end of the sixth century the customs which had developed in the monasteries of the East were generally accepted in the divine service. So some of the icons now had a permanent place in the church. The place selected was the altar rails where the sanctuary was separated from the nave and where most of the rich ornamentation was to be found, as indeed in the oldest Christian churches. But now icons were placed on the balustrade, the *templon*, which stood on the low wall of separation. Pride of place on the *templon* was given to the icons of Christ, the Mother of God and John the Baptist, the three great mediators of the Byzantine Church, with that of Christ in the middle over the entrance to the sanctuary. As well as icons of the three mediators, icons of the church fathers, the archangels and the saints were put up on the *templon*. The icons of the saints were changed according to their anniversaries when they had special mention in the liturgy and extracts from their lives were read and hymns sung in their honour. In the lower row of icons which stood on the screen, were pictures of important church festivals, such as the Crucifixion of Christ, the Ascension, Pentecost and the Dormition (*Koimesis* or Falling Asleep of the Virgin).

The two rows of icons hid the sanctuary from the congregation. From now on the rails were really a wall in front of the altar which came to be called an iconostasis because of the icons placed on it, especially in Russia. The use of the iconostasis was extended in an unusual way in Russian churches, partly in order to give a prominent position to some of the Biblical scenes normally portrayed on the walls of a church. Here it must be borne in mind that the light in a Russian church was liable to be not so good as in a Byzantine church, owing to the narrow span of the domes and the very small windows due to climatic conditions. This meant that the walls and dome could not be used for pictures to the same extent as in a Byzantine church. This is probably why the use of the iconostasis was extended.

The close connection between the icons at the altar rails, the liturgy and even the liturgical vestments, inevitably meant that any liturgical change influenced in turn the composition of the icon and its representation. The reform of the liturgy in the tenth and eleventh centuries and the revision of the whole range of hagiographical literature in the second half of the tenth century had its effect on the iconography of the pictures. Existing icons were subject to scrutiny in precisely the same way as the lives of the saints, and the whole hagiographical tradition was critically reviewed at the imperial command. In the field of hagiographical literature most of the saints' lives were now rewritten and given a 'new look'. A commission was set up under the direction of a senior civil servant, the Logothete Symeon, who was also a distinguished historian. Very little was left as it had been handed down by tradition. Most lives were completely rewritten. It was for this reason that Symeon earned the nickname of 'the Paraphraser' (*Metaphrastes*). There is no similar information about icons, but extant Byzantine icons, and Russian icons influenced by these, provide clear evidence that there was a revision which must be dated to between the first half of the tenth and the eleventh centuries. This may very probably have taken place at the same time as the working over of the saints' lives under the direction of Symeon Metaphrastes. This revision left very few of the saints' pictures with their original form. And it is not irrelevant to mention the heavy losses which icons suffered during the period of iconoclast activity. Famous icons were destroyed at that time. Thus in many cases the iconographic traditions were broken and new creations came into being with the help of copies in miniatures several times removed from the originals. But even when such copies were to be had, changes were made in traditional presentations. This meant the loss of the characteristic details in each faithful copy based on memorial pictures of saints, often going back to portraits made from life. The great care with which the old icons in this tradition were made is amply demonstrated by the sixth-century icons surviving in the monastery of St Catherine on Mt Sinai. The three young men in the fiery furnace are represented in a style otherwise only to be found in the Jewish synagogue of Dura-Europos from the first half of the third century. The Parthian dress with all its detail is more faithfully reproduced here than in the fourth-century representation of the same scene in the *arcosolium* picture in the Catacombs of St Priscilla.

In their range of colour the old icons differ from those found in eleventh-century Byzantium. The harmony of the predominating colours of black and gold turning to a reddish hue is in contrast to the palette of the later icons, which bear a strong resemblance to contemporary fresco painting. The icons on the *templon* and wall in front of the sanctuary give the impression of having been brought into line with the scenes placed on the church walls at the time of the reform which took place at the end of the tenth and beginning of the eleventh centuries. The figures of the icons have obviously suffered the same vigorous adaptation to suit contemporary taste as had befallen the traditional saints' lives, the hymns and canons of the liturgy. Thus the old icons dating from before the iconoclast controversy were only to be found still in use in monasteries and places outside the imperial frontiers, such as Sinai and Rome. It was in their new form that the icons reached the Slav peoples, especially the Russians. One need only compare the head of the Mother of God on an encaustic icon from the Pantheon and on the icon on Sinai, both dating from the sixth century, with the famous icon of Vladimir from the first half of the twelfth century. The break with the old iconographical tradition is obvious. On the icon in Santa Maria Nuova, Mary is carrying the Child Jesus as though he is a sacred being. Her eyes are looking into the distance as though to fix the observer. Her veil flows over a costly garment showing its fine embroidered sleeves and low cut neck. Her hand, decorated with a diamond ring, holds the wand which marked a lady of the palace. The Christ Child holds a book in one hand, the other raised as though to teach and he wears the wide cloak of the ancient philosophers. There is no human link as between mother and child. Both are portrayed as divine beings who can have no earthly relationship.

The Vladimir Mother of God is quite different. She holds a child. She does so as a mother. The Child smiles up at her face and she bends her head down to him, moved by the same deep affection, while her gloved left hand seeks to enfold the Child in a protective embrace.

The great dogmatic controversy which the monophysite movement brought to the Byzantine Church is demonstrated by the almost unbridgeable contrast between the Vladimir icon painted just before 1165 and the icon of Santa Maria Nuova probably dating from the seventh century. The Mother of God in Rome is by a monophysite artist who portrayed not the human, but the divine, nature of Christ, in just the same way as the Council of Ephesus in 431 had called Mary the Mother of God. In contrast, the Vladimir icon shows the portrait of the Christ whose double nature, divine and human, had been acclaimed in 680 at the great Council of Constantinople. The great reform which was carried out, especially after the ending of the iconoclast controversy, rooted out the monophysite representation of the Mother of God and of Christ from the iconographical tradition. Icons of this type only remained in use on the periphery of the Empire, as in Rome and Sinai, or further afield. Similarly this reform had replaced the passive Christ hanging on the Cross and portrayed instead the Saviour as a human being suffering and dying on the Cross.

228

After the reform there was a still closer connection between liturgy and icons. The portrayal of the *deesis,* the supplication, which was found on the *templon,* the rails of the altar wall, was to be seen again on the liturgical vestments of the priest. Pictures of Christ, the Mother of God, John the Baptist and individual apostles and church fathers, were embroidered in gold and silver on his *epitrachilion.* They were seen by the congregation when the priest raised his hands to prayer, thus lifting back the *phelonion* which covered the *epitrachilion.* When he offered this prayer the priest stood before the icon of the *deesis* which portrayed exactly the same scene as could be seen on the *epitrachilion* which he wore as part of his liturgical vestments.

The altar *antependium* which hung before the actual altar, must be distinguished from the iconostasis, the wall of icons which shut off the sanctuary. The altar was covered by a costly cloth or a valuable carpet. This *antependium* was in the sanctuary and therefore mostly not visible to the congregation, and on it the Church's programme of pictures was repeated, only on a smaller scale.

The custom of decorating the altar with costly jewelled pictures was known from Justinian's day onwards. Sometimes these were thin plaques embossed in silver or gold, sometimes enamels, or cloissoné work, which reproduced tiny pictures of the saints or scenes from the life of Christ. In rare cases there were also pictures on the altar rails in enamel or in silver in the form of relief plaques. The former were made for the church inside the palace which the Emperor Basil (867–886) dedicated to St Clement; the latter were originally made for Hagia Sophia in the first half of the sixth century, according to Paul the Silentiary.

One of the finest extant altar frontals is the Pala d'Oro which is now in the church of San Marco in Venice. It was a Venetian commission executed in Constantinople between 976 and 978. But the present composition, measuring 3.40 m. × 1.40 m., does not represent the original work. This was taken to pieces and new plaques were added in complete disregard of the original iconographic plan.

The objects on the altar of a Byzantine church were also richly decorated. There would be a costly reliquary, with a manuscript of the Gospels and the icons of the month, as well as an ex-voto picture which would have its place on the altar on the appropriate festival. The receptacles of relics were usually decorated with enamel plaques and low relief embossed in silver or gold. A costly reliquary of this kind, made about the same time as the oldest part of the Pala d'Oro, is now in the cathedral treasury of Marburg and is the reliquary containing the True Cross (Greek: *staurotheke*). According to its inscription this *staurotheke* was a gift of the Emperor Constantine VII Porphyrogenitus (913–59) and his co-Emperor Romanus (this could refer either to Romanus I, 920–44, or to Romanus II, 945–63). Constantine VII was a versatile and gifted man and during his enforced leisure under the rule of the co-Emperor Romanus I he had learnt the art of the goldsmith, and it is possible that he himself had a hand in making this particular reliquary. When Constantinople was sacked in 1204 this splendid piece was stolen and finally reached Marburg. In the treasury of the cathedral of Aachen there is a somewhat later silver reliquary made in the form of a church and bearing the name of Eustathius.

Like the icons of the iconostasis, the Byzantine altar frontal influenced the development of western altars. The West did not have its sanctuary and altar cut off from the congregation by an iconostasis. Thus the altar frontal was linked with the icons of the iconostasis. This started a development which culminated in the Gothic triptych altar with its combination of altar pictures, reliefs and sculpture.

The Byzantine icons had a special significance for the Italian renaissance. Unlike the

Christian countries of the West which did not regard pictures of the saints as objects of a cult, Rome, like Byzantine South Italy, was familiar with icon veneration. A fresco dating from the first half of the twelfth century in the chapel of San Silvestro in the church of the Quattro Coronati shows the extent to which Rome prized its icons at this time. It portrays Pope Sylvester I handing over to the Emperor Constantine the icons of St Peter and St Paul. Pisa, which had close economic links with Byzantium, also set great store by icons. Here and in other medieval cities an art of the Ducento developed, known as the *maniera greca*. The creations of Coppo di Marcovaldo were closely linked to forms taken over from Byzantine icons. This is particularly true of the portrayal of the Theotokos. And if indeed strong western elements are to be seen fused with Byzantine forms in this old Italian painting inspired by the art of the icons, yet all the same the basic Byzantine prototypes still remain in evidence in the creations of the Ducento, especially in the portrayal of the Madonna. Artists were unable to abandon this; for those who commissioned the work wanted it. But in spite of all this imitation, men often chose genuine Byzantine creations in preference to Italian pictures in the Byzantine style of icon painting. Even as late as the first half of the fourteenth century the Florentines ordered from Constantinople a mosaic diptych that repeated in the form of mosaic icons the cycle of the Twelve Festivals known from the Byzantine iconostasis. According to the views of contemporary art specialists, the Italian painters of the Ducento and Trecento could not compete with the Byzantine icon painters. It was not until the Quattrocento that the Italians, who had originally started out under Byzantine influence, came into their own. It was indeed a long way from the un-mistakably Byzantine Madonna of Guido da Siena in the second half of the thirteenth century to the creations of Raphael in the sixteenth century. With him the last traces of Byzantine style have disappeared.

*Ecclesiastical architecture and church interiors after the
victory of the monastic movement*

Church building was also marked by new forms and these must be seen in the same context as the other radical changes in representational art and in literature. What was now involved was a further development of the basilica with a dome (*cupola*). The decisive phase began directly after the end of the iconoclast controversy with the erection of the so-called Nea, the palace church of Basil I, which was dedicated in 881. This building had the same characteristics as the triconchal throne room built by the Emperor Theophilus. Apart from the connection with imperial official architecture, which had always been a determining factor in Byzantine religious buildings, behind the new types of architecture emerging there stood the liturgical reform of the monastery of Studius and the expansion of the iconographic programme for church interiors. The decisive new element was the elevation of the dome above the body of the church. The drum of the main central dome was raised and the secondary domes were also emphasized by means of a drum. The main central dome could thus give more light to the interior and illuminate surfaces which the previous form of dome and disposition of windows had left completely in the dark. This made it possible to meet the needs of the expanding iconographic programme. The drums of the secondary domes with there carefully sited windows served a similar purpose in lighting up the side aisles. At the same time the system of four supports, by which the main dome with its base rested on four pillars, copied from imperial official architecture, permitted a major extension of the interior. This resulted in joining the main nave (*naos*) and the side aisles into a single *ambiente* in front of the tripartite *bema*, the three apses with the sanctuary in the central apse.

Behind these alterations in the interior of the church there were liturgical changes. The old side aisles of early Byzantine days no longer served any special purpose in the services. The changes in ecclesiastical architecture aimed at an increased use of vaulting in the interior. This was achieved by setting the dome on an octagonal base. The corners and the dome were no longer linked by pendentives but by angled niches. The provision of additional surface space inside the church and the new lighting possibilities through the drum of the dome made practicable the realization in frescoes and mosaics of the greatly expanded iconographic programme of the monastic period.

But the iconographic programme was not the only reason for the transformation of the interior of the church. It was also a question of meeting the special needs of the new church hymns. The canons were sung in unison without any instrumental accompaniment and they needed the resonance of the dome. And the relatively small dome measuring only between 7 to 16 metres in diameter was the fruit of seasoned experience in the science of acoustics. Singing beneath these cupolas the choirs of Byzantine monks achieved a celestial clarity and spiritual concentration that would have been impossible in the interiors of churches constructed on the earlier plan.

Decoration of the interior and of the façade was strongly influenced by the inspiration and experience of the pre-iconoclast period. The rejection of the portrayal of human beings, which the iconoclasts enforced in churches and successfully maintained for a considerable period, resulted in stimulating a highly ornamental art and at the same time strengthened oriental influences on Byzantine church architecture. The imitation of ornamental Persian stucco had been found inside churches as early as Justinian's day. At that time the effect of this stucco decoration was produced in a different medium, marble, and this was found especially in the building establishments and workshops on the west coast of Asia Minor. It was used to provide ornamental foliage on the artistic free-standing capitals which sustained the weight of the walls of the drum of the dome in Justinian's domed churches. As well as these decorative ornamental motifs, figural sculpture in stucco is found. Almost the only surviving instance of this is the procession of virgins in the church of Santa Maria in Valle in Cividale. During the iconoclast controversy sculpture in stucco was completely destroyed, but ornamental stucco continued to be used. Islamic ornamental art provided further stimulus. Without realizing their meaning Byzantine artists even used Kufic sentences as ornamentation to decorate the relief plaques on the lower walls of the church below the beginning of the vaulting.

This Islamic influence was extremely strong during the last years of the iconoclast controversy under the Emperor Theophilus and it showed itself particularly in the appearance of the façade. The wall of the façade was now divided by ornamentation which formed a kind of bonding. Layers of red brick alternated with layers of dull grey freestone. The surface of the exterior walls was decorated with marble plaques, ornamental reliefs and faience plaques. In imitation of the mosques and mausoleums of Islam, artistic grilles, marble window lattices, gave the outside of the church a different appearance from the sacred buildings of Justinian's day.

Anyone coming from the noisy bustle of the outside world and the bright glare of sunlight would find himself in a quite different atmosphere when he passed through the half light of the entrances to the church, the outer and inner narthexes, into the church properly speaking. Here light from the windows of the dome almost poured

231

down on him, as it were, lighting up the mosaics in the body of the dome and guiding the eye in certain directions. The figures on the mosaics, the faces of the saints on the frescoes now seemed to be alive. Then when the holy liturgy began with the priests chanting the opening blessing, each worshipper felt that this was the beginning of a holy mystery. This feeling remained until the end of the service. The alternate singing of priests and congregation, the men standing in the nave under the dome, the women in the galleries, rang out inside the church, echoing back again from the resonant domes in supernatural tone. The supplication of the Cherubic Hymn, one of the most beautiful parts of the Byzantine liturgy, 'Like the cherubim let us cast aside all mortal care', could here be realized in almost complete perfection.

The influence of the monastic movement on secular art

It is difficult to trace the first phase of monastic culture within the central regions of the Byzantine Empire, in Constantinople, in Asia Minor and in Greece, because in these areas the iconoclast controversy has obliterated almost every trace of representational art. It is only in Italy, the refuge of the Byzantine immigrants, that early Byzantine art has been preserved. Here religious pictures were dominated by the statuesque character found as early as the second and third centuries in the ex-voto representation of founders on the frescoes of Dura-Europos. Hellenistic, western elements, which can so often be traced back to Pompeian painting, have completely disappeared. The new religious picture makes clear its oriental origin. In portraying episodes from the Bible, the holy personages stand as statuesque as the figures of the founders at Dura-Europos, lined up without any relationship with each other. The picture was not regarded as a whole, but as presenting a series of individuals as objects of veneration.

The portrait of the ruler, the most important concern of imperial art, was also affected by this change. Since Constantine the imperial portrait had had an established place in the church and it was indeed not removed but radically transformed. In the sixth and seventh centuries the portrait of the ruler kept unchanged the character of secular representational art and it was only at the end of the ninth and beginning of the tenth century that a change took place. At the end of the ninth century a mosaic in the narthex of Hagia Sophia shows the Emperor Leo VI (886–912) kneeling in the act of *proskynesis* before Christ, who is seated on the imperial throne. The imperial portrait has now been removed from the main body of the church and placed in the narthex. But this is not all: the actual portrayal of the Emperor shows a break with the past. Here the Emperor is no longer on his throne. Christ sits in his place as Basileus and the Emperor pays Him the same homage which Byzantine subjects would pay to their Emperor. Half a century later, as ivory tablets show, this representation of the Emperor had been somewhat changed. He was no longer shown as the subject of Christ or of Mary, the Theotokos, the Mother of God. He now stood beside Christ or the Mother of God. The Emperor and Empress were now allowed to occupy the place which in the old secular art would have been taken by the Caesars, the co-Emperors. This is how the Emperor Constantine IX Monomachus (1042–1055) and the Empress Zoe are shown in Hagia Sophia in the eleventh century. During this period there also developed imperial iconography which portrayed the Emperor and Empress being crowned by Christ. Thus the imperial iconography of late antiquity which was still known in the sixth century had been abandoned. The development of monumental imperial art was, however, very different in nature, as can be seen from the evidence of the ivory tablets given to high imperial officials together with the *brabeia*, or sign of office, and the documents of appointment. It is true that the sculptured statues of the Emperor which still existed in late antiquity were no longer found, but the portrayal of the Emperor in mosaic and fresco was widely used. The Emperor was shown being acclaimed, he was portrayed as *triumphator* in the Hippodrome, or as leader in religious processions. Apart from the eleventh-century frescoes in Kiev, practically nothing of this imperial art has survived in the Byzantine world. It is only from the miniatures of the manuscript of John Scylitzes, now in Madrid, that we can get some idea of the extreme vitality and expressiveness of this now vanished secular imperial art.

Italy and Byzantine civilization

The formation of Byzantine spheres of influence in Italian territory

Ecclesiastical influence on Byzantine civilization never implied any measure of exclusiveness. It was indeed during precisely that period when the monastic movement affected almost every aspect of Byzantine cultural life, that it achieved its greatest expansion and not only spread through Italy to affect the whole West, but with the conversion of the Slav peoples deeply influenced the Balkans and South Russia as well. It also extended its influence in Armenia and the Caucasus. The reasons for this cultural expansion were not always the same. In Armenia and in the Balkans it was above all political considerations which opened the door to Byzantine culture. In the Balkans it was a question of forestalling Frankish and papal overtures to the Slavs by giving these peoples the Christianity of the Orthodox Church in the Slavonic tongue. In Armenia the Byzantines wanted to counter the advance of the Arab world and also to bind the country to Byzantium by means of ecclesiastical links. It was only in Italy that the cultural expansion was unconnected with calculated reasons of state. Here it was the result of three great waves of migration which for almost a thousand years turned the southern regions of the peninsula into a Greek-speaking countryside once again. These waves of emigration were particularly noticeable at the time of the Slav penetration into the Peloponnese which compelled a considerable part of the population, particularly the townsfolk, to migrate to Italy. The second great wave came from Syria and Palestine. Some of the Orthodox Christians did not make their way across Asia Minor but went by sea to Sicily and South Italy. The third great wave came from Greece, Asia Minor and Constantinople. The migrants were above all the religious, monks, who were forced to leave their homes because of their icon veneration, and they came to Italy in order to follow their religious beliefs unmolested. It was particularly in the old capital, Rome, that they settled and here they established an influential Greek colony which produced several popes.

The Byzantines had first come to Italy as conquerors. The downfall of Ostrogothic power gave them control over the whole peninsula. But the few decades during which their control was undisputed did not permit political and military conquest to be followed up by cultural supremacy. Cultural influence was at first concentrated in the areas of military and political control, Ravenna and the Adriatic sea ports of North Italy. This first phase of cultural confrontation, which was confined in the main to the coastal area of North Italy, was soon extinguished by a second phase which was linked to the introduction of the theme system into Italy. The settlement of Greek-speaking Byzantine soldiers in South Italy coincided with the first two waves of emigration, thus forming a powerful group of Greeks. Many forts (*castella*) with military settlers gradually won over the villages to the Greek way of life. The Graeco-Byzantine officials in the towns and the regulation of urban economy in accordance with a planned programme had the effect of giving the monopoly of key industries and the various branches of trade to Greek merchants. And in this way the towns in South Italy became permeated with Greek civilization. Above all it was the highly skilled workers, forced by the Arabs to migrate to Italy, who displaced the Italian workers. Thus the Greeks gradually gained control of the economic life of the country.

The third wave of immigration was noticeable for the number of monks which it brought to South Italy. This meant that Greek monasteries were now being founded in the neighbourhood of Greek towns. The era of Latin monastic foundations, such as Cassiodorus' house at Vivarium near Squillace, had now passed. The papacy, which by reason of its enormously valuable estates had been the most powerful economic factor in South Italy and Sicily, saw its influence greatly diminished because of imperial confiscation of its property for political reasons. To meet the needs of the theme organization this property had already been divided up among Byzantine military settlers. But such grants were made in the form of the lease (*emphyteusis*) of private law and the Pope therefore remained the owner of the land and as such continued to receive the rent. But in addition to imperial inroads on the papal patrimony, an imperial law was now issued withdrawing eastern Illyricum and particularly Sicily and Calabria from the jurisdiction of the Roman Pope and placing them under the Patriarch of Constantinople.

Unlike southern Italy, the Latin people of central and northern Italy were not assimilated. On the contrary, developments there took an opposite turn. In northern and central Italy the Roman element showed itself to be considerably stronger than the Greek newcomers. The reasons lay for the most part in a social set-up which differed completely from that of South Italy. Great landowners dominated the scene in South Italy, while the small farmer was the rule in central and northern Italy. The free peasantry proved more impervious to wholesale assimilation than the agrarian proletariat of small leaseholders and slaves on the property of the great landowners. Moreover in South Italy a strong minority had survived from Hellenistic times.

While in South Italy and Sicily the political and military control of the Byzantines was not only connected with the expansion of Graeco-Byzantine culture in the West, but also led to ethnic changes, a similar political situation in central Italy only resulted in establishing islands of Byzantine culture which varied in extent. It did not succeed in bringing out any real demographic change, even if it did create small Greek minorities.

Opposing forces

In the Italian peninsula there was a cultural counter-movement which originated outside Italy. It was the Irish monks, together with African clerics, who played a decisive role in the revival of Latin culture in Italy. By the beginning of the seventh century the Irish under Columban had reached Italy and founded the monastery of Bobbio, the community of monastic ascetes which was to prove a rallying point for the new western culture of North Italy. From year to year the significance of the monastery of Bobbio for the Lombards of North Italy grew. The ascetic emphasis which prevailed in Bobbio was an Irish inheritance which indeed had oriental roots. Christianity had been brought to Ireland very early on by missionaries from Celtic Galatia in Asia Minor, where Celtic was still spoken in the fourth century. The different reckoning of the Easter festival still used in the Irish Church, and particularly at Bobbio, went back to these missionaries from Asia Minor. Later with the heavy exports of tin from Cornwall to Egypt, Egyptian goods, and especially Coptic products, reached the British Isles. These influenced the oldest Christian Irish art. The arrowband ornament of early Irish manuscripts, such as the seventh-century book of Kells, would have been impossible without Coptic models. In the same way representation of stories from the Bible in Irish art reflect Coptic influence which was transmitted either through the miniatures of Coptic manuscripts or through textiles and other art. This was especially true of ivory carving, woodwork and embroidery, on which scenes from the life of Christ or the apostles were represented. This is still to be seen in the painting by the eighth-century monks of the Church of St Proculus of Naturno in the Val Venosta, which shows the flight of the apostle Paul from Damascus. Here the pronounced stylizing reflects the debt to an old, no longer extant, Coptic model from which the painter has also copied the arrowband decoration. In the Lombard kingdom, as in Gaul, these Irish monks created an early Christian culture. This, together with the recently diffused Byzantine influences, was to produce the Carolingian renaissance which laid the foundations of the great romanesque age in the West.

The Latins from Africa brought another culture, differing from that of the Irish. Among these Africans were immigrants carrying with them the bones of St Augustine, which had rested in the cathedral of Carthage until the Arab conquest of the year 700, and they settled in Pavia in the Lombard kingdom. The special development of Latin philology in northern Italy was probably owed to these men. The Lombards certainly had the African emigrants to thank for the cultural stimulus which they experienced earlier than the Franks, thus enabling them to play a leading role in the Carolingian reform movement. The school of grammar and law in Pavia was a particular bulwark of Latin learning in the West. It counted Paul the Deacon among its pupils, and the famous university of Bologna was later to develop from it.

Byzantine culture found it particularly difficult to gain a foothold in northern Italy to begin with because of the cultural independence of this region. This had first come about in an indirect way through Rome by reason of the alliance between the Pope and the Frankish king. There was therefore a noticeable diminution in the Graeco-Byzantine element in northern Italy. Greek inscriptions, such as the late sixth-century dedication of the cathedral of Grado, or the Ravenna documents partly written in Greek, disappear towards the mid-seventh century. This did not, however, disrupt the continuity of certain islands of Graeco-Byzantine culture in northern Italy where late antique art, as in the Umayyad kingdom, still survived throughout the seventh century. But such centres were surrounded by a sea of Irish monastic influence, which produced on Italian soil an abstract style of art, with its stiff forms and its stylized human figures in low relief, such as those on the altar of Pemmo in Cividale with their strange bodies. Hence some authorities have wished to attribute them to a later period. This is also true of the style of the frescoes of Castelseprio near Milan which is almost reminiscent of the illusionism of Pompeian painting, as well as the stucco reliefs on the frieze of Santa Maria in Valle at Cividale. And it must be remembered that these North Italian islands of late antique culture to some extent spread their influence northwards. The fragments of the now lost wall-painting of the Ecclesia Varia, the crypt church of Louis the German (†876), which came to light about twenty years ago in the course of excavations, show neither the Irish-Coptic nor Byzantine-Roman influence. Their models were the paintings of late antiquity, as was also the case with the frescoes of Castelseprio. And the remains of architectural painting in the inner room of the so-called tower hall in Lorch with their obvious Pompeian affinities could only have been conceived through the mediation of these islands of late antique influence in North Italy.

Early Byzantine influence in the West

The bearers of Byzantine culture in the West

Developments in Rome took a different course from those of North Italy. In the sixth century Rome was still a stronghold of Latin culture and Pope Gregory I himself (590–604) admitted that he could not understand Greek, although he had spent some years in Constantinople as papal legate (*apocrisiarius*). After the outbreak of the iconoclast controversy Rome became almost overnight the rallying point of Byzantine culture in the West. The Arab invasion of Egypt, Syria and Palestine had already strengthened the Greek elements in the city. In 642 a Greek from Palestine ascended the papal throne. Pope Agatho (678–681) was a Greek from Sicily, and Zacharias (741–752) who attained the papal tiara came from the Greek population of Calabria. Basilian monasteries were founded in and around Rome. The very names of such churches in Rome as Santa Maria Egiziaca and Santa Maria in Cosmedin point to Byzantine influence in the Eternal City. The mosaics and frescoes in Santa Maria Antiqua, the paintings in the oratorio commissioned by Pope John VII (705–707) and in Santa Maria in Cosmedin are all instances of the Byzantine art which almost completely disappeared in Greece and Asia Minor during the iconoclast controversy.

Rome was now the centre of lively activity in the field of translation. For instance the Greek Pope Zacharias translated into Greek the *Dialogues* of Gregory the Great and in the ninth century a papal official, the librarian Anastasius, made a Latin translation of the chronicle of Theophanes.

The various strands in East Roman and Byzantine culture

At this period it was the Greeks in South Italy and Rome who transmitted Byzantine literature, music and painting to the West. It was above all the Greek immigrants to South Italy and Rome who were responsible for this cultural influence. Greek immigrants to England, Ireland and France had brought knowledge of Greek to these lands. John the Scot (Eriugena) had only been able to undertake the translation of Pseudo-Dionysius the Areopagite because knowledge of Greek had spread in the cathedral schools of the British Isles. Among the Greek immigrants to the Anglo-Saxons was no less a person than a bishop from Tarsus in Cilicia in Asia Minor who had come from Byzantium. In England this Theodore became archbishop of Canterbury (668–693). As archbishop he set up a cathedral school where special attention was given to the study of Greek. The commentary of Hesychius on the book of Leviticus from the Bible is one of the few fragmentary survivals witnessing to the work of translation done at this centre of learning. But it was not only in the field of literature that Anglo-Saxon England felt the influence of Byzantine culture. It can be traced in the art of the early Anglo-Saxon period. As early as the end of the seventh century some of the silver found at Sutton Hoo shows Byzantine stylistic forms.

The kingdom of the Franks felt the influence of Byzantine culture even more than the British Isles. Here Rome was the transmitter. In the Frankish kingdom at this time the currents of the late antique and Byzantino-oriental cultural heritages overlapped with each other, and they both conflicted with the Irish-Celtic influence which the Irish monks brought. During the Carolingian period late antique influence penetrated from Pavia and Ravenna, side by side with the Byzantino-oriental cultural current from Rome. It was these two streams, together with the Irish cultural heritage from late antiquity, which determined the character of the Carolingian renaissance. Thus Charles the Great's circle, the group to which Alcuin, Einhard and Paul the Deacon belonged, experienced the cultural influence not only of the late antique Latin tradition but also of the Byzantino-Greek world. The art of Rome provided it with links with the Byzantine element, that of Ravenna with the late antique. In Ravenna the culture of the age of Justinian was displayed in the art of San Vitale. Rome was the centre of the transmission of Byzantine culture bearing the stamp of the iconophile monks, which found its expression in the frescoes of Santa Maria Antiqua painted by Greeks. The *capella palatina* of Charles the Great, still standing in Aachen, shows the architectural influence of Ravenna. Its builders had as their model the church of San Vitale in Ravenna. But in the decoration of the interior of this church the Byzantine influence of Rome triumphed over that of Ravenna, not in the choice of themes, but in their execution. For the Apocalypse belonged to one of the favourite themes of the early western painting. The cartons which still survive today show the now destroyed mosaics with sketches of the elders of the Apocalypse. They reveal the dramatic sense of movement which is characteristic of the figures in the Greek sixth-century manuscripts on purple parchment, such as the *Codex Rossanensis* (so-called from Rossano in South Italy where the manuscript now is) and the Sinope fragment (now in the Bibliothèque Nationale in Paris). Towards the top of the dome Christ appears enthroned; in another panel there is the figure of the Theotokos. The summit of the dome is adorned with the symbols of the four evangelists. This is not the kind of Byzantine figural decoration found in Rome in the frescoes of Santa Maria Antiqua, which bear the unmistakable stamp of representational conceptions proper to the monastic movement. The mosaics of the *capella palatina* stand halfway between this particular monastic conception of Santa Maria Antiqua and the great late antique art of East Rome in the sixth century.

The influence of the Byzantine monastic art of Rome is more noticeable in the frescoes of the *capella palatina* of Aachen than in its mosaics. The interior of the chapel, as in the Hagia Sophia church of Kiev, is decorated with frescoes as well as mosaics. They are about twenty years later than the mosaics in the dome and they bear witness to the complete breakthrough of Byzantine monastic representational conceptions. In the details of the figures, if not in the composition as a whole, the mosaics show the clear marks of late antique East Roman influence. The frescoes on the contrary show the unmistakable influence of Byzantine monastic art. Their prototypes are the mosaics in the chapel of S. Zeno in Santa Prassede, in Santa Cecilia, San Marco and Santa Maria in Domnica.

The illuminated manuscripts of the Carolingian period were also under the influence of the Byzantine monastic art of Rome. Some of these originating in the palace school of Aachen were probably the work of Greek copyists and painters, or at least were painted and written with the help of a Greek model. The purple Gospel now in Vienna was copied by the priest Demetrius. As the name shows, he was probably a Greek. Here the Byzantine original often reveals itself so clearly that one can even deduce the origin of these Greek painters from the miniatures. This is true for the style of painting, as well as the sequence of individual miniatures which seem to indicate Syrian models. The miniatures of the Ada manuscript and the Godescalc Gospel can be compared with the Syriac Gospel of Etchmiadzin and the Rabula Gospel. Obviously the copyists or painters here were Syrian monks.

It is this Byzantine influence which accounts for the choice of purple for special manuscripts reserved for imperial use.

The influence of the Byzantine monastic culture can be traced outside Aachen in the Frankish Empire and in England. It was the miniatures in manuscripts which transmitted the rich variety of Byzantine models. A good many of the manuscripts were produced

238

by the Greek Basilian monks living in Rome. Here they were seen by high ecclesiastics from the Frankish Empire and the British Isles. The miniatures of such manuscripts served as models for the monumental wall paintings in the churches of these countries. English chronicles tell how many bishops did not hesitate to make more than once the long and hazardous journey to Rome for the sake of acquiring these manuscripts and then had great murals painted in their churches, copied from the manuscripts which they had obtained. There is little now left of this early monumental painting. What has survived points to Byzantine models; for instance, the frescoes in the church of St John in Münster in the Graubünden where there is a cortège in which the knights are wearing the *burnus* of the Arab auxiliary troops of Byzantium. And somewhat later at the end of the ninth century the surviving frescoes of Malles with their square-nimbused founders certainly indicate Byzantine influence.

These Byzantine models were further developed in combination with earlier styles of painting which had been influenced by Coptic conceptions and transmitted by the Irish monks. As early as the end of the ninth century a freer, more individual, style appeared, showing how the older Coptic way of painting was being merged with the more recently acquired Byzantine monastic forms. The most important evidence showing the advance made in this process of fusion is to be found in the pictorial decorations in the church of Oberzell on Reichenau. Here the painting reveals that harmonious fusion which had been attained in the sculpture and miniatures of the late Carolingian period. The tendency to abstraction and the addiction to the ornamental decoration of early Irish art are found side by side with the more vigorous forms and the greater movement in the figures which stem from Byzantine monastic art.

Western and Byzantine music

Developments in the field of music took a similar course. Here too the pattern was provided by the Byzantines. It began when the Emperor Constantine V Copronymus sent the Frankish king Pepin an organ. In Byzantium an organ was only played during ceremonial processions or banquets. Its use during church services was as rare as the use of any other instrument on such occasions. But in the West its development proceeded along different lines. There a detailed study was made of the organ and opportunity for building these instruments soon arose. As early as 873 the Pope asked Anno, then bishop of Freising, to send an organ and an organist. This information shows that in the West the organ was not banned from church services as in Byzantium but on the contrary was already being used.

But the Franks got more than Greek musical instruments from the Byzantines. The Byzantine form of church singing played a decisive part in determining the development of western music. Tradition says that Charles the Great secretly took part in the night service of a Byzantine embassy at his court. The next day he gave the order that the Greek hymns were to be translated into Latin. The truth of this story is supported by extant translations of this kind. A good deal of this work of translation was done at St Gall. It was said that from time to time Greek brothers, *Ellenici fratres*, stayed in the monastery. They were a great help to the German monks in turning the Greek hymns into Latin. Among others, the Acathistus hymn was translated into Latin.

To use Greek music without knowledge of Greek notation was impossible in view of the fact that the West lacked its own notation. Thus the adoption of Byzantine music inevitably meant the use of the Greek system of notation. The present-day Greek names of the Latin neumes and the use of Greek prosody signs are still a reminder of this.

These Byzantine models gave a strong stimulus to western music. But music, like representational art, soon went its own way. Willing use was made of the foreign stimulus: technical aids like musical notation were adopted as well as one of the Byzantine instruments, the organ. But this did not imply that the West continued to imitate Byzantine music. For instance the use of the organ in the services indicated that there was no intention to follow Byzantine church music in every respect.

This deviation and individual development was even more emphatically shown by the departure from unison singing. By about the end of the ninth century harmony is found in western musical theory. In his work *De harmonica institutione* Hugbald of St Amand laid the foundations for voices singing together at regular intervals of a fifth or an octave. Thus a definite break was made with the unison of the Gregorian chant. In Rome unison singing in church music from the East lasted longer. The Frankish Empire, however, went its own way. Probably old musical traditions of church music also continued here, which men like Irenaeus who came from Asia Minor had introduced into the Gallic church. The development of harmony meant changes in notation. Very soon the Byzantine neumes were given up and other musical signs used in their place. This development led from the notation of Herbert the Lame of Reichenau to the great reforms of Guido of Arezzo.

Rome as the centre of Byzantine influence in the West

In figural art as well as in music there is no doubt that Byzantine monastic culture exerted considerable influence in the West. This is not, however, true of the oldest and most individual form of Byzantine art—the icon. Icons and icon veneration were indeed rejected by the Franks, even in their more moderate Roman form. The *Libri Carolini* in a surviving manuscript still preserves notes jotted down in shorthand, giving the views of Charles the Great on the question of icon veneration and showing the profound aversion of governmental circles for this kind of Byzantine devotion. It was only in Rome, where there was a large Greek colony, that icon veneration was possible. It was the icon-venerating monks who brought with them from their old homeland not only their manuscripts, but also those icons which enjoyed special veneration. Among these were very probably the icons still venerated in Rome today, such as that of Christ in the Sancta Sanctorum and of Mary the Theotokos in Santa Maria Maggiore. Both these probably date from the seventh century.

The Byzantine colony in Rome, which in the seventh, eighth, and ninth centuries had its quarters round the old *forum boarium* between the Capitol and the Aventine, influenced not only western art but probably western script as well. Thus it was probably Rome which provided the model for Carolingian minuscule. This made its appearance in the last decade of the eighth century, at first isolated, and then generally accepted throughout the Frankish Empire as the new form of handwriting. At this time Greek minuscule was already in use in the Basilian monasteries of Rome, for Greek scribes had by now completed the change over from the old uncial hand to minuscule. In France it was again the palace of Aachen which was the first to adopt the new script. But there were also Greek scribes at work in the palace school.

Byzantine elements in Ottonian and Salian art

During the Carolingian epoch it was particularly Rome with its large colony of Greek immigrants which transmitted Byzantine influences to the Frankish Empire. In contrast, in Ottonian and Salian art one can speak of an element borrowed directly from Byzantium. Certainly this was by no means as far-reaching as Byzantine influence in the Carolingian period and there were indeed considerable fields of cultural activity, such as music, which remained outside this influence. In the main it was the bishops' sees near the administrative centre of the kingdom and the great imperial monasteries which were receptive to Byzantine influence and introduced it into their works of art.

The door to Byzantium had been opened when Otto the Great was crowned Emperor in Rome in 962. The question of the position of the western Emperor *vis-à-vis* the Byzantine Basileus again came into consideration. Both parties exchanged ambassadors. The German Emperor wanted a marriage alliance with a Byzantine princess for his son in order to set the seal on the legitimacy of his Empire. The Byzantine Emperor wanted to protect his position as Basileus and universal ruler. In the Musée Cluny there is still preserved an ivory tablet which seems to reflect this mutual attempt to find a settlement. It shows Christ crowning Otto II and the Byzantine princess Theophano, a niece of John Tzimisces who was then co-Emperor. This coronation is portrayed in the same way as on a contemporary ivory tablet showing the Byzantine Basileus being crowned by Christ. It is well known that Byzantium frequently stressed the fact that Christ crowned the Emperor, who in turn crowned other kings. The ivory tablet seems to indicate the surrender of this principle, for the Greek inscription gives the Emperor the title *Imperator Romaion* (note that the Greek form *Romaion* is used instead of *Romanorum*). It is however unlikely that the Greek Basileus sent the Western Emperor an ivory tablet bearing this title. Most probably an embassy sent to Otto I by the Byzantine Emperor Nicephorus II Phocas presented him with an ivory tablet showing Nicephorus being crowned by Christ. The West followed the custom of portraying the imperial coronation in this way and Emperors sent ivory tablets showing themselves being crowned by Christ to other kings, especially the West Franks and the Burgundians, thus stressing their own superior authority. And so the ivory tablet showing the coronation of Otto II and Theophano reflects the adoption of the Byzantine form of the imperial cult. This is indeed reflected in many ways. To begin with there was the crown. It was in this period that the Western Emperor stopped using the *kamelaukion* and in its place adopted the existing Byzantine type of crown which consisted of a number of plaques hinged together. The adoption of the crown was followed by taking over imperial iconography. The Carolingians and also Henry I had been portrayed on their seal in profile, but now Otto I copied the Byzantines in having a frontal portrait of the ruler. And then the attempt was also made at using purple for imperial documents as the Byzantines did. Only one such effort of this kind remains (the splendid document in which Otto the Great confirmed the Carolingian Donations to the Roman Pope).

The adoption of Byzantine forms was, however, limited to the narrow field of the symbols of sovereignty. As in the Carolingian period, so now Roman late antiquity again formed a barrier, which meant that here during the Ottonian period the Byzantine element was limited in its influence on culture and was not the determining factor, as in the case of the Slavs. In spite of Byzantine infiltration, particularly in changing the forms in which the symbols of authority were expressed, in portraying the Emperors the Ottonians held fast, both now and in the future, to the symbols of authority handed down to them from Christian Roman late antiquity through Carolingian channels. According to this tradition, the Western Emperor stood on earth as the promised ruler of the *Revelation* of St John (ch. 4) before whom the four and twenty elders cast down their crowns. A mosaic picture of this decorated the dome of the imperial *capella palatina* in Aachen, where the Emperor is shown on the throne placed in the choir and is the living impersonation of the promised ruler of the *Revelation*. In the manuscript of the Gospels dedicated by Abbot Liuthar of Reichenau to either Otto II or Otto III (in the cathedral treasure at Aachen) the imperial throne is surrounded by the symbols of the four evangelists and it is not chance that these have almost the same form and grouping as in the *Revelation* of St John, where they are described as being round the throne of the promised ruler. This points to a gradual exaltation of the western concept of imperial authority. In the mosaic in the dome of Aachen men have not yet had the temerity to place the Emperor on the throne of the promised ruler of the *Revelation* as is done in the miniature. In another miniature (*Codex Aureus, Monac. Cod.lat.*14000) the artist went further and gave the Emperor the throne under the ciborium which adorned the altar itself. The hand of God, or of Christ, appears over the Emperor pointing to his crown, while the nations, in the guise of the ancient civic goddess, pay homage to him. So far western art had not adopted the coronation of the Emperor by Christ, which was the usual way in which the imperial coronation was portrayed in Byzantine miniatures and on ivory tablets. This probably first occurred on the ivory tablet portraying the coronation of Otto II and the Empress Theophano. This development went still further and a few decades later King Henry II commissioned a sacramentary very probably written and illuminated in Regensburg. In one of its miniatures Henry II is shown being crowned by the enthroned Christ and being presented by angels with the holy lance and the imperial sword, while St Ulrich and St Emmeran, the patron saints of Regensburg, are protecting him. Apart from the direct connection of Ottonian with Byzantine imperial art, already revealed in this scene, the style of the figures (as for instance the angel plunging down as it were from heaven) shows the use of Byzantine models. The angels were inspired by the scene of the death of Mary on the Byzantine ivory tablet on the cover of the Gospel of Otto III (in the Bavarian Staatsbibliothek in Munich). What is true of this miniature also holds good for other miniatures in the same manuscript. There are everywhere signs that Byzantine patterns have been followed. The portrayal of the crucifixion (fol.15ʳ) even has a Greek inscription.

The transmission of Byzantine imperial art to the West was achieved through embassies exchanged on both sides. In one of his writings the ambassador Liutprand of Cremona gives a detailed account of his experiences at the imperial court in Byzantium. Ambassadors not only brought back presents as marks of esteem from the Byzantine Basileus, but also valuable textiles and works of art which they had acquired. Liutprand tells of the trouble which he had with the Byzantine customs officials when he wanted to bring back goods which he had bought in Constantinople. Such goods acquired in the Byzantine Empire transmitted Byzantine influence into Central Europe. Thus Bishop Günther of Bamberg obtained in Constantinople and brought back to Germany a valuable wall-hanging which showed the Emperor as *triumphator*; today only fragments of this have survived. It is thought that the two goddesses of Victory on this wall-hanging, as well as the Byzantine Basileus, can be recognized again in the nations paying homage in the imperial picture in the Gospel of Otto III (Munich, *Cod.lat.*4443), the covering of which was decorated with the Byzantine ivory of the death of Mary.

As well as the Emperor being crowned by Christ, Byzantine art knew another and older form of imperial representation. This was the Byzantine Basileus kneeling before Christ, making his submission (*proskynesis*). A mosaic portraying this has survived in the narthex of Hagia Sophia where the Emperor Leo VI is shown prostrating himself before Christ. This form of imperial representation was adopted by Ottonian and Salian art. There is a manuscript of the Gospels copied in Echternach and presented by the Emperor Henry III to the cathedral of Speyer which shows the founders of the cathedral, the imperial couple Conrad II and Gisela, kneeling before Christ, making their *proskynesis*. In this manuscript Byzantine influence is also seen openly expressed in the use of Greek letters in the Latin inscription in the mandorla praising God. The *antependium* presented by Henry II to the cathedral of Basle (today in the Musée Cluny in Paris) represents the imperial couple in the act of *proskynesis* before Christ. In addition this *antependium* clearly shows Byzantine models in the ornamental decoration between the arcades.

In the sphere of religion Byzantine influence was more permanent than in imperial art. The Mother of God with the Christ Child and the dying Christ on the Cross were taken over into western art at this time. It is true that before the Ottonian period Christ on the Cross had been portrayed in the West. But the dying Saviour had none of the characteristics of a man in the agonizing death throes. He was shown hanging on the Cross but without any sign of human suffering, as though all the agony of the Cross and the overwhelming bodily pain could not touch him, as though he were not created of earthly flesh and blood. This portrayal of Christ came from monophysite Syria and Egypt, where the emphasis on the divine nature of Christ could not allow the Saviour to suffer on the Cross as a human being and represented him as being *impatibilis* on the Cross, without corporeal feeling or experience of human pain. This conception of the Crucifixion of Christ is found in a miniature of the Gospels written in 586 in the Mesopotamian city of Zagba by the fine copyist Rabula (today in the Laurentian Library in Florence). It reached Europe from two different sources: from Ireland, where it found its way in late antiquity through the very extensive trade in devotional objects (such as silver *ampullae* with consecrated oil), and on the other hand from Rome, whence it had been brought by Syrian immigrants of the seventh century. In Ireland there were to be found many forms of Coptic and Syrian art and monastic life (one of the most famous Irish monasteries imitated the ground plan of a Syrian monastery down to the last detail) and in addition the Irish had adopted the monophysite representation of Christ on the Cross. The Irish version of the monophysite Christ on the Cross, seen in the sculptured Crucifixion from Athlone (Dublin, National Museum) and repeated in a miniature in the Gospel of St Gall (Cod. 51), was spread on the continent by Irish monks in the seventh and eighth centuries. But this portrayal of the Crucifixion of Christ also reached middle and western Europe from the south, from Rome. A fresco with the Crucifixion scene in the church of Santa Maria Antiqua dating from the first decade of the eighth century shows a Roman version of the monophysite Syrian portrayal of Christ. Coming by way of Rome and the Irish monasteries in Europe, such as Luxeuil and Corbie in the Frankish kingdom, St Gall in Switzerland and Bobbio in Italy, this portrayal of the Crucifixion won a permanent place in Carolingian miniature painting. It was not until the Ottonian period in about the mid-tenth century, when the imperial coronation of Otto I established close cultural relations with Byzantium, that this was replaced by the orthodox portrayal of the Crucifixion showing the Saviour suffering and dying on the Cross as a human being. This portrayal corresponded to Byzantine doctrinal teaching on the two natures of Christ, the divine and human, which had been formulated in 680. According to this belief, Christ suffered on the Cross as a human being and art must portray him thus. The picture of the dying Christ, such as is seen later in the eleventh-century mosaics of Nea Moni and the monastic church of Daphni, influenced Ottonian religious art, particularly through Byzantine ivory tablets. It is to these that the first western imitations can be related, such as the tablet in ivory of 991 on the cover of the *Codex Aureus* coming from the monastery of Echternach. Using this kind of bas-relief work the West achieved the transition to sculpture in full relief which for religious reasons the Byzantines were debarred from using. The result was such works as the Cross of Gero and the later Crucifixion of Werden.

The West borrowed from Byzantium in portraying the Mother of God with the Christ Child as well as the dying Christ. Here too the picture was transmitted to the West from Byzantine originals. These originals are for the most part to be seen in the large number of ivory tablets with the picture of the Hodegetria, the Mother of God with the Child Jesus, found on the covers of western manuscripts. And it was also in portraying this particular subject that the West made its transition from low relief to sculpture in full relief. The first of all the western representations of the Madonna is a work of Ottonian art and is the statue of the Mother of God with the Divine Child, now in the cathedral treasure of Essen. Even though portrayed with somewhat uncertain hand, here is the picture of the Byzantine Mother of God in the medium of free-standing sculpture. This was achieved by the second half of the tenth century.

Byzantine influence in ecclesiastical art was not, however, limited to a brief period determined by political circumstances; it continued unbroken throughout the Salian period of the German Empire. Art in ivory work in the workshops of certain monasteries developed still further, inspired by the Byzantine style of the original models. In Bamberg in the monastery of St Michael, famous for its rich collection of classical manuscripts, there was an atelier with craftsmen whose products were extremely difficult to distinguish from tablets actually made in Byzantium. The tablet with the martyrdom of St Kilian which was made there can be compared to the portrayal of the death of Mary on an ivory tablet on the cover of the Gospel of Otto III (now in the Bavarian Staatsbibliothek in Munich). The filigree decoration and finely ornamental motifs of the frame, and the angel as though plunging down from heaven, are also to be found on the Bamberg tablet. In general, Byzantine ivory tablets exerted considerable influence on the development of western sculpture and this continued well into the Gothic period. In spite of many links with new and often independent interpretations, there is still a very strong relationship between the picture of the death of the Mother of God in relief sculpture on the cathedral of Strasbourg and the same theme handled on the ivory tablet on the cover of the Gospel of Otto III in Munich.

The Byzantine element can be detected in western painting of the early middle ages as well as in sculpture. For instance the miniature of Thuringian-Saxon provenance dating from shortly after 1200 has a portrayal of Christ's Descent into Hell (H.B. II Bibl. 24, Stuttgart, Landesbibliothek) which repeats with very little alteration a similar theme in a wall mosaic in the catholicon of Daphni. Perhaps in this case the picture may have been transmitted through a Byzantine icon, for these were found in the West in the early middle ages. A miniature in a Psalter in Donaueschingen of the first half of the thirteenth century (Fürstl. Fürstenberg. Hofbibl., Ms. 309) coming from the same region is a copy of a Byzantine icon portraying the Mother of God down to almost the last detail. The treatment of the face, the fold of the veil with the star, even the frame of the icon, are all reproduced in the copy. Not only icons, but Greek monks, came to Germany and these were responsible for making more widely known the techniques of Greek art. The Basilian monk Gregory, who came from Byzantine Calabria, was summoned to Aachen by Otto III (983–1002) in order to found a Basilian monastery nearby in Burtscheid. Today the parish church of Burtscheid still has a mosaic icon of St Nicholas, though in a very bad state of preservation.

Links binding the West to Byzantium were forged as early as the Carolingian period. Thus the western Church took over the cult of Byzantine saints, SS. Cosmas, Damian, Christopher, Ephraim, Antony and the Holy Forty Martyrs. This adoption of the cult

244

of Byzantine saints, together with the acquisition of some of their relics, seems to have influenced the architecture of the churches erected for these. It was considered wrong that the bones of a saint should be placed in a building smaller than that in which they had previously been housed. Thus the church of St George in Oberzell on Reichenau, erected in 890 by Hatto III, later archbishop of Mainz, and the proud possessor of the head of its patron saint, was a copy of this saint's *martyrium* in Ortaköi in Cappadocia. It is possible that Greek workmen helped here in the building operations. The vaulting and the building technique of the walls of the crypt are reminiscent of Byzantine work. This kind of participation by Greek workmen in German ecclesiastical buildings is certainly attested for the Ottonian period. The chapel of St Bartholomew in Paderborn, which is still standing today, was erected by Bishop Meinwerk of Paderborn in 1017 'with the help of Greek workmen' (*per operarios graecos*). It is however difficult to believe that this really implies Greek builders, for the ground plan of almost all western churches came from Rome and was inspired by late antiquity. It was not for nothing that almost every church had an altar dedicated to St Peter. Here the difference in the liturgy prevented the adoption of Byzantine types of ground plan. Where similarities are found, as perhaps between the church of the Margrave Gero in Gernrode and the basilica of St Demetrius in Thessalonica, these are due to a common use of types found in late antiquity. Even so, it is not possible to say that the West during the Ottonian and Salian periods borrowed the iconographic programme of the Byzantine church. The small almost completely preserved iconographic scheme of the Carolingian period, as that in St John in Müstair in Switzerland, shows that in the West pictures were borrowed direct from Syrian models without any Byzantine mediation. Details such as the representation of the Ascension in Müstair could have been created directly by Syrian craftsmen. The naturalistic style of painting that was still firmly rooted in late antiquity can be clearly distinguished from contemporary, or only slightly earlier, creations of the Coptic-Irish school of painting, such as the frescoes of the St Proculus church of Naturno in Val Venosta. The naturalistic style of painting found at Müstair has practically nothing in common with the almost abstract presentation of the human figure by the imitators of Irish monastic art working in Naturno.

In the art of the Carolingian and Ottonian periods the influence of late antiquity coming from Syria is clearly perceptible. It was above all in sculpture that the transmission of late classical forms was passed on through Syrian channels. The stucco sculpture in the church of Santa Maria in Valle in Cividale was probably the work of Syrian artists who had had to leave their country as a result of the Arab iconoclast movement at the beginning of the eighth century. To begin with, the West was hesitant about using this new form of art. The first native efforts at sculpture, as for instance that of St Martin in Disentis, were crude and clumsy. But gradually in this field western artists caught up with their Syrian models, as for example in the sculptured reliefs of St Ulrich's chapel in St John in Müstair. This kind of sculpture coming from late antiquity was very closely related to that found in the Umayyad palaces, such as Qasr al-Hayr al-Gharbi in Syria, and together with the reliefs of the Byzantine ivory tablets exercised the strongest influence on romanesque sculpture, which in turn moulded that of the Ottonian period. It was not only in monumental sculpture and painting that this influence from late antiquity acted as a preventive against too extensive an adoption of Byzantine forms. In the art of miniature painting late antique elements were sufficiently strong to stand in the way of the incoming new Byzantine forms in the second half of the tenth century and to prevent a development in the West similar to that which took place among the Slav peoples. In the field of miniature painting late antique influence transmitted through Rome can be most clearly seen in the copying of the late antique pictures of the months in Ottonian miniatures. Here the starting point was the calendar of Philocalus of A.D. 345. As early as the Carolingian period it was being copied as a whole and its pictures of the months soon penetrated into Ottonian and Salian miniatures.

But quite outside ecclesiastical art and the special field of the symbols of imperial authority there was considerable Byzantine influence on western representational art during the romanesque period. This came to the West through the luxury products of the textile industry exported from Constantinople, costly and beautifully embroidered garments and materials. In the matter of clothes and luxury goods Constantinople played a role in the West in the tenth and eleventh centuries similar to that of Paris in Europe of the eighteenth, nineteenth and twentieth centuries. The high aristocracy wished to follow the fashions of the Byzantine magnates. This demand for luxury products was met in the tenth and eleventh centuries by the import of Byzantine textiles. This can be seen from pictures of members of the western aristocracy. In the Rule Book of Niedermünster (Munich, Staatl. Bibl. Ms. lat. 142) there is a miniature showing Henry the Quarrelsome looking just like a Byzantine magnate with his richly decorated tunic with long sleeves and the *paludamentum*, the cloak of a Roman general, over it, as well as long, beautifully embroidered stockings. His footwear consists of fine low-cut leather shoes which allow his stockings to be seen. Not only the tunic but also the shoes and stockings are certainly of Byzantine workmanship.

The figural motifs and the decoration on Byzantine textiles gave an important stimulus to western artists, who took these figures and ornaments from materials and copied them in stone. Thus the export of Byzantine textiles transmitted to the West the motifs of secular Byzantine art. There is for instance the well-known scene from the *Romance of Alexander* in which the hero is shown standing on a chariot with two griffins, tempting them with two pieces of meat attached to a stave and urging them to fly to the heavens with him. This scene is from the story of Pseudo-Callisthenes, which was widely known in late antiquity and in the East and is found on Coptic material of the sixth century. The Byzantine textile industry also included this popular representation in their repertoire of patterns. Byzantine material reached the Rhine valley by way of Venice, the main entrepôt for these goods. The dissemination of this scene corresponded with the route taken by the textiles. It was copied from the material in Venice in the tenth or eleventh centuries and transferred to sculpture. A relief showing Alexander with a tiara and the pair of griffins as described in the story is to be found today on the wall on the north side of the church of San Marco. The next stage was found in the early romanesque part of the cathedral of Basle and then in the late romanesque cathedral of Freiburg im Breisgau in the Rhine valley. In both these churches Alexander is represented on the chariot with the two griffins in the same way.

Some idea of the range of Byzantine cultural influence can be illustrated from another pattern used in textiles which was copied in the West in relief sculpture. This is the picture of a hind being devoured by a wild beast which is found as early as the first century A.D. on a nomad's carpet made for the cemetery of Noin Ula in Mongolia. This came from the nomads of Central Asia to Iran, where it supplied one of the patterns used in the textile industry. Material with this pattern was exported from Iran to Byzantium, where it was copied along with many other Iranian decorative patterns. Textiles with this design found their way into the West, where they were copied, as in the case of material with the apotheosis of Alexander the Great. Almost wherever these textiles penetrated, the designs were also used in sculpture in stone. This had already happened with Iranian exports. Iranian materials with the picture of the hind were copied in sculpture on the façades of churches in Armenia, Georgia and Russia. Through the medium of Byzantine materials this scene reached the early sculpture of French cathedrals.

As well as Byzantine export trade, Greek monks, mostly coming from South Italy to Germany, played a part in spreading Byzantine culture in the West. Otto III had summoned Greek monks to Germany, where they undertook the organization of the new monastic foundations. Amongst these monks may have been the Theophilus who wrote a work in Latin on the techniques of the goldsmith's craft. It is very probable that his literary activity was responsible for the great impetus given to the art of the goldsmith, whether in the production of book covers, reliquaries or altar *antependia*.

The Byzantine element was an important factor in western culture, but it did not stand alone. It was only its fusion with the Roman tradition transmitted through Italy and the Coptic element in its Irish version that could give birth to the unique phenomenon of western art.

Settlements of Graeco-Byzantine peoples in Italy

Byzantine colonization in Italy

Byzantine immigrants in Rome and the considerable Greek settlements in South Italy had no direct relationship. Thus a different liturgy was used in South Italy from that of the Greek immigrants in Rome. As in Constantinople, Greece and Asia Minor, the Greek colony in Rome used the liturgies attributed to St Basil and St John Chrysostom. On the contrary in South Italy the liturgy used was derived partly from Syria and Palestine, partly from a Graeco-Egyptian rite rooted in Alexandria. Immigrants to Rome mostly came from Constantinople, but in South Italy the great majority of the Greek settlements were composed of refugees from the provinces of Syria, Palestine and Egypt which had been conquered by the Arabs. The Greeks in South Italy were prevented from spreading northwards by the powerful Lombard duchy of Beneventum. Under its protection in the ninth century the city states of Gaeta, Amalfi and Naples were able to develop outside the zone of Byzantine official authority. By reason of political circumstances they adhered to the Latin form of the heritage of late antiquity.

The Fatimid conquest of Sicily in the tenth century started off a new wave of immigration to the mainland. The immigrants made for Central Italy and Rome. A Calabrian Greek, John Philagathus from Rossano, held the papal tiara as anti-pope against Gregory V (996–999). He was raised to the papal throne as John XVI (997–998). He had previously belonged to the circle of the German Emperor Otto III (983–1002). As abbot of Nonantola before he became Pope he had transcribed for Otto a medical work (*De Medicina*) by Celsus.

Most of the immigrants who left South Italy because of the Arabs were Basilian monks. They founded monasteries in the neighbourhood of Rome and one of these, Grottoferrata, has survived to the present day. Other Basilian refugee monks of particularly ascetic habits brought their religious outlook to the Latin West. One such ascetic was St Sabas, a refugee from Calabria who founded a monastery near Salerno; and it was St Nilus who settled as a hermit at Serperi near Gaeta. Another Basilian, who had been *hegumenus* (abbot) of the monastery of Cerchiara in Calabria before his flight, was summoned to Aachen by Otto III and he founded the house of Burtscheid. The influence of this ascetic group among the Basilians must have been very considerable. For instance St Nilus was known to Otto III, who often visited him and submitted to the ascetic rules laid down for him by Nilus. This ascetic emphasis was matched by similar tendencies in the West in reaction against the excessive secularization of the life of the Church. Thus side by side with the Basilian Nilus stood the English Abbot Dunstan of Glastonbury and the French Odo of Cluny.

The Greek element in Calabria had got the better of the Arab threat. The real danger to it came later with the Franciscan and Dominican orders. It was through their efforts that the number of Greek episcopal sees was continually being reduced by their submission to Roman Christendom during the period when every effort was being made to achieve reunion. About 1300 Crotone ceased to be a Greek bishopric; Rossano followed in 1364, Santa Ciriaca in 1497 and Bova in 1573. The Greek monasteries were also reduced in number. The most important of these, San Niccolo di Casole, was destroyed by the Turks in 1580. But in spite of the destruction of its cultural centres the Greek character of South Italy has survived down to the present day. In the extreme South of Calabria, in the Aspromonte, as well as in South Apulia in the neighbourhood of Otranto, today there are still villages where Greek is spoken as the mother tongue. But what had once been the tongue of the educated, the language of officials and scholars, has gradually become the speech of shepherds and peasants.

Byzantine civilization in South Italy maintained a standard that could hold its own with that of Constantinople down to the days of Frederick II. It was only then that the decline began. So it came about that in the eleventh century when Psellus died his place as *hypatos ton philosophon* (the head of the philosophical and philological faculty in the University of Constantinople) was taken by a certain John who was nicknamed 'Italus' because he came from Calabria. And when the monastery of Monte Cassino wanted to decorate its church with new mosaics its abbot sent for Greeks from South Italy.

The downfall of Graeco-Byzantine civilization in Italy

By the twelfth century the first signs of decline can be seen. The establishment of the Norman kingdom of South Italy and Sicily could do nothing to alter this. It is certainly true that the founding of the Norman state and the regaining of Sicily for the orthodox Christian faith signified the culminating point of Byzantine civilization in South Italy. The mosaics in the churches of Cefalù and Palermo are among the finest creations of Byzantine art. And after the military conquest of Sicily by the Norman king Roger I the Basilian monks were called in to assist with the conversion and they covered the island with a network of monasteries. Working from the monastery of San Salvatore in Messina founded in 1131, they set up so many new houses that Greek monasteries in Italy at that time numbered about 1500.

The decline of Byzantine civilization was a consequence of the dissolution of that old cosmopolitan culture created by monasticism on the foundations of late antique Christianity. It was this movement, which in the Byzantine Empire gradually led to the displacement of monastic-orientated religious culture, that brought about the disintegration of Byzantine culture in the Norman kingdom. The tolerance which the Norman rulers extended to Islam and to both Orthodox and Latin Christendom alike accorded little with the religious spirit of the old Byzantine culture. Thus the Arab Idrisi (1154) was able to write his famous geographical work at the court of Roger II in the Norman kingdom of Sicily; the work of the great Persian doctor Ali ibn Abbas (Hali Abbas) was the recognized text-book (*Liber Regius*) and the basis of lectures in the medical faculty of the university of Salerno.

In the Norman kingdom Graeco-Byzantine civilization now dominated only within certain limits. The Normans felt that they were a powerful Mediterranean power playing an international role. Arabic, Greek, Latin, and Italian which was then acquiring the status of a language in its own right, were found side by side in this kingdom. The claims of the Greek element to take the lead were thus being continually undermined. Under the Norman kings the administration of the kingdom had been in the hands of high Greek officials but by the days of the Hohenstaufen these were being replaced by Italians. Greek influence in Italy no longer looked to Constantinople. In Italy it was the Norman king and not the Byzantine Basileus who was regarded as the master of the world. It is significant that in an extant poem dating from the time of the Hohenstaufen Frederick II the reason given for lauding the Emperor as ruler of the world was his conquest of the stronghold of Parma.

The decline in Greek influence was also reflected in the decrease in the number of documents in Greek, and the use of this language in protocol constantly diminished. Byzantine imperial documents to high Greek office-holders of the Norman king in the first half of the twelfth century still point to the existence of a cultural link between the Greek civilization of South Italy and the Byzantine Empire, but by the thirteenth century any such connection had been broken. The Hohenstaufen Frederick II still issued his communications in Greek but after his death Greek was no longer one of the recognized languages of public administration. The new masters of South Italy, the Anjou allies of the papacy, attempted to appoint to the bishoprics of the Greek Church. Under their régime the number of private documents in Greek in South Italy declined still further. It was only within monastic walls that Byzantine culture lived on. Thus in the fourteenth century it was possible for a Greek monk Barlaam from Calabria to emerge as the determined opponent of hesychasm. Barlaam made himself the leader of the western-orientated party within the Byzantine Church. This was the last occasion on which the Greek element in South Italy raised its voice on an important issue in the Byzantine Church. But even as late as the sixteenth century, it was through this Greek element in South Italy that knowledge of the Greek language was largely transmitted to the West. The libraries of the South Italian monasteries were the great treasure houses in which western scholars sought out manuscripts of the Greek classics. It was this source which provided the greater number of the valuable Greek codices now in European libraries.

But the Apulian monasteries preserved and did not develop. This is most clearly apparent in the art of the Apulian monks. Their painting, particularly that preserved in the rock monasteries, is characterized by a rigid sterile imitation of old forms expressed in a primitive manner.

Byzantine culture in Armenia and Georgia

Thus Byzantine civilization influenced the West travelling by way of Ravenna, then Rome and finally South Italy, but almost contemporaneously it was also affecting the Slav peoples, Armenia and the races of the Caucasus. There is no doubt that its strongest influence was on the Slavs. But Armenian and Caucasian civilization which was beginning to take shape in the ninth century also owed Byzantium an obvious debt.

Armenian civilization, in so far as it was Christian, was particularly influenced by Syria. But in Armenia, as with the Germanic peoples, there was strong Coptic influence transmitted through exports. Reliefs in stone, particularly the so-called *khachk'ar* used for tombstones, were copied from Coptic carving.

The same elements were evident in early Caucasian civilization, which showed both Syrian and Coptic influences as well as possessing a cultural heritage from the Sassanids. In addition to imports of artistic wares from Syria and Egypt which resulted in ornaments and scenes from Syrian silk being copied on stone, there was also a not inconsiderable Iranian influence. The reliefs of the Sassanid period underwent further transformation in Armenia and in the Caucasus. In these regions an individual form of sculpture developed which also incorporated Christian Hellenistic motifs transmitted through Syrian sources. Here, as also with the Slav peoples and the West, the ninth century was a watershed: it was then that Syrian late antique civilization gave way before Byzantino-monastic influences. The political dependence of the Armenian kings on the Byzantine Emperor was reflected in the cultural sphere. The sources show that in the mid-ninth century Greek miniaturists came to Armenia to copy and illuminate manuscripts of the Gospels for the court. The oldest Armenian miniature painting shows a style closely related to icon painting. Strong oriental influences were also at work, particularly in the field of decoration. Persian textiles with their stylized animals are clearly reflected in the marginal ornamentation of manuscripts.

After the mid-seventh century monumental painting and mosaics, which were originally found in Armenia as in other parts of the Christian *imperium romanum,* became less frequent. In the art of the second Armenian kingdom which grew up from the mid-ninth century there is no longer any trace of the mosaic decoration identical with the Byzantine iconography of the monastic movement which was still to be found in the oldest churches. The break came suddenly and without warning. The church of the palace of the Armenian patriarchs in Zvart'nots dating from the mid-seventh century still has the remains of a wall painting showing the same iconography as the later eighth-century mosaic work of a Byzantine artist working in the Frankish Empire in the church of Germigny-des-Prés. But after the middle of the seventh century mosaic pictures ceased in Armenia for lack of craftsmen from Syria, Egypt or the capital Constantinople. The Arab conquest had disrupted communications between the different parts of the Empire and this made cultural exchanges impossible. For the same reason, that is, lack of technicians and workmen from the provinces Syria and Egypt, or the capital Constantinople, Armenia abandoned the domed church and the basilica. The necessary skilled workmanship for vaulting the dome was no longer available and so Armenian churches, which had drums like the Byzantine churches, were given a pointed roof placed over these drums. Up to the end of the late antique period Armenia, like the rest of the Empire, had built basilicas and domed churches. Here in Armenia the reform in ecclesiastical architecture which was adopted was conditioned by the change-over to another liturgy, coming from Syria. It was only with the Arab conquest of Syria and Egypt that there was a decisive break in architecture and painting. From this time onwards Armenian architecture parted company with that of the Byzantine Empire.

In the sculptured decoration of the façade, the feature which most clearly distinguishes Armenian art from that of contemporary Byzantium, there can be discerned an independent cultural development which was determined by political circumstances. The Armenian church produced rich sculptural decoration placed on the outside walls, sometimes individual figures, sometimes Biblical scenes, corresponding to the iconographic programme found in fresco or mosaic inside Byzantine churches. This representational sculpture on the façade of the church was derived from early Christian cycles. Thus tenth- and eleventh-century churches had figural decoration reminiscent of that of Santa Costanza, the mausoleum of the daughter of the Emperor Constantine, which dated from the first half of the fourth century. And here again the reason for the survival of this kind of figural decoration lay in political separation. In the Byzantine Empire sculpture on the façade of churches is attested (apart from the wealth of surviving sculpture on sarcophagi) by the surviving friezes found in North Italy in Cividale and by evidence about the sculpture on churches and secular public buildings under Constantine. But after the sixth-century reform movement in the church it disappeared. It was only in Armenia that it survived and was even receptive to new influences, mostly from the East, from Sassanid Persia. Thus representations of folk symbols, scenes of animal fights, copied from pictures on old Sassanid bowls and textiles, were used in ecclesiastical sculpture. This kind of decoration on the outside walls of churches is then found all over Christian Caucasia where the same form of ornamentation prevailed, and it was also passed on to early Russian ecclesiastical architecture. Even in the Byzantine Empire, in the church of St Gregory near Skripu not far from Thebes in Boeotia, there is to be found decorative sculpture obviously deriving from an Armenian original. Probably this church was founded by Armenian officers who may have employed some Armenian workmen in its construction.

The same situation held for literature as for representational art. Here the same phenomenon was found, namely, strong Syrian influence in Armenia. The Bible was translated into Armenian from a Syriac text. It was only later on, when Byzantine influence increased, that this translation was revised with the help of the Greek text. In the sixth century, Syrian and Byzantine influences in Armenia were about equal. The chronicle of Eusebius, the homilies of John Chrysostom and a work of Irenaeus were translated from the Greek; the works of Ephraem the Syrian from Syriac.

It was the same in Georgia, where literature was much influenced by Syria. But here too there was soon a strong orientation towards Byzantium, especially in the ninth century. This was particularly assisted by the presence of a Georgian (Iberian) monastery in the Greek Empire. This was the great Iberian house founded on Mount Athos towards the end of the tenth century. This foundation fostered fruitful activity in the field of translation by means of which learned Georgian literature was brought into close contact with Byzantium to which it was much indebted. Georgian hymnography would have been inconceivable without Byzantine models. George, the founder of the Iberian house on Athos, and also the well-known Georgian king, David the Builder, were outstanding hymn-writers. Along with hymns, Byzantine music was also adopted and with it the Byzantine system of notation, the neumes.

Later on, in the eleventh and twelfth centuries, philosophical studies in the Byzantine Empire, particularly the interest in Plato, produced a reaction against the monastic point of view, and this affected Georgian culture. Here there was also a native 'Enlightenment' based on philosophical interests. It was not for nothing, for instance, that Aristotle was translated into Georgian. And it must be remembered that at precisely the time when popular literature was beginning to revive in the eleventh and twelfth centuries in the Byzantine Empire, Georgia and Armenia were producing court poetry inspired by Persian models. This reflects the contemporary political situation, since Georgia was then politically dependent on the Muslim Seljuks who had developed a culture largely influenced by Persia. The rise of this court poetry meant that various oriental, and particularly Persian, elements penetrated into Georgia and Armenia. This was of considerable significance for Byzantine culture because in due course such influences reached Byzantium through these two countries.

Byzantine civilization, the Slavs and the non-Slav peoples in the Balkans

Political conditions

But Byzantine civilization had a stronger influence on the Slav peoples than in Armenia and Georgia. Here there was no competition as there had been in Armenia and Georgia where Byzantium had rivals, first Persian-Sassanid, and then Muslim, civilization.

Byzantine civilization came to the Slavs together with Christianity. The idea of converting the Slavs sprang more from political than religious considerations. The situation in Byzantium was different from the West where the Bohemian Adalbert, later canonized, or Bishop Bruno of Querfurt, each followed the dictates of his religious conscience and began the work of preaching the gospel to the Slavs. Behind the Byzantine apostles to the Slavs stood the Byzantine Basileus. He wanted to counter the Frankish Empire's political penetration of the Balkans. Charles the Great's conquests had pushed forward the Pannonian Mark up to the junction of the Sava and the Danube, and this was threatening Byzantine authority in the Balkans. For the Carolingians had not only established political control over this region but had at the same time begun missionary work among the Slav peoples there. The two great mission centres were the archbishopric of Salzburg and the patriarchate of Aquileia in North Italy. Here they played a role similar to that of the bishoprics of Patras and Sparta in the Peloponnese. The dispute between Aquileia and Salzburg over their respective spheres of influence in this missionary work was settled by drawing a line of demarcation along the river Drava. This meant that Croatia was converted by Aquileia, and the Great Moravian kingdom, that is, Moravia and most of the region of present-day Hungary, by Salzburg.

From the beginning of the ninth century a movement for independence gradually built up among the Slav peoples and led to the formation of the Croat kingdom and the Great Moravian kingdom. This resulted in an attempt to cast off the political links which had been forged when Christianity was accepted from the West. This movement was particularly active among the princes of Great Moravia. The continuing struggles between Great Moravia and the East Frankish kings and Emperors at first led to an understanding between the Moravian princes and the pagan Bulgars, and then with Byzantium as well. Western Christendom had established itself in Moravia with the appointment of several bishops dependent on Salzburg, but an attempt was made to oust it by accepting Byzantine Christendom, which seemed to offer rather less of a political threat. This was the background to the Moravian prince Rastislav's request for Christian priests from Byzantium. But for the Bulgar khan the Moravian prince's acceptance of Christianity constituted a threat to his own authority among the Slav tribes. It was this consideration which finally led him to accept Byzantine Christianity.

The execution of the mission was in the nature of a political enterprise. In Constantinople and other big cities of the Empire there were monasteries whose monks were engaged in publicist activity in support of imperial policy. Commissioned by the Emperor they composed letters and polemic in various languages. Among the contemporaries of Constantine (Cyril) and Methodius were men who knew Slav, Altaic, Arabic and western languages. Constantine and Methodius were two brothers who came from the military circles of Thessalonica. Methodius was born in 820, Constantine in 826. Both had received a good education, probably in the famous school which was directed by Leo of Thessalonica. Both spoke Latin, Arabic and perhaps an Altaic language, as well as the Slav dialect of the region round Thessalonica. Before his mission to the Slavs, Constantine had been active as an ambassador to Samarra. Later he stayed in South Russia at the court of the Khazars where a Turkic dialect was probably spoken. In both Samarra and at the Khazar court he had discussions on religious as well as political matters.

Both brothers were well prepared for their journey to the Slavs in the year 863. They took with them a Slavonic liturgy and part of the Gospels in the Slavonic language. For this purpose they had invented a Slavonic alphabet, the Glagolithic, which was partly written in the Greek cursive script. Neither of the Byzantine apostles to the Slavs had any lasting success in Moravia where they were first sent. Here western Christendom proved the stronger. By 864 the Bulgar khan had been converted to Christianity. He had well weighed the political consequences of such a course and had indeed at the same time conducted negotiations with the western Church in the hope of getting more favourable terms in return for his conversion. It was considered out of the question that the new Slav-Bulgar Church should be under the jurisdiction of the Patriarch of Constantinople. The Bulgar ruler wanted an independent Bulgarian Patriarch. For him this would pave the way for his supremacy over the Slav people. It was the road later taken by the khan Symeon when he assumed the imperial title. Just as the western Emperor thought to rule over all Germanic peoples, so he wished to become overlord of all the Slav tribes by taking the imperial title.

But in spite of such defensive actions as the use of Slavonic as the ecclesiastical language and the creation of an independent Slav patriarchate it proved impossible to keep out Byzantine civilization. Without the conversion of the Bulgar khan Boris to Orthodox Christianity in 864, the later conversion of the grand duke of Kiev, St Vladimir, would have been inconceivable. Both conversions were stages in the process by which Byzantine civilization conquered new provinces. The close bond between Orthodoxy and Empire, the upsurge of literature and representational art in the religious world of Orthodoxy, had created the necessary conditions for building a cultural bridge between Byzantium and the Slav peoples on a religious basis. For together with Christianity in its Byzantine Orthodox form came Byzantine literature, representational art and statecraft. So in the eyes of both the Christian Bulgarian state and the Christian Russian Empire Constantinople was the only true capital and the only centre of the universe. Life was modelled on this city with its imperial palace and its famous churches, its ceremonial and its imperial title.

The Bulgarian khans and the Varangian princes of Kiev adopted the Slavonic form of Christianity brought by Constantine and Methodius as an act of calculated *politique* with their Slav subjects in mind. The available Slavonic translation of the Bible and Slavonic liturgy were of no use to either prince. The Bulgar khan Boris himself spoke a Turkic dialect and used the Greek language for administrative purposes. Thus from the beginning of the eighth century the reports and decrees of the Bulgar khans were drawn up in Greek. And in the early days Christianity had come to them in Greek from the Roman provincial population who were particularly numerous in the lower Danube mouth and the region round Sofia.

Almost the same conditions held for the Varangian grand dukes of Kiev. They themselves spoke a North German dialect but used Greek for communicating with foreigners. There were Greek colonies in Kiev, and by the first half of the tenth century they already had the church of St Elijah, which was the ecclesiastical centre, and they were used by the Varangians as officials and copyists. The point of entry for Greek influence into Kiev was Byzantine Cherson in the Crimea, the Korsun of the Russian chronicles.

The Byzantine imperial conception and Byzantine civilization in Russia and Bulgaria
The khan of the Bulgars and the Russian grand duke had already come into contact with Byzantine provincial civilization before they accepted baptism. By this act they formally adopted the Orthodox Byzantine version of Christianity as their religion and with it Byzantine civilization, which was impregnated with Orthodoxy. From the outset this led to a special development of Byzantine civilization in both these Slav countries. Moreover the provincial Byzantine culture which had been spreading in Russia and Bulgaria before the conversion of their princes found itself cut off from the

main stream of development in the Byzantine Empire by reason of the iconoclast controversy. Although the iconoclasts emerged victorious over the iconophiles, in Bulgaria and the Crimea veneration of icons continued. The Crimea put itself under the ecclesiastical jurisdiction of the Katholikos of Georgia, whose seat was in Mzcheta. The Georgian bishops broke with the heretical patriarchs of Constantinople and recognized the Patriarch of Jerusalem as their spiritual superior. In 759 bishop John of Doros in the Crimea was consecrated by the Georgian Katholikos. Thus close ecclesiastical connections were forged between Georgia and the Byzantine Crimea and these links were also reflected in the exteriors of the churches. This Georgian influence spread from the Byzantine Crimea into those parts of the Russian Varangian kingdom with which it was in contact. Bulgaria also detached itself from the Patriarch of Constantinople, since this prince of the Church supported the iconoclast party, and it sought to establish relations with Rome. This again was not without influence on the character of its ecclesiastical architecture. Thus the basilica was the predominant architectural style of building until the beginning of the tenth century and it was only then that it was gradually superseded by the Byzantine ecclesiastical design, the domed cross-in-square church. So it came about that the Roman architectural tradition was long continued in the Latin-speaking region on the lower Danube as well as on the Black Sea coast. The Constantinian form of ecclesiastical building, the simple basilica with or without pillar supports, and the domed basilica, went on long after Constantinople had adopted the domed cross-in-square church. This Constantinian architecture was still being used in Bulgaria in the ninth and the first half of the tenth centuries, as the building of Aboba Pliska shows.

The same thing happened in Russia. Georgian architecture influenced Russian ecclesiastical building through the medium of the Byzantine art of the Crimea. Thus the ground plan of the Sophia church in Kiev is closely related to that of the Georgian church of Mohkvi. The Russian monastic cave churches are also dependent on Crimean models, which followed the usage of Georgian monastic communities. There were Basilian rock monasteries in Cappadocia and Calabria which seem to have grown up at the time of the iconoclast persecution. According to an old tradition Greeks and Georgians had worked on the mosaics in the Sophia church in Kiev. The ornamental and figural decoration on the façades of early Russian churches also reflects Georgian models.

Besides this particular development, which was in its early days the consequence of the iconoclast controversy, Bulgaria and Russia had their own special imperial art which came through Byzantine channels. They had also adopted the special ceremonial connected with the Byzantine imperial office. This meant that they copied not only the forms of individual churches but adopted a particular group of buildings which was closely linked with the imperial court. This also revealed the political character of the decision of Boris I and St Vladimir to adopt Christianity. With their conversion they entered the Christian *oikoumene* whose centre was Constantinople and whose head was the Byzantine Basileus. They strove to attain both the splendour of the capital and the crown of the Emperor. This is the reason why in 917 Symeon of Bulgaria not only took the title *basileus romaion* but copied the most important buildings of the Byzantine capital in his own residence. He began by erecting the great three-aisled palace near Aboba Pliska which was an imitation of the Magnaura, the Byzantine imperial palace in Constantinople. The next step was the construction of a wide paved ceremonial road leading to his palace. This was copied from the Mese, the great ceremonial avenue of Constantinople.

A hundred years later Yaroslav the Wise (1019–1054) did the same as the Bulgarian ruler. He too took as his model the imperial official buildings of Constantinople. Yaroslav had the new city of Kiev laid out on the hill Kijis in imitation of one of the quarters of Constantinople. The Golden Gate, the most famous part of the city's fortifications and one of the Byzantine official secular buildings, was copied in Kiev. It was from the Golden Gate that the main avenue, the Mese, led to the imperial palace. The Golden Gate of Kiev also had its church of the Holy Virgin like its prototype in Constantinople. This church in Constantinople was in place of the statue of the tutelary goddess of the city. The statue of the city goddess in the form of the Greek goddess Tyche holding a cornucopia in the left hand stood on the propylaion of the gate. When it fell to the ground after an earthquake in 865 a church dedicated to the Holy Virgin was erected on this spot and she now assumed the role of the city's protectress.

In building other sacred edifices in Kiev in imitation of those of Constantinople it was usual to consider their relation to imperial ceremony. It was with this in mind that the Assumption (*Koimesis* or Dormition) church was built in the region of the old Cave Monastery; this was said to be after the model of the *Koimesis* of the Mother of God near the Blachernae Palace in Constantinople. Every year on August 15 a procession went from the imperial palace to this church at the Blachernae Palace and commemorated the death of the Mother of God in solemn liturgy. The Sophia church in Kiev, as its name suggests, had in mind Hagia Sophia in Constantinople, but for lack of technicians and materials it did not copy the architecture of the famous Byzantine building. For this reason the Sophia church in Kiev had to make use of contemporary forms of Byzantine ecclesiastical architecture. Moreover, the Sophia church was begun under St Vladimir (died 1015), and at this time Georgian influence coming via Cherson was stronger than Byzantine. This affected the ground plan, which naturally determined the structure of the building.

In Kiev, as in Bulgaria, the deliberate adoption of the secular and ecclesiastical architecture of Constantinople reflected general political conceptions, which were orientated towards the Byzantine Empire. This orientation towards Byzantine culture and statecraft remained a living factor in Russia after the Kievan era. When Vladimir displaced Kiev as the capital of the kingdom towards the end of the twelfth century the buildings in the new capital were erected in imitation of those of Constantinople, as had been the case in Kiev. The grand duke Andrew who was reigning then had the Golden Gate with a church to the Virgin Mary built in the walls of the city, and as in Kiev a church dedicated to the Assumption (*Koimesis*) was built after the prototype in Constantinople.

Architecture in Constantinople exercised a decisive influence over buildings in Russia. There was a similar development to that which took place in the Arab Empire, when in imitation of the Chalke Palace built by Constantine in Byzantium the Caliph Walid had erected a great mosque in Damascus which was to determine the architectural pattern of a large number of Arab mosques. The influence in Russia of the Assumption church of Kiev was similar to that of the Great Mosque of Damascus in the Muslim world. The prototype of the Assumption was a rotunda in Constantinople, which had in turn been copied by the Emperor Constantine I from a similar rotunda in Jerusalem and therefore differed from Byzantine ecclesiastical architecture in use in the eleventh century. Some idea of the early Christian style of the original Blachernae church can be gained from the mausoleum of Constantina in Rome, which still survives as the church of Santa Costanza. But Russia in the eleventh century no longer had the technical resources to vault in a great rotunda with a dome of similar extent, and so the church was built on a square ground plan with three naves and the dome with a relatively small drum was erected over the central nave. This style found its greatest perfection in the church of St Mary on the river Nerlya near Vladimir (1165–1166) and it did indeed develop into one of the most commonly used architectural forms in early Russian architecture. This can be seen from the Demetrius cathedral (1194–1197) in Vladimir and from the cathedral of St George in Yuryev-Polski.

And so partly under the influence of the original church of St Mary near the Blachernae Palace in Constantinople which was copied in Kiev and Vladimir, partly under Georgian influence, there grew up a distinctive form of building which long influenced Russian ecclesiastical church architecture.

Georgian influence is also evident in the figural and ornamental decoration found on the outside walls of churches. On the façades there was sculpture showing Christian saints fashioned after their stiff icon prototypes, and scenes of fights with animals which were copied from Byzantine and Iranian textiles both here and in the West. In Georgian and Armenian churches decoration of this kind had long been in use. In these countries they had got to know the forms of the Iranian world through the textiles coming from Sassanid Persia. Georgia also exercised some influence over the development of the script of Old Church Slavonic in early Russia. This can be seen in the decoration of the Gospel of Archangel dating from the second half of the eleventh century.

Opposing currents in the Russian world

In the face of Byzantine and what was in fact comparatively weak Georgian influence, the West played a very insignificant part in early Russian culture. Apart from the Korsun door in the cathedral of the Holy Wisdom in Novgorod which was the work of Riquinus, a craftsman from Magdeburg, there was no really noticeable influence until the twelfth century. It then appeared in Halitz and Cernigor after communications between Russia and Constantinople had been broken by the Altaic Polovetzi (the Cumans). The inspiration of the western romanesque style can be seen in the door of the church of St Mary on the Nerlya. This western element in Russian ecclesiastical architecture remained relatively slight in the succeeding period and it was nothing like so pronounced as that of Byzantium. It was however some indication of its force that it managed to spread as far as Novgorod on the threshhold of the Baltic Sea.

As well as Byzantine elements, there was a modest oriental influence coming into Russia from the world of Islam. During the Kievan period this only seems to have affected ceramics. In later Muscovite art it had a far greater range and was particularly noticeable in architecture. Thus in the first half of the sixteenth century the Persian-Islamic funerary towers seem to have inspired churches in the shape of a tower with tent-like roofs, such as is seen in the architecture of the church of the Ascension in Kolomenskoye and the church of St Basil in Moscow. This influence probably came through the Italian master builders employed by the Muscovite tsars. These men had also worked for Muslim princes, such as the Tatar khans of the Crimea, and they had seen this style of architecture and used it in constructing Muscovite churches. Thus before he built the cathedral of the Holy Archangels in the Kremlin in Moscow (1505–1509) Alovisio the Young (Aleviz Novyj) had been employed by the khan of the Crimean Tatars on the palace which still survives today at Bakhshisarai.

But in spite of this oriental influence, Russian art up to the end of the seventeenth century never forgot its Byzantine origins. Foreign builders in the late Muscovite period at the end of the fifteenth and beginning of the sixteenth centuries had to adapt themselves to Byzantine styles which had taken deep root in Russian soil. Thus the Italian Aristotele Fioravanti from Bologna had to use the traditional Byzantine style in the church of the Assumption. It is, however, true that secular buildings did not adopt the same criteria as ecclesiastical ones. Thus the flanged palace (Granovitaya Palata) built in the Kremlin in Moscow, as well as the walls and towers of the Kremlin, were not inspired by Byzantine imperial palaces and city walls but rather by the buildings of Mantua and Ferrara.

The special monastic elements of early Russo-Byzantine culture

Russian architecture, in contrast to that of the Balkan states, was characterized by a certain inflexibility of its own over and above what it had received from early Byzantine sources, and down to the late Muscovite period it kept this immune from any foreign influence. A similar conservatism is found in its other cultural activities. This distinguishes Russian development from that of the Balkans, where elements from both Italy and Constantinople freely mingled together. Thus its development cannot be regarded from the same point of view as the encounter of the Balkan Slavs with Byzantine culture.

In early Russia down to the Muscovite period cultural activity was entirely in the hands of the monks. It is significant that the first beginnings of Russian literature are connected with writings from the Cave Monastery in Kiev. This Russian literature developed out of the Old Bulgarian writings of the tenth and eleventh centuries. Thus the reception of the Byzantine cultural heritage in this field did not come direct from Byzantium but through Bulgarian channels. Translations were made, not only of the saints' lives but of Byzantine chronicles, such as John Malalas and George the Monk (George the Sinner), or popular works such as the story *Barlaam and Joasaph*. From this collection of translations there soon developed an independent body of literature and the centre of this activity was in Kiev. In the first place, the *Russian Primary Chronicle* originated here and was composed in the Cave Monastery. This work, although it certainly used Byzantine sources, had a definite view of Russian history and provided evidence that the Russians had already developed their own conception of the state. The *Instruction of the Grand Duke Vladimir for his sons* also belongs to the same period and this would not have been possible without inspiration from Byzantine models of the same genre. This is equally true of the *Russaya Pravda*, attributed to the grand duke Yaroslav the Wise, which also belongs to the eleventh century and was a work owing an obvious debt to similar Byzantine legal manuals, such as the *Procheiros Nomos*.

The development of a national literature, with the help of Byzantine works transmitted through Bulgarian translations, led to the formation of the old Russian *koine* based on the Kievan dialect. By the eleventh century the Bulgarian translations of Byzantine originals transcribed in Kiev contained idioms from local dialect. The Bulgarian literary language together with Greek had been in existence at the court of the Kievan princes since the beginning of the tenth century (it is attested as early as 912 by Oleg's treaty with the Byzantine Empire). Now in the eleventh century it gradually became the Russian literary language showing a strong Kievan influence. Thus local dialectical differences between the various Slav tribes in the territory under the princes of Kiev were largely eliminated, and so from the linguistic point of view out of a number of different tribes a single people began to emerge.

Byzantine influence on Russia was twofold. There was an indirect cultural current coming by way of Bulgaria, particularly in the literary field, and a direct stream from Cherson in the Crimea, particularly in representational art. The cultural influence of the Byzantine Empire on early Russia was of incalculable importance. It was based on complete monastic domination in the field of cultural activity. Unlike Byzantium, in Russia laymen rarely engaged in literary activity. At the beginning of the twelfth century the *Russian Primary Chronicle* was written by monks in the Kievan Cave Monastery, just as monastic chronicles had been written in Constantinople in the ninth century. But while from the mid-eleventh century onwards new movements emerged in the Byzantine Empire, satire and romance appeared as new literary genres and painting turned to more realistic and naturalistic styles, in Russia the old orthodox Byzantine traditions still prevailed.

It was significant that from the second half of the twelfth century onwards there was a monastery dedicated to St Panteleimon on Mount Athos exclusively for Russian monks. Early Russian literature and representational art with very few exceptions drew their inspiration solely from movements within the circle of orthodox Byzantine monasticism and remained untouched by anything outside this monasticism, such as the new genres of Byzantine representational art and literature. There were no early Russian translations of either the Greek romances and satires of the eleventh and twelfth centuries or of the noted historians of the fifth and sixth centuries, such as Procopius, Menander or Priscus.

Early Russian painting was limited to nothing more than what it found in Greek icons. The pictures on the icons were translated into the language of monumental art. Figures inspired by icons were placed side by side on church walls. The freedom to break away from the prototypes and compose fresh scenes was non-existent and consequently there was no development in art comparable to that found in Byzantium in the twelfth-century frescoes of Nereži, or in Sicily in the mosaics of the *capella palatina* of Roger II in Palermo. The rigidity which characterized early Russian culture was only shaken off with the spiritual movement of hesychasm which came to Russia from Byzantium and made a definite impact. This movement helped early native Russian representational art to achieve a definite breakthrough. In the field of painting it first showed itself in the frescoes in the Dormition (the Assumption) church in Moscow. These were painted in 1408 by Master Daniel and his pupil Andrei Rublev. The same Andrei Rublev painted the Holy Trinity, the most sublime symbol of Orthodoxy, in the church of the Troitsko-Sergievsky monastery near Moscow. Here the artist's brush expressed in painting that which the Byzantine mystic Nicholas Cabasilas had described in his writings on the Holy Liturgy. And it is of course true that this masterpiece of the greatest early Russian master drew inspiration from Byzantine sources. The symbolical meaning which Nicholas found in each divine sacrament, such as Baptism, Confirmation and Eucharist, was expressed by Andrei Rublev through the medium of the picture. This great master of early Russian icon painting himself stood in close relationship to Byzantine art. This was not so much because he was influenced by certain motifs coming from Byzantine sources as by reason of close collaboration with one of the greatest Byzantine masters of that time, the painter Theophanes whom the Russians called Feofan Grek ('the Greek'). Theophanes showed the same mastery alike of icon, fresco and miniature painting. When he came to Russia in 1378 he already had a great reputation due to his work in Constantinople, Chalcedon and the Crimea. According to a contemporary chronicle he alone did the paintings in forty churches. His work was commissioned by Byzantine magnates, Genoese merchants and Russian princes. In Russia he first worked in Novgorod where he was responsible for the frescoes in the church of the Transfiguration. Later he went to Moscow and painted the pictures on the iconostasis in the church of the Annunciation, working in collaboration with Andrei Rublev and the staretz Prochor (Prochoros). Here the Greek master was entrusted with the most important part of the iconostasis, the *Deesis* with the figures of the three great intercessors. Like Domenikos Theotokopoulos (whom the Spanish called 'El Greco'), Feofan Grek belonged to the large group of *pictores graeci* who from the mid-fourteenth century onwards made Byzantine art widely known not only among the Slavs but also in certain romance lands. El Greco came from the circle of the Greek Madonnari resident in Venice. Feofan Grek belonged to the group working in Moscow and Novgorod and went from Italian to Russian service. The third substantial group of *pictores graeci* were especially active at the Serbian court from the first half of the fourteenth century onwards, but the names of individual outstanding artists cannot be distinguished the one from the other, though their creations certainly rank among the masterpieces of European painting in the late middle ages.

The close connection between Byzantine and Russian monasticism endured long, even when the Byzantine Empire had ceased to exist as a political entity. And so the Italian renaissance also reached Russia, in so far as it influenced the holy icons of the Greek Orthodox Church in those parts of the former Byzantine Empire controlled by the Venetians. From Italy came the type of the nursing Madonna, the Maria Galaktophousa, which is first met with in Cretan painting and from there was taken over by Russian icon painting.

Byzantine civilization and the Slav peoples of the Balkans

In brief, it may be said that as long as Russian spiritual life was determined by monks, it was little more than a province of Byzantium. But what was found in early Russia was only one aspect of Byzantine civilization. In this respect the world of the Balkans differed from Russia, for it possessed something which was not simply limited to the world of Byzantine Orthodoxy. The Balkan countries were in contact with the other important aspect of Byzantine life which was closely linked to the upsurge of a new conception of the universe in the mid-eleventh century. And in contrast to Russia, the Slavs in the Balkans were also open to the ways of western influences. This is particularly true of Serbia and Rumania, less so of Bulgaria. Also in contrast to Russia was the influence of Byzantine civilization on social life and on the structure of society and of the state. This was very largely because Byzantium exercised direct control over these regions for several centuries.

Among the Balkan states of Slav nationality, Bulgaria was the bridgehead across which Byzantine civilization entered. It was largely through Bulgarian channels that Byzantine influence was transmitted to Russia and Rumania. In Bulgarian monasteries men worked to translate Byzantine romances and legal works as well as ecclesiastical literature. And the translations of the Greek works were in Church Slavonic.

The decision of the Bulgarian khan Boris to accept Christianity in its Byzantine Orthodox form had linked the Balkan Slavs to Byzantine civilization far more effectively than the conversion of the Kievan grand duke St Vladimir had done for Russia. The social structure of Bulgaria was changed by Byzantine civilization, which was not the case in Russia. The old nomadic tribes of the Altaic proto-Bulgars based on kin had been divided into ten tribal sub-divisions (in Turkic: On ogur) but the acceptance of Byzantine law put an end to this arrangement and also altered the relationship between the Bulgars and the Slav tribes subject to them. The chieftains of the ten proto-Bulgar tribes found a place in the new set-up as military governors, rather like the commanders of the Byzantine themes. The difference between the Slav subject tribes and the proto-Bulgar tribes disappeared. The position of the khan who took the Byzantine title of Basileus in 917 *vis-à-vis* the *boliades* (the chieftains of individual tribes) grew stronger as Byzantine influence penetrated, The *Kormačaya Kniga*, the Byzantine code of public and canon law adopted in the tenth century, together with lawbooks such as the *Ecloga* of Leo III and Constantine V, supplanted old Bulgarian customary law, and gradually the Altaic proto-Bulgars were integrated with the Slavs and the Roman population to form a single nation.

Soon after the adoption of Christianity the social structure of Bulgaria differed little from that of Byzantium. The family of the khan, the princes (*tigin*), were the high aristocracy, the great boyars; the princes of the old tribes and their families belonged to the lesser nobility, the little boyars. The members of these two classes of nobles were the landowners whose estates were worked by *paroikoi*, mainly Slavs, called by the Bulgars *pariči* or *otroči*.

The small towns on the Black Sea coast, the lower Danube and the region of the present day capital Sofia, were entirely occupied by inhabitants of Roman origin. This can be seen from the churches of that period, which at the beginning of the tenth century were still being built in the style of a Constantinian basilica. At first this Roman provincial element, together with the monks coming to Bulgaria from Byzantium, supplied the cultural element. Foreign influences, particularly of Islamic oriental provenance brought in by slaves, were at this time only of secondary importance.

Most of the slaves in Bulgaria had been captured by the Khazars in the raids into North-West Persia and among them were many highly qualified workers from the cities of northern Persia. This explains why at the opening of the tenth century there was a highly developed ceramic industry near Preslav, then the residence of the Bulgar khan, to supply the needs of the court and the monasteries. It was here that the glazed clay tiles in the monastery church of Patleina were made, with pictures of the saints on them. Further, surviving fragments show that many of these glazed plaques were used for decoration, probably on walls. These ornaments originated partly in Samarra, partly in northern Persia, and also in West Turkestan. Ceramics of a similar kind are found in the Byzantine Empire in Constantinople, as well as in Kiev in the early period. This kind of decoration clearly reveals the connection with Islamic ceramics, and the rich tile ornamentation on the façades of Bulgarian churches was due to the work of these oriental craftsmen.

Another factor of importance in Bulgarian culture was Georgian influence. The Georgians had close ties with Byzantine culture through their monasteries in the Empire (their first foundation was that of the monk Hilarion on Bithynian Mount Olympus in 864, followed by the foundation of the Iberian house on Mount Athos between 982 and 985) and in Palestine, and they also established houses in Bulgaria. Thus the monastery of Petritzus, present-day Bačkovo, was built by the Grand Domestic, Gregory Pacurianus. This high-ranking Byzantine imperial official of Georgian origin laid down that his monastery should only receive monks whose mother tongue was Georgian. The unusual architectural feature of Bulgarian churches, that is, the linking of the external façade of the apse to the springing of the roof by arches, can be traced back to the influence of Georgian monastic architecture. A façade of this kind can be seen in the church of St Clement founded about 1295. It is also found as early as the eleventh century in the funerary chapel of the monastery of Bačkovo. From Georgia also came the custom of putting friezes with inscriptions on the façades of churches (as in the eleventh-century Sophia church in Ochrida), and this form was copied by Rumania from Bulgarian churches.

The downfall of the First Bulgarian Empire had the effect of strengthening Byzantine influence in Bulgaria and resulted in the growth of what was almost a Byzantino-Bulgarian civilization. Thus the thunder and lightning books, the dream and oracle books, a kind of pseudo-literature found in every civilization, were translated into Bulgarian. Then followed the Byzantine romances, such as *Stephanites and Ichnelates* and the story of Alexander, the popular story *Barlaam and Joasaph*, the Byzantine satires of *Porikologos* and the animal fables of the *Physiologos*. So in Bulgaria, in contrast to Russia, there grew up a culture based on the new intellectual movement of the mid-eleventh century onwards and not transmitted through Byzantine monastic channels.

The Norman conquest of Sicily and South Italy was of great importance for the development of Byzantine civilization in the Balkans. In relation to the Byzantine Empire the Normans played a role in the Balkans almost identical with that of the victorious Seljuks in Anatolia. From South Italy the Normans laid hands on Albania and Epirus. After the Hohenstaufen interlude, the Anjou followed in their steps. The situation of the Balkans between the Normans, and later the Anjou, on the one hand, and the Byzantines on the other, played a vital part in building up a Serbian state and gave Serbian civilization its singular position between East and West which still determines its present-day character.

Western influence here came from Italy or from the Latin monasteries on the east coast of the Adriatic. Serbian churches built in the fourteenth century were considerably influenced by romanesque architecture. But elements coming from Islamic sources were also present. The architectural style of monastic churches such as Studenica and Dečani combined marked romanesque influences from the Adriatic region with those of the Byzantine world.

Other Serbian churches, such as Kuševač, have grills almost entirely similar to those of Islamic mosques or funerary towers. There is indeed very little difference in the decorative ornamentation of this church and that of an Islamic building such as the Seljuk residence in Konya in Anatolia. This reflects the migratory movement following Seljuk expansion. Many Byzantine craftsmen then moved from Asia Minor to Europe and played a substantial role in the development of Serbian art. These Asia Minor Greeks who helped to build Serbian, and also Dalmatian, churches came from a region that was considerably affected by Islamic culture which had in turn been influenced by Byzantium.

Thus in Irak from the beginning of the thirteenth century there was Arabic miniature painting showing strong stylistic influence from the East Syrian triangular region bounded by the three cities Edessa, Diyarbakr and Mardin. It would be difficult to conceive of the miniatures of the so-called Baghdad school without the twelfth-century Byzantine miniatures produced in this district. Illuminations in this style still lived on, particularly in certain Syriac Gospel manuscripts of the early thirteenth century. It was the immigrants from this Arab-Byzantine border region who were responsible for the remarkable affinity of the illuminations in the Serbian Tetra-Gospel with Islamic miniatures. This affinity derived from a common source on which both the painters at the Baghdad school and those of the Serbian Tetra-Gospel could draw, that is, the work produced in the Edessa-Diyarbakr-Mardin region. The miniatures of the fifteenth-century manuscript of the *Romance of Alexander* also show distinct stylistic links with the Arabic miniatures of the Baghdad school.

In comparison with Bulgaria, Byzantine civilization had nothing like the same foothold in Serbia. One of the main reasons for this lay in the comparatively late confrontation of Serbia with Byzantium. And by then the Byzantine Empire was only a Mediterranean state in the eyes of its neighbours and not the heart of the civilized world. Here in Serbia the social structure of the country was not changed by the reception of Byzantine culture, as was the case in Bulgaria. When Byzantine law reached Serbia it was not able to oust the legal forms of Serbian customary law. The law book of the tsar Dušan, the *Zakonnik*, does indeed use a number of Greek legal terms but the legal conceptions are Serbian. And in any case Byzantine codes, such as the law book of Blastares and the so-called 'Law of the devout and Christ-loving Emperor Justinian', were constantly drawn on to supplement the native legal code, as is attested by the common manuscript tradition of the three works. The *strateia*, the property of the soldier-farmer, and the *pronoia*, the handing over of the fiscal revenue of a certain area to deserving state officials, were both known to the Serbian state. In Serbia, as in the Byzantine Empire, the *pronoia* pointed the way to the imminent disintegration of the state.

Serbia's encounter with Byzantine civilization took place in the shadow of the threat to Byzantium from both East and West. Seljuk penetration into Asia Minor resulted in the displacement of the Greek population, as had happened during the iconoclast controversy four hundred years earlier. These refugees left the lost Byzantine provinces for Europe. This demographic change is reflected in certain aspects of Serbian art, which was however also affected by Italian romanesque influences coming in from the Adriatic. Both these left their imprint on Byzantino-Serbian culture.

Bulgarian development followed a different course. The so-called Second Bulgarian Empire was a national movement growing up in reaction against Byzantine elements which were regarded as a foreign intrusion. But in spite of this conscious detachment of the Bulgarian Empire from Byzantine political control, close cultural links were maintained between the two countries. It is even possible to perceive a strengthening of Byzantine influence at this time.

In the funerary chapel of Boiana built by the Bulgarian magnate Kaloyan, frescoes dating from the first half of the thirteenth century show a close relationship with the frescoes of contemporary Byzantine art. In Boiana the realism first expressed in the frescoes of Nereži and the mosaics of the *capella palatina* of Palermo dating from the twelfth century, is taken a stage further. This development was largely due to an advance in painting technique achieved by the substitution of tempera for fresco. The old fresco painting imposed certain limitations on the colour range: not all colours could be used on the plaster on a wall. And further, fresco painting always became brighter when it dried. With the tempera technique in which the yolk of egg was used as a binding medium it was possible to achieve a far greater luminosity. The colours were softer and far greater spatial effects could now be produced. The realism of the frescoes of Boiana is particularly outstanding in the lifelike portrait of the founder, then the reigning tsar of Bulgaria, while the pictures of the saints are closely linked to iconographic models of the capital.

Influence from the West is also apparent in the frescoes of Boiana; this did not, however, come direct, as in Serbian art, but through Byzantine models. Thus the naves portrayed in the frescoes of Boiana are not those of a Byzantine, but of a crusader, church. In the same way the shields of the knights and the garments of the personages shown are western both in style and cut. This was due to the Latin Empire then set up by the crusaders in Constantinople and to the Venetian lordship over the greater part of the Aegean islands. Venetian influence seemed to be particularly important; it extended even to the minting of coins. Thus Bulgarian gold pieces were partly stamped like the Byzantine *nomisma*, partly like the Venetian zecchino.

In contrast to the Byzantine realism of Bulgarian painting, the naturalism of Serbian painting was stimulated by the West. Some of the frescoes in the church of Sopoćani near Novi Pazor (1265) show Italian influence. Here there is an affinity with the frescoes in the baptistery of Parma. But in later Serbian churches from the beginning of the fourteenth century onwards influence from Central Italy is more noticeable. The Sienese school of painting and Giotto seemed to have considerably influenced the monastery church of Gračanica, although traces of inspiration from North Italy can also be detected here. It is often a question of the Byzantine cultural heritage being transmitted through Italian channels. Thus the violent movement of descending angels in the Deposition of Christ in Santa Maria dell' Arena in Padua seems to have influenced the portrayal of the angels precipitating themselves from heaven in the scene showing the death of Mary in Gračanica. This Italian influence on Serbian representational art reflects the close political and economic links between Serbia and Italy. The fact that the lives of the saints and the Bibles copied in Serbian monasteries from the thirteenth century onwards used Italian paper from Ancona and not Byzantine paper is a significant comment on this economic relationship.

While Serbian fresco painting experienced these western influences, Bulgarian painting encountered eastern forces. There was genuine Islamic influence, particularly on ceramics, and it should be distinguished from the pseudo-Islamic influence in the fields of Bulgarian miniature painting and woodcarving. This pseudo-Islamic style is seen in the Tetra-Gospel of *pop* Dobreišo, dated to 1221, which is decorated with arrow-band and animal motifs showing the same kind of ornamentation as Seljuk woodcarving in Konya. These ornaments figure prominently in the repertoire of patterns found in early Bulgarian woodcarving.

This pseudo-Islamic influence, due to refugees from the Byzantine provinces conquered by the Seljuks, is quite distinct from the genuine Islamic inspiration which at this time was being brought to bear on Bulgarian and Byzantine ceramics. The prototypes of these ceramics were to be found in Persia. There are instances in Kiev of faience dishes of the type found at Ghabri (*c.* 1200) and in Constantinople of faience ware similar to that produced by the North Persian ceramic centre at Rai. The Byzantine and Bulgarian faience industry copied Persian models down to the smallest detail. Bowls coming from the Byzantine ceramic centre of Corinth even copied the Kufic script of their models. To a lesser extent Greek motifs, such as Leda and the swan, are also found on relief ceramics. The finds at the excavations in Trnovo demonstrate that glazed Bulgarian ceramics were not imported from Islamic countries but, as these glazed tiles show, were the products of a native ceramic industry.

Unlike Russia, Bulgaria built up its own native art independently of Byzantium. Almost the only surviving evidence of this art is found in Bulgarian book miniatures. Thus when the Byzantine chronicle of Manasses was translated into Bulgarian it was expanded to include a Bulgarian section. Here information on Bulgarian history is found interpolated into the story of the Trojan war and is illustrated by an excellent series of miniatures. The defeat of Leo III by the Bulgar khan Krum and the Russian invasion of Bulgaria from 967 to 969, as well as later events, such as the death of prince Asen, are all shown in these miniatures. The portrayal of the Bulgar tsar and his family in the so-called Tetra-Gospel (the Tetra-Evangelium of tsar Ivan Alexander of 1356) and in the church of Boiana belong to this kind of native art. The painting at Boiana is probably only a copy of a larger portrait of the tsar.

The year 1393 when the Bulgarian capital Trnovo was captured by the Turks was a turning point in the history of Bulgaro-Byzantine civilization. The Turkish conquest completely changed the social structure of the country. The families of the great Bulgarian magnates were exterminated and the land-owning aristocracy dispossessed, except in so far as they turned Muslim. Even the Bulgarian church was almost exterminated. In the first place the Bulgarian Patriarch was deposed and a Greek bishop appointed instead. Most of the churches were turned into mosques. Only the monasteries and the monastic churches remained.

In spite of this persecution Bulgaro-Byzantine civilization lived on until the first half of the nineteenth century. The Bulgarian monasteries were responsible for this. In any case this culture was, as it were, in a state of arrested development and made no further progress. This is the main characteristic of Bulgarian art after 1393, as is attested both by the few surviving buildings of this period, such as the main church of the monastery of Bačkovo and the church of Christ in Arbanassi, and by the fresco painting. The point of development reached by fresco painting at the time of the Turkish conquest is particularly obvious from later examples of this form of art which preserved their character unchanged up to the beginning of the nineteenth century. A traditional pattern was followed and it is very rare to find any individual touches in the sacred iconography hallowed by tradition. Even miniature painting, which had achieved so high a standard, gradually sank back into servile imitation of its heritage from the pre-Turkish period. The only trace of any genuine development is found in woodcarving. Among the finest examples of this Byzantine art, which is found up to the eve of the nineteenth century, is the iconostasis of the Rila monastery.

In spite of its apparent sterility, Bulgarian art in the epoch after the Turkish conquest played an important role in the development of the other Balkan states. It was indeed Bulgaria which gave Byzantine art to Rumania. Whatever Rumania preserved in the way of Byzantine art came from the Second Bulgarian Empire. Many Bulgarians migrated to Rumania when their metropolis Trnovo fell into Turkish hands in 1393 and likewise after the Bulgarian risings of 1558 and 1688. Just as the Byzantine refugees in Rome in the eighth century made a decisive contribution to the growth of the Carolingian renaissance, so these Bulgarian emigrants laid the foundations of the continued development of Byzantine culture in Rumania.

Byzantine culture in Rumania

The two Rumanian principalities, like Serbia, stood between Byzantine and western influences. What the Dalmatian coastal cities were to Serbia, the Hungarian kingdom was for the Rumanian principalities. Apart from the border region of Argeš in the north-west, where ecclesiastical architecture was influenced by the West, Wallachia was orientated towards Byzantium. In Moldavia, the other Rumanian principality lying to the north-east, Byzantine and western elements were equally balanced. Thus, in Rumania, as in Serbia, western and Byzantine influences were found side by side. In Serbia it was above all the romanesque style from Italy that inspired ecclesiastical architecture. In Rumania, church building in Moldavia was influenced by Gothic inspiration from Hungary. An unusual instance of the mixture of Gothic and Byzantine styles is found on the church of Radautz in Moldavia.

Cultural currents were found mingled together in painting as well as in architecture. In the frescoes in the church of Suceava the portrait of the ruler is copied from a western Gothic model. In other representations of the ruler both western and Byzantine elements were found. Thus the ruler of Moldavia, Stephen the Great, is shown on a gold and silver embroidered standard of the late fifteenth century sitting in western fashion on a throne. But he has a nimbus and two angels hovering above him (goddesses of Victory), as was the custom in the Byzantine portrait of the Emperor.

In Moldavia, Byzantine influence was weaker than in Wallachia. But all the same it was sufficiently strong to effect a far-going transformation of the western elements in its architecture. This accounts for the remarkable marriage of Byzantine and western styles in ecclesiastical building which was responsible for the unusual character which Moldavian churches have kept to this day. Byzantine influence accounts for their tower-like appearance, for the dome set in a drum which has to support a roof shaped like the upturned keel of a boat. This dome was frequently replaced by a roof in the form of a pointed spire recalling western models. In churches such as these the only reminder of Byzantine influence was the round arch springing from under the roof.

While Moldavia showed strong western influence, the Byzantine element was strongest in Wallachia. In spite of obvious western architectural elements the church of Curtea de Argeş, or the church of Targoviste, is in the stream of Byzantine culture. Only the dome here set on a drum on a square socle points to the presence of other elements in the structure of the building.

The portraits of the princes of Wallachia indicate Byzantine influence much more clearly than in Moldavia. Thus the fresco portrait of the Wallachian voivode Negoë Basarab of 1526 shows a style reminiscent of the Bulgarian Tetra-Gospel and comes from Byzantium.

It was only in icon painting that the two countries were completely under Byzantine influence. Here the direct connection between the two Rumanian states and the Greek monasteries of Mount Athos is important. The Athos houses possessed considerable property in the Rumanian principalities. These economic interests proved to have a cultural significance as well. The break in this cultural link only came with the Ottoman deposition of the native princely families at the end of the seventeenth and beginning of the eighteenth centuries. The Greek nobles appointed to the principalities, known as Phanariots by reason of their connection with the Phanar quarter of Constantinople, widened the cleavage between the incoming Byzantine cultural heritage and the native national tradition. The Rumanians regarded the Phanariots as foreign rulers. The change in the government had a fatal effect on the country. The Phanariots, a foreign ruling caste, had no interest in using official commissions, as had previously been done, to promote the art which had developed from Byzantino-Bulgarian roots. So in the Rumanian principalities religious icon painting, formerly undertaken by priests, was now transformed into an art which passed into the hands of the laity, mostly peasants. These laymen copied the old icon pictures, thus creating a folk art which still lived in the first half of the nineteenth century.

Bulgaro-Byzantine influence also determined the further development of literature. Thus the literary language in both principalities was Church Slavonic. The fact that Rumania, a country with a Romance language, chose Church Slavonic as the medium for its literary expression, reflects the weight of political influence in the fourteenth century. The Byzantine Empire was then no longer a great state. Power in the Balkans was divided: on the one hand there were the two Slav kingdoms of Serbia and Bulgaria; on the other there was the western orientated Hungary. Moldavia and Wallachia had then the choice between Hungary under the Anjou—which meant joining forces with western culture—or Bulgaria and Serbia with their links with Byzantino-Bulgarian influences. But as the two principalities had only just freed themselves from Hungarian domination any understanding in this direction was ruled out. If they desired to keep their freedom their only course was a cultural union with Bulgaria.

Church Slavonic remained the written language of the principalities of Moldavia and Rumania up to the seventeenth century. The so-called *Instruction* of the Wallachian prince Basarab IV to his son Theodosius in the first half of the sixteenth century was in Church Slavonic. It was only gradually that the Rumanian people succeeded in freeing themselves from this Slav bondage. Church Slavonic lingered on even longer as the ecclesiastical language. The liturgy in Rumanian was not introduced until the nineteenth century and then, with the national revival, Rumanian was no longer written in the Cyrillic script.

Byzantine influence in Bohemia, Moravia, Hungary and Croatia

Byzantine influence extended beyond the Rumanian principalities and the kingdoms of Serbia and Bulgaria. Constantine and Methodius had indeed gone further West. In their work of winning the Slavs for Byzantine Christianity, and thus for Byzantine culture, their first stage had been in the Empire of Great Moravia, which included part of present-day Slovakia. The subsequent Hungarian conquest of this region meant that the Slav liturgy survived in very few localities. The mission of Constantine and Methodius mostly took root in monasteries situated on the periphery and not in the heart of the Great Moravian kingdom. These did not feel the full force of the Magyar attack which from 895 onwards was gradually infiltrating into the Hungarian plain. Thus at the end of the eleventh century there were still monasteries in Bohemia where Church Slavonic was the language of their literature as well as of their liturgy. And this Church Slavonic included Byzantine literature. In particular the monastery of Sázava in Bohemia kept its liturgy in Church Slavonic up to 1097. This Bohemian house had a rich collection of works in Church Slavonic written in the Glagolithic script. Today only a few fragments of this literature survive in Bohemia. Among them is the legend of Wenceslas written in the tenth century and the slightly later legend of St Ludmila.

The Byzantine art produced in these monasteries is illustrated by certain old frescoes still surviving today. Thus the town church in Znojmo, originally dedicated to the Theotokos (later to St Catherine), contains paintings which entirely conform to the Byzantine Orthodox iconographic programme. The fresco-decorated dome has a dove, the symbol of the Holy Spirit, at the summit. Then a little lower down are the four evangelists together with the cherubim, and underneath are the Annunciation, the Visitation, the Nativity and the shepherds hearing of the birth of Christ. Here Byzantine influence shows itself both in style and iconography, and this remained in Bohemian painting up to the Gothic altar paintings.

In Hungary Byzantine influence was considerably stronger than in Bohemia. It was spread not only by the missions of the apostles to the Slavs but by the Basilian monks in the monastic foundations. Up to 1228 there were Basilian houses in Hungary using the Greek liturgy, and their documents were also written in Greek. It was through these Greek Basilian monasteries that Byzantine imperial art became known at the court of the Arpads, the first Hungarian kings. The close cultural links between Hungary and the Byzantine Empire produced such works as the so-called sarcophagus of St Stephen from Székesfehérvár, as well as the crown of Constantine Monomachus and the horn of Level, an ivory horn with scenes from the Byzantine Hippodrome on it. The vast devastation of the Mongol invasions has left very little in the way of architectural remains of these Greek Basilian houses in Hungary. Capitals and pedestals of pillars and fragments of screens are all that are left from the Byzantine period of the Hungarian kingdom.

Western influence replaced that of Byzantium in Hungary. From the second half of the tenth century to almost the end of the eleventh the predominant cultural force was German. Then with the investiture contest Germany, and with it western culture, withdrew from Hungary which again came under Byzantine influence up to the end of the twelfth century, after which Venice became the dominating factor and Byzantine influence was transmitted through Venetian channels. This transmission is demonstrated by the Cain and Abel cycle in the church at Feldebrö. In North Italy at this time there was distinct evidence of Byzantine influence on iconography.

In certain limited fields, such as ceremonial garments and the diadems of the ruler, Byzantine influence remained noticeably unaltered. An illuminated manuscript of the thirteenth century from Cividale shows the Hungarian king, at that time Andrew II, and his wife in the ceremonial dress and diadems of the Byzantine imperial couple. It was only with Angevin rule in Hungary, following the extinction of the old royal house of the Arpads, that the last traces of this once powerful Byzantine influence also disappeared in these regions.

In Poland there was probably Byzantine influence in the reign of Cracow in the fifteenth century. This is traceable in the ground plan of a church on the Wawel in Cracow. The large Armenian colony in the former Russian principality of Halitz which the Poles had taken was another outpost of Byzantine culture in the fourteenth century. The Armenian cathedral built in Lemberg in the fourteenth century shows Byzantine influence travelling via the Balkan regions.

As well as the Great Moravian Empire, the missionary work of the apostles to the Slavs, Constantine and Methodius, also included the Croat state which was in process of taking shape in the ninth century. The culture of Croatia was orientated towards the West, but it used Church Slavonic in both liturgy and literature up to the fourteenth and fifteenth centuries. The form of writing used was the Glagolithic created by the apostles to the Slavs. But in spite of the Slav liturgy and the Glagolithic alphabet, Byzantine influence was slight in Croatia. Such traces of this as are found mostly came through Venetian channels. In Dalmatia the situation was different, for here there were strong Byzantine cultural elements, transmitted either by way of Venice or directly.

Byzantium and the Bogomil sect

In Croatia as well as the western Church acknowledging the Pope, there was a heretical movement, that of the Bogomils, condemned by the heads of both Churches alike, whether the Patriarch of Constantinople or the Roman Pope.

The religious sect of the Bogomils arose in East Syrian regions. Here it had already set up its own church by the mid-seventh century and the Byzantines called its adherents Paulicians. These men repudiated the Old Testament and the apostle Peter, together with the Christian tradition derived from him. They believed in the existence of two kingdoms, one of good and one of evil, and like the Persian Nestorian church they forbad any figural representation in churches. Under the Syrian Constantine (Silvanus) the movement had by the mid-seventh century assumed that form which it kept in Croatia until the fifteenth century.

The Paulicians were particularly dangerous by reason of their military organization. They were a militant religious movement like the fourth century *circumcelliones* (*milites Christi*) of North Africa. In East Syrian regions manifestations of this kind were not unusual, nor were they confined to Christians. During the same period, the seventh and eighth centuries, there were similar movements among Muslims and Jews characterized by extreme rigorism. In Islam the Charidishites repudiated the Caliphate of Ali. According to them, any Muslim could become Caliph and not only the descendants of the Prophet, while the Muslim who sinned forfeited his right to belong to Islam. Like the Paulicians in Christian regions, they were bitterly persecuted by the government, in their case the Caliphs of Islam.

The Jewish world had to face a movement similar to that of the Charidishites in Islam and the Paulicians in Christendom. Under the leadership of Anan, a particular movement grew up which repudiated the Talmud and wanted to return to the very letter of the Mosaic Law. The members of this group were called Karaïm, that is, witnesses of the Scripture. In common with the Paulicians, they drew a good deal on older religious movements. The Karaïm turned to the Sadducees of Christ's day, the

Paulicians to the Marcionites. All three religious movements were characterized by the fact that they probably arose from the conflict in Irak and East Syria between existing religious movements and Islam.

In the middle of the seventh century Constantine, the religious leader of the Paulicians, under the impact of the religious revelation of Islam, had welded together an exclusive religious body out of the different Marcionite, monophysite and Manichaean groups. In the eighth century the Paulician warriors of the faith were a strong military force courted by both Byzantines and Arabs. Favoured by the iconoclast Leo III, they were able to set foot in Asia Minor. But from the first half of the ninth century they had to face severe persecution. The polemic of monastic theologians went hand in hand with punitive military expeditions against the hated heretics. The great Patriarch Photius dedicated a comprehensive work of polemic against them. As a result of persecution some of the Paulicians crossed into Arab territory. Here they formed the élite corps of the emir of Melitene's cavalry. Another group were evacuated by the Byzantines from the border districts and were transported to Thrace. These Paulicians settled in Thrace were noted for spreading their doctrines in Bulgaria. The European group of Paulicians were called Bogomils, taking their name from their leader, the priest Bogomil. About 1078 the Bogomils, supported by the Turkic Cumans, planned a great rising against the Byzantine Empire, aimed at overturning the existing political system. The revolt, which at first achieved some measure of success, was suppressed by the troops of the future Emperor Alexius I (1081–1118). The undisciplined army of Bogomil peasant soldiers was no match for the regular Byzantine troops. As a result of their defeat and the severe persecution of the sect which followed, part of the Bulgarian Bogomils fled to Serbia and Croatia. In Serbia they had little success in the face of the energetic measures of the tsar Stephen Nemanya, but in what is present-day Bosnia they maintained their hold up to the middle of the fifteenth century.

The Bogomils brought their own culture to Bosnia, and in their art they preserved elements derived from Syrian and Iranian late antiquity. The plants and animals on the unusual stone sarcophagi of Bogomil graves draw inspiration from early Iranian art, as is also seen in the frescoes dating from the iconoclast period in the Cappadocian rock monasteries. Side by side with these, other forms are found, such as the abstract figural motifs which evidently reflect the influence of Coptic art in the East Syrian world.

ICONOCLASM

89 Destruction of icons;
late 9th-century marginal
illustration

90 The stoning of
St Stephen: 9th-century
illustration

91 Ninth- or tenth-century marble relief (possibly Armenian) found in Greece

92 Window of Umayyad palace, Khirbat al-Mafjar, early 8th century

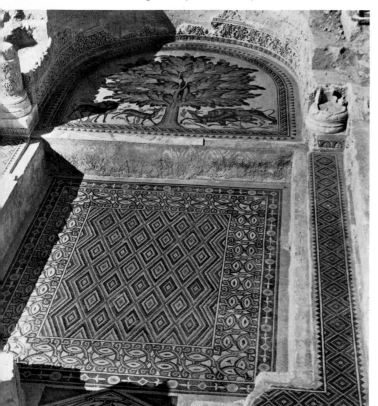

93 Mosaic floor in audience hall of Khirbat al-Mafjar

94 The mihrab of the Great Mosque in Qairawan, 862

95 Elephant pursued by griffin; relief in wall, Konya, c.1221

97 Water clock constructed by Djazari, installed 1200; miniature from treatise of Djazari

96 Portal of the minaret-mosque, Konya, 1258

98 Birth of St John the Baptist; miniature from a Gospel manuscript

99 Two monks in an architectural setting; miniature in a New Testament (? 12th century)

100 The miracle at Chonar; miniature from a manuscript

101 Whitsun; illustrated initial letter from a manuscript, c.1100

102 St Mamas; miniature from 12th-century manuscript

103 An angel, the symbol of the Evangelist Matthew; miniature from Gospels, 13th-14th centuries

104 Adam receiving Eve; mosaic in Monreale
cathedral, Sicily, late 12th century

THE ANCIENT GREEK INHERITANCE
IN BYZANTINE ART

CAOVΛΕΗ
ΧΗΛΗΑCΙ
ΚΑΙΔΑΔ
ΕΝΜΥΡΙ
ΑCΙ

105 Christ as the Good Shepherd; mosaic in Galla Placidia,
Ravenna, 5th century

106 David as a shepherd;
miniature from a Psalter

107 David's return to Jerusalem; miniature from a
9th-century Psalter

108 The rape of Europa;
detail from a Byzantine bridal
casket, 10th century

109 Byzantine enamelled cup,
mid-11th century

110 Head of Eutropius, a high official; early 5th century

111 St Panteleimon; late 9th-century icon

112 Enthroned Mother of God and Child; mosaic, Hagia Sophia, Istanbul

113 Mother of God and the Christ Child; icon, S. Maria Maggiore, Rome

114 St Agnes; tomb relief, Sant'Agnese fuori le mura, Rome

115 The Mother of God; engraved jasper, 11th–12th centuries

116 The Nativity; fresco, S. Maria foris portas, Castelseprio

117 The Annunciation; early 12th-century icon

118 Ascension of Christ; miniature from a Syrian Gospel, 586

119 St Menas; relief from the monastery of St Thecla

120 Mother of God with the Apostles Peter and Paul; fresco from the monastery of St Apollo near Bawit, early 6th century

121 Four saints and a founder; fresco from the monastery of St Jeremiah in Saqqara, Egypt, 7th century

122 Bust of Christ; silver censer,
early 7th century

123 The Crucifixion; jasper plaque,
9th–10th century

124 The Nativity and the Adoration
of the Magi; wood carving from
the church of Abu Sargas, Cairo

◀ 125 Head of an emperor; detail of bronze statue in Barletta, 6th-7th century

127 Head of an empress; marble

128 Head of a queen; early 13th century, Ravello cathedral

◀ 126 The Empress Ariadne; detail of an ivory diptych, late 5th century

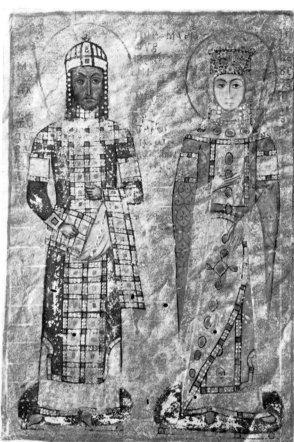

129 Emperor John II Comnenus (1118-43) and his son Alexius; miniature

130 Emperor Manuel I Comnenus (1143-80) and his consort Mary; miniature

131 Emperor John II Comnenus and his wife Irene; mosaic, c.1120, Hagia Sophia, Istanbul

132 Constans II (641-68) 133 Constantine IV (668-85) with his brothers Tiberius and Heraclius

134 Constantine IV

135 Constantine IV and his son
Justinian II (685-95; 705-11)

Justinian II and his son Tiberius II (698-705) 137 Tiberius II

138 Archangels before God, with Satan below; miniature, 905

139 Adoration of the Magi; miniature, c.985

141 The Nativity; miniature, c. 985

140 St Romanus the Melodist, miniature, c.985

142 Christ; detail of mosaic in the Sophia church, Thessalonica

143 The picture of the Redeemer; icon from Constantinople

144 The Mother of God with the Child; icon, second half of 9th century

145 The Mother of God; icon, second half of 9th century

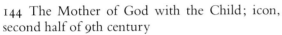

146 John the Baptist; 10th-century ivory

147 Christ giving the blessing; 11th-century ivory

149 Abraham, Isaac and Jacob; miniature, c.985

◀148 The prophet Zacharias; fresco, Brontocheion monastery, Mistra, 1296

150 St Demetrius with a bishop; mosaic,
first half of 7th century

151 The Apostle Paul; mosaic, 1315-20

152 The Annunciation; mosaic, late 11th-century, Daphni, near Athens

153 The Crucifixion; late 11th-century mosaic

154 Head of a martyr; 5th-century mosaic 155 Head of St Demetrius; detail of mosaic, mid-7th centur

156 Apostles at the Dormition of the Mother of God; detail from a mosaic, early 14th century

157 Interior of Hagia Sophia, Istanbul

158 Church of St Sergius and St Bacchus, Istanbul

159 Church of the Myrelaion (Bodrum Cami), Istanbul

160 Interior of the church of St Irene, Istanbul

161 Exterior of the church of St Irene, Istanbul

162 Monastery of Qalat Siman, Syria   163 Baptistery of Qalat Siman

164 Church of St Catherine, Thessalonica   165 Church of the Holy Apostles, Thessalonica

168 Interior of the church of Hosios Loukas of Stiri, Phocis

◀166 Church of the Brontocheion monastery, Mistra

◀167 Church of Pantanassa, Mistra

169 Mosaic cross in the apse of Sant'Apollinare in Classe, Ravenna, early 6th century

Byzantine civilization
in decline

Political decay and cultural flowering

The dissemination of Byzantine civilization among the Slav peoples is of general historical significance—more so even than the transmission of Byzantine culture to the West and to the Armenian and Caucasian peoples—for it has continued to determine their development up to the present day. The mission to the Slavs widened the sphere of Byzantine civilization, and this might seem to be some compensation for the provinces lost to Islam. But cultural penetration is not exactly the same thing as political or military conquest. While the general political situation permitted the Byzantine Empire to consolidate its position in the Balkan peninsula, the broad lines along which it developed pointed towards disintegration rather than towards expansion. It is the peculiarity of Byzantine civilization that obvious symptoms of internal decay coincided with the highest cultural achievements. At the very time when feudalism was taking the place of a social structure that had survived since late antiquity, culture was at the height of its flowering. It is significant that the Emperor Constantine Porphyrogenitus, hampered in the exercise of his authority by the existence of a co-Emperor set up by the feudal magnates, should be the symbol of intellectual revival in the new Byzantine world—a world which succeeded in loosening the grip of the monastic movement on intellectual life by having recourse to its classical inheritance.

In the circle of Constantine Porphyrogenitus there was a return to the earlier method of imperial historiography, which had been abandoned at the beginning of the seventh century with Theophylact Simocattes. The collection of traditional classical material began, which led to the creation of the great encyclopedias bearing the name of the Emperor responsible. Another manifestation of this strange contrast between external decline of power and internal cultural growth, is to be found in the time of Psellus. Michael Psellus was the man to whom the foundation of the Faculty of Philosophy in the university of Constantinople must be attributed. The establishment for philosophy and jurisprudence which had been founded under Caesar Bardas in Photius' time was directed into new channels by Psellus. The old schools of law and Aristotelian philosophy were turned by him into academies. As the very name implies, this indicated a departure from previous practice. 'Academy' meant a turning to Plato, a return to the Platonic Academy, closed by Justinian in the middle of the sixth century so as to open the way for the domination of the monastic movement. In the time of Psellus there was a return to late antiquity and a resumption of the course that had been interrupted for a time.

Now anything that happens in philosophy is significant for intellectual life as a whole. During Psellus' lifetime the visual arts experienced a transition from religious painting that was almost abstract and extremely stylized to a more realistic form of religious art. The object is portrayed as seen. Bodies are represented as such, whereas before they were allowed to be no more than vehicles for movement. Interest in the natural sciences revived. All this happened at a time when the Seljuks were overrunning Asia Minor, when the magnates in alliance with the Seljuk sultans were engaged in a struggle for power and the Norman ruler was marching on Constantinople along the Via Egnatia right across the Balkan peninsula, while the mercantile republic of Venice was exerting economic pressure on the Byzantine Empire. The beginning of the age of this internal decay, followed by that of political disintegration, fell at the turn of the ninth and tenth centuries. It ended with the conquest of the capital, Constantinople, by the crusaders from the West in 1204.

Byzantine culture in bondage to feudalism and the new economic forces

Feudalism as a disintegrating force in the universal empires of East and West

It cannot be said that the decline of the Byzantine Empire was an isolated phenomenon within the context of European and Islamic political history. Events were evolving along the same lines in both East and West. Older powers were abdicating and new ones taking their place. The concept of a universal Empire, the heritage of late antiquity, was demolished by the forces of feudalism as they prepared the way for the new national states. This was so both in Europe and in the East. The Abbasid Caliphate had already fallen in the first half of the ninth century. The emirates on the periphery became independent states. Umayyad Spain, Aghlabid and Fatimid North Africa, Ikshidid and Fatimid Egypt, were the first separatist powers in the western Arab territories. Iran was divided between Samanids and Bugids. Even Irak no longer formed a political entity. East Syria became an independent emirate under the Hamdanids. Disintegration was everywhere apparent and it was characterized by a recession of the Arab element in the population. By the beginning of the tenth century Arabs had everywhere been excluded from political leadership. The rulers of North Africa and Spain were Berbers, those of Egypt and Syria were Turkic and later Kurds, those of Iran were Iranians, and then again Turkic. Even in Arabia proper, the Arabs had forfeited their leadership to the Kurds. Nearly everywhere it was the Turks and Kurds who held political power.

But Europe, too, was developing in the same way. The Carolingian Empire was the last attempt to establish a universal empire on the lines of late antiquity. The German Empire was part of a feudal development from which it could no more stand apart than could the Byzantine Empire in the East.

In Byzantium those responsible for this development were the magnates of Asia Minor, the Phocas, the Maleini, the Scleri and the Curcuas, and in Germany they were the Wettins, Welfs, Babenbergs and Zähringen. In the Byzantine Empire it was the former commanders of military units, the officers of the themes, who became landed rulers. Similarly in Germany the same course of events turned the Carolingian regional officials, counts and margraves, into the hereditary dukes and territorial princes of the new feudal order. The property of the Phocas in Cappadocia, with its centre at Caesarea, is comparable with a German duchy at the time of the Ottos and the Salians. Here too feudalization took place within an external framework of administrative reorganization. The great themes of eastern Asia Minor, the Armeniakon and the Anatolikon, were split up into smaller units. This immediately recalls the partition of the duchy of Bavaria, out of which an independent duchy of Carinthia was formed under Otto II (976); but matters did not end there. The partition went on: Styria, Carniola, Austria and the march of Istria owed their origin as separate entities to the same causes which produced the themes that replaced Armeniakon and Anatolikon in the eastern part of the Byzantine Empire. Thus in the course of the tenth century five new themes were established on the eastern borders of the Byzantine Empire: in the north-east in the Caucasian region there was Chaldia with its centre at Trebizond; adjoining it was Colonea, thus called from the military district with the citadel of that name; then there was Charsianon which, like the southernmost theme on the Mediterranean, Seleucia, was named after a citadel. And in accordance with the wishes of the great Cappadocian landowners, a separate Cappadocian theme was created.

These great landed magnates pursued their own policies, which frequently clashed with those of the Empire. They supported a foreign policy which aimed at the expansion of Byzantine rule in the East. For the sake of this eastern policy, the tasks of the Byzantine Empire in the Mediterranean area, especially in southern Italy and in the Balkan peninsula, were neglected. The landowners of Asia Minor looked only to the East. During the period when their representatives acted as imperial regents for the lawful Emperor, the Byzantine Empire seized·Cilicia, Syria and Armenia. It was the Emperor Nicephorus Phocas, with possessions in the Caesarea district of Cappadocia, who achieved the conquest of Cilicia and Syria. He was followed by John Tzimisces, also a member of the Cappadocian magnate class, who extended his predecessor's conquests in Syria. The legitimate Empire was forced into a policy that was frequently at odds with its own political interests. The great Emperor, Basil II, though he was bent on subduing the Slavs in the Balkan peninsula, was compelled to march eastwards in order to secure/the threatened territories in Syria recently conquered by the co-Emperors Nicephorus Phocas and John Tzimisces, who both belonged to the class of landed magnates.

Here too a parallel may be observed. The independent Italian policy of the Swabian and Bavarian dukes compelled the German king to follow suit to obviate the danger of a new kingdom arising on the periphery. Fearing the rise of feudal powers out of their own imperial federation, the representatives of the central power adopted the political aims of the periphery. Thus Byzantine conquests in this period no longer served to enhance the power of the Empire, as in Justinian's time. The conquered provinces were not, as before, incorporated into the rest of the Empire by the imposition of a special administrative system, but their government was left in the hands of the local ruling magnates. Under Justinian, on the contrary, imperial laws determined the political structure of newly conquered provinces down to the last detail, as for instance the pragmatic sanction promulgated in respect of Italy, and the imperial legislation for Africa. The only concession a newly conquered district could look for was the introduction of one of its own magnates into the government. But now there was no question of setting up an imperial administration in any such region. The conquest of Armenia in the first half of the eleventh century incorporated already existing territories of individual feudal lords into the Byzantine Empire in the form of themes. But only the name had any connection with the former Byzantine administrative organization which was by now only a thin cloak for the new feudal structures.

The natural result of the rapid growth of feudalism was a decline in imperial military power. The great armies of the themes which had been stationed in Asia Minor were no longer the Emperor's willing tools, gathering at assigned places on receipt of mobilization orders, to march along pre-arranged routes into Arab territory. Now armies of the themes rarely marched to the East; more often they made their way to the West in order to precipitate a revolution in the capital, Constantinople. To combat this now unreliable army controlled by great magnates such as the Phocas, the Scleri, the Maleini and the Comneni, the imperial government raised one of its own, obedient only to itself. The divisions of the imperial bodyguard formed the core of this private army. In the sixth century this bodyguard was made up entirely of Germans, and finally of Gepids. In the second half of the ninth century under Basil I, it consisted of men from Ferghana in western Turkestan. These Iranians, like the Germans, were used to a highly developed system of vassalage and were considered to be very reliable. The men of Sogdiana were followed in the ninth century by the Varangian bodyguard. The Varangians were those Scandinavian Germans who were also responsible for the foundation of the Russian and Polish states. These Varangian guards were soon formed into an army which, in return for good pay, obeyed every imperial command. The Emperor's Varangian followers saved the imperial crown for Basil II in his struggle against feudal opposition under Bardas Phocas. The Varangian guards were followed by English Normans in the eleventh century and these in their turn by German troops in the second half of that century. The upkeep of these mercenaries required considerable financial resources. These were in fact far beyond the capacity of the Byzantine Empire which was already in a period of economic decline.

The Byzantine economic crisis

One of the causes of the economic crisis was the loss of markets previously available to Byzantine manufactured goods. The trade monopoly in the West for high quality goods, which continued to be held during the eighth and ninth centuries by the Byzantine Empire, had been lost by the tenth. Only a very limited type of merchandise, mainly luxury goods, still commanded the European market. In the eleventh century Byzantine economic supremacy no longer went uncontested, even in this field.

The loss of outlets in the West resulted from the great economic struggle between Byzantium and the Islamic states, which had been going on since the seventh century.

In 700 the Umayyad Caliph, Abd al-Malik, began himself to mint gold coin, gold dinars, in an attempt to undermine the position of the Byzantine gold *solidus* as a world currency. The Byzantine Empire then put a ban on all Arab goods. Only raw materials were allowed into the Byzantine Empire through a specified port of transit near Attaleia. The Muslim states were thus cut off from direct commercial traffic with the West. As a result, an appreciable quantity of oriental goods vanished from western markets. In particular Egyptian and Syrian manufactured products no longer reached European markets.

The blockade maintained by Byzantium on the commerce of countries under Arabian rule, was dependent on complete command of the seas. The possession of the islands of Cyprus and Crete and more especially control over west Mediterranean islands such as Malta, Lampedusa—between Sicily and Tunis—and Sardinia, together with a strong fleet, made the blockade a workable proposition. It was not till the beginning of the ninth century that the Muslim states were able to break through this fortified barrier. The cordon of the Byzantine blockade was decisively broken by the emirate of Qairawan in North Africa. This North African emirate with a strategic vantage point in Carthage, conquered one Byzantine stronghold after another. Soon the North Africans succeeded in gaining a foothold on the island of Sicily. From the western part of the island which they had occupied, the Carthaginians slowly conquered the whole of Sicily in fierce hand-to-hand encounters.

The Byzantines were well aware of the danger which threatened their commerce from the North African occupation of Sicily. They fought bitterly to defend their positions in Italy. After they had lost control of the maritime route between North Africa and Sicily by the loss of the western part of that island, and of Lampedusa, they were anxious to keep open at least those other routes to western ports which they still commanded. The principal of these were via Messina and Otranto. Through the Straits of Messina, Byzantine commerce reached Naples, Amalfi and Gaeta and, in the north, Pisa, Luni and Genoa. Otranto was the gateway to the Adriatic and the route to the great commercial port of Venice.

The military position of the Byzantines in Italy was however largely dependent on the command of the Via Egnatia, the shortest line of communication between Thessalonica on the Aegean and Durazzo on the Adriatic. The expansion of the Bulgarian kingdom, the encroachment of khan Omurtag, of Krum and subsequently of the tsars Boris-Michael and Symeon, cut off this line of communication. Byzantine military reinforcements for Italy were thus compelled to use the coastal road which reached the isthmus of Corinth by following the Aegean coastline, and led to the West by way of the gulf of Patras. The route taken by Byzantine reinforcements for Italy had been considerably lengthened. This was of decisive importance for the course of military events in Sicily and southern Italy. All too soon the Arabs succeeded in controlling the Straits of Messina and then, by the occupation of Bari, in gaining control over the entry to the Adriatic Sea.

The blockade on Arab commerce had thus become an Arab ban on Byzantine commerce with the West. The sea-ports of Italy, whose economic existence was threatened by this state of affairs, sought a compromise with the Muslim states. It was at this time that the first trade agreements were reached between the Italian ports, the Hamdanids in Syria, and the Fatimids in Egypt. The ports, in particular Venice, supplied the Arab states with the timber they so badly needed for their shipyards, and probably with ore for the manufacture of arms. In return they obtained concessions for the export of oriental luxury goods which were sold very profitably in the West. The Byzantine Emperors, especially John Tzimisces, were fully aware of the part Venice was playing, but were compelled to continue economic co-operation with the Venetians in spite of their duplicity because it was only through Venice and other Italian seaports that western commerce was accessible. Though the Byzantines were aware of what they regarded as the treacherous dealings of the Doge of Venice, he continued to occupy high Byzantine office with its concomitant financial rewards.

Byzantium was never completely cut off from trade with the West. For although the Straits of Messina continued to be controlled by the Arabs until well into the eleventh century, the outlet to the Adriatic was soon reconquered. Bari, Islam's base at the gateway to the Adriatic, was recaptured by the combined armies of the Byzantine and Frankish Emperors, and in this way communications between Byzantium and the West were at least in part restored. But this did not signify the resumption of trade on the former scale. In the West, there was a growing scarcity of all high-quality goods and a demand which the small quantity of Byzantine products reaching Italy failed to satisfy.

Following the turmoil of the migrations, Central Europe had become an area in which the demand for merchandise had increased tenfold. The great trade routes to Italy, for a time interrupted, were now nearly all under unified political control: the Rhine valley, with the route from the North Sea, through the Rhaetian Alps in Italy, and the route over the Brenner; the route to the Rhone valley, under the control of the same political power as the other two since the conquest of the kingdom of Burgundy by the German Empire. All the conditions necessary for intensive trade with the South already existed. This situation, together with Central Europe's unsatisfied demand for merchandise, first brought about the rise of the textile industry in Italy which gradually became the leading source of supply for the markets of the

West. It was a similar situation to that of Europe at the turn of the eighteenth and nine-teenth centuries, when Napoleon's continental blockade against English industrial products brought about the development of heavy industry in Germany. The manu-facturing towns of North Italy produced goods to replace those of Byzantium whose long-distance commerce became restricted to luxury articles; their only monopolies at this time were in silk, purple dye, ivory products and the entrepôt trade in oriental wares.

The decline of Byzantine trade, resulting in diminished returns, was not confined to the Mediterranean area. Changes took place in her commerce with Russia and the Baltic states as a result of which markets were closed to Byzantine manufacturers. The Varan-gians, who were responsible for founding the Russian state in the ninth century, were also the agents for commerce between East and West. The Swedish merchant would travel all the way down to the south of Russia, there to buy Arab goods from the Khazars, who had come by way of West Turkestan or the Caucasian passes. This development resulted in the exclusion of Byzantium from trade with the Baltic states. Thus, through-out the countries on the Baltic seaboard, Norway, Sweden, Finland, Estonia, Latvia and Lithuania, as well as in Denmark, Arab coins were found, but hardly any Byzantine *solidi*. These coins were minted during the eighth, ninth and tenth centuries in West Turkestan and in those parts of the Caucasus under Muslim rule. They testify to intensive commercial exchanges between the Baltic zone and north-east and north-west Persian trade centres, which continued up till 1000. After that year Arab currency disappeared from the Baltic littoral. The cause lay in the great migratory movements of the Turkic nomads, the Cumans, which interrupted communications between the Arab world and the Baltic states. The Cumans were also responsible for disrupting the close economic and cultural relations that had existed until the first half of the eleventh century between Russia and the Byzantine Empire.

Byzantine commerce thus became still more restricted, not only in the Mediterranean area, but also in the East. Consequently there was a considerable economic recession; at the same time military expenditure rose, particularly in relation to the upkeep of mercenaries. The revenues derived from an urban economy of late antiquity which had persisted through the early middle ages now produced revenues that were in-sufficient to meet even the most urgent military commitments. Furthermore, increas-ing feudalization of the machinery of state made urban economy difficult to maintain. Those feudal magnates who, at a time of imperial weakness, had gained control of the Empire's affairs by setting up co-Emperors, had also destroyed Byzantine planned economy and so had undermined one of the foundations of imperial power. They had stopped the compulsory purchase of corn, an indispensable factor in urban state economy, and allowed the grain to be sold on the free market instead. It thus became appreciably more difficult to maintain productivity in the towns. Wages increased, for at this time slaves had begun to play a much smaller part in manufacture. The great landlords, who then controlled the government, failed to see the negative aspect of this policy, which so far as they were concerned, was determined by the fact that the free sale of grain would increase the revenue from their own large estates. The town had now become economically dependent on the magnates.

An attempt to curb this development by a return to the former late antique planned economy was made by those Emperors whose interests were largely bound up with the urban economy. But the wheel of history could not be turned back. The attempt to effect economic reforms by a controlled devaluation of the *solidus* was a particularly disastrous mistake. It was planned to set up an internal currency in which the gold content of the old *nomisma*, which had remained unaltered until the middle of the eleventh century, would be devalued to the rate of 1 : 4. The gold content of the *nomisma*, hitherto 4.48 gr., was in fact reduced. Other metals were added and in consequence there had to be arbitrary rate-fixings to determine the relative value of gold pieces of new and old minting. Those who profited most were the official tax farmers who altered the rate to suit themselves until it was stabilized by imerial decree. After this, the new gold coins were worth only four *miliaresia* instead of twelve in coins of the old value. In practical terms, the new currency regulations meant a reduction in salaries and state pensions; for the state paid in new coin, but at the old rates. The success of these new currency regulations was dependent on economic and political measures which were introduced at the same time.

The attempt to regulate the general rise in prices resulting from the devaluation of the *nomisma* and the free sale of corn was a failure; in the eighth and ninth centuries, grain had been collected by the epibole (*annona*) and brought to the gates of the capital by a system of state-organized deliveries. Now however it was customary for the grain to be purchased in the country by private buyers who conveyed it to the capital, where it was sold at prices which depended on the state of the market. Technically speaking, then, circumstances could hardly have been more unfavourable for the re-introduction of a state monopoly in grain. A rise in grain prices was the inevitable result of the depreciation of the *nomisma*. Even state monopoly in the grain trade could not alter that. The price of bread was four times higher than it had been before currency reform, proportionate to the amount by which the *nomisma* had been devalued. This meant that the attempt to return to the old planned economy had failed along with the currency reform.

The confidence of western states in Byzantine currency was greatly shaken by these financial experiments, and had in no way been restored by the retention, after currency reform, of the old *nomisma* with its former gold content for export currency, while the new, devalued currency was confined to the home market. Byzantine credit had been destroyed and the consequence of the monetary experiment was a further reduction in overseas trade. Gradually a situation arose in which Byzantine gold coins were superseded by those of Italian cities, the Florentine fiorino, the Milanese gold ambrogio and the Venetian zecchino. The large Italian cities which had deprived Byzantine economy of a considerable share of the western market, soon began to extend their supremacy to the field of currency.

The collapse of the official economic system was already making itself felt in the tenth century. It began with a rise in artisans' wages, caused by the de-restriction of grain prices and a drop in the import of slaves. Low wages, only possible when payment in cash was combined with allocations of grain, rose inevitably when the price of grain ceased to be controlled. The wage structure was also greatly affected by the absence of competition from slave labour. The productivity of many factories was jeopardized by this state of affairs. It became impossible for the different trades to pursue their business within the framework of the restrictions set down in the *Book of the Eparch*. Nor was the state any longer in a position to ensure them a supply of raw materials or to distribute these as formerly, for the occupation of Anatolia by the Seljuks had deprived the Byzantine Empire of a large part of those lands which had supplied it with raw materials. Since the battle of Manzikert in which the Seljuks had won control over Asia Minor, the Byzantine textile industry could no longer draw its supply of wool from the Anatolian uplands. On the other hand, the silk industry lost valuable skilled labour, some of it no doubt from the highly industrialized area round Corinth, when it was taken by the Normans to Sicily. Thus a separate Norman silk industry grew up in Sicily which gradually took the place of Byzantine products in the markets of the West. Significantly, in the first half of the twelfth century, the order for the German Emperor's ceremonial robes went, not to Constantinople, but to the Sicilian manufacturers.

These circumstances necessitated the abolition of many of the restrictions involved in a planned economy, and this in turn gave rise to the dissolution of the compulsory associations (*systemata*) of different types of trade. In this way the old restrictions, which dated back to late antiquity, were removed. In the same way that the military holdings gradually went over into the possession of great ecclesiastical or secular landlords, urban economy saw the beginnings of a development in which big entrepreneurs took over different kinds of factory, for instance textiles, or foodstuffs. These capitalists, not usually themselves tradesmen, and having substantial loans, were able to buy a variety of concerns and run them for their own profit.

A document from the end of the thirteenth century contains information about the possessions of one of these Byzantine big capitalists, one Gudeles Tyrannos. It concerns a deed of gift, of which this document was the written record, for a monastery in Constantinople. It contains an inventory of the possessions Gudeles was making over to the monastery and gives an insight into something of the nature of this man's estate. Gudeles' gift to the monastery consisted of: 1. four textile concerns, probably in Smyrna; 2. a tower with a bakehouse and a baker's shop, which were let at the time of the gift; 3. three vineyards; 4. a property with two pairs of draught animals, 4 head of cattle and 2 horses; 5. another bakehouse; 6. half of a bath-house; 7. another vineyard; 8. several parcels of land; 9. houses and other buildings for which 420 *nomismata* were still outstanding (the monastery undertook to pay 150 *nomismata* as soon as possible out of available funds, and the rest by instalments out of the income from the estates they had been given); 10. property and workshops in the town of Nymphaion. All that Gudeles reserved from this gift was a share in a concern manufacturing scent. The inventory reveals that it was quite possible in the Byzantine Empire for one person to possess, not merely a variety of concerns within the capital, but also factories in the provinces. A man like Gudeles Tyrannos could not have attained so powerful a financial status except in a time of complete economic freedom in which the state refrained from any interference that might recall the old planned economy.

The decline of the state in the economic field had serious consequences of another kind. No longer was any attempt made to protect the home market by tariffs, or by limiting exports and imports. In order to meet the need to increase military strength, which could not be paid for out of the revenues from the liberalized economy or from the now feudalized agriculture, the Empire resorted to bartering its sovereign rights in return for military aid from other powers. Thus Venice, by means of special treaties, obtained free trading rights in Byzantine lands, and the privileges exacted on behalf of her subjects destroyed the economic independence of the state on the Bosphorus. In fact the Byzantine Empire had ceased to be a great economic power long before the victory of the crusaders in 1204. From this time onwards Byzantium had no economy independent of the general economy of the Mediterranean area, and was dependent, because politically defenceless, upon every economic fluctuation there.

The disintegration of state control in the provinces

Urban development did not differ essentially from that in the country. Big capitalists of the Gudeles Tyrannos type were to the town what big landlords and magnates were to the country. The formation of large properties was the consequence of military administration, based on the organization of the themes, which very soon succeeded in ousting the former civil administration. In the themes, the rank and file and non-commissioned officers had been given property commensurate with their rank. Its value was determined by the kind of equipment which they had had on active service. Cavalrymen and sailors received better properties than foot-soldiers.

Officers of all arms were excluded from these grants of land. Their high rate of pay and the considerable share of booty to which they were entitled was more than sufficient compensation. They were thus easily able to amass a large amount of capital, and this they sought to invest. Investment in an urban money-market was not very profitable because interest rates were deliberately kept low. It was much more advantageous to own land which could be farmed through tenants, *paroikoi*, or day labourers who were housed on the estate. It thus became the custom to buy up peasants' holdings whose owners, under the burden of taxation, were becoming increasingly in debt. This gave rise to the growth of large properties farmed by once-free peasants who were now in a state of dependency on the new landlords. These peasants, once freemen, enjoyed personal freedom as *paroikoi*, but were bound to the soil of the holdings they had previously owned. When the holding was sold, the *paroikoi* went with it to the new landlord. They could also be exchanged. But it was only the individual *paroikoi* who were bound to the soil, not their families.

The Emperors at first tried to protect the free peasantry against the military aristocracy which had arisen as a result of the greed for land of the officers in the themes. At this time, the *Nomos Georgikos* originating from a commentary on the Justinian Code, was made valid by imperial decree. Generally, however, imperial protection was only extended to the soldiers' holdings which were threatened by the greed of officers who had become landed magnates.

Officers of the armies established in the themes who had become big landed proprietors, were especially interested in enlarging their estates in the area under their command. For the political and social position conferred on them by their military rank enabled them by degrees to become territorial governors. They formed a class which defended its position against all attempts on the part of the central authority to threaten its power. No officer could be dismissed or punished without fear of repercussion from members of this class. Officers of the line were land-owning officers, and the combination of military rank with administration over a large area made of them a rural military aristocracy, whose most powerful members almost had the position of a territorial ruler. The units commanded by these officers, in so far as they consisted of soldiers with military holdings within the boundaries of their estates, always acted in complete accordance with their commander's wishes. In this way the soldier settlers had become members of a private army attached to the military aristocracy.

The officers were now in so powerful a position that the central government was forced to concede important political rights as regards their own private lands and soon after to make further concessions in the field of military command. Complete exemption from state taxation was granted to especially powerful landowners in the form of privileges, called chrysobulls. This meant that the landlord's property was not subject to the authority of the state, thus becoming an immune area which state officials were not permitted to enter. In this way the landlord became a territorial ruler, able to decide whether or not he would comply with an order from the central authority.

The *pronoia* system was also similar to this. By grants in *pronoia*, the Emperor conferred the sovereign rights and revenues of a particular area on deserving supporters; at first this applied only for their lifetime, but later it became hereditary. In return, the beneficiary was bound to give him armed support. Both *pronoia* and chrysobull were measures to secure for the Emperor the support of former army officers who had turned into landowners.

As the *pronoia* or chrysobull systems were extended to an ever wider range of officers' property in the themes, the value of the forces there became increasingly problematical. Not only the areas of command in the themes, but also the organization of military holdings began to disappear. By the tenth century the magnates who, as officers in the themes, conducted the war against the Arabs, were making use of mercenaries. The armies of Nicephorus Phocas and John Tzimisces, though they were still called armies of the themes, consisted of a levy of mercenaries raised by individual officers who had become magnates. In the Byzantine Empire, these mercenaries came mostly from northern Iberia where the Ossetic tribes, to which the present Circassians belong, liked to serve in the Byzantine army. Both the Byzantine *akritai* and the Arab *ghazis*, as the troops stationed on the border were called, were mercenaries.

The far-reaching changes in the social structure of the Byzantine Empire cannot be seen as isolated phenomena in the sphere either of western or of Islamic culture. The disruption of the military system on the one hand, and the emergence from the political order of an urban economy on the other, characterized all three cultural spheres in the eleventh and twelfth centuries. In the Byzantine Empire a land-owning military aristocracy had grown up from the officers' corps which had settled on land in the themes. Some members of this military aristocracy succeeded in obtaining immunities for their property, granted them by imperial chrysobull. In this way they attained the status of landed princes of varying importance. Their relation to the central government depended solely on the Emperor who, as supreme commander of the army of the themes, also had authority over its officers who had become small feudatories. There was no central authority that could wield powers in fiscal or judiciary matters, issue instructions or make decisions in so far as the property of these officers was concerned. This was because they were protected by the privilege of either the chrysobull or the grant in *pronoia*. This process in the Byzantine Empire was similar to that which was taking place in the West, where landowners, great and small, rose from the ranks of high officials and the holders of ministerial benefices. Apart from the appearance of the huge secular estates, another factor was the growth of large ecclesiastical holdings soon after the secularization of ecclesiastical property under Heraclius. In the Byzantine Empire, unlike the West, church land was largely in the hands of the monasteries to whom it had been bestowed by pious donors. These were members of the army of the themes, often soldiers of the rank and file who, in defiance of the current ordinances of imperial law, even transferred their land to the monasteries in the form of a gift. These transfers were not made with the sole object of attaining everlasting salvation through works acceptable to God; very real and worldly considerations were also involved. There was a risk that property, not always acquired by fair means, might be lost through state intervention. In the hands of a monastery, such loss was much less likely.

Another custom was to make over part of a property to a monastery so that some of the owner's relations might be taken in and cared for. By his gift a donor could also secure within the monastery a place for himself, in which to spend his old age.

The institution of *charisticarii*, or secular monastery stewards, made it possible to profit from gifts to a monastery without exchanging the worldly for the religious life. A good example of the monastic security of land tenure is that of the houses on Athos. Part of the property which they held under privilege of the eleventh-century imperial chrysobulls was taken from them by the Greek government, but not until after the

312

first world war, when the land was needed for the resettlement of Greek refugees from Asia Minor. Thus when the Athens government signed an expropriation order, it did what no Byzantine Emperors, and none of the Turkish sultans, had dared to do.

The monasteries too supplied the higher clergy, bishops and metropolitans. This meant that the higher ecclesiastics were also supporters of the military aristocracy.

The political conflict between city and countryside

In the city, big exporters formed the most powerful economic class. Most of them were also owners of important industrial concerns, or lessees of government-owned mines. Byzantine trade was no longer predominantly concerned with luxury articles, as it had been in the period between the sixth and tenth centuries, but with foodstuffs such as grain, or raw materials for the textile industry (wool, flax). But very little of this commerce consisted of exports and imports since most of it was in entrepôt traffic. Constantinople and its overseas trade increasingly played the rôle of supplier to the urban economies of Italy or to the Egyptian luxury trade. Both the Byzantine state and private Byzantine trade subsisted on the Italian factories' consumption of raw materials and foodstuffs. It was then more profitable to take wool to Italy than to supply it to the spinners of the Byzantine capital. Similarly the high toll that had to be paid for transit through the straits was more profitable than taxation from industrial concerns in Constantinople.

Furthermore, the stringent nature of Byzantine tax regulations drove a number of shipping concerns and merchants to transfer their seat of business from Constantinople to one of the maritime cities in Italy or the eastern Adriatic. Their owners became citizens of these cities, returning to Constantinople as foreigners protected by the privileges of the seaports they came from, and so able to pursue their commercial interests without hindrance. Thus in leading economic circles a feeling of indifference towards national issues arose and business interests were the decisive factor. In the capital high-ranking imperial officials were nearly all members of these trading circles, and it was they who dictated foreign and economic policy, so that private interests were better served than those of the state. Everything was planned in the capital from the Constantinopolitan point of view, and in accordance with political and economic circumstances obtaining in the straits. Asia Minor and the Anatolian uplands became increasingly neglected.

In contrast to the financial aristocracy of Constantinople, the military aristocracy of Asia Minor looked to the East. Their political programme consisted in the maintenance of the eastern frontier and the possession or the control of West Syria, or even part of Palestine. Campaigns in this highly-developed area brought in assets which made possible further purchases of land with a consequent increase in power.

This division of interests within the Empire, the result of developments in Asia Minor and in the capital, led to those marked changes in policy characteristic of later Byzantine politics, which sometimes occurred more than once during the reign of the same Emperor. The capital, Constantinople, looked to the West, but Asia Minor, the military heart of the Empire, looked to the East. The European policy of the Byzantine Empire was therefore largely determined by the merchant aristocracy of Constantinople. They saw the principal objective of Byzantine foreign policy in the protection of the Via Egnatia, connecting Thessalonica on the Aegean with Dyrrachium on the Adriatic, and the military command of the route through Adrianople, Plovdiv and Sofia to Belgrade. This would ensure Byzantium's political supremacy in the Balkan peninsula and keep open the possibility of political intervention in Italy and in Hungary.

Pope and Patriarch. The Roman Papacy and
Byzantium in the struggle for the Balkans

Byzantium's western policy was influenced in no small measure by the relations between the Byzantine and Roman Churches. It was a relationship determined less by dogmatic and liturgical differences between the two Churches than by considerations of foreign policy. The withdrawal of southern Italy from the jurisdiction of the Roman Church and the seizure of Roman possessions in Sicily and southern Italy weighed much more heavily in the balance than all dogmatic differences arising out of the concept of the veneration of icons, liturgical differences and theories about the procession of the Holy Spirit. It was the removal of southern Italy from Rome that induced the Pope to make the decisive break with Byzantium, a break which found expression in the alliance with the Frankish Empire and the coronation of a western Emperor.

The great conflict between the two Churches arose out of the problem of defining the spheres of influence of the Byzantine and Roman Churches in the Balkans. The mission of Constantine and Methodius to the Slav peoples was the cause of the great conflict between the Roman Curia and the Patriarch Photius in the second half of the ninth century, a conflict exacerbated by the Pope's efforts to obtain recognition as supreme head of Christendom by the eastern Churches also. Nicholas I, who was then Pope, skilfully chose a moment when Photius, the Patriarch in Constantinople, was in disagreement with the representatives of the monastic movement. Photius himself was by no means a supporter of this movement. He was a man with intellectual, and particularly classical, interests, and his sphere was consequently quite different from that of his opponents, the monks of the monastery of Studius. Photius had been a layman before rising to the rank of Patriarch. Like his predecessor Tarasius he had exchanged the office of imperial secretary for the dignity of Patriarch of Constantinople. This was not unusual in the Byzantine Church. But the representatives of the monastic movement, wishing to exploit their victory over the Emperor in the iconoclast controversy, had in mind a leadership of the Church that would be independent of the Emperor. The head of the Studite monks, the abbot of the monastery, Theodore, proposed that the leadership of the Church should consist of a Pentarchy representing the five Patriarchs. He believed that a corporate body of this kind would be a guarantee against imperial intervention in church matters. When, for reasons of protocol, Photius announced his elevation to the patriarchate to Rome, the Pope assumed the rôle of supreme judge in the conflict between Photius and his monastic opponents. But at this juncture the Byzantine Emperor intervened and rejected Rome's interference. In Byzantium, however, there was no split between the *imperium* and the *sacerdotium*, as there was in the West. The monastic movement did not continue to press its demands. Nor did the Patriarch become, as the Studite monks put it, the Horn of Salvation for the Church, which would relegate the 'God-loving Emperor' to second place in the leadership of the Church.

There were times, however, when the monastic tendency in the Byzantine Church was able to assert its claims more strongly than in this particular instance. This was especially the case with Emperors whose way of life was in conflict with the moral precepts of the Byzantine Church. For instance, when Leo VI married for the fourth time in 906 in defiance of canon law he was forbidden by the Patriarch Nicholas, who had also once been imperial secretary, to enter Hagia Sophia. It was a tremendous victory for the Church when, on the occasion of the two great processions, on Christmas Day and Epiphany, the Emperor arrived in front of the closed doors of Hagia Sophia and together with his whole court and the imperial nobility had to turn round and go away. But Leo VI was able to get his own way with the help of the Roman Pope who gave him a dispensation allowing his fourth marriage. With the support of Rome, he was then able to depose the Patriarch.

In the middle of the tenth century, the Patriarch was again able to impose his will because of the moral turpitude of the reigning monarchs. In 969 the Empress Theophano, daughter of an inn-keeper and wife of the Emperor Nicephorus Phocas by her second marriage, had her husband murdered in order to present both hand and throne to her lover, John Tzimisces. In this case, the Patriarch Polyeuctes demanded that the Emperor should do public penance and that his mistress, the Empress Theophano, should be banished. Here again the Emperor had to bow to the wishes of the Patriarch.

But in general the Patriarch's position was that of a dependent imperial official rather than of the head of the Byzantine Church answerable only to God. It was this division of power that determined the conflict with Rome. The real opponent of the Pope was not the Patriarch, but the Byzantine Emperor. This was the case in the iconoclast controversy under Leo III, and again under Photius, when Caesar Bardas, as actual regent of the Empire, directed imperial policy, and lastly in the conflict half-way through the eleventh century during which the link binding Constantinople to Rome was broken once and for all. This time, too, the conflict broke out on account of South Italy and the presence there of the Normans. Ever since the iconoclast controversy South Italy had been a bone of contention between the two Churches. In the Norman kingdom of South Italy, the Pope saw a unique opportunity of regaining the position which the Roman Church had lost in that region. The Patriarch fought to defend South Italy's adherence to the Byzantine Church, which had come about as a result of the iconoclast controversy. In this instance again, as in the iconoclast controversy and later on in Photius' day, there were dogmatic and liturgical, as well as political differences. The polemicists in the Byzantine cause, the great theologians from the ecclesiastical school of Hagia Sophia, saw only the dogmatic and liturgical differences, such as the western dogma of the double procession of the Holy Spirit, the Roman Sabbath fast, the vow of celibacy and the use of unleavened bread in the Roman Church (the Byzantine Church used leavened bread for communion). The bull of ex-communication which Cardinal Humbert of Silva Candida laid on the altar of Hagia Sophia in 1054, soon to be countered with the Byzantine anathema on the Church of Rome, brought about the schism between the two Churches that has existed until the present day. It was significant that the Patriarchs of the East, those of Alexandria, Jerusalem and Antioch, stood by the Byzantine Patriarch. Thus, East and West went their separate ways.

The attitude of the two Churches was of great significance in the development of the new political world in the Balkans. The Balkan states lay between two great powers, the East Frankish, later German, Empire in the West and the Byzantine Empire in the East. The weakness of the Byzantine Empire was in proportion to the strength of German influence; when the position was reversed Byzantium had the upper hand. In the eleventh century a situation arose where the German Empire was tied up with the investiture contest, while the whole strength of the Byzantine Empire had gathered in Asia Minor to combat the power of the Seljuks. The ex-communication hurled by the Roman Pope against the German king Henry IV (1076) and the decisive defeat of the Byzantines by the Turkish Seljuks at Manzikert in 1071 occurred in the same period. The crippling of the two great powers by conflicts which struck at the very roots of their existence gave the Balkan states an opportunity to snatch their independence. At this time Hungary succeeded in extending her power so far as to include, towards the end of the century, Croatia and Dalmatia. In Serbia, one of the župans in Prizren near the present Albanian frontier had himself crowned tsar of the Serbs and the Pope sent him the crown. In Bulgaria, the Bogomils tried to overthrow Byzantine rule. Not until Byzantium had recovered her strength were the national aspirations of Serbia and Bulgaria crushed.

These movements for independence did not revive until the last two decades of the twelfth century when the military strength of the Byzantine Empire, rocked by internal upheavals, had been substantially weakened. At this time Serbia gained the Byzantine Emperor's official recognition of her independence under Stephen Nemanya. The same thing happened in Bulgaria. Here it began with a demand for a grant of *pronoia* in respect of their estates by two great magnates whose possessions lay between the Balkan mountains and the Lower Danube. This would have meant the virtual secession of this important border country from the Byzantine Empire and the demand was refused. A military insurrection followed. Although the victory went to Byzantium, the struggle ended with a treaty in which the political independence of the new state was recognized. Thus the Second Bulgarian Empire came into being.

Here, as in Serbia, it was the Pope who sent the crown to the newly acclaimed tsar. Both states sought ecclesiastical independence from Byzantium, though not, as the Pope had perhaps hoped, by adherence to the Roman Church, but by the creation of their own national Church. The Serbian Church now had its own patriarchate at Peč, the state of Bulgaria an independent metropolitan at Trnovo. In spite of their political defection, both countries continued to maintain the culture of Byzantium.

Byzantium and the western concept of the crusading movement

The collapse of Byzantine power in the Balkans and also in Asia Minor was not simply the result of internal development, such as the rapid growth of feudalism and economic decline. The western crusading movement played a large share in the destruction of Byzantine power. It was, in fact, the crusaders who dug the grave of the Byzantine Empire. It was not only that a crusade in 1204 brought about the fall of Constantinople, the see of the Eastern Patriarch, and hence the dissolution of the old Byzantine Empire. It also deprived Byzantium of its leading position among other nations, the Slavs, Georgians and Armenians. For in the eyes of the Slav populations in the Balkans, Byzantium had lost the glory of being the only great Christian power. A new Emperor, an Emperor from the West, had marched against it at the head of superbly equipped knights; almost everywhere, Byzantine troops had suffered defeat at their hands. The Byzantine Emperor's inability to withstand these westerners made a deep impression on the Slav peoples and pointed the way to their independence.

The same kind of thing happened in Asia Minor. There too men had witnessed a series of Byzantine defeats in the face of the Turkish Seljuks. Now, out of the distant West, an army had appeared which was nearly everywhere victorious; its way to Palestine and Syria seemed wide open. They could not know that these crusaders had sworn an oath of allegiance to the Byzantine Emperor; all they saw was the army's victorious progress, the retreat of the Turks and a hope of freedom from the Turkish yoke.

The unification of Georgia, previously divided up into many Caucasian states subject either to Byzantium or to the Seljuks, was accomplished as a result of the First Crusade. When the power of the crusaders declined, so also did that of the new Caucasian state. Thus the unsuccessful outcome of the Second Crusade saw the states in that area back under Turkish rule. The Third Crusade brought about a final liberation and the rise in the Caucasus of a Georgian kingdom extending from the Black Sea to the shores of the Caspian and including large tracts of Armenia, together with the old capital Ani.

It was the same in the South. The kingdom of Lesser Armenia, which had grown up in Cilician military border districts under Armenian officers from the mid-eleventh century onwards, became a political factor during the First Crusade and was able to achieve independent national status. In this way it became a national gathering-place for a large proportion of the Armenian people who preferred to emigrate to the Cilician region by the gulf of Adana rather than remain in servitude to the Turk. The kingdom of Lesser Armenia also stood in opposition to Byzantium and looked to the West for support. It is significant in this respect that the ruling monarch of Lesser Armenia ac-knowledged himself vassal to the German Emperor Henry VI. But political opposition to Byzantium here, as in the Balkans, did not denote cultural disaffection. The civiliza-tion of Lesser Armenia, like that of Georgia, was still at this time part of the wider Byzantine culture, although its literature was being enriched by the translation of a number of Latin works and Western motifs had begun to appear with significant fre-quency in art, particularly that of Lesser Armenia. It was only the crusader states in Syria and Palestine which stood in opposition to Byzantium in regard to both politics and culture. In Jerusalem the Franco-Roman style of architecture flourished and there were few reminders of how important a focal point of Byzantine culture the city had once been.

Through the crusades Byzantium lost not only its leading position in Asia Minor and the Balkans, but was driven to ally itself with the Turks and the Islamic opponents of the West. Manuel Comnenus made an alliance with the Sultan of Rum, the enemy of Georgia, Lesser Armenia and the crusader states. The same Emperor also entered into negotiations with the Sultan of Egypt. The Second Crusade, in which the West was defeated in battle by Islam, represented a victory for the Byzantines. The prince of Antioch, and even the king of Jerusalem, bowed down before the Byzantine Emperor, the ally of the infidels. In the eyes of the West, the 'Christ-loving Emperor of Byzantium' had joined the ranks of the Seljuk sultan and the Muslim ruler of Egypt. It is in this context that the Fourth Crusade's choice of objective should be considered. To the West, the Byzantine Emperor who was dethroned was a traitor to the Christian cause. When the crusaders stormed the walls of Constantinople, when they looted churches and palaces, they also set fire to Muslim mosques, which were a living testimony to a Byzantine imperial policy biased in favour of the Islamic East.

The Italian maritime cities as destroyers of Byzantine freedom

The economic policy that brought ruin to the Byzantine Empire had in fact begun early, with the Venetian treaties initiated towards the end of the eleventh century with the purpose of holding in check the threatened advance of the Normans. At that time, when Robert Guiscard's Norman armies had crossed the Straits of Otranto, landed near Durazzo and were marching on Thessalonica along the Via Egnatia, Constantinople was prepared to concede almost anything. All powers were summoned to the Empire's aid. The German Emperor, Henry IV, who was under a ban and engaged in a life and death struggle with the Pope, was asked to go to South Italy to fight the Pope's partisans, the Normans. The Venetians were requested to use their fleet to cut off Norman com-munications between Dyrrachium and the Italian peninsula. Even national minorities previously oppressed by the Byzantines were mobilized. The Albanian, Comiscortes, was put in command of Dyrrachium, while Venetians were allowed to occupy the citadel. In 1082 the župan Constantine Bodin rose in Serbia, the exponent of a new national power.

The treaty made with Venice under the pressure of the Seljuks in the East and the Normans in the West proved to be a noose round the neck of the Byzantine Empire which grew steadily tighter, condemning her to slow death by strangulation. Nearly all the big cities in the Byzantine realm were opened to Venetian free trade. The Venetian settlement in Constantinople grew. Its inhabitants obtained shares or rights of ownership in the most important factories of the capital. This was the time when the great bakery near the quays, which provided bread for ships in transit, fell into Venetian hands, as also a number of other factories, and this in spite of the fact that they had for years belonged to private Byzantine firms. By a single stroke of the Emperor's pen they were transferred without compensation to the Venetians. The merchants of other seaports, such as Amalfi, who co-operated with the Normans, had now to pay a tax (three gold pieces a year for each merchant) to help with the decorations of the church of San Marco. The Doge of Venice was given one of the highest Byzantine court appointments, that of *protosebastus*, and the full salary that went with it. Other Venetian dignitaries, such as the Patricius of Grado, were also given court appointments with the appropriate salary.

Byzantium had difficulty in meeting her Venetian commitments. Immediately after the treaty, the Emperor was compelled to secularize church property. His declaration that it would be restored when the Empire's position improved is unlikely to have been taken seriously at the time.

Byzantium had entered into similar agreements with other Italian ports, less comprehensive than those with Venice. A treaty with Pisa granted the city important privileges, among which was a preferential tariff of four per cent on all goods imported by Pisa from countries not belonging to the Empire. Here too the treaties included an agreement as to quarters on Constantinople's Golden Horn and an important clause on the use of moorings (*skalai*). The treaties involved cultural as well as economic matters; they secured for the Pisans their own seats at the Hippodrome, Constantinople's Circus, and in Hagia Sophia.

Genoa also concluded treaties with the Byzantine Empire. The Byzantines no doubt hoped that by allying themselves with a city hostile to Venice they might, with her aid, divest themselves of the heavy commitments in which their Venetian treaties had involved them. But Genoa did not pledge her help against maritime enemies for nothing. Like Pisa, she received a four per cent preferential tariff. When these treaties had been concluded an attempt was made to repudiate the treaty with Venice. In a single day, 12 March 1171, by order of the imperial government, all Venetians in the Byzantine Empire were arrested and their warehouses seized. The Venetians replied with a display of sea-power. They occupied the Greek island of Chios, important for its production of mastic. The Byzantines were eventually forced to give way. A new treaty between the Byzantine Empire and Venice included further conditions concerning the restoration of Venetian property that had been seized. The return of property to which the Empire was pledged, was to be effected under a joint Byzantino-Venetian commission, which would consider all cases of compensation. In face of these onerous conditions, the undertaking that Venetians should give naval service to the Emperor in return for pay was of little import. The clause which promised that three quarters of all Venetians resident in the Byzantine Empire were to be subject to naval service in return for the appropriate pay, was indeed of little significance when the Byzantine treasury had no money with which to pay. Two years after this treaty had been concluded, the situation moved to a crisis. The Venetians complained that the reparations commission was proceeding too slowly. The Byzantines were then forced to agree to meet Venetian demands by enlarging their quarters in Constantinople and promising annual monetary compensation.

Like Venice, Pisa also made capital out of the Empire's difficult position. During the same period, in 1192, Pisa demanded the repayment of loans made to the Emperor Andronicus Comnenus at a time when he was still opposing the legitimate Byzantine government. Other smaller maritime cities also sought to gain from the bankruptcy of Byzantine power. Even Ragusa, a maritime city of secondary importance, had a treaty with the Byzantine government conceding her free trade within the Empire and in Bulgaria. The next stage in this piecemeal destruction of Byzantine sovereignty by the maritime cities was a treaty whereby all money disputes between Byzantines and Venetians were to be decided in the courts of Venice. At the same time the Supreme Court was also to have jurisdiction at the court of the Emperor, a situation reminiscent of that arising out of the concept of consular jurisdiction towards the end of the nineteenth and the beginning of the twentieth centuries, which served to embitter relations between China and the great western powers. In the circumstances, it is not surprising to learn that a further clause in the treaty went so far as to authorize the transfer of unlimited Venetian forces to Byzantium, so that in the end the Empire also lost its political power.

The end of the supremacy of monastic culture and the beginning of the Byzantine enlightenment

The great Byzantine Encyclopaedists

In spite of the political and economic decline, Byzantine civilization during this period attained heights which it had never achieved even during the times of the Empire's greatest political glory. It is significant that Constantine Porphyrogenitus, the Byzantine Emperor whom the feudal magnates prevented from fulfilling his imperial functions by raising a co-Emperor to the throne, was one of the founders of the Empire's new intellectual culture. It was he who laid the basis of the movement which was to turn its back on the monastic culture. In this he had the support of the literary circles of the capital and the already existing professional schools in Constantinople. The literary salons were always there. Indeed the work of Photius, who lived a hundred years earlier in the middle of the ninth century, can scarcely be imagined without the literary-minded circles that frequented the capital's salons. His *Library*, a commentary on a considerable number of works of late antique literature, could only have been produced in a capital where works of classical and late antique authors were read aloud in literary circles. He and his friend and pupil, Arethas, were especially active in the preservation of classical literature, whether by the compilation of dictionaries, or by copying old and rare manuscripts. Nearly all that has been preserved of Plato can be attributed to Arethas' activities as a collector, for it was he who had copied the manuscript of Plato originally at Patmos.

The professional schools played as important a part as Photius and his circle in the development of the new intellectual culture. This applies equally to the school of philosophy founded in the middle of the ninth century by Caesar Bardas and to the faculties of law and medicine in Constantinople. In particular, the activity of the jurists at the turn of the ninth and tenth centuries reveals a new spirit. Much of the Byzantine legal works, the *Epanagoge* and the *Basilica,* dates from this period. These were works in which already existing old Greek paraphrases of the Latin *Corpus Justiniani* were systematically revised by the selection of laws relevant to the times and the excision of older and now irrelevant sections. Imperial decrees were also included in the law books, thus turning Justinian's out of date code into a new practicable system suited to the needs of the day.

Constantine Porphyrogenitus had a wide circle to assist him in carrying out his cultural programme. He followed the lead of Photius. He too saw his task as the eradication of everything that was irrelevant ballast for his own time and the preservation of all that was of real value. With this in mind he had selections made from the writings of a large number of authors whose works as a whole were no longer in tune with the times. Thus arose the famous encyclopaedias which have preserved a good deal of late antique literature that might otherwise have been lost. The encyclopaedias were planned according to a special programme. For instance, one compilation contained everything concerning diplomatic intrigue, another gave accounts of the journeys of Byzantine ambassadors and foreign diplomats. Others were anthologies of brilliant and incisive speeches which the Emperor and his collaborators believed should be preserved for posterity. These compilations found imitators. The medical faculties at this time also had compilations made. The same is true of the agricultural theorists.

Though it may now be a matter for regret that the works of the past should have survived only in a truncated and incomplete form, it should be realized that force of circumstances necessitated the adoption of a selective method. There were simply not the financial means to employ enough copyists to preserve all these works for posterity or to replace those lost by fire, war and negligence. The budget of the Byzantine schools was restricted, sufficient for no more perhaps than two scribes to copy out those works required for daily use. Often the budget was cancelled and for several years there might be no one to copy manuscripts. The big magnates and dignitaries of the Empire helped in the work of preservation during this time by financing copies of rare ancient works. Their generosity, like that of Arethas, provided funds to enable great and lengthy manuscripts to be copied.

A new secular view of history

The time of Constantine Porphyrogenitus marked the beginning of an epoch of the new, secular historiography. The monastic chronicles disappeared and their place was taken by works by high imperial officials who wrote history from their personal knowledge of the time. Their accounts of contemporary history tend at first to be clumsy and unattractive in presentation. Their forms of expression are both stiff and inelegant. In their reaction against the monastic chronicles, these historians sought to model themselves on the writers of the last era of late antiquity, uncritically imitating their affected descriptions and the clumsy structure of their periods. They quoted indiscriminately and at length from Homer. It was not until the middle of the eleventh century that imperial history attained a standard raising it to the level of a literary work of art. The class of highly-placed officials and jurists gradually grew accustomed to their new literary tasks which afforded them a fresh means of personal expression. Michael Attaleiates, from Attaleia in Pamphylia, is the first really outstanding representative of the new intellectual movement. His history is known. Starting as a lawyer in Constantinople, he acquired a substantial fortune by skilful speculation in real estate in the capital and at Rodosto, and thus attracted official attention. Under the Emperor Constantine Ducas (1059–1067) he was a member of the imperial council and the imperial court of law at the Hippodrome. Later he rose to the rank of military judge and even attained patrician status. Michael of Attaleia, like Photius and also the circle of the Emperor Constantine Porphyrogenitus to begin with, wrote for specific literary salons. He himself belonged to one of these circles. The same literary salon was frequented by Symeon Seth, equally famous as doctor and translator, the statesman Manuel Butumites and archbishop Theophylact of Ochrida, amongst others. Symeon, who was a doctor, wrote medical works such as a report of his investigation into the effect of food on the body—then a new field in medical study—with accounts of the newly imported medical drugs from the Muslim East. He also translated the Indian novel *Stephanites and Ichnelates* from the Syriac. This novel derives from an Indian original, like the novel *Barlaam and Joasaph* which John Damascene had rewritten for the Byzantine world three hundred years earlier. It is the work in Sanskrit *Kalilah va Dimnah*, which is known to have existed in India five hundred years before Christ. It had been translated by the Persian doctor Barzoe from Sanskrit into Pahlevi. The Syriac form of the novel, used by Symeon for his Greek translation, was probably derived from this middle Persian translation. Along with the jurist and statesman Michael Attaleiates, and the doctor and brilliant orientalist Symeon Seth, this literary circle also boasted the theologian, Theophylact of Ochrida. He achieved literary fame largely through his letters from Ochrida, later his archiepiscopal see, to the capital, Constantinople. Distant Ochrida, on the present Albanian-Yugoslav border, felt like banishment to this man, and his letters reveal that the pampered churchman and writer of belles-lettres deprived of the companionship of his own kind, was driven to the verge of breakdown in the isolation of this remote country town.

Michael of Attaleia, the leader of this literary circle, did not owe his fame solely to his activities as an historian. He also produced a legal handbook for use in the Law School of Constantinople. Nor did he confine himself, either, to his personal work. Like Photius and after him his pupil Arethas, he arranged to have important books copied. A statute of a monastery with an almshouse attached and built by him, contains a list of the books which he presented. This means that he also provided the funds enabling these books to be copied.

This Michael Attaleiates was the first of a number of other historians of this period who were not members of the clergy but high officials under imperial command to record the history of their own times. Under the influence of the new secular enthusiasm of their day it was not only officials, but also the Emperor and members of the imperial family, who were inspired to write.

The Caesar Nicephorus Bryennius, who had been associated with the highest power and had shared the imperial authority, was one of these who set down contemporary history. As the Caesar he was the Emperor's representative, the second in the Empire, coming after the Basileus. His wife, the Comnenian princess Anna, twenty-one years younger than her husband, was also avid for literary fame. She had been denied political power as Empress when a strategem aimed at securing the crown for her husband failed. But Nicephorus Bryennius as the second power in the realm had to some extent created history himself. As the holder of the high command he took part in all the great military undertakings of the Byzantines around the turn of the century. In 1097 he defended Constantinople against Godfrey de Bouillon, in 1108 he negotiated the peace between Bohemund of Antioch and the Emperor Alexius Comnenus; and in 1116 he turned the scales against the sultan of Iconium. But his historical writing is disappointing, for it is not contemporary history, but a family chronicle. And this characteristic is precisely what distinguishes the historical writing of these higher civil servants and princes of the eleventh and twelfth centuries from the historians of late antiquity such as Procopius, Agathias and Menander. The Empire is no longer the centre of the historical stage, but the imperial family. For the Caesar Byrennius and Anna Comnena history consists only in the story of the members of the Comnenian house. Events are narrated to redound to their glory. In historical writing of this kind the conception of the Empire has been lost. The successive revolts of parties led by the nobility against the ever victorious Comnenian house take precedence over the major problems of imperial foreign policy. Such is the spirit in which Nicephorus Bryennius wrote history and later on his wife Anna. Their knowledge of the subject is not balanced by objectivity. Their statements and descriptions are vitiated by tendentiousness and personal considerations. Much is left unsaid.

The soldier is discernible in Nicephorus Bryennius; he preferred the sword to the pen. He is not without ability, but in his presentation his style is somewhat unpolished. He himself realized this and he refused to call his work a history, but merely the *Materials of History*, later to be given the form of a historical record. It was otherwise with his wife Anna. She has a literary style that was denied her husband; she was highly educated and better read than he was. The Attic model was the one which this writer most admired and she set herself to imitate Thucydides and Polybius, as also the baroque John of Epiphania, a genuine man of letters from the decadent period of late antiquity. Yet her style remained dry, lifeless and mummified, as if it were a language learnt at school. The Princess shuns the use of vernacular words. Nothing could be further from the demotic speech of the day, as used for instance in the verse of Theodore Prodromus, than the Greek used by this Comnenian princess.

In recording her own times she used not only Byzantine sources, but even works in Latin when direct information was not available. This too is indicative of a great change. The Byzantine sphere of influence now had serious rivals. It was a time when the West was looming larger than ever before on the Byzantine horizon. Princess Anna knew a great deal but she was not prepared to reveal more than the interests of the reigning house demanded. Her *Alexias*, even more than her husband's historical work, is a family chronicle; it is not the history of an Empire. All she writes is intended to emphasize the renown of her father, the great Emperor Alexius Comnenus.

Psellus, the first Byzantine humanist, and
the movement of the enlightenment

At this time, historical writing was not confined to politicians, lawyers and members of the imperial family. Men of learning were also engaged in recording contemporary history. They were however a different type of scholar from the learned men of Justinian's time who were more entitled to the name. Yet Michael Psellus, although more a man of letters than a man of learning, shaped the Byzantine culture of the eleventh century, for which he had the same significance as Photius had for that of the ninth, and Constantine Porphyrogenitus for that of the tenth. He was no philosopher shutting himself away from public life to write books and concentrate on academic matters. He is, for instance, totally unlike Proclus, the head of the neoplatonic school in Athens in the second half of the fifth century, who was equally irreproachable both as a scholarly teacher and as a man of learning.

As a personality Psellus is quite different from Michael Attaleiates or Nicephorus Bryennius and he did not come of any distinguished magnate family of the Byzantine Empire. He was, as he himself admitted, the child of poor parents. By the work of her hands, his mother enabled her son to pursue his studies. It was only at the expense of much privation that he was able to complete the courses in rhetoric and philosophy essential for entry into the higher ranks of the civil service. While he was still a student he got to know others who thought as he did. It was then that he first made friends with John Xiphilinus, who was later to become Patriarch. John, who came from Trebizond, gave Psellus a grounding in jurisprudence. Psellus repaid him by teaching him philosophy. Both men rose rapidly in the world, Xiphilinus to the throne of Patriarch, Psellus to ministerial office. First a judge at Philadelphia in Asia Minor, then imperial secretary and finally professor at the newly-founded philosophical faculty—such was the order of Psellus' advancement.

Psellus was not a man of admirable character; long years as a civil servant and his career at court had made him servile and had brought out the less agreeable side of his nature. His lack of principles, his sycophancy and his cynical and wounding manner in debate made him a far from attractive person. It is difficult to forgive him the letter written to his recent master, the dethroned and blinded Emperor Romanus IV, whose secretary he himself had been. He hypocritically wrote to congratulate the unfortunate man on his good fortune in that, like the saints, he need see nothing henceforth but inner light. Yet this man's human failings should not be allowed to obscure his great significance for Byzantine culture. Psellus was not only an historian, but also a philosopher, a scholar and an organizer of learning. His strength lies in his sharpness of observation and the fluency of his language. He was neither an innovator nor a creator, but a thinker. The scope of his literary activity places him alongside Roger Bacon and Albertus Magnus. But he is never so profound as they are. Even as philosopher, he remained à man of letters. The fact that his philosophy was centred in Plato was characteristic of him.

Ever since the sixth century, with the closing of the university of Athens, Plato as philosopher had been under ban and had almost been forgotten. Nevertheless the theology of late antiquity, fundamental to the life of the Byzantine middle ages almost up to the beginning of modern times, had borrowed from Platonic philosophy virtually all it said about the nature of God, of the Holy Spirit and of Christ. Aristotle, less disturbing, easier to grasp, had taken Plato's place. Even in his case, only a few sections of the *Organon* were read, and these were reserved for higher education. By his revival of Platonic philosophy, Psellus began what was an almost revolutionary development. His return to the teaching on the Platonic ideas, which he also seems to have made the central point of his lectures, introduced a method of observing the world utterly different from anything philosophy had provided within the framework of monastic theology. It gave a new outlook in every form of learned study. In this way investigation and method were freed from the fetters of dogma, the leading position of theology was disputed, and the natural sciences, hitherto much neglected, once more took first place. Platonic teaching on the soul, which Psellus sought to clarify in various writings at this time, was incompatible with Byzantine theology. They were mutually exclusive. To adopt this aspect of Plato's philosophy was to shake the foundations of orthodox dogma.

The revolutionary nature of the new intellectual movement is plainly apparent in the fact that only a few decades after Psellus' lectures on Plato's philosophy, works appeared in Byzantine literature which were directly opposed to the official Church and had indeed a character that was almost anti-Christian. Amongst them was the so-called *Visit to Hades* of the Byzantine Timarion, a work belonging to the middle of the twelfth century. It is an imitation of Lucian's *Necyomanteia*, and the structure of the dialogue anticipates Dante's *Divine Comedy*, but its content is typical of Byzantine satire, which does not stop short of attacking Christianity.

It is the tale of Timarion, a Byzantine, who goes from Constantinople to the great fair at Thessalonica held in honour of the city's patron saint, Demetrius Myroblytes, and who falls sick on his way home and dies soon after. There is a description of Timarion's journey into the underworld where he meets a lawyer whom he had known. The latter takes Timarion under his wing and declares that he, Timarion, has been wrongfully brought to the underworld. His petition on Timarion's behalf is allowed by the underworld's bench of judges, a body that includes pagan gods as well as the iconoclast Emperor Theophilos, and the guides of the dead are convicted of abusing their office. The verdict relies on the evidence of Aesculapius and Hippocrates who, in their capacity as experts, testify that Timarion was summoned from life in defiance of the laws of pathology. Timarion is then allowed to return to earth. The anti-Christian and anti-clerical nature of the tale is clearly shown in Pythagoras' contempt for the Byzantine scholar, John Italus, when he attempts to take his place among the philosophers. If he wishes to live in a circle whose existence is to be based on pure science alone, he must first doff the Galilean cloak, a garment allegedly divine and of heavenly origin. The religious tolerance advocated by this book—on occasion it actually enunciates the principle: Here everyone can belong to whatever sect he wants—is a direct attack on Byzantine orthodoxy.

As a philosopher Psellus still endeavoured to retain the theologian's gown, but he was so indifferent towards traditional religious forms that he prepared the way for the literary movement which later was to give birth to anti-Christian satire. After he had left the monastery on Mount Olympus in Asia Minor where he had resided for a time, he himself became engaged in a literary feud in the course of which he wrote a polemical satire using the form of the ecclesiastical hymn, the canon. It was a symptom, a straw in the wind. The movement which Psellus had started with his revival of Plato's philosophy could not be halted. It was a decisive factor in a large area of intellectual life and was ultimately responsible for creating the conditions which gave rise to the European renaissance. It is true that these ideas were represented by what was a limited literary group, but it was also a powerful group whose importance was enhanced by the study of the natural sciences which accompanied Platonic philosophy.

The renewed interest in the natural sciences was derived from Psellus. In his *Omnifaria Doctrina*, as he called his encyclopaedic compilation, he devoted each section to one of the spheres of natural science which had been neglected during the preceding centuries —astronomy, medicine and mathematics. What he has to say is not original, is full of mistaken ideas and lacking in penetration and profundity. But it was a stimulant, and succeeding generations developed what he had begun.

Orthodox religion recognized the danger inherent in the new philosophy which it sought to combat. Thus at the beginning of the twelfth century, the great theologian Euthymius Zigabenus was commissioned by the Emperor Alexius Comnenus to write a comprehensive polemic in refutation of the heresies of the Platonic freethinkers in the university at Constantinople. It was a literary battle between the partisans of theological orthodoxy and those of the new outlook in philosophy which was to continue unceasingly from then on. The seriousness with which the threat was regarded in orthodox circles can be seen from the increasingly detailed nature of the refutations. For instance analysis and refutation was provided for every sentence of one section of a book by Proclus, the main advocate of scientific neoplatonism in the fifth century.

But neither detailed treatment nor pointed refutation could impede the progress of the dangerous philosophical innovations which had begun to infiltrate even into theology. The previously serried ranks of the guardians of orthodoxy seemed to dissolve as some of them defected to the new philosophical doctrines. A sign of what was on foot was the dismissal for heresy in 1156 of the famous preacher and professor of biblical exegesis at the famous ecclesiastical school of Hagia Sophia, Michael of Thessalonica. A similar fate was shared by Nicephorus Basilaces, also a teacher of biblical exegesis at the same school. In the decree dismissing them, they are accused of over-individual interpretation in their exegesis. There are many secular elements in the writings of these theologians. This gives the impression that the Church prized rhetoric more highly than asceticism. Theologians once more resorted to earlier sophist methods of teaching. But it was out of place for a liberal theologian like Nicephorus Basilaces to occupy himself with over-bold problems of a sophistical nature, such as 'what Danae must have said when Zeus approached her in the form of golden rain.' The autobiographical foreword to the collected works of this scholar shows that he belongs to the new era. Autobiography is the expression of a new universal feeling, a different conception of mankind. This was the beginning of a new development that produced the literary form of memoirs, in which Byzantium itself has an honourable position with the autobiography of its Emperor, John VI Cantacuzenus.

The revival of natural science and its influence on the Italian and Turkish renaissance

Platonic philosophy, especially in its neoplatonic version, provided a system for the study of the world. Here the progressive element was found in the development of the natural sciences. In the eleventh and twelfth centuries men sought to begin again at the point where development had ceased at the end of the sixth and the beginning of the seventh centuries. Mathematics, astronomy and geography were the sciences principally concerned. This, too, looked back to the neoplatonic inspiration of the fifth and sixth centuries. For Proclus himself, the leader of scientific neoplatonism in the university of Athens—subsequently closed by the East Roman Emperor Justinian—had himself written commentaries on Euclid. The mathematicians of the sixth and the beginning of the seventh centuries saw a close relationship between practical application and theoretical scientific research. Isidore of Miletus, the master-builder of Hagia Sophia, also taught pure mathematics. One of his pupils was Eutocius of Ascalon, who wrote commentaries on the famous mathematicians of late antiquity, Archimedes and Apollonius.

When scientific studies were resumed in the eleventh and twelfth centuries the mixture of scientific research and practical application characteristic of sixth-century science was not at first possible. Manuals concerning the natural sciences which have survived from these times show that in mathematics, for instance, scholars were still very far from any real understanding of the original sources, such as the works of Euclid or Archimedes.

The great turning point in the understanding of the natural science of antiquity did not come until the beginning of the fourteenth century with the arrival of Arabic science by way of North-West Persia. The mediator in this case was the Empire of Trebizond which had arisen in 1204 with the fall of Constantinople to the crusaders. In this way Byzantine culture acquired knowledge of the science of the Arabs which had been brought to a high state of development in Persia and West Turkestan. Mathematical learning from India also reached Byzantium through West Turkestan.

At the turn of the thirteenth and fourteenth centuries a doctor, Gregory Chioniades, who lived at the imperial court of Trebizond, travelled through Iran, then under the domination of the Mongol Ilkhans. Chioniades returned from his travels with a large number of Persian books. Close economic contacts had resulted in a general familiarity with the Persian language, and the learning contained in Chioniades' books was passed on to the Greek-speaking world in a handbook, *Introduction to the Learning of the Persians*. At the beginning of the fourteenth century Constantinople already possessed a translation of the astronomical treatise of Shams al-Bukkari, but it was only during the first half of that century that an independent Byzantine body of work on astronomy and mathematics grew up, drawing both on translations from the Persian and on its own Greek sources. But by then the translation of Persian scientific literature had come to an end. The lead in scientific research previously held by the Arab world had now been made up by the Byzantines. Persian manuscripts were no longer needed. But their influence on the development of Byzantine science resembled that which Byzantine science was later to have upon Italy. With the help of the learning of antiquity and of India which she gained by way of Persia, Byzantium was able to complete and develop further her own scientific learning derived from late antiquity.

Classical mathematical knowledge, such as the work of Pappos or Diophantus, came to Florence in the form it had assumed in Byzantium, evolving out of the science of late antiquity and of the Islamic-Persian world. In 1420 this enabled the Florentines to increase the range of their painting by means of the perspective vanishing-point. This was first used in painting by Masaccio and was described in a treatise by Leon Battista Alberti for the first time in 1435.

Another consequence of the mathematical knowledge transmitted through Byzantine culture was the revival in architecture of the large dome. Between 1420 and 1436, Brunelleschi succeeded in constructing a cupola for the duomo in Florence. This achievement would have been impossible without the previous progress in mathematical science. The cupola of the duomo in Florence led in its turn to the creation of the great cupola which Michelangelo set over St Peter's in Rome.

With this great advance in the science of mathematics, Constantinople witnessed the same development as had occurred in Italy. The depleted treasury of the last Byzantine Emperors, however, precluded any building of large cupolas and it was not until after 1453, the year in which the city fell to the Turks, that this was possible. The Ottoman conquest provided Greek architects with patrons rich enough to commission such ambitious projects. Thus barely ten years after the fall of Constantinople, the Greek Christodoulos built the great domed mosque for Mohammed II, named after him Mehmedije. But, as in Italy, this was not the end of the road. Christodoulos was followed by Sinan, as Brunelleschi was followed by Michelangelo. Sinan was a Greek, born in 1489 at Caesarea in Cappadocia. Like his contemporary Michelangelo in Italy, Sinan succeeded in perfecting the construction of the cupola and built a number of mosques with huge domes.

In Byzantine civilization, perspective ran much the same course as in Italy. The wall paintings of the church of St Nicholas at Curtea de Argeş in the principality of Moldavia in present-day Rumania, show representations of incompletely understood perspective forms from a Byzantine model. The mosaics of the church of the Chora, the Kariye Cami, have clearly been influenced by paintings in perspective. The artists who created the mosaics must have seen pictures in which perspective had been fully used. Indeed, the influence of such paintings lasted beyond the Byzantine period into Turkish days. Turkish miniatures of the mid-fifteenth century surprisingly contain perspective which was foreign to the art of Islam. Humans and animals are shown foreshortened, as in the painting of the western renaissance. The landscape itself is not flat in the traditional manner, but is given depth in space. The creators of these miniatures did not proceed only on the basis of models supplied through the Mongols from Chinese painting, but were evidently familiar with Byzantine perspective which they applied to their own pictures.

The birth of a new conception of the world

The way to the renaissance in the West led through Byzantium. The return to late antiquity in the eleventh and twelfth centuries in the Byzantine Empire and the acquisition of mathematical knowledge through Persia had helped to set the stage for the western renaissance. Of hardly less significance than the rediscovery of science, were the new political and social theories which had developed in the Byzantine Empire. For in both these fields the revival of Platonic philosophy in the eleventh century meant the beginning of a new era. Psellus had already concerned himself with the political ideas of Plato, but for all his mockery of religion and his free thought he still remained a Christian. It was not till a generation later that there was any evidence of an anti-Christian movement. Timarion's *Visit to Hades* was a work showing this tendency.

But an actual attack, in the form of a theoretical refutation of Christianity did not come till much later, in the first half of the fifteenth century. The influence of this movement, like that of the revival of the natural sciences, can be seen in the Italian renaissance.

The great exponent of the movement which sought to refute Christianity was Gemistus Pletho. By training he was a lawyer and had occupied influential positions at the court of the Byzantine rulers of Mistra. With the help of Plato's philosophy, Pletho sought to loosen the hold of Christianity on Byzantine society. He insisted that Christian law and Christian world order be replaced by standards derived from classical philosophy. His principal work, the *Nomon Syngraphe*, was however burnt soon after his death by his pupil, the Patriarch Gennadius of Constantinople. But the burning of his writings was not able to lessen his influence in the West. For this was exerted less through his writings than through personal contacts with the leading minds of the Italian renaissance. As the highest legal official of Mistra, he was a member of the Byzantine delegation which took part in the negotiations for the union of the Greek and Latin Churches at the Ferrara-Florence Council of 1438–39. Pletho was thus able to visit other Italian cities besides Ferrara and to give lectures in them. In Florence he met Cosimo de'Medici. The later foundation in 1449 of a Platonic Academy there was the direct outcome of his lectures. His influence was also felt in Rome, where it was to endure for a considerable time at the Academy of Pomponio Leto. Yet it was not only free-thinkers, those already outside the Church, who became his pupils. The man who later became Cardinal Bessarion in Rome, and Gennadius, the first Greek Patriarch of Constantinople after its conquest by the Turks, were as much his pupils as the humanists of Florence and Rome.

But Pletho's influence in the West was not confined to philosophy; he was indeed even better known as a political thinker and social theorist. Thus the philosophy of history of Machiavelli, brought up on Polybius, and also that of Guicciardini, both ultimately derive from the ideas of Pletho. Some of his concepts denied tenets held by the Christian philosophy of history, such as the Christian idea of progress, or the belief that historical events are determined by divine providence. This was replaced by the doctrine of eternal recurrence. In this can be seen an attempt to subject history to the same laws as the natural sciences.

As the last Byzantine exponent of the neoplatonic movement, Pletho also influenced Italian figural art in the second half of the fifteenth and during the first decades of the sixteenth century through his theories relating to a revival of paganism. The artist Leonardo da Vinci was affected by Pletho's ideas. He was the first to attempt a blend of pagan forms with traditional Christian ones which, in the course of the renaissance and even more in the baroque art, was to lead to a disappearance of those forms which had been determined by Christian iconography. The equating of John the Baptist with Dionysus, of the angel with Ganymede and of Mary with Hebe arose during the renaissance out of Pletho's ideas. In Leonardo da Vinci's picture of John the Baptist there is for the first time an attempt to combine the pagan image of Dionysus with the traditional Christian form. Correggio invests his angels with the likeness of Ganymede; they have the beautiful limbs of the pagan boy gods. All the old pagan voluptuousness of the flesh is preserved here in the frescoes, panels, or sculptures of baroque and rococo churches. Similarly in Leonardo's St Anne with Virgin and Child, Mary has all the characteristics of the Greek Hebe, and this representation of her continued to survive in later art.

It must however be admitted that these new forms did not come from Byzantium, which only provided the intellectual stimulus. In Byzantium the old forms of antiquity had not been preserved unchanged as had its literary tradition. The memory of the great pictures and representations of the ancient gods had been lost as early as the end of the seventh century. The Byzantines of the eleventh and twelfth centuries visualized the gods and heroes of antiquity in terms of their own day. Thus a miniature of that time shows the Greek king Midas in the robes worn by the Byzantine Basileus, and the heroes of the Trojan legend are clothed and armed like Byzantine magnates of the eleventh century. The recovery of classical form must be credited entirely to the Italian renaissance. It was through excavations that the true models of antiquity were discovered and artists stimulated to imitate them. This never happened in the field of Byzantine culture. Even where there was a conscious return to antiquity, this related on the whole only to the forms of the final period of late antiquity, which survived to a great extent in miniatures and carved ivories. Byzantium never saw an excavation of classical statues and works of art such as took place in Italy.

Monastic asceticism and the mystic vision of God

The great intellectual movement which, from the middle of the eleventh century onwards, effected a radical revision in the traditional conceptions of the world through its revival of Platonic philosophy, was bound also to awaken those forces aimed at the regeneration of old religious forms which had grown stereotyped and difficult to understand. In Byzantium this revival was almost entirely limited to the monastic movement. Its aim was the spiritual deepening of religious life; its means were the asceticism long familiar in the monastic world. During the fourth and fifth centuries, monks had striven for the vision of God through a particular form of asceticism. Not only in Byzantium, but also in the West and in Islam, this striving for a personal vision of God was known as mysticism, and it was to this that the new movement returned. This mysticism and the movement for a new view of life arising out of Platonic philosophy both have the same spiritual roots, namely the contrast already apparent in the first phase of Christianity resulting from the fusion of elements from the old Hellenistic philosophy with the ascetic forms of early Christianity. The monastic movement, as the radical wing inside Christianity, sought to fulfil the demands of asceticism with all its implications. The early Church, however, chose the middle road. At the universities her leaders had listened to lectures on the ancient philosophers; and as theologians they used the concepts and definitions of the Greek philosophers in their writings and thought.

After the victory of the iconophiles over the iconoclasts in the eighth and ninth centuries, the radical monastic movement had won the leadership of the Church, but by then it was too late. It was now impossible to purge theology of the concepts and definitions derived from the pagan philosophers or to impose the ascetic practices of the few on all the servants of the Church. Herein lies the difference between the Christian Byzantine Church and the Christian Church of the West. In the Byzantine Church asceticism, in so far as sexual abstinence was concerned, was obligatory only for the higher clergy, starting with bishops. All others were allowed to marry. Again, in Byzantium education was not a monopoly of the Church, as in the West. Hence it was not difficult for laymen to become princes of the church. All too often, indeed, imperial private secretaries exchanged their desk for the patriarchal throne. These laymen were then able to win renown as theological writers, notwithstanding their secular education. Thus Maximus the Confessor in the seventh century had first been the Emperor's confidential secretary before taking to the monastic habit and making his name as a theologian and religious leader. The same was true of the Patriarch Photius and not least the great Byzantine theologian John of Damascus, both of whom had been members of a higher civil service.

The split that characterizes the intellectual situation peculiar to the middle of the eleventh century was due basically to the rupture of the ties that bound Christian asceticism and late antique theology, the latter being closely involved with pagan philosophy. One trend, represented by Psellus and his Faculty of Philosophy in Constantinople, aimed at the revival of Platonic philosophy. The other, and more religious, trend was based on an asceticism aiming at a deepened inner spirituality through which it sought to achieve a vision of God. The Byzantine mystic also sought God in his own way and in so doing sometimes departed from the path laid down by the Church. He continued to regard liturgy and prayer as a sacrament, but for him the goal of the Christian life was attainable only through a love of God undisturbed by the temporal world. Here Byzantine and German mysticism have much in common. The same viewpoint is found in Meister Eckhart as in the Byzantine mystic. He too never questioned the sacraments of the Church or the fundamentals of Christian theology. On the one hand in his Latin writings he adheres closely to Christian scholastic theology, while on the other his surviving German writings point to union with God, the *unio mystica*, as the final goal of religion. As far as spiritual development is concerned, Meister Eckhart belongs almost to the end of western Christian mysticism. The same applies to the Byzantine mystic Nicholas Cabasilas. They were virtually contemporaries: Meister Eckhart died in 1327, Nicholas Cabasilas in 1371. Both were representative of the final stage of mysticism, a mysticism which appeared in the West later than in Byzantium. The first Byzantine mystic, Symeon the New Theologian, was already active in the second half of the tenth century, whereas in the West Bernard of Clairvaux (died 1153) and Richard of St Victor were not teaching until the twelfth century. Western mystics regarded suffering as the way to God and in this they perhaps returned more completely than the Byzantines to early Christian precepts. But both western and Byzantine mystics of the eleventh and twelfth centuries had in common the final goal: union with God. This was not always openly stated in their writings, but anyone who follows their trend of thought cannot fail to perceive it.

Nicholas Cabasilas, the Byzantine mystic, unlike Meister Eckhart, was probably never a priest, though in 1354 he was apparently considered for the office of Patriarch. It is just possible that he may have belonged to some kind of community. In his main work *On Life in Christ* he states his goal as being union with the risen Christ. To him this is the meaning of the eucharist. He claims that God can be enjoyed in this life through love for Him. Nicholas Cabasilas differs from Eckhart in that Christ remains the centre of his religious thinking. For Nicholas both Christ and the sacraments are inseparable. But with Eckhart these pass into the background in favour of a *unio mystica* with a universal God of a pantheistic nature.

The fact that mysticism also adopted neoplatonism in its Christian form is significant of the continuity of classical and Christian cultures which survived every upheaval. The writings attributed in the middle ages to Dionysius the Areopagite, allegedly converted by Paul (*Acts*, 17.34) and a member of the Athenian Areopagus, did in fact originate in Syria during the fifth century, and they show a fusion of neoplatonic philosophy and Christian thought. These works of Pseudo-Dionysius the Areopagite reached Byzantine theologians in the middle of the seventh century through Maximus the Confessor, and arrived in the West in the ninth century through the Irish translator John Scotus (or Eriugena). Among Greek works that had been translated into Latin, the writings of John of Damascus, the great Byzantine theologian, and those of Pseudo-Dionysius the Areopagite, were held in equal high esteem.

The influence of neoplatonism which had found expression in the Christian mysticism of Syria travelled from thence to Islam. There, as in Byzantium and the West, it led to the development of a particular doctrine which taught that union with God was attainable through love.Islamic mysticism, called Sufism after the garment (the *suf* or woollen gown) worn by its adherents, the mysticism of Byzantium and that of the West, all started from the same neoplatonic Christian basis, and each independently pursued the same religious goal, the *unio mystica*, union with God. It is the form, not the content of their teaching, that separates Ibn al Arabi, the Islamic mystic who lived at the turn of the twelfth and thirteenth centuries, Meister Eckhart, and the Byzantine Nicholas Cabasilas. The ascetic movement of the Syrian Christians with their monastic communities was the formative element in the development of the Byzantine monk as it was for the Islamic dervish orders. But Muslim dervishes, unlike Christian monks, do not observe strict sexual continence, and they also differ from Byzantine and western ascetics in having no connection with the official Islamic church.

Generally speaking, the quality of the spirituality achieved by the Byzantine monk within the monastic communities was of a much higher order than that of related movements in East and West. In the Islamic East through the orders of dervishes mysticism often became the instrument of political movements and thus brought about the rise of new political entities. The Ottoman state owes its rise to the status of major power not so much to the sword of the Ghazis, to Osman and his successors, as to the Holy War proclaimed by the dervish sheikhs. The rise of the state of the Wahhabis in Arabia was also the work of a religious order. In the West mysticism led to a religious revival but only at the price of the unity of the Church. For although the Christian Churches were revitalized by the reformation and the counter-reformation, they did not retain their unity. In Byzantium, on the other hand, mysticism invested the symbols of the Orthodox Church with a content both new and more profound. The traditional icons of Mary the Mother of God or of the calendar of saints now possessed a mystic significance previously unknown in the Church. The process is less evident in Byzantium itself than on the periphery. The Muscovite school of Rublev, for instance, with its representation of the Holy Trinity, and the Cretan school where Domenikos Theotokopoulos' work had affinities with the West, these were the last splendid flowerings of Byzantine painting inspired by mysticism.

In Byzantium as in the West, the transition to a new age found men either turning to God in their spiritual longing for the unknowable and the transcendental, or else seeking an overrated scientific knowledge which was developing on the basis of work begun in antiquity. Both these trends led away from orthodoxy and from the forms which it had imposed on all spheres of culture. In the West mysticism and science had both contributed to the reformation of the old Church, though at the cost of unity, but in Byzantium the Orthodox Church remained intact. For the Orthodox Church was bound up with national resistance, first to the West and later towards the Turks. The organization and form of the Church were the unique walls and bastions which enabled the Greek world to survive four centuries of Turkish rule.

The beginnings of a literature in the vernacular

The new age heralded by the revival of Platonic philosophy in the Byzantium of the mid-eleventh century also looked to literature and the figural arts for new forms of expression. The decisive turning point was brought about not only by the founding in Constantinople of the Platonic Academy under Psellus. There were great internal social changes in the course of which, during the tenth and eleventh centuries, Byzantine society took on a new aspect and also played a part in the development of the new movements. Much the same had happened during the sixth and seventh centuries when army reform and the monastic movement had laid the foundations of Byzantine civilization for several centuries to come. This time it was the feudalization of the army and the civil service which, together with the intellectual movement arising from the revival of Platonic philosophy, led to the development of new cultural forms.

The magnates of Asia Minor were the agents of the Byzantine state during the tenth and eleventh centuries. It was only gradually that they left their estates in Cappadocia, Armenia or Paphlagonia to come to Constantinople where they assumed political leadership in the central administration. Their contacts with the land from which they came were far more real to them than their contacts with the capital. There they were strangers, instantly recognizable by their almost incomprehensible dialect, the Greek of eastern Asia Minor. The circles of the great merchants and exporters were hostile to them so that they never left their fortified town palaces in Constantinople unless accompanied by a large armed following. They preferred to reside on their estates in Cappadocia, Armenia or Paphlagonia. This led to another development in the life of the time, for alongside the art of the capital, Constantinople, there was now artistic activity in the provinces and the counterpart of Constantinopolitan literature was to be found in the literature of the distant provinces of Asia Minor. In the rock churches in Cappadocia, the oldest frescoes were still closely related to the art of the Syrian and Palestinian regions and were at first quite unconnected with the style of painting practised in the capital. The rock churches lay within the area dominated by the great Byzantine magnate families of the Phocas, Ducas and Maleini, whose support and protection they enjoyed.

In literature it was much the same, except that the divergence from the capital was even more marked than in the representational arts. While Byzantine authors in the capital wrote history, verse and romances in Attic Greek that was artificially kept alive, the language written on the estates of the country magnates was demotic. The wandering performers may have been the first to spread poetic forms. As early as the second half of the ninth century, Arethas mentions the wandering Paphlagonian minstrels. These bards sang about events of recent history and their songs are rightly held to be the forerunners of the later Greek folksongs. But they did not only sing; they also sold copies of their work. In this, they may have resembled the Cypriot minstrels of the last century who sold booklets of their songs to their audiences. It can be assumed that these bards also used themes from districts outside the frontiers of the Byzantine Empire. This would explain the influx of eastern subjects into Byzantine literature, so clearly apparent from the eleventh century onwards.

The visible beginning of the new demotic poetry, which the magnates were probably the first to encourage, was the epic poem *Digenis Akritas*. This work was as significant for the Byzantines as the *Nibelungenlied* for German-speaking lands, and the *Chanson de Roland* for the French. The subject-matter concerns a time when the Byzantine magnates were fighting the Arab emirs. This was the tenth century in the days when the Byzantine Empire was struggling to recover Syria. Behind this poem is an historical figure in the person of the emir of Melitene, Omar al Akta, called Ambro by the Byzantines. The same man was also the hero of an Arabic epic poem which was included in the *Thousand and One Nights* as well as in the Turkish romance *Said Battal*. Thus the character of the emir provided material for the Arab as well as the Byzantine minstrels.

The story of the Byzantine epic runs as follows: The hero of the poem, Basil Digenis, is the son of Mansur, a Syrian emir, and of the daughter of Andronicus Ducas, whom Mansur has carried off. Her five brothers demand her return but in vain. Mansur is converted to Christianity by his bride. The son, Basil Digenis, is already going on dangerous hunting expeditions by the time he is twelve and very soon takes over the struggle against the rough, thieving rabble called the Apelatae. He then wins the love of the beautiful Eudocia—also a member of the Ducas family—and carries her off. Henceforth she accompanies Digenis on all his expeditions, sharing his dangers and privations. Basil Digenis founds a principality on the Euphrates, but death overtakes him at the early age of thirty-three. His wife does not survive him. There is a vivid description of her end; her farewell embrace of the dying Digenis is so close that she suffocates.

The epic poem in its present form is not very old. The oldest versions go back to the thirteenth century or thereabouts, to the period, that is, after Constantinople had fallen to the crusaders in 1204. On the other hand, some shorter epics have survived, indicating that this form goes back even earlier, perhaps as far as the eleventh century.

The *Digenis Akritas* epic, in the form in which it has survived, would seem to have been written by a learned man who not only drew on the traditional material of the minstrels, but also on works in classical Greek. In his poem he used the monastic Byzantine chronicles, the chronicle of Theophanes Continuatus. He must also have been familiar with the contemporary poetry of Constantinople in the learned language. Other sources were the romance of Eustathius Macrembolites, the poem of *Hysmine and Hysminas*, written in the second half of the twelfth century, and the romance of Theodore Meliteniotes, a fourteenth-century work. It is difficult to escape the conclusion that the editor, whose work presumably underlies all surviving versions of the poem, intentionally sought to bridge the gulf between demotic poetry and works in the learned formal language as written in the capital.

The gap between the old and the new literature must at first have been considerable. The new ruling class arriving in the capital from the provinces brought to Constantinople poets who wrote in the vernacular. The littérateurs of the city had to accustom themselves to using demotic speech in poetry if they were to win the favour of the ruling magnates and so ensure a paying audience. It thus came about that individual poets, amongst whom were Theodore Prodromus and Michael Glycas, began to write in demotic as well as in the learned language. The choice of subject matter was also

333

determined by the new ruling class. There were rather coarse farces which dealt in a carefree way with the ordinary man in the street, and there were also imitations of the old sophist romances and satires in the old style and taste going back to Hellenistic times. The literary man, with all the worries and dangers attendant on his profession, emerges as a type as early as the eleventh century. Theodore Prodromus is the archetype of the begging man of letters, dependent on the favour of the powerful and prepared to write anything that is wanted. Farcical satires on the lives of the common people alternate with impossible romances and sycophantic verse addressed to the great men of his time. His writing gives expression to the everyday life of Byzantium. His humour is broad, often bordering on the obscene, whether he is describing his own lot as a penniless poet racked by family quarrels—knock-about fights with his wife, the sons join in and take her part, the poet all too often is driven out of the house into the street— or whether he is writing satires about the prostitutes of Constantinople. He says of a whore whom he would like to consign to hell that she would be an undigestible tit-bit for a hound of hell and that to enjoy her would undoubtedly cost him his teeth; or again, mocking a dandy on account of his excessively long beard, he advises him to cut off his beard so as to restore the symmetry of his outward appearance.

But the magnates were sometimes fickle towards their literary favourites. Often a pension would be taken away because of some violent attack on the patron's faults, or there might even be an official punishment. Prodromus only lost his property; the vindictive pen of Michael Glycas, another writer, cost him his eyes. When in prison, he put forward a moving plea to the Emperor Manuel Comnenus written in demotic Greek, but it did not prevent his being blinded. The careers of men of letters had their ups and downs. Prodromus ended his life in a monastery, but not before giving his imperial patron, who appeared to have forgotten him, a plaintive account in moving terms of this final stage of his life on this earth. But the poet found the peace he longed for no more in the monastery than in marriage. The ruling abbots, father and son, persecuted him mercilessly.

Awareness of the hazards of a writer's existence finds repeated expression in this literature. Authors bewail the fate that made them poets or men of learning instead of bakers, cobblers or butchers, whose life was so much to be preferred to that of the man dedicated to science or to literature. But their writing is often motivated by hatred of a new class with which they had nothing in common, a class that never gave writers any encouragement and they in turn revenged themselves after their own fashion. The city's craftsmen and shopkeepers had grown rich and they, like the country magnates, preferred vernacular writing. Imitations of sophist romances decked out with trappings from the literature of learning, made no appeal at all to such people. They demanded something out of their immediate experience. This accounts for the dual nature of Prodromus' work, on the one hand the sophist romance *Rhodanthe and Dosicles*, on the other, popular farces. This man was evidently seeking desperately to win the favour of a new public. His writings in the formal language betray his fear of being forgotten, for he was also courting the favour of conservative salons where Atticism was still de rigueur. To please that public, he imitated late antique satires. One of these is the humorous tale of a mouse which, having found its way into a dining room, is inspired by the plentiful remains on the table to declaim classical monologues, thereby attracting the attentions of a cat. There follows a dialogue between cat and mouse. Both quote from the Bible. The mouse asserts its right to the title of abbot, which does not however avert its untimely end brought about by the cat. Prodromus also sought to win the favour of the superstitious. To this end he wrote an astrological poem on the

334

power and the meaning of the planets. This man's entire work was motivated by the struggle for existence. Only thus can the mixture of religious verse, obscene farces and romances be explained. He wrote for everyman, and for everyman's money.

The decline of the literature of entertainment in the learned language

Prodromus knew how to move with the times and adapted himself accordingly. Other men of letters were less happy—or less skilled. One of these was John Tzetzes, a contemporary of Prodromus. He was a grammarian who sought to elucidate the literature of antiquity; he was unable to arouse the interest of the magnates. Hence his unending complaints about poverty and lack of recognition. Like Prodromus, he was intemperate in controversy and his self-esteem was enormous; he grossly over-rated his own culture, which by comparison with that of late antiquity was exiguous. Nearly everything he wrote is extremely long. His *Chiliades* contains 12,674 verses. His work is totally lacking in originality and is full of glaring mistakes; the names of places in antiquity are taken for names of people; it is impossible to check up on the allegedly vast extent of his reading which embraces virtually every classical author. But it looks as though a large part of Tzetzes' knowledge may have been derived from learned handbooks which no longer exist today. From the nature of his work, it would appear to have been intended for a small learned circle. His allegories on the *Iliad* and the *Odyssey* preserved much material from works of antiquity which no longer survive today, but all-in-all they are little more than a compilation. It is a pedestrian affair. Furthermore, the bulk of his commentaries are copies of older works with no attempt at any original reconstruction. His commentary on the comedies of Aristophanes turns out to be an almost word for word rendering of the work of earlier scholiasts. Most classical literature was annotated by Tzetzes, including Homer, Aristophanes and Hesiod, as also Porphyry's introduction to Aristotle's *Categories* and Claudius Ptolemy's *Astronomy*.

Tzetzes, like his contemporary Prodromus, was unable to amass worldly wealth. Poor, beset with enemies and filled with bitterness, he too communicates his cruel situation to the rest of the world through dialogue. A dramatic poem describes, in a meeting between a peasant and a man of learning, the difficult life of the scholar. Muses and chorus sing the praises of a life devoted to learning, to which Tzetzes, through the scholar, replies, as Prodromus would have done, with a scathing denunciation of the uselessness of learned endeavour and of study, compared with the material security of other callings.

Tzetzes is part of that intellectual movement associated with the names of Photius, Constantine Porphyrogenitus and lastly that of Psellus. With the object of reviving and preserving the works of antiquity, old manuscripts were copied and compilations made containing extracts from the masterpieces of classical literature. This movement was not only concerned with literature, but also with the representational arts in which it found visible expression. During this time painters began to copy old miniatures from late antiquity. The opponents of this movement were not however confined to those who supported the use of vernacular in poetry or who defended monastic culture. It was rejected by the new social classes who remained unconvinced of the need for a classical revival. By the end of the tenth century voices were actually raised in denunciation of the excessive deference paid to Homer. Arguments raged upon this subject. The deacon Theodosius, who wrote an epic about the Byzantine expulsion of the Arabs from Crete in 961, maintained that the campaign described by Homer was nothing by comparison with that of the Byzantines in Crete, and was indeed hardly worth writing about. Many of the objections to Homer came from members of a literary movement which had the support of a noble feudal circle comprising among others the Emperors Nicephorus Phocas and John Tzimisces. In the circles of the magnates from Asia Minor who had come to power in Constantinople, the general preference was for epics deriving from folk poetry which, like that of *Digenis Akritas,* used contemporary material and were written in demotic Greek.

The influence of the East on the new Byzantine romance

The departure from antiquity came about not only through the use of the vernacular for poetry, to which even Prodromus subscribed by using it in some of his works, but also through chapbooks and oriental romances. Byzantine expansion in Armenia and Syria had brought the East nearer to the Byzantine world, oriental subject-matter was absorbed into folk poetry and also became widely known through Greek translations. It was at this time that romances such as *Stephanites and Ichnelates* and *Syntipas* were translated into Greek, in the first instance into literary Greek. They brought their readers into contact with a world that was unfamiliar, having nothing in common with the world of classical antiquity. These too were Indian romances which had reached the Byzantines by way of translations in Middle Persian (Pahlevi) and in Syriac and Arabic. This literature was usually transmitted through the Syrians of the Edessa and Melitene region.

In the case of the romance *Syntipas,* it is known that the Greek editor, Michael Andreopulus, was commissioned to translate the work by the *dux* Gabriel of Melitene and to adapt it for Byzantine readers. Commissioned by Alexius Comnenus, the famous doctor Symeon Seth, also the author of medical works, translated the romance *Stephanites and Ichnelates* into Greek for the benefit of the Byzantine world. Both works were commissioned by members of the Byzantine magnate class which was beginning to take interest in the world of the Orient.

There had always been an interest in the East in Byzantium, but this had mainly been confined to short-lived fashions such as matters of dress, architecture, objets d'art or circus games and had never extended, as in the eleventh century, to translation of oriental works. It is known that the Emperor Theophilus in the first half of the ninth century had the Bryas Palace built on the model of the Caliph's palaces in Baghdad and Samarra, complete with conical domes and stalactite work. Other palaces, such as the Mouchroutas, were built on Arab lines. The technique and form of the Persian and Mesopotamian ceramics of Rai and Rakka respectively were copied by the Byzantines. From India, by way of Persia, Byzantium had learnt the game of polo, which was played by the Emperor and magnates in the Tzykanisterion in Constantinople, a campus set aside for this purpose.

But there is little in common between such fashions which found expression in sport, design and architectural decoration of oriental origin, and the translation of eastern literature. The translations made known a world that had considerable influence on Byzantine culture. The defeat of the late antique sophist romance which, in the second half of the twelfth century was still being imitated by Prodromus, and after him by Eustathius Macrembolites, was only made possible by these works from the East. This applies to romances such as *Belthandrus and Chrysantza* and *Callimachus and Chrysorrhoe* which show a clear departure from the model of the sophist romance.

Stephanites and Ichnelates derives from the Sanskrit work *Kalilah va Dimnah.* It is an Indian romance of the second century A.D. and was written as a Buddhist work of

336

edification for princes. Towards the end of the sixth century it was translated into Persian. This was a time of close cultural ties between Persia and the Indian states, and an Indian wall painting of this time portrays the arrival of a Persian embassy. From Middle Persian the book was then translated into Syriac, and from Syriac into Greek by Symeon Seth. *Stephanites and Ichnelates* is an animal fable. Animals take the role of humans, explaining how princes ought to govern their peoples. Byzantine animal fables of the thirteenth and fourteenth centuries, and even representational art, drew much inspiration from these tales from the East. The canonical tables of biblical manuscripts include pictures of animals which obviously represent well-known animal fables.

The romance *Syntipas* is of a different kind. It, too, reached the West by way of Persia. The story is as follows: A king had a clever son who had been brought up by a wise teacher. When the years of study were over, the teacher learnt from the stars that danger threatened his pupil whom he ordered, in accordance with the conjunction of the stars, to keep silence for a certain period. (According to one version, this amounted to seven days, ten in another, and forty in a third.) During this time, the boy's step-mother made amorous advances which he rejected. She revenged herself by slandering him to the king. The king condemned him to death. In order to save him, the seven (in another version ten, and in a third forty) wise men of the court each told a story, one every day, about the deceitfulness of women and the inadvisability of a verdict not grounded in proof. Each story was capped by one told by the king's wife, with the object of bringing about the son's execution. By then, his time of silence over, the son could speak at last and was able to prove his innocence. As the story travelled westwards, scenery and costumes changed. In the eastern version, the scene is set in China and India, in the Byzantine version it is set in Persia. Later, when the story reached the West, the king became a Roman Emperor. The Roman *Syntipas* was known throughout the West. Besides the Latin, old French, old Spanish, and Italian versions there are Scandinavian, Slav, and German editions. These books were as significant for the literature of the West as they were for Byzantium, for there, too, the sterile romances of late antiquity were ousted by these oriental folk stories. It is interesting to note that the romance of *Syntipas* was used for the *Gesta Romanorum* as well as for Boccaccio's *Decameron*. This is further evidence of the close ties between Byzantine and European literature.

Besides the translations of eastern romances there are tales either having an oriental original which is not known, or which Byzantines have rearranged to such an extent as to eliminate all trace of the original. The tales mark a stage of transition before the later Byzantine romances. One of the stories belonging to this group is that of poor Leo (*Ptocholeon*). It reached the West in the twelfth century where it served as model for Gautier d'Arras' poem *Heracles*. There are also German and Russian versions of this story, which thus became part of world literature. The tale runs as follows: Leo, a wealthy man, having lost all his property through Arab raids, asks his relations to sell him as a slave. His sons sell him to the imperial treasurer in Constantinople, giving him to understand that the slave is possessed of unusual wisdom. His understanding comprises men, money, precious stones, and horses. At first he is ignored, but soon gives proof of his exceptional wisdom. When the king buys a precious stone, he maintains that it is worthless and contains a worm. On his prophecy proving correct, his treatment improves. He is given two loaves instead of one loaf daily. When the prince wishes to marry, Leo informs him that the bride is of infidel descent, and again he is proved right. The king thereupon asks him the secret of his own provenance. Leo at first refuses to speak, then tells him that he is the son of a mean serf. This too is confirmed. The king enjoins him to silence and restores his fortunes. The tale ends with the moral that wise men are honoured by God.

Farce, satire and erotic poetry

Besides the tales from the East, there was another form of poetry which predominated in Byzantine literature after the middle of the eleventh and during the twelfth century. This was satire, and originated in the mocking verses recited during Brumalia, the Byzantine carnival, which were not then recorded in writing. It was from their fairground origin that these satires derived their tone, broad to the point of obscenity, which has already been noticed in some of Prodromus' work. This kind of verse used demotic Greek almost exclusively and assumed a variety of forms. The animal fable, serving to deride Byzantine officialdom with its self-conscious hierarchy and titles, was a fairly late development. An earlier satire, perhaps belonging to the twelfth century, is one called the *Porikologos* of which the protagonists are different kinds of fruit. The quince is king, the pear protonotary, the melon military judge. This satire depicts a judgment scene in which a bunch of grapes is tried and condemned. The intention of the work is to decry immoderate wine-drinking, but it is directed equally against Byzantine officialdom and the dignitaries of the time.

In contrast to the *Porikologos*, whose tone is still in good taste with a complete absence of crudity, there is another work, the so-called *Mass of the Beardless* which is so coarse as to pass muster only at the Brumalia, when wine has created the right kind of atmosphere. An unidentifiable personage is the object of mockery and attack in this satire. The term 'beardless' indicates a certain degree of inferiority, for the rule of St Sabas excluded beardless men and eunuchs from monastic life. In the form in which it has been preserved, the *Mass of the Beardless* goes back to the thirteenth century. There must presumably have been a much coarser and more outspoken oral version which for obvious reasons would not have been recorded in writing. Enough has been handed down, however, to leave one in no doubt as to the kind of tone that was adopted in the soapbox recitations given at the Brumalia. The very fact that the mass was chosen as the framework of a satire, shows that the time of the supremacy of the monastic world over all spheres of cultural life was at an end. The whole piece parodies the Byzantine mass and closes with a deed of dowry when the priest gives his daughter in marriage to the beardless man. The same attitude that permeates this work also appears in the so-called *Philosophy of the Wine Father*, which even goes so far as to ridicule holy communion and the worship of relics.

Besides satire, the folk epic, the oriental romance, and the sophist romance in classical Greek, the eleventh and twelfth centuries also had the folk song. Part of what have been called the *Rhodian Love Songs*, a collection belonging to the fifteenth century, may date back to this time. Historical events, such as the murder of the Emperor Nicephorus Phocas, also seem to have been the subject of folk song, though of this hardly anything survives. It could be that some of the folk songs whose subjects are taken from episodes in the *Digenis Akritas* epic go back to the eleventh century. The historical matter in Greek folk song does not go back further than the middle of the fifteenth century, the oldest taking the form either of laments on the death of the last Byzantine Emperor or of songs of mourning after the fall of Constantinople. These are the events in Byzantine history which still survive in Greek folk song. Songs about older historical events no longer exist.

World chronicles and imperial history:
the culminating point of Byzantine literature in the learned language

Quite independently of literary movements which in the course of the eleventh, twelfth and thirteenth centuries came more and more to resemble those of Europe, Byzantine imperial history continued to be recorded after the manner of earlier tradition. This historiography, deliberately written in a language other than that in daily use, was far from sterile and indeed possessed characteristics which, at a time when the Empire was in decline, raised it to the level of world literature. Europe in the same period had no comparable historiography.

This position was attained almost without transition. Between the middle of the tenth century and the second half of the eleventh there was no sign in Byzantium of the tremendous step forward that was to take place in imperial historiography which was to endure until the fall of the Empire. The historians of that time were John Cameniates, Leo the Deacon, Michael Attaleiates and Joseph Genesius, and of these only the two latter were laymen. The others were secular clergy closely attached to the imperial court. Their historical writing was somewhat pedestrian, sober and quite without originality. Michael Attaleiates was the first whose writing achieved significance and real distinction, and he was the first highly-placed official to record history. He was followed by the Caesar Bryennius and the imperial princess, Anna Comnena. By comparison with what went before their way of writing history was outstanding.

The same high standard was attained by the philosopher Psellus in his historical work. It is true that his descriptive passages and his affected use of language often obscure the sense and meaning. He was less an historian than a man of letters with a gift for excellent description. Yet always, behind the affectation of style in which his imperial history is written and behind the artificiality of his Attic style, the contemporary world stands out. His description of the two Empresses, of their appearance and character, is on the same high artistic level as the imperial portraits in Hagia Sophia. It is a complex, cultivated style of characterization corresponding to the mode of expression of the artist in mosaic. The art is of the same kind, and the face of the Empress Zoe is like a portrait. The mosaic delineates her characteristics exactly as they are described in Psellus' *Chronographia*. This is in complete contrast to the imperial portrait of Leo VI from the second half of the ninth century in the narthex of the same church, where the style of representation seems designed to withhold the Emperor's characteristics and personality and the whole emphasis is on the event depicted. The Emperor prostrates himself before Christ. In the mosaic portrait of the Empress Zoe she is depicted in the portrait panel next to Christ, as though she was a saint. The eye is drawn immediately to the face, for only that is alive, all the rest consisting of ceremonial state robes.

The historians who came after Psellus and Anna Comnena were either high officials or close collaborators of the Emperor. Thus John Cinnamus was imperial private secretary to Manuel Comnenus and Nicetas Acominatus a general in a theme. Both these men were political leaders and were familiar with the affairs of their time. When Constantinople fell to the crusaders in 1204, Byzantine historiography lost its focal point. During the time of the Comneni, the concept of Empire had been superseded by the dynastic concept, but after the fall of Constantinople this too was absent from historiography. Party politics preponderated. The historians of that time were well-informed, but in their endeavour to depict the intrigues of their own party as essential measures and any opposition to them as tyrannical they showed themselves to be partisans rather than historians whose duty it is to discover the truth. The imperial history of John VI Cantacuzenus is of this kind. Even as Emperor, this man had been a party politician and his historical work, written when he was a monk, is but an attempt to justify himself and his party.

It was a time of doctrinal problems, arising out of the hesychast controversy and the negotiations for the union of the Greek and Latin Churches, and many historians turned from the description of political events and confined their writing to ecclesiastical developments. It was as though the inexorable political decline of the Empire had deflected the interest of the intelligentsia from the politics of their day. Political leadership was abandoned to cliques in the capital and to the landed aristocracy. Thus a man of wide intellectual attainments like Nicephorus Gregoras (1290–1360) devoted the last thirty sections of his Roman history, covering the period from 1204 to 1359, to a comprehensive account of dogmatic controversies which is sometimes little more than a collection of documents. In spite of the bias of his historical work, Nicephorus was a man of wide intellect, combining interests as diverse as theology and astronomy, as well as writing both prayers and iambic verse.

This period of imperial historiography, impregnated as it was with theology and church politics, lasted until the fifteenth century when it was superseded by a view of history consciously seeking to align itself with the classical East Roman historical writing of the Byzantine Empire. It was the time of Byzantine humanism, and this movement cannot be regarded in isolation from the European humanism. The same movement was active in historiography as it was in the sphere of philosophy under the leadership of Gemistus Pletho. Both these forms of humanism, the historical and the philosophical, preceded that of the West. The recognition of a causal principle, which prevailed over the narrow, religious view of history, anticipated the historiography of the West. What Machiavelli achieved in his *Istorie fiorentine* at the beginning of the sixteenth century, complete freedom from Christian bias in historical writing, can already be found in the work of Byzantine historians of the fifteenth century. Among writers of the humanist period was George Sphrantzes (1401–1477). He too reached history by way of politics. As an old man, he took refuge in the Venetian island of Corfu, where he wrote the history of the Byzantine Empire from 1256 to 1476, but he began his career as secretary to the Emperor Manuel II, after which he held high official appointments until the fall of Constantinople in 1453. His work is, as it were, the funeral oration for the Byzantine Empire. His realization of the Empire's great mission in world history is conditioned by the deep ties of affection by which the Byzantine is bound to his country. This carries all the more weight because a large proportion of the Constantinopolitan Byzantine intelligentsia showed all too much alacrity in entering Turkish service where their duties included propaganda on behalf of the sultan's policy. The Byzantine historians, Laonicus Chalcondyles and Critobulus of Imbros wrote history from the Turkish point of view. Laonicus Chalcondyles regarded the Turkish sultan as the focal point of history and to him the Byzantine Empire, which had endured until 1453, was of the same kind as the Christian states of the Balkan peninsula. His writing betrays nothing of the Byzantine's awareness of his country as the first and foremost world power. For Chalcondyles, the Turkish Empire was the new order, the great force that taken the place of the outworn political preeminence of Byzantium.

Critobulus of Imbros went even further than Chalcondyles. He wrote the history of the man who conquered the Byzantines, sultan Mohammed II. As an historian, Critobulus spoke for the circles of the Phanar, a district in Constantinople containing the palaces of the Byzantine aristocracy who, out of political and economic opposition to the party of the Palaeologan Emperors, had aligned themselves with the Turkish sultan.

It was a bitter ending. Instead of voicing the national interests of the Byzantine Empire, these genuinely great historians debased their art to depict the history of the victorious enemy of the Empire. These circles sincerely believed the Turkish people with the sultan at their head to be the heirs of the Byzantine Empire. From this time onwards the intellectual and political representative of the Byzantine nation was her Church. For after the old ruling classes of the Empire had either fled or gone over into the camp of the Turkish conqueror, it was the Church that kept alive the traditions of the historical greatness of the Byzantine Empire.

The monastic chronicles which had taken shape in the ninth century as the expression of the culture of Byzantine monasticism provided the model for the historiography through which the Byzantine Church sought to continue and preserve the history of the nation's past. These two types of historical writing, monastic chronicles and the secular works, existed side by side. The latter were intended for a fairly limited circle, but it would be difficult to overestimate the full extent of the influence of the monastic chronicles. These, and these alone, were translated into other languages, and it was through them that the Slav peoples saw the Byzantine Empire. This explains the apparent contradiction that even in an age when men were beginning to turn from the monastic movement in the middle of the eleventh century, there was no desire to abandon the chronicle as the vehicle of historical writing. Thus in the eleventh century there was a revival of the chronicle. These were no longer written only by monks, but also by high imperial officials. There was now no leaning towards the story-telling, the writing of history almost as though it were fiction, without any feeling for a standard of historical truth. The new standpoint and the method to be pursued in this type of historiography were defined.

John Scylitzes (1018–1079) was the first great historian of this school, and in one of his prefaces he informs his readers of the principles on which his history has been written. Here Scylitzes disassociates himself both from the superficiality of the old monastic chronicles and from the partisanship of some of the works on imperial history, though it must be admitted that he keeps few of the promises made in his foreword. For he, too, was dependent on the Emperor and as a high-ranking officer in the imperial bodyguard he knew exactly what must be left unsaid.

A much finer and more painstaking work than Scylitzes' chronicle is the universal chronicle written in the middle of the twelfth century by Zonaras. This man also belonged to the close entourage of the Emperor; he was head of the Emperor's private chancery as well as commander of the imperial bodyguard. In Zonaras, Byzantine world history reached its zenith, a height never attained either before or after. His work need not fear comparison with world chronicles of the Hellenistic epoch, with the work for instance of an Ephorus. It is indeed clear that in this field the highest achievement of late antiquity has been equalled. In contrast to the world chronicles of Zonaras and Scylitzes, who drew on the historiographical methods of late antiquity, later historical writing reverted to the methods of the monastic chronicles of the ninth century. But the distinctive flavour of the orthodox Christian outlook with its very naive delight in edifying narrative has been discarded in these works in favour of a somewhat woolly enlightenment. It gives the impression that into the world chronicles there has seeped a watered-down version of the new, and increasingly scientific, viewpoint promulgated by the university of Constantinople. The channels along which the chronicle moves are those of an enlightenment that is partly based upon the natural sciences. The historical account, beginning with the story of creation, has an ample store of quotations from the church fathers, and of theological annotations, but to make this dry theological matter palatable to the reader, the description of the creation story is enlivened with animal fables from the *Physiologus*.

The form of speech used by the chronicle stands half way between the vernacular and the learned language which was used more especially in the imperial historical works. Nevertheless the chronicle had to be rewritten in demotic Greek, for the gap between its language and the vernacular had become too great. If the chronicle was to be widely read, it had to be written in the vernacular. The revision of the early imperial and monastic chronicles in this direction led to the accentuation of their anecdotal and legendary characteristics. The imperial history of the chronicles thus became an imperial mythology. This vernacular form was retained in Byzantine imperial and world chronicles until the eve of the nineteenth century, thus successfully preserving the national heritage of Greece throughout the period of Turkish domination. Here was found the story of the mighty Byzantine Emperors who had once reigned in the palaces of Constantinople's Golden Horn until the old imperial city had fallen to the Turk.

Under Turkish domination the Byzantine chronicle was written by the high clergy. They had obtained their theological training in the West at the university of Padua in Venetian territory. The later Byzantine chronicles include the work of Manuel Malaxus (up to 1573) and Bishop Dorotheus of Monemvasia (up to 1629).

Enlightenment and humanism in representational art

4

The new naturalistic style

In the eleventh century, the representational arts experienced the same decisive change as had occurred in literature. Here too the different conception of man and the new outlook on life that had been effected through the Platonic philosophy of the Academy in Constantinople brought about a break with the past.

The old hieratic style in ecclesiastical art was gradually being abandoned. But here the movement was more radical and more in evidence than it was in literature and the break with the past went deeper. The literary salons of the capital had helped to keep alive the memory of late antiquity in literature. This was not so in representational art. Here pictorial decoration in churches seemed to retain little trace of late antiquity. In this field there was no real return to antiquity, either in the time of Photius or in that of the Emperor Constantine Porphyrogenitus, nor was there any recurrence here of what had taken place in literature. The mosaics of Photius' time in the narthex of Hagia Sophia still have forms taken from icons typical of monastic pictorial art. Little difference is to be seen between the stiff, icon-like figures, found as early as the first half of the seventh century in the mosaics in the church of St Demetrius in Thessalonica and later in the frescoes of Santa Maria Antiqua, and the mosaic art of the late ninth and early tenth centuries. The mosaic with the portrait of St John Chrysostom, though dating from the time when literature under the Emperor Constantine Porphyrogenitus was showing a return to classical antiquity, still has the old, severe lines of the monastic icons. The saint's gaze is fixed, the head, as though it were an early icon translated into mosaic, has the characteristics of a portrait, the folds of the garments have the style of an ecclesiastical picture deriving from late antiquity, and only the hands, with their clumsiness and stiff wooden quality, are without a prototype. The passage of time since late antiquity is manifested solely in the hands.

What happened in the mosaics in Hagia Sophia in Constantinople was repeated in the mosaic decoration of the now destroyed Koimesis church (Assumption of the Virgin) in Nicaea. The mosaic in the apse portraying Mary, the Theotokos, has the lines of an old icon. The freedom in depicting bodily form and movement, which persisted along with the art of late antiquity at some places on the Byzantine periphery until the eve of the eighth century, and which is found in the frescoes of Santa Maria Antiqua in Rome and in pictures in the church of Castelseprio near Milan, is here a thing of the past.

The breakthrough of the new art first manifested itself in the miniature. In the Greek Psalter 139, now in the Bibliothèque Nationale in Paris, the great change is already in evidence. The miniatures seem to carry on the development of late antique painting, such as for example, the style of Pompeii. Drapery, dimension, architectural features and landscape are anachronistic in this time of monumental painting determined by the icon. The manuscript which must certainly be dated to the end of the tenth century was undoubtedly inspired by late antique models. The clothes worn by the figures plainly show this. Robes, sandals and ornaments, all indicate the fifth or sixth century. Yet the men who painted the pictures in the Greek Psalter 139 cannot be placed in the same class as the copyists of late antique miniatures at the time of Photius and later of Constantine Porphyrogenitus. Like the old manuscripts, the miniatures of late antiquity were preserved from oblivion by being copied during this period. Thus in a manuscript of St Gregory of Nazianzus' sermons (Paris, Bibl. nat., Cod. graec. 510) there is a miniature depicting the vision of the prophet Ezekiel in which the figures of prophet and angel are seen against an antique background. These two figures are inconceivable without a late antique model, as the clothing alone reveals. This miniature clearly derives from the same time as the pictures from the end of the fourth and beginning of the fifth centuries copied by the miniatures of the Paris Psalter 139. But the old illuminated manuscripts copied in Photius' time, unlike the Paris Psalter 139, evoked no response and contemporary monumental painting, mosaic and fresco remained uninfluenced by them. In the case of the Paris Psalter it was a quite different matter, and its influence on contemporary monumental art is undeniable. The message of the imperial portraits of the eleventh century is plain. They show the development of characteristic forms from late antiquity into an individual style of painting of its own. The pictures of the Emperor and Empress are like portraits, the expressions and the hands are no longer wooden but come to life. The drapery on the figure of Christ has not simply been copied but is an original composition, and the perspective rendering of the throne is the artist's own creation, not a mere imitation.

The new art in Hagia Sophia influenced the great churches elsewhere in the Empire. The superb mosaics in the monastery church of Nea Moni on Chios mark a development of the new style brought into being by the return to late antiquity. In Nea Moni, the old rigidity of the figural groups is no longer found. They have come to life, if only hesitantly. The movements are abrupt and still far removed from the ecstatic intensity of expression found in the illuminated manuscripts of the sixth century (*Cod. Rossanensis*), or in the mosaics of the late Palaeologan era, such as the Kariye Cami mosaics in Constantinople, or the frescoes in the church of the Pantanassa at Mistra. But it was not only the old, stiff forms that had been brought to life in their movement; colour once more came into its own. From late antique prototypes, artists acquired a feeling for colour, for light and shade. Thus the Nea Moni figures in their colouring almost shine with a kind of inner glow. The portrayal of Mary, with her blue robes in brilliant contrast to the purple red of her shoes giving an effect almost as in the renaissance, is something completely new. The facial expression has also been brought into closer harmony with the hands and with the pose of the body.

The full implications of the new art that began with Nea Moni cannot be fully appreciated till this is viewed side by side with other pictures produced at the same time but in the old monastic style. Here again, the old art was not replaced by the new without a period of transition. In the time of the decline of late antique art and the rise of the new monastic art both trends, Christian late antique and monastic-Christian, had for some decades existed side by side. The same was now to happen again. On the Byzantine periphery the old was able to survive longer than in Constantinople and in the more important churches of the Empire. This is why the frescoes in the Sophia church at Ochrida, which belong to about the same period as the Nea Moni mosaics and some of the imperial portraits in Hagia Sophia in Constantinople, still retain the spirit of early monastic art. Angels are earthbound by the weight of their wings, the drapery is copied from models but without understanding, heads seem to exist in separation from the bodies to which they belong. The general impression is one of slavish adherence to an old book of models. Wherever the artist has had to rely on his own imagination, the result is stiff and wooden. A donkey, which carries Christ in the same fresco, looks almost as though carved from wood; the clumsy forms are those of a child's primitive toys. Compared with the frescoes of Ochrida, the mosaics of Nea Moni are like the dawn of a new age.

These forms, revealed for the first time in the mosaics of Nea Moni and in some of the imperial portraits of Hagia Sophia, gradually develop greater freedom. The first steps had been taken in the new art and these were followed by a feeling of confidence and of mastery in handling the new forms. The new, freer style is again apparent in the mosaics of the church at Daphni. The dark colours of Nea Moni become lighter and more luminous here; the movements which are still somewhat compressed at Nea Moni are freer here. Expressive gesture accords harmoniously with the composition of the group. Landscape, earlier on only hinted at, has now acquired depth. Bucolic poetry, the expression of a spoilt urban population's longing for the country, also found in the sophist romances of the twelfth century, is translated into picture in the mosaics of Daphni. Thus in the portrayal of the Nativity there is a landscape designed to still the city dweller's nostalgia for the peace of the countryside. This nostalgia was something that was common to all over-civilized urban cultures. In antiquity, Roman idylls of shepherds and shepherdesses had a counterpart in Pompeian landscape painting and the same is true of all urban cultures since then. The pastoral poems of the eighteenth century, engravings and paintings of country scenes, and pastoral music all belong to the same intellectual movement which gave rise to Beethoven's great Pastoral Symphony. So in the same way in these mosaics at Daphni the artist revels in depicting his countryside; sheep drink from a stream, the little bushes provide shade, and there is a background of mountains and the dark face of the rocks.

The figures reflect the new age. The shepherds are Byzantine peasants; they are the contemporaries of the artist himself. Here we have the beginning of the naturalism which was to characterize this art. And here again Hagia Sophia was to take the lead, once more with imperial mosaic portraits. The mosaic portrays John II Comnenus and the Hungarian Empress Irene. The portrait of the Empress marks yet another step in the direction of the new realism, for here face and hands are related to each other in an unprecedented way. The over-sensitive hands, seeming almost to balance the parchment scroll with its orthodox creed, are in keeping with the softness of the features in the heavily made-up face. The onlooker feels that the artist has succeeded in expressing the temperament of the Empress. Beneath the weighty and over-ample ceremonial robes pleated into heavy folds by a belt, the frail body of a woman is indicated with great beauty of expression.

The realism which governed the new art also revitalized the frescoes of the churches. Whereas the mosaic artist is denied the use of nuances in colour so that the transition from light to shade tends to be somewhat abrupt, the painter of the fresco has at his disposal the most subtle half-tones and in his use of colour is able to achieve in his modelling gradations of the greatest delicacy. This form of shading was a possibility hardly ever exploited in earlier fresco painting, such as that of the Sophia church at Ochrida. Here little more than line drawing is found, mostly coloured in, with somewhat irregular shading to give a more life-like aspect to drapery or to the shapes of faces. Thus the decisive element in the fresco was the transition to the technique of painting.

An instance of this new form of expression in fresco painting is found in the church of St Panteleimon at Nereži, where the interior was decorated soon after 1164. Unlike the mosaic artists of Daphni, the painters at Nereži did not go in for landscape painting; here they still remained entirely within the old monastic tradition. Their own original contribution was the way in which the human figure was portrayed, for instance the light brush-strokes with which different types of people are depicted in the Nativity fresco, almost like a kind of sketch-book on a monumental scale. These Nereži frescoes show observation of nature, a new view of things for which Psellus's revival of Plato's philosophy and his theory of ideas were responsible. In the church at Nereži the heads of the women are painted with an effortlessness almost reminiscent of the figures of the Pompeian wall paintings. Facial expression has grown in intensity to an even greater degree here than at Daphni. In the Pietà the expression of Mary echoed by the movement is almost Gothic in style. The apostles in the Transfiguration seem to have been hurled down by some invisible force, again reminiscent of Gothic painting. To this is added a marked realism that includes women in the dress of the people in the holy scenes. For instance, in the bathing of the Child Jesus there are women in contemporary Byzantine costume carrying pottery of that time who might almost be taken from the daily life of the painter himself.

The humanist element in the art of Byzantium and of the West

The great realistic art of the twelfth century spread to the periphery of the Empire, reaching as far as the Norman kingdom and the coast of the Adriatic where it acquired vital significance for the art of the West. San Marco in Venice, Torcello cathedral and the Capella Palatina of Palermo mark the stages of the triumphant progress of Byzantine art in the West during the twelfth century. Italian painting of the Ducento, at first the product of monastic art of the Byzantine periphery, was fired by the new Byzantine naturalism. The activity of the Maestro di San Martino, of Cimabue, of Duccio and of the Roman school would have been impossible without the Byzantine work at Palermo and San Marco. Cimabue's painting in the upper church at Assisi shows quite marked characteristics of North Italian derivation, but also forms which are clearly borrowed from Byzantine prototypes.

The art of Palermo carried the realism of Daphni a stage further. Here too the subject of the painting is the Nativity. But the peace radiated by the Daphni mosaic is not found in Palermo. The homage of the Magi, the bathing of the Child Jesus, the Christ Child in the crib, are all there. Everything is happening at once. The picture is filled with movement and has lost the zone of peace and silence around the figure of the Divine Child found at Daphni. There is no doubt that the painter at Daphni was the greater artist. But from the point of view of development, Palermo is closer to the new era. The costume worn by Italians at the time determined the clothes of the men and women in the pictures. Thus a noblewoman in the bathing scene is wearing a fashionable turban, then part of aristocratic dress, and the kings on horseback following the star wear the armour of Norman knights. In Palermo too the body was more freely represented. Regardless of their sacred surroundings, the children in the picture of Jesus' entry into Jerusalem throw off their clothes and appear naked. The delight of the mosaic artist in displaying the nude body is reflected in the gesture of one of the children as it flings off its clothes. Again, plants are depicted in almost scientific detail. The palm-tree, for instance, is inspired by that feeling for nature which was made possible by the revival of the natural sciences in the middle of the eleventh century. Architectural forms also show a sense of perspective last in evidence in late antiquity.

Venice forms the connecting link between Sicily and the art of the West. It is true that the Byzantine art of Sicily sometimes shows signs of outside influence, such as the world of Islam, as in Monreale near Palermo, where the treatment of the frieze surrounding the pictures evokes Islamic prototypes. But generally speaking this feature is little more than a suggestion. Though its position is a special one, Norman art is still Byzantine art. The founders of these churches were high Byzantine officials. It is known that the church of the Martorana in Palermo was founded in 1143 by George of Antioch, the grand admiral of the Norman king Roger. It was in Venice that this art first changed, becoming more realistic than it had ever been in Byzantium. The political collapse of 1204 had cast a veil over what was happening in Byzantine art. Half a century was to pass before the great Palaeologan art of Byzantium emerged from the confused trends of different schools of painting to produce the Deesis mosaic of Hagia Sophia. The art of the so-called Macedonian renaissance in its last manifestation ended abruptly with the collapse of the Empire.

The feeling for colour, already apparent in the mosaics of Nea Moni and in those of Daphni, survived in Byzantino-Norman art. A new development in the expressive use of colour can be seen in the bright sulphur yellow used for Lot's wife in the mosaic of the destruction of Sodom in Monreale. There is a foreshadowing here of the perfection found in Grünewald's Isenheim altar with its apocalyptic range of colour.

The church at Torcello is a stepping-stone on the way to Venice. Here the Last Judgment marks an advance on the mosaics of Sicily. Consigned to the fires of hell is a company consisting of the Byzantine Emperor, the Doge, the Patriarch and the German Emperor, together with the sultan and the emirs of the infidel. By thus placing the powerful of this world in the flames of hell the mosaic artists anticipated the social criticism of the urban classes which did not find expression in the Byzantine world, either in painting or in literature, until the fourteenth century. But the artists of Torcello also surpassed the Sicilian Byzantines in their feeling for space, which is especially apparent in the way in which the Theotokos is placed in the dome of the apse. There is nothing like this in Sicily. The figure of Mary with its affinity to the icon which had remained unchanged for more than five hundred years, has been brought to life by its inclusion in the curve of the dome. The Mother of God seems to be advancing towards the onlooker from the unending space of infinity. There is also a third respect in which Torcello marks an advance. The portrayal of the naked body assumes ever greater importance. The damned in hell are naked and anatomically almost perfect. The human figure in art is once again drawn from nature and no longer from pattern books dating back to late antiquity. The Byzantine artists working in San Marco in Venice go even further in this direction. In portraying the creation of man their realism did not shrink even from representing the hairs of the body. From Venice, Byzantine naturalism gradually spread to the rest of Italy. Thus the art of Rome was inspired by Byzantine influence transmitted through Venice. Cavallini, Giotto's older contemporary, drew so much inspiration from Byzantine models that he sometimes gives the impression of having copied late antique frescoes. The same thing applied to Giotto. In his frescoes in the Arena chapel in Padua a Byzantine iconographic scheme is found which he may perhaps have taken from miniatures. But the way in which he portrays his figures, as well as the iconography, shows signs of Byzantine prototypes. The priests in the picture of the rejection of Joachim's sacrifice are wearing the same small cylindrical caps as the priests in the Byzantine mosaics in Constantinople. Here it is possible to recognize the same models which inspired both the Byzantine prototypes preserved in the capital of Constantinople and the mosaic decoration of the monastery of Daphni.

As well as the direct impact of Byzantine forms of expression on Italian painting which came through Sicilian and Venetian channels, considerable Byzantine influence is reflected in the Gothic art of the late middle ages. In the same way as Byzantine art laid the foundations of the great art of the Italian renaissance, it also determined the basic characteristics of western Gothic art. This applied more to sculpture than to architecture, where the different liturgies of the two Churches prevented the adoption of Byzantine ecclesiastical architecture.

The masters of Gothic art translated the compositional schemes of Byzantine sacred iconography, which had come to them through miniatures, into the different medium of sculpture. This influence did not reach them by way of Italy, but through the Fourth Crusade against the Byzantine Empire which culminated in the fall of Constantinople in 1204. In the old Byzantine imperial city, crusaders looted not only the shrines of the saints but also the libraries of monasteries and churches. A large proportion of the finest Byzantine illuminated scripts thus went to the West. It was above all France which profited most from the pillaging of the old imperial city. Some of the plunder consisted in relics, among which was the head of John the Baptist acquired by France complete with reliquary shrine and preserved there until the French Revolution; the saint's arm however remained in Constantinople with its reliquary and is the only remaining Byzantine show-piece in the treasury of the Turkish sultan. In this way miniatures from Byzantine illuminated Bibles and sculptural work in the form of ivory carvings representing scenes from the Holy Scriptures and from the lives of the saints also arrived in the West. Thus there is evidence of very strong Byzantine influence on the iconography of western cathedral sculpture. The Death of Mary on the south portal of Strasbourg Cathedral makes use of the same kind of Byzantine pictorial composition as is found for instance in the frescoes of the monastery of Sopoćani, and earlier at Daphni, and which can also be seen in the ivory tablet preserved in Munich. Doubtless there are important changes and alterations. There is no evidence in any of the Byzantine prototypes of the wonderful flowing drapery of the Strasbourg master. But the form of the composition is the same. At Sopoćani and in the ivory tablet, Christ bears Mary's soul in his arms and this is found again at Strasbourg, as is the apostle bowing down at the foot of Mary's bed. But there are also some differences in the compositional scheme. Sopoćani has figures in the Death of Mary which are not found at Strasbourg and vice versa. The Strasbourg apostles too have an intensity of expression which is lacking in the Byzantine portrayal of Mary's death where everything is more measured, restrained and severe, for it was born of a different hieratic temperament.

The coming of Byzantine art to the Slavs of the East and to Central Europe

During the same period Byzantine art flourished in Russia even more than in the West. There too the new realism that arose at the turn of the tenth and eleventh centuries made its mark on iconographic form. But the transition is not strongly marked, as the earliest surviving Russian frescoes date from a time when the old monastic concept of the holy icon had already been superseded by the new realistic art. Thus the Mother of God in the mosaic in the apse of the Sophia church in Kiev advances from the depths of the dome with hands upraised as in an early Christian Orans. It seems as though the Byzantine master of this mosaic used a late antique miniature as his model in order to free himself from the severe hieratical forms of monastic art. But for Russian artists it was not simply a question of copying early Byzantine forms. They soon cut loose from the old models and achieved an art of their own based on observation of nature.

Kiev is almost the only centre having remains of secular Byzantine wall-painting of this time. These are the frescoes on the staircase to the choir in the north tower of the Sophia church in Kiev. The frescoes belong to the second half of the eleventh century.

348

They depict a bear hunt in which one of the riders turns in the saddle with a lifelike movement to thrust his spear into the bear's chest. The horse is portrayed in a manner that can be compared rather to the forms of late antiquity than to the wooden animals of the Sophia church in Ochrida. Besides the hunting scenes, there are also scenes from everyday life. A driver with a camel recalls the region of Asia Minor and suggests that this may have been the home of the Byzantine artist. Oriental influence is frequently in evidence. The leaping panther and the portrayal of the griffin are clearly copied from paintings on Persian ceramics. Particularly outstanding is the scene from a circus. Here the artist is certainly drawing on his own experience. The musicians whom he paints play instruments that are sometimes still used today in Greek folk music. Among wind-instruments, there is the pipiza, a primitive reedy kind of oboe which is the predecessor of the present-day flute of the Greek peasant. Nor are the stringed instruments different from those used in present-day Greek folk music. A lyre is shown which seems to be an early form of the modern violin, and a dulcimer, of the *santouri*. The musicians in the frescoes, certainly not Byzantine types, appear to come from the Syrian border district which through the dance had already exerted considerable influence on Byzantine music.

Even where Byzantine art in Kiev is not concerned with secular subjects, it still has some of the features of the new realism. Individual personality finds expression in religious painting as well. In the fresco showing the Kievan grand-princess Irene with her three daughters, the women are standing next to each other in a procession with candles in their hands. The individual traits of the features are shown with an almost portrait-like fidelity. Here the realism begins first with the features. It then turns hesitantly, almost timidly, to bodily movement. By comparison with the far more realistic rendering of the faces, this is still reminiscent of early monastic figure-painting. In the monastery of St Michael in Kiev the mosaic depicting Christ with the angel of the Eucharist, the wooden quality of the figure is not quite so marked. Christ is standing, like the priest in the liturgy of the Byzantine church, with a vessel full of bread in front of the altar. Before him lies the paten with the consecrated bread. The angel next to him is holding the ladle (*zeon*) used during the course of the liturgy for pouring the hallowed hot water into the chalice containing the consecrated wine. This liturgical act is supposed to symbolize the union of mankind with Christ in love and faith, and still remains part of the liturgy of the eastern Church. In this portrayal of the liturgical act, a certain freedom has been achieved, a freedom that is even greater in a fresco of Mary at the moment of the Annunciation found in the same monastery. The kind of Mother of God shown here is no longer the old prototype as determined by monastic art. Here Mary is a woman of the people. The old hieratic character has been deliberately discarded.

But the realism of Byzantine art was not confined to the portrayal of faces. Figures and clothing also changed. Miniatures of mythological scenes had put the old Greek heroes into contemporary Byzantine dress; religious pictures now followed suit. In the frescoes of the Sophia cathedral in Novgorod, the prophet Daniel is shown wearing the clothes of a fashionable young Byzantine aristocrat. The prophet is dressed in close-fitting embroidered trousers like tights and a tunic, which miniatures show as the customary wear of Byzantine magnates in the twelfth century.

An inevitable consequence of this new realistic art was the resumption of sculpture in monumental art which from the sixth century onwards had been abandoned. This art, which for the most part took the form of relief sculpture, had been condemned by the monastic movement and had only survived on the periphery of the Empire, in Armenia and the Caucasus, as well as in Italy and the Alpine regions where it was found until the eighth century. What little remains in the Byzantine area proper all belongs to the fifth century; for instance, the ambos of the churches of St George and St Panteleimon and fragments of relief decoration in the basilica of the monastery of Studius. This form of art at first continued to be suppressed within the Empire properly speaking. When it began to appear again it was based on designs belonging to the period of late antiquity, and it must have been late antique sculpture that inspired one of the first attempts, an eleventh-century monumental marble icon in the form of a relief tablet from the district of the Mangana palace (Istanbul, Archaeological Museum). Its late antique derivation is shown in the pose of the Virgin, hands upraised as with an Orans in early Christian art. Probably the model, as also in the case of the eleventh-century portrait of an Emperor of which only a fragment remains, is to be found in contemporary minor objects carved in ivory which preserved a wealth of late antique sculptural design. More of the new sculptural art remains in Kievan Russia than in the Byzantine Empire itself. In a relief depicting St Nestor and St Demetrius even the portrayal of the horses indicates that it is drawn from a smaller carved ivory model. Besides this relief, still preserved today in the Lavra monastery in Kiev, there are other relief pictures from the same area which give evidence of a similar inspiration from ivory carvings. A man fighting with a lion, perhaps Heracles, or a woman resting on a carriage drawn by a lion, possibly the goddess Cybele, by their very subject indicate their derivation from ivory tablets showing mythological scenes.

The influence of eleventh-century art reached Germany by way of Russia. Adam of Bremen regarded Kiev as the brightest ornament of Greece. The town of Regensburg had close ties with Kiev. The wall-paintings of the monastery of Prüfening show Byzantine influence transmitted through Kiev. In this region Byzantine designs were also frequently used in miniature painting. The so-called Psalter of Trier, now preserved in Cividale, shows a blend of western and Byzantine forms.

Byzantine art also affected Germany indirectly at this time, so that its influence continued to be felt in Central Europe up till the time of the Hohenstaufen. Thus the reliefs of the Externstein, dating from the early twelfth century, were based on a Byzantine picture. In 1172 Henry the Lion acquired the head of St Gregory of Nazianzus in Constantinople, and the domed reliquary which he had made for this is still one of the most valuable pieces of the Welf treasure. Objects such as these made by Greek artists stimulated new creations in Germany which elaborated further the Byzantine designs, so that it is often difficult if not impossible to discover when Byzantine influence ceased. Yet the form of the composition, the iconographic scheme, makes it possible to trace the origin of even the most remote inspiration. The influence of the Byzantine art of the eleventh and twelfth centuries on the West must have been considerable. The iconographic models of western religious art, such as scenes from the life of Christ (the Nativity, the Presentation in the Temple, the Baptism, the Raising of Lazarus, the Transfiguration, Entry into Jerusalem, the Crucifixion, the Resurrection and the Ascension) and the life of the Virgin (the Annunciation and the Assumption) were derived from Byzantine models of the eleventh and twelfth centuries. Thus Byzantium's influence in the West was not confined to the sphere of literature, through romances such as *Syntipas* or the *Tale of Poor Leo*, where it gave life to new forms. What happened in literature was repeated in representational art. In the eleventh and twelfth centuries the Byzantine Empire was still a great power in the sphere of culture, sharing its possessions with the Romance peoples as well as with the Slavs and Germans. A decisive turning point came only with the destruction of Constantinople and the disintegration of the Empire in the first half of the thirteenth century.

PART FIVE

The last phase of Byzantine civilization

Culture and public life

The price of the national rebirth

The disintegration of the Byzantine Empire took place in the context of European development as a whole. The development of new national entities out of the old universal political institutions, the heirs of the *imperium romanum* in East and West, was an inevitable trend of the times. The defeat of the old order heralded the final break-through of the new world. The gradual decline of the heritage of the universal Roman Empire before the new forces of the national and communal polities reaches its nadir when in the East the capital Constantinople was conquered in 1204 and in the West the Hohenstaufen Empire collapsed. From then onwards the Byzantine Empire was no more than one of a number of Mediterranean states.

In the same century in which Constantinople fell and the German Empire of the Hohenstaufen broke up, the Papacy, the last universal power, also fulfilled its destiny. The century which had begun with the conquest of Constantinople ended with the French king Philip IV's defeat of the Roman Pope Boniface VIII.

The Lombard cities stood in the same relationship to the German Emperors as did the Italian maritime cities to the Byzantine Emperors. Both possessed economic re-sources against which the political weapons of the two old universal Empires were powerless. Venice aimed at controlling the straits and winning the naval bases necessary for keeping open the sea route to South Russia. As a country which exported grain, South Russia was an important region for supplies to industrial Europe and the carrying trade was in the Venetian hands. Genoa was in a similar position. This rivalry between the two powers was cleverly exploited by the Byzantine Emperors. But all this was no more than a breathing space which could only postpone the threatening disintegra-tion for a few years. Even before the first conquest of the city the political power of the Empire had been so limited by granting concessions and confirming special privileges that it was scarcely possible to speak of a Byzantine state. Every attempt to put the state's economy on a firm basis by economic reforms, and particularly by limiting the concessions made to the Italian maritime cities, was frustrated by Venetian or Genoese naval demonstrations. The end of the Byzantine Empire was the Fourth Crusade diverted to Constantinople by Venice. This destroyed the universal Byzantine Empire and thereby realized Venetian plans for controlling the straits.

But in the dismemberment and administration of the former Byzantine Empire the western powers soon came up against difficulties. In Asia Minor there was a national movement for unification which gave birth to the Empire of Nicaea. Asia Minor did not however achieve complete national unity, since there was a substantial area round Trebizond which maintained an independent existence as an Empire up to the second half of the fifteenth century. But nevertheless the Empire of Nicaea was soon recog-nized by the Greek world as the legitimate successor of the Byzantine Empire. The states which came into being under the Venetian régime, particularly the Latin Empire of Constantinople and its feudal vassals, the principality of Achaia, the duchy of Athens and the kingdom of Thessalonica, were regarded as foreign lordships by the Greeks. This was also true of the former Byzantine provinces now under Venetian rule. Venice controlled a chain of naval bases beginning with the Sea of Marmora and taking in almost all the islands in the Aegean, including Crete and Euboea, as well as all the islands off the west coast of Greece, with the exception of Leukas and Corfu.

The Greek states which had been set up on the soil of the old Byzantine Empire were unable to maintain themselves for long in the face of the Empire of Nicaea. Epirus, which stretched from present-day Alessio to the entry to the gulf of Patras, had to form an alliance with the western powers in order to put up some kind of resistance to the Empire of Nicaea. This Empire was made up of a number of territorial units of the most diverse kind which had escaped the net of the victors of 1204 and it performed the signal service of creating a Byzantine Empire again. It was sustained by the growing Greek national feeling, and it was this feeling which placed the Byzantine Greek world in the main stream of European development. With the rise of vernacular languages, a common phenomenon at this period in almost all European countries, there was a marked growth in national self-consciousness. This can be seen in France in the sirventes of the troubadours and in Germany in the political verse of Walther von der Vogelweide, and it was also present in the Byzantine Empire. But the protagonists of national sentiment were not so much singers and poets as monks. In the Byzantine Empire the national resistance to the West was above all religious in spirit. The West was disowned by reason of its alleged heresies and the true Christian faith was defended against it. This stamped the Greek struggle against the Latins with an implacable bitterness which made collaboration impossible even in the hour of greatest danger. So uncompromising was this antagonism that even on the eve of the Turkish conquest of the Greek capital, any religious understanding with the Christians of the West was rejected and the preservation of their own faith preferred even at the cost of foreign domination by the Turks.

The rebirth of the Byzantine Empire is linked with the name of the Emperor John Vatatzes (1222–1254). His Empire spanned a region stretching at times from Durazzo on the Adriatic coast to the Sea of Marmora and including western Asia Minor. The islands of the Aegean and the greater part of present-day Greece, together with the region round the capital Constantinople and the Byzantine separatist principalities in Epirus and Thessaly, remained outside his control. Without a navy it was impossible to reconquer the old capital. But the Byzantines possessed no fleet. Only a maritime power could help them to regain Constantinople, and this lies behind the alliance between the maritime city Genoa and the Byzantine Emperor resident in Asia Minor. A formal treaty was signed at Nymphaion in 1261. One of the conditions was the cession to the Genoese of the greater part of the customs dues levied at the straits. So after the reconquest of Constantinople 87 per cent of the revenue from the dues paid by vessels passing through the straits went into the pockets of the republic of Genoa.

This treaty granting the income from the customs dues of the narrow straits to foreigners condemned the Byzantine Empire to economic bankruptcy. It was a situation analogous to that of Egypt and the Suez Canal Company in the nineteenth and early twentieth centuries. The rights guaranteed them by the treaty of Nymphaion enabled the Genoese to carry out their policy of acquiring economic bases in South Russia. They were now able to construct settlements in the Crimea and even at the mouth of the Don and to establish themselves at the points where there had been Byzantine trading stations until very recently, for after the fall of Constantinople in 1204 these had been in the hands of the Empire of Trebizond.

The fall of Constantinople in 1204 and the dismemberment of the universal Byzantine Empire had a decisive influence on the development of the Balkan states. For them the effect of 1204 was similar to that of the destruction of the Austro-Hungarian Danube monarchy in 1918. Bulgaria, Serbia, and also the Angevin Hungarian kingdom with its power politics, were able to hold their own because the Byzantine Empire had lost its position as a leading state. The Byzantine Empire restored by Nicaea was only one of a number of south-eastern European powers and was no longer pre-eminent in this region.

The social question

The old universal powers—the Byzantine Empire, the German Empire and the western Church controlled by the Pope—no longer existed. The Byzantine Emperor was fighting for his revenues, the German Emperor was struggling in vain in the German diet against reform, and the Roman Pope was living in exile in Avignon almost reduced to the position of a French prince of the Church. The rise of the great capitalists and the growing strength of groups motivated by economic interests had deprived the old political powers of their authority for good. As early as the Hohenstaufen period the western knights were being increasingly replaced by mercenaries. Armies of mercenaries were the military weapons which the Italian city states used for their political ends. The kings of Aragon and the French Anjou also made use of them to implement their plans. Behind the Anjou stood the capital of the Florentine banking house of the Accia-juoli, and it was this which financed their enterprises in Provence, South Italy, Sicily and the Balkans. It was the capital of the Acciajuoli which in the end even won the Hungarian throne for the Anjou. Side by side with the financial powers stood the captains of the mercenaries. With the support of their armies they too had often enough taken their own steps to turn themselves into feudal lords. Thus the Catalan Company, a mercenary army used by the Byzantines, had possessed itself of the duchy of Athens and had founded its own lordship there. The Italian bankers had also exchanged the counting house for the council chamber of the prince during this period. The Acciajuoli of Florence made themselves dukes of Athens.

It was an age of disintegration, of the transference of power to new forces. The classes which were now coming to the fore were in conflict with the old aristocracy. The social struggles raging in Italy and the contrasts characterizing the cities of Flanders were not unknown in the Byzantine Empire. There too the urban artisans and the landowning magnates were in bitter conflict. The struggles associated in Italy with the names of the two parties, the *populo minuto* and the *populo grasso*, were also the dominating problems in Byzantine territory. The imperial authority did not stand above these conflicts but was involved in them. The Byzantine Emperor himself was a partisan of one of these parties. The Palaeologans supported the *populo minuto*, the Cantacuzeni fought for the *populo grasso*. There were Emperors from both these noble families. Thus after the death of the last Emperor, a Palaeologus, who had favoured the political opponents of the *populo grasso*, the rich magnates went over to the side of the Turkish sultan. This contrast comes out in literature and representational art. In the animal stories, as for instance the *Legend of the Respected Ass*, the supporters of the *populo grasso* are attacked and mocked at: literature was on the side of the *populo minuto*.

Byzantine pietism

In Byzantium, as in the West, political life became more and more dominated by the conflicting economic interests of various groups. This also reacted on religious life. It is not mere chance that in a period when economic prosperity and living standards

354

169 Mosaic cross in the apse of Sant'Apollinare in Classe, Ravenna, early 6th century

168 Interior of the church of Hosios Loukas of Stiri, Phocis

◀166 Church of the Brontocheion monastery, Mistra

◀167 Church of Pantanassa, Mistra

seemed to have reached their peak there was also a return to primitive Christianity. Some, and particularly the thinking element, saw the hand of God in the destruction of the time-honoured institutions of the Byzantine Empire, a clear indication that they should turn their back on worldly affairs. Consequently there was a shift in deployment of energy. In the Byzantine Empire it was as though the leading class had exchanged its armour for the monk's habit and handed over the management of worldly affairs, politics and warfare, to the lower ranks.

This diversion of a wide circle to monastic ways of thinking resulted in a new spiritual movement, hesychasm. Like the mystics, the hesychasts believed that the highest religious goal was knowledge of God. Among the means of obtaining this were certain ascetic practices which involved physical attitudes. Through these practices a state of religious ecstacy was reached at times, as with the dervishes, and then the faithful believed that they perceived the Light of Tabor, so the hesychasts declared. These ascetic practices have no parallel in western mysticism. In this ecstatic approach towards the Godhead, Byzantine hesychasm showed its affinity with oriental movements which can still be found in the Islamic world in the East today. The leaders of hesychasm came from the East. Gregory Sinaites, the most important propagandist, came from the monastery on Mount Sinai. He was the exponent of the movement in Constantinople. Western movements opposed to hesychasm, led by the Greek Calabrian monk Barlaam, proved unsuccessful.

This state of resignation with its religious roots greatly weakened political opposition to the Turkish menace as also did the constantly aggravated social contrasts. Both movements, the social class conflict and the religious controversies, determined the Byzantine situation in the fourteenth and fifteenth centuries.

In Byzantium, however, unlike Italy, this development did not find its outlet along the lines of new political forms. Both phenomena were the expression of the internal disintegration of Byzantine society and they foretold the political catastrophe of 1453 more than a century before it actually took place. Neither the monastic movement of the hesychasts nor the zelots, the artisans representing the *populo minuto* and the small traders, could rejuvenate the state. When the zelots took control in Thessalonica, the second largest city in the Empire, they certainly did not inaugurate a new era. The leaders of the *populo minuto*, or the zelots as they were called in Byzantium, ruled in precisely the same way as the *dynatoi*, the powerful Byzantine magnates. At the head of the city there was a podestà of zelot partisans which wielded authority side by side with the imperial governor. It is true that once the zelots came to power they took over ecclesiastical and secular property, but this did not constitute the introduction of a new social order. The conflicts here in the Byzantine cities were not genuine social struggles. Neither party was fighting for a better standard of living, the struggle was for power. Once they obtained control, the zelots in Thessalonica engaged in the sale of public offices, just as the *dynatoi*, the Byzantine *populo grasso*, had done. The only difference between western and Byzantine class conflicts was that in Byzantium ecclesiastical property was not spared. In Florence when Dante Alighieri and his aristocratic friends went into exile, the bishops and rich prelates were able to remain behind.

Byzantines and Turks

The social and religious movements which pointed to disintegration within Byzantium, were also found in the Islamic world. Here too there were mystics and a religious movement which had affinities with hesychasm. But whereas in the Byzantine Empire all

355

these movements undermined the state, in the Islamic world in Asia Minor they led to a political renewal. To begin with, the régime of the Seljuk emirs in Anatolia indicated the break-up of the old political order and in this respect can be compared with the formation of new Byzantine and Latin polities on the soil of the old Byzantine Empire destroyed by the events of 1204. But in these Islamic lands a rejuvenation set in at the turn of the thirteenth and fourteenth centuries. One of the leaders of the Ghazis, the Turkish border warriors, based his authority on the religious movement of the dervishes, as well as on his military power. He found other supporters among the gilds of merchants and artisans which also had a religious basis. He succeeded in subduing the other Ghazi leaders and getting their recognition of his leadership. Osman, this first leader of a newly-formed state, designated himself as sultan of the Ghazis, as is attested by an inscription of his son Orchan on the Green Mosque built in Broussa in 1334. The expansion of this recently established state in Asia Minor was directed towards the West, since any movement eastwards was inevitably precluded due to the existence at that time of the powerful Mongolian Empire of the Ilkhans. Conditions were, however, favourable in the West, since the reconquest of the capital Constantinople meant that the Byzantine Empire was orientated towards Europe. All its energy was absorbed by the struggle with the Bulgarians and the Serbian tsar Stephen Dušan.

The formation of the Ottoman state took place in a kind of vacuum as far as power politics were concerned. Asia Minor was not attacked by the victorious Mongols represented by the Ilkhan dynasty in Persia. The Empire of Nicaea was orientated towards the West as it wanted to dislodge the Latins in Constantinople and the Greek islands. Therefore the Byzantines did not want a war in Asia Minor. The main issue for the Mongol Ilkhans was the dispute with Egypt which was under Mamluk control. The Mongol khans therefore looked towards Syria and not Asia Minor.

The formation of the Ottoman state was also based on a religious principle, the conception of fighting for the faith. The protagonists of this were the religious confraternities, the so-called dervish orders. These can be regarded as the main supporters of the new Ottoman state, and, like many of the monastic communities in contemporary Byzantium, they sought some kind of mystic revelation. In Islam these men were known as Sufis. This mysticism was particularly active in the dervish order during the early Ottoman period, and Turks and Byzantines appeared to have something in common. It did not seem to matter that they followed different religious persuasions. The characteristics of the two movements were the same. It is significant that some manuscripts of the Persian didactic poem *Rababnama* contain Sufi sentences in the Greek vernacular. It looks as though the Greek population of Asia Minor not only became Muslim converts but took an active part in the Sufi movements, which would explain why Greek sentences of Sufi content in Arabic transcription were inserted into this Persian didactic poem.

On the whole the similarity between the religious and political situation among the Islamic Turks and the Byzantines lay in the fact that both showed a very strong tendency towards mysticism. In Islamic lands the Mongol invasion had led to a marked persecution of the Sunnite Muslims. The Mongols under khan Hulagu had openly favoured the Nestorian Christians. The wife of Hulagu, Doquz Hatun, was indeed a Nestorian Christian, and in 1281 a monk sent to Jerusalem from the court of the East khan Qubilai in North China had even obtained the office of head of the Nestorian Church. At this period Muslims were constrained to defend their faith. The afflictions of the day accelerated the rush to ascetic confraternities. These Islamic brotherhoods of dervishes taught the love of God and they saw the final goal as union with God. But with the Turks this religious mysticism was intimately related to the fight for the true faith, Islam, while the Byzantine mystics remained contemplatives, detached from the world. The Turkish orders of dervishes, and among them the well-known Bektashi, were closely connected to the Sultan's crack troops, the Janissaries. The dervishes were religious leaders. They called for the expansion of Islam. This was so in Asia Minor, as also in Egypt. At almost the same time when the whole of Greek Asia Minor under persecution from this new religious radicalism was forced to succumb to Islam, the last East Christian stronghold in Egypt, in the Sudan, fell. The Christian communities which had been in existence there since the earliest Byzantine days and had possessed their own political organization were now suppressed under pressure from the Mongol persecutions.

Thus Byzantine and Turk confronted each other: the one sunk in resignation and political inactivity, the other moved by fanatical religious zeal and active in politics. The basic foundations of both movements were the same. If an Islamic miniature from the court of these Turkish sultans is compared with a Byzantine miniature of the same period, the same characteristics are apparent. Turkish Islam also had its religious pictures, the saints of Islam; angels and the founder of their religion, Mohammed, are represented, and there are also various types taken from Turkish popular life. If the Turkish and Byzantine are placed side by side it is clear that the spiritual outlook of the men of these two nations does not greatly differ. The Turks were not the barbarians which Byzantine propaganda in the West made them out to be. They had not indeed inherited the tradition of Greek late antiquity, but they were heirs to the Persian cultural inheritance. Thus Byzantine culture under Turkish rule had practically no possibility of future development. It was only architecture that the Turkish conquerors made use of, and here there was a new development going back to the late antique style of building. Here the Turks again picked up the threads of the late antique Byzantine cultural heritage of Justinian's day. The great mosques built by Greeks, such as that of Mohammed II in Constantinople, were copies of the great domed church of Justinian I down to the last detail. But Byzantine literature and Byzantine painting found no echo in Turkish culture. It was otherwise in Spain where Arab art and craftsmanship survived the disappearance of the political independence of the Islamic states and indeed left its stamp on a particular epoch of Spanish art in the *mudejar* style. Thus the conquest of Constantinople in 1453 meant the decline of Byzantine culture. It was only in territories under Venetian control, such as Crete and the Greek islands, that Byzantine provincial culture lived on for a time, though only a shadow of the Byzantine culture which vanished with the conquest of 1453. This disappeared with the Turkish conquest of the islands at the end of the seventeenth and beginning of the eighteenth centuries. So that something in the way of Byzantine culture survived until the threshhold of the eighteenth century. It was then, with the complete Turkish conquest, that Byzantine cultural life died out. Later, with the French revolution and the idea of national liberty at the end of the eighteenth century and beginning of the nineteenth century, a national Greek revival set in, but this had nothing to do with Byzantine civilization.

The destiny and lot of the intellectual élite

The downfall of the old Byzantine Empire that became an accomplished fact with the crusade of 1204 opened the way to the development of national feeling in the Greek world. The idea of a universal Empire disappeared. What mattered now was the national state. For the Greeks, Nicaea, and the opposition against the West building up here, was the symbol of a national rebirth. Patriots from the provinces occupied by the Latins hastened to Nicaea. Thus Gregory, Patriarch of Constantinople, born in Cyprus in 1241, related how he left Cyprus, dominated as it was by foreign Latin rulers, to go to Nicaea to complete his education on Greek soil. The Patriarch tells how he was always left more and more behind at the Frankish (Italian) school because of his inadequate knowledge of the language. He wanted to remain Greek and not to learn Italian and so he left his home. It is at this time that the designation 'Hellenes' is first found for 'Byzantines'. The old name 'Romaioi' was only used now in official imperial statements.

In the early years after the fall of the capital, Constantinople, life in the new residence in Nicaea was on fairly simple lines. There were no celebrated ancient schools like those of the capital here: there were only establishments for elementary grammar and rhetoric which eked out a dreary existence. There was nobody to expound Aristotle or Euclid. The great scholars were scattered in the fortified towns on the west coast of Asia Minor and they showed little inclination to transmit their knowledge to the rising generation. The Gregory already mentioned wished to seek out Nicephorus Blemmydes and he took the dusty and exceedingly arduous way to Ayasoluk where the dwelling of the famous scholar was to be found behind the walls of the Byzantine fort in the shadow of the church of St John built by Justinian I. But Nicephorus, buried beneath the treasures of his salvaged library, had him turned away.

And yet the intellectual élite were found gathered together in Nicea and the last revival of Byzantine culture was owed to them. The decisive element in the formation of this intellectual group was the personality of the Emperor. The Byzantine Emperor Theodore II Lascaris proved himself not only as an efficient ruler but as a highly gifted writer, philosopher and theologian. Before he ascended the throne in 1254 he had already taken up his pen and written a funeral oration for his great contemporary, the German Emperor Frederick II. As well as producing rhetorical works, he occupied himself with philosophical and theological problems. His thoughts on these questions took the form of a kind of theodicy, a defence of the divine cosmology. This work makes it clear that the Emperor had had an excellent classical education and had not confined his studies to classical philosophers and writers but was well able to expound mathematical questions and particularly problems of geometry. Theodore Lascaris was a contemporary of the equally learned and highly educated Frederick II of Hohenstaufen and of Alphonso X of Castile, who had made a name for himself as an astronomer. All three rulers were themselves engaged in literary activity and at the same time the centre of a learned and literary circle. All three stood on the periphery of Europe on the borders of the Islamic world which left its mark on their intellectual activities. Common to them all was the ability to shake off medieval cosmology with the aid of science transmitted from the Islamic East. But Theodore Lascaris did not have the independent scientific outlook of Frederick II and Alphonso X; he remained within Byzantine culture at the time when the decisive breakthrough of natural science occurred.

He was the first of a number of Byzantine Emperors engaged in literary activity. One of these was John VI Cantacuzenus, who not only wrote a brilliant if very prejudiced autobiography but won literary fame with theological works of a polemical nature. In these theological writings he also treats of the problem of the conversion of Byzantine magnates to Islam. Evidently a considerable number of Asia Minor magnates went over to Islam in order to keep their lands. Some of these Byzantine noble families which were converted subsequently appear among the highest aristocracy of the Turkish Empire. The Byzantine Emperor Manuel II (1391–1425) deals with this question in his *Dialogue with a Persian*, not as polemic, as in the case of Cantacuzenus, but on the basis

358

of notes of the religious conversations which he himself had had with Islamic teachers at the Turkish court. In Byzantium the breakthrough of natural science took place within the leading class. The first ministers of the Emperor were supporters of the new movement. The counsellor of Michael VIII and later of his son Andronicus II, Theodore Metochites, the Grand Logothete of the Empire, vigorously pursued astronomy. His pupil in astronomy, Nicephorus Gregoras, was equally outstanding as historian, theologian, philosopher and scientist. Contemporaries told how his house was full of globes and astronomical tables. But preoccupation with scientific studies was only part of the humanist educational programme as it was conceived in Byzantium in the second half of the thirteenth century within a small circle of the ruling class. Classical studies and the sciences were to supplement each other. Nicephorus instructed Theodore Metochites' children in the classical writers while their father introduced them to astronomy.

In contrast to the men of the old enlightenment of the eleventh and twelfth centuries the humanists of the Palaeologan period did not concentrate on Plato. In his philosophical writings Theodore Metochites turned to neoplatonism. Unlike Psellus, he regarded Aristotle as the great philosophical teacher. This change in the emphasis of philosophical studies, which had made a breach in the monastic system of cosmology hitherto prevailing, was conditioned by the much more scientifically based study of the natural sciences. Psellus' knowledge of the natural sciences was derived from the writings of the Egyptian alchemists of late antiquity, which were in his day still carefully copied, and above all Zosimus, whose works are still extant in Byzantine manuscripts of the tenth century. Works of a distinctly alchemic character bear Psellus' name, as for instance the letter on the making of gold. As well as the Egyptian alchemists, the Chaldean writings, going back to the religious founders Zoroaster and Otanes, were used by Psellus and the other men of the enlightenment. A book on the special power of certain stones and metals, or a plant book, would be studied with the same eagerness as the works of Euclid. These works on alchemy derived from late antiquity found credulous readers, particularly among the supporters of the revived platonic philosophy. Even the great Byzantine philosopher Gemistus Pletho, an enthusiastic apostle of Plato's teaching, busied himself with the *logia* of Zoroaster. It is understandable that the circle engaged in serious study of astronomy and mathematics turned their backs on the neoplatonic philosophers who spent time on this pseudo–literature of alchemy.

The rejection of the monastic movement and the cultural programme which they supported was not due solely to the revival of Platonic philosophy inspired by Psellus. Political and social resentment was also responsible. A considerable section of the Byzantine population were antagonistic towards the high aristocracy, the magnates, who particularly favoured the monks, as was later demonstrated in the hesychast movement. Then in the fourteenth century the Emperor John VI Cantacuzenus, the leader of the party of the magnates against the popular party supported by the Palaeologi, was at the same time the protector of the hesychast movement. Similarly in the tenth century the magnates, particularly the Phocas family, were the patrons of the ascetic trend fostered by certain monasteries. It is not by chance that the rock churches of ascetic monks painted with frescoes at this time were in the Cappadocian region where the influence of the Phocas was very strong. But as early as the second half of the tenth century there were also signs of activity other than those coming from a court circle interest in the revival of classical culture. From the dialogue *Philopatris*, which dates from this time, it is clear that there were opposition groups among the people in protest to the government of the Emperor Nicephorus Phocas, who was in fact soon to be murdered. With the downfall of the Emperor it was hoped that the monastic party would also lose its ascendancy. There were also propaganda pamphlets in the tenth century criticizing the alliance of the magnates with the monastic movement and repudiating for political reasons the one-sided way of life laid down by monasticism. The circle of Theodore Metochites and Nicephorus Gregoras was part of the wider European humanism which in Italy is linked to the name of Petrarch. But in spite of everything there were not many meeting points between the East and West at this time. When Barlaam, the learned scholar from the Basilian monasteries of South Italy, who had taught Greek to Petrarch, visited Thessalonica to study the writings of Aristotle there, he was involved in a learned dispute with Nicephorus Gregoras, and the Byzantine scholar won the day over the Greek westerner. It was only when the Byzantine Emperors went on their journeys to ask for help in the fourteenth and fifteenth centuries, going not only to Rome and Venice but to Paris and London as well, that closer intellectual ties between Byzantium and the West were established. By the fourteenth and fifteenth centuries there was a small but influential pro-western party in Byzantium. In this circle western theological works could be read, such as Thomas Aquinas, who was often quoted. These pro-westerners also supported the union of the Byzantine and Roman Churches.

The last manifestation of Byzantine civilization: the Palaeologan renaissance

2

The new realism in representational art

Cultural life in the period between the conquest of Constantinople in 1204 and the fall of the last Venetian stronghold in Greece on the threshhold of the eighteenth century should be considered as a whole. Here the Turkish conquest of Constantinople in 1453 did not mark a break. The movements in literature and art which existed before this conquest still continued to influence cultural life after this event. On the one hand there was the very strong western influence stemming from the conquest of a considerable part of the Byzantine Empire by the French, Italians and Spaniards which inevitably affected Byzantine literature and representational art. But viewed as a whole it shows that the Byzantine element was always stronger than the western influence. This influence was present, but it was not the predominating factor. The strength of the Byzantine element is shown by the fact that in the second generation the foreign conquerors were only speaking Greek. Further, westerners settled on Greek soil married Greek wives, and so their descendants were still more strongly influenced by the Greek world. These children of a Latin father and a Greek mother were known as *gasmuli*, a word which seems to have been made up of *gas* (garçon) and *mulus* (a mule). These gasmules were indeed often strongly opposed to the Greek world of the Byzantines though they spoke their language. The oldest Greek version of the *Chronicle of the Morea*, which describes the Latin attack on Greece and the conquest of Constantinople, was written by a man who hated the Greek Byzantines. He was a gasmule, the son of a Latin father and a Greek mother.

Representational art in the period following the conquest of Constantinople has a special character. In this art there is nothing to suggest any western influence. The mosaic of the Deesis in Hagia Sophia executed by the Byzantines directly after the conquest of Constantinople was in the last analysis a continuation of the great art of the eleventh and twelfth centuries. There are no doubt differences. The style has become that of a painter. It looks as though the artist had no opportunity to work in mosaic during the half century between the fall of the capital to the crusaders and its reconquest by the Byzantines. The Byzantine mosaic ateliers were almost exclusively in the quarter occupied by the Latins. Therefore the tradition in art had been carried on only in the medium of fresco painting. This influenced the style of the new mosaics. Thus the Mary in the Deesis of Hagia Sophia was closely related to the old iconographical type which is found for instance in the Vladimir Mother of God, though the handling of the colours reflects a quite different style. The colouring of the skin, the shadows, the graduations of colouring in the folds of the garments, these all reflect the techniques of painting. This is not the style of a mosaicist but of a painter who has turned to mosaics. In the Deesis not only the Mother of God but John the Baptist reflects the form of the icon portrait. This was not without purpose. Icons were the object of religious veneration. The priest prostrated himself in an act of veneration before the icons on the iconostasis in front of the altar. The Deesis was the place of intercession. It was

361

John the Baptist and the Mother of God who interceded for the people. This was the reason why their figures were placed on each side of the door from which the priest came to give the blessing and to intercede in the presence of the congregation.

Art did not indeed remain untouched by the controversy between the hesychasts and the zelots. In the churches founded by the magnates, who supported the hesychasts, the nature of the frescoes was greatly influenced by hesychast mysticism and its doctrine of the Divine Light. This also had its effects outside the Byzantine Empire and its last off-shoots can be seen in European art, in Feofan Grek in Russia, or later on in Spain in Domenikos Theotokopoulos. The art sponsored by zelot supporters was on the contrary realistic and had a close affinity with the art of the Italian Quattrocento (as for instance the Resurrection of Lazarus at Mistra).

The mosaics in the narthex of the church of the Chora (Kariye Cami) date from the beginning of the fourteenth century, from a period when western influence was indeed very marked, though in Italy the first phase of the renaissance had still not really been reached. The Quattrocento, the first phase of the early renaissance, was only beginning during the period when the mosaics of the Chora were being executed. Western influence was therefore out of the question, and indeed all that it produced before this period was far below the standard of the mosaics in the Chora church.

The mosaic showing the journey of Mary and Joseph to Bethlehem was the last great achievement of Byzantine mosaic art. There is much in this portrayal which was taken from older art. There were the highly stylized mountain tops which were only symbols for the landscape and are found as early as the *Menologion* of Basil II which dates from the end of the tenth century. Then there is the picture, in almost true perspective, of a little Byzantine settlement. The homes of the village are surrounded by a wall, the bright green of the trees shines out between the whitewashed walls, the red tiled roofs and the towers rising in correct perspective. The whole setting looks like a modern landscape and has no parallel in the painting of the eleventh and twelfth centuries. Man feels again a sense of space, and this is the important thing, which did indeed characterize the new art. The city of Nazareth appears on another mosaic. The picture shows the maze of lanes, the towers and the walls of the city, again in almost true perspective. But this picture differs from the work of the twelfth century not only in its mastery of perspective but in the way in which the atmosphere is conveyed. In the scene showing Mary's journey, the horse carrying the Mother of God seems poised in the air, its hoofs do not seem to touch the earth. It seems to soar along by divine impetus, an effect achieved by the great Michelangelo at the height of his powers as seen in the Last Judgment in the Sistine Chapel.

There is also a third scene from the mosaics of the Chora church which points to the rise of a new era. This is the mosaic showing Mary before Quirinius. There is a real connection between all the figures in this scene. They are not just copied from a model and placed side by side but there is an inner relationship between them all, even down to the last servant. The dialogue can be heard, the participation of all present is felt. What each is hearing and seeing can be deduced from the movement and the facial expressions of the figures shown there. One can even tell the time of day. Thus there is meaning in even the smallest detail.

What the mosaics of the Chora church reveal in the field of mosaics is true of the Pantanassa for frescoes, particularly the Resurrection of Lazarus which seems to have been inspired down to the last detail by late antique art. Lazarus is seen wrapped like a mummy walking out of his tomb. Parallels to this can be found in the iconography of late antiquity. What is new here is the execution of the figures. They are human

362

beings from the ranks of the people whom the artist has seen and copied. The long garments of late antiquity showing only the head, hands and extremities of the feet have vanished. The ordinary people wore clothes which left bare their legs from the mid-thigh downwards. And their legs are vigorously portrayed, showing the play of muscle. The bold foreshortening is there, even if it is still not entirely in true perspective. Here the reflection of experience lives even in the facial traits of the apparently secondary characters: the men who have taken away the lid of the coffin, the group who are unwinding the binding strips, the man holding his sleeve in front of his face because of the evil smell from the corpse. The representation of Lazarus is completely new, with his head emerging from the mummy binding. The contrast between the dead, stinking body and the clearly rising life in the facial features is modern. Nowhere else, except in the frescoes of Camposanto in Pisa, is the horror of death more vividly expressed in the language of art.

The expressionist element in representational art

This new realistic Byzantine art expressing itself in forms similar to those of the Italian renaissance did not stand alone. There was another style of painting deep rooted in religious feeling. This underlines the contrast between the hesychasts and contemporary social movement which also dominated political life of that day. Behind the painters of Mistra and the mosaic artists of the church of the Chora, the humanism of Pletho and of Theodore Metochites, there was quite a different style of painting linked to the monasteries, its spiritual content determined by the hesychast movement. That same Mistra contains not only the church of the Pantanassa where the art of the renaissance seems to live, but the church of the Peribleptos which is a witness to the deeply religious art born of hesychasm.

The Nativity is portrayed there: Mary with the Christ Child in the cave, the angels and the three Magi, the preparation of the bath for the Holy Child. It is all as shown in the iconography of the art of the eleventh and twelfth centuries. But even here there is a difference in presentation. The realism of that art is missing. Mary is seen in an almost apocalyptic landscape, the cleft of a mountain which seems to have been reft asunder, whose rock towers high above like a layer of ice and then begins to break. The angels do not hover here. They are painted into the landscape and are yet not part of it. Everywhere there is a mystical significance in the movements of the personages. The artist did not wish to portray anything realistically: for him the picture was only the symbol of a religious conception linked to the birth of the Saviour.

And yet this art so influenced by hesychasm was also inspired by much of the figural style coming from the humanism already pointing towards the renaissance. This can be seen in the manner in which light and shade are treated. The illumination falling from on high on to the saints, especially their heads, has a special vitality of its own. This lighting can be seen earlier in the John the Baptist in the Deesis in Hagia Sophia. And the facial features of the Mary and John in Kariye Cami seem to be dismembered by these restless patches of light. This form of expression in art, somewhat softened here by mosaic technique, was so intensified in fresco painting that it almost became a mannerism. It was particularly the frescoes in monasteries situated on the Byzantine periphery which were executed in this new style of painting with its light effects. This new tendency in painting can be seen as early as the middle of the thirteenth century in the frescoes of Sopoćani, for instance the figure of Andrew. It then spread to Russia, to Novgorod and Pskov, finishing in a style of painting which bathed the facial features in colour effects in an almost expressionist manner. The same is found in the two recently discovered paintings in the cave monastery of Ivanovo in Bulgaria. In using this style, inspired by the new light and shade painting, the hesychast movement showed that it was by no means a conservative factor in Byzantine life but, like the contemporary humanist movement, belonged to the new age.

The two movements did not come into conflict with each other: they co-existed side by side. Hesychasm had supporters even in the highest and best educated court circles, and thus the style of art which it favoured is found in works which are otherwise entirely dominated by the new realistic Byzantine style. There is a famous double portrait of the Emperor John VI Cantacuzenus. This picture is a miniature which shows the Emperor first in his imperial regalia and then as a monk above whom is the Holy Trinity, the symbol of the hesychast movement, which found its finest expression when Andrei Rublev used the iconographic form given here. The Emperor is portrayed almost with the technique of western portrait painting; the celebrated miniatures showing figures at the Burgundian court come to mind. Here is found the same kind of folds; even in the indication of the features of the head, western portraiture seems to live. And yet the representation of the Holy Trinity in the mystical liturgical language of symbolism, well known to Russian painters of the fourteenth and fifteenth centuries, unmistakably indicates the imprint of the hesychast movement.

Representational art on the Byzantine periphery and western influence

With the downfall of the great centres of Byzantine art in Constantinople and Mistra, what had still been outstanding in miniatures and in the Peribleptos church now lived on in Crete and Serbia, Corfu and Russia, translated, as it were, into a primitive art on the periphery. This primitive art presented the pictures of a great art in the simple and almost abstract forms which had characterized the oldest icons. It repeated the process used at the end of the sixth and beginning of the seventh century whereby the monastic movement began to translate material from late antiquity into the simple primitive language of its figural art. Byzantine art on the periphery, which survived Constantinople and Mistra by more than two hundred years, was characterized by this kind of adaptation. But this art was unable to absorb and assimilate foreign influence as the old Byzantine art had done in its great days; it was not in the position to ward off alien influences. Thus from Venetian-occupied Crete, Byzantine art on the periphery came to use the Italian form of the Madonna. It was in Crete that under Italian influence there first developed the type of the nursing Mother of God, the Maria Galaktophousa, which spread from Crete into Byzantino-Russian art.

In architecture the influence of the West is also noticeable. This is particularly true of the church of the Pantanassa in Mistra restored at the beginning of the fifteenth century. The façade there shows not only the Islamic form of arch but also the Gothic pointed arch and is accompanied by decorative ornament in the same style. The inspiration for this Gothic style probably came from the Frankish (French) Cistercians who possessed monasteries in the Peloponnese and from 1203 onwards in Attica. They transmitted western styles into representational art just as the Frankish barons brought the French knightly romance into Byzantine literature.

The art on the periphery was not inferior to that found in the frescoes and pictures of Constantinople and Mistra. But it spoke another language. It began to be difficult to distinguish characteristically Byzantine features in this art. A painter such as Domenikos Theotokopoulos, by reason of his ancestry called in the West El Greco, the Greek, was no Byzantine painter. But his ecstatic mysticism was reminiscent of the frescoes in the caves of Ivanovo in Bulgaria at the turn of the fourteenth and fifteenth centuries. So there lived on in El Greco at least something of the great Palaeologan painting of the thirteenth, fourteenth and fifteenth centuries. El Greco's art may have grown out of the confrontation of western and Byzantine art, as can be seen by his strong affinity with Venetian painting of the sixteenth century, but this confrontation with the West is also seen in the last phase of Palaeologan painting. Even the great frescoes in the mortuary chapel of the church of the Chora (Kariye Cami) go back to Italian models in the division of the frieze and in the decorative arrangement of each panel of the cupola and vaulting. In this church the mosaics of the narthex, inspired by the humanist outlook of the founder Theodore Metochites, and the frescoes in the mortuary chapel, already reflecting the beginnings of the Italian renaissance, stand side by side.

This influence from the West, however strong it was from time to time, never penetrated to the real substance of Byzantine art. Even when Byzantine art used western models, these were so much worked over that it is difficult today to speak either of influence or indeed of dependence. This aversion to accepting foreign elements, which had its roots in the innermost religious conceptions of the Byzantines, is especially evident in the monastic art in the peripheral regions. The monastic art which developed in Greece under the lordship of the western barons, in Apulia under the pressure of the Catholic Angevins, and in Asia Minor under the Turkish yoke, turned its back on all foreign influences. In their hieratic stiffness and their iconography they went back to the monastic models of the ninth and tenth centuries which were known through miniatures in old manuscripts. Similarly in the late chronicles there was a return again to the old monastic chronicles of the ninth century.

The fortunes of representational art were repeated in the literature of that period. Here too development proceded along the same paths. In literature there was something quite modern that can be compared with the great art of the Palaeologan mosaics in Hagia Sophia and Kariye Cami in Constantinople and the frescoes of Mistra. There was also a literature which remained uninfluenced by these new movements, and carried on the old Byzantine forms inspired by the monastic age.

The late Byzantine chronicle, a new form of historical writing

The new style which dominated the literature of the Palaeologan period was, like the art of the period, not an entirely new creation. Here too it is worth while investigating the beginnings out of which this new literature grew. In historiography it was the great chronicles of the eleventh and twelfth centuries, the works of John Scylitzes and Zonaras, which broke with the past. The turning point is clearly revealed in the programme set out in the introduction to Scylitzes' work, where he says that in contrast to earlier superficial and not very thorough historical works he is going to give an account characterized by historical accuracy. In Zonaras' work this goes a stage further. He works over the material provided by earlier accounts and summarizes them. Zonaras was followed by Constantine Manasses and Michael Glycas. Manasses embroidered his history with stories; he was no historian but a writer of fiction. Mythological allusions and moral digressions made the narrative of Byzantine history more entertaining for its readers. The last, Michael Glycas, was a poet, and his world chronicle was influenced by the vernacular then in use in the romances and poetry of his day. His language was lively and bore no relation to the archaic style of the fossilized Atticism which was cultivated by the small class of the so-called erudite. His work circulated among the people and had a great influence on the view of history taken by the vast masses and the lower clergy. Glycas was bold enough to embellish the stereotyped account of the creation of the world at the opening of his chronicle with animal fables from the *Physiologus* and extracts borrowed from Aelian so as to give it a more lively flavour.

From the point of view of social position, a change can also be observed in this series of chroniclers. John Scylitzes and Zonaras were high imperial officials, Constantine Manasses and Michael Glycas on the contrary were men of letters, depending for their livelihood on the patronage of the powerful. They belonged to the same social class as the poet Prodromus or the grammarian Tzetzes.

The manner in which these *literati* lived and produced their creations also marks a new epoch. Like many Byzantines, Zonaras spent his old age in a monastery. Besides his chronicle, he wrote theological works, exegesis on the Holy Scriptures and the writings of the great church fathers. Among his works there is even a treatise on Byzantine church music in which he expounds its terminology. He himself also composed a hymn. The life of this man still followed the same course as that of the older Byzantine chroniclers. Theophanes too had composed his chronicle when he was a monk in a monastery. But then came the break. Constantine Manasses belonged to quite a different walk of life. It is known that as well as his world chronicle he wrote a romance, *Aristander and Callithea*, of which only a few fragments have survived. He also composed a biography of the poet Oppian. For Constantine Manasses secular literary activity was the dominating factor. His chronicle was written in verse which was unusual for a chronicle at this time and in itself marks a break with the past. The other works which he produced reveal him as a literary man whose ancestry goes back to the works of the light muse of Graeco-Roman antiquity. Thus this unusual chronicler wrote a lament for the death of his songster. These were themes unheard of in the Byzantine Empire since the days of Agathias. In any case this unusual return to nature was hardly original but was a version of the moving little poem of Catullus on the death of Lesbia's sparrow, which was known to him through a Greek translation. Another of Manasses' poems describes the capture of a goldfinch, a third the hunting of cranes. The man who wrote these did not compose his chronicle in a monastic cell. He was living in the everyday Byzantine world.

Michael Glycas belonged to the same social class as Manasses. He had already made a name as a poet when he began to write his world chronicle. He was also used to the vernacular as a literary medium. His begging poem to the Emperor Manuel written in prison was in the vernacular and he did not hesitate to use coarse words taken from everyday speech. But he did not succeed in escaping the blinding to which the imperial sentence had condemned him. Perhaps his offence had been a far too daring couplet on the erotic adventures of the Byzantine Basileus or an epigram criticizing the astrological predilections of the ruler. Later he played the part of spiritual consoler to Theodora, the beautiful and frivolous mistress of the Emperor Manuel. In a letter of consolation he offered help to the lady who was despairing of her soul's salvation on account of a murder committed out of jealousy, citing examples from Byzantine imperial history where there was indeed no shortage of such sinners.

So in the chronicles the development of the original monastic and religious view of history was giving way before a freer, almost secular, historical outlook. Here the same is happening as with religious painting. The old stiff forms of the monastic age are brought to life, they are transformed and seem to pick up again the development which was interrupted in the period of late antiquity.

The new Byzantine romance and its oriental and late antique models

The age of Palaeologi also inaugurated a new epoch for the romance. What can be regarded as a kind of foreshadowing of the new period in the chronicles of the eleventh and twelfth centuries, lived on in the romances until the passing of the Byzantine epoch in the first half of the seventeenth century. Chronicles were not continued in the Palaeologan day after the manner of the new form of expression developed in the eleventh and twelfth centuries. The later chronicles reaching to the beginning of the eighteenth century went back to the pattern of the old monastic chronicles and were marked by the same stereotyped characteristics as were the religious paintings of this time.

It was different with the romance. The romances written by Prodromus, and after him Eustathius Macrembolites, were still under the influence of the old sophist romances —or even a continuation of a development broken off at the end of late antiquity. But in contrast the romance of the Palaeologan period produced something new and independent. The oriental romances and stories reached the Byzantine Empire in translations and new versions, which at first came via Melitene and then later through Trebizond, and they played a decisive part in the rise of the new Byzantine romance. It was particularly the oriental fairy stories and poetry which enlivened the inflexible pattern of the old sophist romances refurbished in the eleventh and twelfth centuries. There was an enormous difference between a work of the old form clinging to the cherished patterns, the romances of Tatius and Heliodore, and the new romantic poetry. These sophist romances still survived in the fourteenth century but, like the historical works in the learned Attic language, they only circulated within a very limited section of Byzantine society.

The literary circles and certain families gave strong support to this form of poetry, although others turned to the new romances in the vernacular. An example of the older type of romance is found in the allegorical poem *Sophrosyne* by Theodore Meliteniotes. It begins in an attractive manner with the poet strolling in the open air. He meets a wonderful maiden, Sophrosyne, and at the sight of her falls into a trance. The young poet is trembling with fright and his teeth are chattering and the supernatural being has to use all her eloquence to explain to him the reason for her presence. As soon as she has convinced him that she is not an evil spirit, he follows her. The poet then goes on to describe how he is led into a large park with a castle in it. The entrance to the castle is barred by seven obstacles: a wide stream, a bridge, the door of the bridge, wild beasts, a moat, a thorn hedge and finally a wall. These stand for the seven snares which bar the way to virtue (*sophrosyne*). With the help of Sophrosyne the poet, trembling with fright, overcomes the seven obstacles and then at last he stands before the bed of Sophrosyne. The poem spares the reader no details. He has to tell us how this bed is ornamented with precious jewels. In fact his description reads more like a work on mineralogy than a poem. This kind of work overladen with erudition understandably could only be for the consumption of a very limited circle.

It was different with the new romances in the vernacular, which made considerable use of oriental motifs. A romance of this kind, such as *Callimachus and Chrysorrhoe*, was really a further development of the kind of eastern fairy story found in collections such as the *Thousand and One Nights*. It holds the reader spellbound by its content. This poem tells of a king and his three sons. In choosing his successor the king promises the crown to whichever of his sons performs a heroic deed. All three sons depart to foreign lands to fulfil this command. They find themselves in a magnificent park in which there is a castle. But the castle is inhabited by a dragon. Ignoring the warning of his brothers who stay behind, Callimachus, undaunted, enters the castle. In the empty salons and halls stand heavily laden tables. In one room he finds a maiden hanging by the hair. He scarcely has time to exchange a word with her when heavy sounds announce the approach of the dragon. On the maiden's advice he conceals himself in a silver vessel. He then has evidence as to how the dragon tortures the maiden and then after a heavy meal falls into a deep sleep. Callimachus kills the sleeping dragon. The maiden then reveals herself to him. She is called Chrysorrhoe and has maintained her innocence against the snares of the dragon. The two remain in the castle but their love rhapsody is broken by the arrival of a foreign prince who is intent on conquering the castle and winning Chrysorrhoe. Callimachus is lured out of the castle and with the aid of a magic device is made incapable of fighting. This charm, given to the prince by a sorceress, is an apple which kills if placed on the breast and brings back to life when it touches the lips. Chrysorrhoe is led away by the prince and Callimachus is found by his brothers lying lifeless on the ground. They see the apple on his breast and by chance they let it fall on his mouth and he wakes up, restored to life. He learns of Chrysorrhoe's fate and hastens after her. Employed as a gardener in the prince's residence, he makes himself known to her. Then follows the lovers' meeting by night in a pavilion. Here they are seen, seized and brought to trial. Chrysorrhoe justifies herself in an allegorical story and Callimachus reveals his royal ancestry. Both are forgiven and allowed their freedom. The magician who presented the prince with the apple is burnt in an oven.

This poem has oriental features. There are the same magic charms which are found in the Arabian fairy tales. There is almost always the nocturnal assignation of the lovers which is constantly found in the oriental fairy stories, as for instance the *Thousand and One Nights*. Classical influence in the sense of a return to Hellenistic forms is found only in the descriptions and comparisons, as for instance when the lovers are discovered, and the very awkward story of the surprising of the god Ares with Aphrodite in the net of Hephaistus has to be dragged in for purposes of comparison with the situation in which Chrysorrhoe and Callimachus find themselves.

Callimachus and Chrysorrhoe, although it is a poem written in the vernacular, still makes considerable use of the favourite motifs of the late antique tradition. In contrast to this there were other romances which seem to have been destined less for the aristocratic literary salons of the capital. The reader of *Callimachus and Chrysorrhoe* belonged to circles which were enthusiastic about the new romances with oriental motifs but still wanted to keep the old forms of the sophist romances. Hence the rather pretentious narratives decked out with references to classical mythology. Presentation of this kind can only be understood by those familiar with the classical context.

The romance *Belthandrus and Chrysantza* is quite different. The oriental element is also a prominent feature here but the form of the presentation is far removed from the sophist romance. There are no mythological references. The story again tells of a castle found by the hero who is led thither by a ray of light. It is called *Erotokastron* and it is there that his fate is to be revealed to him. He enters the castle and learns from an inscription that he will fall in love with Chrysantza, the daughter of the prince of Antioch. He is led by the god Eros to the king of Love who gives him a precious staff. Forty maidens are presented to him and he has to choose the most beautiful and hand the staff to her. Belthandrus performs this task, but not in a noble and princely manner. Without any shame he describes the inadequacies of the maidens in detail before he awards the prize to one of them. Then he goes on to Antioch where his destined lover, Chrysantza, the daughter of the prince of that city, lives. The prince accepts him as his vassal. Here too a pavilion is the scene of the nocturnal assignation of the lovers, and it is here that they are discovered. One of Chrysantza's ladies-in-waiting saves Belthandrus by declaring that he came to the park by night to meet her. Thus he has to marry the lady-in-waiting. The marriage gives him the opportunity of continuing to meet his beloved until finally they both take flight. The end of the story tells how the Patriarch blesses their marriage. Here the tone is somewhat coarse. In many respects the subject-matter is reminiscent of the *Decameron* of Boccaccio, though there is no trace of western influence here. The prince of Antioch's acceptance of Belthandrus points to contacts with the crusading states in Syria and Palestine with whom the Byzantine Empire had close relations.

The poem *Lybistrus and Rhodamne* belongs to this same group of Byzantine romances influenced by oriental sources. Here too magic charms play an important role. A magic ring and a sorceress are mentioned. The scene of action changes, passing from Mesopotamia to India and Egypt. The place names are imaginary and show the story to be a Byzantine invention. Unlike *Belthandrus and Chrysantza*, the presentation is excellent. The erotic scenes are restrained and show none of the coarseness and near-obscenity which is found in *Belthandrus and Chrysantza*.

Western influence on the Byzantine romance

Only a relatively small number of romances of this period show western influence. These consist of Byzantine versions of western romances. Thus the Arthurian legend was revised for Byzantine readers. The Celtic names were translated into Greek but here particularly Byzantine customs were taken into account. This particularly concerned the position of women which in Byzantium was quite different from the West. Genevra, the Guinevere of the Celtic romance, was despatched to the women's gynaecium quarters to superintend the maidens spinning. Not only the Arthurian legend, but the Provençal story *Flore et Blanchefleur* was revised for a Byzantine public. The favourite French folk tale *Pierre de Provence et la belle Maguelonne* was also transformed for Byzantine consumption.

It must be remembered that a considerable part of the Byzantine Empire was in the possession of the French aristocracy, and the translations of these romances and the revision of French material must be seen in this context. The Byzantine literature which first used and revised western material arose in regions under foreign control. The Frank barons and Venetians in the Byzantine territories which they ruled also had a determining voice in literary productions. It was the gasmules who played the decisive role in the transmission of western literature. They felt themselves to be westerners. Their literary models were taken from France or Venice.

And of course it is also true that much of their foreign material coming from the West which the gasmules used also awakened echoes in the Byzantine world. These romances were enthusiastically received by the people and circulated widely among them despite a cold reception from Byzantine intellectuals. Thus a work which attained a place in Greek literature similar to that of *Digenis Akritas* was by a Venetian. It was the *Erotocritus*, the candidate for love, by Vincenzo Cornaro from Sitia on the island of Crete. In spite of its immense length—about 11,400 lines of verse—this work had a wide circulation. It almost became a folk epic in Crete, where parts of the poem are still sung today by peasants. But there too the work did not take its inspiration from Byzantine lands. Vincenzo Cornaro had used Italian themes for his celebrated poem. But the vivid and flexible presentation which characterizes the *Erotocritus* seems to have won Greek approval and acquired, as it were, rights of citizenship in Greek lands.

An enormous amount of literature produced foreign western themes for Byzantine Greek consumption. After Constantinople fell in 1453 this took the lead. On Crete, Corfu and also Rhodes western material appeared in its Greek version. It was printed in Venice, thus circulating in a wider circle. It is almost possible to speak of a Venetian-Byzantine literature which survived until the first half of the seventeenth century. Side by side with this, there was also independent Byzantino-Greek literature. It is no small tribute to the vital forces within the Byzantine Greek world that even the Franks living in Greece used Greek as their literary language. The *Chronicle of the Morea*, which makes no secret of its hatred for the Greeks in its earliest form, used the Greek language and in an increasing number of versions almost became a popular work.

During the last centuries of its existence Byzantine literature reflects the struggle of the Greek world against foreign influence coming from the West. In this conflict Byzantine Hellenism often proved itself more potent than what the West had to offer. Above all the national resistance was aggravated by social contrast. For under Venetian and Latin domination the Greeks and Byzantines were reduced to poverty.

The last flash of political splendour

The downfall of the Byzantine Empire after the restoration of Nicaea was only to a small extent a fate which the Byzantines brought upon themselves. The restored state of Nicaea was caught up in the ebb and flow of world politics and this was a far more potent factor inevitably involving it in the fate which befell the Mediterranean countries.

The rise of Nicaea took place in a kind of political vacuum occasioned by the attack on Asia Minor made by the Mongols under the sons of Gengis Khan. The powerful Seljuk state, the dangerous enemy of Byzantium, was rendered impotent and humiliated by becoming the vassal and tributary of the Mongols. The Byzantine enemies in the Balkans, the Bulgars and the Hungarians, were languishing under the Mongol yoke. It was during this period that the Empire succeeded in consolidating its position in Asia Minor and its alliance with Genoa made possible the surprise attack on the old capital, Constantinople. The possession of Constantinople at once brought the Byzantine Empire back into the mainstream of world politics. It now became a desirable ally sought after by the Mamluk sultans of Egypt and the khan of the Golden Horde in South Russia against their common enemy the Mongol Ilkhans whose Empire included Mesopotamia and Iran. The Ilkhans were allied with France and Genoa. Egypt tried to make an alliance with European powers such as Byzantium and Aragon. It was at this time that Egyptian diplomats were negotiating in Constantinople and the fate of the world was decided in the imperial palace. This was the last time that the Byzantine Emperor was to play a role in world politics. Michael VIII, an unscrupulous and ruthless man, determined the fate of the Mediterranean world, and with it indirectly of his own country, with his brilliant diplomatic moves. St Louis IX, one of the greatest medieval French kings, wanted to make his own state preeminent in the Mediterranean. His striking policy revealed him as the first great French colonialist, and by eliminating the Albigensians and annexing the territory of his ally Count Raymond of Toulouse, he had gained a wide area of access to the Mediterranean. Then in alliance with the Mongol Ilkhans he attempted to establish himself in the Nile Delta near Damietta with a view to marching on Cairo. He was not discouraged by the military failure of this enterprise. Shortly afterwards he proceeded to fortify further the French strongholds and those of his allies on the coasts of Syria and Palestine, and counting on his alliance with the Ilkhans he sought to make this the basis for his policy of conquest in the East Mediterranean. Relying on the Pope in Rome and financed by an enormous loan from the Florentine banking house of the Acciajuoli, in 1266 he succeeded in seizing South Italy and Sicily from the Hohenstaufen, and gave them to his brother Charles of Anjou. When he attempted to gain control of the sea route between Sicily and Africa, by leading an expedition to Tunis, he failed. His brother Charles of Anjou in alliance with the Mongol Ilkhan was now trying to take by force the Bosphorus straits and the Dardanelles and thus to annihilate the Byzantine Empire. The Byzantine Empire in alliance with the Mamluk sultan of Egypt and the Golden Horde in South Russia warded off this blow by an understanding with the king of Aragon and the native opposition in Sicily. The popular rising in Sicily (the Sicilian Vespers) had military support from Aragon and this led to the downfall of French Mediterranean policy. The Byzantine Empire was saved. Not long afterwards the last strongholds of the West on the coasts of Palestine and Syria, Tyre, Beirut and Sidon, fell into the hands of Byzantium's allies, the Mamluk sultans.

The Byzantine Emperor as a Turkish vassal

The turn of the fourteenth and fifteenth centuries found the Byzantine Empire in a state of disintegration. The Byzantine Emperor had spent two years in Paris. A regent ruled in the capital which was being blockaded by the Turks. The city's days seemed numbered. But once again the Byzantine Empire was saved—this time by Timur's victory at Angora over the Ottoman sultan Bayezid in 1402. This battle postponed the downfall for more than half a century. But during this period, as also in the second half of the thirteenth century, Byzantium was nothing more than a pawn in the politics of the maritime cities Genoa and Venice, and had no independent will of its own. These cities decided who should reign in Constantinople and placed their candidates on the throne with the help of popular risings stirred up from without.

It was the same in the Empire of Trebizond. This had at first managed to keep its control in the Black Sea by means of the Byzantine possessions in the Crimea. But then the Genoese took over the most important strongholds in the Empire of Trebizond, just as they had done on the Bosphorus and Dardanelles in the Byzantine Empire. In the end the Byzantine Empire in Asia Minor maintained control over only a small coastal strip stretching from Batum through Trebizond up to Kerasunt. Here the magnates ruled almost like the feudal princes of the West. They came from the same families who had so often decided the Empire's fate in the tenth and eleventh centuries. Thus in the Empire of Trebizond, as in Byzantine Thessaly, there was a branch of the family of the Melisseni. The Thessaly branch managed to get control over the whole of Thessaly. In Trebizond the family also governed an enormous area and possessed unlimited power. Like the capital, Constantinople, during the last century of the Byzantine Empire, Trebizond had a history rent by an unending series of civil wars and palace revolutions. By reason of internal weakness both Empires alike suffered the humiliation of being in the position of vassal to their Muslim neighbour. During the final century of the Byzantine Empire the Emperor of Constantinople was the vassal of the Ottoman sultan. He had to accompany him on all campaigns. The Emperor of Trebizond was the vassal of the chief of the Turkic horde of the White Sheep, and he not only owed military service to this prince but often had to provide one of his daughters for his harem.

The last hope: the Morea

Ruin hung over Byzantine rule in Constantinople and Trebizond as something inescapable. Contemporaries regarded this as the death of an old, long worn-out organism. But it was quite different in Byzantine territory in the Peloponnese. In the last days of the Empire this province was governed by sons of the Emperor ruling in Constantinople and it seemed destined to become a rallying point for the Greek nation and a centre for a new and larger Greece. It had indeed cast off the mantle of universal rule which was still being worn by the Byzantine Empire. From the end of the thirteenth century the Greeks in the Peloponnese had been reinforced by the arrival of the Albanians who had migrated southwards. The Albanians were originally transhumants like the Vlachs who moved with their flocks to the high mountains in the summer and came down again to the valleys when winter set in. They had served the rich Byzantine landed magnates either as mercenaries or as agricultural labourers at harvest time. They gradually brought their families to Greece, and since mercenaries and casual labourers only obtained temporary employment they became a settled class of small farmers who survived the downfall of the Graeco-Byzantine landed proprietor brought about by the Turkish conquest.

In the neighbourhood of Corinth an important industry had been built up which had firmly established itself independently of Constantinople. The old silk industry had originally flourished in this district but it was ruined when the Normans carried off its specialist workers. The ceramic industry, however, had developed thanks to the refugee artisans driven out of eastern Asia Minor, and it copied the excellent glass techniques used in Irak and northern Persia, thus filling the gap left by the ruined silk industry. The glass industry in Corinth had achieved a position of considerable importance.

The export trade in wine also added greatly to the prosperity of this region. The wine from Monemvasia in the Peloponnese, the Malvasia of wine lovers in central and western Europe, was much sought after and frequently imitated. Scarcity of grain was met by importing from South Russia through the Genoese. The last remaining Latin principalities in the Peloponnese were gradually reduced by the Byzantines. For a short time Athens was also incorporated into the realm of Mistra, thus marking the first step towards the conquest of central and northern Greece. But the unfortunate outcome of the battle of Varna was decisive for the freedom of Greece. No success on a Greek battlefield could compensate for the annihilation of the army led by the king of Hungary, which was to have liberated Europe from Turkish domination. The Turkish army was soon standing before the Isthmus of Corinth. The fire of Turkish artillery broke through the Byzantine fortifications erected across the Isthmus. Peace terms were imposed and soon after the fall of Constantinople the Graeco-Byzantine polity in the Peloponnese was liquidated.

The basic reason for the disintegration of Byzantine society

Even without the Turkish cannon which laid low the Hexamilion wall, the fortifications across the Isthmus which protected the Morea, this Greek state would probably have fallen. The unhealthy social structure, the existence of a small upper class controlling practically all land, the vast mass of the almost entirely landless populace without opportunity for advancement—all this augured ill for the future. The Byzantine state had been quick to recognize the danger threatening from the ever-growing landed estates. As early as the tenth century the Macedonian dynasty had attempted to protect by legislation both the soldier-farmers settled on the land and the peasantry in general against the landed magnates. They also hoped to raise up a counterbalance against the great proprietors whose constant efforts were directed towards getting all political power into their own hands. This hope was not realized. In the great rebellions of the generals of the themes at the opening of the Emperor Basil II's personal government the soldier-farmers and the peasant populace of the individual themes faithfully supported the rebellious generals. In the light of this experience the imperial government modified the existing system of imperial defence. In the place of the military settlers who had shown that they were entirely under the control of the generals of the themes and impervious to the influence of the imperial government, an attempt was then made to find support for the throne from among the aristocracy, the magnates. With this in mind the *pronoia* was introduced. The *pronoia* consisted in the relinquishment of a number of the state's rights over a particular region to a great magnate, in return for which he gave his support to the Emperor. This concession was usually for life and in return the pronoiar pledged himself to provide the Emperor with a certain contingent of troops. In contrast to the *stratiotai* who worked their land themselves, the holder of a *pronoia* used *paroikoi* to work his property. One result of this grant was that free men might be brought under the control of a great landlord if they happened to belong to land included in the *pronoia* grant. Thus the state itself was sanctioning the destruction of the middle-class peasantry. The Emperors also used this expedient to make monastic property fulfil its military obligations. Earlier on, the office of church steward, *charisticarius*, was only held by ecclesiastics. Then the Emperor granted the management of church property to his supporters who had to fulfil the church's military obligations. Later, foreign western mercenaries were paid not with gold but by grant of a *pronoia* over some small region. These small pronoiars differed from the *stratiotai* in the economic use made of their grant. The *stratiotai* worked their land themselves, the lesser pronoiars lived only from the rent of the land which their *pronoia* yielded them in accordance with the rights over it which had been granted them.

Economic extortion by foreign capitalists

The Byzantine state itself was not spared and suffered in the same way as its individual subjects. In return for military support it had to hand over to the Genoese and Venetians its most important sources of national income, the customs dues of the straits, the monopoly of minerals and the sale of agricultural produce. In order to secure Genoese support during the conquest of old Constantinople, the treaty of Nymphaion made with them in 1261 granted them 85 per cent of the customs dues on the Bosphorus. The important islands and strongholds of the old Byzantine Empire were in the hands of Venetian, Genoese and Florentine capitalists.

The Venetians controlled the export of the famous wines so prized in the West, such as Malvasia, the wine of Monemvasia. It was into their pockets that the revenue flowed. It was a Venetian, Marco Sanudo, who ruled as duke over the Cyclades with the island of Naxos, and his agents worked the emery deposits. This duchy of Naxos managed to survive until 1579, finally ruled by the Crispi. Then the Ottomans handed over the control of the island to a Jew, John Michez, who entrusted its administration and economic exploitation to a Spaniard. In 1304 the Byzantine Emperor had granted the island of Chios to a Genoese merchant in return for a large sum of money. He and his family, the Giustiniani, had almost a European monopoly for the export of mastic from Chios which brought in millions. This Genoese principality also survived the Byzantine Empire by more than a century. In Greek Cyprus, the French dynasty of the Lusignans first ruled, and then from 1489 the Venetians who lost the island to the Turks in 1571. The Venetians held Crete until 1671. On the Greek mainland the situation was no better. In Athens, Thebes and Corinth, the Florentine banking family, the Acciajuoli, were in control. They took the title of dukes. Their tools were the Spanish mercenaries, the Catalan Company and later the Navarrese Company. In certain regions of the Greek mainland these two companies established their own rule, while their vicars administered parts of the Peloponnese.

The hopes roused by the formation of a Greek principality in the Peloponnese are indeed understandable. This was when the Palaeologi, first Theodore, then Constantine

Palaeologus, built up from small beginnings the principality of the Morea, a new and independent Greek kingdom. Mistra, the capital of this principality, brought hope to the Greeks under the domination of Latin lords. It was here that the intellectual élite of the capital gathered, men such as Gemistus Pletho and the painters of the frescoes in the church of the Pantanassa.

The last literary works of the dying Byzantine society (satire, poetry, folk songs)

This economic exhaustion, this constant favouring of foreigners, helped to shape the intellectual life of the Byzantines. The social contrasts can be traced in the poems of Stephen Sachlikes of Crete. Stephen was a noble originally belonging to the governing class and he lived in Chandax, the capital of Crete. This was in the days immediately after the fall of Constantinople; the Venetians were in control of all the important positions. What Stephen gives us is the story of his life, the story of a Byzantine country nobleman under foreign Venetian rule. His account is not very edifying. At school he learnt little; he admits that he hated lessons and books. He then led a dissolute life and was soon without the means to maintain a reasonable standard of life in the capital. So he left the city and lived in the country, where he spent his days with the peasants and occupied himself with dog breeding and hunting. He went back to Chandax, recalled by the Venetian governor to be appointed advocate, but due to the machinations of a lady of doubtful virtue, Kutajotena, he was thrown into prison. Here he ended by learning the hard facts of life.

Sachlikes uses the language of Byzantine everyday life in all its crudity of expression. In prison, where he was guarded by Venetian mercenaries, he composed his autobiographical poem which ends with a satire on the life of prostitutes in the Cretan capital. Even then when Stephen sets himself up as a moralist, as for instance in the exhortations to the son of a friend, he fails to inspire respect. He lacked any moral standards. What he produces is an interesting human document showing life in certain circles of the old Byzantine aristocracy under Venetian rule.

Like the poems of Stephen Sachlikes, the late Byzantine animal fables also deal with the social problems of the age. The struggle between the gilds of the zelots and the aristocracy are treated in literary fashion in the animal fables. This genre follows a development in the Byzantine Empire similar to that found in the West. The western animal tale, the famous *Reinke de Vos*, is also a poem concerned with social contrasts. The work of Hinrek van Alkmar from Flanders in the second half of the fifteenth century arose in an age of class struggles. Whereas the West has a fox, the Byzantines produce an ass. The ass is the hero of the most important Byzantine animal fable, the *Legend of the Respected Ass* from the middle of the fifteenth century. The content of this so-called saint's legend—the work is intentionally described as a *synaxarion*, that is an account of a saint's life—is as follows. An ill-treated donkey has escaped from his tormentors and is grazing in a meadow. A fox and a wolf approach him, meaning to devour him. The ass sees through their intention. His hint that his master is coming along with his fierce dogs persuades them to defer their project. The two then propose to the ass that he should go to the East with them where he could become rich. All three embark in a ship. During the voyage the fox explains that it has been revealed to him in a dream that a terrible storm will shortly break. As good Christians all three then make their confession. The wolf confesses to the fox. In spite of his evil deeds— he has devoured cattle, sheep and pigs—the fox absolves him from all his sins. Then the fox makes his confession and the wolf hears his list of misdeeds. He admits that he has often killed hens and he relates his offences. Then he too is absolved. Both the penitents decide to renounce the world. The wolf is to withdraw to Mount Athos, the Holy Mountain of the Byzantines; the fox explains that he wishes to enter a convent. Then the ass makes his confession. His list of sins is a short one; he confesses that he once unlawfully munched coltsfoot leaf. Both confessors consider that this is a sin punishable by death for which no absolution can be given. In this awkward situation the ass explains that there is a marvellous power in his back hoof which he wishes at least to bestow on his companions before his death. Both rush at him and demand it. Then the ass says that this power can only be handed over under certain conditions. The wolf must kneel on the deck of the ship for three hours saying the 'Our Father'. At the end of the period of prayer the ass gives the kneeling wolf a well directed kick with his hoof and he goes overboard into the sea. The fox is pushed after him and on reaching the bank in safety he praises the ass. And so the story ends. In the wolf and the fox, the two oppressors of the Byzantine populace are easily recognized: the fox stands for the financial officials, the wolf for the magnates. So that this animal poem is really a document on the social conflicts which characterized this period. The poem is written from the point of view of a particular class, the small artisans and traders, the supporters of the Palaeologi.

This social class of Byzantine society is also found in the so-called historical romances. The extant version of the *Romance of Belisarius* must have won the approval of the same social class of the small artisans and traders as are found in the *Legend of the Respected Ass*. The *Romance of Belisarius* is certainly older than this period. The history of the city of Constantinople (*Patria*) dating from the end of the tenth century appears to know of a poem which tells of the fate of Belisarius. According to this story Belisarius was incarcerated for three years in a dark dungeon as a result of the calumnies of the magnates of the Empire. The prison gates were only opened when danger threatened the Empire. The Emperor had equipped a fleet against the enemy, the magnates were disputing the command. The people then rose and shouted only one name—Belisarius. The Emperor gave in. Belisarius sailed at the head of his navy against England, captured the English *kastron* and returned again to Constantinople laden with booty. But the magnates still calumniated Belisarius. The Emperor was convinced by them and had Belisarius blinded. Fresh danger threatened. Saracens and Persians gathered against the Empire. Then the Emperor entrusted the military command to Alexius, the son of Belisarius. There is nothing in this poem recalling the famous general of Justinian. The poem remains a romance lacking any foundation in historical fact. But it is something fresh and marks the coming of age of the new social class which here steps to the fore and gets its own way. It is possible that this historical romance was written for the circle of the zelot party in Thessalonica.

National conflicts between Byzantine Greeks and foreign conquerors also played a significant part in literature. The animal story, used as a weapon of social satire, was only a mouthpiece of these antagonisms. Thus in one of these animal epics there is a description of an assembly of animals called together by the lion as king. Everything is done as in a session of a Byzantine imperial assembly. Much of the work is filled with lengthy disputes between the hostile animals in which national conflicts find expression. For instance the sow complains because the French cleric uses her bristles to sprinkle the holy water with. In another animal poem attacks are made against the western forces of occupation in the Byzantine Empire and one of the animals is accused of adultery with the wife of a French knight and abuse follows. The owl is called a Tatar skull, another animal is branded as being descended from a Bulgar. The atmosphere is that of modern nationalist clashes which are still found in the Balkans in all their sharpness.

Side by side with this political poetry, there were folk songs and folk poetry. The laments on the fall of Constantinople belong to these folk poems. These laments are found both as songs and as poems; the two kinds of poetry shade into each other. One of the most beautiful of the laments on the fall of Constantinople was evidently taken by the poet from a folk song and transformed into a poem. Two ships met during the days when Constantinople was being besieged by the Turks. One is on its way north to the capital and near Tenedos it meets a vessel coming from Constantinople. The ship from the north brings the news of the fall of the city. The descriptions in the poem are true to life and most moving. Other poetry also telling of the downfall of Constantinople lacks this quality found in the ballad or in the folk song. In another poem on the fall of the capital the poet withholds his name and only gives certain indications intelligible to the initiated. This poem appears to belong to the type of Byzantine propaganda which was based on an underground movement and was hoping for intervention by the European powers. Information on the military strength of the Ottomans and the numbers of the Greek population, as well as requests to readers to copy and circulate the poem as widely as possible—all this points to its political aims. The poem does indeed seem to be more in the nature of political propaganda than literature. But the fall of Constantinople had most profoundly moved the Greek spirit. This is clear from every lament, whether simple and homely, or laden with mythological allusions written by a poet with a humanist upbringing. The echoes of this folk poetry were stronger and more enduring than the imperial histories written by high officials in exile after the fall of the Byzantine Empire.

The favourite themes of Greek folk songs today are still the time of the downfall, the death fight with the Turks. Like the conquest of Trebizond and the conquest of Athens, these events live on in poetry and in song.

In this new period, when a wide section of the populace had some share in literature, love poetry came into its own again. Among the new rising classes of artisans and small traders, women did not lead such secluded lives as in the houses of Byzantine governors and magnates. A collection of love poems was made and circulated in the form of stories like the *Decameron* of Boccaccio. The so-called *Rhodian Love Songs* was an anthology containing poetry from all the regions of Greece. Many of the songs in this collection came from the fourteenth century, or at least from the beginning of the fifteenth century. Many of them seem to have been collected and edited by someone interested in folk poetry. These love songs are arranged in the form of a story. A young man is in love with a maiden, and she sets him certain tasks to be performed before she will speak to him of love. The form of arrangement is entirely Byzantine and has no parallel in the West. A certain coarseness of feeling sometimes shows in these poems. When a young man taunts a girl whom he has constrained to his will by brute force it is a sign of the moral decadence occasioned by the political downfall of the Byzantine Empire and the presence of foreign troops. The moral sense was blunted by the continual change in political relations and the simultaneous party struggles and foreign occupation.

The last phase of surviving Graeco-Byzantine literature is in no way comparable to that of the early Byzantine period. The decline was too great. The heroic epic written at the opening of the sixteenth century for one of the Greek condottieri in the service of the renaissance princes has nothing in common with the epic of George of Pisidia on the deeds of the Emperor Heraclius dating from the middle of the seventh century.

This condottiere Mercurius Bua, whose heroic deeds are described by the poet John Koronaios, was one of many: he was a leader of the Greek mercenaries (*stratiotai, estradiots*) who like the Swiss and the German mercenaries, fought for the Italian powers in the early sixteenth century. His tomb is still to be found today in the church of Santa Maria Maggiore in Treviso. The heroic poem of John Koronaios was written during the lifetime of this condottiere and it has nothing in common with genuine poetry, as is shown by its erudite critical use of oral tradition filled out by methodical archivist studies. This kind of learned epic had no longer anything in common with Byzantium. To the modern observer it is only a boundary stone marking the end of Byzantine literature. But these learned epics no doubt still had their heights. They are superior to the clumsy patchwork of Trivoli of Corfu who exalts above the heroes of the *Iliad* the Venetian sea captains who distinguished themselves in the fight against pirates. All else which was written scarcely merits the name of literature. The Venetian printing presses helped to circulate this kind of writing. It continued into the first half of the seventeenth century as a mere shadow of the old Byzantine literature. For the most part it took its material from Italian models and was almost entirely without any original feeling. It may be described as Graeco-Italian, or rather Graeco-Venetian, literature but never as Byzantine poetry.

The end

The downfall of the Byzantine Empire in 1453 was the result of political conflict on a world-wide scale. The Mongol Empire, revived again by Timur Lenk the Lame (Tamurlane), had become the great power in Asia. Timur had defeated the Ottoman sultan Bayezid I in battle. The sultan died the prisoner of the Mongols. But Timur had also intervened in affairs in South Russia and the Empire of the Golden Horde was unable to check him. The Mongol khan of this nomad realm had to take refuge with the Lithuanians. Thus began the Lithuanian drive towards the Black Sea which was eventually to affect economic relations in the Mediterranean. The Lithuanians took possession of the region between the Dnieper and the Dniester. The Mongolian customs officials were now replaced by the counts of the Lithuanian grand duke. Similarly during this period the Rumanian principality of Moldavia became independent under the Basarab family who took their name from Bessarabia. South Russia came into close contact with the Baltic region; the Lithuanians and Poles formed a kingdom. Grain from South Russia now no longer went through the Black Sea and the Bosphorus to Italy but was sent to the North. The straits therefore became less important. On the other hand, the alliance which had once again been formed in the first half of the fifteenth century in order to defend the Byzantine Empire, showed how little concern western Europe still had for the old universal powers of the middle ages. The coalition consisted of the Hungarian king, the voivode of Transylvania, the hospodar of Wallachia, the Serbian despot George Branković and the Albanian leader Skanderbeg (George Kastriota). The Greeks under the despot Constantine Palaeologus' leadership then entered Athens and captured Thebes. But the alliance of the Balkan states could not really overcome any first class power. At the battle of Varna the Hungarian king was killed and the coalition destroyed. The national revival which had began to take shape in the Peloponnese and in Central Greece under Palaeologan leadership was now destroyed at the command of the Turkish victors. Only the guerrilla force of Skanderbeg continued to resist the Turks in Albania.

The help which the European West gave to the Byzantines achieved nothing. The attempt to offer assistance in return for a reunion of the churches was doomed to failure in view of the attitude of the Greek people. The union of the western and Byzantine Church, achieved on 6 July 1439 at Florence, was repudiated by the Orthodox clergy. The Metropolitan of Moscow who, like the Patriarch of Constantinople, had ratified the union was imprisoned on his return to his see. For Moscow the union of Florence meant separation from Byzantium, and with the fall of Constantinople Moscow became the Third Rome. The Muscovite tsar regarded himself as the successor of the Byzantine Emperor. The hand of a Byzantine princess of the Palaeologan house was offered to the tsar of Moscow. The Byzantine double eagle became the symbol of the authority of the Russian tsar and until the October Revolution it remained the national emblem of old Russia.

Thus the abortive union had even deprived the Byzantines of the leadership of the Orthodox Church. The Byzantines had conceded everything to the West and received nothing in return. Just before the fall of the capital Cardinal Isidore, formerly Metropolitan of Moscow, had undertaken to announce the union in Hagia Sophia. But the high Byzantine ecclesiastics had kept aloof. After the fall of the city the patriarchal chair was again held by an Orthodox theologian, Gennadius, who repudiated the ecclesiastical reconciliation.

The siege which was to deliver Constantinople into the hands of the Turks began on 7 April 1453. The heavy Turkish artillery breached at several points the hitherto invincible fortifications of the walls so that the Turkish janissaries were able to launch their attack. The major assault began on 29 May 1453. The Turks penetrated into the city, where they met with bitter resistance from the Greeks. They fought from house to house. In the street battle the last Byzantine Emperor fell. Thus the Byzantine Empire ceased to exist. The Emperor was dead and none dared to name his successor. The Morea followed in 1459 and in 1461 the Empire of Trebizond.

The fall of Constantinople might have been prevented. There were European powers who were in a position to save the Empire, but they lacked the will to do so. Economic interests turned the scale rather than the desire to defend the most important bastion of the West and of Christendom. The most powerful ruler in the Mediterranean at that time, king Alphonso V of Aragon who ruled a considerable part of the Iberian peninsula as well as Naples and Sicily, Sardinia and the Balearics, was not interested in the position of the Byzantine Empire on the narrow straits. To him the Empire of Constantinople was a dependent of Genoa. But once the Venetians were ousted Genoa was the power in almost sole possession of the trade with China and India via South Russia and Central Asia. The free passage of the Bosphorus was vital for Genoa in order to maintain her strongholds on the south coast of the Crimea and at the mouth of the Don. If the gateway to the Bosphorus was shut, Genoese trade with China would be disrupted. Behind Alphonso V stood the Catalan cities. They, like Venice, had trade treaties with the Mamluk sultans who guaranteed them transit passage through Egypt for their supplies of Chinese and Indian goods. Thus they had every reason to be hostile towards Genoese trade with China via South Russia. With the fall of Constantinople and the blocking of this Genoese trade with China, their own revenues inevitably rose to undreamt of sums. Thus the king did not move a finger in the defence of Constantinople. Only the Genoese sent a small auxiliary force.

The accuracy of the king of Aragon's calculations was demonstrated by events after the fall of Constantinople. Twenty-one years after the conquest of the city the last Genoese strongholds in the Crimea had been lost. This did not, however, disrupt trade with China by way of Central Asia and South Russia. The place of the Genoese was taken by the great Muscovite merchants to whom the Stroganovs belonged. Their patron was the grand duke Ivan III, who had expelled foreign merchants and their syndicates from Russian soil. In 1478 the campaign which destroyed the independence of great Novgorod took place. This campaign should be regarded in the same context as the destruction of the last Genoese strongholds in the Crimea. It paved the way for the development of Russia as a great power. The Muscovite merchants now replaced the Genoese in the trade with China. Nišnii Novgorod, which was united with the Muscovite Grand Duchy in 1417, now possessed its own Chinese city (Kitaigorod) where the merchants from China sold their wares. The fall of Constantinople and the end of the Byzantine Empire had cut off the West, and particularly Genoa, from trade with China through Central Asia. In the place of Genoa now stood the Muscovite state. Thus the historical process was initiated which brought about the economic and political penetration of Siberia and this gradually extended the Russian state to the borders of the neighbouring Chinese Empire and turned it into a world power.

Even in the Byzantine Empire itself all forces were not united in defence of the threatened fatherland. Behind the walls of Constantinople there was a pro-Turkish party. The Turks were aware of the internal conflicts, shown for instance in the struggle between magnates and zelots, and they exploited this situation. Emperors of the Palaeologan dynasty supported the cause of the zelots. The monastic orthodox movement with its radical hesychast tendencies was favoured by the magnates. Thus after the fall of Constantinople the sharpest measures of the Turks were directed against the supporters of the zelots, the small artisans and tradesmen. They were settled outside the city and their former quarters within the city were given to members of the Turkish gilds. Churches used by the zelots were at once handed over to the Islamic cult. By way of contrast the magnates were treated with consideration. They were allowed to remain in the city and to erect or expand their palaces in the Phanar quarter.

Similarly the Orthodox views of the Byzantine Church which the magnates favoured suffered no real persecution. After the fall of the city it was a representative of this Orthodox opinion, Gennadius, who became Patriarch. The Turks persecuted the supporters of the union with the Roman Catholic Church and upheld the Greek Orthodox Patriarchs. In general they used the Orthodox Patriarchs to oppress the non-Greek peoples in their Empire, abolishing the Bulgarian patriarchate and placing the Bulgarian Church under a Greek metropolitan who was under the Patriarch of Constantinople. Similarly the Serbian patriarchate was later abolished and the Serbian Church also placed under the patriarchate of Constantinople. Thus under the sign of the sword of Islam the Patriarch of Constantinople was able to make good all the losses which his Church had suffered through the growth of national churches among the Slav peoples in the Balkans.

The patriarchate of Constantinople possessed its own school where Byzantine theology continued to be taught. The use of the Greek language and Greek characters in its documents was permitted. In any case a considerable number of the higher Greek clergy completed their theological studies outside the Turkish Empire in the Venetian university of Padua. Byzantine type was set up in Venice since the Greeks had no printing press of their own in the Ottoman Empire.

The Byzantine magnates had to serve the Ottoman state. They were in charge of the Ottoman financial administration of the conquered Balkan lands. Here they took charge of the government of the country in place of the old dispossessed dynasties. In the Rumanian principalities the Rumanian hospodars were replaced by Byzantine magnates, who were called Phanariots from the Phanar quarter of Constantinople where their

380

palaces stood. They were hated by the native population. In spite of the Byzantine magnates the Greek Orthodox Church under the Ottomans remained a Church of poor people. Even the smaller landowners tended to become Muslim in order to keep their property. The Islamic minority in Bulgaria, Macedonia and Bosnia were for the most part recruited from this class. The Byzantine tenant farmers, the *paroikoi*, possessed no land. They had no inclination to deny their belief in order to keep their land. They maintained an unqualified fidelity to the Greek Orthodox Church, thus keeping their nationality as well as their faith.

The Byzantine Empire suffered a hard fate. But the disintegration of the state remained an unalterable fact. The Greeks lost their freedom and the universal mission of Byzantine civilization was ended.

Byzantium preserved the classical tradition and, more than that, it developed it further and then handed it on in this form to the West. It was not merely a symbolical gesture when the renaissance prince of Rimini, Malatesta, brought the bones of Gemistus Pletho to Italy and had them buried in the outer wall of the church of Rimini. This had the same symbolical significance as the translation of the bones of St Augustine from Carthage to Italy at the beginning of western culture. With his theology and his conception of the world Augustine had given being and form to the spirit of the West. But the work of Gemistus Pletho lived on in the Italian renaissance and through this survived up to the present day. His ideas have been a formative influence in the modern age in Europe.

The Byzantines preserved the cultural heritage of ancient Greece but scarcely developed it further. Above all, they kept the heritage of the thought of late antiquity. The genuine classical spirit, the sleeping Apollo, they left undisturbed. This only came to life again in the modern age, in the Italian renaissance. But Byzantium did indeed guard the treasures of classical science and learning, even though it had kept these in sealed containers waiting until the time came for the seals to be broken and the secrets revealed. Together with Islamic Syria and Egypt, which had also kept something of this knowledge, Byzantium had been able to invigorate it again and thus to provide the modern world with a foundation on which it could build further. This is particularly true of mathematics, astronomy and geography. It was on the basis of the work of the classical geographers handed down by Ptolemy that the Genoese Columbus found a path to the new world; it was with the help of Greek mathematics salvaged by the Byzantines that Michelangelo was able to construct the dome of St Peter. And the revival of the philosophy of Plato not only opened a new epoch in Byzantine culture but, in its last phase, it influenced the rise of a great European renaissance. This Byzantine mission was made possible by its possession of classical Greek literature, including the works of Homer, the tragedians and other poets. The transmission of this was one of Byzantium's greatest gifts to the West. For it was contact with this which stimulated a later day and generation to seek for the works of art of classical antiquity which lay concealed beneath the soil, so that the revival of classical literature was followed by the revival of classical art.

Chronological Table

Byzantine Emperors	Political development	Economics and law
	Construction of the road network in Asia Minor.	
	251: The Emperor Decius falls in the battle of Abrittus (Dacia) against the Goths.	
	260: The Emperor Valerian is taken prisoner by the Persian King Shapur I.	
	Diocletian creates a military zone between the Red Sea and the Euphrates.	The economic crisis reaches its peak. Inflation. The reforms of Diocletian.
324–337 Constantine I	Foundation and development of the state church.	
337–361 Constantius		System of combines. Heavily industrialized cities linked with provisioning regions (Rome-Sicily, Constantinople-Egypt).
361–363 Julian		
363–364 Jovian		
364–378 Valens		
379–395 Theodosius I		
395–408 Arcadius	395: Official separation of the eastern and western halves of the Empire.	*Codex Theodosianus*
408–450 Theodosius II		
	Construction of the wall fortifications of Constantinople.	
	431: Council of Ephesus. Secession of the Nestorians.	
450–457 Marcian		
457–474 Leo I		
474 Leo II		
474–475 Zeno	476: end of the western half of the Empire. Germanic principalities set up in the western half of the Empire.	
475–476 Basiliseos		
476–491 Zeno (again)		
491–518 Anastasius I	System of military settlements in the province of Libya.	*Lex Romana Visigothorum* (506), Spain. Germans outside the *imperium romanum*. The customary law of the Germanic peoples.
518–527 Justin I		
527–565 Justinian I		533: *Corpus juris civilis* of Justinian I (Latin). Early Greek version (paraphrase of Theophilus). The so-called Anonymus' Greek version of the *Digest*. Greek collections of canon law (*nomocanones*).
	Regions regained in Italy and Africa are governed by exarchs. War with Persia. Aim of the war is to secure the trade route to India.	
565–578 Justin II		Changeover to a measure of natural economy. Wages paid in part in kind by the state (officials' and soldiers' wages). Contraction of money economy. Firm control of domestic trade. Increase in planned economy. Little remains outside the system of assignment.
578–582 Tiberius I Constantine		
582–602 Maurice		

Literature and learning	Representational art	Music
c. 200: Clement of Alexandria. The Christian school of Alexandria reaches its peak. c. 240: Sextus Julius Africanus. Fusion of pagan and Christian chronography.	c. 200: Pictorial art in the house of God in spite of orthodox opposition from Christians and Jews. Early monuments: place of Christian cult and the synagogue at Dura-Europos. Painting in Christian and Jewish catacombs. Between 200 and 300: two illustrated redactions of the Scriptures based on the pericopes (lessons). Christian sculpture: bas-relief and full sculpture.	c. 200: Clement of Alexandria. Polemic against contemporary polyphonic music (Alexandrine). Coloratura condemned. Religious hymns sung to secular tunes (sailors' chanties). Instrumental accompaniment. Influence of folklore of the peoples on the periphery of musical life (Arab dance music in Dura-Europos. Negro music from the Sudan in Alexandria). The spiritual song of the eastern religions (Manichaeism and Judaeism), which has no instrumental accompaniment, influences the Christian church song.
University of Constantinople founded by Constantine. Ecclesiastical history of Eusebius.	Basilica and rotunda (mausoleum) determine ecclesiastical architecture which copies imperial secular buildings.	
Basil the Great, Gregory Nazianzus, and Gregory of Nyssa, the great Cappadocian theologians. John Chrysostom. Synesius of Cyrene. Expansion of the University of Constantinople (425).		Secular music (instruments: organ, trumpets, string instruments [lyre], cymbals).
Nonnus of Panopolis, *Dionysiaca*. Priscus, a diplomat turned historian.	End of the fifth century: sculpture banned from churches. Latest evidence: Studius basilica in Constantinople. Ambo of the St Panteleimon church in Thessalonica. Sculpture survives only on the periphery of the Empire: North Italy (Cividale), Armenia and Georgia. Oldest surviving icons: mid-sixth century from Egypt (Sinai, Bawit). The monophysite representation of Christ crucified. Evidence: frescoes in Santa Maria Antiqua in Rome (c. 700). Influence on the West via Ireland and Italy. The same holds for the monophysite picture of Mary: Icons of Santa Maria Maggiore in Rome. In illustrations to the Bible in the East, usually marginal miniatures (e.g. Rabula, Mesopotamia (586); non-Christian, Manichaean manuscripts of Turfan).	Unison hymns. Romanus. Influence of Jewish religious songs – Syriac church poetry – Adoption of Jewish ecphonic notation from which the Byzantine musical notation (neumes) developed.
Justinian closes the schools of Athens (529). Clericalization of higher education. John Malales (beginning of monastic chronicles). Comes Marcellinus (annalist). Corippus (Latin panegyric).	Models: the illustrations of classical manuscripts (Homer and the Roman comedians). Non-figural illustrations. Abandonment of the basilica and gradual change to the domed church. Construction of Hagia Sophia (537–562). The new monastic style, influenced by the icons. Early examples: frescoes of the episcopal church in Stobi in Macedonia, the rotunda of Perustica in Bulgaria (first half of the sixth century) and the church of St Euphemia in Constantinople.	
Annali ravennati John of Antioch (monastic historian).	Late antique naturalism continues on the periphery of the Empire: frescoes of Castelseprio (seventh century) and Qusayr Amrah (Jordan).	

	Byzantine Emperors	Political development	Economics and law
602–610	Phocas		
610–641	Heraclius	Byzantine and Persian Empires attacked by the Arabs spurred on by the new Muslim faith.	
641	Constantine III and Heraclonas		
641	Herclonas		
641–668	Constans II		
668–685	Constantine IV	Reorganization of the Empire with the introduction of themes. 674–678: siege of Constantinople. First use of Greek fire.	Between 600 and 800: private legal codes: *The Farmer's Law* (Georgikos Nomos) and the *Rhodian Sea Law*.
685–695	Justinian II		
695–698	Leontius		
698–705	Tiberius II		
705–711	Justinian II (again)		
711–713	Philippicus		
713–715	Anastasius II		
715–717	Theodosius III		
717–741	Leo III	Successful defence of Constantinople against the Arabs (717). 726: Beginning of the iconoclast controversy. Anti-monastic attitude of the Emperors.	726: the *Ecloga*.
741–775	Constantine V		
775–780	Leo IV		
780–797	Constantine VI		
797–802	Irene		
802–811	Nicephorus I		
811	Stauracius		
811–813	Michael I Rangabe		
813–820	Leo V		
820–829	Michael II		
829–842	Theophilus		
842–867	Michael III		
		842: End of iconoclast controversy. Mission to the Slavs: Constantine and Methodius. 864: Bulgaria, leading Balkan power accepts the Greek Orthodox faith.	*Procheiros Nomos*: between 867 and 879. *Epanagoge*: between 879 and 886. The *Tactica* (military manual), *c*. 900. Revision of canon law.
867–886	Basil I		Development of Byzantine foreign trade with the West. Treaties granting monopolies. Rise of Venice as distributor of Byzantine goods in the West.
886–912	Leo VI		
912–913	Alexander		Beginning of Venetian trading agreements with Muslim states.
913–959	Constantine VII	The legitimate Emperor overshadowed by a co-Emperor from the aristocracy.	
920–944	Romanus I Lecapenus		
956–963	Romanus II	Eastern policy of the Byzantine Empire is directed by the Asia Minor magnates.	Result of blockade of Byzantine and Islamic goods: Beginning of shortage of luxury wares in the West. Development of a western industry in North Italy and the Rhine valley.
963–969	Nicephorus II Phocus		
969–976	John I Tzimisces		
976–1025	Basil II	Russia accepts Orthodox Christianity.	
.1025–1028	Constantine VIII		Emperors from the aristocratic magnate class give up a planned economy. Liberalizing of the grain trade.
1028–1034	Romanus III Argyrus		
1034–1041	Michael IV		
1041–1042	Michael V	Dynastic crisis arises out of a struggle for control of the government.	
1042	Zoe and Theodora		
1042–1055	Constantine IX Monomachus		
1055–1056	Theodora (again)		
1056–1057	Michael VI		
1057–1059	Isaac I Comnenus		
1059–1067	Constantine X Ducas	The Byzantine Empire faces a double threat from Seljuk Turks attacking Asia Minor and from the Normans in Europe.	Economic crisis. The attempt to create a state monopoly of corn overturns price control.
1068–1071	Romanus IV Diogenes		
1071–1078	Michael VII Ducas		

Literature and learning	Representational art	Music
Menander (imperial historian). John of Epiphania (imperial historian). Closing of the University of Constantinople. Reopened under Heraclius. Patriarchal school. Invention of Greek fire. Theophylact Simacattes (imperial historian). George of Pisidia (Greek panegyric).		Patriarch Sergius as hymn-writer.
		Andrew of Crete.
		Cosmas of Jerusalem. John of Damascus. Church hymns in the form of a canon.
730: closing of the university of Constantinople.	Iconoclast controversy.	
Monastic chronicles (world chronicles). Theophanes. Nicephorus. George the Monk. Casia, first Byzantine poetess (religious poetry, aphorisms, maxims, epigrams). University activity in Constantinople under Theophilus. 860: refounding of the university of Constantinople under Bardas Caesar. The literary salon of Photius. The *Bibliotheca* (literary criticism) and dictionary.	Early period of the frescoes in the Cappadocian rock churches.	
	Mosaics of the Koimesis church in Nicaea. Mosaics in the narthex of Hagia Sophia.	
Beginning of a new style of world history. Manual of extracts from historical writings. Encyclopedias of agriculture, medicine and veterinary medicine. Dictionary of the *Suda*. Works on imperial traditions. New hagiographical collection (Symeon Metaphrastes).		
	Mosaics of Hosios Loukas.	
1045: Reorganization of the university of Constantinople. Faculties of Philosophy (rector Psellus) and Law (rector John Xiphelinus) are set up.	Mosaics of Nea Moni on Chios and the Sophia church in Kiev.	
Michael Psellus (1018–?1078). Commentaries on Plato and Aristotle. Treatises on scientific problems. Letters, orations, legal works. Contemporary history (976–1077).		Hymnography ceases with the ending of liturgical development.

Byzantine Emperors		Political development	Economics and law
1078–1081	Nicephorus III Botaneiates		Debasement of the Byzantine currency. Reduction of gold content of the *solidus*. Revision of canon law by Theodore Vestes (*c.* 1090).
1081–1118	Alexius I Comnenus	1082: Alliance with Venice.	
1118–1143	John II Comnenus	Struggle with the Hohenstaufen for control of the Mediterranean.	
1143–1180	Manuel I Comnenus		
1180–1183	Alexias II Comnenus		End of independent Byzantine economy by reason of privileges granted to the Italian maritime cities. Individual treaties with these cities limit Byzantine sovereignty.
1183–1185	Andronicus I Comnenus		
1185–1195	Isaac II Angelus		
1195–1203	Alexius III Angelus		
1203–1204	Isaac II Angelus (again) and Alexius IV Angelus	1202–1204: Fourth Crusade. Capture of Constantinople. Setting up of the Latin Empire.	
1204	Alexius V Murtzuphlus	Political consolidation in Asia Minor: Empire of Nicaea.	Sound economic basis of the Byzantine Empire in Asia Minor.
1204–1222	Theodore I Lascaris		
1222–1254	John III Ducas Vatatzes		
1254–1258	Theodore II Lascaris	1250: Defeat by Louis IX of France at Damietta in Egypt.	
1258–1261	John IV Lascaris	1261: Constantinople rdtaken by the Byzantines.	
1261–1282	Michael VIII Palaeologus	Alliance between the Byzantine Empire and the Ilkhan Hulagu of Persia against the Seljuks of Asia Minor. 1272: alliance with the Tatars of South Russia. 1274: Union between Byzantine and Roman churches.	1261: Treaty of Nymphaeum. Political and economic agreements give the command of the straits to the Genoese.
1282–1328	Andronicus II Palaeologus	1282: Sicilian Vespers and the end of the Latin Empire.	
1328–1341	Andronicus III Palaeologus		
1341–1391	John V Palaeologus	Beginning of the period of decline. Byzantium between the rising Ottoman state and the national states in the Balkans (Serbia, Bulgaria) and Hungary.	The Byzantine Empire is the base for Genoese trade with eastern Asia.
1347–1354	John VI Cantacuzenus		
1376–1379	Andronicus IV Palaeologus		
1390	John VIII Palaeologus		
1391–1425	Manuel II Palaeologus	Internal disintegration: social struggles between magnates and zelots. Failure to change the old universal Byzantine Empire into a national state in the Peloponnese.	
1425–1448	John VIII Palaeologus		
1448–1453	Constantine XI Palaeologus	Conquest of Constantinople by the Turks (1453). Certain Greek regions survive under Venetian rule until the eighteenth century (areas of Byzantine culture).	

Literature and learning	Representational art	Music
High officials as historians: Michael Attaleiates, John Scylitzes, *The history of poor Leo*, John Zonaras.	Mosaics of Daphni. Sculpture reappears in ecclesiastical buildings (marble icons).	
	Mosaics of the *capella palatina* in Palermo, cathedrals of Cefalu and Torcello.	
Theodore Prodromus, representative of Byzantine satirists. Composes in vernacular and in the literary language.	Imperial portraits in the galleries of Hagia Sophia.	
Porikologos.	Frescoes in the church of Nerezi in Macedonia. Naturalistic style.	
	Mosaics of San Marco in Venice.	
First sagas of epic poetry in the vernacular. *Digenis Akritas* (first redaction of this epic), *Bellhandros and Chrysantzas, Callimachus and Chrysorrhoe.*		
Theodore II Lascaris: centre of a circle of scholars. Correspondence with the famous scholars of his day.	Painting of the Palaeologan renaissance: frescoes of the Boiana church in Bulgaria.	
Philosophical, rhetorical and theological writings. Theodorus Metochites (*d.* 1332) donor of the mosaics of the Chora church. Statesman, philosopher and scientist. Collection of writings on philosophical, historical and philological subjects. Further works on philosophy and astronomy. *Chronicle of the Morea. The old knight.* Byzantino–Greek folk songs. *The Rhodian Love Songs. Florius and Platziaphlora.*	Mosaics of the *deesis* in Hagia Sophia. Mosaics in the narthex of the Chora church (Kariye Cami) in Constantinople and the frescoes of its mortuary chapel.	Return to the musical taste of late antiquity. Coloratura and embellishments in church music. Hence the extension and perfection of the system of notation (neumes). Musical forms and the performance of Greek folk songs is influenced by the Albanian migrants (Pidiktos, the leaping dance).
Gemisthus Plethon (1355–?1452): chief justice in the Byzantine province of the Peloponnese and head of the Platonic Academy in Mistra has as pupils Patriarch Gennadius and Cardinal Bessarione. Chief work: *Nomon Syngraphe.* An opponent of Christianity. Political thinker. Influence on the Italian renaissance.	Frecoes in the church of the Pantanassa in Mistra.	
Libistrus and Rhodamne.		
The legend of the respected ass.		
Erotocritus (*c.* 1550).		

Bibliography

1 GENERAL WORKS

G. Ostrogorsky, *History of the Byzantine State,* transl. J. M. Hussey (Oxford 1968)

A. A. Vasiliev, *History of the Byzantine Empire,* 2 vols. (Madison 1958)

Cambridge Medieval History, IV (new ed.) I *Byzantium and its Neighbours* (1966); II *Government, Church and Civilization* (1967)

L. Bréhier, *Le monde byzantin,* 3 vols. (Paris 1947-50)

J. B. Bury, *History of the East Roman Empire from the fall of Irene to the accession of Basil I* (London 1912)

J. B. Bury, *History of the Later Roman Empire from Arcadius to Irene,* 2 vols., 1st ed. (London 1889) (2nd ed., London, 1923, to the end of Justinian's reign)

C. Diehl, *Byzantium: Greatness and Decline,* with introd. by P. Charanis (New Brunswick 1957)

E. Gibbon, *The History of the Decline and Fall of the Roman Empire,* 7 vols., ed. J. B. Bury (London 1896-1900)

J. M. Hussey, *The Byzantine World,* 3rd ed. (London 1967)

R. Jenkins, *Byzantium: the imperial centuries AD 610 to 1071* (London 1966)

M. V. Levchenko, *Byzance des origines à 1453* French transl. by P. Mabille (Paris 1949)

E. Stein, *Histoire de Bas-Empire,* I, French transl. in 2 vols. (Paris 1959); II, ed. by J. R. Palanque (Paris-Brussels-Amsterdam 1949)

2 SPECIAL SUBJECTS

PAPYROLOGY:

A. Bataille, *Les papyrus* (Traité d'études byzantines II), Paris 1955

V. Grumel, *Chronologie* (Traité d'études byzantines I), Paris 1957

DOCUMENTS:

F. Dölger, *Byzantinische Diplomatik* (Munich 1956)

SIGILLOGRAPHY:

G. Schlumberger, *Sigillographie de l'empire byzantin* (Paris 1884)

CHRONOLOGY:

V. Grumel, *Chronologie* (Paris 1957)

PALAEOGRAPHY:

V. Gardthausen, *Griechische Paläographie,* 2nd ed. (Leipzig 1913)

W. Schubart, *Griechische Paläographie* (= Handbuch d. klass. Altert.-Wissenschaft I, 4, I) Munich 1925

HISTORY OF LITERATURE:

K. Krumbacher, *Geschichte der byzantinischen Literatur,* 2nd ed., Munich 1897 (= Handbuch d. klass. Altert.-Wissenschaft IX, I).

Gy. Moravcsik, *Byzantinoturcica,* 2 vols., 2nd ed. (Berlin 1958)

CHURCH HISTORY AND THEOLOGY:

H. G. Beck, *Kirche und theologische Literatur im byzantinischen Reich,* Munich 1959 (= Handbuch d. klass. Altert.-Wissenschaft II, I).

J. Pargoire, *L'Église byzantine de 527 à 847* (Paris 1905)

G. Every, *The Byzantine Patriarchate,* 2nd ed. (London 1962)

R. M. French, *The Eastern Orthodox Church* (London 1951)

T. Ware, *The Orthodox Church* (London 1963)

HISTORY OF ART:

D. Talbot Rice, *The Art of Byzantium* (London 1959)

D. Talbot Rice, *Art of the Byzantine Era* (London 1963)

A. Banck, *Byzantine Art in the Collections of the USSR* (Moscow-Leningrad 1966)

G. Mathew, *Byzantine Aesthetics* (London 1963)

W. F. Volbach and M. Hirmer, *Early Christian Art* (London, New York 1964)

O. Wulff, *Die altchristliche und byzantinische Kunst,* I, Berlin-Neubabelsberg 1913, II, 1918 and Supplement, 1939.

W. Felicetti-Liebenfels, *Geschichte der byzantinischen Ikonenmalerei* (Lausanne 1956)

O. Demus, *Byzantine Mosaic Decoration,* 2nd ed. (London 1953)

M. van Berchem and E. Clouzot, *Mosaïques chrétiennes du IVme au Xme siècle* (Geneva 1924)

T. Whittemore, *The Mosaics of Haghia Sophia at Istanbul,* I-IV (Oxford 1933-52). (For later reports see Dumbarton Oaks Papers IX, 1955 onwards.)

G. Millet, *Broderies religieuses de style byzantin* (= Bibliothèque de l'Ecole des Hautes Études, Sciences religieuses, vol. IV, I-II), Paris 1939

E. Goldschmidt and K. Weitzmann, *Die byzantinischen Elfenbein-skulpturen des 10.-13. Jahrhunderts,* 2 vols., Berlin (I, Elfenbeinkästen, 1930; II, Elfenbeinreliefs, 1934)

L. Brehier, *La Sculpture et les Arts mineurs byzantins* (in Histoire de l'Art byzantin, ed. Ch. Diehl), Paris 1936

K. Weitzmann, *Die byzantinische Buchmalerei des IX. and X. Jahrhunderts* (Berlin 1935)

H. Omont, *Miniatures des plus anciens Manuscrits grecs de la Bibliothèque Nationale du VIe au XIVe siècle,* Paris 1929 (I: Text, II: Plates)

A. Grabar, *Miniatures byzantines de la Bibliothèque Nationale* (Paris 1939)

G. de Jerphanion, *Une nouvelle province de l'art byzantin. Les Églises rupestres de Cap-padoce* (Paris 1925-42), 2 vols. in 2 parts, 3 albums

L. Matzulewitsch, *Byzantinische Antike. Studien auf Grund der Silbergefässe der Ermitage* (= Archäologische Mitteilungen aus russischen Sammlungen, Vol. II), Berlin 1929

D. Talbot Rice, *Byzantine Glazed Pottery* (Oxford 1930)

C. H. Morgan, *Corinth,* Vol. XI, *The Byzantine Pottery.* American School of Classical Studies in Athens (Cambridge, Mass. 1942)

J. Ebersolt, *Monuments d'architecture byzantine* (Paris 1934)

D. Talbot Rice, *The Great Palace of the Byzantine Emperors,* 2 vols. (London 1947-58)

A. Graber, *L'Empereur dans l'art byzantin* (Paris 1936)

A. Xyngopoulos, *Thessalonique et la peinture macédonienne* (Thessalonica 1955)

INFLUENCE OF BYZANTINE ART ON NEIGHBOURING LANDS:

B. Filow, *Geschichte der altbulgarischen Kunst* (Berlin, Leipzig 1932)

A. Grabar, *La Peinture religieuse en Bulgarie* (Paris 1928)

V. N. Lazarev, *Istorija Russkogo Iskusstva,* Part I, II, III (Moscow 1953-55)

G. Millet, *L'Ancien art serbe. Les églises* (Paris 1919)

M. Corović-Ljubinković, *Pećko-Dečanska ikonopisna škola od XIV do XIX veka* (Belgrade 1955)

S. Radojčić, *Majstori starog srpskog slikarstva* (Belgrade 1955)

N. Iorga, *Les arts mineurs en Roumanie,* 2 vols. (Bucarest 1934)

N. Jorga and G. Bals, *Histoire de l'art roumain ancien* (Paris 1922)

C. H. Wendt, *Rumänische Ikonenmalerei* (Eisenach 1953)

D. Ainalov, *Geschichte der russischen Monumentalkunst zur Zeit des Grossfürstentums Moskau* (Berlin-Leipzig 1933)

O. Bihalji-Merin, *Fresken und Ikonen. Mittelalterliche Kunst in Serbien und Makedonien* (Munich 1958)

O. Demus, *The Mosaics of Norman Sicily* (London 1949)

A. Medea, *Gli affreschi delle cripte eremitiche pugliesi,* 2 vols. (Rome 1939)

F. Macler, *L'Architecture arménienne dans ses rapports avec l'art syrien,* I (Syria 1920)

Sirarpie Der Nersessian, *Armenia and the Byzantine Empire* (Cambridge, Mass. 1947)

J. Baltrusaitis, *Études sur l'art médiéval en Géorgie et en Arménie* (Paris 1929)

K. Weitzmann, *Die armenische Buchmalerei des 10. und beginnenden 11. Jahrhunderts* (Bamberg 1933)

J. Baltrusaitis, *L'église cloisonnée en Orient et en Occident* (Paris 1941)

BYZANTINE MUSIC AND THE WEST:

E. Wellesz, *Eastern Elements in Western Chant* (Mon. Mus. Byz., Subs. II), Boston 1947

H. J. W. Tillyard, *Byzantine Music and Hymnography* (London 1928); 2nd ed. (Oxford 1961)

E. Wellesz, *History of Byzantine Music and Hymnography*, 2nd ed. (Oxford 1961)

THE MONASTIC MOVEMENT:

D. J. Chitty, *The Desert a City* (Oxford 1966)

H. Delehaye, *Les Saints stylites* (= Société des Bollandistes, Subsidia Hagiographica, XIV), Brussels 1923

E. Amande de Mendieta, *La presqu'île des caloyers: le Mont-Athos* ((Bruges 1955)

J. M. Hussey, *Church and Learning in the Byzantine Empire 807-1185* (London 1937)

A. M. Ammann, *Die Gottesschau in palamitischen Hesychasmus. Ein Handbuch der spätbyzantinischen Mystik* (= Das östliche Christentum, ed. Georg Wunderle, Heft 6-7), Würzburg 1938

I. Hausherr, *La méthode d'oraison hésychaste* (Orientalia Christiana IX, Teil 2), 1927

J. Meyendorff, *Introduction à l'étude de Grégoire Palamas* (Paris 1959)

V. Lossky, *The Mystical Theology of the Eastern Church* (London 1957)

J. Daniélou, *Platonisme et théologie mystique* (Paris 1944)

D. L. Raschella, *Saggio storico sul Monachismo italo-greco in Calabria* (Messina 1925)

THE BYZANTINE ARMY AND ITS ORGANIZATION:

F. Aussaresses, *L'Armée byzantine* (Paris 1909)

A. Pertusi, 'La Formation des Thèmes Byzantins', *Berichte zum XI. Internationalen Byzantinisten-Kongress* (Munich 1958)

H. W. Haussig, *Anfänge der Themenordnung*, pp. 82-114, in F. Altheim and R. Stiehl, *Finanzgeschichte der Spätantike* (Frankfurt/Main 1957)

THE BYZANTINE NAVY:

H. Ahrweiler, *Byzance et la mer* (Paris 1966)

E. Eickhoff, *Seekrieg und Seepolitik zwischen Islam und Abendland bis zum Aufstiege Pisas und Genuas (650-1040)*, 1954.

AGRARIAN POLICY:

G. Ostrogorsky, in *Cambridge Economic History*, I, 2nd ed., Cambridge 1966, pp. 205-34 and Bibliography, pp. 774-9.

G. Ostrogorsky, *Pour l'histoire de la féodaleté byzantine* (Paris 1954)

G. Ostrogorsky, *Quelques problèmes d'histoire de la paysannerie byzantine* (Brussels 1956)

A. Lemerle, 'Esquisse pour une histoire agraire de Byzance', *Revue Historique*, 219 (1958) and 220 (1958)

THE CAPITAL CONSTANTINOPLE:

R. Janin, *Constantinople byzantine*, 2nd ed. (Paris 1950)

R. Janin, *La Géographie ecclésiastique de l'Empire Byzantin*, Part I, *Le Siège de Constantinople et le Patriarchat Oecuménique*, III, *Les Églises et les Monastères* (Paris 1953)

A. M. Schneider, *Byzanz Vorarbeiten zur Topographie und Archäologie der Stadt* (Berlin 1936)

R. Mayer, *Byzantion, Konstantinopolis, Istanbul. Eine genetische Stadtgeographie*, Vienna 1943 (Akademie der Wissenschaften in Wien, Philosophisch-historische Klasse, Denkschriften, 71 Band, 3. Abhandlung)

INTERNAL ADMINISTRATION:

H. Geiss, *Geld- und naturalwirtschafliche Erscheinungsformen im staatlichen Aussbau Italiens während der Gotenzeit* (= Vierteljahrschrift für Sozial- und Wirtschaftsgeschichte, Beiheft 27), Stuttgart 1931

G. Rouillard, *L'administration civile de l'Egypte byzantine* (Paris 1928)

L. M. Hartmann, *Untersuchungen zur Geschichte der byzantinischen Verwaltung in Italien (540-750)*, Leipzig 1889

G. Ostrogorsky, 'Das Steuersystem im byzantinischen Altertum und Mittelalter', *Byzantion* 6 (1931), pp. 229-40

J. Danstrup, 'Indirect Taxation at Byzantium', *Classica et Mediaevalia 8* (1946)

E. Stein, *Studien zur Geschichte des byzantinischen Reiches* (Stuttgart 1919)

G. Stadtmüller, 'Oströmische Bauern- und Wehrpolitik', *Neue Jahrbücher für deutsche Wissenschaft*, 13 (1937), pp. 421-38.

ECONOMIC HISTORY AND FINANCE:

A. Andréadès, 'Les Finances byzantines', *Revue des sciences politiques*, 3me série, 26e année (1911), pp. 268-86, 620-30.

A. Andréadès, 'De la monnaie et de la puissance, d'achat des métaux précieux dans l'Empire byzantin', *Byzantion*, I (1924), pp. 75-115

G. Ostrogorsky, 'Löhne und Preise in Byzanz', *Byzantinische Zeitschrift*, 32 (1932), pp. 377-87

F. Dölger, *Beiträge zur Geschichte der byzantinischen Finanzverwaltung besonders des 10. und 11. Jahrhunderts* (= Byzantinisches Archiv, ed. A. Heisenberg, Heft 9), Leipzig 1927

A. Stöckle, *Spätrömische und byzantinische Zünfte* (= Klio, Beiheft 9), Leipzig 1911

G. Mickwitz, *Die Kartelfunktionen der Zünfte* (= Societas Scientiarum Fennica, Commentationes Humanarum Litterarum 8, Fasc. 3)

J. Nicole, *Le Livre du Préfet ou l'Edit de L'Empereur Léon le Sage sur les corporations de Constantinople* (Geneva 1894)

F. Dölger, 'Die Frage des Grundeigentums', in *Byzanz und die europäische Staatenwelt* (Ettal 1953), pp. 217-31

F. Dölger, 'Zum Gebührenwesen der Byzantiner', in *op.cit.* (Ettal 1953), pp. 232-60

P. S. Leicht, *Corporazioni romane e arte medievali*, ch. 3 (Turin 1937)

G. Ostrogorsky, 'Die ländliche Steuergemeinde des byzantinischen Reiches im 10. Jahrhundert', *Vierteljahrschrift für Sozial- und Wirtschaftsgeschichte*, 20 (1927), pp. 1-108

R. Gaignerot, *Des Bénéfices militaires dans l'Empire romain et spécialement en Orient et au Xme siècle* (Bordeaux 1896)

A. Ferradou, *Les Biens des monastères à Byzance* (Bordeaux 1896)

G. Ostrogorsky, Die wirtschaftlichen und sozialen Entwicklungsgrundlagen des byzantinischen Reiches, *Vierteljahrschrift für Sozial – und Wirtschaftsgeschichte*, 22 (129-43)

L. C. West, *Byzantine Egypt: Economic Studies*, Princeton Univ. Stud. in Papyr. 6 (Princeton 1949)

S. Lopez, 'La crise du besant au Xe siècle et la date du Livre du Préfet', *Annuaire Inst. de Phil. et d'Hist. Or. et Slav.* 10 (1950), pp. 403 f.

S. Lopez, 'Silk Industry in the Byzantine Empire', *Speculum XX* (1945), pp. 1-42

S. Lopez, *Byzantine Studies* (New Haven 1968)

F. M. Heichelheim, *Byzantinische Seiden*, Ciba-Rundschau, (Basle 1949)

BYZANTINE INTERNATIONAL TRADE:

N. Pigulevskaja, *Byzanz auf den Wegen nach Indien*, German transl. (Berlin 1968)

R. E. M. Wheeler, 'Arikamedu: An Indo-Roman Trading Station on the East Coast of India', *Ancient India 2* (1946).

W. Heyd, *Commerce du Levant au Moyen-âge*, French transl. by F. Raynaud, 2nd ed. (Leipzig 1923)

LANGUAGE AND THE VERNACULAR IN THE BYZANTINE EMPIRE:

H. Zilliacus, *Zum Kampf der Weltsprachen im oströmischen Reich* (Helsinki 1935)

M. Vasmer, *Die Slawen in Griechenland* (Berlin 1941)

A. A. Vasiliev, 'Slavjane v Grecii', *Viz. Vrem.*, 5 (1898), pp. 404-38 and 626-70

IMPERIAL CEREMONIAL:

A. Alföldi, 'Die Ausgestaltung des monarchischen Zeremoniells am römischen Kaiserhofe', *Mitt. d. Deutschen Archäol. Inst., Röm. Abt. 49* (1934), pp. 1-118

A. Alföldi, 'Insignien und Tracht der römischen Kaiser', *Mitt. d. Deutschen Archäol. Inst., Röm. Abt. 50* (1935), pp. 1-171

O. Treitinger, *Die oströmische Kaiser- und Reichsidee nach ihrer Gestaltung im höfischen Zeremoniell* (Jena 1938)

A. Grabar, *L'Empereur dans l'Art byzantin* (Paris 1936)

REGISTERS:

(a) Imperial:

Regesten der Kaiserurkunden des oströmischen Reiches (Corpus der griechischen Urkunden des Mittelalters und der neuren Zeit, Reihe A, Abt. I), I-V (Munich and Berlin 1924-65)

(b) Patriarch of Constantinople:

V. Grumel, *Les Regestes des Actes du Patriarchat de Constantinople*, Vol. I: Les Actes des Patriarches, fasc. I: 381-715; fasc. II: 715-1043; fasc. III: 1043-1206, Socii Assumptionistae Chalcedonenses 1932, 1936, 1947

LAW:

K. E. Zachariä v. Lingenthal, *Geschichte des griechisch-römischen Rechtes* (Berlin 1892)
J. and P. Zepos, *Jus graeco-romanum*, 8 (Athens 1931)

BYZANTINE NUMISMATICS:

W. Wroth, *Catalogue of the Imperial Byzantine Coins in the British Museum*, 2 vols. (London 1908)
H. Goodacre, *A Handbook of the Coinage of the Byzantine Empire*, 3 vols., new ed. (London 1957)
P. Grierson, 'Coinage and Money in the Byzantine Empire 498- c.1090', *Settimani de studio del Centro italiano di studi sull'alto medioevo* (Spoleto 1960), 8 (1961), pp. 411-53

REGIONAL STUDIES:

D. Zakythinos, *Le despotat grec de Morée*, 2 vols. (Paris 1932 and 1950)
A. Bon, *Le Péloponnèse byzantin jusqu'en 1204* (Paris 1951)
H. Ahrweiler, 'L'histoire et la géographie de la région de Smyrne', in *Travaux et Mémoires* I (Paris 1965)
D. M. Nicol, *The despotate of Epiros* (Oxford 1957)
A. Gardiner, *The Lascarids of Nicaea* (London 1912)
W. Miller, *Trebizond: the Last Greek Empire* (London 1926)
W. Miller, *Essays on the Latin Orient* (Cambridge 1921)
W. Miller, *The Latins in the Levant: a History of Frankish Greece (1204-1566)*, London 1908

NEIGHBOURING STATES

Persia:

A. Christensen, *L'Iran sous les Sassanides*, 2nd ed. (Copenhagen 1944)
B. Spuler, *Die Mongolen in Iran* (Berlin 1955)

Seljuks:

F. Taeschner, 'The Turks and the Byzantine Empire to the end of the thirteenth century', *Cambridge Medieval History*, IV, new ed., (1966), Pt. I, pp. 737-52.
T. Talbot Rice, *The Seljuks* (London 1961)

Russia:

D. Obolensky, 'Russia's Byzantine Heritage', *Oxford Slavonic Papers* I (Oxford, 1950)
G. Vernadsky, *The Origins of Russia* (Oxford 1959)

Bulgaria:

S. Runciman, *A History of the First Bulgarian Empire* (London 1930)

Serbia and Bosnia:

M. Miadenovitch, *L'État serbe au Moyen Âge: son caractère* (Paris 1931)
W. Miller, 'The Byzantine Inheritance in South-Eastern Europe', in *Byzantium* (edd. N. H. Baynes and H.St.L.B. Moss), Oxford 1948, pp. 326-37
C. Jireček, *La Civilisation serbe au Moyen Âge* (Paris 1920)
C. Jireček, *Geschichte der Serben*, 2 vols. (Gotha 1911-18)
I. von Bojničić, *Geschichte Bosniens (bis 1463)*, Leipzig 1885
F. Dölger, 'Die mittelalterliche Kultur auf dem Balkan als byzantinisches Erbe', in *Byzanz und die europäische Staatenwelt* (Ettal 1953) pp. 261-81
L. Niederle, *Slovanské starožitnosti*, 4 vols. (Prague 1906-27)
D. Obolensky, *The Bogomils* (Cambridge 1948)

Byzantium and Italy:

C. Diehl, *Études sur l'administration byzantine dans l'Exarchat de Ravenne* (Paris 1888)
J. Gay, *L'Italie méridionale et l'empire byzantin (867-1071)*, Paris 1904
F. Chalandon, *Histoire de la domination normande en Italie et en Sicilie* (Paris 1907)
M. Setton, 'The Byzantine Background to the Italian Renaissance', *Proceedings of the American Philosophical Society*, Vol. 100, Nr. I, February 1956
W. Norden, *Das Papsttum und Byzanz* (Berlin 1903)
D. J. Geanakoplos, *Byzantine East and Latin West* (Oxford 1966)

Byzantium and the Arabs:

M. Amari, *Storia dei Musulmani di Sicilia*, 3 vols. (Florence 1854-68)
A. A. Vasiliev, H. Gregoire, M. Canard and others, *Byzance et les Arabes*, I, II, 1 and 2 (Brussels 1935-68)
G. Marçais, *Le monde oriental de 395 à 1081* (Paris 1936)

Byzantium and Rumania:

N. Jorga, *La Survivance byzantine dans les pays roumains* (Bucarest 1913)

Byzantium and the Ottoman Turks:

H. Gibbons, *The Foundation of the Ottoman Empire* (Oxford 1916)
P. Wittek, *The rise of the Ottoman empire* (London 1938)
F. Babinger, *Beiträge zur Frühgeschichte der Türkenherrschaft in Rumelien (14. and 15. Jahrh.)* Südosteuropäische Arbeiten 34 (Brno-Munich-Vienna 1944)

Byzantium and the Maritime Italian Cities:

G. I. Bratianu, *Recherches sur le commerce génois dans la Mer Noir au XIIIe siècle* (Paris 1929)
E. Č. Skržinskaja, 'Genuezcy v Konstantinopole v XIV v.', *Viz. Vrem.* 26 (1947), pp. 215-34
H. Kretschmayr, *Geschichte von Venedig*, 2 vols (Leipzig 1905-20)

Byzantium and Armenia:

F. Tournebize, *Histoire politique et religieuse de l'Arménie* (Paris 1910)
L. Alishan, *Sissouan ou l'Arméno-Cilicie*, transl. from the Armenian (Venice 1899)
Sirarpie Der Nersessian, *Armenia and the Byzantine Empire* (Cambridge, Mass. 1945)
P. Charanis, *The Armenians in the Byzantine Empire*, Lisbon (n.d.) and in *Byzantinoslavica* 22 (1961)

Byzantium and Georgia:

A. Sanders, *Kaukasien, Geschichtlicher Umriss* (Munich 1944)
G. Brosset, *Histoire de la Géorgie* (Petersburg 1860-61)
W. E. D. Allen, *History of the Georgian People* (London 1932)

Byzantium and the Jews:

J. Starr, *The Jews in the Byzantine Empire, 641-1204* (= Texte und Forschungen zur byzantinisch-neugriechischen Philologie, ed. N. A. Bees, Nr. 30), Athens 1939
P. Browe, 'Die Judengesetzgebung Justinians', *Analecta Gregoriana*, 8 (Rome 1935), pp. 109-46
F. Dölger, 'Die Frage der Judensteuer in Byzanz', *Vierteljahrschrift für Sozial- und Wirtschaftsgeschichte*, 26 (1933), pp. 1-24

Notes to the illustrations

1

THE APSE. SAN VITALE, RAVENNA

San Vitale in Ravenna was dedicated in 547 and, in contrast to the great ecclesiastical imperial edifices in Constantinople which were despoiled by the iconoclasts, it is probably the only church of Justinian's day which has preserved its original mosaics almost intact. At the time of the church's dedication, Ravenna was practically the only Byzantine stronghold in the bitter struggle against the Ostrogoths; moreover, San Vitale was founded not by the Emperor but by Julian, a Syrian banker. In spite of this it has marked stylistic affinities with the style of the capital and its art bears the imperial imprint. In the apse there are mosaic portraits of the imperial couple, Justinian standing on the Gospel side, the Empress Theodora on the Epistle side. In the vaulting of the apse between the two imperial portraits and above the windows Christ sits enthroned on the sphere of the world between two archangels, Vitalis, the patron saint of the church, and Bishop Ecclesius who built it. With a superb gesture, borrowed from an Iranian model of the investiture of Ardashir by Ahura Mazda on a relief in Naksh-i-Rustam, Christ is holding out the ring to St Vitalis as the symbol of his authority over the church. The tones of the different kinds of inlaid marble, also present in the varied ornamentation of the pavement, as well as the mosaic colouring, blend extraordinarily well, and reflect the light penetrating through the windows, thus producing in the interior of the church a highly individual atmosphere. For the West, San Vitale provided the most perfect blending of sacred and imperial responsibilities. It is not surprising that the architect of the Christian West, Charlemagne, took this church as the model for his *capella palatina,* the present church of St Mary in Aachen, though there the mosaics have been subjected to an unfortunate restoration.

2

THE ASCENSION. Miniature from the collection of Homilies on the Virgin by the monk James of Kokkinobaphos. Paris, Bibliothèque Nationale (Cod. gr. 1208).

The miniatures in this manuscript are by an unknown 12th-century artist. His extraordinary feeling for colour places his work in the forefront of Byzantine miniaturists insofar as effects of this kind are concerned. The miniature shown here gives the Ascension. Christ amidst a gloriole of four angels is ascending heavenward, while the Mother of God and the apostles, deeply moved by this supernatural event, stand watching Him. In the miniature the scene is set in a church. It is not difficult to recognize the church of the Holy Apostles with its main dome and four smaller domes, as can be seen today in San Marco in Venice, which was a copy of it. As with the

palace of Theodoric the Ostrogoth in Sant'Apollinare Nuovo in Ravenna, the device of turning back both sides of the building is used, so that the interior is visible (Pl. 4). In the case of Ravenna, this is in order to reveal the peristyle of the palace which here runs round the central courtyard under the main dome. It also shows the marvellous inlaid work of the church which no longer exists, as well as the mosaic of the group of apostles in the vaulting. The church of the Holy Apostles was the imperial burial place, though the tombs in which the Emperors found their last rest were not in the church itself but outside in a *campo santo.* Some, like Justinian, had a special mausoleum erected. Today both imperial tombs and church have vanished to make room for the Sultan Mohammed II mosque.

3

THE NORTH SIDE OF TEKFUR SARAY, ISTANBUL

The ruins known by the Turks as Tekfur Saray are the only remains of a Byzantine palace standing in Constantinople, at least in the outer walls. There is a second palace dating from the Byzantine period, the so-called Palace of Justinian on the sea wall, part of which, with the loggia facing the sea of Marmora, is still preserved, but this permits no more than general conclusions about the original state of the façade. Tekfur Saray has on it monograms of the Palaeologi suggesting that it was probably built by a member of this family in the second half of the 13th century.

The clearly divided façade looks at first sight as if it had links with the Florentine palaces of the early Renaissance. The architecture of Tekfur Saray leads one to believe that there may be a connection between the Byzantine palace architecture of the 13th century and that of the Florentine palazzi of the 15th century similar to that found in the 8th and first half of the 9th centuries between the East Roman buildings of Ravenna and the creations of the Carolingian renaissance (such as the *capella palatina* in Aachen).

The building had two storeys inside it, no longer in existence today. The ground floor opens on to the north side in the form of a portico. The façade of the first floor is closely connected to the pillared hall of the ground floor by its vertical divisions. Three pilasters spring from the ground up to the arch of the first floor. Two further pilasters from the first floor are not continued right down to the ground level of the ground floor but stop just above the pillars of the ground floor. The second floor is separated from that beneath it by a broad ornamental strip running horizontally. This separation is still further emphasized in that the arches in the arcade of the ground floor are the same width across as those of the first floor which stand out sharply from the façade, while the arches on the second floor have a much smaller span. Also in the upper storey the

391

pillars of the arches correspond to the different width of the arches in this floor and so they cannot be continued down into the pillars of the storey underneath. It is this which distinguishes this Byzantine palace building from the Florentine palaces, such as the Pitti and the Strozzi, where the horizontal line of the mouldings is balanced by a vertical arrangement of the windows which is carried right through and not broken.

There is also a striking difference in the bonding. The plain of the wall in the Florentine palaces is treated as *rustica,* rustic work, that is, by means of a strong emphasis, the joints of the hewn stone are brought out into strong relief as part of the construction of the whole wall. In Byzantine palace building the joints are small and the stones smooth and fitted closely into each other. Here the arrangement is in horizontal bands on three layers of narrow bricks. On these are then placed three layers of sandstone. In the arches, layers of brick alternate with hewn stone. In the niches set in these arches are the windows which are also arch-shaped. In the upper storey their size is determined by the outer arch, but in the middle storey this is not so. Here they are considerably smaller than their outer arch and are the same size as the windows in the storey above. Thus the balance between the storeys is maintained. The whole façade is designed with symmetry in mind. The question of balance is seen in the ornaments in the panels between the individual arches. Here checks interchange with lozenges, squares with crosses, zigzags with roundels. The ornaments are in glass, glazed ceramic and stone of various kinds. But here the same ornaments are repeated in both storeys. They have not all survived today but with their original decoration of small glass stones and glazed ceramics they must have shone in the sun like the brilliants in a costly piece of jewellery. In the windows of the upper storey whose soffits are of marble, rectangular alternate with almost square windows. The curve of the arch was lined with stonework to make a circular blind window which would obviously have been filled with bright glass or lustre tiles. On the south façade of the second storey there is an oriel with supports. The roof of the building, as the surviving gable ends show, was comparatively flat. Inside the building all ceilings have fallen in and it is therefore difficult to get any idea what the interior was like, though the surviving ruins support the conclusion that the upper rooms were approached by a staircase placed outside the building, as in Islamic palaces. This staircase was on the east side of the building and gave access to the first floor and then seems to have continued to the upper storey from the inside. The arcades of the ground floor led inside to a slightly vaulted hall. The middle and upper storeys seem to have formed a connected room round which a gallery ran high up by the windows of the second floor. On the south side this was broadened out by the aforementioned oriel. It is possible that this was the box or loggia of the Emperor and Empress who would be present on the occasion of the great court festivals. These enormous rooms running through two storeys were a common feature of Byzantine and Arab palaces – for instance the Zisa Palace in Palermo. Niches built in tiers on each side of the windows, serving for the display of costly vases and other works of art, are also found in Arab palace buildings. It is not clear whether these similarities point to the direct imitation of Islamic architectural styles or whether both alike drew on late antique Roman and Sassanid architecture.

The influence of Byzantine architecture on palace buildings of the Italian Renaissance can be seen in the marked emphasis on the arches with their niches in which there are rectangular windows, as in Byzantine buildings, with circular segments over them filled with masonry. The main difference lies in the continuity of the horizontal and vertical divisions of the façade. The Italian palaces have more of the character of buildings used for purposes of defence.

Thus Byzantine palace architecture shows both late antique and Islamic influences which were later handed on to the West and played their part in the Renaissance.

4

THE PALACE OF THEODORIC THE OSTROGOTH. Mosaic in the nave of the church of Sant'Apollinare Nuovo, Ravenna.

The mosaic of the palace shows the building with the side walls pushed back so that the side aisles seem to be in a line with the centre of the building in front. The mosaic thus portrays a peristyle like that of the imperial buildings of Diocletian's palace still standing in Split (Spalato). But the peristyle of Justinian in the Hormisdas palace with its superb mosaic pavement (Pl. 51) is now only preserved in the wall foundations. In warm weather, imperial audiences were often held in the pillared hall of the peristyle with its open courtyard, though in winter proceedings of this kind would take place in a large closed-in basilica, such as the evangelical church still standing in Trier, dating from the 4th century. Imperial audiences were usually portrayed taking place in the pillared hall of the peristyle. The great *missorium,* or silver votive plate, of the Emperor Theodosius I (now in Madrid) has an imperial scene of this kind showing the Emperor, his two sons and his bodyguard. Thus the Ravenna mosaic of Theodoric follows the normal pattern, although the actual portrait of the Emperor and his entourage have not survived and only the palace background remains. Usually the peristyle where imperial audiences took place had a mosaic pavement decorated with suitable scenes.

5 and 6

THE 'BRUMALIA' AND COUNTRY LIFE. Frescoes from the Umayyad palace of Qusayr Amrah.

Byzantine masters were responsible for painting the remarkable frescoes found in the desert palace of Qusayr Amrah, today lying far from human habitation. These frescoes date from soon after the Arab conquest. The Umayyad princes who had seen the deserted palaces of Byzantine emperors in Palestine and Syria wanted similar dwelling places for themselves, and so they had palaces built with the same kind of interior decoration. Today nothing of the imperial palaces has survived except the external shell, but thanks to their remoteness the Umayyad desert palaces have kept their interior frescoes. These were admittedly devised for Arab princes, but all the same they provide considerable insight into the private taste of the Byzantine aristocracy. They illuminate a side of Byzantine life for which no evidence has survived elsewhere. The decoration consists of different panels divided by crossing garlands. Some of these contain busts of men and women illustrating the different stages in human life. Some pictures illustrate various contemporary occupations: smiths, woodcutters, ivory carvers, dyers, money-changers and masons – to name only a few. Another group of pictures show dancing animals, for instance a bear, playing on a rebeq, a Syrian stringed instrument. Obviously these are scenes from the *Brumalia*, the Byzantine carnival which often had musicians and dancers dressed up as animals, and is known from the protests registered by prominent church fathers. Side by side with scenes taken from the *Brumalia* there are episodes from the life of the ordinary people. For instance, in one panel there is a picture of a man and woman performing a country dance accompanied by a flutist, and, as is still customary in some Greek dances today, the dancing woman is using castanettes.

7

CHARIOTEER IN THE HIPPODROME. Byzantine silk textile from the end of the 8th or beginning of the 9th century with a 6th-century pattern, from the tomb of Charlemagne. Paris, Musée de Cluny.

The medallion (yellow on blue) in compound twill shows a charioteer with his quadriga. He is wearing the armour of a general. The chariot is on the racecourse of the Hippodrome and at the end of this two servants are holding the tape. In the hand of one there is a pennant on a short stick which is used to indicate that the tape has been reached. The other holds an imperial crown instead of the victor's chaplet. In the foreground servants are pouring gold from sacks into a receptacle.

The border of the medallion has stylized flowers with leaves, a motif frequently found in Coptic textiles of the 5th and 6th centuries. The medallion pictures are joined by smaller medallions filled with floral ornamentation, and in the free space between there are pairs of ibex eating branches. This motif of ibex with branches (probably the haoma plant) points to a Sassanid model and is found on silver bowls and textiles from Iranian regions. The yellow colouring of the scenes and ornaments stands out in strong contrast to the blue background.

The picture in the medallion gives a scene taken from part of the ceremonial duties of the Byzantine Emperor, such as had been earlier performed by the Roman consuls and are portrayed on consular diptychs and on the brightly coloured marble (*opus sectile*) in the basilica of Junius Bassus (consul in AD317) in Rome. Here the Byzantine Emperor, like the Roman consul, is driving his quadriga ceremoniously round the course of the Hippodrome. Then he would put on the waiting (victor's) chaplet, the diadem, mount the throne and distribute gold from the already filled receptacles to the people.

But this picture relating to the Emperor also has a parallel with the ceremonial of the charioteer in the Hippodrome. This can be seen by comparing it with the relief on the marble podium of the bronze statue of a charioteer which was erected at the turn of the 5th century as a memorial to the Alexandrian charioteer Porphyrios. It stood originally in the Hippodrome in Constantinople, the present-day site of At Maidan. The bronze statue was damaged and apparently melted down. The podium, however, survived and is now in the Archaeological Museum in Istanbul. This representation of the charioteer shows a clear correspondence with that of the Emperor on the silk textile. Both the Emperor and the charioteer stand in the quadriga in

the 'triumphator' gesture. The picture on the relief indeed goes so far as to show the charioteer surrounded by victory goddesses, who ordinarily were reserved for the Emperor's pictures.

The fact that the silk textile comes from the tomb of Charlemagne suggests that it was a present to the Emperor brought by the Byzantine ambassadors from the Emperor Leo V (813-20) together with his personal recognition of Charlemagne as *imperator*. The picture on the material would be suitable for an occasion of this kind. Since Charlemagne had died shortly before the arrival of the embassy the silk portraying Byzantine imperial ceremonial was placed in his tomb. (See also Pl. 48 and Note.)

8

SESSION OF A CHURCH COUNCIL IN THE PRESENCE OF THE EMPEROR. Miniature from the manuscript of the Homilies of St Gregory of Nazianzus written between 880 and 886. Paris, Bibliothèque Nationale (Cod. gr. 510, f.355).

This miniature is evidently a copy of an icon, perhaps one which belonged to the iconostasis of Hagia Sophia (the frame has been reproduced in the picture), and it shows the interior of the chamber in which a Council was taking place. The members of the Council are seated in a semi-circle. In the centre of this, where the bishop's chair would be in a church, there is an empty throne which has a symbolic meaning. This is the place from which Christ, invisible to human eye, is presiding over the assembly. An opened copy of the Gospels stands on the throne and the liturgy written on a roll. If the Emperor was not present then a symbol of his authority, such as the imperial crown, was laid down on the throne. The empty throne is thus portrayed in a mosaic in S. Maria Maggiore in Rome dating from the time of Pope Sixtus III (432-40). The bronze door of Hagia Sophia also shows the throne with an opened copy of the Gospels on it. The custom of leaving the throne empty with the Holy Writ on it as a sign of Christ's presence is attested as early as the Council of Ephesus in 431. On a table in the middle of the hall was placed a bound book, evidently the *acta* of the earlier councils, and by it were laid rolls containing the exegesis of those who had taken part in the councils. Those taking part in the Council visible in the picture were exclusively bishops and patriarchs recognizable from their *omophoria* embroidered with crosses; with them is the Emperor. He alone is portrayed with a nimbus. The sanctuary was reserved for the Emperor and bishops and in its apse benches were placed for the most distinguished members of the Council, but the other participants, monks, priests and deacons, had also to be indicated. In the bottom left-hand corner a figure is seen turning towards them and speaking to them. The architectural background is conventional and stereotyped. It follows a late antique model and conveys the illusion of buildings in the background rather than independently since these appear to have no connection with the council chamber in the foreground.

The inscription at the top, *synodos deutera*, the Second Council, indicates the second oecumenical Council of Constantinople (381); beneath the figure of the Emperor are the words *Theodosios ho megas* (= Theodosius I the Great, 379-95).

9

PILATE. Detail of a miniature from the Rossano Gospels. Rossano cathedral.

The purple Gospels of Rossano dates from the early 6th century and is a manuscript made for a member of the imperial house, or perhaps even for the Emperor; with its distinguished patron in mind it was written on purple. The miniature here illustrates the meeting of the Roman governor Pilate with Christ (Matthew 27, 2). It shows Pilate seated on the throne before the judgment table. Behind him stand two imperial guards, recognizable from the gold chain worn round their neck. They each hold a banner displaying a portrait of the two Emperors. This presence of two Emperors together in the picture testifies to the antiquity of the model used by the artist which must date from the time of the Emperors Valentinian III (425-55) and Theodosius II (408-50). It was under these rulers that the conception of imperial unity was specially emphasized in the field of law by the publication of the Codex Theodosianus in 438. It is even possible that portrayal of Pilate as judge may be connected with the legal work of the two Emperors. The portrait of the two Emperors is also to be found on the cloth covering the judge's table appliquéd on to the linen with gold thread. It was normal for the imperial portrait to be carried by members of the guard on special occasions and the honours due to the reigning Emperor were also paid to his portrait. When an Emperor came to the throne in Constantinople it was customary for his portrait, together with that of his wife, to be sent to the elder capital Rome. Here the picture was then displayed at the head of a ceremonial procession and the Roman garrison paid it military honours. In this miniature Pilate is sitting on the purple cushion as representative of the Emperor and is wearing the toga. The portrait of Pilate bears a strong resemblance to the Roman portraits found on consular diptychs.

10

THE EMPEROR BASIL II AS 'TRIUMPHATOR'. Miniature from the Psalter of Basil II. Venice, Biblioteca Marciana (Cod. gr. Z17).

This Psalter was commissioned by Basil II and probably dates from the year AD 1017. The Emperor is shown here as *triumphator*. This is the same kind of portrayal which is found as early as the statue of Augustus before the Prima Porta. It seems to find its full expression in the imperial statue of Barletta (Pl. 125) from the second half of the 5th century; if one forgets the clumsy restoration of legs and arms during the early Renaissance there is indeed almost complete similarity. It might even be suggested that the portrayal of Basil II in the Psalter shows what the torso of the imperial statue of Barletta originally looked like. Although separated by almost more than half a century, the ceremonial military garments of the two are similar, except that Basil wears the *palumentum* instead of the toga and his armour is not of metal but of metal plaques which are sewn on to his leather garment. In the miniature in the Psalter there is a bust of Christ holding the imperial crown while the archangel Gabriel is placing another crown on Basil's head and a second archangel presses a spear into his hand. Such angels

correspond closely to the goddesses of victory of pagan imperial times. Prostrate at the Emperor's feet are the Bulgarian boyars whose submission Basil had exacted after his victory over the tsar Samuel. On each side of the Emperor are three circular and square frames containing busts of the military saints.

11

THE LAST JUDGMENT. Detail of mosaic. Torcello cathedral.

This mosaic was done in the 12th century and gives a terrifying picture of the punishment of the damned in hell fire. As in the Inferno of Dante's *Divine Comedy*, the master of this mosaic fills his hell with real personalities. In particular he draws on those whom the Latin West regarded as heretics or infidels. Here pride of place goes to the Byzantine Emperor. Even in hell he is wearing the imperial crown decorated with the Christian cross, but in spite of this an angel tosses him back into the flames. The patriarch of Constantinople – recognizable from his liturgical garments – fares no better. Another angel prods him with a rod in order to push him further down into the flames. A Byzantine patrician, marked out by his white cap and blue ceremonial robes with their gold appliqué, is being seized by the hair and beard by a little devil. The Byzantine Empress, discernible by reason of her crown, is sharing hell fire with a rabbi and a Seljuk sultan. The sultana is facing disaster in another part of the flames of hell, together with a Cuman chieftain and his wife. Among the damned are only two westerners: one, from his tonsure a priest, is being plagued by a devil, while the other is an equally unknown bearded man. Both were almost certainly two specially hated figures in the maritime Venetian republic.

12

THE PRAYER OF THE PROPHET ISAIAH. Miniature from a Constantinopolitan manuscript of a Psalter, mid-tenth century. Paris, Bibliothèque Nationale (Cod. gr. 139, f.435v).

This miniature belongs to the age of the Emperor Constantine VII Porphyrogenitus (913-59) and reflects the revival of the traditions of antiquity. It clearly goes back to a period when attempts were made to portray Biblical Christian scenes in the form of Hellenistic myths, when political toleration, and then recognition, of Christianity were coming to the forefront. The frescoes of the catacombs belong to an era of this kind and the miniature shown here has close affinities with them. The paintings in the catacombs were a branch of the art employed in fresco decoration in the houses of devout Christians. (The Casa Caelimontana in Rome immediately comes to mind as an instance of this heathen tradition of pagan myths closely linked to Christian pictures.) The reason is to be found in the state's attitude towards Christianity which sometimes made it wise not to figure Christian portraits too openly. The miniature shown here might originally have come from fresco decoration in a Roman patrician's palace. When the family migrated to Constantinople they could have taken with them a miniature which was a copy of this scene. The camouflage of the content of the picture is clearly recognizable even on a copy so far removed from the original. The allegorical figures of Night and Dawn signify the cry of the prophet Isaiah. He was indeed the prophet *par excellence* who foretold the coming of the Messiah. The miniature shows that the copyist was not really capable of following the painter of the fresco. He treats his model like a pupil copying a painting, and fails in his treatment of the folds of the garment and the poise of the body. All that the miniature can do is to reveal something of the composition and individuality of a lost masterpiece.

13

THE PRAYER OF ISAIAH. Miniature from the Bristol Psalter. London, British Museum (Add. MS. 40731, f. 252ʳ).

The Bristol Psalter, with its rich collection of miniatures, probably dates from the 11th century. As in the case of the miniatures of the Paris Psalter (Pl. 12), its painter must have copied the pictures of a well-known manuscript of a psalter coming from late antiquity. It is therefore possible to compare the treatment of the Byzantine copyists, even though their original model is no longer extant. This miniature of the Bristol Psalter seems at first sight to be more dependent and in many ways more accurate, and there is no doubt that here a less independent personality was at work. Here the contrast between Night and the praying Isaiah is greater. Then, on the Bristol Psalter the face of Night has not got the Greek features characterizing the work of the Macedonian renaissance. The model used for the face of Night here has the kind of features to be found in perhaps Syrian or Egyptian types. Any Greek characteristics found in the people portrayed here are clearly due to a Byzantine artist who had altered the late antique model.

14

CHRIST WITH ST MENAS. Icon, tempera on wood, from Bawit, 6th century. Paris, Musée du Louvre.

Menas, seen here with Christ, was the national hero of Christian Egypt. He suffered martyrdom under Diocletian in 296. His tomb in the Egyptian region of Marjut was a famous place of pilgrimage and the account of his life and martyrdom was among the most widely circulated of pre-Islamic Egypt.

The icon belongs to the middle of the 6th century and comes from the monastery of Apollo in Bawit, in the neighbourhood of Antinoe. The Christ shown here does not follow the patterns of the Alexandrian and Antiochene redactions and must belong to a period before these versions had penetrated – that is, to the decades shortly after the introduction of icon veneration. Here Christ and St Menas have the appearance of rhetors or philosophers of antiquity. They are reminiscent of the *ex-voto* representations in the sanctuaries of Dura-Europos at the end of the 2nd and beginning of the 3rd centuries. St Menas carries a roll of writing in his right hand while his left is raised as though in teaching. It looks as if this picture was not by a trained icon painter but by an artist well versed in fresco painting, because here he has applied to wood the tempera technique used in fresco painting. To judge from the Sinai icons, the icon masters, being used to encaustic table painting, at first employed this method.

In the case of encaustic icons a preliminary sketch in outline was made with charcoal or crayon. Then the artist spread the hot wax colour on to the wood (poplar or sycamore) with an iron spatula with its end shaped like a key, and worked in the colours with the heated end of the iron. The next stage, the introduction of lighting effects and the addition of minor details, was done in tempera technique with a brush. With tempera technique the colours were mixed and put on with a brush. Here the binding agent played a very different role.

The technique of icon painting did, in the main, represent a further development of tempera painting. From earliest times there had been a close connection between fresco and icon painting which was apparent in composition as well as in technique. Thus the fresco of the enthroned Mother of God surrounded by martyrs in the catacombs of Comodilla in Rome shows almost the same composition as an encaustic icon of the same period in the Sinai monastery. (See also Pl. 119.)

15

CHRIST THE PANTOCRATOR. Mosaic from the church of Hosios Loukas of Stiri in Phocis.

Since this church was an imperial foundation, the mosaic artists would have been from the court and among the finest the Empire could produce. Like the monastic houses on Mount Athos which owed their foundation to the Emperors Nicephorus Phocas and John Tzimisces, Hosios Loukas had its imperial patrons in the Emperors Romanus II and Basil II. Later on Constantine IX Monomachos (1042-55) was to found Nea Moni on Chios. This was indeed the century of great imperial foundations. The sarcophagus of the Emperor Romanus II and his wife still rests in the crypt of Hosios Loukas. The Christ of Hosios Loukas, who seems to have his glance so firmly fixed on the foreground, was related to a particular religious cult which had been stimulated by the recovery of the *mandylion* which was handed over to the Emperor Constantine VII Porphyrogenitus (913-59). The *mandylion* was the portrait of Christ which, according to legend, He had sent to king Abgar of Edessa (see Note 143). According to existing pictures the *mandylion* showed only the head of Christ but it did lead to a new orientation in portraying the Saviour. The Antiochene bearded type of Christ had indeed been known since the 4th century. The stranded, matted hair, the colour of the face and the unnaturally large eyes, as well as the three locks of hair on the forehead, corresponded to the characteristics associated with an outstanding and courageous man, according to the writings of Hellenistic physiognomics (pseudo-Aristotelian works). This type of representation was closely related to the Hellenistic and imperial portraits of a ruler. With the appearance of the *mandylion* certain changes were made, so that it is possible to distinguish between representations of Christ before and after the recovery of the holy portrait. The reproduction of the medallion of Christ in the crown of the dome and vaulting is in the style of the imperial era when the ruler was represented thus enthroned in his mausoleum (as in the Mausoleum of Centcelles). The technique of the mosaic portrait points to icons as models. The juxtaposition of different lines shaded off in different tones of colour to indicate the folds of a garment is found in contemporary icon painting. An 11th-century icon of the apostles Peter and Paul now in Moscow, and preserved only in part, shows precisely the same characteristics. (See also Note 168.)

16

THE MOTHER OF GOD WITH THE CHRIST CHILD, SAINTS AND ANGELS.
From an icon in the monastery of St Catherine, Mount Sinai.

This is part of an icon in St Catherine's monastery on Mount
Sinai dating from the first half of the 6th century and, together
with the icon of the two military saints, St Sergius and St
Bacchus, in Kiev, it belongs to the oldest examples of Byzantine tablet painting. It is also one of the few instances of this kind
of painting in the style of the age of Justinian. The icon is one of
the oldest surviving portraits of the Mother of God. Its composition still clearly shows close affinities with imperial representational art. It might quite well be the portrait of an Empress
holding the future Emperor on her lap. She is wearing an extremely costly blue veil, reminiscent of a garment like the
starred mantle of the Emperor Henry II in the Treasury of
Bamberg, and under this a cap ornamented with pearls is concealed, only just visible under the veil on one side. This was the
same as the formal apparel of the Empresses whose busts have
survived from the second half of the 5th century. The facial
traits of the Mother of God are in no way idealized. She has the
characteristics of the ethnic type of Bedouin woman found in
the Syrian desert. Her features are reminiscent of the Empress
Theodora in the well-known mosaic panel of San Vitale in
Ravenna – the long narrow nose, the disproportionate space
between the nostrils and the eyebrows, and the marked cheek-
bones. It is possible that this may have been used as a model for
a portrait of the Empress Theodora, holding her nephew, the
future Justin II, in her arms. In that case the Empress would
probably be twenty years younger than in the mosaic panel in
San Vitale where her portrait was made shortly before her
death. The Christ Child is wearing the robe of a consul and in
his hand he is holding the scroll which is found in ivory diptychs with their consular portraits. The monastery of St Catherine on Mount Sinai was Justinian's foundation and it is probable
that the icon was an imperial gift to the monastery.

17

THE MOTHER OF GOD OF VLADIMIR. Icon, Moscow, Tretiakov
Gallery.

This icon, now in the Tretiakov Gallery in Moscow, probably
came from a Constantinopolitan workshop and was taken to
Kiev in the early 12th century and thence in 1155 to Vladimir.
It would then be a near contemporary of the mosaic of the
Theotokos with the Christ Child standing between the Emperor
John II Comnenus and the Empress Irene in the gallery of Hagia
Sophia in Constantinople. Various characteristics indicate that
the existing icon is not a later copy but the original commissioned by the Grand Duke of Kiev. Thorough restoration of
the icon after the October 1917 Revolution has revealed that
the head of the Mother and the Child as well as the hands are
undoubtedly the original work. For the rest, only fragments of
the original painting remain. The veil (maphorion) of the Mother
drapes her head and shoulders and like the near-contemporary
mosaic in Hagia Sophia this is blue. The icon as it now is gives
the Mother of God a black veil, but this is not the original. On
the other hand the gold border of the veil is true to the original
picture. Clearly the gold border on a blue veil must have been

extremely effective as it is on the present black veil. The veil
would be fixed by pins to a cap covering the hair and thus the
folds are artistically draped round the face to which particular
emphasis is given by the gold edging. Thus the face of the
wearer of the veil is placed, as it were, within a gold frame like
a picture. The features delineated – the long fine nose, the
regular eyebrows and the small mouth – all these reflect a conception of ideal beauty characteristic of the Macedonian renaissance. The type of Virgin and Child portrayed here is known
as the 'Eleousa', or the Virgin of Tenderness.

18

THE DESCENT OF CHRIST INTO HELL (THE ANASTASIS). Fresco in the
parecclesion (mortuary chapel or side chapel) of the church of
St Saviour in Chora (Kariye Cami), Istanbul.

The church of St Saviour in Chora is one of the oldest in the
capital, but its frescoes and mosaics belong to one of the finest
periods of Byzantine art: the Palaeologan renaissance. The
original church dates from before the erection of the great land
wall under Theodosius II (413) and was outside the city boundary of Constantine the Great. It enjoyed the patronage of Priscus, the general of the Emperor Maurice murdered in 602, and
after a period of decay was restored by Maria Ducaina during
the reign of the Emperor Alexius I Comnenus. It finally owed
its last renovation to Theodore Metochites, the Grand Logothete, or finance minister, of the Emperor Andronicus II
Palaeologus (1282-1328), who died there as a monk in 1331. He
did much to restore the almost thousand-year old church and
had it decorated with mosaics and frescoes. There is a mosaic
portrait of him wearing the ceremonial dress of his high office,
holding a model of the church in his hands. Today the church
has emerged from its whitewash coating and the reconstruction
it underwent while it was a Turkish mosque, and stands revealed in all the glory of its splendid interior decoration. It
served a double purpose: the main church was for the services,
and the parecclesion, or side chapel, was a mausoleum in which
members of the founder's family are buried. The Descent of
Christ into Hell (known in the Greek Church as the Anastasis,
the Resurrection) is in the side chapel. The niches for the tombs
can indeed still be seen in the chapel but they are empty and only
fragments of the paintings in the lunettes above them remain.
But the fresco in which Christ is dragging up the dead from
their graves as they open is connected with the sarcophagi now
absent from the niches, and these must be visualized in order to
realize the full effect of the fresco in its setting at the time when
it was painted. The splendour and almost uniqueness of this
fresco in Byzantine art lies in its essentially dynamic quality.
The earth appears to be reft asunder as if by a terrific shock and
from the deep fissure Christ is dragging up the dead. The force
with which Christ is pulling up the first created human beings,
Adam and Eve, from their shattered tombs is almost over-
powering. His feet seem to be leaping up to the firm ground.
In contrast to this dramatic central episode is the serene calm of
the figures standing on each side. The conception of this picture
is not unique. The church of St Theodore Stratelates in Novgorod built about 1360 has a picture of the Descent of Christ into
Hell which must go back to the same model as that of the Chora
church. But the fresco in the Russian church painted by Greek

artists, in spite of similarity in composition, does show some variations. For instance, although its Christ is pulling up Adam with his right hand, his left hand is only stretching out towards Eve who in the Chora fresco has already been seized. In Novgorod everyone is thronging towards Christ to be brought up by Him, and not just two, but a vast number of graves have opened and the dead are crowding round so that they may reach Christ.

19

THE JOURNEY TO BETHLEHEM. Detail of mosaic in the exonarthex (outer ante-chamber) of the church of the Chora (Kariye Cami), Istanbul, between 1300 and 1320.

This mosaic dates from the time after the Byzantine Empire had played an international role under the Emperor Michael VIII Palaeologus (1259-82) and belongs to the reign of his son Andronicus II (1283-1328). Andronicus was a pious man, deeply rooted in the Orthodox Christian faith. With him there began a period of religious revival. At his side stood the Grand Logothete Theodore Metochites, a representative of this new era, who had strong interests in natural science and was particularly active as an astronomer.

In the mosaics and frescoes of the Chora church the old deep religious feeling of the Emperor still nourished by the monastic movement is seen side by side with his first minister's new interest in the world stimulated by the natural sciences.

The mosaic illustrated here shows Mary with Joseph and one of Joseph's sons on the road to Bethlehem. Behind the slope of the mountain, trees and the houses of a city can be seen. The quality of the artistic mastery shown in this mosaic can only be appreciated when it is compared, not with work from the preceding monastic period, but with that from late antiquity of an earlier date.

The journey to Bethlehem is also the subject of a 7th-century fresco in the church of Castelseprio where there is a scene almost exactly similar to that of the Chora church. The picture in Castelseprio is painted in the flowing style of late antique naturalism. The mule is trotting along. His hoofs touch the ground, while in the mosaic in Constantinople they are not portrayed with attention to exact detail and look as though they are floating in the air; there are also errors in anatomy. For instance, the two left legs are too long. At Castelseprio, Mary is sitting on the mule turning round talking to Joseph who is walking behind. In the Chora mosaic she is indeed turning round as in the fresco but she is not looking at Joseph, but past him. In the fresco Joseph is stretching out his hand in gesticulation as he speaks, while in the mosaic he is catching hold of his garment with it. In the fresco the figure in front of Mary is striding along briskly, his feet firmly planted on the ground. In the mosaic one of his feet is too short and the other is just touching the ground with the tip of his toe. In the fresco the inside of the city gate can be seen drawn in true perspective. In the mosaic the houses are shown in the distance quite unrealistically shaped like chimneys.

The close similarity in the composition of the scene seems to indicate without any doubt that the mosaic in Constantinople and the fresco in Castelseprio both drew on the same late antique model. Compared with the fresco, the mosaic shows a falling off in standard in so far as naturalistic portrayal was concerned. The folds of the garments, the light effects, the movement, were copied from late antiquity, but without real understanding. In fact gross errors in copying from the late antique model can be detected.

But the mosaics of the Chora church should not be judged by their naturalistic qualities. A comparison of the two figures of Mary makes this clear. In spite of her nimbus in the fresco Mary remains a woman who has just left the open city gate with her followers. With his outstanding powers of observation the late antique artist has given this scene the appearance of everyday reality. The mosaic is quite different. Here the Mother of God on the mule has nothing of the appearance of a human being. The hoofs of her mule do not even rest on the earth. They are floating. The figure going before the Mother of God does not seem to be impelled forward by his own strength. He seems to be drawn onwards as if by invisible threads. In the fresco Joseph is in conversation with the Mother of God, here in the mosaic he has veiled his hands as though in the presence of a heavenly being or of the Emperor. The unnaturally elongated bodies of the human beings – they are like the figures of the great Greek master of western painting, El Greco – and the mountain tops piled up like crystal, such as were never seen in this world, place the picture outside the realms of reality and give it the character of a vision created by faith. Herein lies the great difference of the mosaic of the Chora church and the fresco of Castelseprio. The naturalism of Castelseprio is drawn from a culture that has disappeared; but in the Chora, in spite of the intrusion of the secular world revealed by the natural sciences, the old culture rooted in the Christianity of the monastic movement still lives on and has not lost its awareness of the revelations of God.

20

THE RAISING OF LAZARUS. Fresco, church of the Pantanassa, Mistra.

The frescoes in the church of the Pantanassa in Mistra date from the last decades of the independent political life of Byzantium. The church was dedicated in 1428. Thus the frescoes are contemporary with the creations of the Italian Quattrocento. Clearly the question of influence arises, especially as this is so obvious in the architecture of Mistra. The frescoes certainly show signs of having been painted by someone in touch with western forms of artistic expression. But the unique climax of this Byzantine artistic achievement grew up in the environment of the great Palaeologan renaissance. Both in the Byzantine Empire itself and in eastern Europe in the service of the Russian princes this movement developed its own artistic forms which can hold their own with those of the Renaissance in the West. The raising of Lazarus was one of the oldest themes in Christian figural art. It was portrayed in the Antiochene tradition showing Lazarus stepping out of a burial tower of the kind customary in Syria. But he was also shown still swathed as a mummy, after the Alexandrian fashion, as was the case in the Mistra fresco. This was a very late representation of Christ's miracle made during the Palaeologan renaissance and a comparison of it with the oldest reproduction of this same theme on the Pulininus sarcophagus reveals how tenaciously Byzantine artists preserved traditional iconographical forms even in a new and most realistically expressed art.

21

THE PALA D'ORO. Altarpiece in the church of San Marco, Venice.

The oldest part of the famous Pala d'Oro, originally an altar frontal, now in San Marco, dates from the last decade of the 10th century and was made in Constantinople for the Venetian Doge Pietro Orseolo. It shows the superb Byzantine technique in cloisonné enamel work. This oldest part of the Byzantine altar frontal thus dates from the same period as the *staurotheke*, or reliquary, of Limburg designed to contain relics of the True Cross. Today the Pala d'Oro is 1·4 metres high and 3·5 wide and only part of it is the original, since it was frequently worked over between the 12th and 14th centuries and some of the original plaques were enlarged. The additional pieces do not match the quality of those of the original altar frontal made in Constantinople. A lower standard is apparent in the tone and translucence of individual enamel surfaces. The cloisonné enamelling of the Pala d'Oro done in Italy falls short of the Byzantine work in both of the two processes. First the pattern was outlined by strips of metal, and then the enamel in the form of powdered glass, coloured by adding various minerals, was poured into the compartments, or cloisons, and the whole was then fired. As in the case of the oldest coloured glass windows in the cathedrals of the West, individual ateliers had their secret processes, especially for this particular stage of the production. In the process of tracing the pattern or figure with thin strips of metal soldered on to the gold ground, thus forming the compartments into which the enamel was poured, western craftsmen had nothing like the techniques found in the Byzantine workshops. Often all they did was to cut out the design on the gold ground. Both in the setting and in the mounting of the enamels the central section of the Pala d'Oro cannot compare with the form and execution of the original part. The iconography of the enthroned Christ with the Gospel book and the scholar's gesture and the portrayal of the four evangelists points to the middle of the 5th century. The development of these portraits of the evangelists is to be found as early as the 3rd and 4th centuries on early Christian sarcophagi at a time before miniatures and other art forms were in use. The reliefs on the sarcophagi clearly indicate that the models for these portraits of the evangelists were provided by pictures of pagan rhetoricians and philosophers. The porphyry statue of the seated Emperor was copied for the enthroned Christ. The torso of an enthroned ruler found in Alexandria might indeed be either Christ or the Emperor, since almost all the details correspond with the mosaic in the apse of the church of Santa Pudenziana in Rome which portrays Christ enthroned and surrounded by his disciples.

22

THE CROSS OF JUSTIN II. Silver gilt cross. Rome. Museo Sacro Vaticano.

This silver gilt Cross was probably brought to Rome in 577 by the ambassador, the patrician Pamphronius, at a time when the city was being threatened by the Lombards. It is one of the three most important artistic works belonging to the reign of the Emperor Justin II (515-78); the other two are the mosaic in the apse of St Catherine's monastery on Sinai and the imperial palace in Qasr ibn Wardan. The centre of the Cross has a medal-

lion showing the Lamb of God and the arms in either side also have medallions containing portraits of the Emperor and of the Empress. They are shown with uplifted hands, a gesture found in Greek antiquity and associated with Epiphany. This might indicate the festival of the *prokypsis* when the Emperor represented the solar deity in a mime performed on the day of the winter solstice (See Pl. 32 and Note). Emperor and Empress are wearing the coronation ornaments with the plumed crown on the head. This attribute of imperial majesty is comparatively rarely portrayed. It was worn by Justinian in the equestrian statue of him destroyed by the Turks, which is however known from an early renaissance sketch. The Emperor usually took off his crown in church and placed it on the altar as symbolizing his presence there as an ordinary person and not the vice-gerent of Christ. In the same way the crown was removed from the dead Emperor before his final burial as a sign that death had ended his work as the representative of Christ and he was now standing before the throne of the Almighty in all humility as a simple Christian.

The long upright arms of the Cross have medallions containing Christ above and John the Baptist below. The foliage and plant ornamentation decorating the Cross is reminiscent of the surviving fragments of mosaic work in Hagia Sophia dating from the time of Justinian. It is also found in the mosaics of Byzantine masters in the Dome of the Rock in Jerusalem dating from the end of the 7th century.

23

THE CREATION OF MAN. Miniature from an 11th-century manuscript of the Octateuch. Florence, Biblioteca Laurentiana (Pluteus V, Cod. 38, f.4).

This miniature reflects the new spirit of enlightenment which is associated with the scholar Psellus. It shows man being created by a ray of the sun which is falling on a sleeping figure. This sleeping figure is lying in the midst of flowering vegetation, and the vital power of the sun, which gives life to plants and to mankind, is evident. If this representation of the creation is compared with Michelangelo's famous fresco in the Sistine Chapel it looks as if it is much further removed from the Biblical story than the painting of the great Renaissance artist. This miniature is indeed an indication of the extent to which the 11th century had moved away from Aristotelian philosophy and, under the influence of Platonism, was in process of creating a different view of the world.

24

THE ARK OF THE COVENANT. Miniature from a 9th-century manuscript of the *Christian Topography* of Cosmas Indicopleustes. Rome, Biblioteca Vaticana (Cod. Gr. 699, f. 15ᵛ).

The miniatures in this codex were probably copied from the illustrations in the original 6th-century manuscript of this work. Cosmas was an Alexandrian merchant who took part in the trade between Alexandria and India, and visited both the Abyssinian and Indian ports lying on this route. At that time Abyssinia was a Christian kingdom which had links with Byzantium, even though its ruler was known to be monophysite. There is a good deal of evidence, particularly numismatic, to show the considerable extent of Byzantine influence on Abyssinia during the 6th century. While stopping at Adulis, a harbour in the neighbourhood of present-day Massaoua, Cosmas had visited Axum, then the capital of the Abyssinian kingdom. As a result, he left a description of an obelisk with its Greek inscriptions set up in Adulis by a Ptolemaic king, as well as the first drawing of the Ark of the Covenant kept in the cathedral of Axum. This shows the Ark of the Covenant as a throne with pillars round, thus corresponding to the Hebrew text and the frescoes in the synagogue in Dura-Europos. Excavations in the neighbourhood of old Axum have found copies of this throne and also of the so-called Ark of the Covenant belonging to the 5th and 6th centuries. It was remarkable that the Ark of the Covenant was set up in the cathedral of Axum – as it still is today, even if concealed – and was revered in Abyssinia. This is explained, however, by the fact that south Arabia was the southernmost tip of the incense route from Gaza to the Mediterranean and had a considerable Jewish community, which had been reinforced by refugees from Palestine after the destruction of the Temple. It is probable that these refugees brought with them to south Arabia the Ark of the Covenant – or rather what passed for this. As the records of the Abyssinia kings show, this area was conquered by Abyssinia in the 4th century.

The miniature is in the form of a highly stylized map on which individual towns are symbolically represented by their most important monuments.

Other Abyssinian towns apart from Axum are symbolized by ecclesiastical buildings. The architectural type shown here is not that of a basilica but the kind of building seen in San Vitale and the Church of SS. Sergius and Bacchus dating from Justinian's reign. This would seem to imply that the cross-in-square domed church, which developed in Byzantium from the 7th century, was foreshadowed in its early stage by the ecclesiastical buildings of the East, particularly in Syria. In this connection it should be remembered that at this time, in respect of both ecclesiastical architecture and Christian literature, Abyssinia was orientated towards Syria. The oldest Abyssinian translation of the Bible came from Syriac sources.

It is also interesting to note the Abyssinian warrior in this miniature. This would seem to point to the use of the illustrations in a manuscript of the work expressly made for Cosmas. The Abyssinian warrior shown here is carrying the kind of long spear and round shield that is still used by the Negro tribes in eastern Abyssinia today.

25

THE EPISCOPAL CONSECRATION OF GREGORY OF NAZIANZUS. Miniature from Gregory of Nazianzus' *Homilies* on a manuscript copied in Constantinople between 880 and 886. Paris, Bibliothèque Nationale (Cod. Gr. 510).

The consecration of a bishop was effected by touching him with a copy of the Gospels. This form of consecration was to symbolize Christ's ordination of the bishop. It was, for instance, usual to indicate the presence of Christ at a synod or council by placing an open copy of the Gospels on a throne. This miniature shows the bishop standing between two high ecclesiastics who are holding the Gospels in their hands and are touching his

shoulder with it. The holy consecration is taking place inside the sanctuary of the church; marble barriers with a tower can be seen cutting off the sanctuary from the rest of the church. This kind of separation was still usual in the 9th century and can be seen in the altar screens of the Athos monasteries of the following century. During the 9th and 10th centuries in Constantinople it was not yet usual to find an iconastasis with icons on it.

The pillar with a cloth wound round it on the right hand side of the miniature shows the way in which these illustrations were influenced by Hellenistic miniature painting. The same thing is found in the Psalter miniatures which give a purely Hellenistic portrayal of David as a shepherd in a landscape scene. An instance of this can be seen in the miniature of David in the Paris Psalter in the Bibliothèque Nationale.

26

THE EVANGELIST MATTHEW. Miniature from a Constantinopolitan manuscript of about 1150. London, British Museum (Burney, 19, f. 1ᵛ).

Matthew is seated at his writing desk, which is equipped with everything considered necessary for an author at that time. The formal chair of the Evangelist is decorated with horseshoe curves set on little pillars, and this, as well as the writing desk, shows the marked influence of Islamic culture. Both chair and writing desk may have been of Islamic craftsmanship, or at least copied from Islamic models. This kind of wood carving was well known in the Seljuk kingdom in Asia Minor at that time. On the other hand, it was a two-way process and Byzantine influence was felt in the Islamic world; it is seen in the contemporary Arab miniatures of Irak which relied on models taken mostly from Byzantine, or Syrian sources.

The portrayal of the Evangelist is highly stylized but it is clear that a good Hellenistic model had been used. Matthew, in the act of writing, is dipping his *calamus,* or reed pen, into the ink. A Hellenistic model is indicated by the fact that here the Evangelist is not writing on a vellum codex but obviously on a roll. Part of a roll, which has already been written, is lying on the reading desk to dry. Models for this can be found in the miniatures of late antique manuscripts which partly go back to free-standing sculpture. Work of this kind belonging to the 3rd century has been preserved: for instance, the famous statue of Hippolytus in Rome, where the figure is shown sitting down, like the Evangelist in the miniature shown here. Christians, like the various pagan schools of philosophy, usually portrayed their great personalities in this way. Statues were copied in miniatures. The representation of the sitting Peter in the statue in the Vatican Grotto is an instance of one of the few originals of this kind still preserved. Unfortunately it is extensively restored.

27

GREGORY OF NAZIANZUS HEALING A LAME MAN IN THE HOSPITAL IN CAESAREA IN CAPPADOCIA. Miniature from the *Homilies* of Gregory of Nazianzus. Paris, Bibliothèque Nationale (Cod. Gr. 510, f. 149).

Here the bishop is shown together with St Basil taking care of the sick. At this time the church and the Emperor were responsible for the administration of hospitals, geriatric homes and orphanages. There was also an official in the imperial household whose duty it was to supervise the imperial foundations for orphans and the sick. It is possible that this miniature is a copy of a fresco in a building of this kind. The various scenes showing the different activities of the saint are each placed under a separate arch of the arcading. This kind of composition is found in the arcading on early Christian sarcophagi and passed into the tradition of Byzantine early Christian representational art. Here the model might perhaps be placed in the 5th or 6th century. This is indicated by the dominating architectural features in the picture, such as the acanthus capital which was typical of the period. The remarkable fluting on the pillars would support this dating. It is also possible to suggest a regional provenance, since it has affinities with the finds of similar pillar shafts in Diyarbakr on the Anatolian-Irakian borders. The return to the 5th and 6th centuries is typical of the period of the Macedonian renaissance to which this miniature belongs.

28

THE EXPOSITION OF THE HOLY CROSS BY THE PATRIARCH. Miniature in a *Menologion* made for the Emperor Basil II, end of the 10th century. Rome, Biblioteca Vaticana (Cod. Gr. 1613, f. 76).

The Holy Cross consisted of a reliquary containing a fragment of the True Cross of Christ. Crosses of this kind with relics of the True Cross have survived down to the present day. The famous staurotheke of Limburg, dating from the time of Constantine Porphyrogenitus, is one of these. It is fifty years earlier than the miniature shown here. The *Menologion,* like the staurotheke of Limburg was a work specifically commissioned by an Emperor. In the *Menologion* the painters of the miniatures have not remained anonymous. This is one of the few occasions when the creators of Byzantine masterpieces have revealed their quite distinct personalities.

The patriarch is standing in the pulpit and clasping the Cross with both hands while he is being supported by two clerics. This gesture and the white hair of the chief shepherd indicate his extreme old age.

The outstanding artistic quality of the painter is shown by the dramatic character of the scene. The exposition of the Cross was regarded as a manifestation which was in the nature of a supernatural event. This is shown by the grouping and bearing of the persons assisting the patriarch.

The incrustation of the marble plaques is extremely effective and reveals the marked skill of the artist. The miniature also has historical significance. The exposition of the Cross took place before the pillared entrance hall to the palace called the Magnaura, dating from the time of Constantine. It can be seen as early as the *missorium* or votive plate of the Emperor Theodosius I (which is now in Madrid). On this the Emperor is represented with his sons seated under the entrance of the building. The miniature shows that a pulpit was later erected in front of this middle building of the pillared hall and this was where the Emperor used to show himself to the populace. The imperial palace lying behind the Magnaura can be seen through the pillars of the porch.

29

THE DEATH OF ST MARTIN OF TOURS. Miniature from the *Menologion* of Basil II. Rome, Biblioteca Vaticana (Cod. Gr. 1613, f. 176).

The *Menologion* made for the Emperor Basil II has a picture of the death of the Frankish St Martin of Tours. The inclusion of the saint in the Byzantine *Menologion* was for political reasons. It was thought politic for the Byzantines to indicate their respect for the Frankish kingdom. The Byzantine hagiographer acclaims Martin, the bishop of the Frankish realm, a saint.

Martin is lying on his death bed, while a Byzantine patriarch is praying for him. Details of the mourners' clothing indicate the date of the models used here by the artist of the *Menologion*. For instance, the clothing of the painter standing by the side of the bishop has a ring round the neck. Soldiers of the imperial guard wore rings of this kind in late antiquity. Such rings were worn by the body guards in the miniature in the Codex of Rossano where they stand by Pilate's side holding the imperial portraits (Pl. 9). This is also true of the body guards on the *missorium* or votive plate of the Emperor Theodosius I and of the military saints, Sergius and Bacchus, on the icons dating from the 6th century. Such dating is also confirmed by the clothing of the woman standing by the bed of the dead bishop. Her veil is arranged like that of the Mother of God in the icon in the Sinai monastery (Pl. 16), so that the cloth round her hair is visible. In the later period the cloth covering the hair was hidden under the *maphorion*, or veil. The Sinai icon dates from the 6th century, so that it is probable that the model as a whole goes back to this period when Constantinople was particularly anxious to maintain good relations with the Frankish kings by reason of Byzantine policy in Italy. The inclusion of St Martin of Tours in the *Menologion* at such a time would be very understandable.

But to whatever extent a model was followed, the art in the dramatic presentation of the scene was something far beyond a mere copyist. In contrast to the artistic heights reached in the portrayal of the personalities, the landscape appears really poor in quality. The explanation is that the 6th-century models used by the painter had no indications of any landscape. This can be seen in the 6th-century codex of Rossano and in the Vienna *Genesis*. Here the artists of the *Menologion* had to rely on their own resources.

30

THE TRANSLATION OF THE BONES OF THE PATRIARCH JOHN CHRYSOSTOM TO THE CHURCH OF THE HOLY APOSTLES. Miniature from the *Menologion* of Basil II. Rome, Biblioteca Vaticana (Cod. Gr. 1613, f. 653).

This miniature shows the body of the patriarch, who had died in exile, being transferred to the capital. The dead man had to be ceremoniously received into the Church of the Holy Apostles, the burial place of the patriarchs. The Emperor and the patriarch, together with high dignitaries, are receiving the saint's coffin. The bearers of the coffin are in the act of putting down their burden in order to make possible the usual ceremony. The Church of the Holy Apostles, partly enclosed by a wall, can be seen in the background behind trees and bushes. There are parts of the park which surround the church where the imperial tombs lie. In the Church of the Holy Apostles an imperial interment did not take place in the interior as was usual in the West. The imperial tombs were outside the church. Some idea of the building can be gathered from San Marco in Venice whose architecture was extensively modelled on that of the Holy Apostles. Patriarchs as well as Emperors were buried in this church. It was only later on that some Emperors chose to be interred in other churches in the capital, and also adopted the western form of burial in a crypt.

31

THE EMPEROR CONSTANTINE IV GRANTING PRIVILEGES TO ARCH-BISHOP REPARATUS OF RAVENNA. Mosaic from the Church of Sant'Apollinare in Classe in Ravenna.

This mosaic shows the Byzantine Emperor Constantine IV (668–85) and the patriarch of Constantinople with Reparatus, the archbishop of Ravenna, who had stayed in Constantinople in 681. It has obvious affinities with the almost 120 years older representation of the Emperor Justinian I in the Church of San Vitale in Ravenna. It has preserved a portrait of Constantine IV, who was one of the most outstanding of the Byzantine Emperors. It was Constantine IV whose heroic defence of Constantinople first compelled the Arabs to retreat and who defeated them in a naval battle, forcing the Umayyad Caliph of Damascus, the great Muawiya, to make peace and pay tribute to the Byzantines.

Constantine IV had summoned the General Council which sat from 7 November 680 to 16 September 681 and attempted to renew ecclesiastical relations with the West which had been disrupted by the monothelete formula now condemned by the Council. This was the occasion of Reparatus' visit to Constantinople, when he obtained the privileges which the Emperor is seen granting him in this mosaic. The picture shows Constantine with his brothers Theodosius and Tiberius. These two are given a nimbus because they were co-Emperors at this period. A few months later they were deposed by Constantine and their noses were mutilated in order to disqualify them for the imperial office.

The Emperor is seen in his robes of state and toga. He is holding the scroll containing the privilege in his hand and is in the act of handing it over to the archbishop, who is receiving it with his hands veiled as a sign of reverence. In the middle, between the Emperor and the archbishop, stands the patriarch of Constantinople. Next to Reparatus on the left is the Empress with two priests on the other side of her, one of whom is swinging a censer. On the Emperor's right are his two crowned brothers, and next to them is a high imperial dignatory bearing the seal with the imperial monogram which is to be affixed to the document in order to give it legal validity. This is one of the few representations of an imperial seal. Extant originals date from a much later period. This imperial seal of state was a heavy seal made of gold and was only used for special documents. Later on it was customary to give the name of 'gold bull' to documents executed with this special state seal.

32

THE 'PROKYPSIS', THE FESTIVAL OF THE WINTER SOLSTICE. Miniature from a manuscript of the book of Job, 905. Venice, Biblioteca Marciana (Cod. Gr. 538).

The artist who was commissioned to illustrate the book of Job made this an opportunity for portraying the Basileus and magnates of Constantinople. This miniature shows the *prokypsis*, or festival of the winter solstice, when the Emperor presented the birth of the sun god in the form of a mime. This sacral festival is indicated by the posture of the imperial couple. Both Emperor and Empress are shown in the attitude of an Orans. This explains the gesture of their hands which signified the manifestation of a god. The Emperor is wearing the *paludamentum* and has the consular *mappa* over his shoulder. The Empress is also in the ceremonial robes of her high office.

As this manuscript of the book of Job comes from the reign of the Emperor Leo VI it is probable that the Basileus shown here is Leo VI himself. This is supported by the similarity of this portrait with that of Leo VI in the narthex of Hagia Sophia in which he appears as a suppliant kneeling in adoration (*proskynesis*) before Christ. It is also indicated by the person of the Empress. At that time the Empress was Zoe Carbonopsina, a former mistress of Leo, whom he had married, after the birth of his first son, in the face of patriarchal opposition. It was not mere chance that this Emperor was represented as Job. Often enough during the course of his reign he had had to play the role of the Biblical sufferer. It is probable that the artist was following up an imperial hint in likening him to the person of 'the righteous Job'.

33

BISHOP GREGORY OF NAZIANZUS IN CONVERSATION WITH THE EMPEROR THEODOSIUS I. Miniature from the *Homilies* of Gregory of Nazianzus. Paris, Bibliothèque Nationale (Cod. Gr. 510, f. 239ᵛ).

The bishop coming from eastern Asia Minor and the Emperor born in Spain both personified their contrasting racial origins. Nor was this all that divided them. As representative of the imperial Church as conceived by Constantine the great Theodosius stood in sharp contrast to the high ecclesiastics of his Empire. His defeat by Bishop Ambrose of Milan is well known. Ambrose was able to compel the proud Emperor to do humble penance to the Church.

This miniature is obviously based on an old picture of the meeting between the Emperor and the bishop which belonged to the days of Theodosius or his immediate successors. This can be deduced by comparing it with the *missorium* or silver votive plate in Madrid. The similarity in the apparel of the Emperor can only be explained if the miniaturist's copy went back to a contemporary picture. This similarity is also seen in the imperial body guards. Both the chain worn round the neck and the hair style of the soldiers are the same as those of the body guard on the silver shield. The throne, too, points to an old model. It is like a ciborium and is covered by a canopy supported on four pillars, similar to the throne on the diptych of the Empress Ariadne now in Vienna (pl. 126).

401

34

THE CORONATION OF THE EMPEROR CONSTANTINE VII PORPHY-
ROGENITUS (913-39) BY THE PATRIARCH. Miniature from the
chronicle of John Scylitzes. Madrid, Biblioteca Nacional (Cod.
S-3 N-Z).

The Emperor, who was still a child at the time of his coronation, is standing with the patriarch under the ciborium of the
altar on a carpet which is decorating the floor. The senate has
taken up its position on the right, the bishops on the left. The
actual extent of the sanctuary is indicated by the carpet, and
outside this the army and the people have gathered, both also
distinct groups with their own functions at the imperial elevation. The patriarch can be recognized from his *phelonion* with
crosses worn over the *phelonion*. The similarity between the
stretched in the act of placing the crown on the Emperor's head
in the early stages of the ceremony. The other important insignia for the coronation are still being carried by the bishops.
In the next stage of the ceremony – not shown here – the
Emperor is clothed with the *chlamys* and *paludamentum*. With
the exception of the patriarch, all the high dignitaries gathered
in the sanctuary have veiled their hands. It was thus that the
Emperor was approached, as though he were divine. Among
the dignitaries standing in the sanctuary the bishops can be
recognized by reason of the *omophorion* embroidered with
crosses worn over the *phelonion*. The similarity between the
dress of the senators and the bishops – the artist of the miniature
has been misled into giving the bishops the white senatorial
caps – emphasizes the origin of liturgical vestments which were
derived from the formal dress of late Roman imperial officials.
The white cap was the official head-dress of the senators up to
the 13th century and they are shown wearing this up to this date
in imperial scenes. This type of head-dress disappeared in the
Palaeologan period but was retained until the end of the 18th
century in the official dress of the Venetian doges, who originally held the dignity of Byzantine patrician and senator.
Among the representatives of the people shown in the miniature standing outside the sanctuary, the representatives of the
circus parties have been introduced, for in spite of their loss of
political power they continued to play a part on ceremonial
occasions. The representatives of the army probably came from
the detachments of the guards.

35

THE ELEVATION OF THE EMPEROR ON THE SHIELD. Miniature from
the chronicle of John Scylitzes. Madrid, Biblioteca Nacional
(Cod. S-3 N-Z).

This comes from the famous manuscript of the chronicle of
John Scylitzes written and illustrated in the 14th century, and is
probably a copy of a no longer extant monumental painting
from the first half of the 13th century. The picture shows the
Emperor at the elevation of a co-Emperor. Both figures, the
Emperor and the co-Emperor whom he has just designated, are
standing on the shield held aloft to display them to all, while
the senate, army and people shout their acclamation and the
trumpets ring out. The Emperor no longer wears the *paludamentum*, the attribute of the Roman general, and the *chlamys*,
the Macedonian warrior's garment, but is clothed in the *saccus*,

the tunic of the high ecclesiastic. This reflects the increased influence of the Byzantine Church in the age of the Palaeologi.
The style of the magnates' dress shows the remarkable headgear of this last phase of the Byzantine Empire. This new form
of head-dress worn by the aristocracy of the Empire, such as is
seen in the picture of the founder of the Chora church, had
taken the place of the peaked white caps found earlier on.

Before the act shown here, the person designated as co-
Emperor by the Basileus would put on his insignia under the
shelter of the raised shield. When this was done, the two Emperors in full regalia mounted the shield and stood on it while it
was raised aloft. The highest office holders then at once approached the edge of the shield which they touched with their
hands. This symbolic action indicated their recognition that
the Emperor, duly raised on the shield, was then legally elevated
to the throne.

The act of elevation on the shield was known as early as the
Roman Empire. It was adopted from Germanic usage, for this
was how the German tribes recognized their rulers. It was introduced to the Romans by the Emperor's German bodyguard
who, led by their military commanders, all too often determined who should occupy the imperial throne. Both Emperors
still hold the *labarum* in their hands, which is reminiscent of the
old Roman ceremony. The *labarum* was the imperial banner
which, since Constantine's day, had borne the monogram of
Christ. The nimbus also remains and adorns both Emperors.

36

THE EMPEROR PROCESSING. Ivory tablet, Byzantine work of the
5th or 6th century. Trier, Cathedral Treasury.

This ivory tablet, part of a reliquary casket, shows one of the
processions led by the Emperor. The great train of people is
headed by the Emperor, who is accompanied by a carriage in
which there are two ecclesiastics holding a casket containing
relics. The Emperor, like his retinue, is holding a candle in his
hand. He has reached the door of a church still in process of
being built and is being received here by the patriarch bearing
a cross. In the background can be seen part of the many-storeyed
complex of the Great Palace buildings, with the Chalke Gate
above which was the well-known icon of Christ. The people
standing behind the windows of the building are swinging a
censer in their right hands while their heads seems to be resting
on their left hands. This is an attitude copied from Christian
psaltai (church singers) who used it, particularly during their
singing, and it dates from pre-Christian times.

The procession shown in the illustration corresponds to those
mentioned in the imperial *Book of Ceremonies*. This notes all the
details which are seen in this section of the procession, the
Emperor wearing his state robes and the reception by high
imperial officials and ecclesiastics at the different parts of the
palace. Here the relief on the ivory tablet shows that point in
the proceedings when the Cross of Christ was kissed. The
patriarch, at the head of his clergy, stands before the church and
greets the Emperor, holding in his left hand the famous relic of
the Cross, while the Emperor is about to hand over his candle
before he venerates the relic.

It is not possible to identify the procession illustrated here
with any definite event or with the festival of any particular

saint because the artist, contrary to the laws of the unity of time and space, has portrayed in a single representation events which were spread over a number of years, such as the building of the church, the production of the relic for the newly erected house of God, and finally the imperial procession.

The Emperor in procession belongs to one of the firmly established themes of imperial art. One of the most famous representations of this theme is the mosaics in the sanctuary of San Vitale with the portraits of the Emperor Justinian and the Empress Theodora.

37

THE FOUR DAUGHTERS OF THE GRAND DUKE YAROSLAV. Fresco in the Sophia church in Kiev.

Little more than fifty years lay between the procession which the candle-bearing daughters of Yaroslav took part in and the day in 989 when the prince of Kiev, St Vladimir, was received into the Christian Church in the cathedral of Crimean Cherson, now surviving only in its foundation walls. The daughters of Yaroslav are wearing the costly robes of the wives of Byzantine nobles. The unusual kerchiefs, some tied in front, but mostly behind the neck under the knotted hair, are a reminder that these are Russian princesses going to church carrying their candles and not Byzantine aristocrats.

One of the princesses shown here married the king of France, Henry I, a few years later on. She took with her to France a copy of the Gospels in Glagolithic script, and it was on this that almost all the French kings used to take their coronation oath in Rheims. This daughter of the Grand Duke Yaroslav, Anna, astonished the West by her Byzantine-Russian learning. She signed her documents with her name in church Slavonic characters. Her husband, the French king, could not write and in this respect bore no comparison with his wife.

38

THE EMPEROR IN A TRIUMPHAL PROCESSION. Gold medallion of Constantine II (337-61). Berlin, Staatliche Museen, Münzkabinett.

The medallion shows the Emperor as *triumphator* in a six-horse chariot. Items from the booty are displayed in front of him at the feet of the horses. The Emperor is represented as the ruler of the world. In his left hand he is holding the symbol of the world, his right hand is raised in prayer. (It is the old form of prayer customary in the Roman army which is shown here. This is also found on the frescoes in the temple of the Arabian gods in Dura-Europos). On each side of the Emperor the medallion shows a goddess of Victory, and the nimbus round his head is the symbol of the sun's orb, taken over from Iran.

Thus, as the medallion shows, during the first centuries after Constantine, the Emperor took part in the triumphal procession. Later the chariot fell out of use, likewise the Roman toga and the presence of the world orb as a symbol of authority. In later triumphs the Emperor used to ride on horseback and then he wore the *paludamentum*. The rich decoration of the bridles, harness and headgear of the horses on the medallion drawing the imperial chariot suggest an Iranian model. This Iranian

decoration of horses used on ceremonial occasions was borrowed not only by the West; Chinese excavations have revealed models of clay horses showing that China, too, adopted this fashion.

39

THE TRIUMPHANT BASILEUS. Textile, 10th century. Bamberg, Cathedral Treasury.

This textile comes from the tomb of Bishop Günther of Bamberg who died in Hungary on his return journey from visiting the Holy Places and Constantinople. His retinue wrapped his corpse in the silk cloth found in his baggage which he had brought from Constantinople. This was later buried with him in Bamberg. When the tomb was opened in the nineteenth century the material was in a relatively good condition. Today only the two female figures remain undamaged. In the imperial figure only the crown, the nimbus and the left hand holding the *labarum* are undamaged. The work done in the nineteenth century shows the condition of the piece when the tomb was opened; in any case this work is not entirely accurate, as a comparison with surviving fragments of the textile shows. Thus the female figure on the right of the Emperor in the textile is not bearing a crown as shown but a diadem.

The Emperor is mounted and wears a tunic which is richly decorated with precious stones and reaches to his feet. The *paludamentum* hangs from his shoulders. In his left hand he holds the *labarum*, the imperial banner, and in the other the horse's bridle, also decorated with costly stones.

A comparison with the representations on the consular dyptichs makes it clear that the women in this textile are the city goddesses of Rome and Constantinople. As a sign of their submission they are holding out to the Emperor a crown and helmet. The picture implies that the East Roman Emperor rules over West as well as over East Rome. This situation only existed after Justinian's defeat of the East Goths and Vandals. Significantly a medallion issued before the victory over Italy shows the Emperor with only one city goddess. It is possible that this cloth was originally a gift from the Byzantine Emperor to the western Emperor. In that case the gift would be understood to have a political point. The Byzantine Basileus would wish to have indicated that at this time he considered himself the legitimate Emperor of East and West Rome; and this would have been underlined by the appearance of these two city goddesses in the textile. As a sign of their submission they both walk barefoot.

The West did not leave unchallenged the Eastern claims, as they are here iconographically expressed. Emperor Otto III had himself represented sitting on the throne with barefoot goddesses representing the conquered lands showing their submission to him. Among them is the city goddess of Rome.

40

THE EMPEROR AS 'TRIUMPHATOR'. Front view of an ivory casket of the 11th century. Treasury of the Cathedral in Troyes.

This ivory casket (height 14 cm., width 13 cm. and length 26 cm.) came from the booty of a crusader at the conquest of Constantinople in 1204. Jean Langlois, chaplain of the bishop of

Troyes, Garnier Traisnel, brought it back to France from the crusade as a valuable piece of booty and presented it to his bishop's cathedral. On both the long sides is found the old motif, long used in Akkadian and Assyrian imperial art, of the fight of a king with a lion and a wild boar. The two short ends show the picture of the phoenix known from the *Physiologus* which, via Byzantium, found its way into western cathedral sculpture, as did the motif of the apotheosis of Alexander. The illustration here shows the decoration of the lid. The pictures on this casket come from a cycle of imperial portraits firmly established in the repertoire of the art of the Empire. The ivory relief shows the Emperor before a besieged city whose gates are being opened so that the city goddess can go to the imperial camp. In her hands she holds a reliquary. Possibly this scene is in the tradition of the holy towel bearing the portrait of Christ, not painted by human hands, which was handed over after the conquest of Edessa in 944. This Holy Towel made its ceremonial entry into the capital on 15 August 944.

The representation shows that the artist used not only late antique, but also Islamic and Persian, motifs. The portrayal of the besieged city indicates this and also reflects the influence of 6th-century Coptic woodcarving as well as that of contemporary miniatures (the Vienna *Genesis*). But in comparison with these works the representations of the ivory casket already show considerable transformation. The form of the pinnacles has affinities with similar and later Arabic miniatures of the Baghdad school of the first half of the 13th century. The symmetry of the composition, with figures of the Emperor to the right and left of the city, points to a pattern from Persian textiles as a model. This use of foreign motifs is very marked; for instance, it is particularly noticeable in the reliefs of hunting scenes on the two longer sides of the casket which may have been copied from Sassanid silver bowls. But in spite of this, the artist still shows considerable independence of his models. He presents the Emperor in the guise of a *triumphator* of the 11th century. This is true of the crown with its individual plaques and also of the high leather boots borrowed from the Altaic nomads and the stirrups which were originally unknown in Byzantium. (In an imperial portrait on a gold medallion Justinian is shown mounted without them.) The artist also departs from his models in the appearance of the city. The churches do not have Byzantine domes but a pointed roof over the drum, as in Armenia. It is noticeable that the Emperor has no nimbus. In addition to his crown he wears as a sign of office the *chlamys* fastened at the shoulder with a brooch; this was originally the Macedonian warrior's garment and belonged to the official robes of the Byzantine Emperors.

41

THE EMPEROR AS 'TRIUMPHATOR'. Detail from an ivory diptych from the former Barberini collection. Paris, Louvre.

This ivory diptych probably dates from the end of the 6th century and shows the Byzantine Emperor Maurice (590-602). The Emperor is on horseback and his mount is rearing up, while the rider is thrusting his lance into the ground.

The Emperor portrayed here has a striking likeness to the gigantic imperial bronze figure in Barletta (Pl. 125). The re-

semblance even extends to details of the features such as the markedly aquiline nose, the angle of the jaw and the hair falling low on the forehead. It also includes the kind of diadem worn, the toga and the armour. It is tempting to regard the Emperor of the Barberini diptych as the Emperor of Barletta mounted on horseback.

The ruler is portrayed as *triumphator*; this is indicated by his footwear, the field marshal's spurs decorated with young lions' heads. The Emperor has apparently won a victory over the Persians, who are represented here by a man with a Phrygian cap and long trousers. This man, who is directing the imperial lance into the ground, may be seen as a Persian ally in the Emperor's victory. In this case the picture is indicating that the Emperor defeated the Persian Empire with the assistance of a claimant to the Persian throne. A situation of this kind did actually occur and this was during the reign of Maurice. At this time the Persian King Hormizd was defeated by the Byzantines supported by his son Chosroes Parvez. The support of Chosroes Parvez is symbolized here by the way in which he is directing the Emperor's lance. The thrusting of the lance into the ground is the symbol of taking possession.

The female figure beneath the horse is the goddess of the earth who, clinging to the Emperor's foot, begs for mercy. On the right the goddess of victory leans over to bestow the crown of victory on him. The Emperor's horse is wearing the well-known costly ceremonial trappings after the Iranian fashion.

42

THE EMIR PINZARACH (BEN ZARAH) BEING RECEIVED BY THE EMPEROR ROMANUS III ARGYRUS. Miniature from the chronicle of John Scylitzes. Madrid, Biblioteca Nacional (Cod. Gr. S-3 N-Z, f. 203).

The visit shown here took place in 1032 after the Byzantine capture of Edessa. With the loss of the city the Arab emir had to seek peace terms. The illustration shows him being received by the Emperor as a vassal on bent knee.

The conquest of Edessa was the last big military success of the Byzantines against the Arabs. A generation later came the advance of the Seljuk Turks and the end of Byzantine plans for expansion in Mesopotamia. Byzantine military achievements had been linked with the person of the Byzantine general, George Maniaces, who scored marked successes in Mesopotamia, and also on the western front in Sicily (see Note to Pl. 73).

In the miniature, Romanus III is wearing his crown, is clothed in his ceremonial robes and is sitting on his throne in a large peristyled court. The emir and his following would have entered the peristyle through a door facing the throne. The Arabs are wearing the *burnus* and have knee-length leather boots. From their appearance they look like Kurds. The great general, Saif ad Dawla, had made this frontier principality famous. In the background the peristyle along one side of the courtyard can be seen. The architecture of the building shown here is similar to the peristyle of the Hormisdas palace where the foundation walls and the bases of the pillars have been excavated. Above the arcade directly under the roof, a passageway for defenders protected by battlements can be seen. The imperial throne is placed under a *baldachino* in the form of a *ciborium*.

43

CONSTANTINE VI AT THE SEVENTH GENERAL COUNCIL (NICAEA II). Miniature from the *Menologion* of Basil II. Rome, Biblioteca Vaticana (Cod. Gr. 1613, f. 108)

This miniature shows the Seventh General Council which was held from 13 September to 13 October 787 in Nicaea in the presence of the Emperor and the patriarch Tarasius. A Council had originally been held on 31 May 786 in the church of the Holy Apostles in Constantinople, but had been adjourned to Nicaea owing to the hostility of the iconoclast troops in the capital.

In the middle of the picture is a cross, and on one side of it is the 17-year-old Emperor and on the other the patriarch. The Empress Irene, who was directing the work of the Council from the palace, is not present. She was the mother of Constantine VI and was still acting as regent, although according to Byzantine law he was then of age. The Emperor was indeed only present at the Council as the figurehead representing the imperial authority, for all decisions were taken by his mother. She did not hesitate to wear the *paludamentum* of a military commander-in-chief; she occupied the imperial box in the Hippodrome; and she even reviewed the troops mounted on horseback just as a man would have done. But it was not until she required the army to take the oath of allegiance to her that they rebelled, thus enabling the Emperor to take control, at least for a short time. But he was moved by his affection for his mother and reprieved her sentence of exile. Shortly after this Irene overthrew him and had him blinded in the imperial palace in the Porphyry Room in which he had been born. In this picture, however, there is no hint of the cruel fate in store for Constantine, though it is possible to sense the atmosphere in which the deed was to take place. The whole Council gathered here, including the Emperor, were nothing more or less than puppets controlled by the Empress. In view of their impotence it is only a mockery that a heretic lies prostrate on the ground before the bishops and clerics confessing his errors, while his judges themselves are trembling before the despotism of the Empress.

The miniature is a copy of a monumental painting clearly designed for some prominent position in the imperial palace. Even in the copy it is possible to detect the hand of a great master. The way in which the robes of the high ecclesiastics are shown falling in folds is very like the Greek models of classical antiquity. The seated goddesses on the pediment of the Parthenon in Athens, or the statues of seated pagan philosophers, belong to the tradition on which the master of this picture drew.

44

THE EMPEROR MICHAEL V ADDRESSING THE POPULACE IN CONSTANTINOPLE. Miniature from the chronicle of John Scylitzes. Madrid, Biblioteca Nacional (Cod. Gr. S-3 N-Z, f. 220ᵛ).

This miniature shows an episode in the downfall of Michael V (1041-42). He belonged to a Paphlagonian working-class family; as his nickname Calaphates shows, his father had been a ship's caulker. His uncle married the Macedonian Empress Zoe and became the Emperor Michael IV (1034-41); he persuaded the old Empress to adopt his young nephew, who became Michael V on his uncle's death. Michael V soon lost patience with the frivolous and extravagant elderly Zoe and banished her to a nunnery on one of the Princes Islands. At this, the populace of Constantinople rose and the old Empress was hurriedly fetched back.

This illustration shows the Emperor haranguing the crowd from a balcony (see Pl. 81). Zoe is sitting on a throne raised on pillars, wearing the imperial diadem. The Emperor hoped to assuage the fury of the mob by displaying Zoe in this manner, but he failed and soon after this episode fighting broke out. He took refuge in the Studite church but was dragged out by the mob, blinded, deposed and exiled.

45

THE EMPRESS THEODORA DISPLAYING AN ICON OF CHRIST. Miniature from the *Menologion* of Basil II. Rome, Biblioteca Vaticana (Cod. Gr. 1613, f. 392).

This miniature from the *Menologion*, dating from the end of the 10th century, shows the formal act whereby icon veneration was restored in the Byzantine Empire. It portrays the Empress Theodora, wife of the Emperor Theophilus (829-42), who became regent for her six-year-old son when her husband died. In March 843 a synod decided on the restoration of the icons. Here the Empress is seen in front of the Magnaura, the entrance hall of the imperial palace in Constantinople, and she is holding up the icon of Christ which was by tradition 'not made by hand' (*acheiropoietes*).

The Empress is standing under the middle of the building where almost five hundred years earlier the Emperor Theodosius I had sat on his throne and carried out his acts of state, as can be seen from the *missorium* or silver plate now in Madrid. It was here that the purple rota was placed, the round disc which indicated the position on the floor where the Emperor stood. Immediately before the imperial burial in the church of the Holy Apostles the coffin of the dead Emperor would be placed in this purple rota. In the illustration the Empress is seen standing on the rota displaying the famous icon of Christ to the populace. This icon was in the form of the *imago clipeata* and originated from a Syrian tradition, as the bearded Christ shows (see Pl. 89 and Note).

46

THE EMPEROR ROMANUS III DROWNS IN HIS BATH. Miniature from the chronicle of John Scylitzes. Madrid, Biblioteca Nacional (Cod. Gr. S-3 N-Z, f. 220).

This miniature shows the murder of the Emperor Romanus III Argyrus in 1034. He was the husband of the seventy-year-old Empress Zoe. When the Emperor began to neglect his wife she was attracted to the young Paphlagonian Michael, who eventually ascended the throne as Michael IV (see Note to Pl. 44).

As no baths of this period have survived, this miniature provides valuable evidence of their appearance. The earliest bath surviving in its entirety is of Justinian's day and was found in excavations in Ephesus. The frescoes of Qusayr Amrah (Pls. 58, 59) give some idea of bathing activities.

This miniature shows other parts of the imperial palace as well as the bath. There is a tower provided with two circular passages. In towers of this kind there were staircases giving entry to the different floors. The bath itself was not roofed in, but was in a courtyard surrounded by a portico rather like the old Greek peristyle.

47

HEROD SHOWN AS BYZANTINE EMPEROR AT A BANQUET. Mosaic in the sacristy of San Marco, Venice.

The mosaic shows the Emperor at one of the great state banquets such as were perhaps held in the Room of the Nineteen Divans in the imperial palace. This was a continuation of the *convivia publica* of the Roman Emperor. Old Roman customs were so closely adhered to that the Emperor, when he was not eating at the same table with his officials, took his meals reclining on a cushion as in Roman times (see Note to Pl. 55).

In this mosaic the Emperor is seen sitting at table and eating together with the Empress and the Caesar, who can be recognized by his diadem. He is being served by a page, while entertainment is provided by a dancing girl, here Salome with the head of John the Baptist.

An invitation to a state banquet of this kind was followed by the sending of costly clothes. Here a distinction was drawn between a more informal dinner, given for those who stood close to the throne, and the big state banquets. The meal illustrated here was of the kind given only to a small circle. But even here, as in the case when hundreds of guests were present, the Emperor ate alone at a golden table at which only the most highly honoured guests were given a place. At imperial banquets not only were the old Roman traditions preserved but Christian elements were present, emphasizing the close relationship between Christ and the Emperor. Thus during the meal the Emperor partook of the so-called *panhagia*, the blessed bread, as was done in a monastery. In the illustration he is serving his guests, the Caesar, who is thanking him for the wine and then, as at the liturgy, dips the bread into the wine.

The empty place to the right of the Emperor, which is set and has bread put by it, is explained by the Byzantine view that Christ sat to the right of the Emperor and shared his meal. The bread seen here, the *panhagia*, is explained by an old apocryphal tradition according to which, after the Ascension, the apostles left an empty place for Christ at their common meal and then, with special prayers, broke the bread set before his place and regarded it as specially holy bread.

The background of the mosaic shows a palace with a roof garden, indicating that the banquet is taking place in the imperial gardens. The dancing girl bears the dish with the head of John the Baptist in a remarkable position which does not fit in with the usual representation of a dance and its movements. This gives the inescapable impression that the mosaic artist has taken the dancing girl from an unknown model and has himself added to the picture the head of John the Baptist. The dancing girl is wearing a costly garment decorated on the sleeves and sides of the mantle with ermine. It is covered with sequins which glitter in the light of the candles. The fingers of the left hand do not hold a tambourine but are marking time instead. She is dancing in high-heeled shoes. The Caesar and the Empress are wearing costly robes decorated with imperial eagles. Only the Emperor, as host, has taken off his cloak; he is wearing the crown and a tunic embroidered with brilliants. The page, who

is standing on the right in the picture, has a dish in his hand and is wearing close-fitting tights and an over-garment cut away at the shoulders with silver buttons both down the front and on the sleeves. These clothes are similar to the style of male dress also found in the West a little later on and show that Byzantium still played a leading part in influencing western fashions.

48

ELEPHANTS. Byzantine silk from the tomb of Charlemagne, Aachen.

When Charlemagne's tomb was opened by Otto III in 1000, the remains of the Emperor found in the old sarcophagus were wrapped in this silk shroud and re-interred. The material dates from the end of the 10th century. It has a sumptuous pattern of richly ornamented elephants placed in medallions. These are reminiscent of the elephant reliefs 150 years later in date on the city walls of Konya (Pl. 95). The use of animals as symbolic of imperial figures was a very old tradition going back to pagan times. These animal figures were meant to symbolize qualities of strength and skill, which is why Persian magnates in the Sassanian period had pictures of animals in their battle dress; the decoration of a ruler's garments in this way clearly derives from Iranian models.

49

THE IMPERIAL 'REPRESENTATIO' AT THE CIRCUS GAMES. Marble intarsia from the basilica of Junius Bassus, first half of the 4th century. Rome, Capitoline Museum.

Junius Bassus was a city prefect whose sarcophagus is still in the entrance by the tomb of St Peter. He was one of the first imperial officials to become a Christian. The picture gives an example of the duties of the imperial *representatio* at the circus games. The consul can be seen in a richly ornamented show chariot, decorated with scenes from Greek mythology (*hippodamaia*) and drawn by white horses, and having once paraded round the arena he is giving the signal for the games to begin. Supporters of both circus parties are following him on horseback. They are wearing the colours of their party and have the equipment needed for the game which is to begin as soon as the consul declares the proceedings open. The sport in question here is a ball game very like polo, which was played on horseback. (Polo itself was first introduced from Persia. There was a special polo ground near the imperial palace used by magnates and princes.)

The tradition of showing the Emperor in connection with the circus games is a very old one, particularly where chariot racing was concerned. Chariot races, with exact reproductions of the starting and finishing points, can be found from the 2nd century (mosaic of Ampurias) down to the frescoes in the entrance to the steps of the Sophia church in Kiev.

50

BREAKING IN A HORSE. Miniature from a manuscript of the *Cynegetica* of Pseudo-Oppian. Venice, Biblioteca Marciana (Cod. Gr. 479 = 881).

This miniature from a manuscript of Pseudo-Oppian, dating

from towards the end of the 11th century, shows two different stages in the training of horses. On the right, a groom in dress-coat and cap is getting ready for the training by putting on the curb. On the left, the training is shown completed: the master of the horse is leading in a horse and putting him through his paces. The horse has no curb and is simply on a bridle.

The master of the horse is wearing Iranian dress: the long narrow fitting Persian trousers decorated with bands of silk, the almost knee-high leather boots, the Iranian caftan, the upper garment cut short for riding purposes. He has on a fur cap.

The elegant clothes worn by the chief groom indicate the importance of his position, and he was not without influence at the imperial court. He was responsible for the imperial mount, which meant selecting a suitable steed for imperial functions, one that would remain quiet whatever the demands of the ceremonial occasion. He had to provide horses for the personal use of the Emperor, for such activities as playing polo or private riding, without formal obligations.

Before he became Emperor, Basil I had held the position of chief groom and as such had been able to make contact with various influential personages at court.

The very accurate illustrations in this Byzantine riders' handbook influenced the Renaissance in the West. The sketches and notes on the composition of his library show that Leonardo da Vinci, for one, had most carefully studied this manual on horses. His sketches for equestrian statues would appear to be indebted to these illustrations.

51

A LION AND AN ELEPHANT. Part of a mosaic in the peristyle of the Hormisdas palace, Istanbul.

During Justinian's reign the Hormisdas palace was used as a residence. The mosaic in the peristyle belongs to one of the well-known cycles of imperial art. A similar theme is found in the palace of Piazza Armerina.

The detail shown here is from a mosaic divided into two zones. The one displays the *oikoumene* ruled over by the Emperor: here peace reigns between men and beasts, and all is harmony. The other zone shows struggles between wild beasts and between men and beasts. It is from this second zone of bitter fighting that the detail is taken.

The portrayal shows excellent observation of nature, though this should not be pressed to include the lion's attack on an elephant, which is not in fact true to nature. The artist had in mind a symbolic meaning lying behind this particular picture. He wished to contrast an animal personifying courage with the elephant symbolizing brute force.

52

A DANCING GIRL. Enamel plaque from the crown of the Emperor Constantine IX Monomachus, c. 1050. Budapest, National Museum.

The plaque shows a dancing girl wearing a long garment and over it a short tunic with close-fitting sleeves. She has on purple bootees and her hair is adorned with a diadem. Her head is nim-bused. The dancer is surrounded by parakeets and plants, partly climbing tendrils, partly springing from the ground. Her tunic is decorated with geometrical ornaments such as those still seen today in Central Asian carpets. In her hand the dancer is holding a piece of twisted material that has the appearance and movement of a snake. In the dance illustrated here, the dancer is balancing first on one and then on the other foot. One foot remains on the ground while the other is brought across the shin-bone of the leg bearing the main weight, so that the dancer achieves a kind of skipping movement. The dance would be accompanied by an orchestra and one of its musicians would probably beat time on the ground with a *scabellum*, a kind of castanet played on by the foot. Dances like the one shown here are found in the pictures of Greek vases at a very early date, and they still form part of the repertoire of dancing girls in the Islamic East.

Here dancing girls – these are two enamel plaques in the crown of Monomachus – are found side by side with the Emperor Constantine IX Monomachus, the Empress Zoe, her sister Theodora, the apostles Andrew and Peter and the allegories of Truth and Humility, on a crown which was perhaps the most important object of the imperial insignia of the Byzantine state. This emphasizes the specially sacred character of these dancing girls who were also given the nimbus, the old symbol of the sun's disc. One has only to think of the dance of the prophetess Miriam after the victorious Red Sea crossing of the people of Israel (see Pl. 53). The extent to which the prophet Moses is worked into the Byzantine imperial cult is well known. His staff was the highest symbol of authority. It is also possible that the dancing girls in the enamels were derived from pictures of the prophetess Miriam. This does not, however, explain the individual nature of the adjuncts to both the dancing girls, such as the climbing flowers and the parakeets. These show Oriental influence. From the 7th century onwards the form of the Byzantine imperial crown had been derived from Persia. Thus the dynasty of the Heraclians from Persian Armenia had replaced the old diadem which went back to the *corona aurea* of the *triumphator* with a crown consisting of a number of hinged plaques. This is found on the coins of the Kushana kings and also on Sogdianian frescoes of the 9th century. The Byzantine imperial crown was clearly much influenced by the crown in use in Iranian regions, perhaps by the Parthian royal dynasty in Armenia from which Heraclius traced his ancestry. The appearance on a Byzantine crown of a dancing girl with a nimbus in the midst of ornamental plants suggesting a garden might perhaps derive from the model of the Persian goddess Anahita (Ardwi sura) who appears on a Persian silver bowl in the midst of a garden (*paridaeza*). This Persian goddess lived on outside Byzantine culture in Islamic lands. A copper bowl with enamel work inside it belonging to the Ortokid emir Rukr ad-Dawla (which is today in Innsbruck) shows a girl performing the same dance in the midst of ornamental plants suggesting a garden. Here the dancing girls are also linked with the portrait of the ruler who, like the Byzantine Emperor, wears the crown with the separate plaques and holds club and sword in his hands. The seat of the ruler is the state throne. Here the ruler portrait keeps to the Sassanid model. The origin of this enamel with the dancing girl points to the Iranian East and goes back to the same model as the Seljuk enamel owned by the Ortokids.

53

THE DANCE OF MIRIAM. Miniature from the Chludov Psalter, manuscript from the second half of the 9th century. Moscow, Historical Museum (Cod. Gr. 129d, f. 148).

The dancing Miriam comes from Psalm 68, 25 and refers to Exodus 15, 20. The artist shows Miriam dancing in front of the people of Israel who have just successfully crossed the Red Sea. She is dancing a circular dance, swinging castanets, while Moses leads the song of victory. Moses, at the head of his people, staff in hand, is standing nearest to her. The people of Israel are just reaching firm land and leaving the sea, which has parted before them in the shape of a pointed arch.

The form of the illustration from this 9th-century manuscript has close links with Syrian models. The same form of illustration is to be found earlier in Syriac manuscripts of the Gospels in the pictures in the wide margins of the text. Thus the Gospel of Rabula, dating from 586, uses this form of illustration which went back to a very old tradition in the East. It is found outside Christendom in fragments found in Turfan and also in Manichaean manuscripts.

In the Chludov Psalter, scribe and artist were not the same person. Notes for the artist as to what he is to illustrate have been written in Greek capitals. This was an old tradition, for an illustrated fragment of the Itala (the Latin translation of the Bible before Jerome made the Vulgate), which was rescued from the binding of a book in Quedlinburg, also has information meant for the painter of the miniatures.

The painter of the miniatures in the Chludov Psalter was not a particularly outstanding artist and yet it is impossible to deny the deep impression made by these somewhat stiff pictures drawn with a heavy hand. The explanation lies in the way in which the old late antique tradition has been transformed. The break with the naturalism of late antiquity is indicated by the manner in which the sea is represented here by a surface broken by waving lines. This break remains in spite of the fact that the representation of the figures shows close dependence on older models. It is true that the arrangement and movement of the figures, indeed even the very folds of their garments, are copied. Moses, for instance, is shown as a beardless young man, and although the painter of the miniature has placed a staff in his hand, the very hand supposed to be holding it is raised in a speaker's gesture. The painter has taken very little trouble to adapt his model. The same is true with the figure of the oldest man. His foot is positioned as though he were standing in front of the leg of the man before him, which is impossible. One gets the impression that the individual figures were copied from different models and then not very skilfully put together in a group. Nor does the painter show any inventiveness in portraying Miriam. Prototypes of dancing girls and Bacchanalians lay to hand in the artistically woven materials of the Egyptian textile industry. It did not matter that for more than two centuries Egypt had not been part of the Empire. At this period the old Coptic patterns were still being copied by Byzantine weavers. It was almost as if everyone were using the words of a foreign language and trying to make a sentence out of them without understanding their meaning. And yet, in this halting language in which the artist was attempting to express himself, the beginnings of a new epoch in representational art can be

seen. There is the way in which the sea is portrayed, the flying mantle, twirling with the swift twist of the body as it dances, touching one of the waves at the edge of the sea, and the staff of Moses pointing to this spot. This is a new kind of realism, far removed from all naturalism, producing what is almost the idiom of abstract symbolism. And there is something more which is important: the theme of the illustration, Psalm 68. The Greek text to which the illustration belongs, Exodus 15, 1-8, gives Moses' song of victory, and Exodus 15, 21, mentioning the song and dance of Miriam, also belongs to this. In the Byzantine imperial conception this dance of Miriam had a special significance. It stood for the dancing girls who preceded the Emperor at his triumph in the circus. This explains why a dancing girl could be represented even on one of the enamel plaques of the Byzantine crown (Pl. 52). The raised staff of Moses in the miniature, like the holy lance of the West, was one of the most highly prized symbols of the Byzantine imperial dignity. It was kept together with the imperial jewels.

54

JOB WITH HIS CHILDREN. Miniature from the manuscript of the book of Job, 905. Venice, Biblioteca Marciana (Cod. Gr. 538, f. 5ᵛ).

This manuscript illustration, showing Job with his sons and daughters in front of a pillared hall, gives some idea of the appearance of Byzantine nobles in the 10th century. The daughters are wearing the ceremonial robes of a noble's wife, as the gold embroidery of the gowns indicates. This was the usual dress for women at that time. A scarf was put round the shoulders and, in contrast to Justinian's day, the hair was worn without any covering veil. The characteristic item of the men's clothing was the dress-coat which had wide bands of gold embroidery on the edges like the women's gowns. The footwear was reminiscent of puttees which have been found in excavations. They may perhaps have been made of strips of material which were woven together, or constructed out of strips of imported Chinese silk.

55

BYZANTINE MAGNATES AT A BANQUET. Miniature from the manuscript of the book of Job, 905. Venice, Biblioteca Marciana (Cod. Gr. 538, f. 7).

This miniature shows part of one of the great court festivals which were held on appointed days for the great men of the Empire. The banquet illustrated here appears to have been held in the Room of the Nineteen Divans, as is shown by the table in the form of a semi-circle. This chamber was so called because it contained nineteen divans, each seating twelve persons. There were a corresponding number of tables of the same shape as that shown in the miniature. At banquets given in this room Roman table customs were still followed. These differed from the meal-time habits generally in use among the Byzantines. With the method of reclining at table, a custom still found in the late Roman period was carried on (see Note to Pl. 47). For the Byzantines of the 10th century, this was not an anachronism, since it was part of imperial ceremonial. Here in the central period of the Middle Ages, what had once been the daily custom at meals in antiquity, now long abandoned in everyday life, was still continued on certain occasions. But though it was clearly a ceremonial duty for Emperors to recline at table at the various state banquets, the invited courtiers, as this miniature shows, felt less closely bound by the dictates of protocol and took up a rather uncomfortable sitting position on the divan round the meal table. At table the women were seated on one side, the men on the other, and the front of the table was draped with an artistically woven carpet with formal flower patterns.

This miniature does not show very much of the special festive garments of distinguished Byzantine magnates or of the women's jewellery, diadems and earrings. But in another miniature in the same manuscript the guests sitting here at table are seen standing in a hall. Here the effect can be seen of the women's heavy silk dresses sweeping to the ground and the magnates' coats with embroidery almost half a metre wide round the hems and the sleeves richly embroidered round the cuffs. Both men and women wore a broad silk scarf round their shoulders that had taken the place of the *tablion* and in the same way served to drape their hands when the Emperor entered the hall. As this miniature shows, even during the meal the magnates dining at table took care to conceal their hands as far as possible out of reverence for the Emperor. Seating at table was according to age and rank. In the centre of the table the oldest and most distinguished of the men sat and at his side the lady of highest rank.

56

JOB AT TABLE. Miniature from the manuscript of the book of Job, 905. Venice, Biblioteca Marciana (Cod. Gr. 538, f. 7).

Job, in the apparel of a Byzantine magnate, is sitting at table with his friends when the terrible news is brought him. He remains calm, his composure and detachment contrasting with the great agitation among the rest of those present. The magnates are sitting round a semi-circular table, as was usual in antiquity. In the middle there is a large bowl containing the food which has been served up and the guests help themselves and break off pieces to eat. The side of the table show is decorated with fine-spun material, artistically arranged in folds. The messenger who has come in is wearing untanned leather boots like the nomads of the steppes. This kind of footwear was adopted by the Byzantines. The seating at a semi-circular table points to a banquet at the imperial court where tables of this kind were customary.

57

MOSAIC IN THE COURTYARD OF THE GREAT MOSQUE IN DAMASCUS.

These mosaics date from about 715 and, like the frescoes of Qusayr Amrah, dating in part from the mid-9th century, they really belong to Byzantine art. These masterpieces were commissioned by Byzantine magnates living under Arab domination. Members of such families served their new masters in an administrative capacity; an example was the Byzantine church father John of Damascus, who had been in charge of Arab financial departments before he entered the monastery of St Sabas near Jerusalem. The Great Mosque of Damascus was built on the site of the destroyed church of John the Baptist

which, until the city's capture by the Muslims, had contained his tomb. Shortly before the fall of the city his bones had been sent to Constantinople.

The architecture of the Great Mosque of Damascus is closely modelled on that of the oldest Islamic prayer-houses in Medina and Cairo, but the mosaics round the courtyard are certainly the work of a Byzantine master. The scene shown here is that of a country palace, perhaps belonging to an imperial official. In the foreground there is a semi-circular pillared hall. This differs from the usual type of palace building which, from the Hellenistic period onwards, had had a rectangular courtyard with a peristyle. The palace in the mosaic is flanked on each side by a tower. Buildings are attached to it, obviously containing rooms for domestic staff. The towers were probably also used for this purpose as there are stairs leading to the upper storey. The same is found outside the building of the so-called Palace of Theodoric in Ravenna dating from the 7th century (see Note to Pl. 77). In the mosaic the roof is supported by pillars. This meant that the actual area in front of the building was in the shade; a number of doors opened on to this. The space between the pillars of the pillared semi-circular hall was filled with lattice work, thus protecting those living in the palace from the gaze of unannounced visitors.

Behind and in front of the palace there are a number of smaller dwellings mostly looking rather like little kiosks. In the distance there is a fortress which is rather like a western castle. There is a large fortified tower and a tall domed building which is probably a church. As later in the West, this castle is divided into the main building with tower, church and main dwelling apartments and a lower building with the servants' quarters. The presence of this castle in a park with its palace of leisure points to a situation near to the frontier where men had to be on the alert in case of sudden attack and therefore took appropriate precautions.

The artist shows his close powers of observation in his accurate picture of the tall trees in the foreground – perhaps cedars – and the trees behind the palace which have grown into a little wood. This mosaic is one of the few remaining examples of the great skill with which Byzantine artists could portray landscapes. (See also Pl. 81 and Note.)

58 and 59

SCENES OF THE HIPPODROME IN CONSTANTINOPLE. Details of a fresco in Qusayr Amrah, Jordan.

The fresco from which these two details come is earlier than other frescoes in the palace and belongs to the middle of the 9th century. In the part not reproduced here are shown the Emperor Michael III, born 838, with his mother Theodora and his sister Thecla. The fact that the Emperor is presented with his mother and sister indicates that the picture originated during the regency of the mother, Empress Theodora. Along with her name those of the Emperor and his sister appear on coins minted during the regency. Their portraits in Qusayr Amrah are attested by Arabic and Greek inscriptions.

It may seem curious at first that the Byzantine emperor and his family should appear, within the framework of pictures of the Hippodrome, in an Arabian palace. But this is by no means a unique occurrence, for even two hundred years later, in the

Hagia Sophia in Kiev, other Byzantine emperors with their families are shown in the context of scenes of the Hippodrome in Constantinople. As in Kiev, so in Qusayr Amrah, the pictures were executed by Byzantine painters. In view of the close relations which existed between Baghdad and Constantinople during the reign of Emperor Michael III this is not surprising.

The composition of the frescoes, of which only details of performances in the Hippodrome are shown here, is arranged in three scenes. The first, not reproduced here, is the one which shows the imperial family who are in ceremonial procession to the Hippodrome in order to take their places there in the state loges. The second scene shows a pantomime. A woman steps out of a marble bath while being observed by men behind screens. This was a pantomime which evidently exploited an old Greek myth in order to offer the audience an undressing scene similar to a modern striptease. In the third picture one can see acrobats leaping over a rope held by women. Nearby an athlete supports a man in the air with his left arm.

All the scenes indirectly give an impression of the Byzantine style of life in the 9th century. It begins with the Empress Theodora who, like the Empress Irene before her, sought to take upon herself the rights of a Basileus. The portrait in the fresco reveals how great the egotism of this Empress must have been. The picture of the woman stepping out of the bath (Pl. 58) shows the other side of Byzantine civilization, little of which is described in the surviving material: the life behind ceremonial and appearances. The pantomime records episodes in the private life of an aristocratic Byzantine woman who is shown here in one of the women's rooms, not in her splendid garment, but wearing only a transparent shift. This is a counterpart to the presentation of the Byzantine court women, in their stiff brocade clothing laden with jewellery, who appear in the mosaic in San Vitale, Ravenna.

The picture of the leaping acrobats (Pl. 59) is artistically a significant achievement. The movements of the leaping men are masterfully depicted. In contrast to the frescoes on the same theme in Kiev, which represent the practice of acrobats in a wooden, awkward, narrative style, the scene here reveals a mastery which was not to appear again until Michelangelo's cartoons of bathing soldiers.

60 – 63

HUNTING SCENES. Miniatures from a manuscript of Pseudo-Oppian, *Cynegetica*. Venice, Biblioteca Marciana (Cod. Gr. 479 (=881), f. 19ᵛ and 20ʳ).

These pictures show men hunting lions and gazelles, a pursuit which would not be found in the 11th or 12th centuries. It was well-known, however, that the Byzantine Emperors were enthusiastic huntsmen. Hunting on a grand scale, like participation in the Circus shows, had long been regarded as an indispensable imperial activity. It was while he was out hunting that Basil I was attacked by a stag and gored by its antlers. The terribly wounded man was carried some way on the animal before it was caught and the Emperor was dragged off the antler on which he had been impaled.

These miniatures in Pseudo-Oppian reproduce traditional hunting scenes such as would have been found in late antiquity and were a much favoured form of decoration in imperial

villas and palaces, particularly during the iconoclast period. The miniaturists copied these paintings, thus preserving them for posterity. The antiquity of the models copied is shown both by the portrayal of animals no longer available to the Byzantines of the 11th and 12th centuries and by the sparsely indicated trees. These trees are well-known from the Ravenna sarcophagi of the 4th and 5th centuries and they are indirect evidence for the antiquity of the prototypes. The clothing worn by the figures in the pictures provides evidence for the provenance of the model. The shortened caftan and the long close-fitting trousers are characteristic of the East Syrian regions on the Syrio-Parthian frontier. They are reminiscent of the three children in the fiery furnace in the 6th-century icons and in the 4th-century frescoes in the catacombs.

The individual scenes show (60) hunting a lion with a spear, (61) ensnaring a lion with a net, (62) Castor hunting a lion and a stag, (63) Pollux hunting a wild boar and a gazelle.

64

HUNTING SCENE. Detail from an ivory casket of the 10th century. London, British Museum.

Burlesques of hunting scenes, such as are seen on this casket, were found in antiquity. There are, for instance, the hunting pygmies on frescoes in Pompeii and the pygmy hunt on a mosaic at Piazza Armerina. Hunting dwarfs are also found in the 6th-century mosaic in the Hormisdas palace and in the frescoes on the staircase in the Sophia church in Kiev. This little ivory casket shows the extent to which late antique models were still being copied in the middle Byzantine period. There were similar burlesques on horseracing where dwarfs are seen competing in chariots drawn by birds. Instances can be found in the age of Justinian, and also in 11th-century frescoes in Kiev.

65

CONSTANTINE TRIUMPHS WITH THE HELP OF THE CROSS. Miniature from the manuscript of the Chludov Psalter. Moscow, Historical Museum.

This miniature, dated from the second half of the 9th century, shows the Emperor Constantine in the armour of a Byzantine cavalryman at the battle of the Milvian Bridge. He has the long lance and the small shield carried by these troops. His opponents, the soldiers of Maxentius, with their pointed caps and wide breeches and special bows, are most realistically portrayed as Pechenegs from the Russian steppes. The way they are shown drawing their bows indicates that the miniaturist had first-hand knowledge of these Turkic horsemen. The Emperor's horse is rearing up in the manner usually seen in the portrayal of an imperial triumph, as for instance in the ivory diptych from the Barberini collection (Pl. 41).

66

BYZANTINES FIGHTING SELJUK TROOPS. Miniature from a manuscript of the Chronicle of John Scylitzes. Madrid, Biblioteca Nacional (Cod. Gr. S-3 N-Z, f. 234).

This miniature shows a detail from a fight between Byzantines and Seljuk Turks. It illustrates the essential difference between Byzantine and Seljuk arms. The Byzantines rode without stirrups and relied almost exclusively on their lances. The Turks, on the other hand, had both bows and lances. They used stirrups which made it possible to direct their arrows with accuracy while on horseback. On each side of the saddle was a container, one for the bow when the lance or sword was being used, the other for the quiver holding their arrows.

67

THE GERMAN BODYGUARD. Detail from the silver *missorium* of the Emperor Theodosius I (379-95) found in Estremadura in Spain. Madrid, Academia de la Historia.

This *missorium* shows the Emperor Theodosius sitting on the throne with his two sons and was probably destined for the Visigothic king Alaric. Together with the royal treasure it reached Spain, where the Visigothic king founded a new kingdom.

The bodyguards shown here are Germans. The shields, the long hair, the ring round the neck, these all indicate members of a Germanic tribe. By now the Roman Emperor had accepted the allegiance of the Germans and had enrolled them in his bodyguard. Indeed one of the most important Byzantine themes was later on to bear the name 'Opsikion' which came from the Latin 'obsequium' and was called after the German imperial guards. It is in fact known that in the 10th century the ethnic composition of the imperial guards (the *scholae*) was still recognizable. They were called the 'gothogrekoi', that is, the Gothic Greeks. The important role of this bodyguard in imperial ceremonial is made clear in the 10th century by Constantine VII's *De Ceremoniis*. At this time Gothic songs and dances still had their place in the ceremonies.

68

ST DEMETRIUS. Icon in relief in the church of San Marco in Venice.

The 13th-century marble icon of St Demetrius is obviously a copy of the icon of this saint which is now in the Tretiakov Gallery in Moscow. It is an open question as to whether these two or their prototypes were copies of a relief. Like Joshua on the ivory relief (Pl. 71) and in the miniatures in the Joshua Roll, the saint is seated on a folding chair. Roman generals used chairs of this kind when presiding over an assembly in the capacity of judge or political leader (consul).

The garments of Demetrius are not those of a 12th-century Byzantine. The saint's uniform is the same as that on the statue of Constantine, the first Byzantine Emperor. Demetrius was a contemporary of Diocletian, and it is possible that both here and in his portrayal in the mosaic in Thessalonica (Pl. 155) a contemporary prototype was used. The saint is standing in the act of drawing his sword, a particular military situation, that is, the command to attack. It was customary for the Emperor to give the signal with his sword. Bugles relayed this signal to the troops who had already been put on the alert by the warning 'parati', 'ready'. As the bugles signalled, the cry 'Deus' went up from the officers, answered by 'Adiuta' from the ranks. This was the signal to open battle. In the 10th century in the Byzantine army the command to attack was still being given by the Latin words used by the Pannonian Emperors in the 4th and 5th centuries.

69

FIGHTING BETWEEN ROMANS AND GERMANS. Detail from an ivory casket dating from the 8th to the 10th century. London, Victoria and Albert Museum.

Fighting of the kind shown here no longer took place in the Byzantine Empire, and the Byzantine artist copied it from a model dating from the late Roman imperial epoch. These scenes can be compared with the so-called sarcophagus of St Helena, the mother of Constantine the Great, in the Lateran Museum in Rome. This does not, in fact, belong to the Constantinian period, but is older and comes from an imperial mausoleum. It is known that sarcophagi of Roman Emperors which survived were used again. The porphyry sarcophagus of Hadrian was later made use of for a pope. Thus the fighting scenes on the so-called sarcophagus of St Helena probably belong to the 3rd century. These sarcophagi portrayed fighting between Romans and Germans, as on the ivory relief shown here. The long-haired Germans are wearing long trousers and are naked from the waist upwards, while the Romans are equipped with the armour of the early Empire. This is a clear case of imitation of an early model.

70

A MILITARY SAINT. Fresco from the church of the Brontocheion monastery (church of the two Theodores), Mistra.

The church of the two Theodores was erected by the monk Pachomius and his fellow brother David (see Note 166). Pachomius had been prominent in the struggle against Latin domination in the Peloponnese. His services in helping to free the Greeks in the Morea did not pass unnoticed by Constantinople. The Emperor gave considerable help to the church built by the two monks. The wall frescoes, dating from just before the end of Byzantine rule, were unfortunately much damaged by the fall of the roof. Some of them were painted during the reign of the last Byzantine Emperor, Constantine XI, who was crowned Emperor in Mistra on 6 January 1449. These included the Annunciation to the Virgin Mary in the apse and the fresco with two military saints, of which only the left-hand figure has survived. It is possible that the unknown Byzantine painter has portrayed here Constantine XI, who had been ruler of the Morea (he died in Constantinople in 1453).

The saint in the fresco has a reserved, almost resigned, air. He has the curly hair and somewhat dandified moustache which at this time was used both here and in Italy to portray the ideal manly figure. The careless elegance with which he carries his general's cloak, worn over the armour of a cavalry officer, is true to life and the artist has admirably conveyed the aristocratic bearing of his subject. The technique of the artist reveals his high quality; both the handling of the folds and the portrayal of the face can hold their own with the work of the great masters of the Italian Quattrocento.

411

71

JOSHUA RECEIVES AMBASSADORS FROM THE CITY OF GIBEON. Detail from an ivory casket. London, Victoria and Albert Museum.

This detail from a 10th-century ivory casket shows Joshua, the Israelite leader, receiving ambassadors from the city of Gibeon (*Joshua*, 9, 6). This belongs to a series of scenes illustrating Joshua's life, the best known of which is the Joshua Roll in the Vatican Library, presenting the Israelite leader's deeds just as though it were reporting imperial achievements. This particular Biblical hero was specially dear to the Byzantines, as their art shows. Joshua was regarded as being symbolic of the high Byzantine commander who fought against the infidel. He was as it were, the opposite number to an equally beloved Biblical figure, Job. In both these personalities the Byzantines found something which corresponded to their own lives and experiences, and they liked to see them represented in their art.

The event here taken from the book of Joshua illustrates the customary ceremonial when foreign ambassadors were received in a Byzantine camp. Joshua is sitting on a throne surrounded by his body guard. The ambassadors are approaching with veiled hands as a sign of respect and are about to kneel and prostrate themselves. There are many scenes similar to this; for instance, the German chieftains doing homage to the Emperor Marcus Aurelius. Thus the craftsman is following an old tradition in Roman imperial art. Here the military equipment is that of the 10th century. The soldiers are wearing chain armour fastened to the shoulders by leather straps. Their helmets, surrounded by rounded crests, are those of the contemporary imperial body-guard. The straps of the armour are white, hence the name by which these guards were known – *candidati*. Joshua is shown here as a general holding the long staff which, as early as Roman times, was one of the attributes of a commander-in-chief. It is found, for instance, in the hand of Augustus in the statue of the Prima Porta. This staff was originally not merely an attribute, but did in fact serve to call the troops to order.

72

JOSHUA COMMANDS THE SUN TO STAND STILL. Miniature in the Octateuch in Topkapu Saray. Istanbul (Cod. graec. 8).

This miniature from the Octateuch illustrates the story of Joshua, 10, 12, and shows him as a general in battle. His right hand is raised in prayer. This is the same manner of praying as is seen, for instance, in the tempera frescoes of the Palmyrene gods at Dura-Europos. As in the pagan late antique manner, the sun and moon are shown as gods with human faces. This suggests a comparison with the sun and moon gods, Aglibol and Jahribol, worshipped in Dura, who were represented in the same way.

In the illustration the city of Gibeon lies on the left. The city goddess is seated waiting in the gateway following the course of the battle. A band of cavalry have just been given the command to attack, a group of them have surged up a hill, the long lances of the cavalrymen in the first ranks are already taking their toll. The attack takes the enemy unawares, for the lances of its troops are not raised in defence. In the foreground there is a struggle between bands of infantry. Here too the battle is in Joshua's favour. The greater part of the enemy are dead or wounded. One is imploring mercy with upraised hand.

This miniature is one of the best pictures of a battle scene of the Byzantine period. To view it in the context of the development of Byzantine art it is necessary to go back to the late antique archetype preserved in the Joshua Roll now in the Vatican. In all probability this roll dates from the same period as the frescoes of Castelseprio, that is, from the 7th century, but, like these, it derives from a considerably earlier model which in this case can perhaps even be assigned to the first half of the 4th century. This would mean that it is separated from the frescoes of the synagogue of Dura-Europos by only about half a century.

The Joshua Roll of the Vatican shows Joshua in the same pose as in the miniature of the Octateuch. His right hand is raised towards the sun in prayer, his left hand holds spear and shield. The city goddess sits before Gibeon with its gates and towers. In the composition of the battle scene there is also considerable similarity. The infantry battle in the foreground with the fallen soldier begging for mercy and the attack of the cavalry are present. The groups of dead and wounded in the foreground of the miniature in the Octateuch correspond to those in the Vatican Roll. Both show the wounded warriors lying on the ground thrown on to their shields, as found earlier on the east pediment of the temple on Aegina and together with other motifs repeated by the artists of classical and late antiquity. The groups of dead and wounded on the left side of the picture correspond to about half the pediment of the temple. In Aegina the groups of those fighting also occupy the centre, leaving the smaller and diminishing area of the pediment for the dead and wounded. This may possibly indicate that the pediment relief of a Greek classical temple was the earliest model of this miniature transmitted by unknown intermediaries.

Then the question arises of the Byzantine painter's ability as an artist. Here a comparison of the miniature of the Octateuch with the Joshua Roll is favourable to the former. The miniature shows the dramatic moment when the battle turns, the sun is commanded to stand still, the daylight does not fade into evening, the battle can be continued to the destruction of the foe. The Joshua Roll does indeed portray Joshua as the commander on the battlefield but he appears only as the leader in the battle. The miracle achieved by his prayer to God is deprived of all its credibility by reason of its extremely naturalistic portrayal. In the miniature the darkness of the mountains, falling on the groups of cavalry and throwing the bright lights shining on the horses' limbs into sharp relief, creates the atmosphere of approaching night. Then the Byzantine painter has placed Joshua nearer to the sun. Its rays are still shining on groups of foot soldiers, while Joshua and the cavalry are in the dark. The reason for the extremely dramatic presentation of the Octateuch does not lie simply in the colouring. The painter of the Octateuch has refused to copy the massing of the soldiers evidently dominating the picture in the archetype, as can be seen from the Joshua Roll. Only relatively few appear. With his small, easily distinguishable groups he manages to bring to life for the viewer different situations which arise during the battle.

The manuscript of the Octateuch was commissioned by the Sebastocrator Isaac Comnenus and was written and illuminated in 1152. It was for the monastery of the Mother of God the

Saviour of the World at Ferenzik near Dedeagač at the mouth of the Marica. Despite his high office Isaac was distinguished for his literary ability, and he made a new version of the text of the letter of Aristeas with which the manuscript begins. The miniatures have still lost none of the freshness of their original colouring.

73

THE BYZANTINE GENERAL MANIACES DEFENDING EDESSA. Miniature from the chronicle of John Scylitzes. Madrid, Biblioteca Nacional (Cod. Gr. S3 – N2, f. 208).

George Maniaces, one of the most famous Byzantine generals, conquered Edessa in 1032 and held the city against Muslim attacks. As his name suggests, Maniaces was of Iranian origin. He later attempted to gain possession of the Byzantine imperial throne.

This miniature shows the Arab onslaught. Archery is being used to try to dislodge the defenders from the walls of the city. It is interesting to notice the presence of western mercenaries among Maniaces' troops. They are distinguishable by their different shaped shields, like those seen later on the frescoes of Boyana. These shields were carried by Normans and were used by their kinsmen in the Russian Varangian guard. These Varangians first served under the Byzantines in Basil II's reign.

As the miniature shows, the Arabs succeeded in penetrating into the city while the defenders were distracted by an attack of the Arab army outside the walls. The street fighting raged backwards and forwards and some Arabs managed to get possession of part of the city fortifications.

74

A NAVAL BATTLE. Miniature from the *Cynegetica* of Pseudo-Oppian. Venice, Biblioteca Marciana (Cod. Gr. 479, f. 24^r).

This illustration from the manuscript with the *Naumachia*, naval warfare, shows two relatively small Byzantine naval vessels in combat. The type of boat shown here has shields hanging over both sides, on top of the oars, like the Varangian and Norman ships. They are almost the same kind of vessel as those found on the contemporary Bayeux tapestry, illustrating the conquest of England by William the Conqueror's Normans. The similarity is not fortuitous. In the 10th and 11th centuries the Byzantines were known to have used Scandinavian mercenaries in many of their naval battles. This participation of the Vikings in Byzantine campaigns found an echo in Nordic poetry. Byzantium was called Micklegard. Harald Hardrada, who later became king of Norway, was actually one of the Byzantine naval leaders in the fighting over the island of Sicily.

The ships in the illustration have hauled in sails and taken down the masts. By reason of the proximity of the enemy they were moved forward by oar and were therefore much more easily manoeuvrable than in full sail. In both boats the helmsman is recognizable, the signal trumpeter stands beside him. When the boats had manoeuvred fairly close to each other he gave the signal for attack which would be passed on by all boats. Procedure here was similar to that of land fighting. There the commander with the trumpet gave the signal for immediate attack. The command was, in Latin, 'Parati' ('Ready!'), and

this was repeated by the soldiers. Then came the command for the actual attack, 'Deus' ('God'). 'Adiuta' ('Help'), the soldiers replied, completing the phrase and then with lances outstretched they hurled themselves on the enemy.

It was the same with the fleet. They took up a half-moon formation with the heavy squadrons of dromons outside, the light vessels more in the middle and the admiral's flagship right in front in the centre. As soon as the two wings had met the enemy, a passage was made by the ships in the centre to allow boats to slip through. The two horns of the half-moon with the dromons had to surround the enemy fleet and catch them in the rear so that they were encircled. Contrary to present practice, the battle was opened by the heavy squadrons which, as they sailed by, attempted to break their opponents' oars and to overpower them by siphoning Greek fire at them. After this, when the loss of some of their oars and the effect of Greek fire had made it difficult to manoeuvre the enemy ships, they were attacked with rams. The large ships were often unable to disentangle themselves in close-up fighting. Then the light ships took on the attack, as is shown in the miniature.

75

PLAN OF THE PALACE OF QASR IBN WARDAN IN NORTH SYRIA.

This plate gives the ground plan of the extensive surviving ruins of the palace built during the late 6th century in the reign of Justin II. It bears a marked resemblance to that of a Greek house of antiquity and it is especially like those of Pompeii. Its chief characteristic is the great inner courtyard with its peristyle. An example is the palace building of Split erected by Diocletian. There, too, there is the peristyle with arcading.

The ground plan shows the imposing entrance gate. After passing through this, one reached the inner courtyard, giving a direct view on to the throne-room. This is marked black in the plan because the walls are still standing. The throne-room in the form of the Persian *liwan* is like that in the palace of Chosroes Anushirwan. Unlike Iranian palace buildings, Qasr ibn Wardan had an apse in the ceremonial audience room, and today the niche in the apse for the imperial throne can still be seen. There were doors on the right and the left leading out of the *liwan* to two more throne-rooms, which also each had an apse. Clearly rooms were needed which could be used when an imperial council was sitting in the presence of the ruler. There were also doors out of these three larger halls giving entry to smaller rooms, probably used as offices by the imperial secretariat. The rest of the palace (in hatching on the plan) is difficult to identify because very little has survived. These were probably rooms for private use, adjoining those used for official business. There were certainly baths which may have served as a model for Qusayr Amrah. Close to the palace was a domed basilica in which emperor and court could take part in the services.

76

FAÇADE OF 'PALACE OF THEODORIC'. Detail from the so-called Palace of Theodoric in Ravenna (6th and 7th centuries).

The façade of the so-called Palace of Theodoric in Ravenna is still standing and gives some idea of Byzantine palace architecture in the 7th century. Unfortunately, conversion into a church in the 8th and 9th centuries made much of the old palace building unrecognizable. The façade in its present form is the result of the restoration undertaken at the beginning of the 20th century. Originally the lower storey with its arcades on each side of the central door was walled up and lit only by small round windows. The pillars and capitals of the arcades as now restored came from the church of San Michele in Ravenna. But the arches and arcading of the upper storey belong to the original period of the building. The back of the palace (not visible in this illustration) shows that the present façade was part of an arcaded entrance hall with a large central door. This led to an atrium that was adapted by the addition of pillars in order to enlarge the nave when the building was converted into a church. The atrium had a large mosaic pavement like that found in the 6th-century palace of Hormisdas in Istanbul. Surviving fragments of this mosaic show that it was a hunting scene and, like the Hormisdas mosaic (Pl. 51), its theme was the struggle between men and wild beasts. It was obviously a picture of a disordered world meant to contrast with the peaceful regime under beneficent imperial rule.

The front of the palace had two staircases giving entrance to the upper part of the building. This was probably the same kind of arrangement as was found in Hormisdas palace, and later on in Kiev, and it afforded separate entrances to the upper storeys for men and women. After the palace had been converted into a church, the upper storey of the palace whose windows had looked out on to the atrium was used as a gallery. There were no windows on to the street. The arcading placed over the entrance door of the central building was like vaulted apsed niches designed to receive statues of the king and important members of the family. This kind of palace architecture with windows looking inwards and blind windows on the outside to contain statues is known, for instance, from the reliefs on the Arcadius Column copied by Quattrocento artists before its destruction. The palace in its original form would have afforded a view from the street through the great archway of the central door. This was so designed that anyone looking through the doorway of the central building would see the opposite side of the palace with the imperial throne-room and the throne in the apse. Here the architectural arrangements closely follow the protocol of imperial ceremonial carefully preserved by the Gothic king when he built his palace.

77

SOUTH VIEW OF CHURCH AND PALACE, QASR IBN WARDAN, SYRIA.

This Byzantine imperial palace of the 6th century lies between Homs and Aleppo, and the Arabs call it Qasr ibn Wardan. One of the few surviving palace buildings of the age of Justinian, it was erected by Isidore of Miletus, one of the two distinguished architects of Hagia Sophia. Since he was specifically mentioned in an inscription in the palace, there is no doubt about its dating. Isidore had been in Syria since 550, as is attested by an inscription. He probably supervised the great imperial fortifications strengthening the Strata Diocletiana, the line of defence against the Arab desert tribes. Even the palace of Qasr ibn Wardan had its role in this system of military defence; this is true of the basilica as well as the adjoining palace. Only part of the palace has survived, but in contrast to Ravenna and Constantinople

this is not simply the entrance-way but part of the actual palace itself. As the plan shows (Pl. 75), here the palace is built round a courtyard (atrium) which is entered in order to reach the actual imperial palace buildings. Of the three palaces surviving from Justinian's day Qasr ibn Wardan is the only one to give any idea of the buildings used for audiences. The imperial throne-room which opened off the atrium was here in the form of a porticoed hall (liwan), thus showing Iranian influence. The great liwan at Ctesiphon comes to mind, though such a vast complex of buildings as this could not of course be repeated at Qasr ibn Wardan. In Ctesiphon the liwan was designed to contain the throne of the Great King. A chain was suspended from the vaulting and from this hung the almost two hundred-weight heavy Persian crown under which the Greek King took his seat. The effect of this was to make it seem as though the Great King was actually wearing a crown of this kind. The Byzantine Empire did not adopt this Persian ceremonial though it did copy the liwan of Iranian royal palaces. Visitors arriving at the palace could look through the archway of the central building and at once see the inner courtyard with the throne-room in the middle and the imperial throne under a baldachino. Although there is clear Iranian influence here, the actual technical execution and the architectural detail were the work of Byzantine craftsmen. As in the Hormisdas palace, the windows and doors were set in rectangular marble frames surmounted by arches. Unfortunately, apart from the throne-room and the adjoining apartments of the palace, only the foundation walls have survived, but this does at least make it possible to reconstruct the ground plan of the whole complex of buildings.

78

THE RUINS OF AN IMPERIAL PALACE. Hormisdas palace, Istanbul.

The palace of Hormisdas dates from the first half of the 6th century. Hormisdas was a Persian prince who left his own country for political reasons and sought asylum in Constantinople. It was he who first lived in this palace. Later on, in Justinian I's time, it was further enlarged. Justinian's monogram adorns the splendid landing stage which would have been used by visitors arriving by sea. Today only the bare shell is left. During the Byzantine period, most of the building was incorporated into the sea wall built for reasons of defence, and its architectural features were therefore lost. It is only with great difficulty that anything of its original appearance can be reconstructed. As in Ravenna, there was a central arch with arcading on each side, but in contrast these were not blind but genuine openings so designed that the cool sea breezes could blow into the palace. The building was entered by means of a splendid staircase leading to the upper storey. For military reasons the ground floor had neither windows nor doors. Like Ravenna, there was a vaulted arched hall which opened on to the atrium. Viewed from the outside, there is considerable difference between this palace building and that of Ravenna. Under the arcading there are rectangular doorways set in marble framework. Over the markedly projecting upper marble transoms of each doorway was an arched window which was obviously meant to light the interior. The upper windows had glass in them, as can be seen from miniatures of them. This glazing was of coloured glass, thus creating an effective atmosphere inside the building. This was very like the palace building of Darius in Persepolis. It must also be remembered that the present-day bare walls would have been covered with polished marble tiles; these would have given the palace an almost supernatural iridescence as they glittered in the sun. It is a real tragedy that this palace designed by Justinian survived its creator in its original form by only a few years. When the capital was threatened by Avars and Persians, and then by the Arabs, it was inevitable that the arcading should be walled up and the building used for purposes of defence. When the Turkish conqueror, Muhammed II, entered the capital he found only this ruin of the imperial palace left and in a surviving poem he describes the impression it made upon him.

79

EXTERIOR OF THE PALACE QUSAYR AMRAH IN JORDAN.

The silhouette of the palace of Qusayr Amrah stands out sharply against the skyline in the unending desert. Its architecture is quite different from that of the Byzantine imperial castle Qasr ibn Wardan (Pls. 75, 76), though the two are separated by a bare 150 years. Qusayr Amrah belongs to the period of the Arab occupation which has indeed seen a far-reaching deterioration in cultural standards. Only a relatively small minority of the leading architects, craftsmen and artists had chosen to place their services at the disposal of the new Arab regime. Many technical specialists, as for instance the inventor of Greek fire, had elected to emigrate. Thus when the Umayyad caliphs built their castles they could not draw on the expertise of architects and engineers competent to erect stone vaulted domes or buildings of several storeys supported by stone pillars.

When Qasr ibn Wardan was put up, Isidore of Miletus was available to supervise the plans for the building. In the case of Qusayr Amrah there was nobody even remotely approaching him in ability. So it was only possible to erect a single-storeyed building with domes of limited span, constructed with the aid of earthen tubes inserted into each other. The side rooms and niches had to fall back on the old form of barrel vaulting. But it would be misleading to regard this building simply as evidence for the deterioration of Byzantine workmanship in a conquered land. At Qusayr Amrah it was the interior which mattered and all craftsmanship was concentrated on this. Qusayr Amrah was a palace whose leading feature was its dwelling rooms, which offered the caliph respite from the harsh desert climate. The exterior was, as it were, merely a protective and utilitarian shell.

80

TEKFUR SARAY, ISTANBUL.

This Byzantine palace is known by its Turkish name of Tekfur Saray and, in its present form, dates from the second half of the 13th century. It was part of the vast complex of palace buildings in the Blachernae district where Emperors had resided since the mid-7th century. Tekfur Saray was certainly modelled on buildings from the Macedonian period. This is particularly true of the façade shown in this illustration. The oriel can be seen and it was from this projecting bay that the Emperor used to address the populace. This is well known from the miniatures on the Madrid manuscript of John Scylitzes' history. In one of these illustrations (see Pl. 44), Michael V Calaphates is seen speaking

to the crowd who are, however, throwing stones at him. This oriel was part of the original hall supported by pillars like the lower storey and it was here that the Emperor would hold audiences. Today nothing has survived in the almost completely ruined interior except the bases of the pillars and traces of the vaulting. (See also Pl. 3 and Note).

81

MOSAIC IN THE GREAT MOSQUE IN DAMASCUS.

This mosaic shows a different practice from that in Pl. 57. A castle can be seen through a gap in the trees. Comparison with the buildings brings out the enormous height of these trees which may perhaps be the famous cedars of Lebanon. The castle here belongs to a complex of palace buildings; on the right is a pillared hall with an upper storey above it. On the left, buildings with a tower can be seen in the distance. This may have been a water-tower to provide for the fountains in the park. In the central castle the broad gables of the two main wings project over the actual building. The gables are an unusual architectural feature. It is indicative of the function of this building that only the upper storey has windows. It was obviously designed for military purposes. The great square towers of the castle also have windows only in the upper storey. The houses in front of the castle also seem to have been designed with defence in mind. They, too, have no windows in the lower storeys, and on the ground floor the entrance is through a door which could easily be defended. The palace with its open pillared hall on the right of the picture is in marked contrast. Its architectural decoration of the interior is the same as that shown on the mosaics of the rotunda church of St George in baroque style.

82

THE AWAKENING OF NATURE AFTER THE EASTER FESTIVAL. Miniature from the Easter Sermon of Gregory of Nazianzus, 11th century. Paris, Bibliothèque Nationale (Cod. Gr. 533, f. 34).

The farmer is ploughing the field with his span of oxen. This miniature is interesting as showing the comparatively primitive character of the Byzantine plough. The Byzantine farmer used the hook-shaped plough which central and western Europe had abandoned in the early centuries AD in favour of the iron plough with mould board and wheels, which was used up to early modern times. The disadvantage of the hook-shaped plough was that it only touched the surface. The soil was insufficiently turned over and the yield was relatively low. The illustration shows how the farmer is trying to deepen the furrows by walking in the track of the plough.

83

SHEEP-SHEARING. Detail from a miniature in the *Homilies* of St Gregory of Nazianzus. Paris, Bibliothèque Nationale (Cod. Gr. 533, f. 34).

This miniature gives a scene from country life in which a sheep is being shorn. The curly twisted horns of the goat at right indicate the famous angora breed of the Anatolian uplands which were famous for their wool. This suggests that the miniature, or at least its prototype, came from the Asia Minor regions of the Byzantine Empire. It looks as if the artist was using as his model a calendar which illustrated each month with an appropriate rural occupation.

84

THREE FISHERMEN IN A BOAT. Miniature from a manuscript of the *Cynegetica* of Pseudo-Oppian. Venice, Biblioteca Marciana (Cod. Gr. 479 = 881).

These Byzantine fishermen are pulling in their net at night; a light is fixed to the end of the boat. The use of a light to attract fish is well known. The boat in the illustration is small, probably of the kind in general use in shallow coastal waters. The Byzantines called this type of vessel a *karabos,* a word of Cypriot origin. The Byzantine maritime theme of the Carabisiani derives its name from this word. These boats were long and narrow in proportion; they were somewhat like a Venetian gondola. Boats of this kind from the Byzantine period have been found near Commachio, the important Byzantine port on the northern Adriatic coast.

This miniature is probably a copy of a mosaic pavement such as has been preserved in the palace of Piazza Armerina. Fishing as well as hunting was one of the themes found in mosaics in imperial palaces.

85

FARM LABOURERS. Miniatures illustrating Matthew 20, 1-16 from a manuscript of the Gospels, 11th century. Paris, Bibliothèque Nationale (Cod. Gr. 74, f. 39).

This miniature illustrates Christ's parable on the labourers in the vineyard. The Byzantine painter has, however substituted a sunflower field for the vineyard of the Gospel. The bailiff is shown paying the hire of the labourers with gold taken from a pouch. During the payment the householder is sitting nearby in a chair placed there for him, and he signifies his approval by clapping his hands as the labourers come up for their money. The men working for the day, as shown here, were itinerant labourers who hired themselves out for an agreed period for a cash payment. There were special quarters on farmsteads for these labourers rather like the modern itinerant workmen's huts.

86

THE SWINE-HERD. Miniature illustrating the return of the prodigal, from a manuscript of the Gospels, 11th century. Paris, Bibliothèque Nationale (Cod. Gr. 74, f. 143).

This miniature shows two scenes: the prodigal son tending swine, and his reconciliation with his father. On the right-hand side is the prodigal son feeding his herd of swine. He has climbed into a tree and is using his stick to knock down carob pods for them to feed on. On the left of the picture is his father, wearing the garments of a Byzantine magnate, sitting on his throne-like seat greeting his son. In the background is a house looking like a Byzantine palace. It has open arcading supported by pillars on the ground floor as well as on the first floor. There was probably an open portico leading to the main dwelling rooms. There is a gable over a flat roof with trees.

87

GOD SENDS A PLAGUE TO AFFLICT JOB'S FLOCKS. Miniature from book of Job, 905. Venice, Biblioteca Marciana (Cod. Gr. 538).

This manuscript gives a selection of the wealth of calamities and natural disasters, such as plagues, fires and devastation, which must have been only too well known to the populace of the capital. It is understandable that the Byzantines were particularly attached to the book of Job. They saw in it a reflection of their own everyday life.

The miniature shows a plague sent by God to ravage Job's flocks. Men and beasts were laid low; the artist shows great skill in portraying men fleeing before the approach of death. There is a similarity between this picture and the group of the children of Niobe whom Apollo killed, or the affliction of the children of Israel by serpents as painted by Rubens. This is also true of the dying animals. Nothing is stereotyped. The painter has shown great mastery of his art in portraying the animals huddled together in the anguish of death in the process of being overtaken by deadly poison, and on the other hand the patient, almost passive, beasts crouching on the ground.

88

THE DESTRUCTION OF SODOM. Detail from a 12th-century mosaic in the cathedral of Monreale, Sicily.

The Byzantine artist has produced a most terrifying effect in this mosaic. The sun is emitting rays which are setting fire to the city. An earthquake is toppling buildings to the ground. There is a gabled two-storeyed house with its archway crashing down.

The Byzantines, particularly in Asia Minor, had plenty of experience of earthquakes, as is clear from the artist's realistic portrayal. Between cracking walls and broken pillars can be seen a ruined staircase and the severed heads of the dead inhabitants.

This mosaic picture of the disaster can be compared to the rain of fire found in a miniature illustrating the book of Job. This reflects the apprehension about the end of the world which is found in Byzantium as much as in the West. This dread was something which affected all classes, high and low, rich and poor. In the West, for instance, the Emperor Otto III, much under the influence of the Byzantine ascetic St Nilus, believed that the end of the world would come about the year 1000. Comparable to the destruction of Sodom and the scenes from the book of Job are the illustrations to the Apocalypse, the Revelation of St John, whose vivid portrayal reflects Byzantine awareness of the many and constant threats to their very existence.

89

CHRIST ON THE CROSS AND THE ICONOCLASTS. Miniature from Chludov Psalter. Moscow, Historical Museum (Cod. Gr. 129).

This manuscript, written and illustrated in the second half of the 9th century just after the ending of the iconoclast controversy, obviously departs from existing Byzantine traditions. It has marginal illustrations, which were not part of the tradition of book production in antiquity. Without question the models for this practice are to be found outside the frontiers of the Empire in the East. The Manichaeans illustrated their books in this way: it is used exclusively in extant fragments of Manichaean book illustration from Turfan. It was in part adopted by Christians in the East, the Egyptians and Syrians. An early example is to be found in the papyrus of the Alexandrian world chronicle from the second half of the 4th century.

The Byzantine iconophiles' choice of this unusual form of marginal illustration for their works is not unconnected with the place from which their greatest supporter in their struggle came. This was the Umayyad court in Damascus for it was here that John of Damascus, the acknowledged spiritual leader of the iconophiles, lived and wrote. The page format also gives clear indications of eastern influence; that square shape of the parchment sheet suggests the Jewish tradition of book-making.

Here Christ is shown on the cross. The painter has merged two events: the offering of the sponge and the piercing of the right side with the lance. The soldiers in the scene are in the uniform of Byzantine cavalrymen, carrying the long thrusting lance and the small round shield and wearing tunics. They also have the untanned leather boots of the cavalry. Their sword is not the old Roman sword of the legionaries, known from representations of it, but the sabre of the rider used as a cutting weapon. In the foreground there are iconoclasts busily engaged in whitewashing an icon of Christ. The icon is in the form of the *imago clipeata*. It is astonishingly like the icon which the Empress Theodora displayed to the people at the end of the iconoclast controversy (Pl. 45). It is clearly a copy of the famous portrait of Christ, perhaps painted by the apostle Luke, which is reproduced here as a mosaic. It is not by chance that the miniature represents Christ's torturers as Byzantine cavalrymen. The cavalry brigades of the Anatolikon theme were the bitterest enemies of the icons (see Note to Pl. 90).

90

THE STONING OF ST STEPHEN. Miniature from a 9th-century manuscript of *Christian Topography* of Cosmos Indicopleustes. Rome, Biblioteca Vaticana (Cod. Gr. 699, f. 82ᵛ).

This manuscript was copied and illustrated directly after the end of the iconoclast controversy. The stoning to death of the first Christian martyr, Stephen, is used to symbolize the sufferings of the righteous under the iconoclasts. Part of the manuscript has obviously been copied from the original version approved by Cosmas himself, but there are some illustrations which must date from the 9th century. This is true of the martyrdom of St Stephen. The martyr is seen already forced to his knees while his attackers, hurling stones at him, are gathered together in a half-circle in the background. This semi-circle clearly symbolizes the Hippodrome in Constantinople where many iconophiles had been done to death. The identification of the murderers of Stephen with the iconoclasts is supported by the dress of the saint's stone-throwing persecutors. They are shown mostly as soldiers from the Anatolikon theme, recognizable from their small round shield, like those used by Byzantine cavalrymen; but there are also members from high government circles wearing their ceremonial robes for this occasion. The miniature also shows the hand of God bearing the martyr's crown, represented here as being similar to the crown usually worn by the Byzantine Emperor.

91

TWO LIONS TASTING THE FRUIT OF THE HAOMA TREE. Relief slab in pentelic marble; ornamental frieze in imitation Kufic script, 9th or 10th century. Athens, Byzantine Museum.

This relief slab belongs to the sculpture work found in some Byzantine churches in the former theme of Hellas, the Byzantine military zone embracing the greater part of present-day Greece. The Byzantine military commander resided in the capital of this theme, Thebes, and he was frequently an Armenian. These churches with relief decoration on their façade were the foundations of these military governors of Armenian origin, for in Armenia, contrary to practice in the Byzantine Empire, it was customary to decorate the outside of the church with reliefs of this kind. And so Armenian officers who founded churches in Greece wanted them to resemble those of their homeland. It is possible that these churches were built by Armenian workmen. One that survives from this period is the monastery church of Skripu, founded in 873. Today it still has sculpture on its façade in the form of relief slabs as here.

The Armenians had been under the rule of Islam for 200 years before they succeeded in winning their independence. This inevitably influenced the art of the country, as can be seen from this relief slab. It comes from a Byzantine church which no longer exists and it shows unmistakable Islamic features. Here it is not only a question of reproducing individual motifs but of taking over from the model – probably an Islamic prayer rug – animal and flower ornamentation as well as the border composed of a frieze of Kufic script. The flower arabesques of the relief, which the stonemason has translated into marble from his woven model, are found in north Persian medallion carpets of the 17th century. Beneath the highly stylized plant ornamentation, two lotus flowers can be seen; these too are often found on Persian woven carpets. In place of the mihrab in the central panel there is an animal representation. These animal figures later developed into extremely abstract forms. But the motif copied here shows quite clearly two lions tasting the fruit of the haoma tree. This too is of Iranian origin and shows the extent to which the Iranian element was at this time still dominant in Islamic art. Textiles were among the most effective carriers of foreign ornamentation. Kufic letters as ornaments are also found in the West from the end of the 11th century onwards when the crusaders had established direct links with the Islamic East.

92

THE PALACE OF KHIRBAT AL-MAFJAR NEAR JERICHO.

The illustration shows one of the stone carved windows of an Umayyad palace built in the first half of the 8th century. This particular palace is bigger than the older buildings of Qusayr Amrah. In contrast to Qusayr Amrah, only the outer walls are still standing, but in spite of this the extant remains give an excellent impression of what the building must have looked like. The mosaic floors look just like woven carpets placed side by side and they are at their most effective when the light pours through the beautifully worked windows in the outside walls and reaches the interior. There are very few of these windows in the building. There is one large window in the form of a rosette, like the rose windows in medieval cathedrals, which was designed to lighten the great central hall. Today only the shell remains without any glass, which at that period would have been in colours of shining reds, blues and yellows. Only a few fragments of this coloured Byzantine glass have survived and these date from the later period. But it is known that coloured glass, like the organ and other cultural achievements of Byzantium, reached the West in the Carolingian period. The earliest fragments of western glass-work date from the time of Louis the German. The effect of a glass window in an interior cut off from the light must have been exceedingly striking. The ornament of the star with six points circumscribed by a circle had an abstract symbolism perhaps connected with the days of the week. It should be noted that only a few decades after the erection of Khirbat al-Mafjar the Umayyad owners of these palaces had to take refuge in Spain, where they set up a new caliphate in Cordova. It is possible that southern Spain influenced the development of cathedral architecture in northern Spain and in France.

93

MOSAIC FLOOR IN THE AUDIENCE HALL OF THE UMAYYAD CASTLE OF KHIRBAT AL-MAFJAR.

The lighting in the audience hall came through the stone window in Pl. 92. This showed up both the mosaic floor and the wall decoration. The mosaic in the apse had a great tree with two pairs of animals: one an antelope torn by a wild beast and on the other side two antelopes peacefully eating young leaves. There was a symbolic meaning in this scene. It was here in the apse that the caliph's throne stood. The mosaic signified on one side of the tree the land without a ruler where the rule of the strongest prevailed (the powerful wild beast attacking the weak antelope), and on the other the law and order which was maintained by the ruler (the animals can feed in peace and quiet). This kind of symbolical representation of the value of authority was in keeping with Byzantine tradition. There is a similar picture on the great mosaic floor in Hormisdas palace: on the one side there is a country scene with peaceful animals and men engaged in quiet activity, on the other side beasts are fighting with each other and with men (see Note to Pl. 51). This kind of Byzantine palace decoration was adopted in other Umayyad palaces as well as in Khirbat al-Mafjar. In Qusayr Amrah there is a picture of the two different worlds in a fresco.

This theme is also found in the West. The same scenes occur in the so-called Palace of Theodoric (see Note to Pl. 77). In front of the apse with the ruler's throne there was a mosaic floor imitating woven carpets. It might be asked why actual carpets, which were available, could not be used. The answer is found in the function of the floor. It was fitted with hypocausts so that a pleasant warmth might penetrate the floor when the nights got very cold. Carpets laid on top would only have insulated it, thus to some extent blocking the floor heating.

94

THE MIHRAB OF THE GREAT MOSQUE IN QAIRAWAN.

The mihrab of the Great Mosque in Qairawan dates from the year 862 and is one of the oldest Islamic praying pulpits. It was built in Baghdad for the emirs of Qairawan. The horseshoe arch set on pillars and integrated into the architecture of the mihrab was certainly not a feature introduced by the Arabs. The Visigothic churches of Spain have the horseshoe arch. It is an architectural form widespread in North Africa and in Spain and was adopted by the Arabs. Nor are the ornamental plaques worked into the mihrab of Arab origin. This kind of ornamentation was found in East Roman art, and this too was something borrowed by the Arabs; likewise the pillars with capitals supporting an arch set with plaques, which were well known in the churches of Constantinople. The mihrab, with its marble encrusted walls, thus shows a direct continuation of Byzantine art on Muslim soil. The wood-carved minbar can also trace its ancestry back, in this case to Syrian and Egyptian art.

95

ELEPHANT BEING CHASED BY WILD ANIMAL. Relief in the wall of the citadel of Konya.

This relief, dating from about 1221, shows a fight between elephants and griffins. It is tempting to regard this as copied from scenes of fighting animals in the world of the nomads living in Islamic regions. This is the Islamic equivalent of the animal fights found in relief on the outside façades of old Russian churches. In South Russia this clearly derives from the days of the Pecheneg and Cuman disturbances. In Konya it belongs to the tradition brought with them by the Seljuks when they migrated westward from their Central Asian homelands. The elephant in this relief is shown wearing his decorative trappings. This is not a fight between wild beasts, though this may have been an elephant used in warfare; it may reflect memories of the elephants ridden into battle by the great Turkic conqueror Mahmud of Gazna, who subdued Afghanistan and India. In the Seljuks' homeland on the northern edge of the Gobi, griffins were the symbol of the strength of the nomads vanquishing the animals of the steppes, and so the elephants are made to flee before them. The victory of the griffin over an animal from the steppes is shown on a carpet from the tomb of the prince Noin Uland dating from the 1st century BC.

Konya was the place where Byzantine animal motifs come into contact with those brought from the steppes by the Seljuks. The Byzantine tradition goes back to the palace of Piazza Armerina. Animal fights are seen on the mosaic in the 6th-century Hormisdas palace (Pl. 51) and on the frescoes on the staircase walls of the Sophia church in Kiev dating from the 11th century. Byzantine silk material shows an elephant with the same trappings as in this illustration (Pl. 48), and it looks as though this Konya relief and the Byzantine silk have drawn on a common prototype whose origin is to be found in the Islamic-Indian frontier region. Thus, after Sassanian Persia came under Islamic domination, Byzantine links with eastern Iran and northern India were not broken.

96

THE PORTAL OF A SELJUK MINARET-MOSQUE. Konya, Ince Minareli Medrese (1258).

The entrance door of the minaret-mosque is one of the most significant monuments built by the Seljuk conquerors of Byzantine Anatolia. This art does not derive from Byzantine but from Central Asian models. Its influence spread beyond the Anatolian lands and is indeed noticeable in Byzantine art.

The portal is framed in bands of writing, and these are also found round the inner doorway. These inscriptions consist of Surah from the Koran. They reflect an eastern style which the Turks had found in West Turkestan and had stamped with an Islamic religious imprint. They are also reminiscent of the sacral forms of the Manichaean 'opening of the door', the reading of the Holy Writ. In Byzantine art it was ornamentation which showed this Seljuk influence, for instance the bands of the framework separated by knot decoration are found in the canonical tables of Byzantine Gospels as well as in reliefs on steatite and ivory. Byzantine art also has instances of pillars flanking an inner gateway and flowering plants like those here climbing over the vaulting of the inner doorway. Clearly Byzantine art cannot be regarded in isolation; it was influenced by Islam as well as by the West.

97

THE MECHANICAL CLOCK OF DJAZARI, A COPY AND FURTHER DEVELOPMENT OF A BYZANTINE MECHANICAL CLOCK IN THE HOROLOGION OF HAGIA SOPHIA. Islamic miniature, first decade of the 13th century. Museum of Fine Arts, Boston.

This miniature comes from the fragment of a treatise of Djazari on mechanical clocks, and gives a picture of a water clock constructed by the author, a famous mechanic. This clock was installed in 1200 in the residence of the Ortokid Nur ed-Din Mohammed. The treatise contains a detailed description of all the parts of the clock and its mechanism. The Ortokids ruled the regions round Amida and Mardin on the upper Tigris, then on the Byzantine-Arab frontiers. This region had long played a particularly important role in cultural cross-fertilization between Byzantium and the parts of Irak under Islamic control.

The water clock of Djazari probably copied clocks constructed by the Byzantines which were well known in the East through reports of Arab visitors. In Constantinople there were twelve public clocks. The best known was that at Hagia Sophia which had its role in the processions in which the Emperor took part. It was at the Horologion that the Emperor was received by the citizens organized into the two circus parties. The sites of the other clocks were equally well known. These had been specially selected to make it possible for processions to keep to a timing carefully planned beforehand. There was a clock of this kind, among others, in the imperial palace, one at the Milion, the milestone and the centre of the city from which all the main streets began, and also at the Church of the Holy Apostles and at the forum of Constantine.

The Horologion at Hagia Sophia was well known from two Arab accounts coming from different periods. According to the oldest, written by Harun ibn-Yahya who stayed in Constantinople about 900, it stood to the right of the exonarthex (the outer ante-hall). The time was told with the help of twenty-four small four-cornered gates, one of which opened each time an hour had passed. This water clock, which was working about 900, was later further improved upon. The account of an Arab prisoner of war in the 13th century describes a new clock which told the time by means of twelve gates corresponding to the

hours of the day. Each time a new hour began a door opened and a figure appeared which remained there until the hour had passed.

Djazari seems to have known this last clock and copied it in various respects. But there was a new feature which may well have been his own invention. This was the Turkish orchestra, illustrated in the miniature, which was connected to the mechanism of the clock, and also the introduction of two falcons holding a ring in their beaks which fell into the bowl standing in front of them as each hour passed. The Turkish orchestra is playing beneath the archway of a gate. Their clothes and hair style show eastern influence which must still have been very strong among the Seljuks in the second half of the 12th century. The Turks are wearing boots and festive garments like the east Turkic Onogurs, some of whom practised Manichaeism, others Buddhism. Their hair, plaited in a pigtail and worn without a turban, is also reminiscent of these east Turkic peoples. The nimbus round the heads of all five musicians in the scene shown here is also like the Buddhist model; it arises out of the so-called celestial music which played a great role in Buddhist iconography. The influence of the Far East is also responsible for the presence of a circle of animals in the miniature by means of which the Karachanids ruling West Turkestan still date their documents. West Turkestan was the home of the Seljuks who migrated to Asia Minor. Thus a link between Byzantine and Far Eastern motifs is found in this miniature.

The Byzantines, as also the Arabs, derived their knowledge of mechanics from late antiquity. At this time the complete works of Heron and Archimedes on mechanics were still available and commented on. Archimedes was one of the Hellenistic scholars who had already combined the water clock with an automatic mechanism. The Arabs had done detailed work on Hellenistic mechanics, as the catalogues of the book markets of Baghdad in the form of the *Fihrist* show. All the same, the similarity between the construction of the Arab and Byzantine water clocks is so marked that there can scarcely be any doubts that the Arabs copied Byzantine models.

98

THE BIRTH OF JOHN THE BAPTIST. Miniature from the manuscript of the Gospel of St Luke. Parma, Biblioteca Palatina (Cod. Gr. 5, f. 137^r).

This manuscript belongs to the period between the end of the Macedonian dynasty, with its sustained cultural programme, and the new western-orientated era of the Comneni. The first impression made by this picture is its similarity to enamel decoration and the ornamentation of carpets. A comparison of the centre panel which copies the indentation of an enamel at once brings to mind the Pala d'Oro (Pl. 22). This centrepiece is mounted in ornamentation very like an Iranian medallioned carpet and this setting itself has a border with decoration of Iranian provenance. It looks, therefore, as if the manuscript came from the north-east frontiers of Byzantium.

The gospel theme of the miniature is handled with real aesthetic feeling and tenderness. The houses are in perspective. The men stand in front of the midwife, the father of the child is sitting down. But in spite of its artistic qualities the representation is far removed from realism. Everything is subordinated to the markedly symbolic content of the picture. In looking at it one is reminded of the icon of the Holy Trinity of Rublev. It can also be compared to the icon of Poganovo, now in the National Museum in Sofia. Here, too, the figures are characterized by their unnatural height as in the miniature. It would seem that in the second half of the 11th century there were already the first stirrings of that mystic outlook which is found in the hesychast movement in the Palaeologan period.

99

TWO MONKS IN AN ARCHITECTURAL SETTING. Miniature from a manuscript of the New Testament. Oxford, Bodleian Library (Cod. Ebnerianus, f. 16ʳ).

The picture of two monks is set in an elaborate architectural framework. A large ornamental ground covered with decoration is supported by three pillars. The capitals of each pillar have on them jugglers and musicians, and the sockets of the pillars also have such figures. These capitals can be compared with Romanesque sculptured capitals and indeed the fluting of the pillar shafts can also be found on western architectural sculpture. And the decorated ground with the lunette supported on three pillars is a well known feature of European cathedral sculpture. It is only the way in which the lunette is filled in with ornamental motifs that is characteristic of Byzantine decoration.

The adoption of western motifs in Byzantine art frequently occurred after the Latin capture of Constantinople in 1204 – the churches of Mistra, for instance – but it can also be seen from the 12th century onwards. This was not simply due to the temperament of the Emperor Manuel Comnenus who was known to like the Latins. The influence of western art had immeasurably increased since the arrival of the crusaders in the Holy Land. The examples of western cathedral sculpture erected during the early period of the Latin kingdom of Jerusalem were like the Romanesque cathedrals of France and Germany.

The monks in the miniature have the mystic look and bearing found in icons of the Palaeologan period. Like the icon of Poganovo in Sofia this miniature is characterized by its mystic spirituality. The bareness of the background landscape shows a desire to break with late antique landscape painting; and it would indeed be at home on the icons of the hesychasts.

100

THE MIRACLE OF CHONAR. Miniature from a manuscript of the work of Symeon Metaphrastes. London, British Museum (Cod. Gr. Add. 11870, f. 60ʳ).

This miniature is taken from a manuscript copied at the turn of the 11th and 12th centuries containing the work of Symeon Metaphrastes, 'the Paraphraser', who was commissioned by imperial command to undertake a revision of the traditional text and illustrations of the lives of the saints and the *acta* of the martyrs.

The manuscript was made only a few years after the battle of Manzikert (1071), a victory over the Byzantines which gave the Muslim Seljuks control of the greater part of Asia Minor which had previously been in Byzantine hands. This led to a direct confrontation with Islamic civilization in Byzantium. The victor was now the immediate neighbour of the Empire and his

civilization was studied and copied. This is true also of manuscripts originating in Bithynia, which was later to become the heart of the Ottoman Empire.

The meeting of the archangel and the saint takes place beneath the archway of a door. The decoration of the tower has marked Islamic characteristics with its mixture of Iranian faience and woven carpets in its ornamentation. Architectural decoration of this kind was well known in Moorish Spain. On the other hand, the style of the figural composition still reflects the spirit of the Macedonian renaissance. The movement and dress of the archangel indicate Hellenistic motifs in their models which could only have been partially understood. In contrast the picture of the saint follows the recognized iconography of Byzantine monastic miniatures.

101

WHITSUN. Miniature from a manuscript of the *Homilies* of St Gregory of Nazianzus. Oxford, Bodleian Library (Canon Gr. 103, f. 35ʳ).

This miniature shows the outstanding mastery of the Byzantines in the art of combining illustration with the initial letter of the text. The manuscript, written in Constantinople about 1100, is one of the great masterpieces of Byzantine art. The miracle of Pentecost, the outpouring of the Holy Spirit on the assembly, is portrayed here. The kind of composition seen in this miniature is found in earlier reliefs in Coptic wood carving decorating the doors of the iconastasis (the reliefs of Abu Sargas – Pl. 124). Its iconographical models are derived from the East. This kind of initial and its integration with the calligraphy of the actual text was well established there. Again there are similarities with Manichaen manuscripts. It was not for nothing that the Greek letter Pi was given the form of a pillared doorway. For the Manichaeans the open door was a symbolic way of proclaiming the good news of the holy writings. It was under the influence of this idea that the apostles in the mosaics and frescoes of the early Christian period had a key fastened to their robes to symbolize the prophecy of the Holy Bible (the key was, as it were, to open the doors of the divine truth of the holy text). Even the form of the handwriting has a symbolic meaning. The heading at the top is in the uncial hand, the oldest script of the Bible, and the text itself is in the minuscule hand which had come into use from the beginning of the 9th century.

102

ST MAMAS. Manuscript of the *Homilies* of St Gregory of Nazianzus dating from the 12th century. Paris, Bibliothèque Nationale (Cod. Gr. 550, f. 30).

Affinity in the lacquer work of the Far East (China) can be found in the elegantly interwoven flowers encircling the star-shaped central medallion. As early as the 1st century AD this lacquer work had reached the eastern regions of Iran by way of Afghanistan. Here Chinese patterns were known from lacquer bowls and they were copied in Persian silk embroidery and in a coarser and much simplified version on woven carpets. The influence of Far Eastern motifs is indicated not only by the interwoven floral decoration but by the pictures in the individual motifs. Thus the medallion on the left shows the Chinese motif of the dragon fight: the dragon is in the form of a serpent and is shown with two wings. The medallion on the right shows, on the other hand, the Iranian motif of the fight between two ibex. In the big star-shaped central medallion both the encircling ornamentation and the arrangement of the group of figures in the middle show the influence of the lustre tiles from the north Persian ceramic centre of Rai. Even the focal point, the portrait of St Mamas, almost smothered as it is with surrounding floral decoration, shows that even here the artist did not allow rein to his own feelings but was dominated by outside influences. The hands of the saint are not raised to heaven, as would be expected if portraying the early Christian attitude of prayer; they are holding something not actually portrayed but beneath which it is not difficult to make out the shape of a lyre. The scene thus represents a rather clumsy adaptation of a picture of Orpheus whose music charmed the wild beasts of the woods. The bust of Christ above the saint is somewhat similar to the monumental representation in mosaic at Daphni.

Viewed as a whole with its wealth of decorative ornament, the miniature is reminiscent of an Oriental carpet. But the border is missing. In its place the framework is ornamented with animals and groups of figures almost impishly thrown down on to the parchment. The top corners have two highly stylized Buddhas with aureole and edged with flames. The sitting Buddha has almost been turned into an ornament. In the middle of the top edge is an eagle. The lower left edge provides decoration for the initial capital letter with which the text, written in minuscule, begins. It shows the shepherd Mamas milking a sheep. The lower right-hand corner shows the harvesting of dates. The fruit, still green, are being cut off the tree by one of the workers who has climbed up it. Other workers are collecting them and taking them away in baskets.

On the question of the division of labour between scribe and miniature painter, this manuscript gives the impression that the miniatures were added only after the text had been written, for the painting of the miniature runs over part of the accents on the words in the first line of handwriting. In larger manuscripts, such as the Octateuch in the Saray Library in Istanbul, it is not unusual to find blank spaces left for miniatures which were never painted in.

103

AN ANGEL, THE SYMBOL OF THE EVANGELIST MATTHEW. Miniature from a manuscript of the four Gospels. Oxford, Bodleian Library (Cod. Gr. Selden supra 6, f. 15ʳ).

This manuscript dates from the turn of the 13th and 14th centuries, that is, the first decades of Palaeologan rule, and it already shows traces of the characteristic feature of the later Palaeologan renaissance. This is the unusual combination of a mystical spirituality with a revived interest in classical Greek antiquity. The angel, the symbol of the evangelist Matthew, placed at the head of his Gospel, is like a kind of mystic secret sign. This impression is deepened by the ornamental border. The circles and square figures surrounding the picture of the angel in the rectangle produce the effect of some kind of sign of secret knowledge. They bring to mind the signs of the astrologer. In this ornamental framework the flowers blooming within the circles and squares lose their own significance. In the picture

of the angel the poise of the body and the inclination of the head and the expression on the face have an astonishing similarity with the icon of the Holy Trinity by Rublev. The composition of Rublev's icon was borrowed from Byzantine models. This is proved by the representation of the Holy Trinity found on a miniature showing the Emperor John Cantacuzenus as both monk and emperor. The similarity can only be explained on the assumption that the miniature came from the scriptorium of a hesychast monastery in Constantinople, which was connected with a school of painters. This manuscript of the Gospel was probably commissioned for use by the supporters of the hesychast party.

104

ADAM RECEIVING EVE. Mosaic from the cathedral of Monreale, Sicily.

This mosaic was made in the 12th century during the rule of the Norman kings. Some of the mosaics in the interior of the cathedral show both Byzantine and Arab characteristics. It is true that Islam had been defeated, but Arab influence was by no means entirely discarded under the Norman kings. There was almost a kind of fusion of the Byzantino-Arab elements.

This mosaic, which shows the meeting of the first two human beings, is notable for the very careful portrayal of the three different species of trees; the master mosaicist must have had an excellent model. Adam and Eve, too, give the impression of having been copied from a miniature in an Arabic manuscript. Despite Islam's ban on pictorial representation, Arabic natural history manuscripts did have such representation if it were essential in order to clarify the text. Thus medical books would contain pictures of nude figures. And in other manuscripts the various plants were illustrated as well as described. This is true of codices made in the region of Baghdad in the first half of the 13th century. It is obvious that work of this kind would also be produced in Sicily which had for a time come under Arab rule. It was at the court of the Norman king Roger II that the distinguished Muslim geographer Idrisi wrote his great work in Arabic. In the mosaic in Monreale it is only God the Father who is portrayed in Byzantine style. He is clothed in the robe of a Roman consul.

Arab influence in Byzantine Sicilian art penetrated further north. In the cathedral of San Marco in Venice there are mosaics probably made from Arab models. Possibly the mosaics of San Marco were executed by Byzantine mosaic craftsmen from Sicily, who were familiar with Arab civilization.

105

CHRIST AS THE GOOD SHEPHERD. Mosaic in the mausoleum of Galla Placidia, Ravenna.

This mosaic picture of the Good Shepherd is in the 5th-century imperial mausoleum dedicated to St Lawrence. It has been placed in the lunette over the entrance door and this gives the impression that Christ is keeping watch over Galla Placidia who is buried here. This kind of representation of Christ is closely related to work found in the catacombs in Rome, and is by no means fortuitous. The art of the catacombs was only part of a wider contemporary development which used frescoes and mosaics to decorate the palaces and houses of the living. And it was thought right that the dead should enjoy the same as the living, at least to some extent, so the model for this mosaic is almost certainly to be found in a fresco in the palace of a Christian patrician. Some frescoes of this kind have survived. For instance, in the Casa Caelimontana the motifs of pagan decorative painting are found together with Christian themes as in the mosaic shown here. Galla Placidia's second husband was a Roman patrician. She may have had some of the frescoes in her Roman palace copied in her mausoleum.

The full effect of the colours of the mosaics is brought out by the atmosphere of the interior. They are shown up by the cleverly planned way in which the light comes through the small windows. These windows are not glazed but covered with thin plates of gold coloured marble. The light pours through to produce a kind of mellow atmosphere subduing the outlines of the people and objects portrayed in the mosaics. Thus the softness of evening pervades the mosaic showing Christ in the midst of his flock. This impression is further heightened by the contrast with the deep blue of the vaulting. The small mosaic stones of the vaulting produce a chilling effect and so does the mesembryanthemum ornamentation. But the coldness of the vaulting in the arches brings out the warmth of the colours of the mosaic picture.

106

DAVID AS A SHEPHERD. Miniature from a Psalter, 10th or 11th century. Milan, Biblioteca Ambrosiana (Cod. Gr. 54 sup., f. 2ᵛ).

This miniature shows David playing a lyre in a country landscape. He is evidently being inspired by a Muse who stands behind him. The picture is framed in a pillared archway, indicating a Hellenistic model. This is also clear from the resemblance of David to Orpheus in the Hellenistic tradition, as well as from other details of the picture. The stringed instrument being played by David was unknown in the Byzantine world, nor was the Muse really characteristic of this era, even though she is given a nimbus here. The prototype of this picture, transmitted through the medium of earlier miniatures, was clearly some fresco from the private house of a distinguished family. This would account for the architectural framework in which the picture itself is placed.

107

DAVID'S RETURN TO JERUSALEM. Miniature from a manuscript of the Psalter. Paris, Bibliothèque Nationale (Cod. Gr. 139, f. 5ᵛ).

The illustrations of this 9th-century Psalter reach the high water mark of Byzantine miniature painting after the end of the iconoclast controversy. This particular manuscript belongs to the period when the Macedonian renaissance was attempting to pick up the threads of classical antiquity, that is, antiquity of the 5th and 6th centuries. This presented various difficulties, as the miniatures show, for there was a gap of two hundred years between the end of the great days of early Byzantine art and the Macedonian renaissance. Models were certainly used. This is evident from details in this miniature. For instance, the dancing girl, who is representing David dancing before the Ark of the

Covenant, is holding castanets and is performing in a manner often seen in 5th-century figural art. It is also clear that this figure has been copied from two different models. The upper half of the body does not fit the lower half. Both halves are extremely well drawn and indicate the quality of the models used. The draping of the folds in the lower half is almost classical in style. The robe enfolds the body with great elegance. It is all the more astonishing that the figure changes from the waist upwards to show the body of a dancing girl viewed from the front. The ram behind the dancing girl indicates that the model copied was of a Bacchanalian scene.

The man accompanying Saul, who is represented as a Byzantine Emperor, fares no better. His feet belong to someone being viewed from behind, the upper half of his body is turned and faces towards the right. Here again the painter betrays his blind dependence on his models. The dress of the Basileus indicates the period to which the model belonged. The Emperor is wearing the same armour as the giant of Barletta, which is one of the last great bronze figures of east Roman art (Pl. 125). The architectural decoration, the building furnished with a roof and supported by pillars also dates from this period. It still has a feeling for perspective which was no longer known in the 9th century.

108

THE RAPE OF EUROPA. Detail from the Veroli casket. London, Victoria and Albert Museum.

It was a custom going back to Roman times for the bride on marriage to bring her jewels and valuables with her in a richly decorated casket. The scenes on these bridal chests were either something taken from Greek mythology having a direct bearing on the marriage ceremony, or they would illustrate interludes in the life of a lady of rank having some connection with the contents of the casket. A silver bridal casket was found in the Esquiline dating from about 380. This shows a lady at her toilet. One of her maids is holding up a mirror in front of her and another is bringing her the jewellery which she requires. On another bridal casket, now in the Coptic Museum in Cairo, all the arcades decorating it have the figure of a lady beneath them, each wearing a different dress from her wardrobe according to the needs of various different occasions.

The 10th-century Byzantine ivory casket shown here is decorated with mythological scenes. There were no inhibitions to using crudely erotic episodes, stressing the obscene, as in this particular casket. Here, amidst other scenes, is Zeus in the guise of a bull raping Europa amid the dances of drunken centaurs and putti. Europa's maidens are vainly trying to pull her back and her servants are throwing stones at the bull in an attempt to make him desist from his purpose. The movement of the scene is dynamic in the extreme. In contrast to the clumsy adaptation of antique models in Pl. 107, here the old patterns have been followed with astonishing ease. The explanation lies in the continuity of the antique collegia or gilds (the Byzantine systemata). Thus – at least in the gilds of the ivory carvers and the gem cutters – it was possible to preserve something of late antique tradition in the forms and motifs which were handed down from generation to generation. This is why the ivory diptychs of the Emperors in the 9th and 10th centuries were not so far removed in quality from the work of the 5th and 6th centuries.

109

BYZANTINE ENAMELLED CUP. Venice, Treasury of San Marco.

This enamelled glass dating from the mid-11th century obviously belonged to the imperial household. It was probably brought to Venice after the crusaders captured and looted Constantinople in 1204. The cup is in a silver gilt mount with beautifully wrought handles. A costly drinking goblet of this kind would be used by the Emperor and members of his family at state banquets. Full knowledge of the techniques employed in this work remained the secret of the Byzantines and Arabs in the Middle Ages. The Arabs made great use of this enamelled glass work in the lamps used in mosques. The enamelled medallions on this glass show pagan gods, such as Mercury and Aesculapius, indicating the vitality of the antique tradition.

At this time the West, too, looked for its models in antiquity. Book covers are one example of this; there, antique gems were set in goldsmith's work. But, as on the goblet shown here, the Byzantines were able to produce enamelled medallions in glass of a quality which at superficial glance looked like the work of antiquity. Only the ornamentation at the base of the cup in the form of a Kufic inscription points to a later origin. Byzantine art in the mid-11th century was not content simply to imitate the artistic work of antiquity; with the utmost skill it combined the forms of Greek antiquity with those of the Iranian East. Here it was simply repeating what was to be found in Byzantine silks, or in the architectural sculpture of Mshatter in the 7th century. It was Byzantine art which preserved and developed both the forms of Greek and Roman antiquity and those of pre-Islamic Iran.

110

PORTRAIT OF A HIGH OFFICIAL. Sculptured head. Vienna Kunsthistorisches Museum.

This portrait of the high East Roman dignitary Eutropius comes from the first half of the 5th century. It belongs to a series of sculptured portraits demonstrating East Rome's ability to produce work which could hold its own with the portraiture of the Roman imperial epoch. Among such works are the head of an Empress in Milan (perhaps Pulcheria, wife of Marcian, but probably not Theodora), the colossal bronze statue of Barletta and the portraits of East Roman officials in the Museum in Brussels. This succession of imperial and official portraits ends with that of Justinian II (685-95 and 705-11). In the reign of Leo III (717-41) the iconoclast controversy broke out. Sculptured portraiture was then forbidden on religious grounds. The reaction in favour of icons did not bring back any revival of this form of imperial portrait.

Eutropius is in official court dress, as his hair style indicates. This same hair style is found in the mosaic in San Vitale which shows the Emperor Justinian I with his court, and it is also seen in the mosaics in the church of St Demetrius in Thessalonica (Pl. 150). Work of this kind had freed itself from the restrictive rules laid down for the representation of distinguished personages by Hellenistic physiognomists which had continued to dominate imperial portraiture in the late Roman period. Thus in the head shown here, the hair falls naturally and the eyes are not so exaggerated in size that the eyelids seem to be almost completely pushed into the background.

Eutropius was the East Roman counterpart of Aetius whose ivory diptych (now in the cathedral of Monza in northern Italy) shows him in similar official court dress with a similar style of hair dress. Both portraits have the same kind of beard, so this was presumably the fashion of the day. In both cases likeness to the subject is achieved by means of a certain amount of caricature. This is seen in the exaggerated raised eyebrows, the overemphasis of the folds springing from the roots of the nostrils and the closed lips turned down at the corners, and the modelling of the face in such a way as to avoid any suggestion of weakness. This is still further stressed by the hair, which comes down in a sharp line across the forehead, and the strong jaw and striking narrowness of the head.

111

ST PANTELEIMON, PATRON SAINT OF DOCTORS. Icon. Kiev, National Museum.

This icon dates from the second half of the 9th century. Like the icon of the Mother of God (Pl. 113) it is one of the few portable pictures which has survived from the period of the Macedonian renaissance. Panteleimon was for the Byzantino-Greek world what Aba Kyros (Father Kyros) was for the Syrians and Egyptians. Both are shown with the distinctive attributes of their profession – the doctor's case and the spoon for salves or medicines. Among the early icons of this saint there is a kind of toy, or miniature, icon which was so tiny that it could be carried everywhere. In the church of Santa Maria Antiqua in Rome there is a fresco with a picture of Aba Kyros, the eastern patron saint of doctors. In the Kievan icon the saint holds in his right hand a little rod which he used to take the holy salve out of his medicine case and in his left hand he holds his professional instruments covered with a cloth. But however great the similarities in representing this particular saint, the icon clearly reflects the stylistic characteristics of the Macedonian renaissance with its partiality for Hellenistic models. These models were not, however, those of classical antiquity but of the 5th century. For instance, the face on the icon resembles the marble head of Eutropius (Pl. 110). Panteleimon's face is framed in just the same way by the fringe of his hair, almost as though it had been cut straight across. There is similarity in the treatment of eyes and nose. The same marked symmetry dominates his face as in the case of Eutropius. The portrait is set on the frame of the icon in such a way that the head is almost touching the upper edge of the frame, a mannerism also to be found in the work of the classical Italian Renaissance.

According to M. W. Alpatov, this icon was destroyed during the Second World War.

112

THE ENTHRONED MOTHER OF GOD AND CHILD. Mosaic in the apse of Hagia Sophia, Istanbul.

This mosaic may be regarded as the most significant monumental work of art of the Macedonian renaissance. Exactly how much of the original work has survived later Byzantine restoration is comparatively irrelevant here. To judge from the materials used, the archangels (of whom only one has been preserved) are not from the same hand or from the same period. These archangels stand on each side of the Mother of God. An inscription dates the mosaic to the reigns of the Emperors Michael III (842-67) and Basil I (867-86). It thus belongs to the Macedonian renaissance at its height. Like the icon of Panteleimon, it reflects the tendency to look back to the 5th and 6th centuries. This is seen in the unnaturally long straight nose, the strong chin, and the clearly marked line of the hair, or rather, of the kerchief covering the hair. The garments worn are similar to those of the Mother of God on the mid-6th century icon of Sinai (Pl. 16). There is also a similarity in the features of the face. It seems probable that this mosaic was copied from an icon of Justinian's day which had managed to survive the iconoclast controversy. The garments also indicate the age of Justinian. Here the Mother of God is not wearing a veil covering part of her forehead, such as is found on the Mother of God in Santa Maria Maggiore in Rome which dates from the time of the Macedonian renaissance (Pl. 113). Instead she has a veil drawn back so that the edge of the silk kerchief covering her hair is visible, as in the case of Mary on the Sinai icon. Other details also point to a 6th-century prototype. For instance, textile finds date the pattern of the cushions to this period, also the throne and the footstool, which are like those found on an imperial statue in porphyry (Archaeological Museum in Alexandria). The Child is shown in the dress of a Roman consul.

However much it owes to its prototype, this is undoubtedly the work of a great artist. The outlining which produces the billowing of the folds with all the exactness of a silhouette is unique for this period.

113

THE MOTHER OF GOD AND THE CHRIST CHILD. Icon, the so-called Madonna of St Luke. Rome, Santa Maria Maggiore.

Pious tradition attributed this icon to St Luke but it is probably more than 200 years later than the 6th-century icon of the Mother of God on Sinai (Pl. 16). In contrast to the Sinai icon, Mary is shown here in the apparel of a lady of the Byzantine court and not as an Empress. In her right hand she is carrying a wand, the mark of a lady of rank. She has idealized features, markedly Greek in character, such as were favoured in the Macedonian renaissance. This icon of the Mother of God has close stylistic affinities with the almost contemporary icon of Panteleimon, the patron saint of doctors, in Kiev (Pl. 111). The portrait of the Mother of God created during the Macedonian renaissance had far-reaching influence on later Byzantine art. It was this kind of representation which characterizes two of the finest icons of the Mother of God which date from the first half of the 12th century, the Mother of God of Vladimir (Pl. 17) and the figure of Mary in the so-called Annunciation of Ustyug (Pl. 117), both of which are now in the Tretiakov Gallery in Moscow. The icon in Santa Maria Maggiore has suffered a good deal from the metal covering placed over it. This has now been removed but the icon has unfortunately not been restored. The figure of the Christ Child in its present form is very probably a re-painting of the original and, judging by its stylistic characteristics, dates from the first half of the 12th century.

114

ST AGNES. Relief from the tomb of St Agnes. Rome, Sant' Agnese fuori le mura.

This portrait of St Agnes is still completely imbued with the spirit of the catacomb paintings and is in sharp contrast to the other picture of her in the apse of the same church where she is portrayed in the ceremonial robes of a Byzantine Empress. In the history of art this relief can be described as belonging to a time which saw a revival of Roman influence, supported by Pope Damasus (†384) and some of the influential senatorial families. This was, however, characterized by a return to the art of the 3rd century AD and not to that of the republican period. This is borne out by this particular relief, which has close affinities with similar portraits on 3rd-century Roman sarcophagi. In the Museum for Christian Archaeology in Tarragona there are sarcophagi which might well have come from the same Roman atelier as the relief on St Agnes' tomb in Rome. The saints on them seem to be standing up in their tombs and showing themselves to the faithful praying before them. There are hints here of later portrayals of the Raising of Lazarus. The robe, falling in folds round the body, is an exceedingly fine piece of modelling, giving the illusion of free-standing sculpture. It is tempting to suppose the use of a contemporary portrait of the saint by a sculptor. If the portrait used had been one of the saint at an early age this would explain the fact that the legs are too long for the body.

115

THE MOTHER OF GOD. Engraved jasper. London, British Museum.

This gem, which dates from the turn of the 11th and 12th centuries shows the Mother of God Orans, i.e. with hands raised like the priest in benediction. The engraving shows that at this period it was still usual to copy the old 4th-century models. This can be seen by comparing this stone with the relief on St Agnes' tomb (Pl. 114).

116

THE NATIVITY. Fresco. Castelseprio, near Milan, Santa Maria foris portas.

The unique frescoes in the church of Santa Maria, possibly dating from the late 6th century, were discovered in 1944 during the fighting in northern Italy in the Second World War. Castrum Seprum, the fort itself, was built to protect Milan and the Via Emilia. The military reason for selecting this particular site was neither to defend Ostrogothic settlers in northern Italy nor to meet the defence needs of the Lombard kingdom founded there in 568. The fort must therefore be dated to the period of Byzantine rule in this region from 558 to 572. The Byzantines used it to protect themselves from the Franks breaking through the Alpine passes. The church and its frescoes may thus be assigned to this time.

The frescoes are based on the text of the apocryphal Infancy Gospel (the Protoevangelium) of the apostle James. In this respect they have affinities with the frescoes of another slightly earlier church at Peruštica near Plovdiv (Philippopolis).

The Protoevangelium is an apocryphal work based on a variety of sources including the Gospels of St Mark and St Luke. It was particularly popular in North Syria, whence it spread into Cappadocia and is found in the rock churches in this region. It was also brought from North Syria to Italy and Bulgaria by Byzantine soldiers who liked to see pictures of their favourite stories around them in their military settlements. And so Byzantine garrisons in small places like Castelseprio or Peruštica got painters from the East to paint frescoes for them, such as those in Castelseprio.

This fresco shows the Mother of God lying back on her pallet exhausted while two maidservants are getting a bath ready for the Child. Joseph is sitting nearby, sunk in thought, with an almost philosophical look. One of the shepherds surrounded by his flock is approaching the scene of the holy event while an angel in the heavens is flying away to announce the good tidings. In the distance the towers and walls of Bethlehem can be seen. On the left-hand side of the Mother of God is the maidservant whose arm was withered.

The artistic feeling of the painter is superb. This is particularly apparent in the way the figure of the Mother of God is made to stand out as the central focus of the picture. The secret of the effect of the fresco on the spectator lies in the solitude which seems to surround the Mother of God, despite the bustling activity in the zone reserved for the Divine Child. The landscape has an almost bucolic character. The delicacy of colouring and masterly painting, which often indicates only the outlines of the figures, links this work to the great days of antique landscape painting.

117

THE ANNUNCIATION. Icon from Ustyug, early 12th century Moscow, Tretiakov Gallery.

The Annunciation was one of the first themes to be portrayed in Byzantine monumental art. One of the earliest examples is the Annunciation in the basilica of Bishop Euphrasius at Poreč (Parenzo) which dates from the mid-6th century; there the Mother of God is shown seated on a throne. This theme also appears in a miniature in a manuscript, dating from about 600, probably of Syrian origin, which is bound up with the Etchmiadzin Gospel of 989 (now in Erivan); the Mother of God is shown standing. This type of portrayal appears to indicate the apocryphal Protoevangelium of James which enjoyed great popularity in the 6th century – witness the frescoes in the church of Castelseprio and at Peruštica near Plovdiv in Bulgaria. Almost six hundred years lie between these frescoes and the icon of Ustyug, but there is scarcely any alteration in the composition. The angel is holding a staff in just the same way as in the miniature of Etchmiadzin and the gesture with the right hand has scarcely changed at all from that of the 6th century. The appearance of the Child Jesus in a picture of the Annunciation is new. Here the artist has evidently been influenced by the text of the Liturgy which assumes a material manifestation simultaneously with the words of the angel. The appearance of God the Father seated on his throne surrounded by the seraphim refers to the vision of Daniel (Daniel, 7, 9: 13, 22). This provides some indirect evidence about the painter himself, who was probably a monk of considerable theological training.

The icon of Ustyug dates from the same period as the Mother of God of Vladimir. This latter came to Kiev in the first half of the 12th century soon after it was painted and the former evidently reached Novgorod about the same time. Both icons were inspired by the classical spirit of the Macedonian renaissance which enjoyed a new lease of life in the revival of the second half of the 11th century. This style is also seen in the icons of the 9th century, as for instance the icon of the Mother of God in Santa Maria Maggiore in Rome (Pl. 113), or in the icon of St Panteleimon in Kiev (Pl. 111).

Like the icon of the Mother of God of Vladimir, the Annunciation of Ustyug is now only a torso. Reconstruction of the original colours does not, of course, give the same impression as the original. Only the outline, a network of lines, has survived the ravages of time. Almost all expression in the figure of the Mother of God is concentrated in the face and hands. The features of the face with their intent awareness reflect the hearing of the angel's message, and the right hand is raised in a gesture signifying the conception of the Child.

The portrayal of the archangel is masterly. His staff rests on the ground at his feet. His garment, falling in folds as he moves, seems to raise his body from the flat surface of the picture as though in sculptured relief. Only traces of the colours can be seen under the re-painting, but the techniques used are clearly recognizable. The paint of the robe was put on in layers, different colours next to each other so that the folds are emphasized. This is something like 19th-century pointillism which gives an effect of material billowing in folds. This method is clearly distinguishable from the flat colour used by the later copyist.

Novgorod seems to have possessed other Greek icons as well as this one, such as the icon of St George now in the church of the Koimesis in the Kremlin in Moscow. There is also an icon of St Peter and St Paul which came from the Sophia church in Moscow and is now in the History and Architecture Museum in Novgorod; here only part of the robes have survived in the original. This is from the mid-11th century and is the oldest Byzantine icon made in Constantinople for the Russian princes.

118

THE ASCENSION OF CHRIST. From a miniature in the Rabula Gospel. Florence, Biblioteca Lorenziana (Pluteus I, cod. 56, f. 136).

This Syrian Gospel, dating from 586, has a colophon stating that it was copied by Rabula in Zagba in Mesopotamia. It is not known who commissioned it, but it would appear to be a high Byzantine dignitary of Syrian origin living in this Byzantine frontier province. The frontier between the Byzantine Empire and Sassanian-ruled Iran at that time ran through Mesopotamia. The note about the completion of the manuscript only refers to the copyist's work. The miniatures were added later in the spaces left for this purpose. Usually copyists would leave notes on the subject-matter of the illustrations which had to be added. There are, for instance, notes of this kind in Roman cursive left for the painter by the copyist of the Quedlinburg Itala.

The work of the miniaturist of the Rabula Gospel must have been completed in the 6th century. In this illustration of the

Ascension, Christ in a gloriole is placed on a chariot borne by cherubim. The Hellenistic style is the same as that of the miniatures found in the Cotton Bible which dates from the same century. But it is not only the style which follows a particular tradition; the composition of the picture showing Christ in a gloriole embodies Hellenistic features. Clearly the gloriole is regarded as the disc of the sun. Like the god Helios, Christ is being borne on his way through the heavens in the chariot of the sun. The connection between Christ and the god Helios goes back to the 3rd century when the sun god of Emesa was one of the strongest rivals to Christianity. The representation of Christ in the sun's chariot in a mosaic in the mausoleum destroyed when the Constantinian church of St Peter was built in Rome illustrates this development, as also does the choice of the winter solstice, the birthday of the sun, for the day of Christ's nativity.

This miniature also illustrates the influence of the imperial cult on Christian iconography. As in the ceremonial surrounding the Emperor *triumphator*, the two angels on each side of Christ are crowning Him. He stands in the gloriole wearing the state robes of the Emperor about to sacrifice. This can be seen in the well-known relief of Augustus sacrificing in the temple of the Ara Pacis. The bearing of Christ also follows pagan models. One hand lies on the altar and the other is raised as in prayer.

119

ST MENAS. Relief from the monastery of St Thecla. Cairo, Coptic Museum.

St Menas is shown on this relief as an Orans, with hands uplifted, as was usual in portraying the manifestation of a god. He is standing between two dromedaries. The saint suffered martyrdom in Egypt under Diocletian; although he was only a soldier he is shown here in the dress of a Roman general wearing the *paludamentum*. This indicates how greatly he was venerated in Egypt and to the south in Nubia. The account of his martyrdom was among the religious works most widely circulated in Egypt. In Nubia his passion is the only substantial surviving monument of the old Nubian language.

The monastery of Menas in the Libyan desert was founded by the Emperor Anastasius and was the goal of pilgrims from all over the Christian world. They wanted to pray at the saint's tomb and then to take home with them ampullae decorated with his portrait and filled with holy water drawn from the cisterns by his tomb. (See also Pl. 14).

120

THE MOTHER OF GOD ORANS WITH THE APOSTLES PETER AND PAUL. Fresco from the monastery of St Apollo near Bawit. Cairo, Coptic Museum.

The frescoes from Bawit should be dated to the first half of the 6th century. This monastery was founded by St Apollo and, like that of St Menas in the Libyan desert, consisted of a great complex of buildings. It was one of the places of pilgrimage in Christian Egypt and was inhabited by monks until its destruction during the Fatimid regime in the 11th century.

These frescoes followed the iconographical pattern which had been increasingly accepted from Theodosian times onwards. But the reproduction here was markedly stereotyped

and had been altered in the direction of drastic simplification. This was due to the social background of the monks who opposed the imperial ecclesiastical policy and who were responsible for the kind of frescoes shown here. It reflects a tendency which can also be discerned in literary work. The chronicle of Malalas and the imperial history of Procopius are as different in their own way as these frescoes are from the contemporaneous icon of the Mother of God between Peter and Paul (Pl. 16). It is the difference in social *milieux* which accounts for the contrasting standards. It is only necessary to compare the Peter of the Sinai icon with the figure in this fresco. The one is a portrait with features and beard reproduced with almost photographic accuracy. But in the fresco these are simply indicated by a line and it is only possible to identify the personage with the help of the inscription and attribute. Thus Peter is recognized because he is holding a key.

121

FOUR SAINTS AND A FOUNDER. Fresco from the monastery of St Jeremiah in Saqqara, Egypt.

The frescoes in Saqqara are later than those in the neighbouring monastery of St Apollo. The fresco shown here probably dates from the second half of the 7th century. Compared with the frescoes in St Apollo the standard of these has considerably worsened. They were painted soon after the Arab invasion. The monastery would thus have been isolated and out of reach of any Constantinopolitan influence. The extent of the deterioration can be seen in the extraordinary way the founder is twisted round the saints' feet. The saints themselves are copied from old models, but are more stereotyped compared with the St Apollo frescoes. There is no background at all here, and the figures are one-dimensional, being almost like symbols painted on the wall. The indication of the folds of the garments is noticeable: they seem to have been painted in afterwards without any attempt at integration.

122

BUST OF CHRIST IN FORM OF THE 'IMAGO CLIPEATA'. From a silver censer. London, British Museum.

This silver censer, found in Cyprus, dates from the reign of the Byzantine Emperor Phocas (602-10). It is hexagonal and, round its rim, has three loops for its chains so that it could be swung backwards and forwards at Mass. The way in which it was used can be seen from the big mosaic panel of Justinian and his followers in San Vitale: on the left-hand side stands an ecclesiastic holding a censer similar to this one. That was only about fifty years before the date of the censer shown here. The sides of this censer are decorated with embossed busts of Christ, the Mother of God, Peter, Paul and the evangelists John and James. These are in the form of the *imago clipeata*, crowned with laurels, as was usual on pictures of the Emperor. Christ is shown between Peter and Paul. The features of the Saviour are those of Antiochene portraiture. Peter's face has the characteristics associated with him; they are found also on the Sinai icon of St Peter.

The *imago clipeata* is evidently linked with old pictures preserved on icons. Icons of this kind no longer exist in the original but in very early copies. Such are the papal portraits on the walls of the nave of San Paolo fuori le mura in Rome beginning with Peter. These too are in the form of the *imago clipeata*. Probably the great number of pictures surviving here in fresco went back to portrait icons of the popes which had long been in possession of the Romans. The early Christians clearly adopted the pagan Roman habit of paying special honour to the portraits of important persons and kept their likenesses in a special place. Pagan Romans had the *lararium* in their houses; Christians had a space reserved as a kind of sacristy. It is even possible that the pictures of some apostles go back to original portraits, for instance those of Peter and Paul in Rome, and John in Ephesus.

123

THE CRUCIFIXION. Plaque engraved on jasper. London, Victoria and Albert Museum.

This Crucifixion is engraved on jasper, a semi-precious stone similar to chalcedony. It belongs to the mid-9th–10th centuries, that is, the transitional hundred years after the end of the iconoclast controversy. The iconography of this theme is very like that found in the miniatures of the Chludov Psalter, and it indicates a break with the traditional portrayal of the Crucifixion. Christ is standing between the Mother of God and St John and the details in the Gospel narrative are not closely followed. The soldiers mentioned there are missing – the one with the sponge of vinegar and the other piercing the Saviour's side with a spear. The portrayal given here raises the death on the Cross to the level of a sacrament. Christ on the Cross holds up his hands as an Orans and stands as the vanquisher of all human suffering. Here the gesture of the Orans signifies the conquest of suffering. At this period the death on the Cross was the symbol of liberation and therefore Christ could not hang from the Cross. The Mother of God has unveiled her face and with his right hand St John is crossing himself. This new iconographical development in portraying the Crucifixion can be seen as an expression of a different religious outlook which arose after the iconoclast controversy. On the other hand, there was also greater freedom in handling material, since the older pictures showing the Crucifixion had been destroyed.

124

THE NATIVITY AND THE ADORATION OF THE MAGI. Wood carving from the door of the iconostasis in the church of Abu Sargas (Father Sergius) in Cairo.

This wood carving from the door of the iconostasis is one of five with pictures from the Bible which have survived. The relief dates from the same time as the Crucifixion engraved in jasper (Pl. 123). A comparison with other pictures of the same theme show that in spite of different doctrinal developments (such as Monophysitism) and different political systems (such as that of Islam) there was nevertheless in Byzantine art a *koine* which was understood in countries as far apart as Nubia and Spain. Pictures achieved what writing and speech could not do.

This piece of relief in wood shows how the carver has translated a Byzantine model of high artistic quality into the language of his own medium. The nearest comparisons would be with the doors of St Ambrose in Milan and Santa Sabina in Rome.

It is true that such a comparison emphasizes the fact that the work in Abu Sargas is 500 years later, but it also brings out certain common elements, for all this work followed the same Hellenistic Greek model. Above all, the marked symmetry clearly points to the composition of a Hellenistic prototype with its careful arrangement of Mary resting on her bed exhausted after childbirth, Joseph sunk deep in thought, the shepherds and the magi following the star. It looks just as if the wood carver, in copying a well-known picture, had cut out the holy figures and placed them into a rectangle, using the sides of the altar door to form the frame of the picture.

125

HEAD OF AN EMPEROR. Detail from the bronze statue of 'the giant of Barletta'. Barletta, in front of church of San Sepolcro.

This statue of an Emperor was found as a torso without legs or arms. It was so clumsily restored in the 15th century that only the head and body can give any idea of the effect of the original. Scholars differ widely in the identification of the statue, even by as much as 150 years.

The face, with its jutting chin, large nose and prominent eyebrows, seems to indicate an Armenian. There is much to suggest that the Emperor portrayed here might be Maurice, who was of Cappadocian origin. This Emperor was murdered in 602 and the political revolution after his death might well have led to the mutilation of the arms and legs of the deposed ruler. Maurice was much disliked in Italy and the general rejoicing at his downfall was celebrated by erecting a triumphal column to his successor Phocas. This feeling is further illustrated by a letter from Pope Gregory I congratulating Phocas on the fall of the hated tyrant.

The face of the statue is not very sympathetically portrayed. The artist has viewed the features of the Emperor with an exceedingly penetrating eye and has made no attempt to idealize his subject. This kind of realism is almost reminiscent of old Roman portraiture. The only concession to the aesthetic demands of the time is to be seen in the excessively large eyes which convention required in the portrayal of an important personage. The diadem of the Emperor has a shield, in the centre of which Christ was probably shown. According to Byzantine political thought it was indeed Christ who appointed the Emperor as his vice-gerent. (The crowns of the German kings now in the Imperial Treasury in Vienna have the same centre shields with a picture of Christ.) In some respects this diadem shows the transition to the imperial crown which became usual later on. It has the pendants, and between the rows of pearls there are enamel plaques bearing pictures of circus life and also personifications of imperial virtues, similar to those which can still be seen on the crown which the Emperor Constantine IX Monomachus sent to the Hungarian king.

126

THE EMPRESS ARIADNE. From a detail on a panel of an ivory diptych. Vienna, Kunsthistorisches Museum.

The diptych of the Empress Ariadne can be compared with that of an Empress (perhaps Eudoxia) which is now in the Bargello in Florence. Ariadne was the daughter of Leo I and the wife, first of the Emperor Zeno, and then of his successor Anastasius.

Like Eudoxia, and later on Theodora, she was one of those Byzantine Empresses who were not content simply to play their part in court ceremonial. She was frequently involved in politics and steered the ship of state with a firm hand. After the death of Zeno, Ariadne had a decisive voice in the choice of his successor whom she then married. This ivory panel well reflects the authoritative position of the Empress. Ariadne is shown seated under the *ciborium* where the throne of Solomon stood. In her hand she is holding the world orb, the symbol of universal authority, which later on in the Byzantine Empire, after the iconoclast controversy, was to be replaced by the parchment scroll with the Credo and the pouch of dust symbolizing human mortality.

This portrait seems to indicate a ceremonial state occasion. The Empress is in front of the *ciborium* between the two pillars, the curtains are drawn back. At the beginning of an audience they would remain closed and would be opened only after the music had begun to play. The Empress is wearing the kind of crown known from the portrait busts of the 5th century. Her body is enveloped in her heavy coronation robes in an almost strikingly similar manner to those of the Empress Theodora in the mosaic panel in San Vitale. There is in fact very little difference between the ceremonial garments of Theodora and those of Ariadne. What does distinguish the two portraits is Ariadne's clearly recognizable way of indicating her position of authority. Her right hand is outstretched in the moment of indicating her will.

127

HEAD OF AN EMPRESS. Marble head. Milan, Castello Sforzesco.

Only the head remains from this marble statue of an Empress, often regarded as a portrait of the Empress Theodora, the wife of Justinian I. The hair style, however, makes this unlikely. It is more probable that it is a portrait of the Empress Galla Placidia who built the mausoleum in Ravenna. She had been forced to marry the Visigothic king Ataulf in 414; on his death she left Barcelona, at that time the Visigothic royal residence, and came back again to Italy. In 417 she married a patrician (who became Constantius III in 421) and their son was Valentinian III. She was a woman distinguished for her singular beauty and roused the passion of her step-brother Honorius, the unfortunate West Roman Emperor whose seat was Ravenna. She died in 450 and was probably buried only for a short time in her mausoleum in Ravenna before being taken to Rome and laid to rest in the imperial mausoleum near St Peter's.

This portrait shows a woman who has still kept her beauty. The marks of old age are less noticeable here than on her ivory diptych which is now in the treasury of the cathedral of Monza in North Italy. There she is portrayed with her small son Valentinian while nearby stands the all-powerful general, Aetius.

128

HEAD OF A QUEEN. From a sculptured bust. Ravello, Cathedral of San Pantaleon.

It is only in her royal attributes that this early 13th-century queen shows Byzantine influence. The pendants of the crown and indeed the crown itself are of Byzantine ancestry. The resemblance comes out very clearly if they are compared with those of the Empress Irene standing with the Emperor John II Comnenus in the mosaic panel in the gallery of Hagia Sophia (Pl. 131). It can also be seen in the queen's style of hair dressing, but not, however, in her face. Here she closely resembles the Countess Uta on the cathedral of Naumburg, a product of western sculpture. The Byzantine artist working at the Hohenstaufen court faithfully reproduced the features of a queen of northern origin. The face is most expressive; it is no mere reproduction of the features. The eyes are fixed on the beholder. The mouth reflects the attitude of the listener, and even the neck, which is really too long, seems to be in keeping with the rest of the portrait.

It is possible that the princess shown here is the Empress Constance, the mother of the Hohenstaufen Frederick II. This portrait of an empress is a piece of statuary sculpture, a form of art which had been revived again from the Comnenian period onwards and which was used for imperial portraits. In Byzantium only half-relief was used, as can be seen from the portraits of individual emperors carved in stone of which fragments have survived. Here Turkish hostility to figural portraiture has been responsible for much destruction. More has been preserved in Italy. An instance of this kind of sculpture was the statue of the Emperor Frederick II which stood on the famous city gate of Capua before its destruction in 1557.

129

THE EMPEROR JOHN II COMNENUS AND HIS SON ALEXIUS. Miniature from a manuscript. Rome, Biblioteca Vaticana (Cod. Gr. Urbin. 2, f. 19ᵛ).

This miniature shows John, the most outstanding of the Comnenian dynasty, with his son Alexius, whom he himself crowned as co-Emperor. The son is seen here wearing the crown, but in actual fact he died before his father and the successor to the throne was a younger brother, Manuel.

John II (1118-43) can be recognized by the larger sceptre which he is holding. He and his son are both receiving their thrones from Christ. This is in keeping with the Byzantine conception of the imperial office, which regarded the Basileus as the representative of Christ, appointed by him through the inspired acclamation of the people, army and senate at the imperial election. Mercy and Justice are personified in the figures of two counsellors in the guise of Byzantine Empresses standing on each side of Christ and apparently guiding his decision. Here a secular, rationalist conception of the imperial office was forcing its way in, thus consciously desecrating the myth of the divine appointment. This was in keeping with the rationalist view of life found in intellectual circles during the Comnenian period.

The miniature was designed in colours of blue, red and purple, and the figures are almost symmetrically arranged. The Emperor and co-Emperor stand side by side, just like pieces on a chessboard. This marks a reappraisal of the religious element in the imperial conception which was indeed characteristic of this age. There was an agnostic trend in the air. This was the result of the upsurge of a new philosophical movement inspired by Platonism.

428

130

THE EMPEROR MANUEL I COMNENUS AND HIS WIFE MARY OF ANTIOCH. Miniature from a manuscript. Rome, Biblioteca Vaticana (Cod. Gr. 1176, f. 11).

The Emperor Manuel was the fourth son of John II. He survived his elder brother Alexius, who had been crowned co-Emperor, and on his father's death in 1143 he succeeded to the throne of the Byzantine Empire.

The faces of the Emperor and Empress look lost amid the stiff folds of their ceremonial robes. This seems to be of symbolical significance. It is as if the human element is entirely submerged beneath the all-powerful ceremonial. But appearances are deceptive. Ceremonial was the language of mime whereby something of the nature of the Byzantine imperial office could be conveyed to each subject.

Even so, a break with tradition can be detected in the picture, as also in the miniature of the Emperor John and his son Alexius (Pl. 129). There the two imperial figures were likened to chessmen; here Christ is not represented, and the Emperor and Empress give the impression of being marionettes, worked by hidden strings. This impression of being controlled like a marionette is heightened by the living character of the faces which look like portraits and seem to have been placed almost arbitrarily on bodies enveloped in ceremonial garments.

Already a dreadful fate seems to be hanging over the imperial couple. Manuel was spared this by his death, but the Empress Mary of Antioch could not escape it. After Manuel's death she took over the regency and was displaced in a political upheaval when the late Emperor's cousin, Andronicus, gained control of the government. It was then that the Dowager Empress suffered a terrible death on the scaffold. Under extreme physical pressure her twelve-year-old son, who was then Emperor, was forced to sign her death warrant. A few days later he too met his death at the hands of Andronicus' executioners.

131

PORTRAIT OF THE EMPEROR JOHN II COMNENUS AND HIS WIFE IRENE, A HUNGARIAN PRINCESS. Mosaic on the east wall of the south gallery in Hagia Sophia, Istanbul c. 1120.

John II was one of the most active and successful of the Byzantine Emperors. He distinguished himself by his energetic policy both in the Balkans and in Syria. Of all the imperial portraits in Hagia Sophia, that of the Empress Irene is perhaps the most expressive. Her features and bearing express the tragic circumstances in which she had to live, for the Emperor, her husband, found himself at war with Hungary, her homeland.

The Emperor and Empress stand on each side of the Mother of God who is holding the Christ Child. The Child is wearing the garments of a Hellenistic philosopher. Both poise and attributes point to pagan models: for instance, the right hand outstretched as if teaching and the left hand holding a parchment roll. In contrast to the almost contemporary Vladimir Mother of God, there is no trace here of a human relationship between Mary and the Christ Child, such as could be seen as early as the 7th-century Byzantine icon in Santa Maria Maggiore. This indicates that the model for the Theotokos was an old mono-

physite icon which sought to emphasize, not the human, but the divine nature of Christ and Mary. This old icon which the mosaic artist copied was probably a picture of the Mother of God and the Christ Child said by tradition to have been painted by the evangelist Luke. This was known as the Hodegetria, or 'She who points the way', and it was in the monastery in Constantinople founded by Pulcheria, the sister of the Emperor Theodosius II. During the Easter festival this icon was brought to the imperial palace and venerated. Later it was kept in the sanctuary of Hagia Sophia. It was left untouched by the icon reformers after the iconoclast controversy, probably because of its association with the evangelist.

The portraits of the imperial couple correspond to the *imagines imperiales,* in use since Roman times, which played an important part in the ruler cult. Since Caligula's time the imperial portrait enjoyed divine worship. When a new Emperor came to the throne his portrait was ceremonially received in the big cities. In the 7th century the imperial annals still recorded the date when the city of Rome received the imperial portrait. Amid crowning and acclamation, the honoured portrait was carried round all the public places in the city, the Emperor was acclaimed as *triumphator* and then, after visiting the Capitol, it was placed in the *oratorium* of Caesarius in the imperial palace on the Palatine. This was the ceremony that still took place with the portraits of the Emperor Phocas and the Empress Leontia.

The mosaic in Hagia Sophia recalls the position of the portraits of the imperial couple in the sanctuary on each side of the cult icon. Here the Emperor is holding the pouch containing dust and the Empress the *akakia,* the parchment roll signifying orthodox belief. The names and title of the Emperor and Empress are written in a mixture of capitals and uncials, a style of writing normally used only in liturgical rolls.

132 – 137

COINS SHOWING MEMBERS OF THE HERACLIAN DYNASTY. 132 Constans II (641-68); 133 Constantine IV (668-85) with his brothers Tiberius and Heraclius (co-Emperors 681); 134 Constantine IV; 135 Constantine IV and his son Justinian II (685-95; 705-11); 136 Justinian II and his son Tiberius II (698-705); 137 Tiberius II. London, British Museum.

The coins shown here cover a period of more than sixty years. This was a time which saw far-reaching changes, a kind of internal revolution which left its mark on much of the cultural and spiritual life of the Empire, and was due to the monastic movement. These coins with imperial portraits belong to the decisive last phase of the period during which the monastic element established its authority. At that time monks gained control of the patriarchate, the episcopal sees and the university chairs. They also exerted their influence over Byzantine literature and art. The *acta* of the General Council of 681 are charateristic of this period: it was then that the church fathers strongly denounced student customs and the disorderly festivities of the city populace during the Brumalia when women went about in men's clothing and men impersonated animals. Even art bore the stamp of this period, though not much of it managed to survive the iconoclast controversy. This gives special significance to the imperial portraits on the coins of this age. Here the significant fact is not so much a change in portraiture as a rejection of the kind of work in relief which is found in the cameo-like imperial portrait. The coins shown here illustrate the rejection of this kind of representation which was still found in the portraits of Justinian on coins and medallions. The coins of the period 641-711 show imperial portraits which are linear in character, thus reflecting the transition from relief work to engraving. This was part of the general rejection of relief and free-standing sculpture. Neither were to play any part in Byzantine art again until the Macedonian period. It is significant that the last portrait head of a Byzantine Emperor which has been preserved is from the reign of Justinian II and shows the Emperor himself.

The portraits on the coins show a somewhat caricatured style which almost amounts to a rather naive standardization. It is very reminiscent of the portrayal of rulers found on the coins of the German kings in the Roman provinces. For instance the coins of the Vandal king Gunthamund can be compared with those of Tiberius II. What can almost be described as a barbarization of the portraits found on coins is not without parallel in other forms of figural art, such, for instance, as the so-called portrait head of Queen Theodelinda and the crest associated with King Agilulf (in the Bargello in Florence). In the field of panel painting the icon of the Mother of God of San Francesco falls into this category.

The fundamental reason for this development is to be found in the rise of a new social class after the extinction of the old aristocracy under the terrible regime of the usurper Phocas. But the style of art during the age of Justinian, the art of late antiquity, was not entirely extinguished. It no longer took the lead, but later on it did once more come to the fore under the Macedonian dynasty.

138

THE OPENING SCENE IN THE BOOK OF JOB. Miniature from a manuscript of the book of Job. Venice, Biblioteca Marciana (Cod. Gr. 538).

This miniature of 905 illustrates the prologue to the book of Job. The angels are drawn up in front of God, and beneath them stands Satan. He can be seen to the right of the three archangels Michael, Raphael and Gabriel, who are looking towards God, while he has turned away. The scene is reminiscent of Goethe's Prologue in *Faust*. Satan makes a bargain with God concerning Job. He is to have full power over all Job's worldly possessions and Job is to be left with no more than his life. This means that Job is to be sorely tried and the question is, 'Will Job curse God who has allowed him to be deprived of all his many blessings?'

The composition of this scene reveals a gifted master of miniature painting. There is no other instance of Satan, the angel of evil, turning from God in this way while the three archangels lift up their faces to Him. God is not shown in this picture, except for His hand which can be seen coming out of the clouds. Like the archangels who have not fallen away from God, the angel of evil has the nimbus of a saint. It is tempting to find an analogy here with the Byzantine Emperors who were given haloes by posterity irrespective of their moral worth.

139

THE ADORATION OF THE MAGI. Miniature from the *Menologion* of Basil II. Rome, Biblioteca Vaticana (Cod. Gr. 1613, f. 272).

This illustration is an instance of the extent to which Byzantine pictures in the Gospels, both in composition and in detail, are indebted to Iranian models. Here is a Persian homage scene like that on the great relief of Persepolis. On the Persian relief those bringing tribute are recognizing the overlordship of the Great King Darius, while the names of their various peoples are announced by the grand vizier. In this miniature the place of the grand vizier is taken by the angel. Like vassals before the Great King, the three magi in the miniature are in the act of abasing themselves at the foot of the Mother of God with the gifts they have brought. Though the Mother of God and the Divine Child are placed in a cave there is clear evidence of Iranian influence. The three magi, as elsewhere, are wearing long Persian trousers and the kaftan, or long oriental garment, tucked up for riding. They have the same crowns as the priests in the frescoes of Castelseprio.

The painter has used traditional forms to create a masterpiece. His artistry is shown by the way in which he has placed the Virgin with the Child on a throne of rock in the cave. She has lost the divine detachment which is found in the prototypes used by the painter. Her bearing is not that demanded by a ceremonial occasion such as the adoration of the three magi, for she is looking at the strangers with genuine human curiosity. The angel also seems to be announcing the embassy in a different way, introducing each of the magi separately. The manner in which the mountainous folds of the angel's garment conceal his body is characteristic of the marked individuality of the painter. The right wing of the angel is stretched out as if protectively over the magi. The miniature is characterized by a superb combination of symbolic suggestion and artistic expression.

140

ST ROMANUS THE MELODIST. Miniature from the *Menologian* of Basil II. Rome, Biblioteca Vaticana (Cod. Gr. 1613, f. 78).

This miniature shows Romanus, the greatest of the Byzantine hymn-writers, receiving the gift of writing *kontakia* from the Mother of God in a wonderful vision. He is portrayed lying asleep while the Mother of God appears to him in a dream. In the background can be seen the church of the Resurrection in Beirut where he was serving as a deacon at the time of his dream. He probably came to Constantinople during the reign of the Emperor Anastasius I (491-518) and became a priest at the church of Mary the Mother of God.

In the miniature the church of the Resurrection in Beirut has the form of a basilica with an apse. This architectural style is known from Syrian churches surviving from the time of Anastasius. Syrian churches of this period also have portals like that seen in the miniature. It is thus possible that the *Menologion* of Basil drew on a biography dating from shortly after the saint's death and illustrated in this way. It probably belonged to the church of Mary the Mother of God where Romanus' tomb was and where his literary work was preserved.

141

THE NATIVITY. Miniature from the *Menologion* of Basil II. Rome, Biblioteca Vaticana (Cod. Gr. 1613, f. 78).

This miniature shows the Mother of God lying on her bed exhausted after childbirth, while Jesus is seen being bathed by a maidservant and the three magi are approaching with their gifts. The iconography follows an old tradition found as early as the 5th century, and indeed the early pictures of this scene clearly reveal the extent to which they in turn were indebted to pagan iconography. The same is found in the portrayal of the Ascension of Christ which has a close affinity with the pictures of the apotheosis of the Emperor. In the miniature shown here the iconography points to the use of the illustrations of the Alexander myth. The scenes from Baalbek come to mind in this connection. In their announcement of the birth of Alexander to the Olympians and the bathing of the infant after his birth, the iconography is almost identical with that of the Nativity scene. So once again there is evidence of far-reaching continuity stretching from the pagan Hellenistic world to Christian Byzantium. It is also noticeable that the sequence illustrating the life of Christ originated in those same Syrian regions where the Alexander pictures are found.

142

THE ASCENSION OF CHRIST. Detail from a mosaic in the Sophia church in Thessalonica.

This illustration gives only the head of the Redeemer. In the mosaic Christ is shown in the circular framework of an *imago clipeata,* sitting on a semi-circular band in the midst of the firmament, while this whole picture of the Saviour is being borne heavenwards by angels.

The mosaic dates from the beginning of the 10th century, not long after the end of the iconoclast controversy, and it follows a famous prototype: the enthroned Christ shown in the top of the dome of the church of St George in Thessalonica. Only very few fragments have survived but the picture is in the form of an *imago clipeata.* Only vestiges of the angels can be seen – the hands bearing the picture, the heads and part of the feet. But there is sufficient to indicate that the dome mosaic of St George's church in Thessalonica was similar to the mosaic in the Sophia church in presentation with almost identical detail. Only parts of the decoration were not taken over, such as flowers and fruit as symbols of eternity. The mosaic decorating the church of St George, which had formerly been the mausoleum of the Emperor Galerius, dates from the time of Theodosius the Great.

This means that at least a copy has been preserved of one of the most important themes of Christian iconography from the formative period of Christian imperial art. The model for the portrayal of the Ascension of Christ was no doubt taken from pagan representations of the apotheosis of the Emperor.

The significance of this mosaic is brought out by the existence of an early icon in the Sinai monastery of St Catherine which also shows Christ Emmanuel enthroned on a band encircling the firmament. This icon gives some idea of the lost picture in the dome of the church of St George and indicates that the master of the Sophia church must have known this mosaic.

Here Christ has the large eyes characteristic of late Roman imperial portraiture, which in Roman times were supposed to indicate courage, as well as the three strands of hair hanging over the forehead.

There is additional evidence suggesting that the enthroned Christ in the Sophia church is a copy of a representation of Christ dating from the Theodosian period. This is a porphyry statue of Christ now in the Archaeological Museum in Alexandria which bears a marked similarity to the mosaic in the Sophia church.

143

THE PICTURE OF THE REDEEMER. Icon. Rome, Sancta Sanctorum (chapel of San Lorenzo at the Scala Santa).

This icon came from Constantinople. Only the head is visible, as the rest of it is protected by a covering of precious metal. According to legend, this is the picture which was once sent by Christ as a present to Abgar, king of Edessa. After the crusaders conquered the imperial city in 1204 they presented this icon to the powerful Pope Innocent III as the most valuable part of their loot and as a token of his victory over the heretical Emperor of Constantinople. The metal covering the icon dates from this time.

It is difficult to establish whether the crusaders actually brought back to Rome the real icon kept in the imperial palace. On the back of the icon there is a silver cross, like that of the 6th-century icon in the monastery on Sinai. This alone, however, is not decisive in the problem of whether it can be identified with the famous portrait of Christ. In Constantinople there were two famous portraits of the Saviour. One came from Camuliana and was brought to Constantinople in 574: this was the wonder-working palladium which protected the city when it was invaded by Avars and Persians in 625. The other portrait of Christ was the *mandylion*: up to the first half of the 10th century it was kept in the main church of Edessa, then it seems to have been handed over to the Byzantines. There is an icon in the monastery of St Catherine on Sinai which shows the Emperor Constantine VII Porphyrogenitus displaying it to the populace. Like the portrait of Camuliana, the *mandylion* was painted on linen material and was not stretched and mounted. But this is not so with the icon of the Sancta Sanctorum. In any case there are early representations of the *mandylion*, such as that from the 12th century now in the Tretiakov Gallery in Moscow, which is painted on a wooden panel like the one in Rome with a cross on the reverse side. A decisive factor is the lack of similarity between the icon in the Sancta Sanctorum and either the portrait of Christ on the *mandylion* or the one from Camuliana. All that can be seen of the icon in Rome is the head, and that resembles a portrait of John the Baptist. The Deesis on a Byzantine iconostasis consisted of three icons (the Saviour, the Mother of God and John the Baptist); it is possible that the looting westerners confused the picture of Christ with that of John the Baptist when they were plundering the palace chapel containing the most holy Treasure of the Orthodox Church.

This icon may belong to the 8th century, but its identification must be treated with great caution since it has not yet been available for a thorough examination.

144

THE MOTHER OF GOD WITH THE CHILD. Icon of the Nicoplya Mother of God. Venice, Treasury of San Marco.

This icon belongs to the second half of the 9th century. Almost entirely protected with a covering of precious metal, it is a miracle-working icon and as such can only be the object of scholarly investigation to a limited extent. The decoration of the nimbus dates from the 10th century. It is enamel cloisonné ornamented with semi-precious stones projecting from the surface of the nimbus. All that can really be seen is the face with the Hellenistic features so characteristic of the Macedonian school of painting. In this respect there is a similarity with the Madonna attributed to St Luke (Pl. 113) which dates from the same period. The prototype of this picture of the Mother of God may well have been the holy icon kept in a special chapel in the imperial palace and only displayed to the people by the Emperor himself on very special occasions. Here it is probably not a case of a 6th-century prototype. The achievement of the 9th-century artist lies in the outstanding mastery with which he has used the traditional form and has produced a living, eloquent picture where the moving expression of the eyes seems to strike each beholder. The face of the Christ Child is obviously later and does not come from the hand of such a master.

145

THE MOTHER OF GOD. Icon. Venice, Treasury of San Marco.

This icon is painted in a strangely un-Byzantine and almost Hellenistic style. Like the icons of the Theotokos in Santa Maria Maggiore in Rome and of St Panteleimon in Kiev, it is a masterpiece of the Macedonian renaissance. Despite the considerable damage it has suffered in the course of restoration, it has not lost the magic powers of attraction bestowed on it by an unknown master of the second half of the 9th century. All of the original which remains undamaged or not repainted is the face, part of the head veil, the neck, the hands, and the Child's head.

Obviously comparison with other icons of the Mother of God in the Treasury of San Marco dating from the same period destroys the legend that this particular icon is an actual portrait of Mary, from which all other pictures of her are derived. This icon differs from that of the Nicoplya Mother of God in that the face looks out as though through the veil of a mysterious twilight; it is also unlike that of the Mother of God of Vladimir (Pl. 17) with her human maternal fondling of the Child. This Mary presents the emanation of the Divinity. The very movement of the hands clasping the Child – the touch of the right hand, and the left hand lying protectively on the shoulder of the Child – indicates the manifestation of the Divinity in which all power in the world rests. The blue shades lightly indicated on the nose and cheeks, as well as the dark lines between the face and the blue of the veil give the painted head almost the effect of sculpture. The veil, too, is so painted that one can almost feel the texture of the fine silk material. The picture is of such outstanding quality that it is tempting to think it may have been the famous icon in the palace chapel which was lost at the time of the conquest of Constantinople in 1204.

146

JOHN THE BAPTIST. Ivory relief, 10th century. Liverpool, Public Museum.

This relief may perhaps show what the famous icon of the Baptist on the iconostasis of Hagia Sophia was like. It is possible that the relief is the same as the icon, now in Rome, of which only the head is visible (Pl. 143 and Note). The ivory carver would have translated that masterpiece into the medium of work in relief. It should be remembered that an ivory carved tablet was originally painted; this would have heightened the similarity with the original icon.

The figure of the Baptist is so elongated as to seem out of proportion. But this is not simply an artist's mannerism, as is found during the Palaeologan period. Nor is it the result of any religious mystic revelation of the Divine Light, such as that experienced by the hesychasts. The reason lies in the deliberate intention of the artist who created the original model, for the icon would probably be on the altar screen and therefore be seen from a height. Hence the proportions had to be such that they would appear normal when viewed from below. The almost classical treatment of the folds of the garments reflects the influence of monumental sculpture at that period. (Here the torso of a relief of the praying Mother of God from the church of St George in Thessalonica comes to mind.)

On this relief the Baptist is holding in his left hand a scroll bearing the words, 'Behold the Lamb of God, which taketh away the sin of the world.'

147

CHRIST GIVING THE BLESSING. Ivory relief, 11th century. Oxford, Bodleian Library.

This work is one of the few surviving copies of the famous icon of the enthroned Christ which was placed over the gateway of the Chalke (the Bronze Gate) of the imperial palace in Constantinople. In 726, in obedience to the Emperor Leo III's iconoclast policy, an officer of the imperial bodyguard destroyed the icon with an axe; he was immediately lynched by Byzantine women.

The icon was copied very early on by mosaic artists. One of the earliest examples was in the dome of the church of St George in Thessalonica, dating from the reign of the Emperor Theodosius I. Only a few fragments have survived.

This relief shows the enthroned Christ holding the Holy Scriptures in his veiled left hand, while his right hand is raised in blessing. Christ is wearing the ceremonial robes of a Roman consul. In contrast to other representations of this kind, he is not seated on an imperial throne with a back and arms, but on a stool richly decorated with ivory plaques and semi-precious jewels with an equally richly ornamental footstool. He is presiding in the midst of the firmament, as is shown by the stars placed on the surface on which the relief is mounted.

148

THE PROPHET ZACHARIAS. Fresco in the church of the monastery of Brontocheion, Mistra.

This fresco, dating from 1296, was probably executed by a

Constantinopolitan master who was commissioned by the founder, a high imperial official resident in the capital. It belongs to the early frescoes of the Palaeologan age, and is particularly important as affording insight into the style of Constantinopolitan artists of this period. Two decades later the frescoes of the church of the Chora (Kariye Cami) showed different trends in style. This is still more noticeable in the frescoes of Feofan Grek in the church of the Redeemer in Novgorod. Here there is a common approach shown in the composition and the presentation of the picture of the prophet in the *imago clipeata*. The similarity with Feofan is shown by the similarity of treatment found in the blues used for the beard and hair. In the church of the Redeemer in Novgorod almost all the blues remain, while the other colours have been virtually destroyed by the plaster on which they were applied. Thus these frescoes make an impression now that was certainly not visualized by their creator. They give the effect of being impressionist in a sense known only in the 20th century. But the shades of colour which have been lost in Novgorod are still there in the Mistra frescoes. The technique of the painter consisted in an almost deliberate juxtaposition of different shades so as to give the illusion of sculpture to a distant viewer. In particular, the blues used on the beard and hair leave the impression of light shining down on them and give the individual strands of hair a kind of sculptured effect. It is this device which makes the face look as if it is encircled by a double nimbus. This is because it is surrounded by a crown of flaming hair. Here some role must be assigned to the mysticism of the Divine Light found in the Palaeologan period, for it was an important factor in art as well as in Byzantine spirituality.

149

ABRAHAM, ISAAC AND JACOB. Miniature from the *Menologion* of Basil II. Rome, Biblioteca Vaticana (Cod. Gr. 1613, f. 250).

The portrayal of the three patriarchal fathers Abraham, Isaac and Jacob, illustrates the way in which Byzantine masters adapted the forms of the antique world to Christian use. In this case not only the style but the Christian tradition had its roots in antiquity. This goes right back to the frescoes of the catacombs. Here, to begin with, it was not strictly speaking the frescoes of the catacombs but their prototypes in the houses and palaces of distinguished Christians. The patriarch Isaac in this illustration is seen in the guise of the apostle Paul on a fresco in the catacombs under the via Latina in Rome. The patriarch Abraham has also been given the same attributes of the apostle, though the scroll and wax tablet were an anachronism. For obvious reasons the old patriarchs had not hitherto been portrayed with writing materials or books. In the case of Abraham and Isaac a prototype closely connected with the fresco under the via Latina had obviously been used. This is indicated not only by the scroll and wax tablet given to the patriarch Abraham but by the way in which Isaac's garment is arranged over his bent arm. All this points to a prototype closely related to the representation of the apostles. This is also shown by the broad band (*clavus*) which is worn by the patriarch in the miniature as also by the apostles in the catacombs. Such bands were also worn by the priests in the frescoes of the synagogue at Dura-Europos, but were no longer intelligible in the period of the *Menologion*.

150

ST DEMETRIUS WITH A BISHOP. Mosaic from the church of St Demetrius in Thessalonica.

This mosaic, dating from the first half of the 7th century, shows St Demetrius with the bishop who had the church built and commissioned the mosaic. The bishop's head has a square nimbus, a sign that he was still alive at the time when the mosaic was made.

Here St Demetrius has his hand on the bishop's shoulder in the same way as, on the porphyry group of the Tetrarchs, Diocletian is laying his hand on the co-Emperor's shoulder and thereby installing him. Demetrius is endowing the bishop with authority over the diocese, his left hand is raised in prayer calling down God's blessing.

The saint is wearing the same court robe of a man of rank as the imperial official to the left of Justinian in the mosaic in San Vitale in Ravenna. It looks as if this is meant to indicate the high secular status of the saint.

A comparison of the various pictures of the saint in the church reveals that Demetrius is not always portrayed with the same features. Only some of the mosaics show the same characteristics. It would appear that only the master of these mosaics worked from a portrait. (It follows that these mosaics are the later ones.) This conclusion can also be applied to the materials found on some of the pictures. One of the mosaics portraying Demetrius with bishop John and a founder shows the saint wearing Chinese silk that can be dated to the 3rd century. He could well have been wearing this, and it suggests that this picture showing him as a youth with a very narrow chin went back to a contemporary portrait of him. It is not so with the pictures of the saint as a protector of children. The master here had no special use for an original portrait. The same is true of the picture of St Sergius which clearly comes from the same hand. Here, too, one misses the likeness which is found in the eighty-years-older icon of the saint which is now in the Museum in Cairo. This raises the question of the artist's freedom. Although there was an authentic portrait of St Demetrius on one of the pillars (Pl. 155), the creator clearly preferred to create his own idealized picture. His aesthetic pleasure in the repetition of the ornament on the material of the robes is characteristic. The same is true of the garment of the military St Sergius for, though he belonged to the imperial bodyguard, he is shown in the dress of a patrician. There is an obvious inconsistency, for the saint is wearing the golden neck chain of the guards over the cloak of a patrician, a discrepancy brought out by a glance at the mosaic of Justinian in San Vitale where a guardsman and a patrician are seen side by side.

151

THE APOSTLE PAUL. Mosaic from the church of the Chora (Kariye Cami), Istanbul.

Like all the mosaics in the church of the Chora (Kariye Cami), this dates from the half decade after 1315 which saw the last brief blossoming of the mosaic art in the Palaeologan period. It shows how strongly the Byzantines were influenced in this field by Hellenistic antiquity. We must not, however, assume from this any direct imitation of pictures of the late antique period; it is rather a question of a living tradition of late antique forms already absorbed into Byzantine art as early as the Macedonian and Comnenian periods. Traces of this process can also certainly be detected in surviving monuments. The pillars in the basilica of St Demetrius have standing saints in mosaic in the same tradition as that to which the Apostle Paul in the Chora church belongs. And this process is not only seen in mosaic work. Icons were also used here, serving the same purpose and corresponding to the mosaic figures on the pillars of a Byzantine church. Such icons can be recognized by their unusual size, corresponding to that of the mosaic portraits on the pillars with which they alternated. Among the oldest icons of this kind dating from the 11th century are those of the Apostles Peter and Paul, now in the Museum for Architecture and History in Novgorod. They measure 2·36 x 1·47 metres. As Lazarev recognized, these were not icons from the iconostasis but had decorated the pillars of the Sophia church in Novgorod. Here it was usual to have both mosaic portraits and painted icons on the pillars. The production of mosaic icons was ruled out by reason of their large size. Byzantine mosaic icons are all small. The glass cubes used in the making of icons had to be imbedded in a layer of wax so that with the extension of the surface there was the danger of cracks, and this has indeed been responsible for the destruction of many mosaic icons. Thus icons on pillars were much used. The figures were lengthened in order to give the viewer the illusion of natural proportions. A comparison of the icons of Novgorod with the mosaic of the Apostle in the Chora reveals more than a common theme. It shows a similarity in the handling of the folds. In Novgorod the sculptured effect of the folds is achieved by a juxtaposition of different thin strips of colour which, to the distant viewer, create the appearance of a figure in relief. The master of the Chora church has translated this into the mosaic medium, for he has taken mosaic cubes of different colours and smaller format and has used them side by side in the folds of the garment.

The Apostle Paul is portrayed in the attitude of a teacher. The close connection between this mosaic and the icon of Novgorod can also be seen in the treatment of the face. The Deesis mosaic in Hagia Sophia had already provided a clear instance of the use of an icon as a model and its painterly style is translated into mosaic work. So too, in the Chora church, the rendering of the face was influenced by the icon model used. It is difficult, however, to compare this mosaic with the icon of Novgorod since the 15th-century restoration of the latter has preserved the heads of the Apostles only in outline.

152

THE ANNUNCIATION. Mosaic, c.1090, from the church of the Dormition at Daphni near Athens.

The monastery and church of Daphni with its splendid mosaics are part of an imperial foundation. The mosaics were planned by the finest artists and executed by the greatest masters from the ateliers of the capital; they are among the finest examples of Byzantine art.

This mosaic shows the Annunciation which very early gained a secure place in the themes of Christian iconography. It is found in a mosaic as early as the mid-6th century in the cathedral of Bishop Euphrasius in Poreč (Parenzo). (See Note

117 for the development of this theme.)

The period to which the Annunciation of Daphni belongs is distinguished by its new interpretation of traditional iconography. Evidence of this can also be seen by comparison with the icon of the Annunciation of Ustyug (Pl. 117), which may be half a century earlier. In Daphni the angel can be seen moving swiftly down. In the face of this wonderful event the Mother of God has risen from her throne and has placed her hand on her breast as a sign of submission. Unlike the icon of Ustyug, the symbolic gesture is plain here. The movement of the hand is at the same time a symbol of the fulfilment of that which the Annunciation has declared.

The folds of the garments are treated with great mastery and show that, as between the icon of Ustyug and the mosaic of Daphni, there is no difference in the artistic heights reached. The faces of the angel and the Mother of God reflect the influence of antiquity which is found as early as the second half of the 9th century in the Macedonian renaissance.

153

THE CRUCIFIXION. Mosaic, c.1090, from the church of the Dormition at Daphni near Athens.

This mosaic shows Christ on the Cross, with the Mother of God and John, the beloved disciple, on each side. An angel is hovering over the arms of the Cross. From the right side of the Saviour's body blood is spurting on to the skull of Adam at the foot of the Cross, a reminder of the significance of Christ's death on the Cross. The eyes of the Saviour are still open in the rigidity of death, and in spite of all the signs of death in the mosaic it is not clear whether those open eyes are not still living, triumphant over the death and agony of the Cross. Blood is running from the hands nailed to the Cross and is falling on to the Mother of God and John.

This mosaic has about it something of the special mystique of the Cross which had developed then. It was the symbol and sign of the Emperor Basil II in his campaigns in Syria and the Holy Land, which were in a special sense Byzantine crusades. This was a time when fragments of the True Cross of Christ in reliquaries had a special significance. Evidence of this can still be seen in the many costly surviving reliquaries of the Cross, staurothekes.

On the other hand the iconographical tradition of the Crucifixion was very old, though it was unknown during the early Christian period down to the 6th century. It was the monks of Syria and Palestine who first secured it a firm place in Christian iconography. But to begin with they did not dare portray Christ on the Cross. A revealing instance of this is found in the *ampullae* of Monza and Bobbio. Both were articles made in Palestine shortly before 600 for sale to the devout. On them, only the bust of Christ was shown on the Cross. In contrast to the crosses of the two robbers, that of the Saviour remains empty. It was only gradually that Christ's body began to be portrayed on the Cross. Later on, this was to become almost a symbol of the monastic movement. It was not for nothing that in the Chludov Psalter (Pl. 89) the Crucifixion of Christ was shown closely linked to the iconophile monks during the iconoclast movement which the Emperor initiated. It was especially in monastic churches that the Crucifixion was found.

434

The earliest known portrayals showing Christ hanging on the Cross begin with an ivory painted picture in the Museo Sacro in the Vatican. At most it can only be two decades later than the *ampullae* of Monzo and Bobbio. It was about 700 that the first known example of a monumental painting of the Crucifixion is found on a fresco in the church of Santa Maria Antiqua in Rome. Here there were monks who had fled from Syria and Palestine and it is to their influence that the first surviving large-scale picture of the Cross is owed. In Byzantine territory the portrayal of the Crucifixion began about 900 on the frescoes of the rock churches of Göreme in Cappadocia. In their churches the monks of Göreme had, side by side, frescoes of the Last Supper, the Crucifixion and the Ascension. There is a mosaic of the Crucifixion in the monastery church of Nea Moni on Chios, founded in the mid-11th century by Constantine IX (1048-55). The mosaics of Nea Moni and Daphni are not so far separated in time and obviously invite comparison. The master of Nea Moni keeps more closely to the text of St John's Gospel (19, 26-27) in contrast to the artist of the mosaic at Daphni. In Nea Moni, Mary Cleophas, Mary Magdalena and the Roman centurion are found together with the Mother of God and John. But in the mosaic at Daphni there are only the Mother of God and John, so that the glance of the beholder is concentrated on the crucified Saviour, thus giving this event for the first time the supreme significance of a sacrament.

154

HEAD OF A MARTYR. Mosaic from the church of St George in Thessalonica.

This mosaic is important in the development of the style of the work at Thessalonica. This picture of a saint is very like the portrait heads found in western Asia Minor and Egypt in the second half of the 5th century.

In general the style of Byzantine art in Thessalonica was extremely conservative. In contrast to what happened in the capital a good many of the pre-iconoclast mosaics of Thessalonica have survived. The monastery church of Latomos illustrates the unbroken continuity of artistic development from the second half of the 5th to the 14th century. Dating from the second half of the 5th century is the mosaic in the apse showing Christ in a gloriole which is being borne by the symbols of the four evangelists. In the foreground are the prophets Ezekiel and Habbakuk. A similar composition is found on the reverse side of the icon of Poganovo dating from the last years of the 14th century. The survival of early Byzantine composition in Thessalonica is all the more important since the city greatly influenced the art of Macedonia, Serbia and Bulgaria. It is instructive, for instance, to consider the extent to which the Ascension in the Sophia church in Ochrida or in the lower church in San Clemente in Rome depends on the treatment of the same theme in the mosaic of Thessalonica. The explanation of this continuity lies in the internal resources of the city. It was a famous goal for pilgrims. It held a fair of international proportions frequented by merchants from all over the Slav South-east Europe as well as by Byzantine traders.

The mosaic with the picture of the martyr is a characteristic example of this development. It has stylistic links with the 5th century imperial portraits already mentioned. The saint has unnaturally large eyes, a particularly firm chin and hair with stylized spiral curls. A comparison of this with the head of a martyr from an early Russian icon of the 12th century shows how widespread was the influence of Thessalonica. Russian icons of this kind are the famous ones of St Demetrius in the Tretiakov Gallery in Moscow and of St George in the Kremlin.

It was characteristic of art in Thessalonica that it so extensively preserved a style which had developed in the 4th and 5th centuries out of both eastern and western elements. Western Asia Minor, with its Hellenistic past, and the West Roman traditions still alive in South-east Europe provided the foundations on which Thessalonican art developed. This mingling of various influences was the result of the occupation of the provinces of Pannonia, Moesia and Illyria by Germanic peoples, and then by the Altaic nomad horsemen. The town populations of these regions, including craftsmen and artists, gravitated to a great extent towards Thessalonica. Added to West Roman, originally Latin, elements were the Graeco-Hellenistic peoples coming from western Asia Minor. Under pressure of Germanic pirate raids in the 3rd and 4th centuries they had abandoned the old maritime cities, such as Pergamon, Miletus and Ephesus and had sought refuge behind the walls of Thessalonica.

155

THE HEAD OF ST DEMETRIUS. Detail from a mosaic in the church of St Demetrius in Thessalonica.

This is from a mosaic dating from the mid-7th century on one of the pillars in the church of St Demetrius. The saint is shown as the protector of children. The children have veiled their hands before him as though in ceremonial reverence. His left hand is placed protectively on the shoulder of a small child, the right hand is raised in prayer. In this picture he is not wearing his great robes of state with the ceremonial tunic showing his sign of office, as in the mosaic illustrating his investiture (Pl. 150). Here he has on a light purple silk garment drawn in by a golden girdle. Over it he has put a simple version of his official robes, informal dress as it were, suited to this particular occasion when he is taking children under his protection.

156

APOSTLES AT THE DORMITION OF THE MOTHER OF GOD. Detail from a mosaic in the church of the Holy Apostles in Thessalonica.

This mosaic dates from the early years of the 14th century. Like the mosaics in the church of the Chora (Kariye Cami) in Constantinople, it is one of the last great achievements of Byzantine mosaicists. The masters creating this came from the imperial ateliers in the capital, and it is no surprise to learn that the work was given by Patriarch Niphon of Constantinople.

The detail shows a group of apostles gazing at the dying Mother of God. It is the moment of her soul's passing over, which a 12th century Russian icon tried to indicate by the restless flicker of a candle at the bed of the dying woman. The outlines of the figures in the mosaic are hard, lacking the painterly, almost modelled, half-tones found in early Palaeologan mosaic work of which the example *par excellence* is the Deesis in Hagia Sophia. But this harshness of outline does not imply any lack of technique. The cartoon shows not only the sketched figures but the numbers of the cubes to be used, so that the mosaicist knew exactly which colour to take. Often the cubes were of a special format in order to get a particular nuance. The harshness of the outline was intentional. The clear-cut contours emphasized the feeling of despair which surrounded the passing away of the Saviour's mother.

The iconography of the group follows an old tradition, such as is found on a 10th-century ivory relief on the Gospel of Emperor Otto III in Munich. In the mosaic a master hand is seen at work in the superb way that dominating outline is used to express feeling. A lattice-work of lines seems to outline the figures of the apostles. At the moment when the Mother of God dies, their feelings are expressed, not by any bodily movement, but by the look on their faces, the fixed gaze of their eyes.

The art of Thessalonica reached new heights in the days of the Palaeologi. It was a formative element in the developing Serbian art which was much influenced by Byzantine artists. Greek painters from Thessalonica, such as Michael Astrapas and Eutychius, were in the service of the Serbian rulers in Ochrida, Skoplje and Prizren.

157

INTERIOR OF HAGIA SOPHIA IN ISTANBUL.

The 6th-century Hagia Sophia, even in the form in which it has survived, represents a highlight in Byzantine ecclesiastical architecture, and reveals the perfection which can be attained by the domed church. It should not, however, be concluded that this meant the abandonment of the basilican form. In the early Christian period the two styles of architecture are found side by side.

In connection with the domed church it is possible to speak of a pre-Christian development. The Villa Hadriana in Tivoli has vaulted rooms with a dome built on an octagonal ground plan. The next stage is seen in the mausoleum of Galerius, the Rotunda or church of St George in Thessalonica. This was built as a mausoleum in Galerius' day and altered into a domed church under Theodosius. When it was converted, it was decorated with mosaics as is characteristic of later Byzantine churches. In the crown of the dome there are still traces of a picture of Christ inside an *imago clipeata*. This is probably the picture found in the portrayal of the Ascension in the Rabula Gospel. In Thessalonica the Ascension of Christ is also portrayed. This is clear from the surviving fragments of the head, hands and feet of the angels bearing aloft the *imago clipeata* with Christ within it. So that in the age of Theodosius there was mosaic decoration which could afford a pattern for the Byzantine art of Justinian's day and later on after the iconoclast controversy. The portrayal of the Ascension required the architectural setting of a dome. This was true also of other Gospel scenes. The beginnings of this development, which was to lead to the use of small domes grouped round the main dome, can be seen in the Theodosian period. Examples of this can be found in Milan and particularly in the church building of San Aquilino.

When the old church in Constantinople was destroyed in the Nika riots and Justinian commissioned a new one, the basilical architecture of Arcadius' church was given up in favour of a domed building. Behind this there no doubt lay a political reason. The basilica had been particularly linked with the com-

munal life of the city and was perhaps not so well suited to support imperial absolution as was the domed church which had long had its place in the imperial cult. From the technical point of view Hagia Sophia was a triumph for late antique statics; it was remarkable that so vast a dome could yet survive all the shocks of the frequent earthquakes in Constantinople. Nothing is left of the old mosaic decoration of the interior except the four cherubim bearing the picture of Christ in the dome. This picture of Christ has not itself survived. One distinct result of the change-over from the basilican style was to deprive the apse of its importance. The liturgy in Justinian's day was concentrated in the space under the vaulted dome.

158

EXTERIOR OF THE CHURCH OF ST SERGIUS AND ST BACCHUS, ISTANBUL.

This church is dedicated to the two military saints, Sergius and Bacchus, whose icons have survived from the age of Justinian, when the building was erected. It is indeed one of the finest surviving examples of the architecture of this period. The view given here shows the dome almost disappearing behind the square block of the main building. This was intentional. It was so designed that as anyone approached, the dome should seem to rise up from the main building, as did the vaulting of the heavens. Later on it became usual for domes to have a raised drum and this architectural subtlety was lost. The original intention can be much better seen from St Sergius and St Bacchus than from the later domed cross-in-square church. Like Hagia Sophia, St Sergius and St Bacchus still had an atrium which played a considerable role in ecclesiastical life. Funeral obsequies took place here, as well as the mass of the catechumens. Directly connected with the atrium was the baptistery. Hagia Sophia still has its baptistery; it is now the place where Mehmet Fati, the conqueror of Constantinople, is buried. The atrium was also used as a burial place. In the course of later developments it became necessary to enlarge the actual interior of the church. In the West the atrium was incorporated into the nave and in this way a basilica could be lengthened. This architectural device is particularly noticeable in Italy. In the East the domed church was enlarged by building out the narthex and by grouping separate domes round the main dome. In the case of St Sergius and St Bacchus the problem was solved by leaving the old basilica with the dome as an octagon in the centre and by enlarging the rectangle in which it was set, with the dome being supported on eight pillars. In this way the interior was expanded into the surrounding rectangle. In the church of St Sergius and St Bacchus this rectangle already contained an apse and within the four corners there was apse-like vaulting in the form of half domes, thus clearly pointing the way to the four domed church. Thus the transition from the domed church to the domed cross-in-square gradually came about and was indeed determined by the eastern preference for the domed church.

159

THE CHURCH OF THE MYRELAION (BUDRUM CAMI), ISTANBUL.

The church of the Myrelaion was founded by Romanus I Lecapenus (920-44), the representative of the magnate class who

436

was co-Emperor with Constantine VII Porphyrogenitus (913-59). He designated the crypt, now used as a cistern, as his burial place. In the Byzantine Empire at this time, as in the West, it was customary for the founder of a church to have a special crypt built for his own tomb. Similarly, twenty years later, the Emperor Romanus II (959-63) had a crypt erected in the church of St Luke in which his sarcophagus together with that of the Empress were to be placed in the immediate neighbourhood of the saint's tomb. Today this crypt still contains these two sarcophagi.

The church of the Myrelaion, later converted by the Turks into a mosque and called Budrum Cami, is an excellent example of the type of church architecture which developed after the confusion of the iconoclast controversy. The photograph shows the three entrances to the church of which only the middle one remains unblocked. They led into the narthex, the passage or entrance hall which stood in front of the actual church built on the cross-in-square ground plan. As in the Nea, the *capella palatina* of Basil I, the system of four supports was used in order to carry the dome. Thus the constructional element in the building was still strongly emphasized, for the drum rested on supports which could carry a dome of far greater span. The constructional element of late antique ecclesiastical building has been changed here to a decorative form. What was still a constructional necessity in Hagia Sophia in order to distribute the pressure of the dome serves here only to divide up the drum. The next step was the substitution of columns for supports.

Thus one of the decisive turning-points in Byzantine church architecture was reached: the relation of the dome to the drum and the connection of both to the building as a whole. Balance between dome and drum characterized the last days of late antiquity. Thus the dome was regarded as an organic continuation of the drum. Such is above all the case with Hagia Sophia, the greatest domed building of this period. The beholder sees the drum almost as part of the dome.

The departure from this balance between dome and drum was one of the signs of the break between Byzantine ecclesiastical architecture and that of late antiquity. The drum was almost always higher than the dome above it. In the Renaissance, Michelangelo reverted to the late antique form of the dome. But St Peter's itself shows how ecclesiastical architecture of the Renaissance was influenced not only by the domed church of late antiquity but by the domed cross-in-square church which developed during the time when the monastic movement was dominant. Bramante's design for the new building of St Peter's would have been inconceivable without the knowledge of Byzantine church architecture. The two side spaces behind the *confessio* to the right and left of the high altar correspond to the *diakonikon* and the *prothesis* of the Byzantine church. And the erection of the great dome over the *confessio* is also copied from a Byzantine *katholikon* vaulted over by its dome. The narthex projects as an independent building with three doors, which can be seen as early as the Myrelaion church, and a special storey is placed over it in the façade of St Peter's. There are, however, pillars for the vertical supports of the façade at St Peter's instead of the pilasters of the Myrelaion church.

In the Myrelaion church the space round the dome shows new features. The barrel-vaulting, which had hitherto been usual, was replaced by cross-vaulting. The windows of the narthex, which are over entrance doors, have been blocked up. These windows were originally of marble pierced by ornaments. The size of the openings was so calculated that only a certain amount of bright light entered. The iconographic programme was so sited that the light would fall upon it. Unlike the West, Byzantium did not have many-coloured glass windows which shed many varieties and graduations of colour upon the interior of the church. But the Byzantines carefully directed their light so that it caught and lit up the surface of the individual glass cubes used in their mosaics.

The façade of the Myrelaion church was divided vertically by half-rounded abutments in the form of pilasters. On the front of the church they are worn almost down to the ground. It is only on each side of the central doorway that remains can be seen at ground level. On the other side of the building these pilasters have been preserved and, together with a horizontal running and narrow projecting middle cornice, determine the arrangement of the façade.

160

INTERIOR OF THE CHURCH OF ST IRENE IN ISTANBUL.

This interior shows the changes which came about with the iconoclast controversy. Even more than in the period of Justinian, all liturgical action was concentrated in the space in front of the altar. The altar stands out, visible, almost on the threshold between the sanctuary and the vast space under the dome. It is significant that there is no trace of any altar-rail. The altar is in full sight of all, clergy and laity. It should also be noted that, contrary to usual practice in a Byzantine church, the presbyterium in the apse had been brought back in accordance with the practice of the early Church. This enabled a large number of clergy to be accommodated on benches rising up like an amphitheatre behind the altar. In the early Church the priests would be seated in the apse behind the altar. The iconoclasts made a point of returning to the early Church, as for instance in their repudiation of icons, based on the commandment, 'Thou shalt make no graven image'. The use of the presbyterium is another example of this.

The exits under the semi-circle of the priests' benches in the apse are new. These were necessary for liturgical reasons, since the space between the altar and the benches was narrow. This arrangement of the apse was abandoned by the Byzantine Church after the end of the iconoclast controversy.

161

EXTERIOR OF THE CHURCH OF ST IRENE IN ISTANBUL.

The church of St Irene was built by Justinian in place of an older church destroyed in the Nika riot of 532. During the 8th century both interior and exterior were so altered that this building can no longer be regarded as belonging to the age of Justinian. The main difference lies in the height of the dome and the arrangement of the apse and side rooms. Apart from the four central supports of the dome, all that remains of the church of Justinian's day is the narthex. By reason of its reconstruction this church is as important for the development of Byzantine ecclesiastical architecture as Hagia Sophia. In contrast to 6th-century architecture the dome has a raised drum which gives more window space. And unlike Hagia Sophia the dome and the drum are set in sharp contrast to each other. The reason lies in the extension of the interior by additions which had to be lit from the dome. This reconstruction took place under the iconoclast Emperors and it is one of the few instances of ecclesiastical building during this period.

162

SOUTH FAÇADE OF THE MONASTERY OF ST SYMEON STYLITES. Qalat Siman, north-east of Antioch in Syria, monastery built round the pillar of St Symeon Stylites.

Qalat Siman is the name of the sanctuary built about 480 round the pillar on which St Symeon spent most of his life. Its designation in Arabic is a reminder that what was once a martyrium in the centre of a Byzantine and Christian Syria is now in an Arab and Islamic land. The central shrine in the form of an octagon was built round the place where the saint's pillar used to be, and it protected his tomb. It was a mausoleum fit for an emperor that was erected round the simple coffin of the saint. Famous craftsmen from Constantinople drafted the design and superintended the work. The saint on the pillar was as dear to the Emperors on the Bosphorus as he was to the monks of the Syrian desert. This veneration lasted more than a thousand years. When the Byzantines, under their great Emperor Basil II, once again took possession of Qalat Siman, the first concern of the Emperor was to restore the sanctuary. The remains of a mosaic from this period still survive. There was also a monastery attached to the tomb of the saint at the foot of the column. Its monks were responsible for the liturgy and offices said at the tomb and they looked after the thronging crowds of pilgrims.

Qalat Siman had been erected by the Emperor Zeno, the Isaurian on the Byzantine throne. His successor Anastasius founded the monastery and church at the tomb of St Menas in the desert west of Alexandria. Justinian I had a monastery built round the tomb of St Catherine on Sinai. These three monasteries were imperial foundations, as were the later houses on Mount Athos endowed by rulers during the Macedonian period. (It is only the monastery on Sinai, by reason of its more isolated and protected position, which has been able to preserve the greater part of its valuable treasure of manuscripts, icons and frescoes. Of the two other monasteries, Qalat Siman and St Menas, only the walls remain.) The imperial interest in these foundations meant that they were the work of Constantinopolitan masters. In so far as they have survived, these buildings can fill gaps in our knowledge of architectural development in Constantinople during the transition from the 5th to the 6th century.

The south façade of the monastery of Qalat Siman still makes a striking impression. It is closely related to the Magnaura. If it is compared to the *missorium*, the silver plate of Theodosius I, which shows the Emperor and his two sons sitting in the Magnaura, the strong resemblance is apparent. It can be seen even in the details, such as the particular kind of arcading and the façade of the roof. The arrangement of the doors round the central portal – it is flanked on each side by a smaller door – influenced later architectural features found on the façades of Romanesque churches. This kind of façade ceased in the 5th century in Constantinople (one of the last monumental buildings in this

style was the Hagia Sophia built under Arcadius and destroyed in the Nika riots in Justinian's reign), but in the West it enjoyed a revival.

163

THE BAPTISTERY OF QALAT SIMAN.

Pilgrims coming from a distance can see from afar the dome of the baptistery of Qalat Siman. Dating from about 470 this is one of the best examples of 5th-century pre-Justinian architecture. Like the point of a pyramid the octagon, which carried the dome, towers up out of the square main building. This building is arranged in two stages, the rectangular outside part and the square inner core which carries the octagon of the dome. This kind of arrangement is possible only with outstanding craftsmanship and mastery of building techniques. To fit the huge stone blocks into each other almost without joints demands an extraordinary mastery of the law of statics, for it is only this that enables the builder to distribute the immense weight of the dome among the various supports in the body of the building. The art of fitting great blocks of hewn stone together in this way is only to be found in Europe in the mausoleum of Theodoric in Ravenna and in the tomb of Diocletian in Split. Broad edges fashioned like bands frame the window arches and these soften the contrast between the vertical lines of the façade, which are particularly stressed by the rectangular shape of the building and the octagon of the dome opposite. The building was something which lived. When the rays of the sun struck the smooth stone, the whole building seemed to light up like the flickering flame of a burning candle. The stone reflected back the sun, so that it was impossible to gaze at it for long. To the approaching visitor the building, thus lit up, looked like some vision raised up out of the desert sand. It demonstrates the brilliant intuition with which Byzantine architects were able to blend landscape and architecture.

From the architectural point of view this baptistery is of considerable significance as preparing the way for the domed church of Justinian's day. It can be regarded as the forerunner of St Sergius and St Bacchus in Istanbul. And from the domed church of Justinian the way leads to the domed cross-in-square church.

164

THE CHURCH OF ST CATHERINE IN THESSALONICA.

The church of St Catherine in Thessalonica, together with the church of the Apostles in the same city, represents some of the finest architecture of the Palaeologan period.

The architectural style of this building can only be understood in the light of the beginnings and development of the domed cross-in-square church from the 7th century onwards. In keeping the square ground plan of the domed church, which had previously been roofed over by barrel-vaulting, the cross-in-square church had vaulted over the space round the central dome with domes of smaller span. This meant a reduction in the amount of space in front of the altar available for liturgical purposes. In order to meet this need the adjoining rooms were deprived of their upper storeys and given smaller domes, thus providing extra space and extending the room beneath the central dome. There were of course other factors, such as the expansion of the iconographic programmes and the views about the universe coming from the East. The work of the traveller Cosmas Indicopleustes did much to spread these new cosmic views which were penetrating the Byzantine Empire during the second half of the 6th century. Such ideas did in fact imply a different conception of the cosmos which was divided into four cardinal points. This cosmic view was like the arrangement of Jewish family vaults. Probably all these factors combined to produce the new architectural structure found in the cross-in-square church. Later on, in the 10th century, the supports of the dome were increased from four to eight. This change arose out of the need for more space inside the church and it meant the adoption of the octagon which had originally been used when the domed building was first introduced. An example of this is the Rotunda, the church of St George in Thessalonica, where the dome is supported by an octagon-shaped structure. The changeover from four to eight supports was no doubt connected with the general change in architectural orientation which took place within the framework of the Macedonian renaissance with its interest in late antique and early Christian worlds. This movement can be inferred from the ornamentation on the altar rails and the sarcophagi, as also from the pictures – mosaics, frescoes and miniatures – of this period.

The architectural changes found in the Palaeologan period also show a preference for late antique forms. On the outside façade of the church of St Catherine there is an almost complete disruption of the vertical line. The rectangle which can be regarded as the first stage of the building has its façade so arranged that it is almost covered with arches breaking up the vertical lines. Behind it the dome can be seen stretching up close behind the façade. The dome has two storeys, the upper one seeming to grow out of the lower one. Here too, in the storeys of the dome, the vertical line is obliterated. The effect is rather like that of a flower; the arches of the upper storey surround the dome like the sepals of the opening bud of a growing blossom. The line of the arches is further stressed by the triple crown of arches round the windows and still more by the arches repeated on the outside of the dome. By reason of their brick ornamentation these arches are projected so that they stretch over the windows like eyebrows raised over the eyes. The analogy with the world of nature can be extended to the window grills which consist of sheets of marble cut into ornamental shapes, sometimes like the honeycomb of a bee-hive, sometimes like the twigs of a dense hedge. This reveals Byzantine mastery of the art of glazing. Instead of simple thin sheets in narrow windows, the marble grill was used making it possible for the light to reach the interior through this network of ornamentation. Thus the kind of glazing used in western cathedrals played a relatively subordinate role here. But it should be remembered that this cathedral glass, which the West had got from the Byzantines in the Carolingian period, was still used in churches under the Palaeologans. This is specially true of windows in the dome. Here, as in the West, the windows were decorated with saints portrayed in coloured glass. Fragments of this kind of art were found when the Palaeologan church Fetiye Cami was restored. On the pillars and capitals of the outside, façade ornamentation from the age of Justinian was re-introduced.

165

THE CHURCH OF THE HOLY APOSTLES IN THESSALONICA.

The church of the Holy Apostles in Thessalonica dates from between 1312 and 1315 and is one of the finest domed cross-in-square churches in the Palaeologan period. It was founded by the Patriarch Niphon I of Constantinople and can be regarded as an example of Constantinopolitan court art. Here, in contrast to the church of St Catherine, the vertical lines of the main building from which the dome springs are preserved throughout. There is an interesting connection between the shape of the arches and the vertical lines, similar to the baptistery of Qalat Siman (Pl. 163). A certain tendency to look back to pre-Justinian architecture can be observed here, as well as in the use of pillars with capitals in the style of Justinian's period. The treatment of the windows is like that of the church of St John the Divine in Ephesus. The plaques added to the capitals also point in this direction. The same is true of the setting of the doors, which is reminiscent of the marble surrounds to the portals of the pre-Justinian period. And there is also the horseshoe arch of the windows which is characteristic of the early Christian period. The Christian churches of North Africa, which were uninfluenced by Islam, come to mind. Here too the technique is used of surrounding the window with a raised arch in ceramic.

166

THE CHURCH OF THE BRONTOCHEION MONASTERY, MISTRA.

This church of the two SS. Theodores was built about 1295 and is contemporary with the Tekfur-Saray palace in Constantinople. Both buildings made use of techniques derived from Islamic models, for instance in the coloured faience decoration on the façade. This can still be seen firmly embedded in plaster on the irregularly hewn stones on the part of the façade which has survived. This faience decoration would have greatly altered the present-day appearance of the church. But it is not only this which distinguished the churches of Mistra from other Byzantine churches. The structure of the façade also marks a break with previous architectural styles. Here the dome towers above a roof which consists of a series of gables. It is only over the entrance doors that arches instead of gables are found. The gabled roof is in three storeys and the central storey rises up sharply. This divided gable is in keeping with the strange effect of effortlessness which characterizes the whole building. This use of the gable points to the infiltration of western influence. The Morea and indeed Mistra were in the hands of Frankish barons. As in politics, so in architecture the situation lent itself to a combination of Byzantine and western elements. The enormous size of the dome in comparison with the rest of the building is not in the Byzantine tradition and would seem to indicate the influence of French cathedral architecture.

167

THE CHURCH OF THE PANTANASSA AT MISTRA. Dedicated 1428.

One of the latest Byzantine churches, this shows even more western influence than the church of the two Theodores in Mistra. French Romanesque influence from the South is there

439

as well as French Gothic. The façade has Gothic arches and finial ornament of Gothic cathedrals can be seen in a slightly altered form. The church tower is without Byzantine precedent. On the other hand, the dome and the setting of the upper windows are clear evidence of Byzantine influence.

168

INTERIOR OF THE MAIN CATHOLICON OF HOSIOS LOUKAS OF STIRI IN PHOCIS.

The church of St Luke was built over the tomb of a 10th-century ascetic of this name who had come to live in this neighbourhood. Even in his own day he had become an almost legendary figure. He foretold the liberation of Crete from Arab control and thus became almost a Byzantine hero. His monastery and its churches were endowed by the Emperor Romanus II (†963) who found his last rest in the crypt, together with his Empress.

Romanus II was in no sense a particularly distinguished Emperor, nor did his wife belong to the ranks of those Empresses who played a leading political role in Byzantine history. She was Theophano, originally a barmaid, who became Empress by reason of her beauty. Her second husband was the Emperor Nicephorus II Phocas, whom she had murdered, in the hopes of marrying the general John Tzimisces as her third husband.

The church of Hosios Loukas has one of the most beautiful of Byzantine interiors. The mosaic decoration here was largely due to the patronage of the Emperor Basil II (†1025) during whose reign Byzantine art reached new heights.

This illustration gives a view of the interior looking towards the iconostasis and the sanctuary. It shows the characteristic arrangement with the altar barriers on each side of the entrance used by the priest.

169

THE CROSS FROM THE MOSAIC IN THE APSE OF SANT'APOLLINARE IN CLASSE IN RAVENNA.

The cross of Sant'Apollinare in Classe is one of the three large representations of the cross surviving from the period of Ostrogothic rule in Ravenna. The other two are in the arch-episcopal chapel and in the dome of the mausoleum of Theodoric the Ostrogoth. Only the outline of the cross can now be seen on the stonework of the vaulting of the dome in the tomb of Theodoric but in the apse of Sant'Apollinare in Classe and in the archepiscopal chapel the mosaic work of the picture has survived.

In external form and decoration the cross of Sant'Apollinare corresponds closely to the gold cross which Justin II sent in 576 to the Pope in Rome (Pl. 21). Both have a central medallion on which there is a picture of the Redeemer, and the arms of the crosses are decorated with precious stones. The inscription in its present form may not be from the same period as the cross itself. But the alpha and omega, symbolizing the beginning and the end of life, are part of the original mosaic. The head of Christ in the medallion is the bearded Syrian type. This use of a Syrian model for Christ is not mere chance. The pictures decorating the cross fall into two groups illustrating the teaching and miracles of Christ and the stations of the Cross. They indicate a selection of pericopes (lessons from the Gospels) particularly favoured in Syria. The sub-divisions of the story of the Passion correspond to those found in the Jacobite rite. This fits in with the fact that Syrians acted as bankers in Ravenna and took a prominent part in two ecclesiastical foundations. Here the founder is named as Julian the Banker (*Julianus Argentarius*).

PHOTOGRAPHIC ACKNOWLEDGMENTS

Except for those provided by the author, the illustrations in this book were supplied by: De Antonis 21; Emil Bauer 39; Osvaldo Böhm 32, 55, 56, 74, 87, 138; British Museum 13, 26, 64; Bulloz 127; Courtesy of the Byzantine Institute Inc. 18, 112; J. E. Dayton 5, 6, 79; Direction Générale des Antiquités et des Musées, Damascus 57, 76, 80, 162, 163; Ecole Pratique des Hautes Etudes Collection Chrétienne et Byzantine, Paris 65, 89, 120; Alison Frantz 168; German Archaeological Institute, Istanbul 159; German Archaeological Institute, Rome 49; Giraudon 67; Graeco-Roman Museum, Alexandria 119; National Tourist Organization of Greece 91, 154, 155, 156, 164, 165, 166; Hirmer Fotoarchiv, Munich 9, 10, 19, 40, 72, 77, 81, 105, 116, 118, 125, 131, 157; Martin Hürlimann 78, 161; Israel Department of Antiquities and Museums 92, 93; Pamela Jacobson 3; Jordan Department of Antiquities 58, 59; Kiev National Museum 111; Lykides 142; Mansell Collection 31, 47, 68, 88, 104, 113, 114, 128, 169; Marzari 4; Ann Münchow 48; Novosti Press Agency 17; G. B. Pineider 23; Josephine Powell 15, 20, 51, 150, 151, 152, 153, 160; Scala 1, 22; Helga Schmidt-Glassner 36; Service de Documentation Photographique de la Réunion des Musées Nationaux, Versailles 7; Albert Shoucair 124; Sparta Museum 70; T. Talbot Rice 95; Tosi 98; Turkish Tourist Office 96; Roger Wood 94; Yan 158.

Illustration 75 is from H. C. Butler, *Ancient Architecture in Syria,* Publications of the Princeton University Archaeological Expeditions to Syria in 1907 (Leyden 1907-21); illustrations 16 and 41 are from A. Grabar, *Byzantium* (London 1966); illustration 148 is from G. Millet, *Monuments byzantins de Mistra* (Paris 1910) and illustration 121 is from J. E. Quibell, *Excavations at Saqqara 1905-1906* (Cairo 1907).

Pompeian art 76, 88, 232, 236, 343, 345–6, 410
Pontifex Maximus 119
populo grasso 354–5
populo minuto 354–5
porcelain 173, 204
Poreč 425, 434
Porikologos 261, 338
Porphyrios 393
Porphyry 113, 335
porphyry 199
portraiture 42, 123, 125, 186–7, 194, 213, 223–4, 226, 232–3, 241, 339, 343–5, 364; in Balkans and Russia 263, 264–5, 349–50; in Roman Empire 30, 123, 195, 394
postal service 52, 180
praefectus praetorio 52, 56, 97–8, 180; *per Orientem* 103
praefectus urbis 60–1, 180
praetor 42, 175–6
praetorium 52
precious stones 62–3, 172, 197, 229
Preslav 260
printing 378, 380
Priscus, diplomat 104, 118, 257
Prizren 315–6, 436
Procheiros Nomos 257
Prochor (Prochoros) 258
Proclus 49, 122, 323, 325–6
Procopius of Caesarea 115–20, 125, 215–6, 258, 322, 426; *De Aedificiis* 119; *History of the Wars* 116–7; *Secret History* 99, 116–7
Procopius of Gaza 218
Prodromus *see* Theodore Prodromus
prokypsis 38, 55, 193, 398, 401
pronoia 262, 311–2, 316, 374
Prophetologion 48
proskynesis 123, 189–91, 232, 242–3
proto-Bulgars 259–60
Protoevangelium 424, 425
protonotarius 175
protos apostolos 55, 112
Provence, Provençal 110, 354, 369
Psalter 169, 223–5, 244, 343, 350
Psellus 217, 248, 302, 323–5, 327, 330, 332, 335, 339, 346, 359, 398
Pseudo-Dionysius the Areopagite 36, 86, 237, 330–1
Pseudo-Oppian 406, 410, 413
Pskov 363
Ptocholeon (*Tale of Poor Leo*) 337–8, 350
Ptolemy, Claudius 122, 205, 335, 381
Pulcheria 40, 200, 423
purple 58, 60, 172, 187, 189, 194, 199, 238, 241, 308
Pythagoras 324
Pythagorean basilica 41

QAIRAWAN 205, 306, 418
Qalat Siman, Syria, monastery of St Symeon Stylites and baptistery 438, 439
Qasr al-Hayr al-Gharbi 245
Qasr ibn Wardan 86, 398, 413, 414, 415
Quadi 31, 109
Qubilai 356
Qumran 48, 224
Qunduz 204
Quqāya *see* Simon the Potter
Quraysh 203
Qusayr Amrah 127, 392, 405, 409, 413, 415, 417, 418

RABABNAMA 356
Rabbinic schools 47
Rabula Gospels 162, 223, 238, 243, 408, 425, 436
Ragusa 319
Rai 263, 336, 421
Rakka 63, 336
Rangabe family 98
Raphael 230

Ratislav of Moravia 252
Ravenna 117, 119, 122, 214, 234, 236, 237–8, 249, 391, 414; archbishop of 94, 119; economy 28, 57, 93, 109–10, 172
—, church of Sant'Apollinare in Classe 401, 440
—, church of Sant'Apollinare Nuovo 391, 392
—, church of San Vitale 42, 88–9, 123, 197, 238, 391, 396, 399, 401, 403, 410, 423, 426, 428, 433
—, mausoleum of Galla Placidia 421
—, mausoleum of Theodoric 438
—, Palace of Theodoric 409, 413–14, 418
—, San Michele 414
Raymond of Toulouse 371
Red Sea 44, 62, 91, 105–6, 212, 407, 408
Regensburg 242, 350
Reichenau 239–40, 241, 245
Reinke de Vos 375
relics, reliquaries 41, 84, 112, 229, 236, 245, 247, 338, 348, 350
reliefs 170, 186, 191, 213, 229, 231, 236, 243–6, 249–50, 263, 349–50
renaissance, Carolingian 165, 226, 236, 237–8, 264
renaissance, Italian (European) 229–30, 259, 325, 326–9, 348, 362–3, 365, 377, 381
Reparatus, archbishop of Ravenna 401
reservoirs 52
Revelation of St John 201, 241–2; *cf.* Apocalypse
Rhine 27, 31–2, 109–10
Rhine valley 27, 172, 246, 307
Rhodanthe and Desicles 334
Rhodes 61, 95, 203, 207, 370
Rhodian Love Songs 338, 377
Rhône valley 26, 307
Richard of St Victor 330
Rila monastery (Bulgaria) 264
Rimini 381
Riquinus 256
roads 32–3, 91, 93, 96, 180; *see* trade routes
Robert Guiscard 317
rock churches 332, 359
rock monasteries 249, 254, 268
Roger I of Sicily 248
Roger II of Sicily 248, 258, 347
Romaioi 200–1, 241, 254, 358
Roman Church 29, 36, 39, 44–5, 55, 79–80, 112, 248, 252–4, 261, 314–6, 329, 331 *and see* papacy; attempt at union with Greek Church 328, 340, 360, 379–80; liturgy and music 240, 314, 348
Romance of Alexander 246
Romance of Belisarius 376
romances, novels 125, 216, 258–61, 321, 332–3, 334–5, 336–8, 345, 350, 364–6, 367–70, 376
romanesque 230, 245–6, 256, 261–2, 264
Romanus, poet and saint 47–8, 219, 430
Romanus I Lecapenus, co-emperor 229, 436
Romanus II, emperor 229, 395, 437, 440
Romanus III Argyrus, emperor 404, 405
Romanus IV, emperor 323–4
Rome, Romans 31, 34, 35, 104, 109, 118, 201, 234, 241, 360, 429; architecture 30, 41–2, 86–7, 245; art and culture 64, 83, 228, 237–9, 240, 243, 247, 249, 264, 345, 347, 427; economy and communications 28, 57, 93, 109–10, 172, 202; Romans in old provinces 111, 113–4, 163, 206–7, 253, 260; traditions

30, 111, 124–5, 191–3, 195, 199–201
Rome, Academy of Pomponio Leto 328
—, *Ara Pacis Augustae* 123, 426
—, Capella Greco 36–7
—, Capitol 87, 240
—, Casa Caelimontana 394, 422
—, catacombs 36–7, 228, 395, 421, 433
—, Circus 30, 123
—, Circus Maximus 87
—, Forum Boarium 240
—, Pantheon 228
—, Porta Maggiore 41
—, Prima Porta 123, 412
—, S. Agnese fuori le mura 424
—, S. Cecilia 238
—, S. Clemente 435
—, S. Costanza 41, 250, 255
—, S. Maria Antiqua 223, 237–8, 243, 343, 423, 435
—, S. Maria in Cosmedin 237
—, S. Maria in Domnica 238
—, S. Maria Egiziaca 237
—, S. Maria Maggiore 192, 240, 393, 424, 425, 429, 432
—, S. Maria Nuova 228
—, S. Paolo fuori le mura 427
—, St Peter's 327, 381, 426, 437
—, S. Prassede, chapel of S. Zeno in 238
—, S. Pudenziana 398
—, SS. Quattro Coronati, Capella di S. Silvestro 230
—, S. Sabina 427
—, Sancta Sanctorum 240, 431
—, Sistine chapel 362, 398
—, Torre Pignatara 41
—, Vatican Grotto 399
Rossano 238, 247–8; *Codex Rossanensis* 89, 124, 238, 344, 394, 400
Rothari 173
rotunda 87, 255
Rublev, Andrei 258, 331, 364, 420, 421
Rufinus 78
Rum, sultanate of 317; *see* Seljuks
Rumania 31, 104, 108, 163, 259–60, 264–5, 327, 378, 380–1
Russia, Russians 35, 215, 267, 306, 337, 410; art and architecture 227–8, 247, 251, 254–9, 263, 348–50, 362, 363–4; trade 64, 101, 105–6, 108–10, 169, 308, 352–3, 373, 378–9; tribes of South Russia 33, 43, 95, 163, 186–7, 234, 252–3, 271
Russian Primary Chronicle 257

SABAS, ST 247, 338; monastery of 79, 127, 203, 211–2, 219, 222, 409
sacellum 98, 175, 181, 198
Sadducees 267
Said Battal 333
St Gall 239, 243; Gospel 243
saints' lives 221–2, 224–8, 257, 263
Salerno 247–8
Salian period 240, 242, 244–6, 304
saloi 78, 222
Salvian 113
Salzburg 209, 252
Samanids 304
Samarkand 64, 169, 204
Samarra 169, 173, 197, 252, 260, 336
Samland 27
Samuel, tsar 394
San Niccolo di Casole, monastery 248
Sanskrit 222, 321, 336
Santa Ciriaca 240
Saqqara, monastery of St Jeremiah 426
sarcophagus 199, 250, 266, 268
Sardinia 110, 206, 208, 306, 379
Sarjun ibn Mansur 210
Sarmatians 28, 31, 109
Sassanids, *see s.v.* Persia
satire 126, 221, 258, 261, 324–5, 334, 338, 375–7

Sava 163, 252
Saxons 110, 244
Sázava, monastery 266
Scandinavia 26–7, 64, 101, 173, 306, 337
Schleswig 110, 173
scholae 53, 100, 411
Sciri 110
Scleri 98, 304–5
script, *scriptoria* 102, 169, 194, 205, 214, 243, 252, 256, 265–7, 380 *and see* Kufic; western (Latin) 195, 214, 240
sculpture 221, 231, 245, 247, 250–1, 256, 349–50; portrait sculpture 30, 123, 125, 233; in West 299, 239, 243–7, 250, 328, 348
Scythia Maior 97
Scythopolis 58
Sebasteia (Sivas) 78
Seleucia, on Euphrates 44, 63; theme 305
Seleucids 38, 54
Seljuks 195, 251, 261–3, 303, 309, 315, 316–8, 356, 371, 399, 404, 407, 410, 418, 419
sellisternium 192
senate, senators 29–30, 49, 187–9, 194, 199
Septimius Severus 30
Septuagint 47, 217
Serapis 76
Serbia, Serbs 201, 207, 215, 259, 264–6, 268, 315–6, 318, 354, 356, 378, 380; art and architecture 261–3, 364, 435
Serdica *see* Sofia
Sergiopolis 162
Sergius, Patriarch 211, 215, 219
Sergius, sanctuary of, at Rusapha 86
Sergius and Bacchus, martyrs 89, 400, 433
Severus of Antioch 79, 81–2, 219
shamans 103
Shams al-Bukkari 326
Shapur I 31, 205
Shen-si 104
Shipka pass 92
shipowners, shipping 61–2, 64, 95, 106, 110, 170–1, 307, 313
shorthand 103, 240
Siberia 64, 380
Sicilian Vespers 372
Sicily 109, 202, 208, 234–5, 237, 314, 354, 371–2, 379; Arab conquest 206, 208, 247, 306–7; art 30, 187, 248, 258, 346–7, 421; and Normans 248, 261, 309–10, 413; trade 28, 57, 61, 110, 309–10
Sidon 221, 372
Siena 262
Silesia 27
silk 58, 61–3, 99, 102–6, 172–3, 249, 308, 309–10, 373
silver 64, 103, 187, 197, 204, 223, 237, 243; coinage 59–60, 100, 173; embroidery 229, 264
Simon the Potter (Quqāya) 219
Simplicius 122
Sinai, Sinai peninsula 88–9, 210–2, 214, 222, 223, 228; monastery of St Catherine 228, 355, 395, 396, 398, 400, 424, 431, 438
Singidunum (Belgrade) 32
Sinope fragment 238
Sivas *see* Sebasteia
Sixtus III, pope 393
skalai 172, 318
Skanderberg (George Kastriota) 378
Skripu, church of St Gregory near 251, 417
slaves 27–8, 46, 48, 56, 59, 100, 168–70, 182, 185, 235, 260, 308; slave trade 29, 195, 309
Slavonic, Church 215, 234, 252–3, 256, 259, 265–7

447